In Praise of *Digital Design and Computer Architecture*

ARM® Edition

Harris and Harris have done a remarkable and commendable job in creating a true textbook which clearly shows their love and passion for teaching and educating. The students who read this book will be thankful to Harris and Harris for many years after graduation. The writing style, the clearness, the detailed diagrams, the flow of information, the gradual increase in the complexity of the subjects, the great examples throughout the chapters, the exercises at the end of the chapters, the concise yet clear explanations, the useful real-world examples, the coverage of all aspects of each topic—all of these things are done very well. If you are a student using this book for your course get ready to have fun, be impressed, and learn a great deal as well!

Mehdi Hatamian, Sr. Vice President, Broadcom

Harris and Harris have done an excellent job creating this ARM version of their popular book, *Digital Design and Computer Architecture*. Retargeting to ARM is a challenging task, but the authors have done it successfully while maintaining their clear and thorough presentation style, as well as their outstanding documentation quality. I believe this new edition will be very much welcomed by both students and professionals.

Donald Hung, San Jose State University

Of all the textbooks I've reviewed and assigned in my 10 years as a professor, *Digital Design and Computer Architecture* is one of only two that is unquestionably worth buying. (The other is *Computer Organization and Design*.) The writing is clear and concise; the diagrams are easy to understand; and the CPU the authors use as a running example is complex enough to be realistic, yet simple enough to be thoroughly understood by my students.

Zachary Kurmas, Grand Valley State University

Digital Design and Computer Architecture brings a fresh perspective to an old discipline. Many textbooks tend to resemble overgrown shrubs, but Harris and Harris have managed to prune away the deadwood while preserving the fundamentals and presenting them in a contemporary context. In doing so, they offer a text that will benefit students interested in designing solutions for tomorrow's challenges.

Jim Frenzel, University of Idaho

Harris and Harris have a pleasant and informative writing style. Their treatment of the material is at a good level for introducing students to computer engineering with plenty of helpful diagrams. Combinational circuits, microarchitecture, and memory systems are handled particularly well.

James Pinter-Lucke, Claremont McKenna College

Harris and Harris have written a book that is very clear and easy to understand. The exercises are well-designed and the real-world examples are a nice touch. The lengthy and confusing explanations often found in similar textbooks are not seen here. It's obvious that the authors have devoted a great deal of time and effort to create an accessible text. I strongly recommend *Digital Design and Computer Architecture*.

Peiyi Zhao, Chapman University

Digital Design and
Computer Architecture

ARM® Edition

Digital Design and Computer Architecture

ARM® Edition

Sarah L. Harris
David Money Harris

AMSTERDAM • BOSTON • HEIDELBERG • LONDON
NEW YORK • OXFORD • PARIS • SAN DIEGO
SAN FRANCISCO • SINGAPORE • SYDNEY • TOKYO

Morgan Kaufmann is an imprint of Elsevier

Acquiring Editor: Steve Merken
Development Editor: Nate McFadden
Project Manager: Punithavathy Govindaradjane
Designer: Vicky Pearson

Morgan Kaufmann is an imprint of Elsevier
225 Wyman Street, Waltham, MA 02451, USA

ISBN: 978-0-12-800056-4

British Library Cataloguing-in-Publication Data
A catalogue record for this book is available from the British Library

Library of Congress Cataloging-in-Publication Data
A catalog record for this book is available from the Library of Congress

For Information on all Morgan Kaufmann publications,
visit our website at www.mkp.com

Transferred to Digital Printing, 2015
Printed and bound in the United States of America

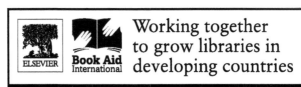

Working together
to grow libraries in
developing countries

www.elsevier.com • www.bookaid.org

To our families

Contents

Preface

This book is unique in its treatment in that it presents digital logic design from the perspective of computer architecture, starting at the beginning with 1's and 0's, and leading through the design of a microprocessor.

We believe that building a microprocessor is a special rite of passage for engineering and computer science students. The inner workings of a processor seem almost magical to the uninitiated, yet prove to be straightforward when carefully explained. Digital design in itself is a powerful and exciting subject. Assembly language programming unveils the inner language spoken by the processor. Microarchitecture is the link that brings it all together.

The first two editions of this increasingly popular text have covered the MIPS architecture in the tradition of the widely used architecture books by Patterson and Hennessy. As one of the original Reduced Instruction Set Computing architectures, MIPS is clean and exceptionally easy to understand and build. MIPS remains an important architecture and has been infused with new energy after Imagination Technologies acquired it in 2013.

Over the past two decades, the ARM architecture has exploded in popularity because of its efficiency and rich ecosystem. More than 50 billion ARM processors have been shipped, and more than 75% of humans on the planet use products with ARM processors. At the time of this writing, nearly every cell phone and tablet sold contains one or more ARM processors. Forecasts predict tens of billions more ARM processors soon controlling the Internet of Things. Many companies are building high-performance ARM systems to challenge Intel in the server market. Because of the commercial importance and student interest, we have developed this ARM edition of this book.

Pedagogically, the learning objectives of the MIPS and ARM editions are identical. The ARM architecture has a number of features including addressing modes and conditional execution that contribute to its efficiency but add a small amount of complexity. The microarchitectures also are very similar, with conditional execution and the program counter being the largest changes. The chapter on I/O provides numerous examples using the Raspberry Pi, a very popular ARM-based embedded Linux single board computer.

We expect to offer both MIPS and ARM editions as long as the market demands.

FEATURES

Side-by-Side Coverage of SystemVerilog and VHDL

Hardware description languages (HDLs) are at the center of modern digital design practices. Unfortunately, designers are evenly split between the two dominant languages, SystemVerilog and VHDL. This book introduces HDLs in Chapter 4 as soon as combinational and sequential logic design has been covered. HDLs are then used in Chapters 5 and 7 to design larger building blocks and entire processors. Nevertheless, Chapter 4 can be skipped and the later chapters are still accessible for courses that choose not to cover HDLs.

This book is unique in its side-by-side presentation of SystemVerilog and VHDL, enabling the reader to learn the two languages. Chapter 4 describes principles that apply to both HDLs, and then provides language-specific syntax and examples in adjacent columns. This side-by-side treatment makes it easy for an instructor to choose either HDL, and for the reader to transition from one to the other, either in a class or in professional practice.

ARM Architecture and Microarchitecture

Chapters 6 and 7 offer the first in-depth coverage of the ARM architecture and microarchitecture. ARM is an ideal architecture because it is a real architecture shipped in millions of products yearly, yet it is streamlined and easy to learn. Moreover, because of its popularity in the commercial and hobbyist worlds, simulation and development tools exist for the ARM architecture. All material relating to ARM® technology has been reproduced with permission from ARM Limited.

Real-World Perspectives

In addition to the real-world perspective in discussing the ARM architecture, Chapter 6 illustrates the architecture of Intel x86 processors to offer another perspective. Chapter 9 (available as an online supplement) also describes peripherals in the context of the Raspberry Pi single-board computer, a hugely popular ARM-based platform. These real-world perspective chapters show how the concepts in the chapters relate to the chips found in many PCs and consumer electronics.

Accessible Overview of Advanced Microarchitecture

Chapter 7 includes an overview of modern high-performance microarchitectural features including branch prediction, superscalar, and out-of-order operation, multithreading, and multicore processors. The treatment is accessible to a student in a first course and shows how the microarchitectures in the book can be extended to modern processors.

End-of-Chapter Exercises and Interview Questions

The best way to learn digital design is to do it. Each chapter ends with numerous exercises to practice the material. The exercises are followed by a set of interview questions that our industrial colleagues have asked students who are applying for work in the field. These questions provide a helpful glimpse into the types of problems that job applicants will typically encounter during the interview process. Exercise solutions are available via the book's companion and instructor websites.

ONLINE SUPPLEMENTS

Supplementary materials are available online at http://textbooks.elsevier. com/9780128000564. This companion site (accessible to all readers) includes the following:

▶ Solutions to odd-numbered exercises

▶ Links to professional-strength computer-aided design (CAD) tools from Altera®

▶ Link to Keil's ARM Microcontroller Development Kit (MDK-ARM), a tool for compiling, assembling, and simulating C and assembly code for ARM processors

▶ Hardware description language (HDL) code for the ARM processor

▶ Altera Quartus II helpful hints

▶ Lecture slides in PowerPoint (PPT) format

▶ Sample course and laboratory materials

▶ List of errata

The instructor site (linked to the companion site and accessible to adopters who register at http://textbooks.elsevier.com/9780128000564) includes the following:

▶ Solutions to all exercises

▶ Links to professional-strength computer-aided design (CAD) tools from Altera®

▶ Figures from the text in PDF and PPT formats

Additional details on using the Altera, Raspberry Pi, and MDK-ARM tools in your course are provided. Details on the sample laboratory materials are also provided here.

HOW TO USE THE SOFTWARE TOOLS IN A COURSE

Altera Quartus II

Quartus II Web Edition is a free version of the professional-strength Quartus™ II FPGA design tools. It allows students to enter their digital designs in schematic or using either the SystemVerilog or the VHDL hardware description language (HDL). After entering the design, students can simulate their circuits using ModelSim™-Altera Starter Edition, which is available with the Altera Quartus II Web Edition. Quartus II Web Edition also includes a built-in logic synthesis tool supporting both SystemVerilog and VHDL.

The difference between Web Edition and Subscription Edition is that Web Edition supports a subset of the most common Altera FPGAs. The difference between ModelSim-Altera Starter Edition and ModelSim commercial versions is that the Starter Edition degrades performance for simulations with more than 10,000 lines of HDL.

Keil's ARM Microcontroller Development Kit (MDK-ARM)

Keil's MDK-ARM is a tool for developing code for an ARM processor. It is available for free download. The MDK-ARM includes a commercial ARM C compiler and a simulator that allows students to write both C and assembly programs, compile them, and then simulate them.

LABS

The companion site includes links to a series of labs that cover topics from digital design through computer architecture. The labs teach students how to use the Quartus II tools to enter, simulate, synthesize, and implement their designs. The labs also include topics on C and assembly language programming using the MDK-ARM and Raspberry Pi development tools.

After synthesis, students can implement their designs using the Altera DE2 (or DE2-115) Development and Education Board. This powerful and competitively priced board is available from www.altera.com. The board contains an FPGA that can be programmed to implement student designs. We provide labs that describe how to implement a selection of designs on the DE2 Board using Quartus II Web Edition.

To run the labs, students will need to download and install Altera Quartus II Web Edition and either MDK-ARM or the Raspberry Pi tools. Instructors may also choose to install the tools on lab machines. The labs include instructions on how to implement the projects on the DE2 Board. The implementation step may be skipped, but we have found it of great value.

We have tested the labs on Windows, but the tools are also available for Linux.

BUGS

As all experienced programmers know, any program of significant complexity undoubtedly contains bugs. So, too, do books. We have taken great care to find and squash the bugs in this book. However, some errors undoubtedly do remain. We will maintain a list of errata on the book's webpage.

Please send your bug reports to ddcabugs@gmail.com. The first person to report a substantive bug with a fix that we use in a future printing will be rewarded with a $1 bounty!

ACKNOWLEDGMENTS

We appreciate the hard work of Nate McFadden, Joe Hayton, Punithavathy Govindaradjane, and the rest of the team at Morgan Kaufmann who made this book happen. We love the art of Duane Bibby, whose cartoons enliven the chapters.

We thank Matthew Watkins, who contributed the section on Heterogeneous Multiprocessors in Chapter 7. We greatly appreciate the work of Joshua Vasquez, who developed code for the Raspberry Pi in Chapter 9. We also thank Josef Spjut and Ruye Wang, who class-tested the material.

Numerous reviewers substantially improved the book. They include Boyang Wang, John Barr, Jack V. Briner, Andrew C. Brown, Carl Baumgaertner, A. Utku Diril, Jim Frenzel, Jaeha Kim, Phillip King, James Pinter-Lucke, Amir Roth, Z. Jerry Shi, James E. Stine, Luke Teyssier, Peiyi Zhao, Zach Dodds, Nathaniel Guy, Aswin Krishna, Volnei Pedroni, Karl Wang, Ricardo Jasinski, Josef Spjut, Jörgen Lien, Sameer Sharma, John Nestor, Syed Manzoor, James Hoe, Srinivasa Vemuru, K. Joseph Hass, Jayantha Herath, Robert Mullins, Bruno Quoitin, Subramaniam Ganesan, Braden Phillips, John Oliver, Yahswant K. Malaiya, Mohammad Awedh, Zachary Kurmas, Donald Hung, and an anonymous reviewer. We appreciate Khaled Benkrid and his colleagues at ARM for their careful review of the ARM-related material.

We also appreciate the students in our courses at Harvey Mudd College and UNLV who have given us helpful feedback on drafts of this textbook. Of special note are Clinton Barnes, Matt Weiner, Carl Walsh, Andrew Carter, Casey Schilling, Alice Clifton, Chris Acon, and Stephen Brawner.

And last, but not least, we both thank our families for their love and support.

From Zero to One

1

1.1 THE GAME PLAN

Microprocessors have revolutionized our world during the past three decades. A laptop computer today has far more capability than a room-sized mainframe of yesteryear. A luxury automobile contains about 100 microprocessors. Advances in microprocessors have made cell phones and the Internet possible, have vastly improved medicine, and have transformed how war is waged. Worldwide semiconductor industry sales have grown from US $21 billion in 1985 to $306 billion in 2013, and microprocessors are a major segment of these sales. We believe that microprocessors are not only technically, economically, and socially important, but are also an intrinsically fascinating human invention. By the time you finish reading this book, you will know how to design and build your own microprocessor. The skills you learn along the way will prepare you to design many other digital systems.

We assume that you have a basic familiarity with electricity, some prior programming experience, and a genuine interest in understanding what goes on under the hood of a computer. This book focuses on the design of digital systems, which operate on 1's and 0's. We begin with digital logic gates that accept 1's and 0's as inputs and produce 1's and 0's as outputs. We then explore how to combine logic gates into more complicated modules such as adders and memories. Then we shift gears to programming in assembly language, the native tongue of the microprocessor. Finally, we put gates together to build a microprocessor that runs these assembly language programs.

A great advantage of digital systems is that the building blocks are quite simple: just 1's and 0's. They do not require grungy mathematics or a profound knowledge of physics. Instead, the designer's challenge is to combine these simple blocks into complicated systems. A microprocessor may be the first system that you build that is too complex to fit in

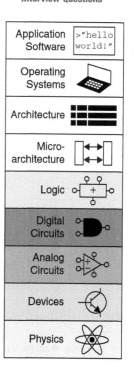

your head all at once. One of the major themes weaved through this book is how to manage complexity.

1.2 THE ART OF MANAGING COMPLEXITY

One of the characteristics that separates an engineer or computer scientist from a layperson is a systematic approach to managing complexity. Modern digital systems are built from millions or billions of transistors. No human being could understand these systems by writing equations describing the movement of electrons in each transistor and solving all of the equations simultaneously. You will need to learn to manage complexity to understand how to build a microprocessor without getting mired in a morass of detail.

1.2.1 Abstraction

The critical technique for managing complexity is *abstraction*: hiding details when they are not important. A system can be viewed from many different levels of abstraction. For example, American politicians abstract the world into cities, counties, states, and countries. A county contains multiple cities and a state contains many counties. When a politician is running for president, the politician is mostly interested in how the state as a whole will vote, rather than how each county votes, so the state is the most useful level of abstraction. On the other hand, the Census Bureau measures the population of every city, so the agency must consider the details of a lower level of abstraction.

Figure 1.1 illustrates levels of abstraction for an electronic computer system along with typical building blocks at each level. At the lowest level of abstraction is the physics, the motion of electrons. The behavior of electrons is described by quantum mechanics and Maxwell's equations. Our system is constructed from electronic *devices* such as transistors (or vacuum tubes, once upon a time). These devices have well-defined connection points called *terminals* and can be modeled by the relationship between voltage and current as measured at each terminal. By abstracting to this device level, we can ignore the individual electrons. The next level of abstraction is *analog circuits*, in which devices are assembled to create components such as amplifiers. Analog circuits input and output a continuous range of voltages. *Digital circuits* such as logic gates restrict the voltages to discrete ranges, which we will use to indicate 0 and 1. In logic design, we build more complex structures, such as adders or memories, from digital circuits.

Microarchitecture links the logic and architecture levels of abstraction. The *architecture* level of abstraction describes a computer from the programmer's perspective. For example, the Intel x86 architecture used by microprocessors in most *personal computers* (PCs) is defined by a set of

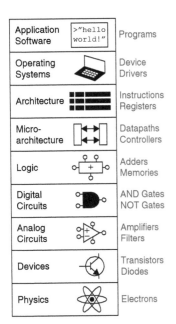

Figure 1.1 Levels of abstraction for an electronic computing system

instructions and registers (memory for temporarily storing variables) that the programmer is allowed to use. Microarchitecture involves combining logic elements to execute the instructions defined by the architecture. A particular architecture can be implemented by one of many different microarchitectures with different price/performance/power trade-offs. For example, the Intel Core i7, the Intel 80486, and the AMD Athlon all implement the x86 architecture with different microarchitectures.

Moving into the software realm, the operating system handles low-level details such as accessing a hard drive or managing memory. Finally, the application software uses these facilities provided by the operating system to solve a problem for the user. Thanks to the power of abstraction, your grandmother can surf the Web without any regard for the quantum vibrations of electrons or the organization of the memory in her computer.

This book focuses on the levels of abstraction from digital circuits through computer architecture. When you are working at one level of abstraction, it is good to know something about the levels of abstraction immediately above and below where you are working. For example, a computer scientist cannot fully optimize code without understanding the architecture for which the program is being written. A device engineer cannot make wise trade-offs in transistor design without understanding the circuits in which the transistors will be used. We hope that by the time you finish reading this book, you can pick the level of abstraction appropriate to solving your problem and evaluate the impact of your design choices on other levels of abstraction.

Each chapter in this book begins with an abstraction icon indicating the focus of the chapter in deep blue, with secondary topics shown in lighter shades of blue.

1.2.2 Discipline

Discipline is the act of intentionally restricting your design choices so that you can work more productively at a higher level of abstraction. Using interchangeable parts is a familiar application of discipline. One of the first examples of interchangeable parts was in flintlock rifle manufacturing. Until the early 19th century, rifles were individually crafted by hand. Components purchased from many different craftsmen were carefully filed and fit together by a highly skilled gunmaker. The discipline of interchangeable parts revolutionized the industry. By limiting the components to a standardized set with well-defined tolerances, rifles could be assembled and repaired much faster and with less skill. The gunmaker no longer concerned himself with lower levels of abstraction such as the specific shape of an individual barrel or gunstock.

In the context of this book, the digital discipline will be very important. Digital circuits use discrete voltages, whereas analog circuits use continuous voltages. Therefore, digital circuits are a subset of analog circuits and in some sense must be capable of less than the broader class of analog circuits. However, digital circuits are much simpler to design. By limiting ourselves to digital circuits, we can easily combine components into sophisticated systems that ultimately outperform those built from analog components in many applications. For example, digital televisions, compact disks (CDs), and cell phones are replacing their analog predecessors.

1.2.3 The Three-Y's

In addition to abstraction and discipline, designers use the three "-y's" to manage complexity: hierarchy, modularity, and regularity. These principles apply to both software and hardware systems.

- ▸ *Hierarchy* involves dividing a system into modules, then further subdividing each of these modules until the pieces are easy to understand.

- ▸ *Modularity* states that the modules have well-defined functions and interfaces, so that they connect together easily without unanticipated side effects.

- ▸ *Regularity* seeks uniformity among the modules. Common modules are reused many times, reducing the number of distinct modules that must be designed.

To illustrate these "-y's" we return to the example of rifle manufacturing. A flintlock rifle was one of the most intricate objects in common use in the early 19th century. Using the principle of hierarchy, we can break it into components shown in Figure 1.2: the lock, stock, and barrel.

The barrel is the long metal tube through which the bullet is fired. The lock is the firing mechanism. And the stock is the wooden body that holds the parts together and provides a secure grip for the user. In turn, the lock contains the trigger, hammer, flint, frizzen, and pan. Each of these components could be hierarchically described in further detail.

Modularity teaches that each component should have a well-defined function and interface. A function of the stock is to mount the barrel and lock. Its interface consists of its length and the location of its mounting pins. In a modular rifle design, stocks from many different manufacturers can be used with a particular barrel as long as the stock and barrel are of the correct length and have the proper mounting mechanism. A function of the barrel is to impart spin to the bullet so that it travels more accurately. Modularity dictates that there should be no side effects: the design of the stock should not impede the function of the barrel.

Regularity teaches that interchangeable parts are a good idea. With regularity, a damaged barrel can be replaced by an identical part. The barrels can be efficiently built on an assembly line, instead of being painstakingly hand-crafted.

We will return to these principles of hierarchy, modularity, and regularity throughout the book.

Captain Meriwether Lewis of the Lewis and Clark Expedition was one of the early advocates of interchangeable parts for rifles. In 1806, he explained:

The guns of Drewyer and Sergt. Pryor were both out of order. The first was repared with a new lock, the old one having become unfit for use; the second had the cock screw broken which was replaced by a duplicate which had been prepared for the lock at Harpers Ferry where she was manufactured. But for the precaution taken in bringing on those extra locks, and parts of locks, in addition to the ingenuity of John Shields, most of our guns would at this moment be entirely unfit for use; but fortunately for us I have it in my power here to record that they are all in good order.

See Elliott Coues, ed., *The History of the Lewis and Clark Expedition...* (4 vols), New York: Harper, 1893; reprint, 3 vols, New York: Dover, 3:817.

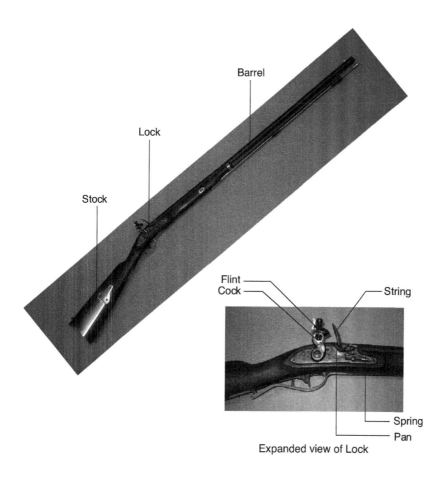

Expanded view of Lock

Figure 1.2 **Flintlock rifle with a close-up view of the lock**
(Image by Euroarms Italia. *www.euroarms.net* © 2006.)

1.3 THE DIGITAL ABSTRACTION

Most physical variables are continuous. For example, the voltage on a wire, the frequency of an oscillation, or the position of a mass are all continuous quantities. Digital systems, on the other hand, represent information with *discrete-valued variables*—that is, variables with a finite number of distinct values.

An early digital system using variables with ten discrete values was Charles Babbage's Analytical Engine. Babbage labored from 1834 to 1871, designing and attempting to build this mechanical computer. The Analytical Engine used gears with ten positions labeled 0 through 9, much like a mechanical odometer in a car. Figure 1.3 shows a prototype of the Analytical Engine, in which each row processes one digit. Babbage chose 25 rows of gears, so the machine has 25-digit precision.

Charles Babbage, 1791–1871. Attended Cambridge University and married Georgiana Whitmore in 1814. Invented the Analytical Engine, the world's first mechanical computer. Also invented the cowcatcher and the universal postage rate. Interested in lock-picking, but abhorred street musicians (image courtesy of Fourmilab Switzerland, *www.fourmilab.ch*).

Figure 1.3 Babbage's Analytical Engine, under construction at the time of his death in 1871 (image courtesy of Science Museum/Science and Society Picture Library)

George Boole, 1815–1864. Born to working-class parents and unable to afford a formal education, Boole taught himself mathematics and joined the faculty of Queen's College in Ireland. He wrote *An Investigation of the Laws of Thought* (1854), which introduced binary variables and the three fundamental logic operations: AND, OR, and NOT (image courtesy of the American Institute of Physics).

Unlike Babbage's machine, most electronic computers use a binary (two-valued) representation in which a high voltage indicates a '1' and a low voltage indicates a '0', because it is easier to distinguish between two voltages than ten.

The *amount of information D* in a discrete valued variable with N distinct states is measured in units of *bits* as

$$D = \log_2 N \text{ bits} \tag{1.1}$$

A binary variable conveys $\log_2 2 = 1$ bit of information. Indeed, the word bit is short for *binary digit*. Each of Babbage's gears carried $\log_2 10 = 3.322$ bits of information because it could be in one of $2^{3.322} = 10$ unique positions. A continuous signal theoretically contains an infinite amount of information because it can take on an infinite number of values. In practice, noise and measurement error limit the information to only 10 to 16 bits for most continuous signals. If the measurement must be made rapidly, the information content is lower (e.g., 8 bits).

This book focuses on digital circuits using binary variables: 1's and 0's. George Boole developed a system of logic operating on binary variables that is now known as *Boolean logic*. Each of Boole's variables could be TRUE or FALSE. Electronic computers commonly use a positive voltage to represent '1' and zero volts to represent '0'. In this book, we will use the terms '1', TRUE, and HIGH synonymously. Similarly, we will use '0', FALSE, and LOW interchangeably.

The beauty of the *digital abstraction* is that digital designers can focus on 1's and 0's, ignoring whether the Boolean variables are physically represented with specific voltages, rotating gears, or even hydraulic fluid levels. A computer programmer can work without needing to know the intimate details of the computer hardware. On the other hand, understanding the details of the hardware allows the programmer to optimize the software better for that specific computer.

An individual bit doesn't carry much information. In the next section, we examine how groups of bits can be used to represent numbers. In later chapters, we will also use groups of bits to represent letters and programs.

1.4 NUMBER SYSTEMS

You are accustomed to working with decimal numbers. In digital systems consisting of 1's and 0's, binary or hexadecimal numbers are often more convenient. This section introduces the various number systems that will be used throughout the rest of the book.

1.4.1 Decimal Numbers

In elementary school, you learned to count and do arithmetic in *decimal*. Just as you (probably) have ten fingers, there are ten decimal digits: 0, 1, 2, ..., 9. Decimal digits are joined together to form longer decimal numbers. Each column of a decimal number has ten times the weight of the previous column. From right to left, the column weights are 1, 10, 100, 1000, and so on. Decimal numbers are referred to as *base 10*. The base is indicated by a subscript after the number to prevent confusion when working in more than one base. For example, Figure 1.4 shows how the decimal number 9742_{10} is written as the sum of each of its digits multiplied by the weight of the corresponding column.

An N-digit decimal number represents one of 10^N possibilities: 0, 1, 2, 3, ..., $10^N - 1$. This is called the *range* of the number. For example, a three-digit decimal number represents one of 1000 possibilities in the range of 0 to 999.

1.4.2 Binary Numbers

Bits represent one of two values, 0 or 1, and are joined together to form *binary numbers*. Each column of a binary number has twice the weight of the previous column, so binary numbers are *base 2*. In binary, the

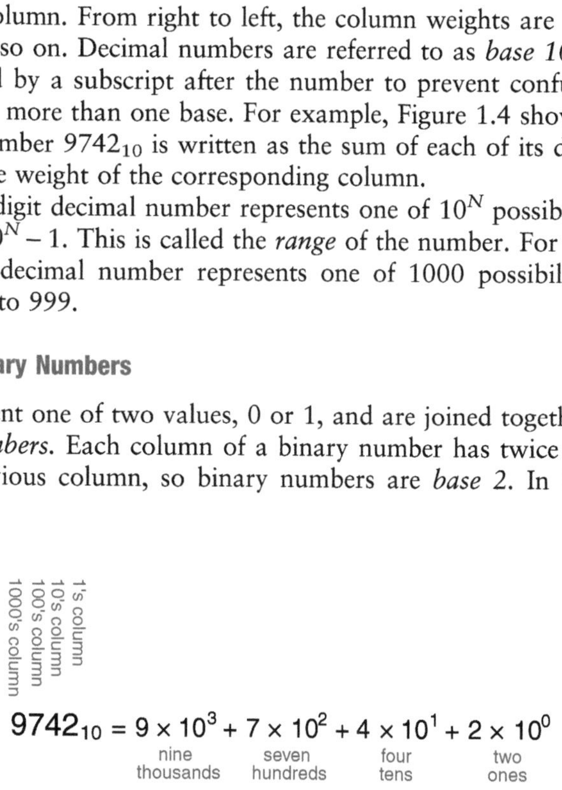

$$9742_{10} = 9 \times 10^3 + 7 \times 10^2 + 4 \times 10^1 + 2 \times 10^0$$

1's column
10's column
100's column
1000's column

nine thousands   seven hundreds   four tens   two ones

Figure 1.4 Representation of a decimal number

column weights (again from right to left) are 1, 2, 4, 8, 16, 32, 64, 128, 256, 512, 1024, 2048, 4096, 8192, 16384, 32768, 65536, and so on. If you work with binary numbers often, you'll save time if you remember these powers of two up to 2^{16}.

An N-bit binary number represents one of 2^N possibilities: 0, 1, 2, 3, ..., $2^N - 1$. Table 1.1 shows 1, 2, 3, and 4-bit binary numbers and their decimal equivalents.

Example 1.1 BINARY TO DECIMAL CONVERSION

Convert the binary number 10110_2 to decimal.

Solution: Figure 1.5 shows the conversion.

Table 1.1 **Binary numbers and their decimal equivalent**

1-Bit Binary Numbers	2-Bit Binary Numbers	3-Bit Binary Numbers	4-Bit Binary Numbers	Decimal Equivalents
0	00	000	0000	0
1	01	001	0001	1
	10	010	0010	2
	11	011	0011	3
		100	0100	4
		101	0101	5
		110	0110	6
		111	0111	7
			1000	8
			1001	9
			1010	10
			1011	11
			1100	12
			1101	13
			1110	14
			1111	15

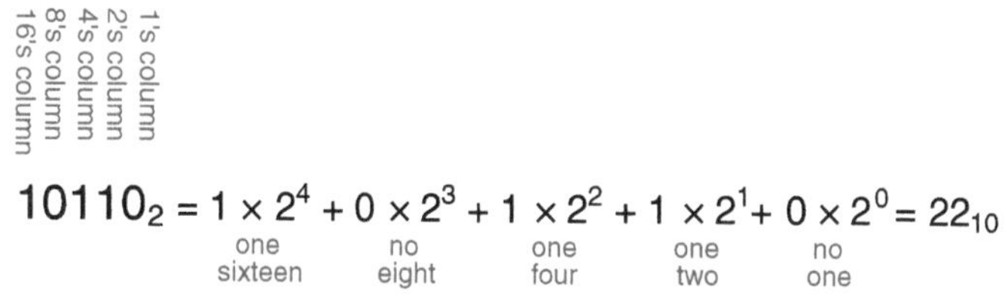

$$10110_2 = 1 \times 2^4 + 0 \times 2^3 + 1 \times 2^2 + 1 \times 2^1 + 0 \times 2^0 = 22_{10}$$

one   no   one   one   no
sixteen eight   four   two   one

Figure 1.5 **Conversion of a binary number to decimal**

Example 1.2 DECIMAL TO BINARY CONVERSION

Convert the decimal number 84_{10} to binary.

Solution: Determine whether each column of the binary result has a 1 or a 0. We can do this starting at either the left or the right column.

Working from the left, start with the largest power of 2 less than or equal to the number (in this case, 64). $84 \geq 64$, so there is a 1 in the 64's column, leaving $84 - 64 = 20$. $20 < 32$, so there is a 0 in the 32's column. $20 \geq 16$, so there is a 1 in the 16's column, leaving $20 - 16 = 4$. $4 < 8$, so there is a 0 in the 8's column. $4 \geq 4$, so there is a 1 in the 4's column, leaving $4 - 4 = 0$. Thus there must be 0's in the 2's and 1's column. Putting this all together, $84_{10} = 1010100_2$.

Working from the right, repeatedly divide the number by 2. The remainder goes in each column. $84/2 = 42$, so 0 goes in the 1's column. $42/2 = 21$, so 0 goes in the 2's column. $21/2 = 10$ with a remainder of 1 going in the 4's column. $10/2 = 5$, so 0 goes in the 8's column. $5/2 = 2$ with a remainder of 1 going in the 16's column. $2/2 = 1$, so 0 goes in the 32's column. Finally $1/2 = 0$ with a remainder of 1 going in the 64's column. Again, $84_{10} = 1010100_2$.

1.4.3 Hexadecimal Numbers

Writing long binary numbers becomes tedious and prone to error. A group of four bits represents one of $2^4 = 16$ possibilities. Hence, it is sometimes more convenient to work in *base 16*, called *hexadecimal*. Hexadecimal numbers use the digits 0 to 9 along with the letters A to F, as shown in Table 1.2. Columns in base 16 have weights of 1, 16, 16^2 (or 256), 16^3 (or 4096), and so on.

"Hexadecimal," a term coined by IBM in 1963, derives from the Greek *hexi* (six) and Latin *decem* (ten). A more proper term would use the Latin *sexa* (six), but *sexadecimal* sounded too risqué.

Example 1.3 HEXADECIMAL TO BINARY AND DECIMAL CONVERSION

Convert the hexadecimal number $2ED_{16}$ to binary and to decimal.

Solution: Conversion between hexadecimal and binary is easy because each hexadecimal digit directly corresponds to four binary digits. $2_{16} = 0010_2$, $E_{16} = 1110_2$ and $D_{16} = 1101_2$, so $2ED_{16} = 001011101101_2$. Conversion to decimal requires the arithmetic shown in Figure 1.6.

Table 1.2 Hexadecimal number system

Hexadecimal Digit	Decimal Equivalent	Binary Equivalent
0	0	0000
1	1	0001
2	2	0010
3	3	0011
4	4	0100
5	5	0101
6	6	0110
7	7	0111
8	8	1000
9	9	1001
A	10	1010
B	11	1011
C	12	1100
D	13	1101
E	14	1110
F	15	1111

Figure 1.6 Conversion of a hexadecimal number to decimal

$$2ED_{16} = 2 \times 16^2 + E \times 16^1 + D \times 16^0 = 749_{10}$$

256's column · 16's column · 1's column

two
two hundred
fifty six's

fourteen
sixteens

thirteen
ones

Example 1.4 BINARY TO HEXADECIMAL CONVERSION

Convert the binary number 1111010_2 to hexadecimal.

Solution: Again, conversion is easy. Start reading from the right. The four least significant bits are $1010_2 = A_{16}$. The next bits are $111_2 = 7_{16}$. Hence $1111010_2 = 7A_{16}$.

Example 1.5 DECIMAL TO HEXADECIMAL AND BINARY CONVERSION

Convert the decimal number 333_{10} to hexadecimal and binary.

Solution: Like decimal to binary conversion, decimal to hexadecimal conversion can be done from the left or the right.

Working from the left, start with the largest power of 16 less than or equal to the number (in this case, 256). 256 goes into 333 once, so there is a 1 in the 256's column, leaving $333 - 256 = 77$. 16 goes into 77 four times, so there is a 4 in the 16's column, leaving $77 - 16 \times 4 = 13$. $13_{10} = D_{16}$, so there is a D in the 1's column. In summary, $333_{10} = 14D_{16}$. Now it is easy to convert from hexadecimal to binary, as in Example 1.3. $14D_{16} = 101001101_2$.

Working from the right, repeatedly divide the number by 16. The remainder goes in each column. $333/16 = 20$ with a remainder of $13_{10} = D_{16}$ going in the 1's column. $20/16 = 1$ with a remainder of 4 going in the 16's column. $1/16 = 0$ with a remainder of 1 going in the 256's column. Again, the result is $14D_{16}$.

1.4.4 Bytes, Nibbles, and All That Jazz

A group of eight bits is called a *byte*. It represents one of $2^8 = 256$ possibilities. The size of objects stored in computer memories is customarily measured in bytes rather than bits.

A group of four bits, or half a byte, is called a *nibble*. It represents one of $2^4 = 16$ possibilities. One hexadecimal digit stores one nibble and two hexadecimal digits store one full byte. Nibbles are no longer a commonly used unit, but the term is cute.

Microprocessors handle data in chunks called *words*. The size of a word depends on the architecture of the microprocessor. When this chapter was written in 2015, most computers had 64-bit processors, indicating that they operate on 64-bit words. At the time, older computers handling 32-bit words were also widely available. Simpler microprocessors, especially those used in gadgets such as toasters, use 8- or 16-bit words.

Within a group of bits, the bit in the 1's column is called the *least significant bit* (*lsb*), and the bit at the other end is called the *most significant bit* (*msb*), as shown in Figure 1.7(a) for a 6-bit binary number. Similarly, within a word, the bytes are identified as *least significant byte* (*LSB*) through *most significant byte* (*MSB*), as shown in Figure 1.7(b) for a four-byte number written with eight hexadecimal digits.

A *microprocessor* is a processor built on a single chip. Until the 1970's, processors were too complicated to fit on one chip, so mainframe processors were built from boards containing many chips. Intel introduced the first 4-bit microprocessor, called the 4004, in 1971. Now, even the most sophisticated supercomputers are built using microprocessors. We will use the terms microprocessor and processor interchangeably throughout this book.

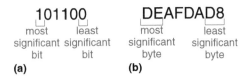

Figure 1.7 **Least and most significant bits and bytes**

By handy coincidence, $2^{10} = 1024 \approx 10^3$. Hence, the term *kilo* (Greek for thousand) indicates 2^{10}. For example, 2^{10} bytes is one kilobyte (1 KB). Similarly, *mega* (million) indicates $2^{20} \approx 10^6$, and *giga* (billion) indicates $2^{30} \approx 10^9$. If you know $2^{10} \approx 1$ thousand, $2^{20} \approx 1$ million, $2^{30} \approx 1$ billion, and remember the powers of two up to 2^9, it is easy to estimate any power of two in your head.

Example 1.6 ESTIMATING POWERS OF TWO

Find the approximate value of 2^{24} without using a calculator.

Solution: Split the exponent into a multiple of ten and the remainder.

$2^{24} = 2^{20} \times 2^4$. $2^{20} \approx 1$ million. $2^4 = 16$. So $2^{24} \approx 16$ million. Technically, $2^{24} = 16,777,216$, but 16 million is close enough for marketing purposes.

1024 bytes is called a *kilobyte* (KB). 1024 bits is called a *kilobit* (Kb or Kbit). Similarly, MB, Mb, GB, and Gb are used for millions and billions of bytes and bits. Memory capacity is usually measured in bytes. Communication speed is usually measured in bits/sec. For example, the maximum speed of a dial-up modem is usually 56 kbits/sec.

1.4.5 Binary Addition

Binary addition is much like decimal addition, but easier, as shown in Figure 1.8. As in decimal addition, if the sum of two numbers is greater than what fits in a single digit, we *carry* a 1 into the next column. Figure 1.8 compares addition of decimal and binary numbers. In the right-most column of Figure 1.8(a), $7 + 9 = 16$, which cannot fit in a single digit because it is greater than 9. So we record the 1's digit, 6, and carry the 10's digit, 1, over to the next column. Likewise, in binary, if the sum of two numbers is greater than 1, we carry the 2's digit over to the next column. For example, in the right-most column of Figure 1.8(b),

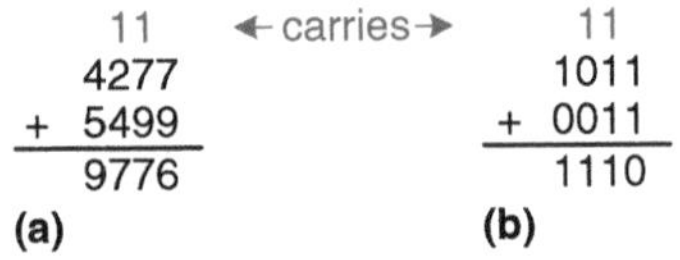

Figure 1.8 **Addition examples showing carries: (a) decimal (b) binary**

```
        11   ← carries →      11
      4277                  1011
   +  5499               +  0011
   ───────               ───────
      9776                  1110
      (a)                    (b)
```

the sum $1 + 1 = 2_{10} = 10_2$ cannot fit in a single binary digit. So we record the 1's digit (0) and carry the 2's digit (1) of the result to the next column. In the second column, the sum is $1 + 1 + 1 = 3_{10} = 11_2$. Again, we record the 1's digit (1) and carry the 2's digit (1) to the next column. For obvious reasons, the bit that is carried over to the neighboring column is called the *carry bit*.

Example 1.7 BINARY ADDITION

Compute $0111_2 + 0101_2$.

Solution: Figure 1.9 shows that the sum is 1100_2. The carries are indicated in blue. We can check our work by repeating the computation in decimal. $0111_2 = 7_{10}$. $0101_2 = 5_{10}$. The sum is $12_{10} = 1100_2$.

```
  111
  0111
+ 0101
------
  1100
```

Figure 1.9 Binary addition example

Digital systems usually operate on a fixed number of digits. Addition is said to *overflow* if the result is too big to fit in the available digits. A 4-bit number, for example, has the range [0, 15]. 4-bit binary addition overflows if the result exceeds 15. The fifth bit is discarded, producing an incorrect result in the remaining four bits. Overflow can be detected by checking for a carry out of the most significant column.

Example 1.8 ADDITION WITH OVERFLOW

Compute $1101_2 + 0101_2$. Does overflow occur?

Solution: Figure 1.10 shows the sum is 10010_2. This result overflows the range of a 4-bit binary number. If it must be stored as four bits, the most significant bit is discarded, leaving the incorrect result of 0010_2. If the computation had been done using numbers with five or more bits, the result 10010_2 would have been correct.

```
  11 1
   1101
+  0101
-------
  10010
```

Figure 1.10 Binary addition example with overflow

1.4.6 Signed Binary Numbers

So far, we have considered only *unsigned* binary numbers that represent positive quantities. We will often want to represent both positive and negative numbers, requiring a different binary number system. Several schemes exist to represent *signed* binary numbers; the two most widely employed are called sign/magnitude and two's complement.

Sign/Magnitude Numbers

Sign/magnitude numbers are intuitively appealing because they match our custom of writing negative numbers with a minus sign followed by the magnitude. An N-bit sign/magnitude number uses the most significant

The $7 billion Ariane 5 rocket, launched on June 4, 1996, veered off course 40 seconds after launch, broke up, and exploded. The failure was caused when the computer controlling the rocket overflowed its 16-bit range and crashed.

The code had been extensively tested on the Ariane 4 rocket. However, the Ariane 5 had a faster engine that produced larger values for the control computer, leading to the overflow.

(Photograph courtesy of ESA/CNES/ARIANESPACE-Service Optique CS6.)

bit as the sign and the remaining $N-1$ bits as the magnitude (absolute value). A sign bit of 0 indicates positive and a sign bit of 1 indicates negative.

Example 1.9 SIGN/MAGNITUDE NUMBERS

Write 5 and -5 as 4-bit sign/magnitude numbers

Solution: Both numbers have a magnitude of $5_{10} = 101_2$. Thus, $5_{10} = 0101_2$ and $-5_{10} = 1101_2$.

Unfortunately, ordinary binary addition does not work for sign/magnitude numbers. For example, using ordinary addition on $-5_{10} + 5_{10}$ gives $1101_2 + 0101_2 = 10010_2$, which is nonsense.

An N-bit sign/magnitude number spans the range $[-2^{N-1} + 1, 2^{N-1} - 1]$. Sign/magnitude numbers are slightly odd in that both $+0$ and -0 exist. Both indicate zero. As you may expect, it can be troublesome to have two different representations for the same number.

Two's Complement Numbers

Two's complement numbers are identical to unsigned binary numbers except that the most significant bit position has a weight of -2^{N-1} instead of 2^{N-1}. They overcome the shortcomings of sign/magnitude numbers: zero has a single representation, and ordinary addition works.

In two's complement representation, zero is written as all zeros: $00...000_2$. The most positive number has a 0 in the most significant position and 1's elsewhere: $01...111_2 = 2^{N-1} - 1$. The most negative number has a 1 in the most significant position and 0's elsewhere: $10...000_2 = -2^{N-1}$. And -1 is written as all ones: $11...111_2$.

Notice that positive numbers have a 0 in the most significant position and negative numbers have a 1 in this position, so the most significant bit can be viewed as the sign bit. However, the overall number is interpreted differently for two's complement numbers and sign/magnitude numbers.

The sign of a two's complement number is reversed in a process called *taking the two's complement*. The process consists of inverting all of the bits in the number, then adding 1 to the least significant bit position. This is useful to find the representation of a negative number or to determine the magnitude of a negative number.

Example 1.10 TWO'S COMPLEMENT REPRESENTATION
OF A NEGATIVE NUMBER

Find the representation of -2_{10} as a 4-bit two's complement number.

Solution: Start with $+2_{10} = 0010_2$. To get -2_{10}, invert the bits and add 1. Inverting 0010_2 produces 1101_2. $1101_2 + 1 = 1110_2$. So -2_{10} is 1110_2.

Example 1.11 VALUE OF NEGATIVE TWO'S COMPLEMENT NUMBERS

Find the decimal value of the two's complement number 1001_2.

Solution: 1001_2 has a leading 1, so it must be negative. To find its magnitude, invert the bits and add 1. Inverting $1001_2 = 0110_2$. $0110_2 + 1 = 0111_2 = 7_{10}$. Hence, $1001_2 = -7_{10}$.

Two's complement numbers have the compelling advantage that addition works properly for both positive and negative numbers. Recall that when adding N-bit numbers, the carry out of the Nth bit (i.e., the $N + 1^{\text{th}}$ result bit) is discarded.

Example 1.12 ADDING TWO'S COMPLEMENT NUMBERS

Compute (a) $-2_{10} + 1_{10}$ and (b) $-7_{10} + 7_{10}$ using two's complement numbers.

Solution: (a) $-2_{10} + 1_{10} = 1110_2 + 0001_2 = 1111_2 = -1_{10}$. (b) $-7_{10} + 7_{10} = 1001_2 + 0111_2 = 10000_2$. The fifth bit is discarded, leaving the correct 4-bit result 0000_2.

Subtraction is performed by taking the two's complement of the second number, then adding.

Example 1.13 SUBTRACTING TWO'S COMPLEMENT NUMBERS

Compute (a) $5_{10} - 3_{10}$ and (b) $3_{10} - 5_{10}$ using 4-bit two's complement numbers.

Solution: (a) $3_{10} = 0011_2$. Take its two's complement to obtain $-3_{10} = 1101_2$. Now add $5_{10} + (-3_{10}) = 0101_2 + 1101_2 = 0010_2 = 2_{10}$. Note that the carry out of the most significant position is discarded because the result is stored in four bits. (b) Take the two's complement of 5_{10} to obtain $-5_{10} = 1011$. Now add $3_{10} + (-5_{10}) = 0011_2 + 1011_2 = 1110_2 = -2_{10}$.

The two's complement of 0 is found by inverting all the bits (producing $11...111_2$) and adding 1, which produces all 0's, disregarding the carry out of the most significant bit position. Hence, zero is always represented with all 0's. Unlike the sign/magnitude system, the two's complement system has no separate -0. Zero is considered positive because its sign bit is 0.

Like unsigned numbers, N-bit two's complement numbers represent one of 2^N possible values. However the values are split between positive and negative numbers. For example, a 4-bit unsigned number represents 16 values: 0 to 15. A 4-bit two's complement number also represents 16 values: -8 to 7. In general, the range of an N-bit two's complement number spans $[-2^{N-1}, 2^{N-1} - 1]$. It should make sense that there is one more negative number than positive number because there is no -0. The most negative number $10...000_2 = -2^{N-1}$ is sometimes called the *weird number*. Its two's complement is found by inverting the bits (producing $01...111_2$) and adding 1, which produces $10...000_2$, the weird number, again. Hence, this negative number has no positive counterpart.

Adding two N-bit positive numbers or negative numbers may cause overflow if the result is greater than $2^{N-1} - 1$ or less than -2^{N-1}. Adding a positive number to a negative number never causes overflow. Unlike unsigned numbers, a carry out of the most significant column does not indicate overflow. Instead, overflow occurs if the two numbers being added have the same sign bit and the result has the opposite sign bit.

Example 1.14 ADDING TWO'S COMPLEMENT NUMBERS WITH OVERFLOW

Compute $4_{10} + 5_{10}$ using 4-bit two's complement numbers. Does the result overflow?

Solution: $4_{10} + 5_{10} = 0100_2 + 0101_2 = 1001_2 = -7_{10}$. The result overflows the range of 4-bit positive two's complement numbers, producing an incorrect negative result. If the computation had been done using five or more bits, the result $01001_2 = 9_{10}$ would have been correct.

When a two's complement number is extended to more bits, the sign bit must be copied into the most significant bit positions. This process is called *sign extension*. For example, the numbers 3 and -3 are written as 4-bit two's complement numbers 0011 and 1101, respectively. They are sign-extended to seven bits by copying the sign bit into the three new upper bits to form 0000011 and 1111101, respectively.

Comparison of Number Systems

The three most commonly used binary number systems are unsigned, two's complement, and sign/magnitude. Table 1.3 compares the range of N-bit numbers in each of these three systems. Two's complement numbers are convenient because they represent both positive and negative integers and because ordinary addition works for all numbers. Subtraction is performed by negating the second number (i.e., taking the two's

Table 1.3 Range of N-bit numbers

System	Range
Unsigned	$[0, 2^N - 1]$
Sign/Magnitude	$[-2^{N-1} + 1, 2^{N-1} - 1]$
Two's Complement	$[-2^{N-1}, 2^{N-1} - 1]$

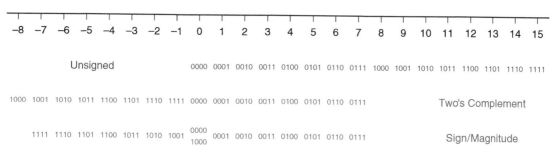

Figure 1.11 Number line and 4-bit binary encodings

complement), and then adding. Unless stated otherwise, assume that all signed binary numbers use two's complement representation.

Figure 1.11 shows a number line indicating the values of 4-bit numbers in each system. Unsigned numbers span the range [0, 15] in regular binary order. Two's complement numbers span the range [−8, 7]. The nonnegative numbers [0, 7] share the same encodings as unsigned numbers. The negative numbers [−8, −1] are encoded such that a larger unsigned binary value represents a number closer to 0. Notice that the weird number, 1000, represents −8 and has no positive counterpart. Sign/magnitude numbers span the range [−7, 7]. The most significant bit is the sign bit. The positive numbers [1, 7] share the same encodings as unsigned numbers. The negative numbers are symmetric but have the sign bit set. 0 is represented by both 0000 and 1000. Thus, N-bit sign/magnitude numbers represent only $2^N - 1$ integers because of the two representations for 0.

1.5 LOGIC GATES

Now that we know how to use binary variables to represent information, we explore digital systems that perform operations on these binary variables. *Logic gates* are simple digital circuits that take one or more binary inputs and produce a binary output. Logic gates are drawn with a symbol showing the input (or inputs) and the output. Inputs are usually drawn on the left (or top) and outputs on the right (or bottom). Digital designers typically use letters near the beginning of the alphabet for gate inputs and the letter Y for the gate output. The relationship between the inputs and the output can be described with a truth table or a Boolean equation. A *truth table* lists inputs on the left and the corresponding output on the right. It has one row for each possible combination of inputs. A *Boolean equation* is a mathematical expression using binary variables.

1.5.1 NOT Gate

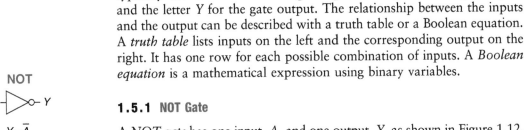

A *NOT gate* has one input, A, and one output, Y, as shown in Figure 1.12. The NOT gate's output is the inverse of its input. If A is FALSE, then Y is TRUE. If A is TRUE, then Y is FALSE. This relationship is summarized by the truth table and Boolean equation in the figure. The line over A in the Boolean equation is pronounced *NOT*, so $Y=\overline{A}$ is read "Y equals NOT A." The NOT gate is also called an *inverter*.

Other texts use a variety of notations for NOT, including $Y = A'$, $Y = \neg A$, $Y = !A$ or $Y = {\sim}A$. We will use $Y = \overline{A}$ exclusively, but don't be puzzled if you encounter another notation elsewhere.

1.5.2 Buffer

The other one-input logic gate is called a *buffer* and is shown in Figure 1.13. It simply copies the input to the output.

From the logical point of view, a buffer is no different from a wire, so it might seem useless. However, from the analog point of view, the buffer might have desirable characteristics such as the ability to deliver large amounts of current to a motor or the ability to quickly send its output to many gates. This is an example of why we need to consider multiple levels of abstraction to fully understand a system; the digital abstraction hides the real purpose of a buffer.

The triangle symbol indicates a buffer. A circle on the output is called a *bubble* and indicates inversion, as was seen in the NOT gate symbol of Figure 1.12.

1.5.3 AND Gate

Two-input logic gates are more interesting. The *AND gate* shown in Figure 1.14 produces a TRUE output, Y, if and only if both A *and* B are TRUE. Otherwise, the output is FALSE. By convention, the inputs are listed in the order 00, 01, 10, 11, as if you were counting in binary. The Boolean equation for an AND gate can be written in several ways: $Y = A \bullet B$, $Y = AB$, or $Y = A \cap B$. The $\cap$ symbol is pronounced "intersection" and is preferred by logicians. We prefer $Y = AB$, read "Y equals A and B," because we are lazy.

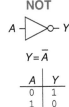

Figure 1.12 NOT gate

NOT

$$Y = \overline{A}$$

A	Y
0	1
1	0

BUF

$$Y = A$$

A	Y
0	0
1	1

Figure 1.13 Buffer

AND

$$Y = AB$$

A	B	Y
0	0	0
0	1	0
1	0	0
1	1	1

Figure 1.14 AND gate

According to Larry Wall, inventor of the Perl programming language, "the three principal virtues of a programmer are Laziness, Impatience, and Hubris."

1.5.4 OR Gate

The *OR gate* shown in Figure 1.15 produces a TRUE output, Y, if either
A or B (or both) are TRUE. The Boolean equation for an OR gate is written as $Y = A + B$ or $Y = A \cup B$. The $\cup$ symbol is pronounced union and
is preferred by logicians. Digital designers normally use the $+$ notation,
$Y = A + B$ is pronounced "Y equals A or B."

1.5.5 Other Two-Input Gates

Figure 1.16 shows other common two-input logic gates. *XOR* (exclusive
OR, pronounced "ex-OR") is TRUE if A or B, but not both, are TRUE.
The XOR operation is indicated by $\oplus$, a plus sign with a circle around
it. Any gate can be followed by a bubble to invert its operation. The
NAND gate performs NOT AND. Its output is TRUE unless both inputs
are TRUE. The *NOR gate* performs NOT OR. Its output is TRUE if
neither A nor B is TRUE. An N-input XOR gate is sometimes called a
parity gate and produces a TRUE output if an odd number of inputs
are TRUE. As with two-input gates, the input combinations in the truth
table are listed in counting order.

OR

$$Y = A + B$$

A	B	Y
0	0	0
0	1	1
1	0	1
1	1	1

Figure 1.15 OR gate

A silly way to remember the
OR symbol is that its input
side is curved like Pacman's
mouth, so the gate is hungry
and willing to eat any TRUE
inputs it can find!

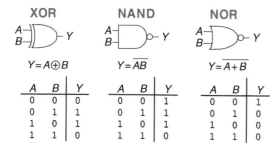

XOR				NAND				NOR		
$Y = A \oplus B$				$Y = \overline{AB}$				$Y = \overline{A + B}$		
A	B	Y		A	B	Y		A	B	Y
0	0	0		0	0	1		0	0	1
0	1	1		0	1	1		0	1	0
1	0	1		1	0	1		1	0	0
1	1	0		1	1	0		1	1	0

Figure 1.16 More two-input logic gates

Example 1.15 XNOR GATE

Figure 1.17 shows the symbol and Boolean equation for a two-input *XNOR gate*
that performs the inverse of an XOR. Complete the truth table.

Solution: Figure 1.18 shows the truth table. The XNOR output is TRUE if both
inputs are FALSE or both inputs are TRUE. The two-input XNOR gate is sometimes
called an *equality* gate because its output is TRUE when the inputs are equal.

1.5.6 Multiple-Input Gates

Many Boolean functions of three or more inputs exist. The most common
are AND, OR, XOR, NAND, NOR, and XNOR. An N-input AND gate

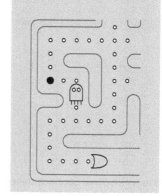

XNOR

$$Y = \overline{A \oplus B}$$

A	B	Y
0	0	
0	1	
1	0	
1	1	

Figure 1.17 XNOR gate

A	B	Y
0	0	1
0	1	0
1	0	0
1	1	1

Figure 1.18 **XNOR truth table**

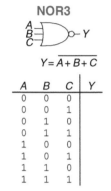

$$Y = \overline{A + B + C}$$

A	B	C	Y
0	0	0	
0	0	1	
0	1	0	
0	1	1	
1	0	0	
1	0	1	
1	1	0	
1	1	1	

Figure 1.19 **Three-input NOR gate**

A	B	C	Y
0	0	0	1
0	0	1	0
0	1	0	0
0	1	1	0
1	0	0	0
1	0	1	0
1	1	0	0
1	1	1	0

Figure 1.20 **Three-input NOR truth table**

$$Y = ABCD$$

Figure 1.21 **Four-input AND gate**

produces a TRUE output when all *N* inputs are TRUE. An *N*-input OR gate produces a TRUE output when at least one input is TRUE.

Example 1.16 THREE-INPUT NOR GATE

Figure 1.19 shows the symbol and Boolean equation for a three-input NOR gate. Complete the truth table.

Solution: Figure 1.20 shows the truth table. The output is TRUE only if none of the inputs are TRUE.

Example 1.17 FOUR-INPUT AND GATE

Figure 1.21 shows the symbol and Boolean equation for a four-input AND gate. Create a truth table.

Solution: Figure 1.22 shows the truth table. The output is TRUE only if all of the inputs are TRUE.

1.6 BENEATH THE DIGITAL ABSTRACTION

A digital system uses discrete-valued variables. However, the variables are represented by continuous physical quantities such as the voltage on a wire, the position of a gear, or the level of fluid in a cylinder. Hence, the designer must choose a way to relate the continuous value to the discrete value.

For example, consider representing a binary signal *A* with a voltage on a wire. Let 0 volts (V) indicate *A* = 0 and 5 V indicate *A* = 1. Any real system must tolerate some noise, so 4.97 V probably ought to be interpreted as *A* = 1 as well. But what about 4.3 V? Or 2.8 V? Or 2.500000 V?

1.6.1 Supply Voltage

Suppose the lowest voltage in the system is 0 V, also called *ground* or GND. The highest voltage in the system comes from the power supply and is usually called V_{DD}. In 1970's and 1980's technology, V_{DD} was generally 5 V. As chips have progressed to smaller transistors, V_{DD} has dropped to 3.3 V, 2.5 V, 1.8 V, 1.5 V, 1.2 V, or even lower to save power and avoid overloading the transistors.

1.6.2 Logic Levels

The mapping of a continuous variable onto a discrete binary variable is done by defining *logic levels*, as shown in Figure 1.23. The first gate is called the *driver* and the second gate is called the *receiver*. The output of the driver is connected to the input of the receiver. The driver produces a LOW (0) output in the range of 0 to V_{OL} or a HIGH (1) output in the range of V_{OH} to V_{DD}. If the receiver gets an input in the range of 0 to V_{IL}, it will consider the input to be LOW. If the receiver gets an input in the range of V_{IH} to V_{DD}, it will consider the input to be HIGH. If, for some reason such as noise or faulty components, the receiver's input should fall in the *forbidden zone* between V_{IL} and V_{IH}, the behavior of the gate is unpredictable. V_{OH}, V_{OL}, V_{IH}, and V_{IL} are called the output and input high and low logic levels.

1.6.3 Noise Margins

If the output of the driver is to be correctly interpreted at the input of the receiver, we must choose $V_{OL} < V_{IL}$ and $V_{OH} > V_{IH}$. Thus, even if the output of the driver is contaminated by some noise, the input of the receiver will still detect the correct logic level. The *noise margin* is the amount of noise that could be added to a worst-case output such that the signal can still be interpreted as a valid input. As can be seen in Figure 1.23, the low and high noise margins are, respectively

$$NM_L = V_{IL} - V_{OL} \tag{1.2}$$

$$NM_H = V_{OH} - V_{IH} \tag{1.3}$$

A	B	C	D	Y
0	0	0	0	0
0	0	0	1	0
0	0	1	0	0
0	0	1	1	0
0	1	0	0	0
0	1	0	1	0
0	1	1	0	0
0	1	1	1	0
1	0	0	0	0
1	0	0	1	0
1	0	1	0	0
1	0	1	1	0
1	1	0	0	0
1	1	0	1	0
1	1	1	0	0
1	1	1	1	1

Figure 1.22 **Four-input AND truth table**

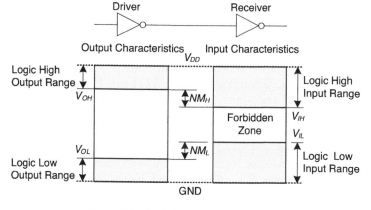

Figure 1.23 **Logic levels and noise margins**

Example 1.18 CALCULATING NOISE MARGINS

Consider the inverter circuit of Figure 1.24. V_{O1} is the output voltage of inverter I1, and V_{I2} is the input voltage of inverter I2. Both inverters have the following characteristics: $V_{DD} = 5$ V, $V_{IL} = 1.35$ V, $V_{IH} = 3.15$ V, $V_{OL} = 0.33$ V, and $V_{OH} = 3.84$ V. What are the inverter low and high noise margins? Can the circuit tolerate 1 V of noise between V_{O1} and V_{I2}?

V_{DD} stands for the voltage on the *drain* of a metal-oxide-semiconductor transistor, used to build most modern chips. The power supply voltage is also sometimes called V_{CC}, standing for the voltage on the *collector* of a bipolar junction transistor used to build chips in an older technology. Ground is sometimes called V_{SS} because it is the voltage on the *source* of a metal-oxide-semiconductor transistor. See Section 1.7 for more information on transistors.

Figure 1.24 Inverter circuit

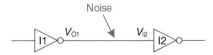

Solution: The inverter noise margins are: $NM_L = V_{IL} - V_{OL} = (1.35 \text{ V} - 0.33 \text{ V}) = 1.02 \text{ V}$, $NM_H = V_{OH} - V_{IH} = (3.84 \text{ V} - 3.15 \text{ V}) = 0.69 \text{ V}$. The circuit can tolerate 1 V of noise when the output is LOW ($NM_L = 1.02$ V) but not when the output is HIGH ($NM_H = 0.69$ V). For example, suppose the driver, I1, outputs its worst-case HIGH value, $V_{O1} = V_{OH} = 3.84$ V. If noise causes the voltage to droop by 1 V before reaching the input of the receiver, $V_{I2} = (3.84 \text{ V} - 1 \text{ V}) = 2.84 \text{ V}$. This is less than the acceptable input HIGH value, $V_{IH} = 3.15$ V, so the receiver may not sense a proper HIGH input.

DC indicates behavior when an input voltage is held constant or changes slowly enough for the rest of the system to keep up. The term's historical root comes from direct current, a method of transmitting power across a line with a constant voltage. In contrast, the transient response of a circuit is the behavior when an input voltage changes rapidly. Section 2.9 explores transient response further.

1.6.4 DC Transfer Characteristics

To understand the limits of the digital abstraction, we must delve into the analog behavior of a gate. The DC *transfer characteristics* of a gate describe the output voltage as a function of the input voltage when the input is changed slowly enough that the output can keep up. They are called transfer characteristics because they describe the relationship between input and output voltages.

An ideal inverter would have an abrupt switching threshold at $V_{DD}/2$, as shown in Figure 1.25(a). For $V(A) < V_{DD}/2$, $V(Y) = V_{DD}$. For $V(A) > V_{DD}/2$, $V(Y) = 0$. In such a case, $V_{IH} = V_{IL} = V_{DD}/2$. $V_{OH} = V_{DD}$ and $V_{OL} = 0$.

A real inverter changes more gradually between the extremes, as shown in Figure 1.25(b). When the input voltage $V(A)$ is 0, the output voltage $V(Y) = V_{DD}$. When $V(A) = V_{DD}$, $V(Y) = 0$. However, the transition between these endpoints is smooth and may not be centered at exactly $V_{DD}/2$. This raises the question of how to define the logic levels.

A reasonable place to choose the logic levels is where the slope of the transfer characteristic $dV(Y)/dV(A)$ is -1. These two points are called the *unity gain points*. Choosing logic levels at the unity gain points usually maximizes the noise margins. If V_{IL} were reduced, V_{OH} would only increase by a small amount. But if V_{IL} were increased, V_{OH} would drop precipitously.

1.6.5 The Static Discipline

To avoid inputs falling into the forbidden zone, digital logic gates are designed to conform to the *static discipline*. The static discipline requires that, given logically valid inputs, every circuit element will produce logically valid outputs.

By conforming to the static discipline, digital designers sacrifice the freedom of using arbitrary analog circuit elements in return for the simplicity and robustness of digital circuits. They raise the level of abstraction

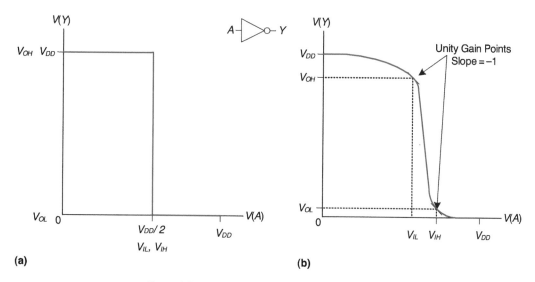

Figure 1.25 **DC transfer characteristics and logic levels**

from analog to digital, increasing design productivity by hiding needless detail.

The choice of V_{DD} and logic levels is arbitrary, but all gates that communicate must have compatible logic levels. Therefore, gates are grouped into *logic families* such that all gates in a logic family obey the static discipline when used with other gates in the family. Logic gates in the same logic family snap together like Legos in that they use consistent power supply voltages and logic levels.

Four major logic families that predominated from the 1970's through the 1990's are Transistor-Transistor Logic (TTL), Complementary Metal-Oxide-Semiconductor Logic (CMOS, pronounced sea-moss), Low Voltage TTL Logic (LVTTL), and Low Voltage CMOS Logic (LVCMOS). Their logic levels are compared in Table 1.4. Since then, logic families have balkanized with a proliferation of even lower power supply voltages. Appendix A.6 revisits popular logic families in more detail.

Table 1.4 **Logic levels of 5 V and 3.3 V logic families**

Logic Family	V_{DD}	V_{IL}	V_{IH}	V_{OL}	V_{OH}
TTL	5 (4.75–5.25)	0.8	2.0	0.4	2.4
CMOS	5 (4.5–6)	1.35	3.15	0.33	3.84
LVTTL	3.3 (3–3.6)	0.8	2.0	0.4	2.4
LVCMOS	3.3 (3–3.6)	0.9	1.8	0.36	2.7

Table 1.5 Compatibility of logic families

		Receiver			
		TTL	CMOS	LVTTL	LVCMOS
Driver	TTL	OK	NO: $V_{OH} < V_{IH}$	MAYBE[a]	MAYBE[a]
	CMOS	OK	OK	MAYBE[a]	MAYBE[a]
	LVTTL	OK	NO: $V_{OH} < V_{IH}$	OK	OK
	LVCMOS	OK	NO: $V_{OH} < V_{IH}$	OK	OK

[a] As long as a 5 V HIGH level does not damage the receiver input.

Example 1.19 LOGIC FAMILY COMPATIBILITY

Which of the logic families in Table 1.4 can communicate with each other reliably?

Solution: Table 1.5 lists which logic families have compatible logic levels. Note that a 5 V logic family such as TTL or CMOS may produce an output voltage as HIGH as 5 V. If this 5 V signal drives the input of a 3.3 V logic family such as LVTTL or LVCMOS, it can damage the receiver, unless the receiver is specially designed to be "5-volt compatible."

1.7 CMOS TRANSISTORS*

This section and other sections marked with a * are optional and are not necessary to understand the main flow of the book.

Babbage's Analytical Engine was built from gears, and early electrical computers used relays or vacuum tubes. Modern computers use transistors because they are cheap, small, and reliable. *Transistors* are electrically controlled switches that turn ON or OFF when a voltage or current is applied to a control terminal. The two main types of transistors are *bipolar junction transistors* and *metal-oxide-semiconductor field effect transistors* (*MOSFETs* or *MOS transistors*, pronounced "moss-fets" or "M-O-S", respectively).

In 1958, Jack Kilby at Texas Instruments built the first integrated circuit containing two transistors. In 1959, Robert Noyce at Fairchild Semiconductor patented a method of interconnecting multiple transistors on a single silicon chip. At the time, transistors cost about $10 each.

Thanks to more than four decades of unprecedented manufacturing advances, engineers can now pack roughly three billion MOSFETs onto a 1 cm^2 chip of silicon, and these transistors cost less than 1 microcent apiece. The capacity and cost continue to improve by an order of magnitude every 8 years or so. MOSFETs are now the building blocks of almost all digital

Robert Noyce, 1927–1990. Born in Burlington, Iowa. Received a B. A. in physics from Grinnell College and a Ph.D. in physics from MIT. Nicknamed "Mayor of Silicon Valley" for his profound influence on the industry.

Cofounded Fairchild Semiconductor in 1957 and Intel in 1968. Coinvented the integrated circuit. Many engineers from his teams went on to found other seminal semiconductor companies (photograph © 2006, Intel Corporation. Reproduced by permission).

systems. In this section, we will peer beneath the digital abstraction to see
how logic gates are built from MOSFETs.

1.7.1 Semiconductors

MOS transistors are built from silicon, the predominant atom in rock and
sand. Silicon (Si) is a group IV atom, so it has four electrons in its valence
shell and forms bonds with four adjacent atoms, resulting in a crystalline
lattice. Figure 1.26(a) shows the lattice in two dimensions for ease of
drawing, but remember that the lattice actually forms a cubic crystal. In
the figure, a line represents a covalent bond. By itself, silicon is a poor
conductor because all the electrons are tied up in covalent bonds. However, it becomes a better conductor when small amounts of impurities,
called *dopant* atoms, are carefully added. If a group V dopant such as
arsenic (As) is added, the dopant atoms have an extra electron that is
not involved in the bonds. The electron can easily move about the lattice,
leaving an ionized dopant atom (As^+) behind, as shown in Figure 1.26(b).
The electron carries a negative charge, so we call arsenic an *n-type* dopant.
On the other hand, if a group III dopant such as boron (B) is added, the
dopant atoms are missing an electron, as shown in Figure 1.26(c). This
missing electron is called a *hole*. An electron from a neighboring silicon
atom may move over to fill the missing bond, forming an ionized dopant
atom (B^-) and leaving a hole at the neighboring silicon atom. In a similar
fashion, the hole can migrate around the lattice. The hole is a lack of negative charge, so it acts like a positively charged particle. Hence, we call
boron a *p-type* dopant. Because the conductivity of silicon changes over
many orders of magnitude depending on the concentration of dopants, silicon is called a *semiconductor*.

1.7.2 Diodes

The junction between p-type and n-type silicon is called a *diode*. The
p-type region is called the *anode* and the n-type region is called the *cathode*, as illustrated in Figure 1.27. When the voltage on the anode rises
above the voltage on the cathode, the diode is *forward biased*, and current

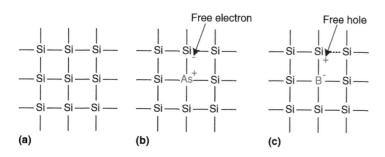

Figure 1.26 Silicon lattice and dopant atoms

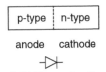

anode   cathode

Figure 1.27 The p-n junction diode structure and symbol

$\dashv\vdash C$

Figure 1.28 Capacitor symbol

Technicians in an Intel clean room wear Gore-Tex bunny suits to prevent particulates from their hair, skin, and clothing from contaminating the microscopic transistors on silicon wafers (photograph © 2006, Intel Corporation. Reproduced by permission).

A 40-pin dual-inline package (DIP) contains a small chip (scarcely visible) in the center that is connected to 40 metal pins, 20 on a side, by gold wires thinner than a strand of hair (photograph by Kevin Mapp. © 2006 Harvey Mudd College).

flows through the diode from the anode to the cathode. But when the anode voltage is lower than the voltage on the cathode, the diode is *reverse biased*, and no current flows. The diode symbol intuitively shows that current only flows in one direction.

1.7.3 Capacitors

A *capacitor* consists of two conductors separated by an insulator. When a voltage V is applied to one of the conductors, the conductor accumulates electric *charge* Q and the other conductor accumulates the opposite charge $-Q$. The *capacitance* C of the capacitor is the ratio of charge to voltage: $C = Q/V$. The capacitance is proportional to the size of the conductors and inversely proportional to the distance between them. The symbol for a capacitor is shown in Figure 1.28.

Capacitance is important because charging or discharging a conductor takes time and energy. More capacitance means that a circuit will be slower and require more energy to operate. Speed and energy will be discussed throughout this book.

1.7.4 nMOS and pMOS Transistors

A MOSFET is a sandwich of several layers of conducting and insulating materials. MOSFETs are built on thin flat *wafers* of silicon of about 15 to 30 cm in diameter. The manufacturing process begins with a bare wafer. The process involves a sequence of steps in which dopants are implanted into the silicon, thin films of silicon dioxide and silicon are grown, and metal is deposited. Between each step, the wafer is *patterned* so that the materials appear only where they are desired. Because transistors are a fraction of a micron[1] in length and the entire wafer is processed at once, it is inexpensive to manufacture billions of transistors at a time. Once processing is complete, the wafer is cut into rectangles called *chips* or *dice* that contain thousands, millions, or even billions of transistors. The chip is tested, then placed in a plastic or ceramic *package* with metal pins to connect it to a circuit board.

The MOSFET sandwich consists of a conducting layer called the *gate* on top of an insulating layer of *silicon dioxide* (SiO_2) on top of the silicon wafer, called the *substrate*. Historically, the gate was constructed from metal, hence the name metal-oxide-semiconductor. Modern manufacturing processes use polycrystalline silicon for the gate because it does not melt during subsequent high-temperature processing steps. Silicon dioxide is better known as glass and is often simply called *oxide* in the semiconductor industry. The metal-oxide-semiconductor sandwich forms a capacitor, in which a thin layer of insulating oxide called a *dielectric* separates the metal and semiconductor plates.

[1] $1\ \mu m = 1\ micron = 10^{-6}\ m$.

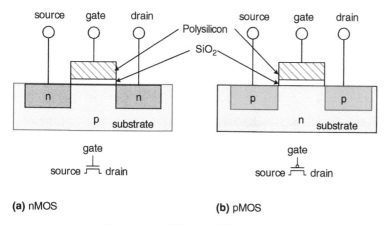

Figure 1.29 nMOS and pMOS transistors

There are two flavors of MOSFETs: nMOS and pMOS (pronounced "n-moss" and "p-moss"). Figure 1.29 shows cross-sections of each type, made by sawing through a wafer and looking at it from the side. The n-type transistors, called *nMOS*, have regions of n-type dopants adjacent to the gate called the *source* and the *drain* and are built on a p-type semiconductor substrate. The *pMOS* transistors are just the opposite, consisting of p-type source and drain regions in an n-type *substrate.*

A MOSFET behaves as a voltage-controlled switch in which the gate voltage creates an electric field that turns ON or OFF a connection between the source and drain. The term *field effect transistor* comes from this principle of operation. Let us start by exploring the operation of an nMOS transistor.

The substrate of an nMOS transistor is normally tied to GND, the lowest voltage in the system. First, consider the situation when the gate is also at 0 V, as shown in Figure 1.30(a). The diodes between the source or drain and the substrate are reverse biased because the source or drain voltage is nonnegative. Hence, there is no path for current to flow between the source and drain, so the transistor is OFF. Now, consider when the gate is raised to V_{DD}, as shown in Figure 1.30(b). When a positive voltage is applied to the top plate of a capacitor, it establishes an electric field that attracts positive charge on the top plate and negative charge to the bottom plate. If the voltage is sufficiently large, so much negative charge is attracted to the underside of the gate that the region *inverts* from p-type to effectively become n-type. This inverted region is called the *channel*. Now the transistor has a continuous path from the n-type source through the n-type channel to the n-type drain, so electrons can flow from source to drain. The transistor is ON. The gate voltage required to turn on a transistor is called the *threshold voltage,* V_t, and is typically 0.3 to 0.7 V.

The source and drain terminals are physically symmetric. However, we say that charge flows from the source to the drain. In an nMOS transistor, the charge is carried by electrons, which flow from negative voltage to positive voltage. In a pMOS transistor, the charge is carried by holes, which flow from positive voltage to negative voltage. If we draw schematics with the most positive voltage at the top and the most negative at the bottom, the source of (negative) charges in an nMOS transistor is the bottom terminal and the source of (positive) charges in a pMOS transistor is the top terminal.

A technician holds a 12-inch wafer containing hundreds of microprocessor chips (photograph © 2006, Intel Corporation. Reproduced by permission).

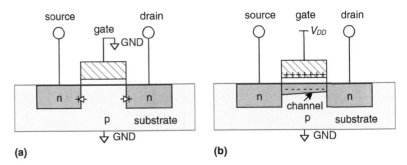

Figure 1.30 nMOS transistor operation

pMOS transistors work in just the opposite fashion, as might be guessed from the bubble on their symbol shown in Figure 1.31. The substrate is tied to V_{DD}. When the gate is also at V_{DD}, the pMOS transistor is OFF. When the gate is at GND, the channel inverts to p-type and the pMOS transistor is ON.

Unfortunately, MOSFETs are not perfect switches. In particular, nMOS transistors pass 0's well but pass 1's poorly. Specifically, when the gate of an nMOS transistor is at V_{DD}, the drain will only swing between 0 and $V_{DD} - V_t$. Similarly, pMOS transistors pass 1's well but 0's poorly. However, we will see that it is possible to build logic gates that use transistors only in their good mode.

nMOS transistors need a p-type substrate, and pMOS transistors need an n-type substrate. To build both flavors of transistors on the same chip, manufacturing processes typically start with a p-type wafer, then implant n-type regions called *wells* where the pMOS transistors should go. These processes that provide both flavors of transistors are called Complementary MOS or CMOS. CMOS processes are used to build the vast majority of all transistors fabricated today.

In summary, CMOS processes give us two types of electrically controlled switches, as shown in Figure 1.31. The voltage at the gate (g) regulates the flow of current between the source (s) and drain (d). nMOS

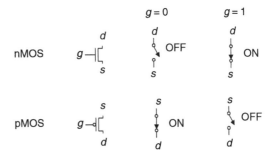

Figure 1.31 Switch models of MOSFETs

transistors are OFF when the gate is 0 and ON when the gate is 1. pMOS transistors are just the opposite: ON when the gate is 0 and OFF when the gate is 1.

1.7.5 CMOS NOT Gate

Figure 1.32 shows a schematic of a NOT gate built with CMOS transistors. The triangle indicates GND, and the flat bar indicates V_{DD}; these labels will be omitted from future schematics. The nMOS transistor, N1, is connected between GND and the Y output. The pMOS transistor, P1, is connected between V_{DD} and the Y output. Both transistor gates are controlled by the input, A.

If $A = 0$, N1 is OFF and P1 is ON. Hence, Y is connected to V_{DD} but not to GND, and is pulled up to a logic 1. P1 passes a good 1. If $A = 1$, N1 is ON and P1 is OFF, and Y is pulled down to a logic 0. N1 passes a good 0. Checking against the truth table in Figure 1.12, we see that the circuit is indeed a NOT gate.

1.7.6 Other CMOS Logic Gates

Figure 1.33 shows a schematic of a two-input NAND gate. In schematic diagrams, wires are always joined at three-way junctions. They are joined at four-way junctions only if a dot is shown. The nMOS transistors N1 and N2 are connected in series; both nMOS transistors must be ON to pull the output down to GND. The pMOS transistors P1 and P2 are in parallel; only one pMOS transistor must be ON to pull the output up to V_{DD}. Table 1.6 lists the operation of the pull-down and pull-up networks and the state of the output, demonstrating that the gate does function as a NAND. For example, when $A = 1$ and $B = 0$, N1 is ON, but N2 is OFF, blocking the path from Y to GND. P1 is OFF, but P2 is ON, creating a path from V_{DD} to Y. Therefore, Y is pulled up to 1.

Figure 1.34 shows the general form used to construct any inverting logic gate, such as NOT, NAND, or NOR. nMOS transistors are good at passing 0's, so a pull-down network of nMOS transistors is placed between the output and GND to pull the output down to 0. pMOS transistors are

Figure 1.32 NOT gate schematic

Figure 1.33 Two-input NAND gate schematic

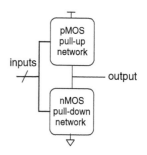

Figure 1.34 General form of an inverting logic gate

Table 1.6 NAND gate operation

A	B	Pull-Down Network	Pull-Up Network	Y
0	0	OFF	ON	1
0	1	OFF	ON	1
1	0	OFF	ON	1
1	1	ON	OFF	0

Experienced designers claim that electronic devices operate because they contain *magic smoke*. They confirm this theory with the observation that if the magic smoke is ever let out of the device, it ceases to work.

good at passing 1's, so a pull-up network of pMOS transistors is placed between the output and V_{DD} to pull the output up to 1. The networks may consist of transistors in series or in parallel. When transistors are in parallel, the network is ON if either transistor is ON. When transistors are in series, the network is ON only if both transistors are ON. The slash across the input wire indicates that the gate may receive multiple inputs.

If both the pull-up and pull-down networks were ON simultaneously, a *short circuit* would exist between V_{DD} and GND. The output of the gate might be in the forbidden zone and the transistors would consume large amounts of power, possibly enough to burn out. On the other hand, if both the pull-up and pull-down networks were OFF simultaneously, the output would be connected to neither V_{DD} nor GND. We say that the output *floats*. Its value is again undefined. Floating outputs are usually undesirable, but in Section 2.6 we will see how they can occasionally be used to the designer's advantage.

In a properly functioning logic gate, one of the networks should be ON and the other OFF at any given time, so that the output is pulled HIGH or LOW but not shorted or floating. We can guarantee this by using the rule of *conduction complements*. When nMOS transistors are in series, the pMOS transistors must be in parallel. When nMOS transistors are in parallel, the pMOS transistors must be in series.

Example 1.20 THREE-INPUT NAND SCHEMATIC

Draw a schematic for a three-input NAND gate using CMOS transistors.

Solution: The NAND gate should produce a 0 output only when all three inputs are 1. Hence, the pull-down network should have three nMOS transistors in series. By the conduction complements rule, the pMOS transistors must be in parallel. Such a gate is shown in Figure 1.35; you can verify the function by checking that it has the correct truth table.

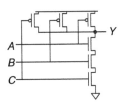

Figure 1.35 Three-input NAND gate schematic

Example 1.21 TWO-INPUT NOR SCHEMATIC

Draw a schematic for a two-input NOR gate using CMOS transistors.

Solution: The NOR gate should produce a 0 output if either input is 1. Hence, the pull-down network should have two nMOS transistors in parallel. By the conduction complements rule, the pMOS transistors must be in series. Such a gate is shown in Figure 1.36.

Figure 1.36 Two-input NOR gate schematic

Example 1.22 TWO-INPUT AND SCHEMATIC

Draw a schematic for a two-input AND gate.

Solution: It is impossible to build an AND gate with a single CMOS gate. However, building NAND and NOT gates is easy. Thus, the best way to build an AND gate using CMOS transistors is to use a NAND followed by a NOT, as shown in Figure 1.37.

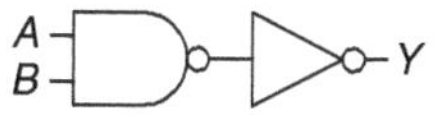

Figure 1.37 **Two-input AND gate schematic**

1.7.7 Transmission Gates

At times, designers find it convenient to use an ideal switch that can pass both 0 and 1 well. Recall that nMOS transistors are good at passing 0 and pMOS transistors are good at passing 1, so the parallel combination of the two passes both values well. Figure 1.38 shows such a circuit, called a *transmission gate* or *pass gate*. The two sides of the switch are called *A* and *B* because a switch is bidirectional and has no preferred input or output side. The control signals are called *enables*, *EN* and $\overline{EN}$. When $EN = 0$ and $\overline{EN} = 1$, both transistors are OFF. Hence, the transmission gate is OFF or disabled, so *A* and *B* are not connected. When $EN = 1$ and $\overline{EN} = 0$, the transmission gate is ON or enabled, and any logic value can flow between *A* and *B*.

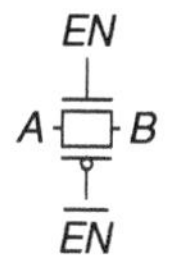

Figure 1.38 **Transmission gate**

1.7.8 Pseudo-nMOS Logic

An *N*-input CMOS NOR gate uses *N* nMOS transistors in parallel and *N* pMOS transistors in series. Transistors in series are slower than transistors in parallel, just as resistors in series have more resistance than resistors in parallel. Moreover, pMOS transistors are slower than nMOS transistors because holes cannot move around the silicon lattice as fast as electrons. Therefore the parallel nMOS transistors are fast and the series pMOS transistors are slow, especially when many are in series.

Pseudo-nMOS logic replaces the slow stack of pMOS transistors with a single weak pMOS transistor that is always ON, as shown in Figure 1.39. This pMOS transistor is often called a *weak pull-up*. The physical dimensions of the pMOS transistor are selected so that the pMOS transistor will pull the output *Y* HIGH weakly—that is, only if none of the nMOS transistors are ON. But if any nMOS transistor is ON, it overpowers the weak pull-up and pulls *Y* down close enough to GND to produce a logic 0.

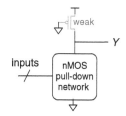

Figure 1.39 **Generic pseudo-nMOS gate**

The advantage of pseudo-nMOS logic is that it can be used to build fast NOR gates with many inputs. For example, Figure 1.40 shows a pseudo-nMOS four-input NOR. Pseudo-nMOS gates are useful for certain memory and logic arrays discussed in Chapter 5. The disadvantage is that a short circuit exists between V_{DD} and GND when the output is LOW; the weak pMOS and nMOS transistors are both ON. The short circuit draws continuous power, so pseudo-nMOS logic must be used sparingly.

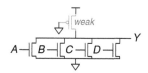

Figure 1.40 **Pseudo-nMOS four-input NOR gate**

Pseudo-nMOS gates got their name from the 1970's, when manufacturing processes only had nMOS transistors. A weak nMOS transistor was used to pull the output HIGH because pMOS transistors were not available.

1.8 POWER CONSUMPTION*

Power consumption is the amount of energy used per unit time. Power consumption is of great importance in digital systems. The battery life of portable systems such as cell phones and laptop computers is limited by power consumption. Power is also significant for systems that are plugged in, because electricity costs money and because the system will overheat if it draws too much power.

Digital systems draw both *dynamic* and *static* power. Dynamic power is the power used to charge capacitance as signals change between 0 and 1. Static power is the power used even when signals do not change and the system is idle.

Logic gates and the wires that connect them have capacitance. The energy drawn from the power supply to charge a capacitance C to voltage V_{DD} is CV_{DD}^2. If the voltage on the capacitor switches at frequency f (i.e., f times per second), it charges the capacitor $f/2$ times and discharges it $f/2$ times per second. Discharging does not draw energy from the power supply, so the dynamic power consumption is

$$P_{\text{dynamic}} = \frac{1}{2}CV_{DD}^2 f \tag{1.4}$$

Electrical systems draw some current even when they are idle. When transistors are OFF, they leak a small amount of current. Some circuits, such as the pseudo-nMOS gate discussed in Section 1.7.8, have a path from V_{DD} to GND through which current flows continuously. The total static current, I_{DD}, is also called the *leakage current* or the *quiescent supply current* flowing between V_{DD} and GND. The static power consumption is proportional to this static current:

$$P_{\text{static}} = I_{DD}V_{DD} \tag{1.5}$$

Example 1.23 POWER CONSUMPTION

A particular cell phone has a 6 watt-hour (W-hr) battery and operates at 1.2 V. Suppose that, when it is in use, the cell phone operates at 300 MHz and the average amount of capacitance in the chip switching at any given time is 10 nF (10^{-8} Farads). When in use, it also broadcasts 3 W of power out of its antenna. When the phone is not in use, the dynamic power drops to almost zero because the signal processing is turned off. But the phone also draws 40 mA of quiescent current whether it is in use or not. Determine the battery life of the phone (a) if it is not being used, and (b) if it is being used continuously.

Solution: The static power is $P_{static} = (0.040 \text{ A})(1.2 \text{ V}) = 48$ mW. (a) If the phone is not being used, this is the only power consumption, so the battery life is (6 Whr)/ (0.048 W) = 125 hours (about 5 days). (b) If the phone is being used, the dynamic power is $P_{dynamic} = (0.5)(10^{-8} \text{ F})(1.2 \text{ V})^2(3 \times 10^8 \text{ Hz}) = 2.16$ W. Together with the static and broadcast power, the total active power is 2.16 W + 0.048 W + 3 W = 5.2 W, so the battery life is 6 W-hr/5.2 W = 1.15 hours. This example somewhat oversimplifies the actual operation of a cell phone, but it illustrates the key ideas of power consumption.

1.9 SUMMARY AND A LOOK AHEAD

There are 10 kinds of people in this world: those who can count in binary and those who can't.

This chapter has introduced principles for understanding and designing complex systems. Although the real world is analog, digital designers discipline themselves to use a discrete subset of possible signals. In particular, binary variables have just two states: 0 and 1, also called FALSE and TRUE or LOW and HIGH. Logic gates compute a binary output from one or more binary inputs. Some of the common logic gates are:

▸ **NOT:** TRUE when input is FALSE

▸ **AND:** TRUE when all inputs are TRUE

▸ **OR:** TRUE when any inputs are TRUE

▸ **XOR:** TRUE when an odd number of inputs are TRUE

Logic gates are commonly built from CMOS transistors, which behave as electrically controlled switches. nMOS transistors turn ON when the gate is 1. pMOS transistors turn ON when the gate is 0.

In Chapters 2 through 5, we continue the study of digital logic. Chapter 2 addresses *combinational logic*, in which the outputs depend only on the current inputs. The logic gates introduced already are examples of combinational logic. You will learn to design circuits involving multiple gates to implement a relationship between inputs and outputs specified by a truth table or Boolean equation. Chapter 3 addresses *sequential logic*, in which the outputs depend on both current and past inputs. *Registers* are common sequential elements that remember their previous input. *Finite state machines*, built from registers and combinational logic, are a powerful way to build complicated systems in a systematic fashion. We also study timing of digital systems to analyze how fast a system can operate. Chapter 4 describes hardware description languages (HDLs). HDLs are related to conventional programming languages but are used to simulate and build hardware rather than software. Most digital systems today are designed with HDLs. SystemVerilog and VHDL are the two prevalent languages, and they are covered side-by-side in this book. Chapter 5 studies other combinational and sequential building blocks such as adders, multipliers, and memories.

Chapter 6 shifts to computer architecture. It describes the ARM processor, an industry-standard microprocessor used in almost all smart phones and tablets and many other devices, from pinball machines to cars and servers. The ARM architecture is defined by its registers and assembly language instruction set. You will learn to write programs in assembly language for the ARM processor so that you can communicate with the processor in its native language.

Chapters 7 and 8 bridge the gap between digital logic and computer architecture. Chapter 7 investigates microarchitecture, the arrangement of digital building blocks, such as adders and registers, needed to construct a processor. In that chapter, you learn to build your own ARM processor. Indeed, you learn three microarchitectures illustrating different trade-offs of performance and cost. Processor performance has increased exponentially, requiring ever more sophisticated memory systems to feed the insatiable demand for data. Chapter 8 delves into memory system architecture. Chapter 9 (available as a web supplement, see Preface) describes how computers communicate with peripheral devices such as monitors, Bluetooth radios, and motors.

Exercises

Exercise 1.1 Explain in one paragraph at least three levels of abstraction that are used by

(a) biologists studying the operation of cells.

(b) chemists studying the composition of matter.

Exercise 1.2 Explain in one paragraph how the techniques of hierarchy, modularity, and regularity may be used by

(a) automobile designers.

(b) businesses to manage their operations.

Exercise 1.3 Ben Bitdiddle is building a house. Explain how he can use the principles of hierarchy, modularity, and regularity to save time and money during construction.

Exercise 1.4 An analog voltage is in the range of 0–5 V. If it can be measured with an accuracy of ±50 mV, at most how many bits of information does it convey?

Exercise 1.5 A classroom has an old clock on the wall whose minute hand broke off.

(a) If you can read the hour hand to the nearest 15 minutes, how many bits of information does the clock convey about the time?

(b) If you know whether it is before or after noon, how many additional bits of information do you know about the time?

Exercise 1.6 The Babylonians developed the *sexagesimal* (base 60) number system about 4000 years ago. How many bits of information is conveyed with one sexagesimal digit? How do you write the number 4000_{10} in sexagesimal?

Exercise 1.7 How many different numbers can be represented with 16 bits?

Exercise 1.8 What is the largest unsigned 32-bit binary number?

Exercise 1.9 What is the largest 16-bit binary number that can be represented with

(a) unsigned numbers?

(b) two's complement numbers?

(c) sign/magnitude numbers?

Exercise 1.10 What is the largest 32-bit binary number that can be represented with

(a) unsigned numbers?

(b) two's complement numbers?

(c) sign/magnitude numbers?

Exercise 1.11 What is the smallest (most negative) 16-bit binary number that can be represented with

(a) unsigned numbers?

(b) two's complement numbers?

(c) sign/magnitude numbers?

Exercise 1.12 What is the smallest (most negative) 32-bit binary number that can be represented with

(a) unsigned numbers?

(b) two's complement numbers?

(c) sign/magnitude numbers?

Exercise 1.13 Convert the following unsigned binary numbers to decimal. Show your work.

(a) 1010_2

(b) 110110_2

(c) 11110000_2

(d) 000100010100111_2

Exercise 1.14 Convert the following unsigned binary numbers to decimal. Show your work.

(a) 1110_2

(b) 100100_2

(c) 11010111_2

(d) 011101010100100_2

Exercise 1.15 Repeat Exercise 1.13, but convert to hexadecimal.

Exercise 1.16 Repeat Exercise 1.14, but convert to hexadecimal.

Exercise 1.17 Convert the following hexadecimal numbers to decimal. Show your work.

(a) $A5_{16}$

(b) $3B_{16}$

(c) $FFFF_{16}$

(d) $D0000000_{16}$

Exercise 1.18 Convert the following hexadecimal numbers to decimal. Show your work.

(a) $4E_{16}$

(b) $7C_{16}$

(c) $ED3A_{16}$

(d) $403FB001_{16}$

Exercise 1.19 Repeat Exercise 1.17, but convert to unsigned binary.

Exercise 1.20 Repeat Exercise 1.18, but convert to unsigned binary.

Exercise 1.21 Convert the following two's complement binary numbers to decimal.

(a) 1010_2

(b) 110110_2

(c) 01110000_2

(d) 10011111_2

Exercise 1.22 Convert the following two's complement binary numbers to decimal.

(a) 1110_2

(b) 100011_2

(c) 01001110_2

(d) 10110101_2

Exercise 1.23 Repeat Exercise 1.21, assuming the binary numbers are in sign/magnitude form rather than two's complement representation.

Exercise 1.24 Repeat Exercise 1.22, assuming the binary numbers are in sign/magnitude form rather than two's complement representation.

Exercise 1.25 Convert the following decimal numbers to unsigned binary numbers.

(a) 42_{10}

(b) 63_{10}

(c) 229_{10}

(d) 845_{10}

Exercise 1.26 Convert the following decimal numbers to unsigned binary numbers.

(a) 14_{10}

(b) 52_{10}

(c) 339_{10}

(d) 711_{10}

Exercise 1.27 Repeat Exercise 1.25, but convert to hexadecimal.

Exercise 1.28 Repeat Exercise 1.26, but convert to hexadecimal.

Exercise 1.29 Convert the following decimal numbers to 8-bit two's complement numbers or indicate that the decimal number would overflow the range.

(a) 42_{10}

(b) -63_{10}

(c) 124_{10}

(d) -128_{10}

(e) 133_{10}

Exercise 1.30 Convert the following decimal numbers to 8-bit two's complement numbers or indicate that the decimal number would overflow the range.

(a) 24_{10}

(b) -59_{10}

(c) 128_{10}

(d) -150_{10}

(e) 127_{10}

Exercise 1.31 Repeat Exercise 1.29, but convert to 8-bit sign/magnitude numbers.

Exercise 1.32 Repeat Exercise 1.30, but convert to 8-bit sign/magnitude numbers.

Exercise 1.33 Convert the following 4-bit two's complement numbers to 8-bit two's complement numbers.

(a) 0101_2

(b) 1010_2

Exercise 1.34 Convert the following 4-bit two's complement numbers to 8-bit two's complement numbers.

(a) 0111_2

(b) 1001_2

Exercise 1.35 Repeat Exercise 1.33 if the numbers are unsigned rather than two's complement.

Exercise 1.36 Repeat Exercise 1.34 if the numbers are unsigned rather than two's complement.

Exercise 1.37 Base 8 is referred to as *octal*. Convert each of the numbers from Exercise 1.25 to octal.

Exercise 1.38 Base 8 is referred to as *octal*. Convert each of the numbers from Exercise 1.26 to octal.

Exercise 1.39 Convert each of the following octal numbers to binary, hexadecimal, and decimal.

(a) 42_8

(b) 63_8

(c) 255_8

(d) 3047_8

Exercise 1.40 Convert each of the following octal numbers to binary, hexadecimal, and decimal.

(a) 23_8

(b) 45_8

(c) 371_8

(d) 2560_8

Exercise 1.41 How many 5-bit two's complement numbers are greater than 0? How many are less than 0? How would your answers differ for sign/magnitude numbers?

Exercise 1.42 How many 7-bit two's complement numbers are greater than 0? How many are less than 0? How would your answers differ for sign/magnitude numbers?

Exercise 1.43 How many bytes are in a 32-bit word? How many nibbles are in the word?

Exercise 1.44 How many bytes are in a 64-bit word?

Exercise 1.45 A particular DSL modem operates at 768 kbits/sec. How many bytes can it receive in 1 minute?

Exercise 1.46 USB 3.0 can send data at 5 Gbits/sec. How many bytes can it send in 1 minute?

Exercise 1.47 Hard disk manufacturers use the term "megabyte" to mean 10^6 bytes and "gigabyte" to mean 10^9 bytes. How many real GBs of music can you store on a 50 GB hard disk?

Exercise 1.48 Estimate the value of 2^{31} without using a calculator.

Exercise 1.49 A memory on the Pentium II microprocessor is organized as a rectangular array of bits with 2^8 rows and 2^9 columns. Estimate how many bits it has without using a calculator.

Exercise 1.50 Draw a number line analogous to Figure 1.11 for 3-bit unsigned, two's complement, and sign/magnitude numbers.

Exercise 1.51 Draw a number line analogous to Figure 1.11 for 2-bit unsigned, two's complement, and sign/magnitude numbers.

Exercise 1.52 Perform the following additions of unsigned binary numbers. Indicate whether or not the sum overflows a 4-bit result.

(a) $1001_2 + 0100_2$

(b) $1101_2 + 1011^2$

Exercise 1.53 Perform the following additions of unsigned binary numbers. Indicate whether or not the sum overflows an 8-bit result.

(a) $10011001_2 + 01000100_2$

(b) $11010010_2 + 10110110_2$

Exercise 1.54 Repeat Exercise 1.52, assuming that the binary numbers are in two's complement form.

Exercise 1.55 Repeat Exercise 1.53, assuming that the binary numbers are in two's complement form.

Exercise 1.56 Convert the following decimal numbers to 6-bit two's complement binary numbers and add them. Indicate whether or not the sum overflows a 6-bit result.

(a) $16_{10} + 9_{10}$

(b) $27_{10} + 31_{10}$

(c) $-4_{10} + 19_{10}$

(d) $3_{10} + -32_{10}$

(e) $-16_{10} + -9_{10}$

(f) $-27_{10} + -31_{10}$

Exercise 1.57 Repeat Exercise 1.56 for the following numbers.

(a) $7_{10} + 13_{10}$

(b) $17_{10} + 25_{10}$

(c) $-26_{10} + 8_{10}$

(d) $31_{10} + -14_{10}$

(e) $-19_{10} + -22_{10}$

(f) $-2_{10} + -29_{10}$

Exercise 1.58 Perform the following additions of unsigned hexadecimal numbers. Indicate whether or not the sum overflows an 8-bit (two hex digit) result.

(a) $7_{16} + 9_{16}$

(b) $13_{16} + 28_{16}$

(c) $AB_{16} + 3E_{16}$

(d) $8F_{16} + AD_{16}$

Exercise 1.59 Perform the following additions of unsigned hexadecimal numbers. Indicate whether or not the sum overflows an 8-bit (two hex digit) result.

(a) $22_{16} + 8_{16}$

(b) $73_{16} + 2C_{16}$

(c) $7F_{16} + 7F_{16}$

(d) $C2_{16} + A4_{16}$

Exercise 1.60 Convert the following decimal numbers to 5-bit two's complement binary numbers and subtract them. Indicate whether or not the difference overflows a 5-bit result.

(a) $9_{10} - 7_{10}$

(b) $12_{10} - 15_{10}$

(c) $-6_{10} - 11_{10}$

(d) $4_{10} - -8_{10}$

Exercise 1.61 Convert the following decimal numbers to 6-bit two's complement binary numbers and subtract them. Indicate whether or not the difference overflows a 6-bit result.

(a) $18_{10} - 12_{10}$

(b) $30_{10} - 9_{10}$

(c) $-28_{10} - 3_{10}$

(d) $-16_{10} - 21_{10}$

Exercise 1.62 In a *biased* N-bit binary number system with bias B, positive and negative numbers are represented as their value plus the bias B. For example, for 5-bit numbers with a bias of 15, the number 0 is represented as 01111, 1 as 10000, and so forth. Biased number systems are sometimes used in floating point mathematics, which will be discussed in Chapter 5. Consider a biased 8-bit binary number system with a bias of 127_{10}.

(a) What decimal value does the binary number 10000010_2 represent?

(b) What binary number represents the value 0?

(c) What is the representation and value of the most negative number?

(d) What is the representation and value of the most positive number?

Exercise 1.63 Draw a number line analogous to Figure 1.11 for 3-bit biased numbers with a bias of 3 (see Exercise 1.62 for a definition of biased numbers).

Exercise 1.64 In a *binary coded decimal* (BCD) system, 4 bits are used to represent a decimal digit from 0 to 9. For example, 37_{10} is written as 00110111_{BCD}.

(a) Write 289_{10} in BCD

(b) Convert 100101010001_{BCD} to decimal

(c) Convert 01101001_{BCD} to binary

(d) Explain why BCD might be a useful way to represent numbers

Exercise 1.65 Answer the following questions related to BCD systems (see Exercise 1.64 for the definition of BCD).

(a) Write 371_{10} in BCD

(b) Convert 000110000111_{BCD} to decimal

(c) Convert 10010101_{BCD} to binary

(d) Explain the disadvantages of BCD when compared to binary representations of numbers

Exercise 1.66 A flying saucer crashes in a Nebraska cornfield. The FBI investigates the wreckage and finds an engineering manual containing an equation in the Martian number system: $325 + 42 = 411$. If this equation is correct, how many fingers would you expect Martians to have?

Exercise 1.67 Ben Bitdiddle and Alyssa P. Hacker are having an argument. Ben says, "All integers greater than zero and exactly divisible by six have exactly two 1's in their binary representation." Alyssa disagrees. She says, "No, but all such numbers have an even number of 1's in their representation." Do you agree with Ben or Alyssa or both or neither? Explain.

Exercise 1.68 Ben Bitdiddle and Alyssa P. Hacker are having another argument. Ben says, "I can get the two's complement of a number by subtracting 1, then inverting all the bits of the result." Alyssa says, "No, I can do it by examining each bit of the number, starting with the least significant bit. When the first 1 is found, invert each subsequent bit." Do you agree with Ben or Alyssa or both or neither? Explain.

Exercise 1.69 Write a program in your favorite language (e.g., C, Java, Perl) to convert numbers from binary to decimal. The user should type in an unsigned binary number. The program should print the decimal equivalent.

Exercise 1.70 Repeat Exercise 1.69 but convert from an arbitrary base b_1 to another base b_2, as specified by the user. Support bases up to 16, using the letters of the alphabet for digits greater than 9. The user should enter b_1, b_2, and then the number to convert in base b_1. The program should print the equivalent number in base b_2.

Exercise 1.71 Draw the symbol, Boolean equation, and truth table for

(a) a three-input OR gate

(b) a three-input exclusive OR (XOR) gate

(c) a four-input XNOR gate

Exercise 1.72 Draw the symbol, Boolean equation, and truth table for

(a) a four-input OR gate

(b) a three-input XNOR gate

(c) a five-input NAND gate

Exercise 1.73 A *majority gate* produces a TRUE output if and only if more than half of its inputs are TRUE. Complete a truth table for the three-input majority gate shown in Figure 1.41.

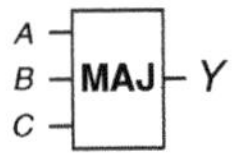

$$A$$
$$B - \boxed{\textbf{MAJ}} - Y$$
$$C$$

Figure 1.41 **Three-input majority gate**

Exercise 1.74 A three-input *AND-OR (AO) gate* shown in Figure 1.42 produces a TRUE output if both *A* and *B* are TRUE, or if *C* is TRUE. Complete a truth table for the gate.

Figure 1.42 **Three-input AND-OR gate**

Exercise 1.75 A three-input *OR-AND-INVERT (OAI) gate* shown in Figure 1.43 produces a FALSE output if *C* is TRUE and *A* or *B* is TRUE. Otherwise it produces a TRUE output. Complete a truth table for the gate.

Figure 1.43 **Three-input OR-AND-INVERT gate**

Exercise 1.76 There are 16 different truth tables for Boolean functions of two variables. List each truth table. Give each one a short descriptive name (such as OR, NAND, and so on).

Exercise 1.77 How many different truth tables exist for Boolean functions of N variables?

Exercise 1.78 Is it possible to assign logic levels so that a device with the transfer characteristics shown in Figure 1.44 would serve as an inverter? If so, what are the input and output low and high levels (V_{IL}, V_{OL}, V_{IH}, and V_{OH}) and noise margins (NM_L and NM_H)? If not, explain why not.

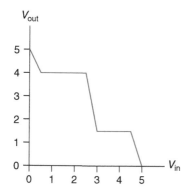

Figure 1.44 **DC transfer characteristics**

Exercise 1.79 Repeat Exercise 1.78 for the transfer characteristics shown in Figure 1.45.

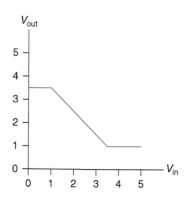

Figure 1.45 **DC transfer characteristics**

Exercise 1.80 Is it possible to assign logic levels so that a device with the transfer characteristics shown in Figure 1.46 would serve as a buffer? If so, what are the input and output low and high levels (V_{IL}, V_{OL}, V_{IH}, and V_{OH}) and noise margins (NM_L and NM_H)? If not, explain why not.

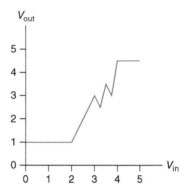

Figure 1.46 DC transfer characteristics

Exercise 1.81 Ben Bitdiddle has invented a circuit with the transfer characteristics shown in Figure 1.47 that he would like to use as a buffer. Will it work? Why or why not? He would like to advertise that it is compatible with LVCMOS and LVTTL logic. Can Ben's buffer correctly receive inputs from those logic families? Can its output properly drive those logic families? Explain.

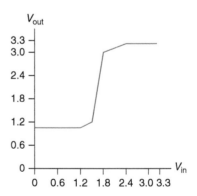

Figure 1.47 Ben's buffer DC transfer characteristics

Exercise 1.82 While walking down a dark alley, Ben Bitdiddle encounters a two-input gate with the transfer function shown in Figure 1.48. The inputs are A and B and the output is Y.

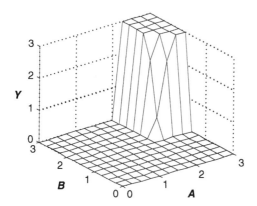

Figure 1.48 Two-input DC transfer characteristics

(a) What kind of logic gate did he find?

(b) What are the approximate high and low logic levels?

Exercise 1.83 Repeat Exercise 1.82 for Figure 1.49.

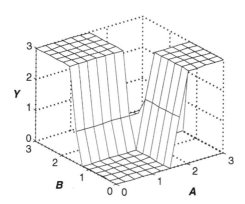

Figure 1.49 Two-input DC transfer characteristics

Exercise 1.84 Sketch a transistor-level circuit for the following CMOS gates. Use a minimum number of transistors.

(a) four-input NAND gate

(b) three-input OR-AND-INVERT gate (see Exercise 1.75)

(c) three-input AND-OR gate (see Exercise 1.74)

Exercise 1.85 Sketch a transistor-level circuit for the following CMOS gates. Use a minimum number of transistors.

(a) three-input NOR gate

(b) three-input AND gate

(c) two-input OR gate

Exercise 1.86 A *minority gate* produces a TRUE output if and only if fewer than half of its inputs are TRUE. Otherwise it produces a FALSE output. Sketch a transistor-level circuit for a three-input CMOS minority gate. Use a minimum number of transistors.

Exercise 1.87 Write a truth table for the function performed by the gate in Figure 1.50. The truth table should have two inputs, A and B. What is the name of this function?

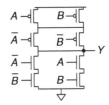

Figure 1.50 Mystery schematic

Exercise 1.88 Write a truth table for the function performed by the gate in Figure 1.51. The truth table should have three inputs, A, B, and C.

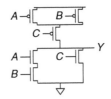

Figure 1.51 Mystery schematic

Exercise 1.89 Implement the following three-input gates using only pseudo-nMOS logic gates. Your gates receive three inputs, A, B, and C. Use a minimum number of transistors.

(a) three-input NOR gate

(b) three-input NAND gate

(c) three-input AND gate

Exercise 1.90 *Resistor-Transistor Logic (RTL)* uses nMOS transistors to pull the gate output LOW and a weak resistor to pull the output HIGH when none of the paths to ground are active. A NOT gate built using RTL is shown in Figure 1.52. Sketch a three-input RTL NOR gate. Use a minimum number of transistors.

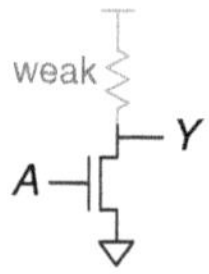

Figure 1.52 RTL NOT gate

Interview Questions

These questions have been asked at interviews for digital design jobs.

Question 1.1 Sketch a transistor-level circuit for a CMOS four-input NOR gate.

Question 1.2 The king receives 64 gold coins in taxes but has reason to believe that one is counterfeit. He summons you to identify the fake coin. You have a balance that can hold coins on each side. How many times do you need to use the balance to find the lighter, fake coin?

Question 1.3 The professor, the teaching assistant, the digital design student, and the freshman track star need to cross a rickety bridge on a dark night. The bridge is so shaky that only two people can cross at a time. They have only one flashlight among them and the span is too long to throw the flashlight, so somebody must carry it back to the other people. The freshman track star can cross the bridge in 1 minute. The digital design student can cross the bridge in 2 minutes. The teaching assistant can cross the bridge in 5 minutes. The professor always gets distracted and takes 10 minutes to cross the bridge. What is the fastest time to get everyone across the bridge?

Combinational Logic Design

2.1 INTRODUCTION

In digital electronics, a *circuit* is a network that processes discrete-valued variables. A circuit can be viewed as a black box, shown in Figure 2.1, with

▶ one or more discrete-valued *input terminals*

▶ one or more discrete-valued *output terminals*

▶ a *functional specification* describing the relationship between inputs and outputs

▶ a *timing specification* describing the delay between inputs changing and outputs responding.

Peering inside the black box, circuits are composed of nodes and elements. An *element* is itself a circuit with inputs, outputs, and a specification. A *node* is a wire, whose voltage conveys a discrete-valued variable. Nodes are classified as *input, output,* or *internal.* Inputs receive values from the external world. Outputs deliver values to the external world. Wires that are not inputs or outputs are called internal nodes. Figure 2.2

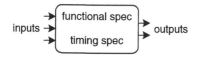

Figure 2.1 Circuit as a black box with inputs, outputs, and specifications

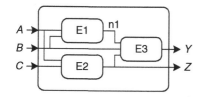

Figure 2.2 Elements and nodes

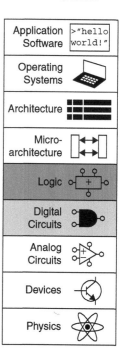

illustrates a circuit with three elements, E1, E2, and E3, and six nodes. Nodes A, B, and C are inputs. Y and Z are outputs. n1 is an internal node between E1 and E3.

Digital circuits are classified as *combinational* or *sequential*. A combinational circuit's outputs depend only on the current values of the inputs; in other words, it combines the current input values to compute the output. For example, a logic gate is a combinational circuit. A sequential circuit's outputs depend on both current and previous values of the inputs; in other words, it depends on the input sequence. A combinational circuit is *memoryless*, but a sequential circuit has *memory*. This chapter focuses on combinational circuits, and Chapter 3 examines sequential circuits.

The functional specification of a combinational circuit expresses the output values in terms of the current input values. The timing specification of a combinational circuit consists of lower and upper bounds on the delay from input to output. We will initially concentrate on the functional specification, then return to the timing specification later in this chapter.

Figure 2.3 shows a combinational circuit with two inputs and one output. On the left of the figure are the inputs, A and B, and on the right is the output, Y. The symbol $\mathcal{C}$ inside the box indicates that it is implemented using only combinational logic. In this example, the function F is specified to be OR: $Y = F(A, B) = A + B$. In words, we say the output Y is a function of the two inputs, A and B, namely $Y = A$ OR B.

Figure 2.4 shows two possible *implementations* for the combinational logic circuit in Figure 2.3. As we will see repeatedly throughout the book, there are often many implementations for a single function. You choose which to use given the building blocks at your disposal and your design constraints. These constraints often include area, speed, power, and design time.

Figure 2.5 shows a combinational circuit with multiple outputs. This particular combinational circuit is called a *full adder* and we will revisit it in Section 5.2.1. The two equations specify the function of the outputs, S and C_{out}, in terms of the inputs, A, B, and C_{in}.

To simplify drawings, we often use a single line with a slash through it and a number next to it to indicate a *bus*, a bundle of multiple signals. The number specifies how many signals are in the bus. For example, Figure 2.6(a) represents a block of combinational logic with three inputs and two outputs. If the number of bits is unimportant or obvious from the context, the slash may be shown without a number. Figure 2.6(b) indicates two blocks of combinational logic with an arbitrary number of outputs from one block serving as inputs to the second block.

The rules of *combinational composition* tell us how we can build a large combinational circuit from smaller combinational circuit elements.

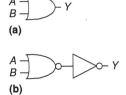

$$Y = F(A, B) = A + B$$

Figure 2.3 Combinational logic circuit

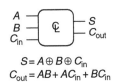

(a)

(b)

Figure 2.4 Two OR implementations

$$S = A \oplus B \oplus C_{in}$$
$$C_{out} = AB + AC_{in} + BC_{in}$$

Figure 2.5 Multiple-output combinational circuit

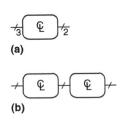

(a)

(b)

Figure 2.6 Slash notation for multiple signals

A circuit is combinational if it consists of interconnected circuit elements such that

▸ Every circuit element is itself combinational.

▸ Every node of the circuit is either designated as an input to the circuit or connects to exactly one output terminal of a circuit element.

▸ The circuit contains no cyclic paths: every path through the circuit visits each circuit node at most once.

The rules of combinational composition are sufficient but not strictly necessary. Certain circuits that disobey these rules are still combinational, so long as the outputs depend only on the current values of the inputs. However, determining whether oddball circuits are combinational is more difficult, so we will usually restrict ourselves to combinational composition as a way to build combinational circuits.

Example 2.1 COMBINATIONAL CIRCUITS

Which of the circuits in Figure 2.7 are combinational circuits according to the rules of combinational composition?

Solution: Circuit (a) is combinational. It is constructed from two combinational circuit elements (inverters I1 and I2). It has three nodes: n1, n2, and n3. n1 is an input to the circuit and to I1; n2 is an internal node, which is the output of I1 and the input to I2; n3 is the output of the circuit and of I2. (b) is not combinational, because there is a cyclic path: the output of the XOR feeds back to one of its inputs. Hence, a cyclic path starting at n4 passes through the XOR to n5, which returns to n4. (c) is combinational. (d) is not combinational, because node n6 connects to the output terminals of both I3 and I4. (e) is combinational, illustrating two combinational circuits connected to form a larger combinational circuit. (f) does not obey the rules of combinational composition because it has a cyclic path through the two elements. Depending on the functions of the elements, it may or may not be a combinational circuit.

Large circuits such as microprocessors can be very complicated, so we use the principles from Chapter 1 to manage the complexity. Viewing a circuit as a black box with a well-defined interface and function is an application of abstraction and modularity. Building the circuit out of

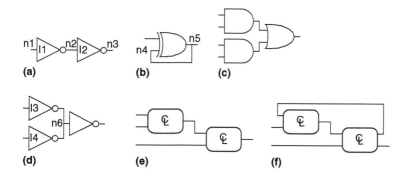

Figure 2.7 Example circuits

smaller circuit elements is an application of hierarchy. The rules of combinational composition are an application of discipline.

The functional specification of a combinational circuit is usually expressed as a truth table or a Boolean equation. In the next sections, we describe how to derive a Boolean equation from any truth table and how to use Boolean algebra and Karnaugh maps to simplify equations. We show how to implement these equations using logic gates and how to analyze the speed of these circuits.

2.2 BOOLEAN EQUATIONS

Boolean equations deal with variables that are either TRUE or FALSE, so they are perfect for describing digital logic. This section defines some terminology commonly used in Boolean equations, then shows how to write a Boolean equation for any logic function given its truth table.

2.2.1 Terminology

The *complement* of a variable A is its inverse $\overline{A}$. The variable or its complement is called a *literal*. For example, A, $\overline{A}$, B, and $\overline{B}$ are literals. We call A the *true form* of the variable and $\overline{A}$ the *complementary form*; "true form" does not mean that A is TRUE, but merely that A does not have a line over it.

The AND of one or more literals is called a *product* or an *implicant*. $\overline{A}B$, $A\overline{B}\,\overline{C}$, and B are all implicants for a function of three variables. A *minterm* is a product involving all of the inputs to the function. $A\overline{B}\,\overline{C}$ is a minterm for a function of the three variables A, B, and C, but $\overline{A}B$ is not, because it does not involve C. Similarly, the OR of one or more literals is called a *sum*. A *maxterm* is a sum involving all of the inputs to the function. $A+\overline{B}+C$ is a maxterm for a function of the three variables A, B, and C.

The *order of operations* is important when interpreting Boolean equations. Does $Y = A + BC$ mean $Y = (A$ OR $B)$ AND C or $Y = A$ OR $(B$ AND $C)$? In Boolean equations, NOT has the highest *precedence*, followed by AND, then OR. Just as in ordinary equations, products are performed before sums. Therefore, the equation is read as $Y = A$ OR $(B$ AND $C)$. Equation 2.1 gives another example of order of operations.

$$\overline{A}B + BC\overline{D} = ((\overline{A})B) + (BC(\overline{D})) \qquad (2.1)$$

A	B	Y	minterm	minterm name
0	0	0	$\overline{A}\,\overline{B}$	m_0
0	1	1	$\overline{A}\,B$	m_1
1	0	0	$A\,\overline{B}$	m_2
1	1	0	$A\,B$	m_3

Figure 2.8 Truth table and minterms

2.2.2 Sum-of-Products Form

A truth table of N inputs contains 2^N rows, one for each possible value of the inputs. Each row in a truth table is associated with a minterm that is TRUE for that row. Figure 2.8 shows a truth table of two inputs, A and B. Each row shows its corresponding minterm. For example, the minterm for the first row is $\overline{A}\,\overline{B}$ because $\overline{A}\,\overline{B}$ is TRUE when $A = 0$, $B = 0$. The minterms are numbered starting with 0; the top row corresponds to minterm 0, m_0, the next row to minterm 1, m_1, and so on.

We can write a Boolean equation for any truth table by summing each of the minterms for which the output, Y, is TRUE. For example, in Figure 2.8, there is only one row (or minterm) for which the output Y is TRUE, shown circled in blue. Thus, $Y = \overline{A}B$. Figure 2.9 shows a truth table with more than one row in which the output is TRUE. Taking the sum of each of the circled minterms gives $Y = \overline{A}B + AB$.

This is called the *sum-of-products canonical form* of a function because it is the sum (OR) of products (ANDs forming minterms). Although there are many ways to write the same function, such as $Y = B\overline{A} + BA$, we will sort the minterms in the same order that they appear in the truth table, so that we always write the same Boolean expression for the same truth table.

The sum-of-products canonical form can also be written in *sigma notation* using the summation symbol, Σ. With this notation, the function from Figure 2.9 would be written as:

$$F(A, B) = \Sigma(m_1, m_3)$$

or

$$F(A, B) = \Sigma(1, 3)$$

(2.2)

A	B	Y	minterm	minterm name
0	0	0	$\overline{A}\,\overline{B}$	m_0
0	1	1	$\overline{A}\,B$	m_1
1	0	0	$A\,\overline{B}$	m_2
1	1	1	$A\,B$	m_3

Figure 2.9 Truth table with multiple TRUE minterms

Canonical form is just a fancy word for standard form. You can use the term to impress your friends and scare your enemies.

Example 2.2 SUM-OF-PRODUCTS FORM

Ben Bitdiddle is having a picnic. He won't enjoy it if it rains or if there are ants. Design a circuit that will output TRUE *only* if Ben enjoys the picnic.

Solution: First define the inputs and outputs. The inputs are A and R, which indicate if there are ants and if it rains. A is TRUE when there are ants and FALSE when there are no ants. Likewise, R is TRUE when it rains and FALSE when the sun smiles on Ben. The output is E, Ben's enjoyment of the picnic. E is TRUE if Ben enjoys the picnic and FALSE if he suffers. Figure 2.10 shows the truth table for Ben's picnic experience.

Using sum-of-products form, we write the equation as: $E = \overline{A}\,\overline{R}$ or $E = \Sigma(0)$. We can build the equation using two inverters and a two-input AND gate, shown in Figure 2.11(a). You may recognize this truth table as the NOR function from Section 1.5.5: $E = A$ NOR $R = \overline{A + R}$. Figure 2.11(b) shows the NOR implementation. In Section 2.3, we show that the two equations, $\overline{A}\,\overline{R}$ and $\overline{A + R}$, are equivalent.

The sum-of-products form provides a Boolean equation for any truth table with any number of variables. Figure 2.12 shows a random three-input truth table. The sum-of-products form of the logic function is

$$Y = \overline{A}\,\overline{B}\,\overline{C} + A\overline{B}\,\overline{C} + A\overline{B}C$$

or

$$Y = \Sigma(0, 4, 5)$$

(2.3)

A	R	E
0	0	1
0	1	0
1	0	0
1	1	0

Figure 2.10 Ben's truth table

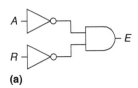

(a)

(b)

Figure 2.11 Ben's circuit

A	B	C	Y
0	0	0	1
0	0	1	0
0	1	0	0
0	1	1	0
1	0	0	1
1	0	1	1
1	1	0	0
1	1	1	0

Figure 2.12 Random three-input truth table

A	B	Y	maxterm	maxterm name
0	0	0	$A + B$	M_0
0	1	1	$A + \overline{B}$	M_1
1	0	0	$\overline{A} + B$	M_2
1	1	1	$\overline{A} + \overline{B}$	M_3

Figure 2.13 Truth table with multiple FALSE maxterms

Unfortunately, sum-of-products form does not necessarily generate the simplest equation. In Section 2.3 we show how to write the same function using fewer terms.

2.2.3 Product-of-Sums Form

An alternative way of expressing Boolean functions is the *product-of-sums canonical form*. Each row of a truth table corresponds to a maxterm that is FALSE for that row. For example, the maxterm for the first row of a two-input truth table is $(A + B)$ because $(A + B)$ is FALSE when $A = 0$, $B = 0$. We can write a Boolean equation for any circuit directly from the truth table as the AND of each of the maxterms for which the output is FALSE. The product-of-sums canonical form can also be written in *pi notation* using the product symbol, Π.

Example 2.3 PRODUCT-OF-SUMS FORM

Write an equation in product-of-sums form for the truth table in Figure 2.13.

Solution: The truth table has two rows in which the output is FALSE. Hence, the function can be written in product-of-sums form as $Y = (A + B)(\overline{A} + B)$ or, using pi notation, $Y = \Pi(M_0, M_2)$ or $Y = \Pi(0, 2)$. The first maxterm, $(A + B)$, guarantees that $Y = 0$ for $A = 0$, $B = 0$, because any value AND 0 is 0. Likewise, the second maxterm, $(\overline{A} + B)$, guarantees that $Y = 0$ for $A = 1$, $B = 0$. Figure 2.13 is the same truth table as Figure 2.9, showing that the same function can be written in more than one way.

Similarly, a Boolean equation for Ben's picnic from Figure 2.10 can be written in product-of-sums form by circling the three rows of 0's to obtain $E = (A + R)(\overline{A} + R)(\overline{A} + \overline{R})$ or $E = \Pi(1, 2, 3)$. This is uglier than the sum-of-products equation, $E = \overline{A}\,\overline{R}$, but the two equations are logically equivalent.

Sum-of-products produces a shorter equation when the output is TRUE on only a few rows of a truth table; product-of-sums is simpler when the output is FALSE on only a few rows of a truth table.

2.3 BOOLEAN ALGEBRA

In the previous section, we learned how to write a Boolean expression given a truth table. However, that expression does not necessarily lead to the simplest set of logic gates. Just as you use algebra to simplify mathematical equations, you can use *Boolean algebra* to simplify Boolean equations. The rules of Boolean algebra are much like those of ordinary algebra but are in some cases simpler, because variables have only two possible values: 0 or 1.

Boolean algebra is based on a set of axioms that we assume are correct. Axioms are unprovable in the sense that a definition cannot be proved. From these axioms, we prove all the theorems of Boolean algebra.

Table 2.1 **Axioms of Boolean algebra**

	Axiom		Dual	Name
A1	$B = 0$ if $B \neq 1$	A1′	$B = 1$ if $B \neq 0$	Binary field
A2	$\overline{0} = 1$	A2′	$\overline{1} = 0$	NOT
A3	$0 \cdot 0 = 0$	A3′	$1 + 1 = 1$	AND/OR
A4	$1 \cdot 1 = 1$	A4′	$0 + 0 = 0$	AND/OR
A5	$0 \cdot 1 = 1 \cdot 0 = 0$	A5′	$1 + 0 = 0 + 1 = 1$	AND/OR

These theorems have great practical significance, because they teach us how to simplify logic to produce smaller and less costly circuits.

Axioms and theorems of Boolean algebra obey the principle of *duality*. If the symbols 0 and 1 and the operators • (AND) and + (OR) are interchanged, the statement will still be correct. We use the prime symbol (′) to denote the *dual* of a statement.

2.3.1 Axioms

Table 2.1 states the axioms of Boolean algebra. These five axioms and their duals define Boolean variables and the meanings of NOT, AND, and OR. Axiom A1 states that a Boolean variable B is 0 if it is not 1. The axiom's dual, A1′, states that the variable is 1 if it is not 0. Together, A1 and A1′ tell us that we are working in a Boolean or binary field of 0's and 1's. Axioms A2 and A2′ define the NOT operation. Axioms A3 to A5 define AND; their duals, A3′ to A5′ define OR.

2.3.2 Theorems of One Variable

Theorems T1 to T5 in Table 2.2 describe how to simplify equations involving one variable.

The *identity* theorem, T1, states that for any Boolean variable B, B AND $1 = B$. Its dual states that B OR $0 = B$. In hardware, as shown in Figure 2.14, T1 means that if one input of a two-input AND gate is always 1, we can remove the AND gate and replace it with a wire connected to the variable input (B). Likewise, T1′ means that if one input of a two-input OR gate is always 0, we can replace the OR gate with a wire connected to B. In general, gates cost money, power, and delay, so replacing a gate with a wire is beneficial.

The *null element theorem*, T2, says that B AND 0 is always equal to 0. Therefore, 0 is called the *null* element for the AND operation, because it nullifies the effect of any other input. The dual states that B OR 1 is always equal to 1. Hence, 1 is the null element for the OR operation. In hardware,

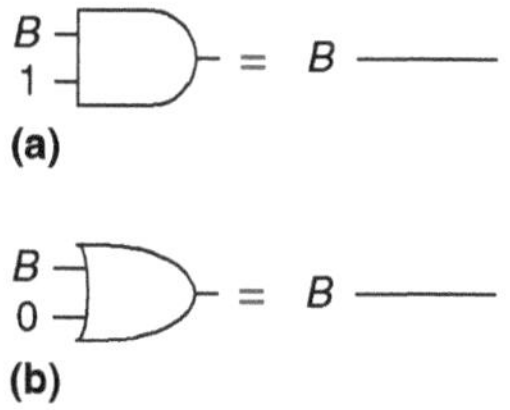

Figure 2.14 **Identity theorem in hardware: (a) T1, (b) T1′**

The null element theorem leads to some outlandish statements that are actually true! It is particularly dangerous when left in the hands of advertisers: YOU WILL GET A MILLION DOLLARS or we'll send you a toothbrush in the mail. (You'll most likely be receiving a toothbrush in the mail.)

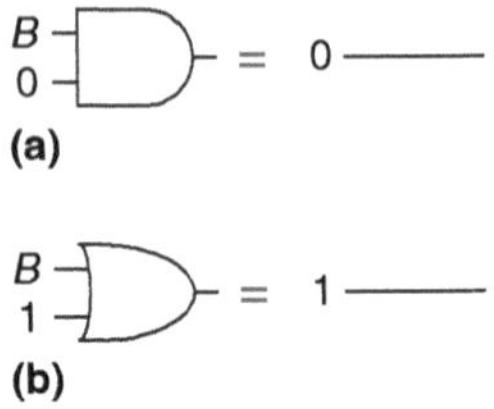

Figure 2.15 **Null element theorem in hardware: (a) T2, (b) T2′**

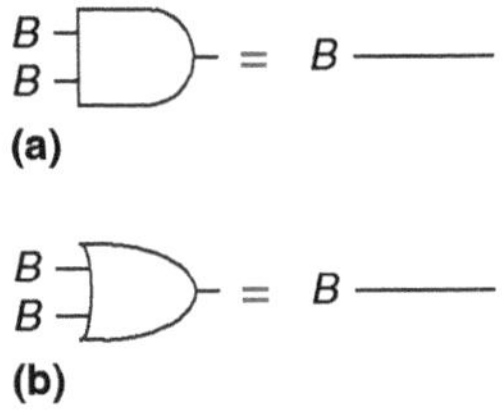

Table 2.2 Boolean theorems of one variable

	Theorem		Dual	Name
T1	$B \bullet 1 = B$	T1′	$B + 0 = B$	Identity
T2	$B \bullet 0 = 0$	T2′	$B + 1 = 1$	Null Element
T3	$B \bullet B = B$	T3′	$B + B = B$	Idempotency
T4	$\overline{\overline{B}} = B$			Involution
T5	$B \bullet \overline{B} = 0$	T5′	$B + \overline{B} = 1$	Complements

Figure 2.16 **Idempotency theorem in hardware: (a) T3, (b) T3′**

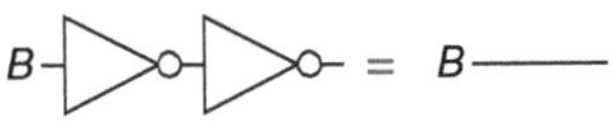

as shown in Figure 2.15, if one input of an AND gate is 0, we can replace the AND gate with a wire that is tied LOW (to 0). Likewise, if one input of an OR gate is 1, we can replace the OR gate with a wire that is tied HIGH (to 1).

Idempotency, T3, says that a variable AND itself is equal to just itself. Likewise, a variable OR itself is equal to itself. The theorem gets its name from the Latin roots: *idem* (same) and *potent* (power). The operations return the same thing you put into them. Figure 2.16 shows that idempotency again permits replacing a gate with a wire.

Involution, T4, is a fancy way of saying that complementing a variable twice results in the original variable. In digital electronics, two wrongs make a right. Two inverters in series logically cancel each other out and are logically equivalent to a wire, as shown in Figure 2.17. The dual of T4 is itself.

Figure 2.17 **Involution theorem in hardware: T4**

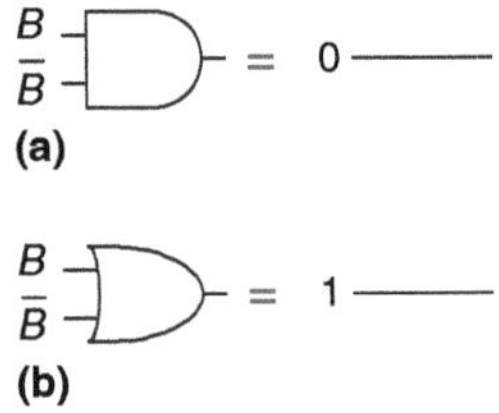

The *complement theorem*, T5 (Figure 2.18), states that a variable AND its complement is 0 (because one of them has to be 0). And by duality, a variable OR its complement is 1 (because one of them has to be 1).

2.3.3 Theorems of Several Variables

Theorems T6 to T12 in Table 2.3 describe how to simplify equations involving more than one Boolean variable.

Commutativity and *associativity*, T6 and T7, work the same as in traditional algebra. By commutativity, the *order* of inputs for an AND or OR function does not affect the value of the output. By associativity, the specific groupings of inputs do not affect the value of the output.

The *distributivity theorem*, T8, is the same as in traditional algebra, but its dual, T8′, is not. By T8, AND distributes over OR, and by T8′, OR distributes over AND. In traditional algebra, multiplication distributes over addition but addition does not distribute over multiplication, so that $(B + C) \times (B + D) \neq B + (C \times D)$.

Figure 2.18 **Complement theorem in hardware: (a) T5, (b) T5′**

The *covering*, *combining*, and *consensus* theorems, T9 to T11, permit us to eliminate redundant variables. With some thought, you should be able to convince yourself that these theorems are correct.

Table 2.3 Boolean theorems of several variables

	Theorem		Dual	Name
T6	$B \cdot C = C \cdot B$	T6'	$B + C = C + B$	Commutativity
T7	$(B \cdot C) \cdot D = B \cdot (C \cdot D)$	T7'	$(B + C) + D = B + (C + D)$	Associativity
T8	$(B \cdot C) + (B \cdot D) = B \cdot (C + D)$	T8'	$(B + C) \cdot (B + D) = B + (C \cdot D)$	Distributivity
T9	$B \cdot (B + C) = B$	T9'	$B + (B \cdot C) = B$	Covering
T10	$(B \cdot C) + (B \cdot \overline{C}) = B$	T10'	$(B + C) \cdot (B + \overline{C}) = B$	Combining
T11	$(B \cdot C) + (\overline{B} \cdot D) + (C \cdot D)$ $= B \cdot C + \overline{B} \cdot D$	T11'	$(B + C) \cdot (\overline{B} + D) \cdot (C + D)$ $= (B + C) \cdot (\overline{B} + D)$	Consensus
T12	$\overline{B_0 \cdot B_1 \cdot B_2 ...}$ $= (\overline{B}_0 + \overline{B}_1 + \overline{B}_2 ...)$	T12'	$\overline{B_0 + B_1 + B_2 ...}$ $= (\overline{B}_0 \cdot \overline{B}_1 \cdot \overline{B}_2 ...)$	De Morgan's Theorem

De Morgan's Theorem, T12, is a particularly powerful tool in digital design. The theorem explains that the complement of the product of all the terms is equal to the sum of the complement of each term. Likewise, the complement of the sum of all the terms is equal to the product of the complement of each term.

According to De Morgan's theorem, a NAND gate is equivalent to an OR gate with inverted inputs. Similarly, a NOR gate is equivalent to an AND gate with inverted inputs. Figure 2.19 shows these *De Morgan equivalent gates* for NAND and NOR gates. The two symbols shown for each function are called *duals*. They are logically equivalent and can be used interchangeably.

The inversion circle is called a *bubble*. Intuitively, you can imagine that "pushing" a bubble through the gate causes it to come out at the other side

Augustus De Morgan, died 1871. A British mathematician, born in India. Blind in one eye. His father died when he was 10. Attended Trinity College, Cambridge, at age 16, and was appointed Professor of Mathematics at the newly founded London University at age 22. Wrote widely on many mathematical subjects, including logic, algebra, and paradoxes. De Morgan's crater on the moon is named for him. He proposed a riddle for the year of his birth: "I was x years of age in the year x^2."

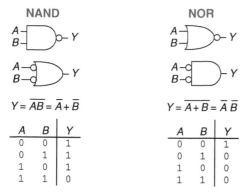

NAND

$Y = \overline{AB} = \overline{A} + \overline{B}$

A	B	Y
0	0	1
0	1	1
1	0	1
1	1	0

NOR

$Y = \overline{A + B} = \overline{A}\,\overline{B}$

A	B	Y
0	0	1
0	1	0
1	0	0
1	1	0

Figure 2.19 De Morgan equivalent gates

and flips the body of the gate from AND to OR or vice versa. For example, the NAND gate in Figure 2.19 consists of an AND body with a bubble on the output. Pushing the bubble to the left results in an OR body with bubbles on the inputs. The underlying rules for bubble pushing are

▸ Pushing bubbles backward (from the output) or forward (from the inputs) changes the body of the gate from AND to OR or vice versa.

▸ Pushing a bubble from the output back to the inputs puts bubbles on all gate inputs.

▸ Pushing bubbles on *all* gate inputs forward toward the output puts a bubble on the output.

Section 2.5.2 uses bubble pushing to help analyze circuits.

Example 2.4 DERIVE THE PRODUCT-OF-SUMS FORM

Figure 2.20 shows the truth table for a Boolean function Y and its complement $\overline{Y}$. Using De Morgan's Theorem, derive the product-of-sums canonical form of Y from the sum-of-products form of $\overline{Y}$.

Solution: Figure 2.21 shows the minterms (circled) contained in $\overline{Y}$. The sum-of-products canonical form of $\overline{Y}$ is

$$\overline{Y} = \overline{A}\,\overline{B} + \overline{A}B \tag{2.4}$$

Taking the complement of both sides and applying De Morgan's Theorem twice, we get:

$$\overline{\overline{Y}} = Y = \overline{\overline{A}\,\overline{B} + \overline{A}B} = (\overline{\overline{A}\,\overline{B}})(\overline{\overline{A}B}) = (A+B)(A+\overline{B}) \tag{2.5}$$

A	B	Y	$\overline{Y}$
0	0	0	1
0	1	0	1
1	0	1	0
1	1	1	0

Figure 2.20 Truth table showing Y and $\overline{Y}$

A	B	Y	$\overline{Y}$	minterm
0	0	0	1	$\overline{A}\,\overline{B}$
0	1	0	1	$\overline{A}\,B$
1	0	1	0	$A\,\overline{B}$
1	1	1	0	$A\,B$

Figure 2.21 Truth table showing minterms for $\overline{Y}$

2.3.4 The Truth Behind It All

The curious reader might wonder how to prove that a theorem is true. In Boolean algebra, proofs of theorems with a finite number of variables are easy: just show that the theorem holds for all possible values of these variables. This method is called *perfect induction* and can be done with a truth table.

Example 2.5 PROVING THE CONSENSUS THEOREM USING PERFECT INDUCTION

Prove the consensus theorem, T11, from Table 2.3.

Solution: Check both sides of the equation for all eight combinations of B, C, and D. The truth table in Figure 2.22 illustrates these combinations. Because $BC + \overline{B}D + CD = BC + \overline{B}D$ for all cases, the theorem is proved.

B	C	D	$BC + \overline{B}D + CD$	$BC + \overline{B}D$
0	0	0	0	0
0	0	1	1	1
0	1	0	0	0
0	1	1	1	1
1	0	0	0	0
1	0	1	0	0
1	1	0	1	1
1	1	1	1	1

Figure 2.22 Truth table proving T11

2.3.5 Simplifying Equations

The theorems of Boolean algebra help us simplify Boolean equations. For example, consider the sum-of-products expression from the truth table of Figure 2.9: $Y = \overline{A}B + AB$. By Theorem T10, the equation simplifies to $Y = B$. This may have been obvious looking at the truth table. In general, multiple steps may be necessary to simplify more complex equations.

The basic principle of simplifying sum-of-products equations is to combine terms using the relationship $PA + P\overline{A} = P$, where P may be any implicant. How far can an equation be simplified? We define an equation in sum-of-products form to be *minimized* if it uses the fewest possible implicants. If there are several equations with the same number of implicants, the minimal one is the one with the fewest literals.

An implicant is called a *prime implicant* if it cannot be combined with any other implicants in the equation to form a new implicant with fewer literals. The implicants in a minimal equation must all be prime implicants. Otherwise, they could be combined to reduce the number of literals.

Example 2.6 EQUATION MINIMIZATION

Minimize Equation 2.3: $\overline{A}\,\overline{B}\,\overline{C} + A\overline{B}\,\overline{C} + A\overline{B}C$.

Solution: We start with the original equation and apply Boolean theorems step by step, as shown in Table 2.4.

Have we simplified the equation completely at this point? Let's take a closer look. From the original equation, the minterms $\overline{A}\,\overline{B}\,\overline{C}$ and $A\overline{B}\,\overline{C}$ differ only in the variable A. So we combined the minterms to form $\overline{B}\,\overline{C}$. However, if we look at the original equation, we note that the last two minterms $A\overline{B}\,\overline{C}$ and $A\overline{B}C$ also differ by a single literal (C and $\overline{C}$). Thus, using the same method, we could have combined these two minterms to form the minterm $A\overline{B}$. We say that implicants $\overline{B}\,\overline{C}$ and $A\overline{B}$ *share* the minterm $A\overline{B}\,\overline{C}$.

So, are we stuck with simplifying only one of the minterm pairs, or can we simplify both? Using the idempotency theorem, we can duplicate terms as many times as we want: $B = B + B + B + B \ldots$. Using this principle, we simplify the equation completely to its two prime implicants, $\overline{B}\,\overline{C} + A\overline{B}$, as shown in Table 2.5.

Table 2.4 Equation minimization

Step	Equation	Justification
	$\overline{A}\,\overline{B}\,\overline{C} + A\overline{B}\,\overline{C} + A\overline{B}C$	
1	$\overline{B}\,\overline{C}(\overline{A} + A) + A\overline{B}C$	T8: Distributivity
2	$\overline{B}\,\overline{C}(1) + A\overline{B}C$	T5: Complements
3	$\overline{B}\,\overline{C} + A\overline{B}C$	T1: Identity

Table 2.5 Improved equation minimization

Step	Equation	Justification
	$\overline{A}\,\overline{B}\,\overline{C} + A\overline{B}\,\overline{C} + A\overline{B}C$	
1	$\overline{A}\,\overline{B}\,\overline{C} + A\overline{B}\,\overline{C} + A\overline{B}\,\overline{C} + A\overline{B}C$	T3: Idempotency
2	$\overline{B}\,\overline{C}(\overline{A} + A) + A\overline{B}(\overline{C} + C)$	T8: Distributivity
3	$\overline{B}\,\overline{C}(1) + A\overline{B}(1)$	T5: Complements
4	$\overline{B}\,\overline{C} + A\overline{B}$	T1: Identity

Although it is a bit counterintuitive, *expanding* an implicant (for example, turning AB into $ABC + AB\overline{C}$) is sometimes useful in minimizing equations. By doing this, you can repeat one of the expanded minterms to be combined (shared) with another minterm.

You may have noticed that completely simplifying a Boolean equation with the theorems of Boolean algebra can take some trial and error. Section 2.7 describes a methodical technique called Karnaugh maps that makes the process easier.

Why bother simplifying a Boolean equation if it remains logically equivalent? Simplifying reduces the number of gates used to physically implement the function, thus making it smaller, cheaper, and possibly faster. The next section describes how to implement Boolean equations with logic gates.

2.4 FROM LOGIC TO GATES

The labs that accompany this textbook (see Preface) show how to use *computer-aided design* (CAD) tools to design, simulate, and test digital circuits.

A *schematic* is a diagram of a digital circuit showing the elements and the wires that connect them together. For example, the schematic in Figure 2.23 shows a possible hardware implementation of our favorite logic function, Equation 2.3:

$$Y = \overline{A}\,\overline{B}\,\overline{C} + A\overline{B}\,\overline{C} + A\overline{B}C$$

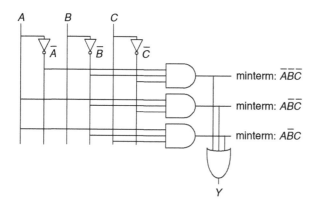

Figure 2.23 Schematic of
$Y = \overline{A}\,\overline{B}\,\overline{C} + A\overline{B}\,\overline{C} + \overline{A}\overline{B}C$

By drawing schematics in a consistent fashion, we make them easier to read and debug. We will generally obey the following guidelines:

▸ Inputs are on the left (or top) side of a schematic.

▸ Outputs are on the right (or bottom) side of a schematic.

▸ Whenever possible, gates should flow from left to right.

▸ Straight wires are better to use than wires with multiple corners (jagged wires waste mental effort following the wire rather than thinking of what the circuit does).

▸ Wires always connect at a T junction.

▸ A dot where wires cross indicates a connection between the wires.

▸ Wires crossing *without* a dot make no connection.

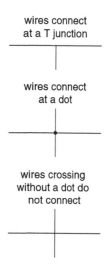

wires connect
at a T junction

wires connect
at a dot

wires crossing
without a dot do
not connect

Figure 2.24 Wire connections

The last three guidelines are illustrated in Figure 2.24.

Any Boolean equation in sum-of-products form can be drawn as a schematic in a systematic way similar to Figure 2.23. First, draw columns for the inputs. Place inverters in adjacent columns to provide the complementary inputs if necessary. Draw rows of AND gates for each of the minterms. Then, for each output, draw an OR gate connected to the minterms related to that output. This style is called a *programmable logic array (PLA)* because the inverters, AND gates, and OR gates are arrayed in a systematic fashion. PLAs will be discussed further in Section 5.6.

Figure 2.25 shows an implementation of the simplified equation we found using Boolean algebra in Example 2.6. Notice that the simplified circuit has significantly less hardware than that of Figure 2.23. It may also be faster, because it uses gates with fewer inputs.

We can reduce the number of gates even further (albeit by a single inverter) by taking advantage of inverting gates. Observe that $\overline{B}\,\overline{C}$ is an

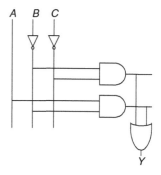

Figure 2.25 Schematic of
$Y = \overline{B}\,\overline{C} + AB$

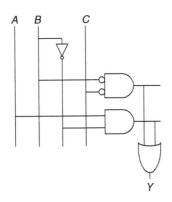

Figure 2.26 Schematic using fewer gates

AND with inverted inputs. Figure 2.26 shows a schematic using this optimization to eliminate the inverter on C. Recall that by De Morgan's theorem the AND with inverted inputs is equivalent to a NOR gate. Depending on the implementation technology, it may be cheaper to use the fewest gates or to use certain types of gates in preference to others. For example, NANDs and NORs are preferred over ANDs and ORs in CMOS implementations.

Many circuits have multiple outputs, each of which computes a separate Boolean function of the inputs. We can write a separate truth table for each output, but it is often convenient to write all of the outputs on a single truth table and sketch one schematic with all of the outputs.

Example 2.7 MULTIPLE-OUTPUT CIRCUITS

The dean, the department chair, the teaching assistant, and the dorm social chair each use the auditorium from time to time. Unfortunately, they occasionally conflict, leading to disasters such as the one that occurred when the dean's fundraising meeting with crusty trustees happened at the same time as the dorm's BTB[1] party. Alyssa P. Hacker has been called in to design a room reservation system.

The system has four inputs, $A_3, \ldots, A_0$, and four outputs, $Y_3, \ldots, Y_0$. These signals can also be written as $A_{3:0}$ and $Y_{3:0}$. Each user asserts her input when she requests the auditorium for the next day. The system asserts at most one output, granting the auditorium to the highest priority user. The dean, who is paying for the system, demands highest priority (3). The department chair, teaching assistant, and dorm social chair have decreasing priority.

Write a truth table and Boolean equations for the system. Sketch a circuit that performs this function.

Solution: This function is called a four-input *priority circuit.* Its symbol and truth table are shown in Figure 2.27.

We could write each output in sum-of-products form and reduce the equations using Boolean algebra. However, the simplified equations are clear by inspection from the functional description (and the truth table): Y_3 is TRUE whenever A_3 is asserted, so $Y_3 = A_3$. Y_2 is TRUE if A_2 is asserted and A_3 is not asserted, so $Y_2 = \overline{A_3} A_2$. Y_1 is TRUE if A_1 is asserted and neither of the higher priority inputs is asserted: $Y_1 = \overline{A_3}\overline{A_2}A_1$. And Y_0 is TRUE whenever A_0 and no other input is asserted: $Y_0 = \overline{A_3}\overline{A_2}\overline{A_1}A_0$. The schematic is shown in Figure 2.28. An experienced designer can often implement a logic circuit by inspection. Given a clear specification, simply turn the words into equations and the equations into gates.

---

[1] Black light, twinkies, and beer.

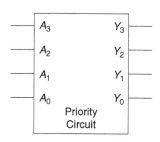

A_3	A_2	A_1	A_0	Y_3	Y_2	Y_1	Y_0
0	0	0	0	0	0	0	0
0	0	0	1	0	0	0	1
0	0	1	0	0	0	1	0
0	0	1	1	0	0	1	0
0	1	0	0	0	1	0	0
0	1	0	1	0	1	0	0
0	1	1	0	0	1	0	0
0	1	1	1	0	1	0	0
1	0	0	0	1	0	0	0
1	0	0	1	1	0	0	0
1	0	1	0	1	0	0	0
1	0	1	1	1	0	0	0
1	1	0	0	1	0	0	0
1	1	0	1	1	0	0	0
1	1	1	0	1	0	0	0
1	1	1	1	1	0	0	0

Figure 2.27 **Priority circuit**

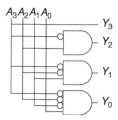

Figure 2.28 **Priority circuit schematic**

A_3	A_2	A_1	A_0	Y_3	Y_2	Y_1	Y_0
0	0	0	0	0	0	0	0
0	0	0	1	0	0	0	1
0	0	1	X	0	0	1	0
0	1	X	X	0	1	0	0
1	X	X	X	1	0	0	0

Figure 2.29 **Priority circuit truth table with don't cares (X's)**

Notice that if A_3 is asserted in the priority circuit, the outputs *don't care* what the other inputs are. We use the symbol X to describe inputs that the output doesn't care about. Figure 2.29 shows that the four-input priority circuit truth table becomes much smaller with don't cares. From this truth table, we can easily read the Boolean equations in sum-of-products form by ignoring inputs with X's. Don't cares can also appear in truth table outputs, as we will see in Section 2.7.3.

> X is an overloaded symbol that means "don't care" in truth tables and "contention" in logic simulation (see Section 2.6.1). Think about the context so you don't mix up the meanings. Some authors use D or ? instead for "don't care" to avoid this ambiguity.

2.5 MULTILEVEL COMBINATIONAL LOGIC

Logic in sum-of-products form is called *two-level logic* because it consists of literals connected to a level of AND gates connected to a level of OR gates. Designers often build circuits with more than two levels of logic gates. These multilevel combinational circuits may use less hardware than their two-level counterparts. Bubble pushing is especially helpful in analyzing and designing multilevel circuits.

2.5.1 Hardware Reduction

Some logic functions require an enormous amount of hardware when built using two-level logic. A notable example is the XOR function of multiple variables. For example, consider building a three-input XOR using the two-level techniques we have studied so far.

Recall that an N-input XOR produces a TRUE output when an odd number of inputs are TRUE. Figure 2.30 shows the truth table for a three-input XOR with the rows circled that produce TRUE outputs. From the truth table, we read off a Boolean equation in sum-of-products form in Equation 2.6. Unfortunately, there is no way to simplify this equation into fewer implicants.

$$Y = \overline{A}\,\overline{B}C + \overline{A}B\overline{C} + A\overline{B}\,\overline{C} + ABC \qquad (2.6)$$

On the other hand, $A \oplus B \oplus C = (A \oplus B) \oplus C$ (prove this to yourself by perfect induction if you are in doubt). Therefore, the three-input XOR can be built out of a cascade of two-input XORs, as shown in Figure 2.31.

Similarly, an eight-input XOR would require 128 eight-input AND gates and one 128-input OR gate for a two-level sum-of-products implementation. A much better option is to use a tree of two-input XOR gates, as shown in Figure 2.32.

Figure 2.30 Three-input XOR: (a) functional specification and (b) two-level logic implementation

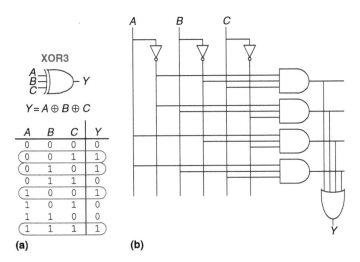

Selecting the best multilevel implementation of a specific logic function is not a simple process. Moreover, "best" has many meanings: fewest gates, fastest, shortest design time, least cost, least power consumption. In Chapter 5, you will see that the "best" circuit in one technology is not necessarily the best in another. For example, we have been using ANDs and ORs, but in CMOS, NANDs and NORs are more efficient. With some experience, you will find that you can create a good multilevel design by inspection for most circuits. You will develop some of this experience as you study circuit examples through the rest of this book. As you are learning, explore various design options and think about the trade-offs. Computer-aided design (CAD) tools are also available to search a vast space of possible multilevel designs and seek the one that best fits your constraints given the available building blocks.

Figure 2.31 **Three-input XOR using two-input XORs**

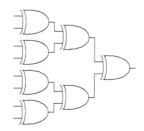

Figure 2.32 **Eight-input XOR using seven two-input XORs**

2.5.2 Bubble Pushing

You may recall from Section 1.7.6 that CMOS circuits prefer NANDs and NORs over ANDs and ORs. But reading the equation by inspection from a multilevel circuit with NANDs and NORs can get pretty hairy. Figure 2.33 shows a multilevel circuit whose function is not immediately clear by inspection. Bubble pushing is a helpful way to redraw these circuits so that the bubbles cancel out and the function can be more easily determined. Building on the principles from Section 2.3.3, the guidelines for bubble pushing are as follows:

▸   Begin at the output of the circuit and work toward the inputs.

▸   Push any bubbles on the final output back toward the inputs so that you can read an equation in terms of the output (for example, Y) instead of the complement of the output ($\overline{Y}$).

▸   Working backward, draw each gate in a form so that bubbles cancel. If the current gate has an input bubble, draw the preceding gate with an output bubble. If the current gate does not have an input bubble, draw the preceding gate without an output bubble.

Figure 2.34 shows how to redraw Figure 2.33 according to the bubble pushing guidelines. Starting at the output Y, the NAND gate has a bubble on the output that we wish to eliminate. We push the output bubble back to form an OR with inverted inputs, shown in

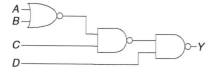

Figure 2.33 **Multilevel circuit using NANDs and NORs**

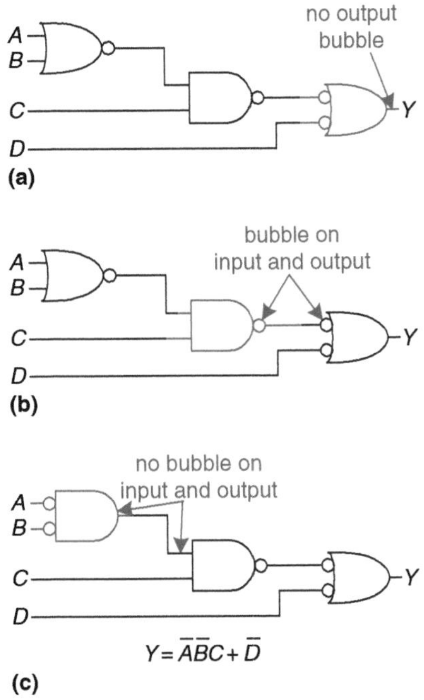

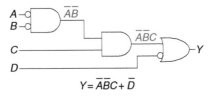

Figure 2.34 Bubble-pushed circuit

Figure 2.34(a). Working to the left, the rightmost gate has an input bubble that cancels with the output bubble of the middle NAND gate, so no change is necessary, as shown in Figure 2.34(b). The middle gate has no input bubble, so we transform the leftmost gate to have no output bubble, as shown in Figure 2.34(c). Now all of the bubbles in the circuit cancel except at the inputs, so the function can be read by inspection in terms of ANDs and ORs of true or complementary inputs: $Y = \overline{A}\,\overline{B}C + \overline{D}$.

For emphasis of this last point, Figure 2.35 shows a circuit logically equivalent to the one in Figure 2.34. The functions of internal nodes are labeled in blue. Because bubbles in series cancel, we can ignore the bubbles on the output of the middle gate and on one input of the rightmost gate to produce the logically equivalent circuit of Figure 2.35.

Figure 2.35 Logically equivalent bubble-pushed circuit

Example 2.8 BUBBLE PUSHING FOR CMOS LOGIC

Most designers think in terms of AND and OR gates, but suppose you would like to implement the circuit in Figure 2.36 in CMOS logic, which favors NAND and NOR gates. Use bubble pushing to convert the circuit to NANDs, NORs, and inverters.

Solution: A brute force solution is to just replace each AND gate with a NAND and an inverter, and each OR gate with a NOR and an inverter, as shown in Figure 2.37. This requires eight gates. Notice that the inverter is drawn with the bubble on the front rather than back, to emphasize how the bubble can cancel with the preceding inverting gate.

For a better solution, observe that bubbles can be added to the output of a gate and the input of the next gate without changing the function, as shown in Figure 2.38(a). The final AND is converted to a NAND and an inverter, as shown in Figure 2.38(b). This solution requires only five gates.

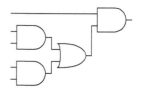

Figure 2.36 Circuit using ANDs and ORs

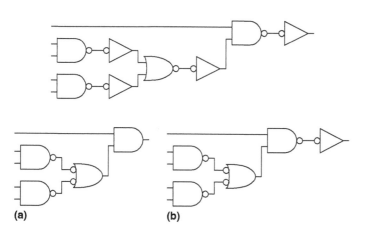

(a) (b)

Figure 2.37 Poor circuit using NANDs and NORs

Figure 2.38 Better circuit using NANDs and NORs

2.6 X'S AND Z'S, OH MY

Boolean algebra is limited to 0's and 1's. However, real circuits can also have illegal and floating values, represented symbolically by X and Z.

2.6.1 Illegal Value: X

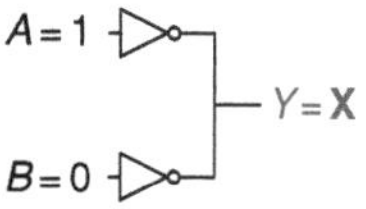

The symbol X indicates that the circuit node has an *unknown* or *illegal* value. This commonly happens if it is being driven to both 0 and 1 at the same time. Figure 2.39 shows a case where node Y is driven both HIGH and LOW. This situation, called *contention*, is considered to be

$A = 1$

$B = 0$

$Y = X$

Figure 2.39 Circuit with contention

an error and must be avoided. The actual voltage on a node with contention may be somewhere between 0 and V_{DD}, depending on the relative strengths of the gates driving HIGH and LOW. It is often, but not always, in the forbidden zone. Contention also can cause large amounts of power to flow between the fighting gates, resulting in the circuit getting hot and possibly damaged.

X values are also sometimes used by circuit simulators to indicate an uninitialized value. For example, if you forget to specify the value of an input, the simulator may assume it is an X to warn you of the problem.

As mentioned in Section 2.4, digital designers also use the symbol X to indicate "don't care" values in truth tables. Be sure not to mix up the two meanings. When X appears in a truth table, it indicates that the value of the variable in the truth table is unimportant (can be either 0 or 1). When X appears in a circuit, it means that the circuit node has an unknown or illegal value.

2.6.2 Floating Value: Z

The symbol Z indicates that a node is being driven neither HIGH nor LOW. The node is said to be *floating, high impedance,* or *high Z.* A typical misconception is that a floating or undriven node is the same as a logic 0. In reality, a floating node might be 0, might be 1, or might be at some voltage in between, depending on the history of the system. A floating node does not always mean there is an error in the circuit, so long as some other circuit element does drive the node to a valid logic level when the value of the node is relevant to circuit operation.

One common way to produce a floating node is to forget to connect a voltage to a circuit input, or to assume that an unconnected input is the same as an input with the value of 0. This mistake may cause the circuit to behave erratically as the floating input randomly changes from 0 to 1. Indeed, touching the circuit may be enough to trigger the change by means of static electricity from the body. We have seen circuits that operate correctly only as long as the student keeps a finger pressed on a chip.

The *tristate buffer,* shown in Figure 2.40, has three possible output states: HIGH (1), LOW (0), and floating (Z). The tristate buffer has an input A, output Y, and *enable E.* When the enable is TRUE, the tristate buffer acts as a simple buffer, transferring the input value to the output. When the enable is FALSE, the output is allowed to float (Z).

The tristate buffer in Figure 2.40 has an *active high* enable. That is, when the enable is HIGH (1), the buffer is enabled. Figure 2.41 shows a tristate buffer with an *active low* enable. When the enable is LOW (0),

Tristate
Buffer

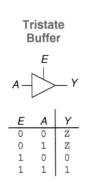

E	A	Y
0	0	Z
0	1	Z
1	0	0
1	1	1

Figure 2.40 Tristate buffer

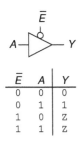

$\bar{E}$	A	Y
0	0	0
0	1	1
1	0	Z
1	1	Z

Figure 2.41 Tristate buffer with active low enable

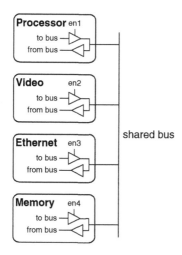

Figure 2.42 Tristate bus connecting multiple chips

the buffer is enabled. We show that the signal is active low by putting a bubble on its input wire. We often indicate an active low input by drawing a bar over its name, $\overline{E}$, or appending the letters "b" or "bar" after its name, *Eb* or *Ebar*.

Tristate buffers are commonly used on *busses* that connect multiple chips. For example, a microprocessor, a video controller, and an Ethernet controller might all need to communicate with the memory system in a personal computer. Each chip can connect to a shared memory bus using tristate buffers, as shown in Figure 2.42. Only one chip at a time is allowed to assert its enable signal to drive a value onto the bus. The other chips must produce floating outputs so that they do not cause contention with the chip talking to the memory. Any chip can read the information from the shared bus at any time. Such tristate busses were once common. However, in modern computers, higher speeds are possible with *point-to-point links*, in which chips are connected to each other directly rather than over a shared bus.

2.7 KARNAUGH MAPS

After working through several minimizations of Boolean equations using Boolean algebra, you will realize that, if you're not careful, you sometimes end up with a completely *different* equation instead of a simplified equation. *Karnaugh maps* (*K-maps*) are a graphical method for simplifying Boolean equations. They were invented in 1953 by Maurice Karnaugh, a telecommunications engineer at Bell Labs. K-maps work well for problems

Maurice Karnaugh, 1924–. Graduated with a bachelor's degree in physics from the City College of New York in 1948 and earned a Ph.D. in physics from Yale in 1952.

Worked at Bell Labs and IBM from 1952 to 1993 and as a computer science professor at the Polytechnic University of New York from 1980 to 1999.

Gray codes were patented (U.S. Patent 2,632,058) by Frank Gray, a Bell Labs researcher, in 1953. They are especially useful in mechanical encoders because a slight misalignment causes an error in only one bit.

Gray codes generalize to any number of bits. For example, a 3-bit Gray code sequence is:

```
000, 001, 011, 010,
110, 111, 101, 100
```

Lewis Carroll posed a related puzzle in *Vanity Fair* in 1879.

"The rules of the Puzzle are simple enough. Two words are proposed, of the same length; and the puzzle consists of linking these together by interposing other words, each of which shall differ from the next word in one letter only. That is to say, one letter may be changed in one of the given words, then one letter in the word so obtained, and so on, till we arrive at the other given word."

For example, SHIP to DOCK:

```
SHIP, SLIP, SLOP,
SLOT, SOOT, LOOT,
LOOK, LOCK, DOCK.
```

Can you find a shorter sequence?

with up to four variables. More important, they give insight into manipulating Boolean equations.

Recall that logic minimization involves combining terms. Two terms containing an implicant P and the true and complementary forms of some variable A are combined to eliminate A: $PA + P\overline{A} = P$. Karnaugh maps make these combinable terms easy to see by putting them next to each other in a grid.

Figure 2.43 shows the truth table and K-map for a three-input function. The top row of the K-map gives the four possible values for the A and B inputs. The left column gives the two possible values for the C input. Each square in the K-map corresponds to a row in the truth table and contains the value of the output Y for that row. For example, the top left square corresponds to the first row in the truth table and indicates that the output value $Y = 1$ when $ABC = 000$. Just like each row in a truth table, each square in a K-map represents a single minterm. For the purpose of explanation, Figure 2.43(c) shows the minterm corresponding to each square in the K-map.

Each square, or minterm, differs from an adjacent square by a change in a single variable. This means that adjacent squares share all the same literals except one, which appears in true form in one square and in complementary form in the other. For example, the squares representing the minterms $\overline{A}\,\overline{B}\,\overline{C}$ and $\overline{A}\,\overline{B}C$ are adjacent and differ only in the variable C. You may have noticed that the A and B combinations in the top row are in a peculiar order: 00, 01, 11, 10. This order is called a *Gray code*. It differs from ordinary binary order (00, 01, 10, 11) in that adjacent entries differ only in a single variable. For example, 01 : 11 only changes A from 0 to 1, while 01 : 10 would change A from 0 to 1 and B from 1 to 0. Hence, writing the combinations in binary order would not have produced our desired property of adjacent squares differing only in one variable.

The K-map also "wraps around." The squares on the far right are effectively adjacent to the squares on the far left, in that they differ only in one variable, A. In other words, you could take the map and roll it into a cylinder, then join the ends of the cylinder to form a torus (i.e., a donut), and still guarantee that adjacent squares would differ only in one variable.

2.7.1 Circular Thinking

In the K-map in Figure 2.43, only two minterms are present in the equation, $\overline{A}\,\overline{B}\,\overline{C}$ and $\overline{A}\,\overline{B}C$, as indicated by the 1's in the left column. Reading the minterms from the K-map is exactly equivalent to reading equations in sum-of-products form directly from the truth table.

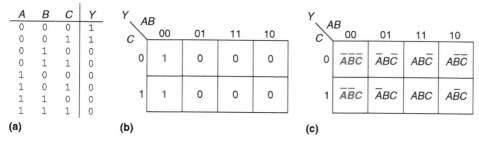

Figure 2.43 **Three-input function: (a) truth table, (b) K-map, (c) K-map showing minterms**

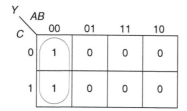

Figure 2.44 **K-map minimization**

As before, we can use Boolean algebra to minimize equations in sum-of-products form.

$$Y = \overline{A}\,\overline{B}\,\overline{C} + \overline{A}\,\overline{B}C = \overline{A}\,\overline{B}(\overline{C} + C) = \overline{A}\,\overline{B} \tag{2.7}$$

K-maps help us do this simplification graphically by *circling* 1's in adjacent squares, as shown in Figure 2.44. For each circle, we write the corresponding implicant. Remember from Section 2.2 that an implicant is the product of one or more literals. Variables whose true *and* complementary forms are both in the circle are excluded from the implicant. In this case, the variable C has both its true form (1) and its complementary form (0) in the circle, so we do not include it in the implicant. In other words, Y is TRUE when $A = B = 0$, independent of C. So the implicant is $\overline{A}\,\overline{B}$. The K-map gives the same answer we reached using Boolean algebra.

2.7.2 Logic Minimization with K-Maps

K-maps provide an easy visual way to minimize logic. Simply circle all the rectangular blocks of 1's in the map, using the fewest possible number of circles. Each circle should be as large as possible. Then read off the implicants that were circled.

More formally, recall that a Boolean equation is minimized when it is written as a sum of the fewest number of prime implicants. Each circle on the K-map represents an implicant. The largest possible circles are prime implicants.

For example, in the K-map of Figure 2.44, $\overline{A}\,\overline{B}\,\overline{C}$ and $\overline{A}\,\overline{B}C$ are implicants, but *not* prime implicants. Only $\overline{A}\,\overline{B}$ is a prime implicant in that K-map. Rules for finding a minimized equation from a K-map are as follows:

▶ Use the fewest circles necessary to cover all the 1's.

▶ All the squares in each circle must contain 1's.

▶ Each circle must span a rectangular block that is a power of 2 (i.e., 1, 2, or 4) squares in each direction.

▶ Each circle should be as large as possible.

▶ A circle may wrap around the edges of the K-map.

▶ A 1 in a K-map may be circled multiple times if doing so allows fewer circles to be used.

Example 2.9 MINIMIZATION OF A THREE-VARIABLE FUNCTION
                USING A K-MAP

Suppose we have the function $Y = F(A, B, C)$ with the K-map shown in Figure 2.45. Minimize the equation using the K-map.

Solution: Circle the 1's in the K-map using as few circles as possible, as shown in Figure 2.46. Each circle in the K-map represents a prime implicant, and the dimension of each circle is a power of two (2×1 and 2×2). We form the prime implicant for each circle by writing those variables that appear in the circle only in true or only in complementary form.

For example, in the 2×1 circle, the true and complementary forms of B are included in the circle, so we *do not* include B in the prime implicant. However, only the true form of A (A) and complementary form of C ($\overline{C}$) are in this circle, so we include these variables in the prime implicant $A\overline{C}$. Similarly, the 2×2 circle covers all squares where $B = 0$, so the prime implicant is $\overline{B}$.

Notice how the top-right square (minterm) is covered twice to make the prime implicant circles as large as possible. As we saw with Boolean algebra techniques, this is equivalent to sharing a minterm to reduce the size of the implicant. Also notice how the circle covering four squares wraps around the sides of the K-map.

Figure 2.45 K-map for Example 2.9

Y $\diagdown$ AB C	00	01	11	10
0	1	0	1	1
1	1	0	0	1

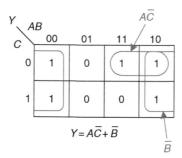

Figure 2.46 **Solution for Example 2.9**

$$Y = A\overline{C} + \overline{B}$$

Example 2.10 SEVEN-SEGMENT DISPLAY DECODER

A *seven-segment display decoder* takes a 4-bit data input $D_{3:0}$ and produces seven outputs to control light-emitting diodes to display a digit from 0 to 9. The seven outputs are often called segments a through g, or S_a–S_g, as defined in Figure 2.47. The digits are shown in Figure 2.48. Write a truth table for the outputs, and use K-maps to find Boolean equations for outputs S_a and S_b. Assume that illegal input values (10–15) produce a blank readout.

Solution: The truth table is given in Table 2.6. For example, an input of 0000 should turn on all segments except S_g.

Each of the seven outputs is an independent function of four variables. The K-maps for outputs S_a and S_b are shown in Figure 2.49. Remember that adjacent squares may differ in only a single variable, so we label the rows and columns in Gray code order: 00, 01, 11, 10. Be careful to also remember this ordering when *entering* the output values into the squares.

Next, circle the prime implicants. Use the fewest number of circles necessary to cover all the 1's. A circle can wrap around the edges (vertical *and* horizontal), and a 1 may be circled more than once. Figure 2.50 shows the prime implicants and the simplified Boolean equations.

Note that the minimal set of prime implicants is not unique. For example, the 0000 entry in the S_a K-map was circled along with the 1000 entry to produce the $\overline{D}_2\overline{D}_1\overline{D}_0$ minterm. The circle could have included the 0010 entry instead, producing a $\overline{D}_3\overline{D}_2\overline{D}_0$ minterm, as shown with dashed lines in Figure 2.51.

Figure 2.52 (see page 82) illustrates a common error in which a nonprime implicant was chosen to cover the 1 in the upper left corner. This minterm, $\overline{D}_3\overline{D}_2\overline{D}_1\overline{D}_0$, gives a sum-of-products equation that is *not* minimal. The minterm could have been combined with either of the adjacent ones to form a larger circle, as was done in the previous two figures.

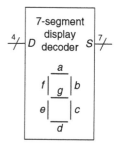

Figure 2.47 **Seven-segment display decoder icon**

Figure 2.48 **Seven-segment display digits**

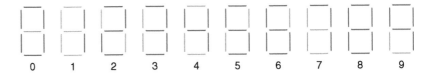

Table 2.6 **Seven-segment display decoder truth table**

$D_{3:0}$	S_a	S_b	S_c	S_d	S_e	S_f	S_g
0000	1	1	1	1	1	1	0
0001	0	1	1	0	0	0	0
0010	1	1	0	1	1	0	1
0011	1	1	1	1	0	0	1
0100	0	1	1	0	0	1	1
0101	1	0	1	1	0	1	1
0110	1	0	1	1	1	1	1
0111	1	1	1	0	0	0	0
1000	1	1	1	1	1	1	1
1001	1	1	1	0	0	1	1
others	0	0	0	0	0	0	0

Figure 2.49 **Karnaugh maps for S_a and S_b**

S_a

$D_{1:0}$ \ $D_{3:2}$	00	01	11	10
00	1	0	0	1
01	0	1	0	1
11	1	1	0	0
10	1	1	0	0

S_b

$D_{1:0}$ \ $D_{3:2}$	00	01	11	10
00	1	1	0	1
01	1	0	0	1
11	1	1	0	0
10	1	0	0	0

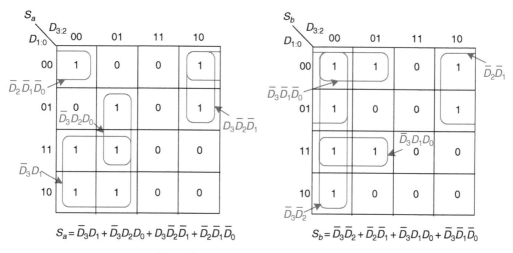

$$S_a = \bar{D}_3 D_1 + \bar{D}_3 D_2 D_0 + D_3 \bar{D}_2 \bar{D}_1 + \bar{D}_2 \bar{D}_1 \bar{D}_0$$

$$S_b = \bar{D}_3 \bar{D}_2 + \bar{D}_2 \bar{D}_1 + \bar{D}_3 D_1 D_0 + \bar{D}_3 \bar{D}_1 \bar{D}_0$$

Figure 2.50 K-map solution for Example 2.10

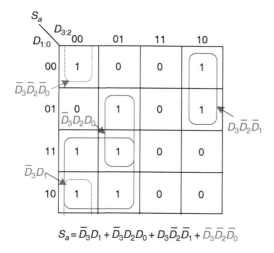

$$S_a = \bar{D}_3 D_1 + \bar{D}_3 D_2 D_0 + D_3 \bar{D}_2 \bar{D}_1 + \bar{D}_3 \bar{D}_2 \bar{D}_0$$

Figure 2.51 Alternative K-map for S_a showing different set of prime implicants

2.7.3 Don't Cares

Recall that "don't care" entries for truth table inputs were introduced in Section 2.4 to reduce the number of rows in the table when some variables do not affect the output. They are indicated by the symbol X, which means that the entry can be either 0 or 1.

Don't cares also appear in truth table outputs where the output value is unimportant or the corresponding input combination can never

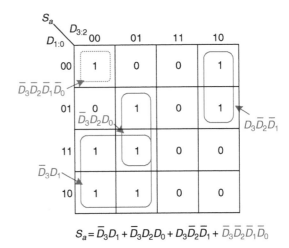

Figure 2.52 Alternative K-map for S_a showing incorrect nonprime implicant

$$S_a = \bar{D}_3 D_1 + \bar{D}_3 D_2 D_0 + D_3 \bar{D}_2 \bar{D}_1 + \bar{D}_3 \bar{D}_2 \bar{D}_1 \bar{D}_0$$

happen. Such outputs can be treated as either 0's or 1's at the designer's discretion.

In a K-map, X's allow for even more logic minimization. They can be circled if they help cover the 1's with fewer or larger circles, but they do not have to be circled if they are not helpful.

Example 2.11 SEVEN-SEGMENT DISPLAY DECODER WITH DON'T CARES

Repeat Example 2.10 if we don't care about the output values for illegal input values of 10 to 15.

Solution: The K-map is shown in Figure 2.53 with X entries representing don't care. Because don't cares can be 0 or 1, we circle a don't care if it allows us to cover the 1's with fewer or bigger circles. Circled don't cares are treated as 1's, whereas uncircled don't cares are 0's. Observe how a 2 × 2 square wrapping around all four corners is circled for segment S_a. Use of don't cares simplifies the logic substantially.

2.7.4 The Big Picture

Boolean algebra and Karnaugh maps are two methods of logic simplification. Ultimately, the goal is to find a low-cost method of implementing a particular logic function.

In modern engineering practice, computer programs called *logic synthesizers* produce simplified circuits from a description of the logic function, as we will see in Chapter 4. For large problems, logic synthesizers are much more efficient than humans. For small problems, a

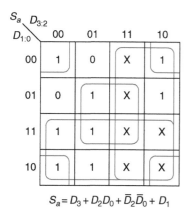

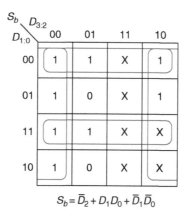

$$S_a = D_3 + D_2D_0 + \bar{D}_2\bar{D}_0 + D_1$$

$$S_b = \bar{D}_2 + D_1D_0 + \bar{D}_1\bar{D}_0$$

Figure 2.53 **K-map solution with don't cares**

human with a bit of experience can find a good solution by inspection. Neither of the authors has ever used a Karnaugh map in real life to solve a practical problem. But the insight gained from the principles underlying Karnaugh maps is valuable. And Karnaugh maps often appear at job interviews!

2.8 COMBINATIONAL BUILDING BLOCKS

Combinational logic is often grouped into larger building blocks to build more complex systems. This is an application of the principle of abstraction, hiding the unnecessary gate-level details to emphasize the function of the building block. We have already studied three such building blocks: full adders (from Section 2.1), priority circuits (from Section 2.4), and seven-segment display decoders (from Section 2.7). This section introduces two more commonly used building blocks: multiplexers and decoders. Chapter 5 covers other combinational building blocks.

2.8.1 Multiplexers

Multiplexers are among the most commonly used combinational circuits. They choose an output from among several possible inputs based on the value of a *select* signal. A multiplexer is sometimes affectionately called a *mux*.

2:1 Multiplexer

Figure 2.54 shows the schematic and truth table for a 2:1 multiplexer with two data inputs D_0 and D_1, a select input S, and one output Y. The multiplexer chooses between the two data inputs based on the select: if $S = 0$, $Y = D_0$, and if $S = 1$, $Y = D_1$. S is also called a *control signal* because it controls what the multiplexer does.

A 2:1 multiplexer can be built from sum-of-products logic as shown in Figure 2.55. The Boolean equation for the multiplexer may be derived

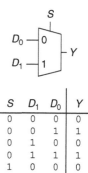

S	D_1	D_0	Y
0	0	0	0
0	0	1	1
0	1	0	0
0	1	1	1
1	0	0	0
1	0	1	0
1	1	0	1
1	1	1	1

Figure 2.54 **2:1 multiplexer symbol and truth table**

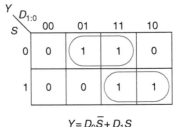

$$Y = D_0\overline{S} + D_1 S$$

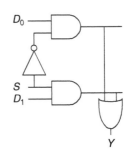

Figure 2.55 2:1 multiplexer implementation using two-level logic

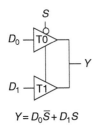

$$Y = D_0\overline{S} + D_1 S$$

Figure 2.56 Multiplexer using tristate buffers

Shorting together the outputs of multiple gates technically violates the rules for combinational circuits given in Section 2.1. But because exactly one of the outputs is driven at any time, this exception is allowed.

Figure 2.57 4:1 multiplexer

with a Karnaugh map or read off by inspection (Y is 1 if $S = 0$ AND D_0 is 1 OR if $S = 1$ AND D_1 is 1).

Alternatively, multiplexers can be built from tristate buffers as shown in Figure 2.56. The tristate enables are arranged such that, at all times, exactly one tristate buffer is active. When $S = 0$, tristate T0 is enabled, allowing D_0 to flow to Y. When $S = 1$, tristate T1 is enabled, allowing D_1 to flow to Y.

Wider Multiplexers

A 4:1 multiplexer has four data inputs and one output, as shown in Figure 2.57. Two select signals are needed to choose among the four data inputs. The 4:1 multiplexer can be built using sum-of-products logic, tristates, or multiple 2:1 multiplexers, as shown in Figure 2.58.

The product terms enabling the tristates can be formed using AND gates and inverters. They can also be formed using a decoder, which we will introduce in Section 2.8.2.

Wider multiplexers, such as 8:1 and 16:1 multiplexers, can be built by expanding the methods shown in Figure 2.58. In general, an N:1 multiplexer needs $\log_2 N$ select lines. Again, the best implementation choice depends on the target technology.

Multiplexer Logic

Multiplexers can be used as *lookup tables* to perform logic functions. Figure 2.59 shows a 4:1 multiplexer used to implement a two-input

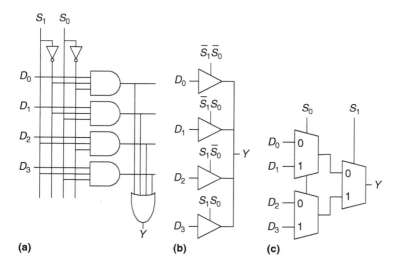

Figure 2.58 4:1 multiplexer implementations: (a) two-level logic, (b) tristates, (c) hierarchical

AND gate. The inputs, A and B, serve as select lines. The multiplexer data inputs are connected to 0 or 1 according to the corresponding row of the truth table. In general, a 2^N-input multiplexer can be programmed to perform any N-input logic function by applying 0's and 1's to the appropriate data inputs. Indeed, by changing the data inputs, the multiplexer can be reprogrammed to perform a different function.

With a little cleverness, we can cut the multiplexer size in half, using only a 2^{N-1}-input multiplexer to perform any N-input logic function. The strategy is to provide one of the literals, as well as 0's and 1's, to the multiplexer data inputs.

To illustrate this principle, Figure 2.60 shows two-input AND and XOR functions implemented with 2:1 multiplexers. We start with an ordinary truth table, and then combine pairs of rows to eliminate the rightmost input variable by expressing the output in terms of this variable. For example, in the case of AND, when $A = 0$, $Y = 0$, regardless of B. When $A = 1$, $Y = 0$ if $B = 0$ and $Y = 1$ if $B = 1$, so $Y = B$. We then use the multiplexer as a lookup table according to the new, smaller truth table.

A	B	Y
0	0	0
0	1	0
1	0	0
1	1	1

$Y = AB$

Figure 2.59 4:1 multiplexer implementation of two-input AND function

Example 2.12 LOGIC WITH MULTIPLEXERS

Alyssa P. Hacker needs to implement the function $Y = A\overline{B} + \overline{B}\,\overline{C} + \overline{A}BC$ to finish her senior project, but when she looks in her lab kit, the only part she has left is an 8:1 multiplexer. How does she implement the function?

Solution: Figure 2.61 shows Alyssa's implementation using a single 8:1 multiplexer. The multiplexer acts as a lookup table where each row in the truth table corresponds to a multiplexer input.

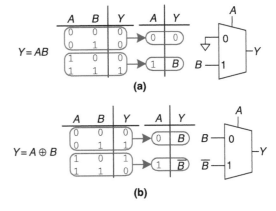

Figure 2.60 Multiplexer logic using variable inputs

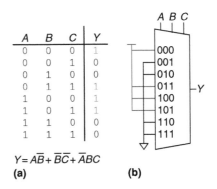

Figure 2.61 Alyssa's circuit: (a) truth table, (b) 8:1 multiplexer implementation

---

Example 2.13 LOGIC WITH MULTIPLEXERS, REPRISED

Alyssa turns on her circuit one more time before the final presentation and blows up the 8:1 multiplexer. (She accidently powered it with 20 V instead of 5 V after not sleeping all night.) She begs her friends for spare parts and they give her a 4:1 multiplexer and an inverter. Can she build her circuit with only these parts?

Solution: Alyssa reduces her truth table to four rows by letting the output depend on C. (She could also have chosen to rearrange the columns of the truth table to let the output depend on A or B.) Figure 2.62 shows the new design.

2.8.2 Decoders

A decoder has N inputs and 2^N outputs. It asserts exactly one of its outputs depending on the input combination. Figure 2.63 shows a 2:4 decoder. When $A_{1:0} = 00$, Y_0 is 1. When $A_{1:0} = 01$, Y_1 is 1. And so forth. The outputs are called *one-hot*, because exactly one is "hot" (HIGH) at a given time.

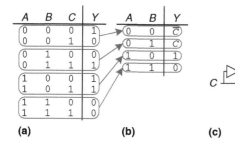

A	B	C	Y
0	0	0	1
0	0	1	0
0	1	0	0
0	1	1	1
1	0	0	1
1	0	1	1
1	1	0	0
1	1	1	0

A	B	Y
0	0	$\overline{C}$
0	1	C
1	0	1
1	1	0

(a)   **(b)**   **(c)**

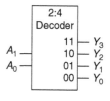

Figure 2.62 **Alyssa's new circuit**

Example 2.14 DECODER IMPLEMENTATION

Implement a 2:4 decoder with AND, OR, and NOT gates.

Solution: Figure 2.64 shows an implementation for the 2:4 decoder using four AND gates. Each gate depends on either the true or the complementary form of each input. In general, an N:2^N decoder can be constructed from 2^N N-input AND gates that accept the various combinations of true or complementary inputs. Each output in a decoder represents a single minterm. For example, Y_0 represents the minterm $\overline{A_1}\,\overline{A_0}$. This fact will be handy when using decoders with other digital building blocks.

A_1	A_0	Y_3	Y_2	Y_1	Y_0
0	0	0	0	0	1
0	1	0	0	1	0
1	0	0	1	0	0
1	1	1	0	0	0

Figure 2.63 **2:4 decoder**

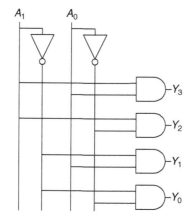

Figure 2.64 **2:4 decoder implementation**

Decoder Logic

Decoders can be combined with OR gates to build logic functions. Figure 2.65 shows the two-input XNOR function using a 2:4 decoder and a single OR gate. Because each output of a decoder represents a single minterm, the function is built as the OR of all the minterms in the function. In Figure 2.65, $Y = \overline{A}\,\overline{B} + AB = \overline{A \oplus B}$.

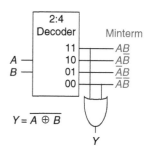

Figure 2.65 **Logic function using decoder**

When using decoders to build logic, it is easiest to express functions as a truth table or in canonical sum-of-products form. An N-input function with M 1's in the truth table can be built with an $N:2^N$ decoder and an M-input OR gate attached to all of the minterms containing 1's in the truth table. This concept will be applied to the building of Read Only Memories (ROMs) in Section 5.5.6.

2.9 TIMING

In previous sections, we have been concerned primarily with whether the circuit works—ideally, using the fewest gates. However, as any seasoned circuit designer will attest, one of the most challenging issues in circuit design is *timing*: making a circuit run fast.

An output takes time to change in response to an input change. Figure 2.66 shows the *delay* between an input change and the subsequent output change for a buffer. The figure is called a *timing diagram*; it portrays the *transient response* of the buffer circuit when an input changes. The transition from LOW to HIGH is called the *rising edge*. Similarly, the transition from HIGH to LOW (not shown in the figure) is called the *falling edge*. The blue arrow indicates that the rising edge of Y is caused by the rising edge of A. We measure delay from the *50% point* of the input signal, A, to the *50% point* of the output signal, Y. The 50% point is the point at which the signal is half-way (50%) between its LOW and HIGH values as it transitions.

2.9.1 Propagation and Contamination Delay

> When designers speak of calculating the *delay* of a circuit, they generally are referring to the worst-case value (the propagation delay), unless it is clear otherwise from the context.

Combinational logic is characterized by its *propagation delay* and *contamination delay*. The propagation delay t_{pd} is the maximum time from when an input changes until the output or outputs reach their final value. The contamination delay t_{cd} is the minimum time from when an input changes until any output starts to change its value.

Figure 2.66 Circuit delay

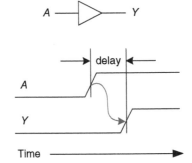

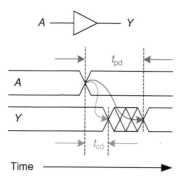

Figure 2.67 Propagation and contamination delay

Figure 2.67 illustrates a buffer's propagation delay and contamination delay in blue and gray, respectively. The figure shows that A is initially either HIGH or LOW and changes to the other state at a particular time; we are interested only in the fact that it changes, not what value it has. In response, Y changes some time later. The arcs indicate that Y may start to change t_{cd} after A transitions and that Y definitely settles to its new value within t_{pd}.

The underlying causes of delay in circuits include the time required to charge the capacitance in a circuit and the speed of light. t_{pd} and t_{cd} may be different for many reasons, including

▸ different rising and falling delays

▸ multiple inputs and outputs, some of which are faster than others

▸ circuits slowing down when hot and speeding up when cold

Calculating t_{pd} and t_{cd} requires delving into the lower levels of abstraction beyond the scope of this book. However, manufacturers normally supply data sheets specifying these delays for each gate.

Along with the factors already listed, propagation and contamination delays are also determined by the *path* a signal takes from input to output. Figure 2.68 shows a four-input logic circuit. The *critical path*, shown in blue, is the path from input A or B to output Y. It is the longest, and

Circuit delays are ordinarily on the order of picoseconds (1 ps = 10^{-12} seconds) to nanoseconds (1 ns = 10^{-9} seconds). Trillions of picoseconds have elapsed in the time you spent reading this sidebar.

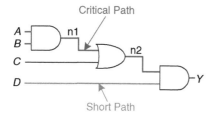

Figure 2.68 Short path and critical path

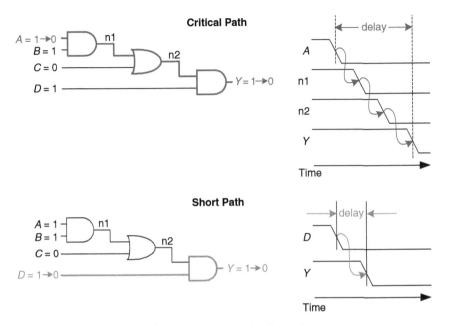

Figure 2.69 Critical and short path waveforms

therefore the slowest, path, because the input travels through three gates to the output. This path is critical because it limits the speed at which the circuit operates. The *short path* through the circuit, shown in gray, is from input D to output Y. This is the shortest, and therefore the fastest, path through the circuit, because the input travels through only a single gate to the output.

The propagation delay of a combinational circuit is the sum of the propagation delays through each element on the critical path. The contamination delay is the sum of the contamination delays through each element on the short path. These delays are illustrated in Figure 2.69 and are described by the following equations:

$$t_{pd} = 2t_{pd\_AND} + t_{pd\_OR} \tag{2.8}$$

$$t_{cd} = t_{cd\_AND} \tag{2.9}$$

Although we are ignoring wire delay in this analysis, digital circuits are now so fast that the delay of long wires can be as important as the delay of the gates. The speed of light delay in wires is covered in Appendix A.

Example 2.15 FINDING DELAYS

Ben Bitdiddle needs to find the propagation delay and contamination delay of the circuit shown in Figure 2.70. According to his data book, each gate has a propagation delay of 100 picoseconds (ps) and a contamination delay of 60 ps.

Solution: Ben begins by finding the critical path and the shortest path through the circuit. The critical path, highlighted in blue in Figure 2.71, is from input A or B through three gates to the output Y. Hence, t_{pd} is three times the propagation delay of a single gate, or 300 ps.

The shortest path, shown in gray in Figure 2.72, is from input C, D, or E through two gates to the output Y. There are only two gates in the shortest path, so t_{cd} is 120 ps.

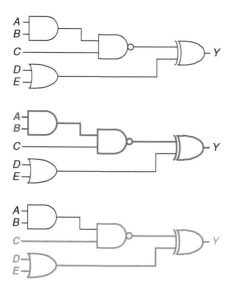

Figure 2.70 **Ben's circuit**

Figure 2.71 **Ben's critical path**

Figure 2.72 **Ben's shortest path**

Example 2.16 MULTIPLEXER TIMING: CONTROL-CRITICAL
VS. DATA-CRITICAL

Compare the worst-case timing of the three four-input multiplexer designs shown in Figure 2.58 in Section 2.8.1. Table 2.7 lists the propagation delays for the components. What is the critical path for each design? Given your timing analysis, why might you choose one design over the other?

Solution: One of the critical paths for each of the three design options is highlighted in blue in Figures 2.73 and 2.74. t_{pd_sy} indicates the propagation delay from input S to output Y; t_{pd_dy} indicates the propagation delay from input D to output Y; t_{pd} is the worst of the two: $\max(t_{pd\_sy}, t_{pd\_dy})$.

For both the two-level logic and tristate implementations in Figure 2.73, the critical path is from one of the control signals S to the output Y: $t_{pd} = t_{pd\_sy}$. These circuits are *control critical*, because the critical path is from the control signals to the output. Any additional delay in the control signals will add directly to the worst-case delay. The delay from D to Y in Figure 2.73(b) is only 50 ps, compared with the delay from S to Y of 125 ps.

Figure 2.74 shows the hierarchical implementation of the 4:1 multiplexer using two stages of 2:1 multiplexers. The critical path is from any of the D inputs to the output. This circuit is *data critical*, because the critical path is from the data input to the output: $t_{pd} = t_{pd\_dy}$.

If data inputs arrive well before the control inputs, we would prefer the design with the shortest control-to-output delay (the hierarchical design in Figure 2.74). Similarly, if the control inputs arrive well before the data inputs, we would prefer the design with the shortest data-to-output delay (the tristate design in Figure 2.73(b)).

The best choice depends not only on the critical path through the circuit and the input arrival times, but also on the power, cost, and availability of parts.

Table 2.7 **Timing specifications for multiplexer circuit elements**

Gate	t_{pd} (ps)
NOT	30
2-input AND	60
3-input AND	80
4-input OR	90
tristate (A to Y)	50
tristate (enable to Y)	35

2.9.2 Glitches

So far we have discussed the case where a single input transition causes a single output transition. However, it is possible that a single input transition can cause *multiple* output transitions. These are called *glitches* or *hazards*. Although glitches usually don't cause problems, it is important to realize that they exist and recognize them when looking at timing diagrams. Figure 2.75 shows a circuit with a glitch and the Karnaugh map of the circuit.

The Boolean equation is correctly minimized, but let's look at what happens when $A = 0$, $C = 1$, and B transitions from 1 to 0. Figure 2.76 (see page 94) illustrates this scenario. The short path (shown in gray) goes through two gates, the AND and OR gates. The critical path (shown in blue) goes through an inverter and two gates, the AND and OR gates.

Hazards have another meaning related to microarchitecture in Chapter 7, so we will stick with the term *glitches* for multiple output transitions to avoid confusion.

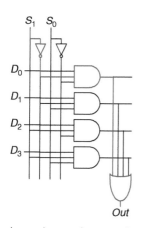

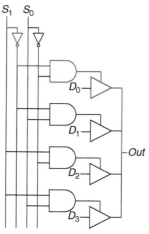

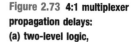

Figure 2.73 4:1 multiplexer propagation delays: (a) two-level logic, (b) tristate

(a)

$$t_{pd\_sy} = t_{pd\_INV} + t_{pd\_AND3} + t_{pd\_OR4}$$
$$= 30 \text{ ps} + 80 \text{ ps} + 90 \text{ ps}$$
$$= 200 \text{ ps}$$
$$t_{pd\_dy} = t_{pd\_AND3} + t_{pd\_OR4}$$
$$= 170 \text{ ps}$$

(b)

$$t_{pd\_sy} = t_{pd\_INV} + t_{pd\_AND2} + t_{pd\_TRI\_sy}$$
$$= 30 \text{ ps} + 60 \text{ ps} + 35 \text{ ps}$$
$$= 125 \text{ ps}$$
$$t_{pd\_dy} = t_{pd\_TRI\_ay}$$
$$= 50 \text{ ps}$$

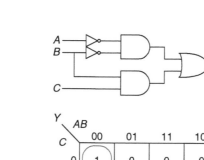

$$t_{pd\_s0y} = t_{pd\_TRI\_sy} + t_{pd\_TRI\_ay} = 85 \text{ ps}$$
$$t_{pd\_dy} = 2 \, t_{pd\_TRI\_ay} = 100 \text{ ps}$$

Figure 2.74 4:1 multiplexer propagation delays: hierarchical using 2:1 multiplexers

Y \ AB C	00	01	11	10
0	1	0	0	0
1	1	1	1	0

$$Y = \overline{A}\overline{B} + BC$$

Figure 2.75 Circuit with a glitch

As *B* transitions from 1 to 0, n2 (on the short path) falls before n1 (on the critical path) can rise. Until n1 rises, the two inputs to the OR gate are 0, and the output *Y* drops to 0. When n1 eventually rises, *Y* returns to 1. As shown in the timing diagram of Figure 2.76, *Y* starts at 1 and ends at 1 but momentarily glitches to 0.

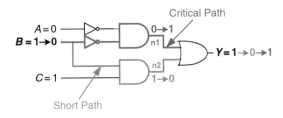

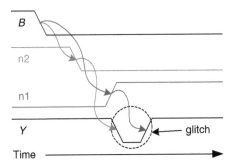

Figure 2.76 Timing of a glitch

As long as we wait for the propagation delay to elapse before we depend on the output, glitches are not a problem, because the output eventually settles to the right answer.

If we choose to, we can avoid this glitch by adding another gate to the implementation. This is easiest to understand in terms of the K-map. Figure 2.77 shows how an input transition on B from $ABC = 011$ to $ABC = 001$ moves from one prime implicant circle to another. The transition across the boundary of two prime implicants in the K-map indicates a possible glitch.

As we saw from the timing diagram in Figure 2.76, if the circuitry implementing one of the prime implicants turns *off* before the circuitry of the other prime implicant can turn *on*, there is a glitch. To fix this, we add another circle that *covers* that prime implicant boundary, as shown in Figure 2.78. You might recognize this as the consensus theorem, where the added term, $\overline{A}C$, is the consensus or redundant term.

Figure 2.77 Input change crosses implicant boundary

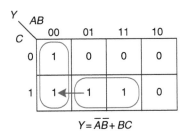

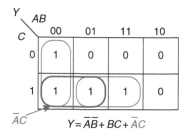

Figure 2.78 **K-map without glitch**

$$Y = \overline{A}\,\overline{B} + BC + \overline{A}C$$

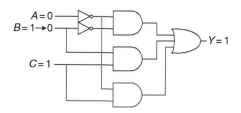

Figure 2.79 **Circuit without glitch**

Figure 2.79 shows the glitch-proof circuit. The added AND gate is highlighted in blue. Now a transition on B when $A = 0$ and $C = 1$ does not cause a glitch on the output, because the blue AND gate outputs 1 throughout the transition.

In general, a glitch can occur when a change in a single variable crosses the boundary between two prime implicants in a K-map. We can eliminate the glitch by adding redundant implicants to the K-map to cover these boundaries. This of course comes at the cost of extra hardware.

However, simultaneous transitions on multiple inputs can also cause glitches. These glitches cannot be fixed by adding hardware. Because the vast majority of interesting systems have simultaneous (or near-simultaneous) transitions on multiple inputs, glitches are a fact of life in most circuits. Although we have shown how to eliminate one kind of glitch, the point of discussing glitches is not to eliminate them but to be aware that they exist. This is especially important when looking at timing diagrams on a simulator or oscilloscope.

2.10 SUMMARY

A digital circuit is a module with discrete-valued inputs and outputs and a specification describing the function and timing of the module. This chapter has focused on combinational circuits, circuits whose outputs depend only on the current values of the inputs.

The function of a combinational circuit can be given by a truth table or a Boolean equation. The Boolean equation for any truth table can be obtained systematically using sum-of-products or product-of-sums form. In sum-of-products form, the function is written as the sum (OR) of one or more implicants. Implicants are the product (AND) of literals. Literals are the true or complementary forms of the input variables.

Boolean equations can be simplified using the rules of Boolean algebra. In particular, they can be simplified into minimal sum-of-products form by combining implicants that differ only in the true and complementary forms of one of the literals: $PA + P\overline{A} = P$. Karnaugh maps are a visual tool for minimizing functions of up to four variables. With practice, designers can usually simplify functions of a few variables by inspection. Computer-aided design tools are used for more complicated functions; such methods and tools are discussed in Chapter 4.

Logic gates are connected to create combinational circuits that perform the desired function. Any function in sum-of-products form can be built using two-level logic: NOT gates form the complements of the inputs, AND gates form the products, and OR gates form the sum. Depending on the function and the building blocks available, multilevel logic implementations with various types of gates may be more efficient. For example, CMOS circuits favor NAND and NOR gates because these gates can be built directly from CMOS transistors without requiring extra NOT gates. When using NAND and NOR gates, bubble pushing is helpful to keep track of the inversions.

Logic gates are combined to produce larger circuits such as multiplexers, decoders, and priority circuits. A multiplexer chooses one of the data inputs based on the select input. A decoder sets one of the outputs HIGH according to the inputs. A priority circuit produces an output indicating the highest priority input. These circuits are all examples of combinational building blocks. Chapter 5 will introduce more building blocks, including other arithmetic circuits. These building blocks will be used extensively to build a microprocessor in Chapter 7.

The timing specification of a combinational circuit consists of the propagation and contamination delays through the circuit. These indicate the longest and shortest times between an input change and the consequent output change. Calculating the propagation delay of a circuit involves identifying the critical path through the circuit, then adding up the propagation delays of each element along that path. There are many different ways to implement complicated combinational circuits; these ways offer trade-offs between speed and cost.

The next chapter will move to sequential circuits, whose outputs depend on current as well as previous values of the inputs. In other words, sequential circuits have *memory* of the past.

Exercises

Exercise 2.1 Write a Boolean equation in sum-of-products canonical form for each of the truth tables in Figure 2.80.

(a)

A	B	Y
0	0	1
0	1	0
1	0	1
1	1	1

(b)

A	B	C	Y
0	0	0	1
0	0	1	0
0	1	0	0
0	1	1	0
1	0	0	0
1	0	1	0
1	1	0	0
1	1	1	1

(c)

A	B	C	Y
0	0	0	1
0	0	1	0
0	1	0	1
0	1	1	0
1	0	0	1
1	0	1	1
1	1	0	0
1	1	1	1

(d)

A	B	C	D	Y
0	0	0	0	1
0	0	0	1	1
0	0	1	0	1
0	0	1	1	1
0	1	0	0	0
0	1	0	1	0
0	1	1	0	0
0	1	1	1	0
1	0	0	0	1
1	0	0	1	0
1	0	1	0	1
1	0	1	1	0
1	1	0	0	0
1	1	0	1	0
1	1	1	0	1
1	1	1	1	0

(e)

A	B	C	D	Y
0	0	0	0	1
0	0	0	1	0
0	0	1	0	0
0	0	1	1	1
0	1	0	0	0
0	1	0	1	1
0	1	1	0	1
0	1	1	1	0
1	0	0	0	0
1	0	0	1	1
1	0	1	0	1
1	0	1	1	0
1	1	0	0	1
1	1	0	1	0
1	1	1	0	0
1	1	1	1	1

Figure 2.80 Truth tables for Exercises 2.1 and 2.3

Exercise 2.2 Write a Boolean equation in sum-of-products canonical form for each of the truth tables in Figure 2.81.

(a)

A	B	Y
0	0	0
0	1	1
1	0	1
1	1	1

(b)

A	B	C	Y
0	0	0	0
0	0	1	1
0	1	0	1
0	1	1	1
1	0	0	1
1	0	1	0
1	1	0	1
1	1	1	0

(c)

A	B	C	Y
0	0	0	0
0	0	1	1
0	1	0	0
0	1	1	0
1	0	0	0
1	0	1	0
1	1	0	1
1	1	1	1

(d)

A	B	C	D	Y
0	0	0	0	1
0	0	0	1	0
0	0	1	0	1
0	0	1	1	1
0	1	0	0	0
0	1	0	1	0
0	1	1	0	1
0	1	1	1	1
1	0	0	0	1
1	0	0	1	0
1	0	1	0	1
1	0	1	1	0
1	1	0	0	0
1	1	0	1	0
1	1	1	0	0
1	1	1	1	0

(e)

A	B	C	D	Y
0	0	0	0	0
0	0	0	1	0
0	0	1	0	0
0	0	1	1	1
0	1	0	0	0
0	1	0	1	0
0	1	1	0	1
0	1	1	1	1
1	0	0	0	1
1	0	0	1	1
1	0	1	0	1
1	0	1	1	1
1	1	0	0	0
1	1	0	1	0
1	1	1	0	0
1	1	1	1	0

Figure 2.81 Truth tables for Exercises 2.2 and 2.4

Exercise 2.3 Write a Boolean equation in product-of-sums canonical form for the truth tables in Figure 2.80.

Exercise 2.4 Write a Boolean equation in product-of-sums canonical form for the truth tables in Figure 2.81.

Exercise 2.5 Minimize each of the Boolean equations from Exercise 2.1.

Exercise 2.6 Minimize each of the Boolean equations from Exercise 2.2.

Exercise 2.7 Sketch a reasonably simple combinational circuit implementing each of the functions from Exercise 2.5. Reasonably simple means that you are not wasteful of gates, but you don't waste vast amounts of time checking every possible implementation of the circuit either.

Exercise 2.8 Sketch a reasonably simple combinational circuit implementing each of the functions from Exercise 2.6.

Exercise 2.9 Repeat Exercise 2.7 using only NOT gates and AND and OR gates.

Exercise 2.10 Repeat Exercise 2.8 using only NOT gates and AND and OR gates.

Exercise 2.11 Repeat Exercise 2.7 using only NOT gates and NAND and NOR gates.

Exercise 2.12 Repeat Exercise 2.8 using only NOT gates and NAND and NOR gates.

Exercise 2.13 Simplify the following Boolean equations using Boolean theorems. Check for correctness using a truth table or K-map.

(a) $Y = AC + \overline{A}\,\overline{B}C$

(b) $Y = \overline{A}\,\overline{B} + A\overline{B}C + \overline{(A + \overline{C})}$

(c) $Y = \overline{A}\,\overline{B}\,\overline{C}\,\overline{D} + A\overline{B}\,\overline{C} + A\overline{B}C\overline{D} + ABD + \overline{A}\,\overline{B}C\overline{D} + B\overline{C}D + \overline{A}$

Exercise 2.14 Simplify the following Boolean equations using Boolean theorems. Check for correctness using a truth table or K-map.

(a) $Y = \overline{A}BC + \overline{A}B\overline{C}$

(b) $Y = \overline{ABC} + A\overline{B}$

(c) $Y = AB\overline{C}\overline{D} + A\overline{B}\,\overline{C}D + \overline{(A + B + C + D)}$

Exercise 2.15 Sketch a reasonably simple combinational circuit implementing each of the functions from Exercise 2.13.

Exercise 2.16 Sketch a reasonably simple combinational circuit implementing each of the functions from Exercise 2.14.

Exercise 2.17 Simplify each of the following Boolean equations. Sketch a reasonably simple combinational circuit implementing the simplified equation.

(a) $Y = BC + \overline{A}\,\overline{B}\,\overline{C} + B\overline{C}$

(b) $Y = \overline{A + \overline{A}B + \overline{A}\,\overline{B} + \overline{A + \overline{B}}}$

(c) $Y = ABC + ABD + ABE + ACD + ACE + (\overline{A + D + E}) + \overline{B}\,CD$
$\quad + \overline{B}\,CE + \overline{B}\,\overline{D}\,\overline{E} + \overline{C}\,\overline{D}\,\overline{E}$

Exercise 2.18 Simplify each of the following Boolean equations. Sketch a reasonably simple combinational circuit implementing the simplified equation.

(a) $Y = \overline{A}BC + \overline{B}\,\overline{C} + BC$

(b) $Y = (\overline{A + B + C})D + AD + B$

(c) $Y = ABCD + \overline{A}B\overline{C}D + (\overline{B + D})E$

Exercise 2.19 Give an example of a truth table requiring between 3 billion and 5 billion rows that can be constructed using fewer than 40 (but at least 1) two-input gates.

Exercise 2.20 Give an example of a circuit with a cyclic path that is nevertheless combinational.

Exercise 2.21 Alyssa P. Hacker says that any Boolean function can be written in minimal sum-of-products form as the sum of all of the prime implicants of the function. Ben Bitdiddle says that there are some functions whose minimal equation does not involve all of the prime implicants. Explain why Alyssa is right or provide a counterexample demonstrating Ben's point.

Exercise 2.22 Prove that the following theorems are true using perfect induction. You need not prove their duals.

(a) The idempotency theorem (T3)

(b) The distributivity theorem (T8)

(c) The combining theorem (T10)

Exercise 2.23 Prove De Morgan's Theorem (T12) for three variables, B_2, B_1, B_0, using perfect induction.

Exercise 2.24 Write Boolean equations for the circuit in Figure 2.82. You need not minimize the equations.

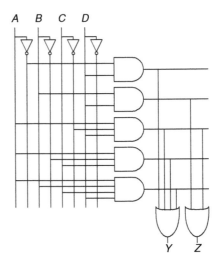

Figure 2.82 Circuit schematic

Exercise 2.25 Minimize the Boolean equations from Exercise 2.24 and sketch an improved circuit with the same function.

Exercise 2.26 Using De Morgan equivalent gates and bubble pushing methods, redraw the circuit in Figure 2.83 so that you can find the Boolean equation by inspection. Write the Boolean equation.

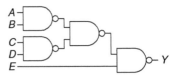

Figure 2.83 Circuit schematic

Exercise 2.27 Repeat Exercise 2.26 for the circuit in Figure 2.84.

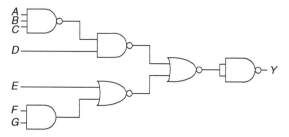

Figure 2.84 Circuit schematic

Exercise 2.28 Find a minimal Boolean equation for the function in Figure 2.85. Remember to take advantage of the don't care entries.

A	B	C	D	Y
0	0	0	0	X
0	0	0	1	X
0	0	1	0	X
0	0	1	1	0
0	1	0	0	0
0	1	0	1	X
0	1	1	0	0
0	1	1	1	X
1	0	0	0	1
1	0	0	1	0
1	0	1	0	X
1	0	1	1	1
1	1	0	0	1
1	1	0	1	1
1	1	1	0	X
1	1	1	1	1

Figure 2.85 Truth table for Exercise 2.28

Exercise 2.29 Sketch a circuit for the function from Exercise 2.28.

Exercise 2.30 Does your circuit from Exercise 2.29 have any potential glitches when one of the inputs changes? If not, explain why not. If so, show how to modify the circuit to eliminate the glitches.

Exercise 2.31 Find a minimal Boolean equation for the function in Figure 2.86. Remember to take advantage of the don't care entries.

A	B	C	D	Y
0	0	0	0	0
0	0	0	1	1
0	0	1	0	X
0	0	1	1	X
0	1	0	0	0
0	1	0	1	X
0	1	1	0	X
0	1	1	1	X
1	0	0	0	1
1	0	0	1	0
1	0	1	0	0
1	0	1	1	1
1	1	0	0	0
1	1	0	1	1
1	1	1	0	X
1	1	1	1	1

Figure 2.86 Truth table for Exercise 2.31

Exercise 2.32 Sketch a circuit for the function from Exercise 2.31.

Exercise 2.33 Ben Bitdiddle will enjoy his picnic on sunny days that have no ants. He will also enjoy his picnic any day he sees a hummingbird, as well as on days where there are ants and ladybugs. Write a Boolean equation for his enjoyment (E) in terms of sun (S), ants (A), hummingbirds (H), and ladybugs (L).

Exercise 2.34 Complete the design of the seven-segment decoder segments S_c through S_g (see Example 2.10):

(a) Derive Boolean equations for the outputs S_c through S_g assuming that inputs greater than 9 must produce blank (0) outputs.

(b) Derive Boolean equations for the outputs S_c through S_g assuming that inputs greater than 9 are don't cares.

(c) Sketch a reasonably simple gate-level implementation of part (b). Multiple outputs can share gates where appropriate.

Exercise 2.35 A circuit has four inputs and two outputs. The inputs $A_{3:0}$ represent a number from 0 to 15. Output P should be TRUE if the number is prime (0 and 1 are not prime, but 2, 3, 5, and so on, are prime). Output D should be TRUE if the number is divisible by 3. Give simplified Boolean equations for each output and sketch a circuit.

Exercise 2.36 A *priority encoder* has 2^N inputs. It produces an N-bit binary output indicating the most significant bit of the input that is TRUE, or 0 if none of the inputs are TRUE. It also produces an output *NONE* that is TRUE if none of the inputs are TRUE. Design an eight-input priority encoder with inputs $A_{7:0}$ and outputs $Y_{2:0}$ and *NONE*. For example, if the input is 00100000, the output Y should be 101 and *NONE* should be 0. Give a simplified Boolean equation for each output, and sketch a schematic.

Exercise 2.37 Design a modified priority encoder (see Exercise 2.36) that receives an 8-bit input, $A_{7:0}$, and produces two 3-bit outputs, $Y_{2:0}$ and $Z_{2:0}$ Y indicates the most significant bit of the input that is TRUE. Z indicates the second most significant bit of the input that is TRUE. Y should be 0 if none of the inputs are TRUE. Z should be 0 if no more than one of the inputs is TRUE. Give a simplified Boolean equation for each output, and sketch a schematic.

Exercise 2.38 An M-bit *thermometer code* for the number k consists of k 1's in the least significant bit positions and $M - k$ 0's in all the more significant bit positions. A *binary-to-thermometer code converter* has N inputs and 2^N-1 outputs. It produces a 2^N-1 bit thermometer code for the number specified by the input. For example, if the input is 110, the output should be 0111111. Design a 3:7 binary-to-thermometer code converter. Give a simplified Boolean equation for each output, and sketch a schematic.

Exercise 2.39 Write a minimized Boolean equation for the function performed by the circuit in Figure 2.87.

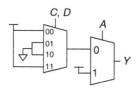

Figure 2.87 Multiplexer circuit

Exercise 2.40 Write a minimized Boolean equation for the function performed by the circuit in Figure 2.88.

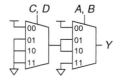

Figure 2.88 Multiplexer circuit

Exercise 2.41 Implement the function from Figure 2.80(b) using

(a) an 8:1 multiplexer

(b) a 4:1 multiplexer and one inverter

(c) a 2:1 multiplexer and two other logic gates

Exercise 2.42 Implement the function from Exercise 2.17(a) using

(a) an 8:1 multiplexer

(b) a 4:1 multiplexer and no other gates

(c) a 2:1 multiplexer, one OR gate, and an inverter

Exercise 2.43 Determine the propagation delay and contamination delay of the circuit in Figure 2.83. Use the gate delays given in Table 2.8.

Exercise 2.44 Determine the propagation delay and contamination delay of the circuit in Figure 2.84. Use the gate delays given in Table 2.8.

Table 2.8 Gate delays for Exercises 2.43–2.47

Gate	t_{pd} (ps)	t_{cd} (ps)
NOT	15	10
2-input NAND	20	15
3-input NAND	30	25
2-input NOR	30	25
3-input NOR	45	35
2-input AND	30	25
3-input AND	40	30
2-input OR	40	30
3-input OR	55	45
2-input XOR	60	40

Exercise 2.45 Sketch a schematic for a fast 3:8 decoder. Suppose gate delays are given in Table 2.8 (and only the gates in that table are available). Design your decoder to have the shortest possible critical path, and indicate what that path is. What are its propagation delay and contamination delay?

Exercise 2.46 Design an 8:1 multiplexer with the shortest possible delay from the data inputs to the output. You may use any of the gates from Table 2.7 on page 92. Sketch a schematic. Using the gate delays from the table, determine this delay.

Exercise 2.47 Redesign the circuit from Exercise 2.35 to be as fast as possible. Use only the gates from Table 2.8. Sketch the new circuit and indicate the critical path. What are its propagation delay and contamination delay?

Exercise 2.48 Redesign the priority encoder from Exercise 2.36 to be as fast as possible. You may use any of the gates from Table 2.8. Sketch the new circuit and indicate the critical path. What are its propagation delay and contamination delay?

Interview Questions

The following exercises present questions that have been asked at interviews for digital design jobs.

Question 2.1 Sketch a schematic for the two-input XOR function using only NAND gates. How few can you use?

Question 2.2 Design a circuit that will tell whether a given month has 31 days in it. The month is specified by a 4-bit input $A_{3:0}$. For example, if the inputs are 0001, the month is January, and if the inputs are 1100, the month is December. The circuit output Y should be HIGH only when the month specified by the inputs has 31 days in it. Write the simplified equation, and draw the circuit diagram using a minimum number of gates. (Hint: Remember to take advantage of don't cares.)

Question 2.3 What is a tristate buffer? How and why is it used?

Question 2.4 A gate or set of gates is universal if it can be used to construct any Boolean function. For example, the set {AND, OR, NOT} is universal.

(a) Is an AND gate by itself universal? Why or why not?

(b) Is the set {OR, NOT} universal? Why or why not?

(c) Is a NAND gate by itself universal? Why or why not?

Question 2.5 Explain why a circuit's contamination delay might be less than (instead of equal to) its propagation delay.

Sequential Logic Design

3.1 INTRODUCTION

In the last chapter, we showed how to analyze and design combinational logic. The output of combinational logic depends only on current input values. Given a specification in the form of a truth table or Boolean equation, we can create an optimized circuit to meet the specification.

In this chapter, we will analyze and design *sequential* logic. The outputs of sequential logic depend on both current and prior input values. Hence, sequential logic has memory. Sequential logic might explicitly remember certain previous inputs, or it might distill the prior inputs into a smaller amount of information called the *state* of the system. The state of a digital sequential circuit is a set of bits called *state variables* that contain all the information about the past necessary to explain the future behavior of the circuit.

The chapter begins by studying latches and flip-flops, which are simple sequential circuits that store one bit of state. In general, sequential circuits are complicated to analyze. To simplify design, we discipline ourselves to build only synchronous sequential circuits consisting of combinational logic and banks of flip-flops containing the state of the circuit. The chapter describes finite state machines, which are an easy way to design sequential circuits. Finally, we analyze the speed of sequential circuits and discuss parallelism as a way to increase speed.

3.2 LATCHES AND FLIP-FLOPS

The fundamental building block of memory is a *bistable* element, an element with two stable states. Figure 3.1(a) shows a simple bistable element consisting of a pair of inverters connected in a loop. Figure 3.1(b) shows the same circuit redrawn to emphasize the symmetry. The inverters are *cross-coupled*, meaning that the input of I1 is the output of I2 and vice versa. The circuit has no inputs, but it does have two outputs, Q and $\overline{Q}$.

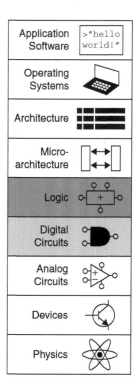

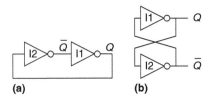

Figure 3.1 Cross-coupled inverter pair

Analyzing this circuit is different from analyzing a combinational circuit because it is cyclic: Q depends on $\overline{Q}$, and $\overline{Q}$ depends on Q.

Consider the two cases, Q is 0 or Q is 1. Working through the consequences of each case, we have:

▸ *Case I: $Q = 0$*
As shown in Figure 3.2(a), I2 receives a FALSE input, Q, so it produces a TRUE output on $\overline{Q}$. I1 receives a TRUE input, $\overline{Q}$, so it produces a FALSE output on Q. This is consistent with the original assumption that $Q = 0$, so the case is said to be *stable*.

▸ *Case II: $Q = 1$*
As shown in Figure 3.2(b), I2 receives a TRUE input and produces a FALSE output on $\overline{Q}$. I1 receives a FALSE input and produces a TRUE output on Q. This is again stable.

Because the cross-coupled inverters have two stable states, $Q = 0$ and $Q = 1$, the circuit is said to be bistable. A subtle point is that the circuit has a third possible state with both outputs approximately halfway between 0 and 1. This is called a *metastable* state and will be discussed in Section 3.5.4.

An element with N stable states conveys $\log_2 N$ bits of information, so a bistable element stores one bit. The state of the cross-coupled inverters is contained in one binary state variable, Q. The value of Q tells us everything about the past that is necessary to explain the future behavior of the circuit. Specifically, if $Q = 0$, it will remain 0 forever, and if $Q = 1$, it will remain 1 forever. The circuit does have another node, $\overline{Q}$, but $\overline{Q}$ does not contain any additional information because if Q is known, $\overline{Q}$ is also known. On the other hand, $\overline{Q}$ is also an acceptable choice for the state variable.

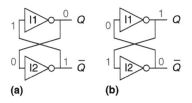

Figure 3.2 Bistable operation of cross-coupled inverters

When power is first applied to a sequential circuit, the initial state is unknown and usually unpredictable. It may differ each time the circuit is turned on.

Although the cross-coupled inverters can store a bit of information, they are not practical because the user has no inputs to control the state. However, other bistable elements, such as *latches* and *flip-flops*, provide inputs to control the value of the state variable. The remainder of this section considers these circuits.

3.2.1 SR Latch

One of the simplest sequential circuits is the *SR latch*, which is composed of two cross-coupled NOR gates, as shown in Figure 3.3. The latch has two inputs, S and R, and two outputs, Q and $\overline{Q}$. The SR latch is similar to the cross-coupled inverters, but its state can be controlled through the S and R inputs, which *set* and *reset* the output Q.

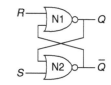

Figure 3.3 SR latch schematic

A good way to understand an unfamiliar circuit is to work out its truth table, so that is where we begin. Recall that a NOR gate produces a FALSE output when either input is TRUE. Consider the four possible combinations of R and S.

▸ *Case I: R = 1, S = 0*
N1 sees at least one TRUE input, R, so it produces a FALSE output on Q. N2 sees both Q and S FALSE, so it produces a TRUE output on $\overline{Q}$.

▸ *Case II: R = 0, S = 1*
N1 receives inputs of 0 and $\overline{Q}$. Because we don't yet know $\overline{Q}$, we can't determine the output Q. N2 receives at least one TRUE input, S, so it produces a FALSE output on $\overline{Q}$. Now we can revisit N1, knowing that both inputs are FALSE, so the output Q is TRUE.

▸ *Case III: R = 1, S = 1*
N1 and N2 both see at least one TRUE input (R or S), so each produces a FALSE output. Hence Q and $\overline{Q}$ are both FALSE.

▸ *Case IV: R = 0, S = 0*
N1 receives inputs of 0 and $\overline{Q}$. Because we don't yet know $\overline{Q}$, we can't determine the output. N2 receives inputs of 0 and Q. Because we don't yet know Q, we can't determine the output. Now we are stuck. This is reminiscent of the cross-coupled inverters. But we know that Q must either be 0 or 1. So we can solve the problem by checking what happens in each of these subcases.

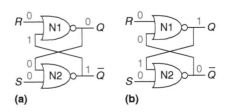

Figure 3.4 Bistable states of SR latch

> ▸ *Case IVa:* $Q = 0$
> Because S and Q are FALSE, N2 produces a TRUE output on $\overline{Q}$, as shown in Figure 3.4(a). Now N1 receives one TRUE input, $\overline{Q}$, so its output, Q, is FALSE, just as we had assumed.

> ▸ *Case IVb:* $Q = 1$
> Because Q is TRUE, N2 produces a FALSE output on $\overline{Q}$, as shown in Figure 3.4(b). Now N1 receives two FALSE inputs, R and $\overline{Q}$, so its output, Q, is TRUE, just as we had assumed.

Putting this all together, suppose Q has some known prior value, which we will call Q_{prev}, before we enter Case IV. Q_{prev} is either 0 or 1, and represents the state of the system. When R and S are 0, Q will remember this old value, Q_{prev}, and $\overline{Q}$ will be its complement, $\overline{Q}_{prev}$. This circuit has memory.

Case	S	R	Q	$\overline{Q}$
IV	0	0	Q_{prev}	$\overline{Q}_{prev}$
I	0	1	0	1
II	1	0	1	0
III	1	1	0	0

Figure 3.5 SR latch truth table

The truth table in Figure 3.5 summarizes these four cases. The inputs S and R stand for *Set* and *Reset*. To *set* a bit means to make it TRUE. To *reset* a bit means to make it FALSE. The outputs, Q and $\overline{Q}$, are normally complementary. When R is asserted, Q is reset to 0 and $\overline{Q}$ does the opposite. When S is asserted, Q is set to 1 and $\overline{Q}$ does the opposite. When neither input is asserted, Q remembers its old value, Q_{prev}. Asserting both S and R simultaneously doesn't make much sense because it means the latch should be set and reset at the same time, which is impossible. The poor confused circuit responds by making both outputs 0.

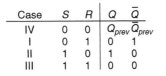

Figure 3.6 SR latch symbol

The SR latch is represented by the symbol in Figure 3.6. Using the symbol is an application of abstraction and modularity. There are various ways to build an SR latch, such as using different logic gates or transistors. Nevertheless, any circuit element with the relationship specified by the truth table in Figure 3.5 and the symbol in Figure 3.6 is called an SR latch.

Like the cross-coupled inverters, the SR latch is a bistable element with one bit of state stored in Q. However, the state can be controlled through the S and R inputs. When R is asserted, the state is reset to 0. When S is asserted, the state is set to 1. When neither is asserted, the state retains its old value. Notice that the entire history of inputs can be accounted for by the single state variable Q. No matter what pattern of setting and resetting occurred in the past, all that is needed to predict the future behavior of the SR latch is whether it was most recently set or reset.

3.2.2 D Latch

The SR latch is awkward because it behaves strangely when both S and R are simultaneously asserted. Moreover, the S and R inputs conflate the issues of *what* and *when*. Asserting one of the inputs determines not only *what* the state should be but also *when* it should change. Designing circuits becomes easier when these questions of what and when are separated. The D latch in Figure 3.7(a) solves these problems. It has two inputs. The *data* input, D, controls what the next state should be. The *clock* input, CLK, controls when the state should change.

Again, we analyze the latch by writing the truth table, given in Figure 3.7(b). For convenience, we first consider the internal nodes $\overline{D}$, S, and R. If $CLK = 0$, both S and R are FALSE, regardless of the value of D. If $CLK = 1$, one AND gate will produce TRUE and the other FALSE, depending on the value of D. Given S and R, Q and $\overline{Q}$ are determined using Figure 3.5. Observe that when $CLK = 0$, Q remembers its old value, Q_{prev}. When $CLK = 1$, $Q = D$. In all cases, $\overline{Q}$ is the complement of Q, as would seem logical. The D latch avoids the strange case of simultaneously asserted R and S inputs.

Putting it all together, we see that the clock controls when data flows through the latch. When $CLK = 1$, the latch is *transparent*. The data at D flows through to Q as if the latch were just a buffer. When $CLK = 0$, the latch is *opaque*. It blocks the new data from flowing through to Q, and Q retains the old value. Hence, the D latch is sometimes called a *transparent latch* or a *level-sensitive* latch. The D latch symbol is given in Figure 3.7(c).

The D latch updates its state continuously while $CLK = 1$. We shall see later in this chapter that it is useful to update the state only at a specific instant in time. The D flip-flop described in the next section does just that.

Some people call a latch open or closed rather than transparent or opaque. However, we think those terms are ambiguous—does *open* mean transparent like an open door, or opaque, like an open circuit?

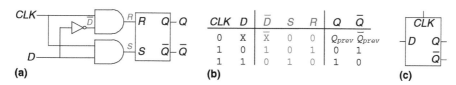

CLK	D	$\overline{D}$	S	R	Q	$\overline{Q}$
0	X	$\overline{X}$	0	0	Q_{prev}	$\overline{Q}_{prev}$
1	0	1	0	1	0	1
1	1	0	1	0	1	0

(a)   (b)   (c)

Figure 3.7 **D latch: (a) schematic, (b) truth table, (c) symbol**

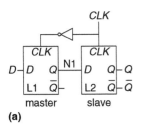

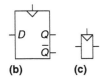

(b)   **(c)**

Figure 3.8 D flip-flop:
(a) schematic, (b) symbol,
(c) condensed symbol

The precise distinction between *flip-flops* and *latches* is somewhat muddled and has evolved over time. In common industry usage, a flip-flop is *edge-triggered*. In other words, it is a bistable element with a *clock* input. The state of the flip-flop changes only in response to a clock edge, such as when the clock rises from 0 to 1. Bistable elements without an edge-triggered clock are commonly called latches.

The term flip-flop or latch by itself usually refers to a *D flip-flop* or *D latch*, respectively, because these are the types most commonly used in practice.

3.2.3 D Flip-Flop

A *D flip-flop* can be built from two back-to-back D latches controlled by complementary clocks, as shown in Figure 3.8(a). The first latch, L1, is called the *master*. The second latch, L2, is called the *slave*. The node between them is named N1. A symbol for the D flip-flop is given in Figure 3.8(b). When the $\overline{Q}$ output is not needed, the symbol is often condensed as in Figure 3.8(c).

When $CLK = 0$, the master latch is transparent and the slave is opaque. Therefore, whatever value was at D propagates through to N1. When $CLK = 1$, the master goes opaque and the slave becomes transparent. The value at N1 propagates through to Q, but N1 is cut off from D. Hence, whatever value was at D immediately before the clock rises from 0 to 1 gets copied to Q immediately after the clock rises. At all other times, Q retains its old value, because there is always an opaque latch blocking the path between D and Q.

In other words, *a D flip-flop copies D to Q on the rising edge of the clock, and remembers its state at all other times.* Reread this definition until you have it memorized; one of the most common problems for beginning digital designers is to forget what a flip-flop does. The rising edge of the clock is often just called the *clock edge* for brevity. The D input specifies what the new state will be. The clock edge indicates when the state should be updated.

A D flip-flop is also known as a *master-slave flip-flop*, an *edge-triggered flip-flop*, or a *positive edge-triggered flip-flop*. The triangle in the symbols denotes an edge-triggered clock input. The $\overline{Q}$ output is often omitted when it is not needed.

Example 3.1 FLIP-FLOP TRANSISTOR COUNT

How many transistors are needed to build the D flip-flop described in this section?

Solution: A NAND or NOR gate uses four transistors. A NOT gate uses two transistors. An AND gate is built from a NAND and a NOT, so it uses six transistors. The SR latch uses two NOR gates, or eight transistors. The D latch uses an SR latch, two AND gates, and a NOT gate, or 22 transistors. The D flip-flop uses two D latches and a NOT gate, or 46 transistors. Section 3.2.7 describes a more efficient CMOS implementation using transmission gates.

3.2.4 Register

An N-bit register is a bank of N flip-flops that share a common CLK input, so that all bits of the register are updated at the same time. Registers are the key building block of most sequential circuits. Figure 3.9

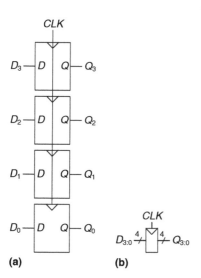

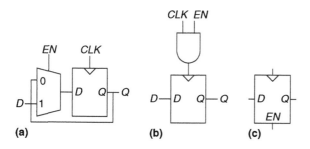

Figure 3.9 **A 4-bit register: (a) schematic and (b) symbol**

shows the schematic and symbol for a four-bit register with inputs $D_{3:0}$ and outputs $Q_{3:0}$. $D_{3:0}$ and $Q_{3:0}$ are both 4-bit busses.

3.2.5 Enabled Flip-Flop

An *enabled flip-flop* adds another input called *EN* or *ENABLE* to determine whether data is loaded on the clock edge. When *EN* is TRUE, the enabled flip-flop behaves like an ordinary D flip-flop. When *EN* is FALSE, the enabled flip-flop ignores the clock and retains its state. Enabled flip-flops are useful when we wish to load a new value into a flip-flop only some of the time, rather than on every clock edge.

Figure 3.10 shows two ways to construct an enabled flip-flop from a D flip-flop and an extra gate. In Figure 3.10(a), an input multiplexer chooses whether to pass the value at *D*, if *EN* is TRUE, or to recycle the old state from *Q*, if *EN* is FALSE. In Figure 3.10(b), the clock is *gated*. If *EN* is TRUE, the *CLK* input to the flip-flop toggles normally. If *EN* is

Figure 3.10 **Enabled flip-flop: (a, b) schematics, (c) symbol**

FALSE, the *CLK* input is also FALSE and the flip-flop retains its old value. Notice that *EN* must not change while *CLK* = 1, lest the flip-flop see a clock *glitch* (switch at an incorrect time). Generally, performing logic on the clock is a bad idea. Clock gating delays the clock and can cause timing errors, as we will see in Section 3.5.3, so do it only if you are sure you know what you are doing. The symbol for an enabled flip-flop is given in Figure 3.10(c).

3.2.6 Resettable Flip-Flop

A *resettable flip-flop* adds another input called *RESET*. When *RESET* is FALSE, the resettable flip-flop behaves like an ordinary D flip-flop. When *RESET* is TRUE, the resettable flip-flop ignores *D* and resets the output to 0. Resettable flip-flops are useful when we want to force a known state (i.e., 0) into all the flip-flops in a system when we first turn it on.

Such flip-flops may be *synchronously* or *asynchronously resettable*. Synchronously resettable flip-flops reset themselves only on the rising edge of *CLK*. Asynchronously resettable flip-flops reset themselves as soon as *RESET* becomes TRUE, independent of *CLK*.

Figure 3.11(a) shows how to construct a synchronously resettable flip-flop from an ordinary D flip-flop and an AND gate. When $\overline{RESET}$ is FALSE, the AND gate forces a 0 into the input of the flip-flop. When $\overline{RESET}$ is TRUE, the AND gate passes *D* to the flip-flop. In this example, $\overline{RESET}$ is an *active low* signal, meaning that the reset signal performs its function when it is 0, not 1. By adding an inverter, the circuit could have accepted an active high reset signal instead. Figures 3.11(b) and 3.11(c) show symbols for the resettable flip-flop with active high reset.

Asynchronously resettable flip-flops require modifying the internal structure of the flip-flop and are left to you to design in Exercise 3.13; however, they are frequently available to the designer as a standard component.

As you might imagine, settable flip-flops are also occasionally used. They load a 1 into the flip-flop when SET is asserted, and they too come in synchronous and asynchronous flavors. Resettable and settable flip-flops may also have an enable input and may be grouped into *N*-bit registers.

3.2.7 Transistor-Level Latch and Flip-Flop Designs*

Example 3.1 showed that latches and flip-flops require a large number of transistors when built from logic gates. But the fundamental role of a latch is to be transparent or opaque, much like a switch. Recall from

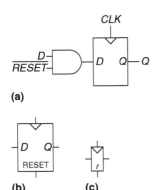

(a)

(b)   **(c)**

Figure 3.11 Synchronously resettable flip-flop: (a) schematic, (b, c) symbols

Section 1.7.7 that a transmission gate is an efficient way to build a CMOS switch, so we might expect that we could take advantage of transmission gates to reduce the transistor count.

A compact D latch can be constructed from a single transmission gate, as shown in Figure 3.12(a). When $CLK = 1$ and $\overline{CLK} = 0$, the transmission gate is ON, so D flows to Q and the latch is transparent. When $CLK = 0$ and $\overline{CLK} = 1$, the transmission gate is OFF, so Q is isolated from D and the latch is opaque. This latch suffers from two major limitations:

▸ *Floating output node:* When the latch is opaque, Q is not held at its value by any gates. Thus Q is called a *floating* or *dynamic* node. After some time, noise and charge leakage may disturb the value of Q.

▸ *No buffers:* The lack of buffers has caused malfunctions on several commercial chips. A spike of noise that pulls D to a negative voltage can turn on the nMOS transistor, making the latch transparent, even when $CLK = 0$. Likewise, a spike on D above V_{DD} can turn on the pMOS transistor even when $CLK = 0$. And the transmission gate is symmetric, so it could be driven backward with noise on Q affecting the input D. The general rule is that neither the input of a transmission gate nor the state node of a sequential circuit should ever be exposed to the outside world, where noise is likely.

Figure 3.12(b) shows a more robust 12-transistor D latch used on modern commercial chips. It is still built around a clocked transmission gate, but it adds inverters I1 and I2 to buffer the input and output. The state of the latch is held on node N1. Inverter I3 and the tristate buffer, T1, provide feedback to turn N1 into a *static node*. If a small amount of noise occurs on N1 while $CLK = 0$, T1 will drive N1 back to a valid logic value.

Figure 3.13 shows a D flip-flop constructed from two static latches controlled by $\overline{CLK}$ and CLK. Some redundant internal inverters have been removed, so the flip-flop requires only 20 transistors.

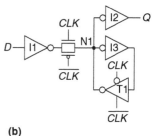

(a)

(b)

Figure 3.12 D latch schematic

This circuit assumes CLK and $\overline{CLK}$ are both available. If not, two more transistors are needed for a CLK inverter.

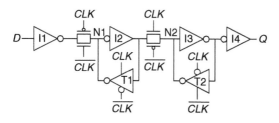

Figure 3.13 D flip-flop schematic

3.2.8 Putting It All Together

Latches and flip-flops are the fundamental building blocks of sequential circuits. Remember that a D latch is level-sensitive, whereas a D flip-flop is edge-triggered. The D latch is transparent when $CLK = 1$, allowing the input D to flow through to the output Q. The D flip-flop copies D to Q on the rising edge of CLK. At all other times, latches and flip-flops retain their old state. A register is a bank of several D flip-flops that share a common CLK signal.

Example 3.2 FLIP-FLOP AND LATCH COMPARISON

Ben Bitdiddle applies the D and CLK inputs shown in Figure 3.14 to a D latch and a D flip-flop. Help him determine the output, Q, of each device.

Solution: Figure 3.15 shows the output waveforms, assuming a small delay for Q to respond to input changes. The arrows indicate the cause of an output change. The initial value of Q is unknown and could be 0 or 1, as indicated by the pair of horizontal lines. First consider the latch. On the first rising edge of CLK, $D = 0$, so Q definitely becomes 0. Each time D changes while $CLK = 1$, Q also follows. When D changes while $CLK = 0$, it is ignored. Now consider the flip-flop. On each rising edge of CLK, D is copied to Q. At all other times, Q retains its state.

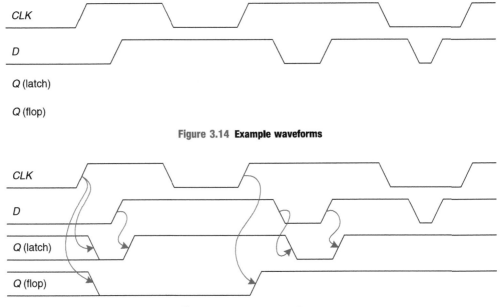

Figure 3.14 Example waveforms

Figure 3.15 Solution waveforms

3.3 SYNCHRONOUS LOGIC DESIGN

In general, sequential circuits include all circuits that are not combinational—that is, those whose output cannot be determined simply by looking at the current inputs. Some sequential circuits are just plain kooky. This section begins by examining some of those curious circuits. It then introduces the notion of synchronous sequential circuits and the dynamic discipline. By disciplining ourselves to synchronous sequential circuits, we can develop easy, systematic ways to analyze and design sequential systems.

3.3.1 Some Problematic Circuits

Example 3.3 ASTABLE CIRCUITS

Alyssa P. Hacker encounters three misbegotten inverters who have tied themselves in a loop, as shown in Figure 3.16. The output of the third inverter is *fed back* to the first inverter. Each inverter has a propagation delay of 1 ns. Help Alyssa determine what the circuit does.

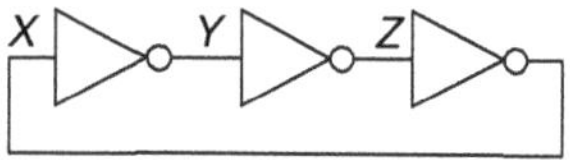

Figure 3.16 Three-inverter loop

Solution: Suppose node X is initially 0. Then $Y = 1$, $Z = 0$, and hence $X = 1$, which is inconsistent with our original assumption. The circuit has no stable states and is said to be *unstable* or *astable*. Figure 3.17 shows the behavior of the circuit. If X rises at time 0, Y will fall at 1 ns, Z will rise at 2 ns, and X will fall again at 3 ns. In turn, Y will rise at 4 ns, Z will fall at 5 ns, and X will rise again at 6 ns, and then the pattern will repeat. Each node oscillates between 0 and 1 with a *period* (repetition time) of 6 ns. This circuit is called a *ring oscillator*.

The period of the ring oscillator depends on the propagation delay of each inverter. This delay depends on how the inverter was manufactured, the power supply voltage, and even the temperature. Therefore, the ring oscillator period is difficult to accurately predict. In short, the ring oscillator is a sequential circuit with zero inputs and one output that changes periodically.

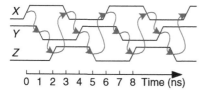

Figure 3.17 Ring oscillator waveforms

Example 3.4 RACE CONDITIONS

Ben Bitdiddle designed a new D latch that he claims is better than the one in Figure 3.7 because it uses fewer gates. He has written the truth table to find the

CLK	D	Q_{prev}	Q
0	0	0	0
0	0	1	1
0	1	0	0
0	1	1	1
1	0	0	0
1	0	1	0
1	1	0	1
1	1	1	1

$$Q = CLK \cdot D + \overline{CLK} \cdot Q_{prev}$$

Figure 3.18 An improved (?) D latch

$N1 = CLK \cdot D$

$N2 = \overline{CLK} \cdot Q_{prev}$

output, Q, given the two inputs, D and CLK, and the old state of the latch, Q_{prev}. Based on this truth table, he has derived Boolean equations. He obtains Q_{prev} by feeding back the output, Q. His design is shown in Figure 3.18. Does his latch work correctly, independent of the delays of each gate?

Solution: Figure 3.19 shows that the circuit has a *race condition* that causes it to fail when certain gates are slower than others. Suppose $CLK = D = 1$. The latch is transparent and passes D through to make $Q = 1$. Now, CLK falls. The latch should remember its old value, keeping $Q = 1$. However, suppose the delay through the inverter from CLK to $\overline{CLK}$ is rather long compared to the delays of the AND and OR gates. Then nodes N1 and Q may both fall before $\overline{CLK}$ rises. In such a case, N2 will never rise, and Q becomes stuck at 0.

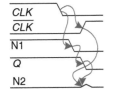

Figure 3.19 Latch waveforms illustrating race condition

This is an example of *asynchronous* circuit design in which outputs are directly fed back to inputs. Asynchronous circuits are infamous for having race conditions where the behavior of the circuit depends on which of two paths through logic gates is fastest. One circuit may work, while a seemingly identical one built from gates with slightly different delays may not work. Or the circuit may work only at certain temperatures or voltages at which the delays are just right. These malfunctions are extremely difficult to track down.

3.3.2 Synchronous Sequential Circuits

The previous two examples contain loops called *cyclic paths*, in which outputs are fed directly back to inputs. They are sequential rather than combinational circuits. Combinational logic has no cyclic paths and no races. If inputs are applied to combinational logic, the outputs will always settle to the correct value within a propagation delay. However, sequential circuits with cyclic paths can have undesirable races or unstable behavior. Analyzing such circuits for problems is time-consuming, and many bright people have made mistakes.

To avoid these problems, designers break the cyclic paths by inserting registers somewhere in the path. This transforms the circuit into a collection of combinational logic and registers. The registers contain the state of the system, which changes only at the clock edge, so we say the state is *synchronized* to the clock. If the clock is sufficiently slow, so that the inputs to all registers settle before the next clock edge, all races are eliminated. Adopting this discipline of always using registers in the feedback path leads us to the formal definition of a synchronous sequential circuit.

Recall that a circuit is defined by its input and output terminals and its functional and timing specifications. A sequential circuit has a finite set of discrete *states* $\{S_0, S_1,..., S_{k-1}\}$. A *synchronous sequential circuit* has a clock input, whose rising edges indicate a sequence of times at which state transitions occur. We often use the terms *current state* and *next state* to distinguish the state of the system at the present from the state to which it will enter on the next clock edge. The functional specification details the next state and the value of each output for each possible combination of current state and input values. The timing specification consists of an upper bound, t_{pcq}, and a lower bound, t_{ccq}, on the time from the rising edge of the clock until the *output* changes, as well as *setup* and *hold* times, t_{setup} and t_{hold}, that indicate when the *inputs* must be stable relative to the rising edge of the clock.

The rules of *synchronous sequential circuit composition* teach us that a circuit is a synchronous sequential circuit if it consists of interconnected circuit elements such that

▶ Every circuit element is either a register or a combinational circuit

▶ At least one circuit element is a register

▶ All registers receive the same clock signal

▶ Every cyclic path contains at least one register.

Sequential circuits that are not synchronous are called *asynchronous*.

A flip-flop is the simplest synchronous sequential circuit. It has one input, D, one clock, CLK, one output, Q, and two states, $\{0, 1\}$. The functional specification for a flip-flop is that the next state is D and that the output, Q, is the current state, as shown in Figure 3.20.

We often call the current state variable S and the next state variable S'. In this case, the prime after S indicates next state, not inversion. The timing of sequential circuits will be analyzed in Section 3.5.

Two other common types of synchronous sequential circuits are called finite state machines and pipelines. These will be covered later in this chapter.

t_{pcq} stands for the time of propagation from clock to Q, where Q indicates the output of a synchronous sequential circuit. t_{ccq} stands for the time of contamination from clock to Q. These are analogous to t_{pd} and t_{cd} in combinational logic.

This definition of a synchronous sequential circuit is sufficient, but more restrictive than necessary. For example, in high-performance microprocessors, some registers may receive delayed or gated clocks to squeeze out the last bit of performance or power. Similarly, some microprocessors use latches instead of registers. However, the definition is adequate for all of the synchronous sequential circuits covered in this book and for most commercial digital systems.

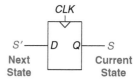

Figure 3.20 **Flip-flop current state and next state**

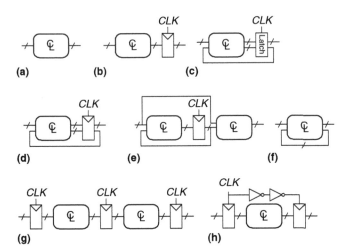

Figure 3.21 Example circuits

Example 3.5 SYNCHRONOUS SEQUENTIAL CIRCUITS

Which of the circuits in Figure 3.21 are synchronous sequential circuits?

Solution: Circuit (a) is combinational, not sequential, because it has no registers. (b) is a simple sequential circuit with no feedback. (c) is neither a combinational circuit nor a synchronous sequential circuit, because it has a latch that is neither a register nor a combinational circuit. (d) and (e) are synchronous sequential logic; they are two forms of finite state machines, which are discussed in Section 3.4. (f) is neither combinational nor synchronous sequential, because it has a cyclic path from the output of the combinational logic back to the input of the same logic but no register in the path. (g) is synchronous sequential logic in the form of a pipeline, which we will study in Section 3.6. (h) is not, strictly speaking, a synchronous sequential circuit, because the second register receives a different clock signal than the first, delayed by two inverter delays.

3.3.3 Synchronous and Asynchronous Circuits

Asynchronous design in theory is more general than synchronous design, because the timing of the system is not limited by clocked registers. Just as analog circuits are more general than digital circuits because analog circuits can use any voltage, asynchronous circuits are more general than synchronous circuits because they can use any kind of feedback. However, synchronous circuits have proved to be easier to design and use than asynchronous circuits, just as digital are easier than analog circuits. Despite decades of research on asynchronous circuits, virtually all digital systems are essentially synchronous.

Of course, asynchronous circuits are occasionally necessary when communicating between systems with different clocks or when receiving inputs at arbitrary times, just as analog circuits are necessary when communicating with the real world of continuous voltages. Furthermore, research in asynchronous circuits continues to generate interesting insights, some of which can improve synchronous circuits too.

3.4 FINITE STATE MACHINES

Synchronous sequential circuits can be drawn in the forms shown in Figure 3.22. These forms are called *finite state machines* (*FSMs*). They get their name because a circuit with k registers can be in one of a finite number (2^k) of unique states. An FSM has M inputs, N outputs, and k bits of state. It also receives a clock and, optionally, a reset signal. An FSM consists of two blocks of combinational logic, *next state logic* and *output logic*, and a register that stores the state. On each clock edge, the FSM advances to the next state, which was computed based on the current state and inputs. There are two general classes of finite state machines, characterized by their functional specifications. In *Moore machines*, the outputs depend only on the current state of the machine. In *Mealy machines*, the outputs depend on both the current state and the current inputs. Finite state machines provide a systematic way to design synchronous sequential circuits given a functional specification. This method will be explained in the remainder of this section, starting with an example.

3.4.1 FSM Design Example

To illustrate the design of FSMs, consider the problem of inventing a controller for a traffic light at a busy intersection on campus. Engineering students are moseying between their dorms and the labs on Academic Ave. They are busy reading about FSMs in their favorite textbook and aren't

Moore and Mealy machines are named after their promoters, researchers who developed *automata theory*, the mathematical underpinnings of state machines, at Bell Labs.

Edward F. Moore (1925–2003), not to be confused with Intel founder Gordon Moore, published his seminal article, *Gedanken-experiments on Sequential Machines* in 1956. He subsequently became a professor of mathematics and computer science at the University of Wisconsin.

George H. Mealy (1927–2010) published *A Method of Synthesizing Sequential Circuits* in 1955. He subsequently wrote the first Bell Labs operating system for the IBM 704 computer. He later joined Harvard University.

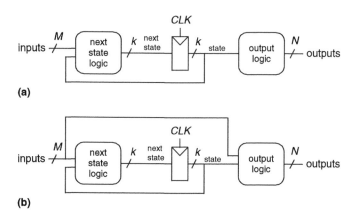

(a)

(b)

Figure 3.22 **Finite state machines: (a) Moore machine, (b) Mealy machine**

looking where they are going. Football players are hustling between the athletic fields and the dining hall on Bravado Boulevard. They are tossing the ball back and forth and aren't looking where they are going either. Several serious injuries have already occurred at the intersection of these two roads, and the Dean of Students asks Ben Bitdiddle to install a traffic light before there are fatalities.

Ben decides to solve the problem with an FSM. He installs two traffic sensors, T_A and T_B, on Academic Ave. and Bravado Blvd., respectively. Each sensor indicates TRUE if students are present and FALSE if the street is empty. He also installs two traffic lights, L_A and L_B, to control traffic. Each light receives digital inputs specifying whether it should be green, yellow, or red. Hence, his FSM has two inputs, T_A and T_B, and two outputs, L_A and L_B. The intersection with lights and sensors is shown in Figure 3.23. Ben provides a clock with a 5-second period. On each clock tick (rising edge), the lights may change based on the traffic sensors. He also provides a reset button so that Physical Plant technicians can put the controller in a known initial state when they turn it on. Figure 3.24 shows a black box view of the state machine.

Ben's next step is to sketch the *state transition diagram*, shown in Figure 3.25, to indicate all the possible states of the system and the transitions between these states. When the system is reset, the lights are green on Academic Ave. and red on Bravado Blvd. Every 5 seconds, the controller examines the traffic pattern and decides what to do next. As long as

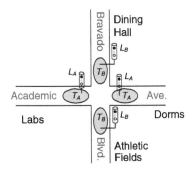

Figure 3.23 Campus map

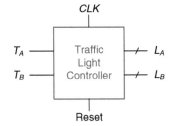

Figure 3.24 Black box view of finite state machine

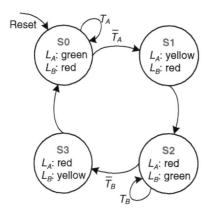

Figure 3.25 State transition diagram

traffic is present on Academic Ave., the lights do not change. When there is no longer traffic on Academic Ave., the light on Academic Ave. becomes yellow for 5 seconds before it turns red and Bravado Blvd.'s light turns green. Similarly, the Bravado Blvd. light remains green as long as traffic is present on the boulevard, then turns yellow and eventually red.

In a state transition diagram, circles represent states and arcs represent transitions between states. The transitions take place on the rising edge of the clock; we do not bother to show the clock on the diagram, because it is always present in a synchronous sequential circuit. Moreover, the clock simply controls when the transitions should occur, whereas the diagram indicates which transitions occur. The arc labeled Reset pointing from outer space into state S0 indicates that the system should enter that state upon reset, regardless of what previous state it was in. If a state has multiple arcs leaving it, the arcs are labeled to show what input triggers each transition. For example, when in state S0, the system will remain in that state if T_A is TRUE and move to S1 if T_A is FALSE. If a state has a single arc leaving it, that transition always occurs regardless of the inputs. For example, when in state S1, the system will always move to S2. The value that the outputs have while in a particular state are indicated in the state. For example, while in state S2, L_A is red and L_B is green.

Ben rewrites the state transition diagram as a *state transition table* (Table 3.1), which indicates, for each state and input, what the next state, S', should be. Note that the table uses don't care symbols (X) whenever the next state does not depend on a particular input. Also note that Reset is omitted from the table. Instead, we use resettable flip-flops that always go to state S0 on reset, independent of the inputs.

The state transition diagram is abstract in that it uses states labeled {S0, S1, S2, S3} and outputs labeled {red, yellow, green}. To build a real circuit, the states and outputs must be assigned *binary encodings*. Ben chooses the simple encodings given in Tables 3.2 and 3.3. Each state and each output is encoded with two bits: $S_{1:0}$, $L_{A1:0}$, and $L_{B1:0}$.

Notice that states are designated as S0, S1, etc. The subscripted versions, S_0, S_1, etc., refer to the state bits.

Table 3.1 State transition table

Current State S	Inputs T_A	T_B	Next State S'
S0	0	X	S1
S0	1	X	S0
S1	X	X	S2
S2	X	0	S3
S2	X	1	S2
S3	X	X	S0

Table 3.2 State encoding

State	Encoding $S_{1:0}$
S0	00
S1	01
S2	10
S3	11

Table 3.3 Output encoding

Output	Encoding $L_{1:0}$
green	00
yellow	01
red	10

Ben updates the state transition table to use these binary encodings, as shown in Table 3.4. The revised state transition table is a truth table specifying the next state logic. It defines next state, S', as a function of the current state, S, and the inputs.

From this table, it is straightforward to read off the Boolean equations for the next state in sum-of-products form.

$$S_1' = \overline{S}_1 S_0 + S_1 \overline{S}_0 \overline{T}_B + S_1 \overline{S}_0 T_B$$
$$S_0' = \overline{S}_1 \overline{S}_0 \overline{T}_A + S_1 \overline{S}_0 \overline{T}_B \tag{3.1}$$

The equations can be simplified using Karnaugh maps, but often doing it by inspection is easier. For example, the T_B and $\overline{T}_B$ terms in the S_1' equation are clearly redundant. Thus S_1' reduces to an XOR operation. Equation 3.2 gives the simplified *next state equations*.

Table 3.4 State transition table with binary encodings

Current State S_1	S_0	Inputs T_A	T_B	Next State S_1'	S_0'
0	0	0	X	0	1
0	0	1	X	0	0
0	1	X	X	1	0
1	0	X	0	1	1
1	0	X	1	1	0
1	1	X	X	0	0

Table 3.5 Output table

Current State		Outputs			
S_1	S_0	L_{A1}	L_{A0}	L_{B1}	L_{B0}
0	0	0	0	1	0
0	1	0	1	1	0
1	0	1	0	0	0
1	1	1	0	0	1

$$S_1' = S_1 \oplus S_0$$
$$S_0' = \overline{S_1}\,\overline{S_0}\,\overline{T_A} + S_1\overline{S_0}\,\overline{T_B} \tag{3.2}$$

Similarly, Ben writes an *output table* (Table 3.5) indicating, for each state, what the output should be in that state. Again, it is straightforward to read off and simplify the Boolean equations for the outputs. For example, observe that L_{A1} is TRUE only on the rows where S_1 is TRUE.

$$L_{A1} = S_1$$
$$L_{A0} = \overline{S_1}S_0$$
$$L_{B1} = \overline{S_1} \tag{3.3}$$
$$L_{B0} = S_1S_0$$

Finally, Ben sketches his Moore FSM in the form of Figure 3.22(a). First, he draws the 2-bit state register, as shown in Figure 3.26(a). On each clock edge, the state register copies the next state, $S_{1:0}'$, to become the state $S_{1:0}$. The state register receives a synchronous or asynchronous reset to initialize the FSM at startup. Then, he draws the next state logic, based on Equation 3.2, which computes the next state from the current state and inputs, as shown in Figure 3.26(b). Finally, he draws the output logic, based on Equation 3.3, which computes the outputs from the current state, as shown in Figure 3.26(c).

Figure 3.27 shows a timing diagram illustrating the traffic light controller going through a sequence of states. The diagram shows *CLK*, Reset, the inputs T_A and T_B, next state S', state S, and outputs L_A and L_B. Arrows indicate causality; for example, changing the state causes the outputs to change, and changing the inputs causes the next state to change. Dashed lines indicate the rising edges of *CLK* when the state changes.

The clock has a 5-second period, so the traffic lights change at most once every 5 seconds. When the finite state machine is first turned on, its state is unknown, as indicated by the question marks. Therefore, the system should be reset to put it into a known state. In this timing diagram, *S*

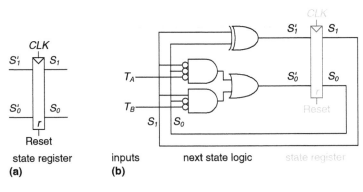

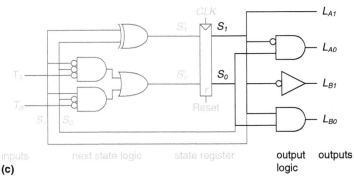

This schematic uses some AND gates with bubbles on the inputs. They might be constructed with AND gates and input inverters, with NOR gates and inverters for the non-bubbled inputs, or with some other combination of gates. The best choice depends on the particular implementation technology.

Figure 3.26 State machine circuit for traffic light controller

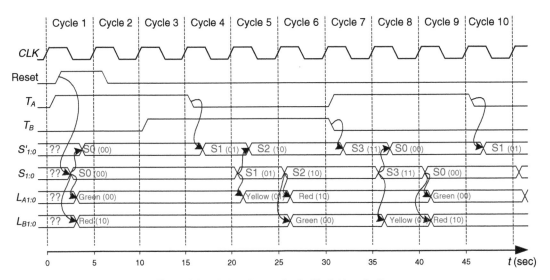

Figure 3.27 Timing diagram for traffic light controller

immediately resets to S0, indicating that asynchronously resettable flip-flops are being used. In state S0, light L_A is green and light L_B is red.

In this example, traffic arrives immediately on Academic Ave. Therefore, the controller remains in state S0, keeping L_A green even though traffic arrives on Bravado Blvd. and starts waiting. After 15 seconds, the traffic on Academic Ave. has all passed through and T_A falls. At the following clock edge, the controller moves to state S1, turning L_A yellow. In another 5 seconds, the controller proceeds to state S2 in which L_A turns red and L_B turns green. The controller waits in state S2 until all the traffic on Bravado Blvd. has passed through. It then proceeds to state S3, turning L_B yellow. 5 seconds later, the controller enters state S0, turning L_B red and L_A green. The process repeats.

Despite Ben's best efforts, students don't pay attention to traffic lights and collisions continue to occur. The Dean of Students next asks him and Alyssa to design a catapult to throw engineering students directly from their dorm roofs through the open windows of the lab, bypassing the troublesome intersection all together. But that is the subject of another textbook.

3.4.2 State Encodings

In the previous example, the state and output encodings were selected arbitrarily. A different choice would have resulted in a different circuit. A natural question is how to determine the encoding that produces the circuit with the fewest logic gates or the shortest propagation delay. Unfortunately, there is no simple way to find the best encoding except to try all possibilities, which is infeasible when the number of states is large. However, it is often possible to choose a good encoding by inspection, so that related states or outputs share bits. Computer-aided design (CAD) tools are also good at searching the set of possible encodings and selecting a reasonable one.

One important decision in state encoding is the choice between binary encoding and one-hot encoding. With *binary encoding*, as was used in the traffic light controller example, each state is represented as a binary number. Because K binary numbers can be represented by $\log_2 K$ bits, a system with K states only needs $\log_2 K$ bits of state.

In *one-hot encoding*, a separate bit of state is used for each state. It is called one-hot because only one bit is "hot" or TRUE at any time. For example, a one-hot encoded FSM with three states would have state encodings of 001, 010, and 100. Each bit of state is stored in a flip-flop, so one-hot encoding requires more flip-flops than binary encoding. However, with one-hot encoding, the next-state and output logic is often simpler, so fewer gates are required. The best encoding choice depends on the specific FSM.

Example 3.6 FSM STATE ENCODING

A *divide-by-N counter* has one output and no inputs. The output Y is HIGH for one clock cycle out of every N. In other words, the output divides the frequency of the clock by N. The waveform and state transition diagram for a divide-by-3 counter is shown in Figure 3.28. Sketch circuit designs for such a counter using binary and one-hot state encodings.

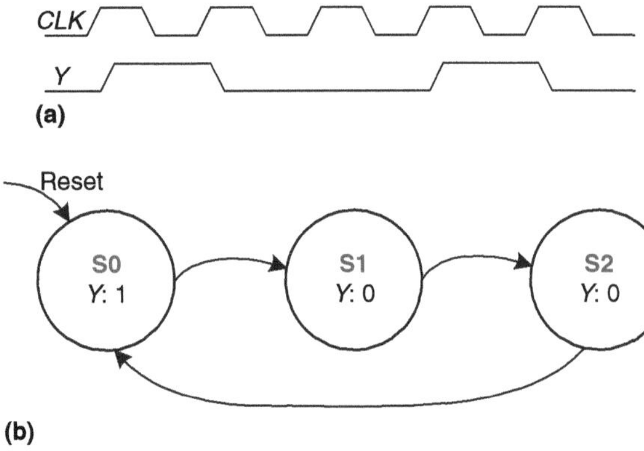

Figure 3.28 Divide-by-3 counter (a) waveform and (b) state transition diagram

Table 3.6 Divide-by-3 counter state transition table

Current State	Next State
S0	S1
S1	S2
S2	S0

Table 3.7 Divide-by-3 counter output table

Current State	Output
S0	1
S1	0
S2	0

Solution: Tables 3.6 and 3.7 show the abstract state transition and output tables before encoding.

Table 3.8 compares binary and one-hot encodings for the three states.

The binary encoding uses two bits of state. Using this encoding, the state transition table is shown in Table 3.9. Note that there are no inputs; the next state depends only on the current state. The output table is left as an exercise to the reader. The next-state and output equations are:

$$S_1' = \overline{S}_1 S_0$$
$$S_0' = \overline{S}_1 \overline{S}_0 \tag{3.4}$$

$$Y = \overline{S}_1 \overline{S}_0 \tag{3.5}$$

The one-hot encoding uses three bits of state. The state transition table for this encoding is shown in Table 3.10 and the output table is again left as an exercise to the reader. The next-state and output equations are as follows:

$$S_2' = S_1$$
$$S_1' = S_0 \tag{3.6}$$
$$S_0' = S_2$$

$$Y = S_0 \tag{3.7}$$

Figure 3.29 shows schematics for each of these designs. Note that the hardware for the binary encoded design could be optimized to share the same gate for Y and S_0'. Also observe that the one-hot encoding requires both settable (s) and resettable (r) flip-flops to initialize the machine to S0 on reset. The best implementation choice depends on the relative cost of gates and flip-flops, but the one-hot design is usually preferable for this specific example.

A related encoding is the *one-cold* encoding, in which K states are represented with K bits, exactly one of which is FALSE.

Table 3.8 One-hot and binary encodings for divide-by-3 counter

State	One-Hot Encoding			Binary Encoding	
	S_2	S_1	S_0	S_1	S_0
S0	0	0	1	0	0
S1	0	1	0	0	1
S2	1	0	0	1	0

Table 3.9 State transition table with binary encoding

Current State		Next State	
S_1	S_0	S_1'	S_0'
0	0	0	1
0	1	1	0
1	0	0	0

Table 3.10 State transition table with one-hot encoding

Current State			Next State		
S_2	S_1	S_0	S_2'	S_1'	S_0'
0	0	1	0	1	0
0	1	0	1	0	0
1	0	0	0	0	1

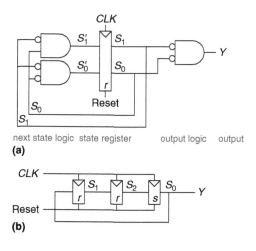

(a)

next state logic   state register   output logic   output

(b)

Figure 3.29 Divide-by-3 circuits for (a) binary and (b) one-hot encodings

3.4.3 Moore and Mealy Machines

An easy way to remember the difference between the two types of finite state machines is that a Moore machine typically has *more* states than a Mealy machine for a given problem.

So far, we have shown examples of Moore machines, in which the output depends only on the state of the system. Hence, in state transition diagrams for Moore machines, the outputs are labeled in the circles. Recall that Mealy machines are much like Moore machines, but the outputs can depend on inputs as well as the current state. Hence, in state transition diagrams for Mealy machines, the outputs are labeled on the arcs instead of in the circles. The block of combinational logic that computes the outputs uses the current state and inputs, as was shown in Figure 3.22(b).

Example 3.7 MOORE VERSUS MEALY MACHINES

Alyssa P. Hacker owns a pet robotic snail with an FSM brain. The snail crawls from left to right along a paper tape containing a sequence of 1's and 0's. On each clock cycle, the snail crawls to the next bit. The snail smiles when the last two bits that it has crawled over are 01. Design the FSM to compute when the snail should smile. The input A is the bit underneath the snail's antennae. The output Y is TRUE when the snail smiles. Compare Moore and Mealy state machine designs. Sketch a timing diagram for each machine showing the input, states, and output as Alyssa's snail crawls along the sequence 0100110111.

Solution: The Moore machine requires three states, as shown in Figure 3.30(a). Convince yourself that the state transition diagram is correct. In particular, why is there an arc from S2 to S1 when the input is 0?

In comparison, the Mealy machine requires only two states, as shown in Figure 3.30(b). Each arc is labeled as A/Y. A is the value of the input that causes that transition, and Y is the corresponding output.

Tables 3.11 and 3.12 show the state transition and output tables for the Moore machine. The Moore machine requires at least two bits of state. Consider using a binary state encoding: S0 = 00, S1 = 01, and S2 = 10. Tables 3.13 and 3.14 rewrite the state transition and output tables with these encodings.

From these tables, we find the next state and output equations by inspection. Note that these equations are simplified using the fact that state 11 does not exist. Thus, the corresponding next state and output for the non-existent state are don't cares (not shown in the tables). We use the don't cares to minimize our equations.

$$S_1' = S_0 A$$
$$S_0' = \overline{A}$$

(3.8)

$$Y = S_1$$

(3.9)

Table 3.15 shows the combined state transition and output table for the Mealy machine. The Mealy machine requires only one bit of state. Consider using a binary state encoding: S0 = 0 and S1 = 1. Table 3.16 rewrites the state transition and output table with these encodings.

From these tables, we find the next state and output equations by inspection.

$$S_0' = \overline{A} \tag{3.10}$$

$$Y = S_0 A \tag{3.11}$$

The Moore and Mealy machine schematics are shown in Figure 3.31. The timing diagrams for each machine are shown in Figure 3.32 (see page 135). The two machines follow a different sequence of states. Moreover, the Mealy machine's output rises a cycle sooner because it responds to the input rather than waiting for the state change. If the Mealy output were delayed through a flip-flop, it would match the Moore output. When choosing your FSM design style, consider when you want your outputs to respond.

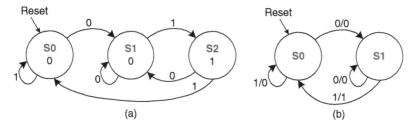

Figure 3.30 FSM state transition diagrams: (a) Moore machine, (b) Mealy machine

Table 3.11 Moore state transition table

Current State S	Input A	Next State S'
S0	0	S1
S0	1	S0
S1	0	S1
S1	1	S2
S2	0	S1
S2	1	S0

Table 3.12 Moore output table

Current State S	Output Y
S0	0
S1	0
S2	1

Table 3.13 **Moore state transition table with state encodings**

| Current State | | Input | Next State | |
S_1	S_0	A	S'_1	S'_0
0	0	0	0	1
0	0	1	0	0
0	1	0	0	1
0	1	1	1	0
1	0	0	0	1
1	0	1	0	0

Table 3.14 **Moore output table with state encodings**

| Current State | | Output |
S_1	S_0	Y
0	0	0
0	1	0
1	0	1

Table 3.15 **Mealy state transition and output table**

Current State S	Input A	Next State S'	Output Y
S0	0	S1	0
S0	1	S0	0
S1	0	S1	0
S1	1	S0	1

Table 3.16 **Mealy state transition and output table with state encodings**

Current State S_0	Input A	Next State S'_0	Output Y
0	0	1	0
0	1	0	0
1	0	1	0
1	1	0	1

3.4.4 Factoring State Machines

Designing complex FSMs is often easier if they can be broken down into multiple interacting simpler state machines such that the output of some machines is the input of others. This application of hierarchy and modularity is called *factoring* of state machines.

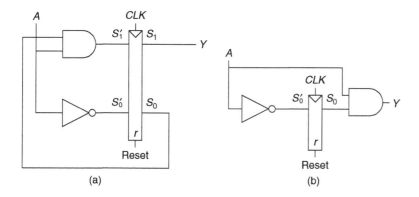

Figure 3.31 FSM schematics for (a) Moore and (b) Mealy machines

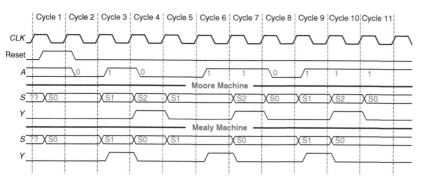

Figure 3.32 Timing diagrams for Moore and Mealy machines

Example 3.8 UNFACTORED AND FACTORED STATE MACHINES

Modify the traffic light controller from Section 3.4.1 to have a parade mode, which keeps the Bravado Boulevard light green while spectators and the band march to football games in scattered groups. The controller receives two more inputs: P and R. Asserting P for at least one cycle enters parade mode. Asserting R for at least one cycle leaves parade mode. When in parade mode, the controller proceeds through its usual sequence until L_B turns green, then remains in that state with L_B green until parade mode ends.

First, sketch a state transition diagram for a single FSM, as shown in Figure 3.33(a). Then, sketch the state transition diagrams for two interacting FSMs, as shown in Figure 3.33(b). The Mode FSM asserts the output M when it is in parade mode. The Lights FSM controls the lights based on M and the traffic sensors, T_A and T_B.

Solution: Figure 3.34(a) shows the single FSM design. States S0 to S3 handle normal mode. States S4 to S7 handle parade mode. The two halves of the diagram are almost identical, but in parade mode, the FSM remains in S6 with a green light on Bravado Blvd. The P and R inputs control movement between these two halves. The FSM is messy and tedious to design. Figure 3.34(b) shows the factored FSM design. The mode FSM has two states to track whether the lights are in normal or parade mode. The Lights FSM is modified to remain in S2 while M is TRUE.

**Figure 3.33 (a) single and
(b) factored designs for modified
traffic light controller FSM**

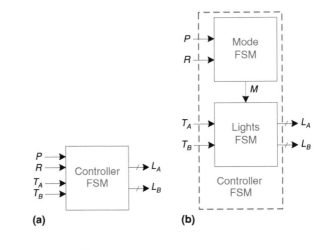

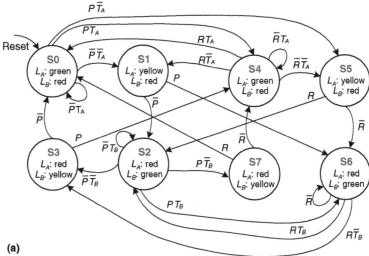

**Figure 3.34 State transition
diagrams: (a) unfactored,
(b) factored**

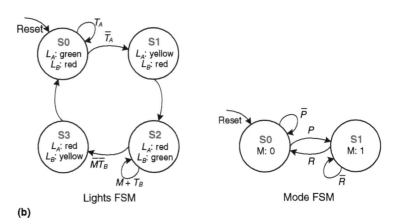

3.4.5 Deriving an FSM from a Schematic

Deriving the state transition diagram from a schematic follows nearly the reverse process of FSM design. This process can be necessary, for example, when taking on an incompletely documented project or reverse engineering somebody else's system.

▶ Examine circuit, stating inputs, outputs, and state bits.

▶ Write next state and output equations.

▶ Create next state and output tables.

▶ Reduce the next state table to eliminate unreachable states.

▶ Assign each valid state bit combination a name.

▶ Rewrite next state and output tables with state names.

▶ Draw state transition diagram.

▶ State in words what the FSM does.

In the final step, be careful to succinctly describe the overall purpose and function of the FSM—do not simply restate each transition of the state transition diagram.

Example 3.9 DERIVING AN FSM FROM ITS CIRCUIT

Alyssa P. Hacker arrives home, but her keypad lock has been rewired and her old code no longer works. A piece of paper is taped to it showing the circuit diagram in Figure 3.35. Alyssa thinks the circuit could be a finite state machine and decides to derive the state transition diagram to see if it helps her get in the door.

Solution: Alyssa begins by examining the circuit. The input is $A_{1:0}$ and the output is *Unlock*. The state bits are already labeled in Figure 3.35. This is a Moore

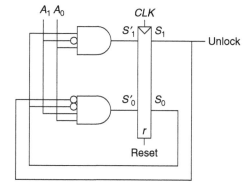

Figure 3.35 Circuit of found FSM for Example 3.9

machine because the output depends only on the state bits. From the circuit, she writes down the next state and output equations directly:

$$S'_1 = S_0 \overline{A_1} A_0$$
$$S'_0 = \overline{S_1}\, \overline{S_0} A_1 A_0 \qquad\qquad (3.12)$$
$$Unlock = S_1$$

Next, she writes down the next state and output tables from the equations, as shown in Tables 3.17 and 3.18, first placing 1's in the tables as indicated by Equation 3.12. She places 0's everywhere else.

Alyssa reduces the table by removing unused states and combining rows using don't cares. The $S_{1:0} = 11$ state is never listed as a possible next state in Table 3.17, so rows with this current state are removed. For current state $S_{1:0} = 10$, the next

Table 3.17 Next state table derived from circuit in Figure 3.35

Current State		Input		Next State	
S_1	S_0	A_1	A_0	S'_1	S'_0
0	0	0	0	0	0
0	0	0	1	0	0
0	0	1	0	0	0
0	0	1	1	0	1
0	1	0	0	0	0
0	1	0	1	1	0
0	1	1	0	0	0
0	1	1	1	0	0
1	0	0	0	0	0
1	0	0	1	0	0
1	0	1	0	0	0
1	0	1	1	0	0
1	1	0	0	0	0
1	1	0	1	1	0
1	1	1	0	0	0
1	1	1	1	0	0

Table 3.18 Output table derived from circuit in Figure 3.35

Current State		Output
S_1	S_0	$Unlock$
0	0	0
0	1	0
1	0	1
1	1	1

Table 3.19 Reduced next state table

Current State		Input		Next State	
S_1	S_0	A_1	A_0	S_1'	S_0'
0	0	0	0	0	0
0	0	0	1	0	0
0	0	1	0	0	0
0	0	1	1	0	1
0	1	0	0	0	0
0	1	0	1	1	0
0	1	1	0	0	0
0	1	1	1	0	0
1	0	X	X	0	0

Table 3.20 Reduced output table

Current State		Output
S_1	S_0	Unlock
0	0	0
0	1	0
1	0	1

Table 3.21 Symbolic next state table

Current State S	Input A	Next State S'
S0	0	S0
S0	1	S0
S0	2	S0
S0	3	S1
S1	0	S0
S1	1	S2
S1	2	S0
S1	3	S0
S2	X	S0

Table 3.22 Symbolic output table

Current State S	Output Unlock
S0	0
S1	0
S2	1

state is always $S_{1:0} = 00$, independent of the inputs, so don't cares are inserted for the inputs. The reduced tables are shown in Tables 3.19 and 3.20.

She assigns names to each state bit combination: S0 is $S_{1:0} = 00$, S1 is $S_{1:0} = 01$, and S2 is $S_{1:0} = 10$. Tables 3.21 and 3.22 show the next state and output tables with state names.

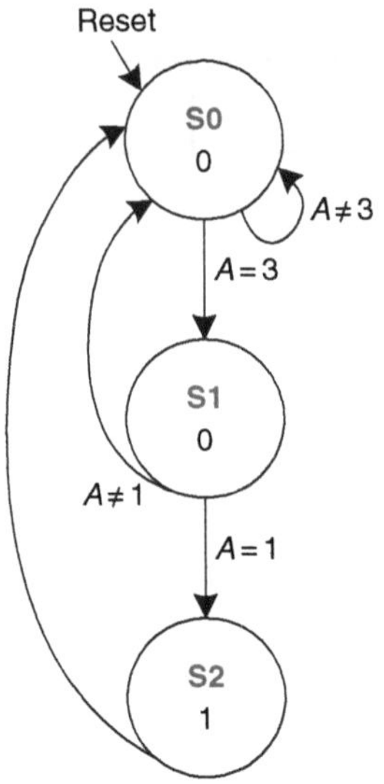

Reset

Figure 3.36 State transition diagram of found FSM from Example 3.9

Alyssa writes down the state transition diagram shown in Figure 3.36 using Tables 3.21 and 3.22. By inspection, she can see that the finite state machine unlocks the door only after detecting an input value, $A_{1:0}$, of three followed by an input value of one. The door is then locked again. Alyssa tries this code on the door key pad and the door opens!

3.4.6 FSM Review

Finite state machines are a powerful way to systematically design sequential circuits from a written specification. Use the following procedure to design an FSM:

▶ Identify the inputs and outputs.

▶ Sketch a state transition diagram.

▶ For a Moore machine:
  – Write a state transition table.
  – Write an output table.

▶ For a Mealy machine:
  – Write a combined state transition and output table.

▶ Select state encodings—your selection affects the hardware design.

▶ Write Boolean equations for the next state and output logic.

▶ Sketch the circuit schematic.

We will repeatedly use FSMs to design complex digital systems throughout this book.

3.5 TIMING OF SEQUENTIAL LOGIC

Recall that a flip-flop copies the input D to the output Q on the rising edge of the clock. This process is called *sampling* D on the clock edge. If D is *stable* at either 0 or 1 when the clock rises, this behavior is clearly defined. But what happens if D is changing at the same time the clock rises?

This problem is similar to that faced by a camera when snapping a picture. Imagine photographing a frog jumping from a lily pad into the lake. If you take the picture before the jump, you will see a frog on a lily pad. If you take the picture after the jump, you will see ripples in the water. But if you take it just as the frog jumps, you may see a blurred image of the frog stretching from the lily pad into the water. A camera is characterized by its *aperture time*, during which the object must remain still for a sharp image to be captured. Similarly, a sequential element has an aperture time around the clock edge, during which the input must be stable for the flip-flop to produce a well-defined output.

The aperture of a sequential element is defined by a *setup* time and a *hold* time, before and after the clock edge, respectively. Just as the static discipline limited us to using logic levels outside the forbidden zone, the *dynamic discipline* limits us to using signals that change outside the aperture time. By taking advantage of the dynamic discipline, we can think of time in discrete units called clock cycles, just as we think of signal levels as discrete 1's and 0's. A signal may glitch and oscillate wildly for some bounded amount of time. Under the dynamic discipline, we are concerned only about its final value at the end of the clock cycle, after it has settled to a stable value. Hence, we can simply write $A[n]$, the value of signal A at the end of the *nth* clock cycle, where n is an integer, rather than $A(t)$, the value of A at some instant t, where t is any real number.

The clock period has to be long enough for all signals to settle. This sets a limit on the speed of the system. In real systems, the clock does not reach all flip-flops at precisely the same time. This variation in time, called clock skew, further increases the necessary clock period.

Sometimes it is impossible to satisfy the dynamic discipline, especially when interfacing with the real world. For example, consider a circuit with an input coming from a button. A monkey might press the button just as the clock rises. This can result in a phenomenon called metastability, where the flip-flop captures a value partway between 0 and 1 that can take an unlimited amount of time to resolve into a good logic value. The solution to such asynchronous inputs is to use a synchronizer, which has a very small (but nonzero) probability of producing an illegal logic value.

We expand on all of these ideas in the rest of this section.

3.5.1 The Dynamic Discipline

So far, we have focused on the functional specification of sequential circuits. Recall that a synchronous sequential circuit, such as a flip-flop or FSM, also has a timing specification, as illustrated in Figure 3.37. When the clock rises, the output (or outputs) may start to change after the clock-to-Q *contamination delay*, t_{ccq}, and must definitely settle to the final value within the clock-to-Q *propagation delay*, t_{pcq}. These represent the fastest and slowest delays through the circuit, respectively. For the circuit to sample its input correctly, the input (or inputs) must have stabilized at least some *setup time*, t_{setup}, before the rising edge of the clock and must remain stable for at least some *hold time*, t_{hold}, after the rising edge of the clock. The sum of the setup and hold times is called the *aperture time* of the circuit, because it is the total time for which the input must remain stable.

The *dynamic discipline* states that the inputs of a synchronous sequential circuit must be stable during the setup and hold aperture time around the clock edge. By imposing this requirement, we guarantee that the flip-flops sample signals while they are not changing. Because we are concerned only about the final values of the inputs at the time they are sampled, we can treat signals as discrete in time as well as in logic levels.

3.5.2 System Timing

The *clock period* or *cycle time*, T_c, is the time between rising edges of a repetitive clock signal. Its reciprocal, $f_c = 1/T_c$, is the *clock frequency*. All else being the same, increasing the clock frequency increases the work that a digital system can accomplish per unit time. Frequency is measured in units of Hertz (Hz), or cycles per second: 1 megahertz (MHz) = 10^6 Hz, and 1 gigahertz (GHz) = 10^9 Hz.

Figure 3.38(a) illustrates a generic path in a synchronous sequential circuit whose clock period we wish to calculate. On the rising edge of the clock, register R1 produces output (or outputs) Q1. These signals enter a block of combinational logic, producing D2, the input (or inputs) to register R2. The timing diagram in Figure 3.38(b) shows that each output signal may start to change a contamination delay after its input

In the three decades from when one of the authors' families bought an Apple II+ computer to the present time of writing, microprocessor clock frequencies have increased from 1 MHz to several GHz, a factor of more than 1000. This speedup partially explains the revolutionary changes computers have made in society.

Figure 3.37 Timing specification for synchronous sequential circuit

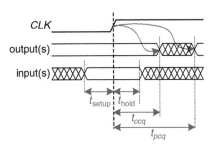

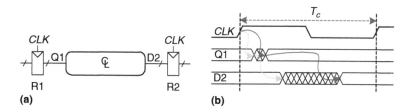

Figure 3.38 Path between registers and timing diagram

changes and settles to the final value within a propagation delay after its input settles. The gray arrows represent the contamination delay through R1 and the combinational logic, and the blue arrows represent the propagation delay through R1 and the combinational logic. We analyze the timing constraints with respect to the setup and hold time of the second register, R2.

Setup Time Constraint

Figure 3.39 is the timing diagram showing only the maximum delay through the path, indicated by the blue arrows. To satisfy the setup time of R2, $D2$ must settle no later than the setup time before the next clock edge. Hence, we find an equation for the minimum clock period:

$$T_c \geq t_{pcq} + t_{pd} + t_{setup} \tag{3.13}$$

In commercial designs, the clock period is often dictated by the Director of Engineering or by the marketing department (to ensure a competitive product). Moreover, the flip-flop clock-to-Q propagation delay and setup time, t_{pcq} and t_{setup}, are specified by the manufacturer. Hence, we rearrange Equation 3.13 to solve for the maximum propagation delay through the combinational logic, which is usually the only variable under the control of the individual designer.

$$t_{pd} \leq T_c - (t_{pcq} + t_{setup}) \tag{3.14}$$

The term in parentheses, $t_{pcq} + t_{setup}$, is called the *sequencing overhead*. Ideally, the entire cycle time T_c would be available for useful

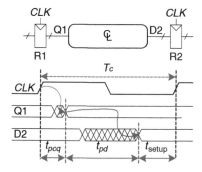

Figure 3.39 Maximum delay for setup time constraint

computation in the combinational logic, t_{pd}. However, the sequencing overhead of the flip-flop cuts into this time. Equation 3.14 is called the *setup time constraint* or *max-delay constraint*, because it depends on the setup time and limits the maximum delay through combinational logic.

If the propagation delay through the combinational logic is too great, $D2$ may not have settled to its final value by the time R2 needs it to be stable and samples it. Hence, R2 may sample an incorrect result or even an illegal logic level, a level in the forbidden region. In such a case, the circuit will malfunction. The problem can be solved by increasing the clock period or by redesigning the combinational logic to have a shorter propagation delay.

Hold Time Constraint

The register R2 in Figure 3.38(a) also has a *hold time constraint*. Its input, $D2$, must not change until some time, t_{hold}, after the rising edge of the clock. According to Figure 3.40, $D2$ might change as soon as $t_{ccq} + t_{cd}$ after the rising edge of the clock. Hence, we find

$$t_{ccq} + t_{cd} \geq t_{hold} \qquad (3.15)$$

Again, t_{ccq} and t_{hold} are characteristics of the flip-flop that are usually outside the designer's control. Rearranging, we can solve for the minimum contamination delay through the combinational logic:

$$t_{cd} \geq t_{hold} - t_{ccq} \qquad (3.16)$$

Equation 3.16 is also called the *hold time constraint* or *min-delay constraint* because it limits the minimum delay through combinational logic.

We have assumed that any logic elements can be connected to each other without introducing timing problems. In particular, we would expect that two flip-flops may be directly cascaded as in Figure 3.41 without causing hold time problems.

Figure 3.40 Minimum delay for hold time constraint

In such a case, $t_{cd} = 0$ because there is no combinational logic between flip-flops. Substituting into Equation 3.16 yields the requirement that

$$t_{hold} \leq t_{ccq} \qquad (3.17)$$

In other words, a reliable flip-flop must have a hold time shorter than its contamination delay. Often, flip-flops are designed with $t_{hold} = 0$, so that Equation 3.17 is always satisfied. Unless noted otherwise, we will usually make that assumption and ignore the hold time constraint in this book.

Nevertheless, hold time constraints are critically important. If they are violated, the only solution is to increase the contamination delay through the logic, which requires redesigning the circuit. Unlike setup time constraints, they cannot be fixed by adjusting the clock period. Redesigning an integrated circuit and manufacturing the corrected design takes months and millions of dollars in today's advanced technologies, so *hold time violations* must be taken extremely seriously.

Putting It All Together

Sequential circuits have setup and hold time constraints that dictate the maximum and minimum delays of the combinational logic between flip-flops. Modern flip-flops are usually designed so that the minimum delay through the combinational logic is 0—that is, flip-flops can be placed back-to-back. The maximum delay constraint limits the number of consecutive gates on the critical path of a high-speed circuit, because a high clock frequency means a short clock period.

Example 3.10 TIMING ANALYSIS

Ben Bitdiddle designed the circuit in Figure 3.42. According to the data sheets for the components he is using, flip-flops have a clock-to-Q contamination delay of 30 ps and a propagation delay of 80 ps. They have a setup time of 50 ps and a hold time of 60 ps. Each logic gate has a propagation delay of 40 ps and a

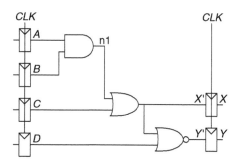

Figure 3.42 **Sample circuit for timing analysis**

contamination delay of 25 ps. Help Ben determine the maximum clock frequency and whether any hold time violations could occur. This process is called *timing analysis.*

Solution: Figure 3.43(a) shows waveforms illustrating when the signals might change. The inputs, *A* to *D*, are registered, so they only change shortly after *CLK* rises.

The critical path occurs when $B = 1$, $C = 0$, $D = 0$, and A rises from 0 to 1, triggering n1 to rise, X' to rise, and Y' to fall, as shown in Figure 3.43(b). This path involves three gate delays. For the critical path, we assume that each gate requires its full propagation delay. Y' must setup before the next rising edge of the *CLK*. Hence, the minimum cycle time is

$$T_c \geq t_{pcq} + 3\,t_{pd} + t_{\text{setup}} = 80 + 3 \times 40 + 50 = 250\text{ps} \qquad (3.18)$$

The maximum clock frequency is $f_c = 1/T_c = 4$ GHz.

A short path occurs when $A = 0$ and C rises, causing X' to rise, as shown in Figure 3.43(c). For the short path, we assume that each gate switches after only a contamination delay. This path involves only one gate delay, so it may occur after $t_{ccq} + t_{cd} = 30 + 25 = 55$ ps. But recall that the flip-flop has a hold time of

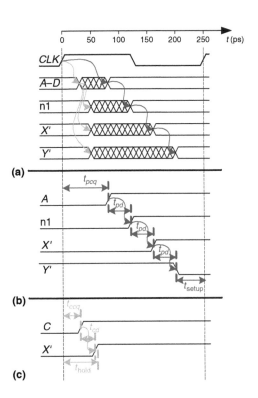

Figure 3.43 Timing diagram:
(a) general case, (b) critical path,
(c) short path

60 ps, meaning that X' must remain stable for 60 ps after the rising edge of CLK for the flip-flop to reliably sample its value. In this case, $X' = 0$ at the first rising edge of CLK, so we want the flip-flop to capture $X = 0$. Because X' did not hold stable long enough, the actual value of X is unpredictable. The circuit has a hold time violation and may behave erratically at any clock frequency.

Example 3.11 FIXING HOLD TIME VIOLATIONS

Alyssa P. Hacker proposes to fix Ben's circuit by adding buffers to slow down the short paths, as shown in Figure 3.44. The buffers have the same delays as other gates. Help her determine the maximum clock frequency and whether any hold time problems could occur.

Solution: Figure 3.45 shows waveforms illustrating when the signals might change. The critical path from A to Y is unaffected, because it does not pass through any buffers. Therefore, the maximum clock frequency is still 4 GHz. However, the short paths are slowed by the contamination delay of the buffer. Now X' will not change until $t_{ccq} + 2t_{cd} = 30 + 2 \times 25 = 80$ ps. This is after the 60 ps hold time has elapsed, so the circuit now operates correctly.

This example had an unusually long hold time to illustrate the point of hold time problems. Most flip-flops are designed with $t_{hold} < t_{ccq}$ to avoid such problems.

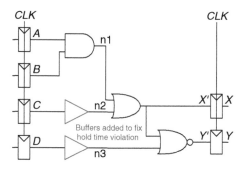

Figure 3.44 **Corrected circuit to fix hold time problem**

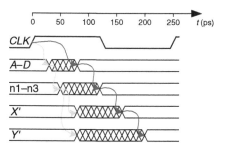

Figure 3.45 **Timing diagram with buffers to fix hold time problem**

However, some high-performance microprocessors, including the Pentium 4, use an element called a *pulsed latch* in place of a flip-flop. The pulsed latch behaves like a flip-flop but has a short clock-to-Q delay and a long hold time. In general, adding buffers can usually, but not always, solve hold time problems without slowing the critical path.

3.5.3 Clock Skew*

In the previous analysis, we assumed that the clock reaches all registers at exactly the same time. In reality, there is some variation in this time. This variation in clock edges is called *clock skew*. For example, the wires from the clock source to different registers may be of different lengths, resulting in slightly different delays, as shown in Figure 3.46. Noise also results in different delays. Clock gating, described in Section 3.2.5, further delays the clock. If some clocks are gated and others are not, there will be substantial skew between the gated and ungated clocks. In Figure 3.46, $CLK2$ is *early* with respect to $CLK1$, because the clock wire between the two registers follows a scenic route. If the clock had been routed differently, $CLK1$ might have been early instead. When doing timing analysis, we consider the worst-case scenario, so that we can guarantee that the circuit will work under all circumstances.

Figure 3.47 adds skew to the timing diagram from Figure 3.38. The heavy clock line indicates the latest time at which the clock signal might reach any register; the hashed lines show that the clock might arrive up to t_{skew} earlier.

First, consider the setup time constraint shown in Figure 3.48. In the worst case, R1 receives the latest skewed clock and R2 receives the earliest skewed clock, leaving as little time as possible for data to propagate between the registers.

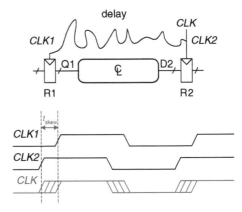

Figure 3.46 Clock skew caused by wire delay

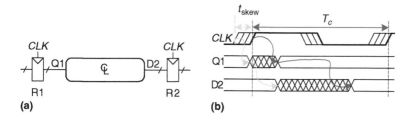

Figure 3.47 Timing diagram with clock skew

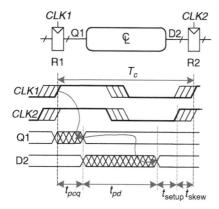

Figure 3.48 Setup time constraint with clock skew

The data propagates through the register and combinational logic and must setup before R2 samples it. Hence, we conclude that

$$T_c \geq t_{pcq} + t_{pd} + t_{\text{setup}} + t_{\text{skew}} \tag{3.19}$$

$$t_{pd} \leq T_c - (t_{pcq} + t_{\text{setup}} + t_{\text{skew}}) \tag{3.20}$$

Next, consider the hold time constraint shown in Figure 3.49. In the worst case, R1 receives an early skewed clock, $CLK1$, and R2 receives a late skewed clock, $CLK2$. The data zips through the register and combinational logic but must not arrive until a hold time after the late clock. Thus, we find that

$$t_{ccq} + t_{cd} \geq t_{\text{hold}} + t_{\text{skew}} \tag{3.21}$$

$$t_{cd} \geq t_{\text{hold}} + t_{\text{skew}} - t_{ccq} \tag{3.22}$$

In summary, clock skew effectively increases both the setup time and the hold time. It adds to the sequencing overhead, reducing the time available for useful work in the combinational logic. It also increases the required minimum delay through the combinational logic. Even if $t_{\text{hold}} = 0$, a pair of back-to-back flip-flops will violate Equation 3.22 if $t_{\text{skew}} > t_{ccq}$. To prevent

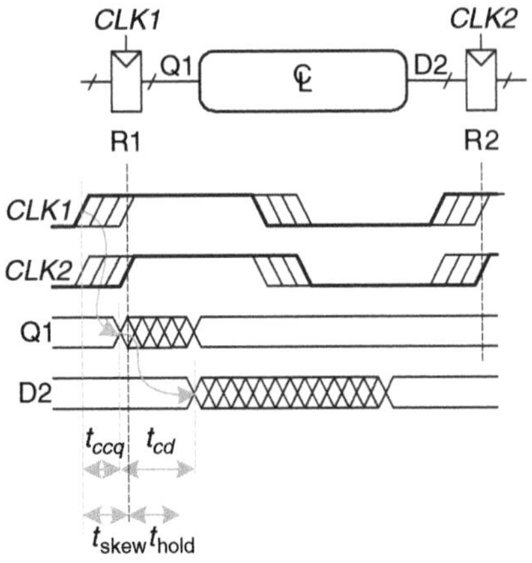

Figure 3.49 Hold time constraint with clock skew

serious hold time failures, designers must not permit too much clock skew. Sometimes flip-flops are intentionally designed to be particularly slow (i.e., large t_{ccq}), to prevent hold time problems even when the clock skew is substantial.

Example 3.12 TIMING ANALYSIS WITH CLOCK SKEW

Revisit Example 3.10 and assume that the system has 50 ps of clock skew.

Solution: The critical path remains the same, but the setup time is effectively increased by the skew. Hence, the minimum cycle time is

$$
\begin{aligned}
T_c &\geq t_{pcq} + 3t_{pd} + t_{setup} + t_{skew} \\
&= 80 + 3\times40 + 50 + 50 = 300\text{ps}
\end{aligned}
\tag{3.23}
$$

The maximum clock frequency is $f_c = 1/T_c = 3.33$ GHz.

The short path also remains the same at 55 ps. The hold time is effectively increased by the skew to $60 + 50 = 110$ ps, which is much greater than 55 ps. Hence, the circuit will violate the hold time and malfunction at any frequency. The circuit violated the hold time constraint even without skew. Skew in the system just makes the violation worse.

Example 3.13 FIXING HOLD TIME VIOLATIONS

Revisit Example 3.11 and assume that the system has 50 ps of clock skew.

Solution: The critical path is unaffected, so the maximum clock frequency remains 3.33 GHz.

The short path increases to 80 ps. This is still less than $t_{hold} + t_{skew} = 110$ ps, so the circuit still violates its hold time constraint.

To fix the problem, even more buffers could be inserted. Buffers would need to be added on the critical path as well, reducing the clock frequency. Alternatively, a better flip-flop with a shorter hold time might be used.

3.5.4 Metastability

As noted earlier, it is not always possible to guarantee that the input to a sequential circuit is stable during the aperture time, especially when the input arrives from the external world. Consider a button connected to the input of a flip-flop, as shown in Figure 3.50. When the button is not pressed, $D = 0$. When the button is pressed, $D = 1$. A monkey presses the button at some random time relative to the rising edge of CLK. We want to know the output Q after the rising edge of CLK. In Case I, when the button is pressed much before CLK, $Q = 1$. In Case II, when the button is not pressed until long after CLK, $Q = 0$. But in Case III, when the button is pressed sometime between t_{setup} before CLK and t_{hold} after CLK, the input violates the dynamic discipline and the output is undefined.

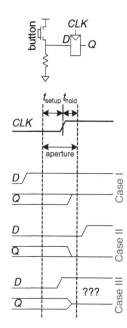

Figure 3.50 Input changing before, after, or during aperture

Metastable State

When a flip-flop samples an input that is changing during its aperture, the output Q may momentarily take on a voltage between 0 and V_{DD} that is in the forbidden zone. This is called a *metastable* state. Eventually, the flip-flop will resolve the output to a *stable state* of either 0 or 1. However, the *resolution time* required to reach the stable state is unbounded.

The metastable state of a flip-flop is analogous to a ball on the summit of a hill between two valleys, as shown in Figure 3.51. The two valleys are stable states, because a ball in the valley will remain there as long as it is not disturbed. The top of the hill is called metastable because the ball would remain there if it were perfectly balanced. But because nothing is perfect, the ball will eventually roll to one side or the other. The time required for this change to occur depends on how nearly well balanced the ball originally was. Every bistable device has a metastable state between the two stable states.

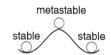

Figure 3.51 Stable and metastable states

Resolution Time

If a flip-flop input changes at a random time during the clock cycle, the resolution time, t_{res}, required to resolve to a stable state is also a random variable. If the input changes outside the aperture, then $t_{res} = t_{pcq}$. But if the input happens to change within the aperture, t_{res} can be substantially longer. Theoretical and experimental analyses (see Section 3.5.6) have shown that the probability that the resolution time, t_{res}, exceeds some arbitrary time, t, decreases exponentially with t:

$$P(t_{res} > t) = \frac{T_0}{T_c} e^{-\frac{t}{\tau}} \qquad (3.24)$$

where T_c is the clock period, and T_0 and τ are characteristic of the flip-flop. The equation is valid only for t substantially longer than t_{pcq}.

Intuitively, T_0/T_c describes the probability that the input changes at a bad time (i.e., during the aperture time); this probability decreases with the cycle time, T_c. τ is a time constant indicating how fast the flip-flop moves away from the metastable state; it is related to the delay through the cross-coupled gates in the flip-flop.

In summary, if the input to a bistable device such as a flip-flop changes during the aperture time, the output may take on a metastable value for some time before resolving to a stable 0 or 1. The amount of time required to resolve is unbounded, because for any finite time, t, the probability that the flip-flop is still metastable is nonzero. However, this probability drops off exponentially as t increases. Therefore, if we wait long enough, much longer than t_{pcq}, we can expect with exceedingly high probability that the flip-flop will reach a valid logic level.

3.5.5 Synchronizers

Asynchronous inputs to digital systems from the real world are inevitable. Human input is asynchronous, for example. If handled carelessly, these asynchronous inputs can lead to metastable voltages within the system, causing erratic system failures that are extremely difficult to track down and correct. The goal of a digital system designer should be to ensure that, given asynchronous inputs, the probability of encountering a metastable voltage is sufficiently small. "Sufficiently" depends on the context. For a cell phone, perhaps one failure in 10 years is acceptable, because the user can always turn the phone off and back on if it locks up. For a medical device, one failure in the expected life of the universe (10^{10} years) is a better target. To guarantee good logic levels, all asynchronous inputs should be passed through *synchronizers*.

A synchronizer, shown in Figure 3.52, is a device that receives an asynchronous input D and a clock CLK. It produces an output Q within a bounded amount of time; the output has a valid logic level with extremely high probability. If D is stable during the aperture, Q should take on the same value as D. If D changes during the aperture, Q may take on either a HIGH or LOW value but must not be metastable.

Figure 3.53 shows a simple way to build a synchronizer out of two flip-flops. F1 samples D on the rising edge of CLK. If D is changing at that time, the output D2 may be momentarily metastable. If the clock

Figure 3.52 Synchronizer symbol

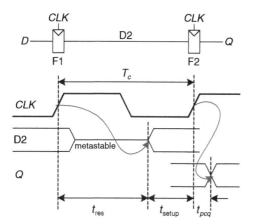

Figure 3.53 **Simple synchronizer**

period is long enough, D2 will, with high probability, resolve to a valid logic level before the end of the period. F2 then samples D2, which is now stable, producing a good output Q.

We say that a synchronizer *fails* if Q, the output of the synchronizer, becomes metastable. This may happen if D2 has not resolved to a valid level by the time it must setup at F2—that is, if $t_{res} > T_c - t_{setup}$. According to Equation 3.24, the probability of failure for a single input change at a random time is

$$P(\text{failure}) = \frac{T_0}{T_c} e^{-\frac{T_c - t_{setup}}{\tau}} \qquad (3.25)$$

The probability of failure, $P(\text{failure})$, is the probability that the output Q will be metastable upon a single change in D. If D changes once per second, the probability of failure per second is just $P(\text{failure})$. However, if D changes N times per second, the probability of failure per second is N times as great:

$$P(\text{failure})/\text{sec} = N \frac{T_0}{T_c} e^{-\frac{T_c - t_{setup}}{\tau}} \qquad (3.26)$$

System reliability is usually measured in *mean time between failures* (*MTBF*). As the name suggests, MTBF is the average amount of time between failures of the system. It is the reciprocal of the probability that the system will fail in any given second

$$MTBF = \frac{1}{P(\text{failure})/\text{sec}} = \frac{T_c e^{\frac{T_c - t_{setup}}{\tau}}}{NT_0} \qquad (3.27)$$

Equation 3.27 shows that the MTBF improves exponentially as the synchronizer waits for a longer time, T_c. For most systems, a synchronizer that waits for one clock cycle provides a safe MTBF. In exceptionally high-speed systems, waiting for more cycles may be necessary.

Example 3.14 SYNCHRONIZER FOR FSM INPUT

The traffic light controller FSM from Section 3.4.1 receives asynchronous inputs from the traffic sensors. Suppose that a synchronizer is used to guarantee stable inputs to the controller. Traffic arrives on average 0.2 times per second. The flip-flops in the synchronizer have the following characteristics: $\tau = 200$ ps, $T_0 = 150$ ps, and $t_{\text{setup}} = 500$ ps. How long must the synchronizer clock period be for the MTBF to exceed 1 year?

Solution: 1 year $\approx \pi \times 10^7$ seconds. Solve Equation 3.27.

$$\pi \times 10^7 = \frac{T_c e^{\frac{T_c - 500 \times 10^{-12}}{200 \times 10^{-12}}}}{(0.2)(150 \times 10^{-12})} \tag{3.28}$$

This equation has no closed form solution. However, it is easy enough to solve by guess and check. In a spreadsheet, try a few values of T_c and calculate the MTBF until discovering the value of T_c that gives an MTBF of 1 year: $T_c = 3.036$ ns.

3.5.6 Derivation of Resolution Time*

Equation 3.24 can be derived using a basic knowledge of circuit theory, differential equations, and probability. This section can be skipped if you are not interested in the derivation or if you are unfamiliar with the mathematics.

A flip-flop output will be metastable after some time, t, if the flip-flop samples a changing input (causing a metastable condition) and the output does not resolve to a valid level within that time after the clock edge. Symbolically, this can be expressed as

$$P(t_{res} > t) = P(\text{samples changing input}) \times P(\text{unresolved}) \tag{3.29}$$

We consider each probability term individually. The asynchronous input signal switches between 0 and 1 in some time, t_{switch}, as shown in Figure 3.54. The probability that the input changes during the aperture around the clock edge is

$$P(\text{samples changing input}) = \frac{t_{\text{switch}} + t_{\text{setup}} + t_{\text{hold}}}{T_c} \tag{3.30}$$

If the flip-flop does enter metastability—that is, with probability $P(\text{samples changing input})$—the time to resolve from metastability depends on the inner workings of the circuit. This resolution time determines $P(\text{unresolved})$, the probability that the flip-flop has not yet resolved

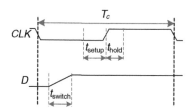

Figure 3.54 **Input timing**

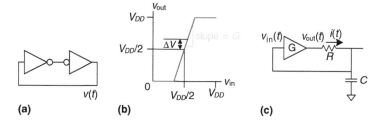

Figure 3.55 **Circuit model of bistable device**

to a valid logic level after a time t. The remainder of this section analyzes a simple model of a bistable device to estimate this probability.

A bistable device uses storage with positive feedback. Figure 3.55(a) shows this feedback implemented with a pair of inverters; this circuit's behavior is representative of most bistable elements. A pair of inverters behaves like a buffer. Let us model the buffer as having the symmetric DC transfer characteristics shown in Figure 3.55(b), with a slope of G. The buffer can deliver only a finite amount of output current; we can model this as an output resistance, R. All real circuits also have some capacitance C that must be charged up. Charging the capacitor through the resistor causes an RC delay, preventing the buffer from switching instantaneously. Hence, the complete circuit model is shown in Figure 3.55(c), where $v_{\text{out}}(t)$ is the voltage of interest conveying the state of the bistable device.

The metastable point for this circuit is $v_{\text{out}}(t) = v_{\text{in}}(t) = V_{DD}/2$; if the circuit began at exactly that point, it would remain there indefinitely in the absence of noise. Because voltages are continuous variables, the chance that the circuit will begin at exactly the metastable point is vanishingly small. However, the circuit might begin at time 0 near metastability at $v_{\text{out}}(0) = V_{DD}/2 + \Delta V$ for some small offset ΔV. In such a case, the positive feedback will eventually drive $v_{\text{out}}(t)$ to V_{DD} if $\Delta V > 0$ and to 0 if $\Delta V < 0$. The time required to reach V_{DD} or 0 is the resolution time of the bistable device.

The DC transfer characteristic is nonlinear, but it appears linear near the metastable point, which is the region of interest to us. Specifically, if $v_{\text{in}}(t) = V_{DD}/2 + \Delta V/G$, then $v_{\text{out}}(t) = V_{DD}/2 + \Delta V$ for small ΔV. The current through the resistor is $i(t) = (v_{\text{out}}(t) - v_{\text{in}}(t))/R$. The capacitor charges at a rate $dv_{in}(t)/dt = i(t)/C$. Putting these facts together, we find the governing equation for the output voltage.

$$\frac{dv_{out}(t)}{dt} = \frac{(G-1)}{RC}\left[v_{out}(t) - \frac{V_{DD}}{2}\right] \tag{3.31}$$

This is a linear first-order differential equation. Solving it with the initial condition $v_{out}(0) = V_{DD}/2 + \Delta V$ gives

$$v_{out}(t) = \frac{V_{DD}}{2} + \Delta V e^{\frac{(G-1)t}{RC}} \tag{3.32}$$

Figure 3.56 plots trajectories for $v_{out}(t)$ given various starting points. $v_{out}(t)$ moves exponentially away from the metastable point $V_{DD}/2$ until it saturates at V_{DD} or 0. The output eventually resolves to 1 or 0. The amount of time this takes depends on the initial voltage offset (ΔV) from the metastable point ($V_{DD}/2$).

Solving Equation 3.32 for the resolution time t_{res}, such that $v_{out}(t_{res}) = V_{DD}$ or 0, gives

$$|\Delta V| e^{\frac{(G-1)t_{res}}{RC}} = \frac{V_{DD}}{2} \tag{3.33}$$

$$t_{res} = \frac{RC}{G-1}\ln\frac{V_{DD}}{2|\Delta V|} \tag{3.34}$$

In summary, the resolution time increases if the bistable device has high resistance or capacitance that causes the output to change slowly. It decreases if the bistable device has high *gain*, G. The resolution time also increases logarithmically as the circuit starts closer to the metastable point ($\Delta V \rightarrow 0$).

Define τ as $\frac{RC}{G-1}$. Solving Equation 3.34 for ΔV finds the initial offset, ΔV_{res}, that gives a particular resolution time, t_{res}:

$$\Delta V_{res} = \frac{V_{DD}}{2}e^{-t_{res}/\tau} \tag{3.35}$$

Suppose that the bistable device samples the input while it is changing. It measures a voltage, $v_{in}(0)$, which we will assume is uniformly distributed

Figure 3.56 Resolution trajectories

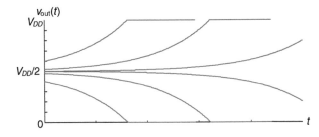

between 0 and V_{DD}. The probability that the output has not resolved to a legal value after time t_{res} depends on the probability that the initial offset is sufficiently small. Specifically, the initial offset on v_{out} must be less than ΔV_{res}, so the initial offset on v_{in} must be less than $\Delta V_{res}/G$. Then the probability that the bistable device samples the input at a time to obtain a sufficiently small initial offset is

$$P(\text{unresolved}) = P\left(\left|v_{in}(0)-\frac{V_{DD}}{2}\right|<\frac{\Delta V_{res}}{G}\right)=\frac{2\Delta V_{res}}{GV_{DD}} \tag{3.36}$$

Putting this all together, the probability that the resolution time exceeds some time t is given by the following equation:

$$P(t_{res}>t) = \frac{t_{switch} + t_{setup} + t_{hold}}{GT_c}e^{-\frac{t}{\tau}} \tag{3.37}$$

Observe that Equation 3.37 is in the form of Equation 3.24, where $T_0 = (t_{switch} + t_{setup} + t_{hold})/G$ and $\tau = RC/(G-1)$. In summary, we have derived Equation 3.24 and shown how T_0 and τ depend on physical properties of the bistable device.

3.6 PARALLELISM

The speed of a system is characterized by the latency and throughput of information moving through it. We define a *token* to be a group of inputs that are processed to produce a group of outputs. The term conjures up the notion of placing subway tokens on a circuit diagram and moving them around to visualize data moving through the circuit. The *latency* of a system is the time required for one token to pass through the system from start to end. The *throughput* is the number of tokens that can be produced per unit time.

Example 3.15 COOKIE THROUGHPUT AND LATENCY

Ben Bitdiddle is throwing a milk and cookies party to celebrate the installation of his traffic light controller. It takes him 5 minutes to roll cookies and place them on his tray. It then takes 15 minutes for the cookies to bake in the oven. Once the cookies are baked, he starts another tray. What is Ben's throughput and latency for a tray of cookies?

Solution: In this example, a tray of cookies is a token. The latency is 1/3 hour per tray. The throughput is 3 trays/hour.

As you might imagine, the throughput can be improved by processing several tokens at the same time. This is called *parallelism*, and it comes in two forms: spatial and temporal. With *spatial parallelism*, multiple copies of the hardware are provided so that multiple tasks can be done at the same time. With *temporal parallelism*, a task is broken into stages, like an assembly line. Multiple tasks can be spread across the stages. Although each task must pass through all stages, a different task will be in each stage at any given time so multiple tasks can overlap. Temporal parallelism is commonly called *pipelining*. Spatial parallelism is sometimes just called parallelism, but we will avoid that naming convention because it is ambiguous.

Example 3.16 COOKIE PARALLELISM

Ben Bitdiddle has hundreds of friends coming to his party and needs to bake cookies faster. He is considering using spatial and/or temporal parallelism.

Spatial Parallelism: Ben asks Alyssa P. Hacker to help out. She has her own cookie tray and oven.

Temporal Parallelism: Ben gets a second cookie tray. Once he puts one cookie tray in the oven, he starts rolling cookies on the other tray rather than waiting for the first tray to bake.

What is the throughput and latency using spatial parallelism? Using temporal parallelism? Using both?

Solution: The latency is the time required to complete one task from start to finish. In all cases, the latency is 1/3 hour. If Ben starts with no cookies, the latency is the time needed for him to produce the first cookie tray.

The throughput is the number of cookie trays per hour. With spatial parallelism, Ben and Alyssa each complete one tray every 20 minutes. Hence, the throughput doubles, to 6 trays/hour. With temporal parallelism, Ben puts a new tray in the oven every 15 minutes, for a throughput of 4 trays/hour. These are illustrated in Figure 3.57.

If Ben and Alyssa use both techniques, they can bake 8 trays/hour.

Consider a task with latency L. In a system with no parallelism, the throughput is $1/L$. In a spatially parallel system with N copies of the hardware, the throughput is N/L. In a temporally parallel system, the task is ideally broken into N steps, or stages, of equal length. In such a case, the throughput is also N/L, and only one copy of the hardware is required. However, as the cookie example showed, finding N steps of equal length is often impractical. If the longest step has a latency L_1, the pipelined throughput is $1/L_1$.

Pipelining (temporal parallelism) is particularly attractive because it speeds up a circuit without duplicating the hardware. Instead, registers are placed between blocks of combinational logic to divide the logic into shorter stages that can run with a faster clock. The registers prevent a

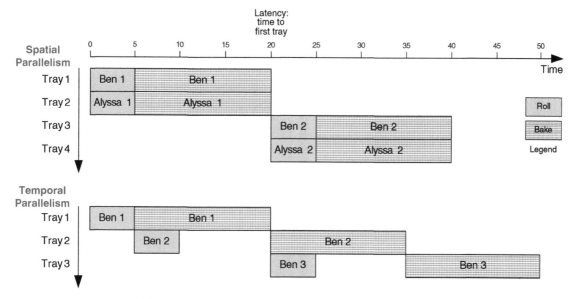

Figure 3.57 **Spatial and temporal parallelism in the cookie kitchen**

token in one pipeline stage from catching up with and corrupting the token in the next stage.

Figure 3.58 shows an example of a circuit with no pipelining. It contains four blocks of logic between the registers. The critical path passes through blocks 2, 3, and 4. Assume that the register has a clock-to-Q propagation delay of 0.3 ns and a setup time of 0.2 ns. Then the cycle time is $T_c = 0.3 + 3 + 2 + 4 + 0.2 = 9.5$ ns. The circuit has a latency of 9.5 ns and a throughput of 1/9.5 ns = 105 MHz.

Figure 3.59 shows the same circuit partitioned into a two-stage pipeline by adding a register between blocks 3 and 4. The first stage has a minimum clock period of $0.3 + 3 + 2 + 0.2 = 5.5$ ns. The second stage has a minimum clock period of $0.3 + 4 + 0.2 = 4.5$ ns. The clock must be slow enough for all stages to work. Hence, $T_c = 5.5$ ns. The latency

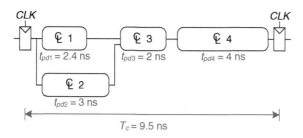

Figure 3.58 **Circuit with no pipelining**

Figure 3.59 **Circuit with two-stage pipeline**

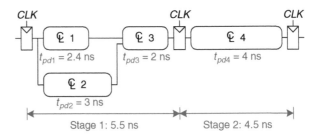

Figure 3.60 **Circuit with three-stage pipeline**

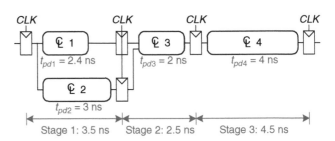

is two clock cycles, or 11 ns. The throughput is 1/5.5 ns = 182 MHz. This example shows that, in a real circuit, pipelining with two stages almost doubles the throughput and slightly increases the latency. In comparison, ideal pipelining would exactly double the throughput at no penalty in latency. The discrepancy comes about because the circuit cannot be divided into two exactly equal halves and because the registers introduce more sequencing overhead.

Figure 3.60 shows the same circuit partitioned into a three-stage pipeline. Note that two more registers are needed to store the results of blocks 1 and 2 at the end of the first pipeline stage. The cycle time is now limited by the third stage to 4.5 ns. The latency is three cycles, or 13.5 ns. The throughput is 1/4.5 ns = 222 MHz. Again, adding a pipeline stage improves throughput at the expense of some latency.

Although these techniques are powerful, they do not apply to all situations. The bane of parallelism is *dependencies*. If a current task is dependent on the result of a prior task, rather than just prior steps in the current task, the task cannot start until the prior task has completed. For example, if Ben wants to check that the first tray of cookies tastes good before he starts preparing the second, he has a dependency that prevents pipelining or parallel operation. Parallelism is one of the most important techniques for designing high-performance digital systems. Chapter 7 discusses pipelining further and shows examples of handling dependencies.

3.7 SUMMARY

This chapter has described the analysis and design of sequential logic. In contrast to combinational logic, whose outputs depend only on the current inputs, sequential logic outputs depend on both current and prior inputs. In other words, sequential logic remembers information about prior inputs. This memory is called the *state* of the logic.

Sequential circuits can be difficult to analyze and are easy to design incorrectly, so we limit ourselves to a small set of carefully designed building blocks. The most important element for our purposes is the flip-flop, which receives a clock and an input D and produces an output Q. The flip-flop copies D to Q on the rising edge of the clock and otherwise remembers the old state of Q. A group of flip-flops sharing a common clock is called a register. Flip-flops may also receive reset or enable control signals.

Although many forms of sequential logic exist, we discipline ourselves to use synchronous sequential circuits because they are easy to design. Synchronous sequential circuits consist of blocks of combinational logic separated by clocked registers. The state of the circuit is stored in the registers and updated only on clock edges.

Finite state machines are a powerful technique for designing sequential circuits. To design an FSM, first identify the inputs and outputs of the machine and sketch a state transition diagram, indicating the states and the transitions between them. Select an encoding for the states, and rewrite the diagram as a state transition table and output table, indicating the next state and output given the current state and input. From these tables, design the combinational logic to compute the next state and output, and sketch the circuit.

Synchronous sequential circuits have a timing specification including the clock-to-Q propagation and contamination delays, t_{pcq} and t_{ccq}, and the setup and hold times, t_{setup} and t_{hold}. For correct operation, their inputs must be stable during an aperture time that starts a setup time before the rising edge of the clock and ends a hold time after the rising edge of the clock. The minimum cycle time T_c of the system is equal to the propagation delay t_{pd} through the combinational logic plus $t_{pcq} + t_{\text{setup}}$ of the register. For correct operation, the contamination delay through the register and combinational logic must be greater than t_{hold}. Despite the common misconception to the contrary, hold time does not affect the cycle time.

Overall system performance is measured in latency and throughput. The latency is the time required for a token to pass from start to end. The throughput is the number of tokens that the system can process per unit time. Parallelism improves system throughput.

> Anyone who could invent logic whose outputs depend on future inputs would be fabulously wealthy!

Exercises

Exercise 3.1 Given the input waveforms shown in Figure 3.61, sketch the output, *Q*, of an SR latch.

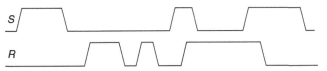

Figure 3.61 **Input waveforms of SR latch for Exercise 3.1**

Exercise 3.2 Given the input waveforms shown in Figure 3.62, sketch the output, *Q*, of an SR latch.

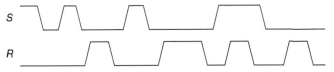

Figure 3.62 **Input waveforms of SR latch for Exercise 3.2**

Exercise 3.3 Given the input waveforms shown in Figure 3.63, sketch the output, *Q*, of a D latch.

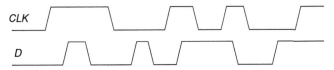

Figure 3.63 **Input waveforms of D latch or flip-flop for Exercises 3.3 and 3.5**

Exercise 3.4 Given the input waveforms shown in Figure 3.64, sketch the output, *Q*, of a D latch.

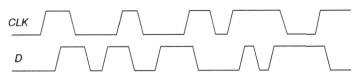

Figure 3.64 **Input waveforms of D latch or flip-flop for Exercises 3.4 and 3.6**

Exercise 3.5 Given the input waveforms shown in Figure 3.63, sketch the output, Q, of a D flip-flop.

Exercise 3.6 Given the input waveforms shown in Figure 3.64, sketch the output, Q, of a D flip-flop.

Exercise 3.7 Is the circuit in Figure 3.65 combinational logic or sequential logic? Explain in a simple fashion what the relationship is between the inputs and outputs. What would you call this circuit?

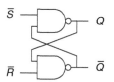

Figure 3.65 Mystery circuit

Exercise 3.8 Is the circuit in Figure 3.66 combinational logic or sequential logic? Explain in a simple fashion what the relationship is between the inputs and outputs. What would you call this circuit?

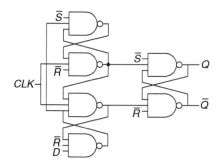

Figure 3.66 Mystery circuit

Exercise 3.9 The *toggle (T) flip-flop* has one input, CLK, and one output, Q. On each rising edge of CLK, Q toggles to the complement of its previous value. Draw a schematic for a T flip-flop using a D flip-flop and an inverter.

Exercise 3.10 *A JK flip-flop* receives a clock and two inputs, J and K. On the rising edge of the clock, it updates the output, Q. If J and K are both 0, Q retains its old value. If only J is 1, Q becomes 1. If only K is 1, Q becomes 0. If both J and K are 1, Q becomes the opposite of its present state.

(a) Construct a JK flip-flop using a D flip-flop and some combinational logic.

(b) Construct a D flip-flop using a JK flip-flop and some combinational logic.

(c) Construct a T flip-flop (see Exercise 3.9) using a JK flip-flop.

Exercise 3.11 The circuit in Figure 3.67 is called a *Muller C-element*. Explain in a simple fashion what the relationship is between the inputs and output.

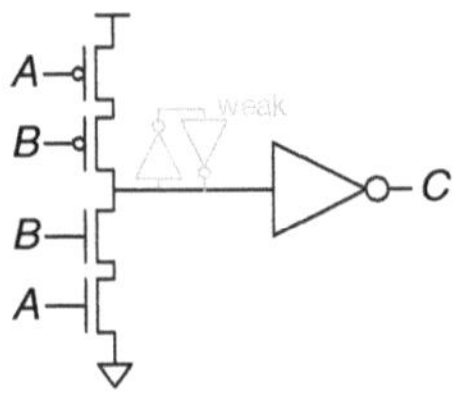

Figure 3.67 Muller C-element

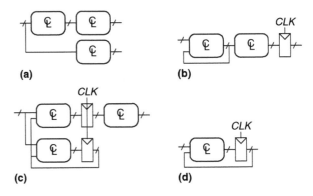

Exercise 3.12 Design an asynchronously resettable D latch using logic gates.

Exercise 3.13 Design an asynchronously resettable D flip-flop using logic gates.

Exercise 3.14 Design a synchronously settable D flip-flop using logic gates.

Exercise 3.15 Design an asynchronously settable D flip-flop using logic gates.

Exercise 3.16 Suppose a ring oscillator is built from N inverters connected in a loop. Each inverter has a minimum delay of t_{cd} and a maximum delay of t_{pd}. If N is odd, determine the range of frequencies at which the oscillator might operate.

Exercise 3.17 Why must N be odd in Exercise 3.16?

Exercise 3.18 Which of the circuits in Figure 3.68 are synchronous sequential circuits? Explain.

Figure 3.68 Circuits

Exercise 3.19 You are designing an elevator controller for a building with 25 floors. The controller has two inputs: *UP* and *DOWN*. It produces an output indicating the floor that the elevator is on. There is no floor 13. What is the minimum number of bits of state in the controller?

Exercise 3.20 You are designing an FSM to keep track of the mood of four students working in the digital design lab. Each student's mood is either HAPPY (the circuit works), SAD (the circuit blew up), BUSY (working on the circuit), CLUELESS (confused about the circuit), or ASLEEP (face down on the circuit board). How many states does the FSM have? What is the minimum number of bits necessary to represent these states?

Exercise 3.21 How would you factor the FSM from Exercise 3.20 into multiple simpler machines? How many states does each simpler machine have? What is the minimum total number of bits necessary in this factored design?

Exercise 3.22 Describe in words what the state machine in Figure 3.69 does. Using binary state encodings, complete a state transition table and output table for the FSM. Write Boolean equations for the next state and output and sketch a schematic of the FSM.

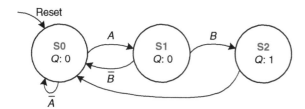

Figure 3.69 **State transition diagram**

Exercise 3.23 Describe in words what the state machine in Figure 3.70 does. Using binary state encodings, complete a state transition table and output table for the FSM. Write Boolean equations for the next state and output and sketch a schematic of the FSM.

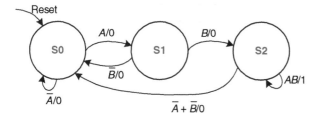

Figure 3.70 **State transition diagram**

Exercise 3.24 Accidents are still occurring at the intersection of Academic Avenue and Bravado Boulevard. The football team is rushing into the intersection the moment light B turns green. They are colliding with sleep-deprived CS majors who stagger into the intersection just before light A turns red. Extend the traffic light controller from Section 3.4.1 so that both lights are red for 5 seconds before either light turns green again. Sketch your improved Moore machine state transition diagram, state encodings, state transition table, output table, next state and output equations, and your FSM schematic.

Exercise 3.25 Alyssa P. Hacker's snail from Section 3.4.3 has a daughter with a Mealy machine FSM brain. The daughter snail smiles whenever she slides over the pattern 1101 or the pattern 1110. Sketch the state transition diagram for this happy snail using as few states as possible. Choose state encodings and write a combined state transition and output table using your encodings. Write the next state and output equations and sketch your FSM schematic.

Exercise 3.26 You have been enlisted to design a soda machine dispenser for your department lounge. Sodas are partially subsidized by the student chapter of the IEEE, so they cost only 25 cents. The machine accepts nickels, dimes, and quarters. When enough coins have been inserted, it dispenses the soda and returns any necessary change. Design an FSM controller for the soda machine. The FSM inputs are *Nickel*, *Dime*, and *Quarter*, indicating which coin was inserted. Assume that exactly one coin is inserted on each cycle. The outputs are *Dispense*, *ReturnNickel*, *ReturnDime*, and *ReturnTwoDimes*. When the FSM reaches 25 cents, it asserts *Dispense* and the necessary *Return* outputs required to deliver the appropriate change. Then it should be ready to start accepting coins for another soda.

Exercise 3.27 Gray codes have a useful property in that consecutive numbers differ in only a single bit position. Table 3.23 lists a 3-bit Gray code representing the numbers 0 to 7. Design a 3-bit modulo 8 Gray code counter FSM with no inputs and three outputs. (A modulo N counter counts from 0 to $N - 1$, then

Table 3.23 3-bit Gray code

Number	Gray code		
0	0	0	0
1	0	0	1
2	0	1	1
3	0	1	0
4	1	1	0
5	1	1	1
6	1	0	1
7	1	0	0

repeats. For example, a watch uses a modulo 60 counter for the minutes and seconds that counts from 0 to 59.) When reset, the output should be 000. On each clock edge, the output should advance to the next Gray code. After reaching 100, it should repeat with 000.

Exercise 3.28 Extend your modulo 8 Gray code counter from Exercise 3.27 to be an UP/DOWN counter by adding an UP input. If $UP = 1$, the counter advances to the next number. If $UP = 0$, the counter retreats to the previous number.

Exercise 3.29 Your company, Detect-o-rama, would like to design an FSM that takes two inputs, A and B, and generates one output, Z. The output in cycle n, Z_n, is either the Boolean AND or OR of the corresponding input A_n and the previous input A_{n-1}, depending on the other input, B_n:

$$Z_n = A_n A_{n-1} \quad \text{if } B_n = 0$$
$$Z_n = A_n + A_{n-1} \quad \text{if } B_n = 1$$

(a) Sketch the waveform for Z given the inputs shown in Figure 3.71.

(b) Is this FSM a Moore or a Mealy machine?

(c) Design the FSM. Show your state transition diagram, encoded state transition table, next state and output equations, and schematic.

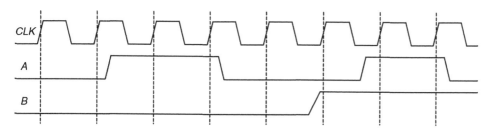

Figure 3.71 FSM input waveforms

Exercise 3.30 Design an FSM with one input, A, and two outputs, X and Y. X should be 1 if A has been 1 for at least three cycles altogether (not necessarily consecutively). Y should be 1 if A has been 1 for at least two consecutive cycles. Show your state transition diagram, encoded state transition table, next state and output equations, and schematic.

Exercise 3.31 Analyze the FSM shown in Figure 3.72. Write the state transition and output tables and sketch the state transition diagram. Describe in words what the FSM does.

Figure 3.72 FSM schematic

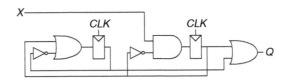

Exercise 3.32 Repeat Exercise 3.31 for the FSM shown in Figure 3.73. Recall that the *s* and *r* register inputs indicate set and reset, respectively.

Figure 3.73 FSM schematic

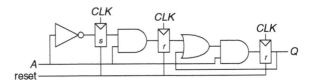

Exercise 3.33 Ben Bitdiddle has designed the circuit in Figure 3.74 to compute a registered four-input XOR function. Each two-input XOR gate has a propagation delay of 100 ps and a contamination delay of 55 ps. Each flip-flop has a setup time of 60 ps, a hold time of 20 ps, a clock-to-*Q* maximum delay of 70 ps, and a clock-to-*Q* minimum delay of 50 ps.

(a) If there is no clock skew, what is the maximum operating frequency of the circuit?

(b) How much clock skew can the circuit tolerate if it must operate at 2 GHz?

(c) How much clock skew can the circuit tolerate before it might experience a hold time violation?

(d) Alyssa P. Hacker points out that she can redesign the combinational logic between the registers to be faster *and* tolerate more clock skew. Her improved circuit also uses three two-input XORs, but they are arranged differently. What is her circuit? What is its maximum frequency if there is no clock skew? How much clock skew can the circuit tolerate before it might experience a hold time violation?

Figure 3.74 Registered four-input XOR circuit

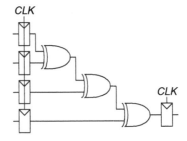

Exercise 3.34 You are designing an adder for the blindingly fast 2-bit RePentium Processor. The adder is built from two full adders such that the carry out of the first adder is the carry in to the second adder, as shown in Figure 3.75. Your adder has input and output registers and must complete the addition in one clock cycle. Each full adder has the following propagation delays: 20 ps from C_{in} to C_{out} or to *Sum* (S), 25 ps from A or B to C_{out}, and 30 ps from A or B to S. The adder has a contamination delay of 15 ps from C_{in} to either output and 22 ps from A or B to either output. Each flip-flop has a setup time of 30 ps, a hold time of 10 ps, a clock-to-Q propagation delay of 35 ps, and a clock-to-Q contamination delay of 21 ps.

(a) If there is no clock skew, what is the maximum operating frequency of the circuit?

(b) How much clock skew can the circuit tolerate if it must operate at 8 GHz?

(c) How much clock skew can the circuit tolerate before it might experience a hold time violation?

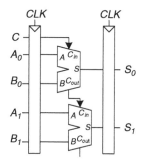

Figure 3.75 **2-bit adder schematic**

Exercise 3.35 A *field programmable gate array* (FPGA) uses *configurable logic blocks* (CLBs) rather than logic gates to implement combinational logic. The Xilinx Spartan 3 FPGA has propagation and contamination delays of 0.61 and 0.30 ns, respectively, for each CLB. It also contains flip-flops with propagation and contamination delays of 0.72 and 0.50 ns, and setup and hold times of 0.53 and 0 ns, respectively.

(a) If you are building a system that needs to run at 40 MHz, how many consecutive CLBs can you use between two flip-flops? Assume there is no clock skew and no delay through wires between CLBs.

(b) Suppose that all paths between flip-flops pass through at least one CLB. How much clock skew can the FPGA have without violating the hold time?

Exercise 3.36 A synchronizer is built from a pair of flip-flops with $t_{setup} = 50$ ps, $T_0 = 20$ ps, and $\tau = 30$ ps. It samples an asynchronous input that changes 10^8 times per second. What is the minimum clock period of the synchronizer to achieve a mean time between failures (MTBF) of 100 years?

Exercise 3.37 You would like to build a synchronizer that can receive asynchronous inputs with an MTBF of 50 years. Your system is running at 1 GHz, and you use sampling flip-flops with $\tau = 100$ ps, $T_0 = 110$ ps, and $t_{setup} = 70$ ps. The synchronizer receives a new asynchronous input on average 0.5 times per second (i.e., once every 2 seconds). What is the required probability of failure to satisfy this MTBF? How many clock cycles would you have to wait before reading the sampled input signal to give that probability of error?

Exercise 3.38 You are walking down the hallway when you run into your lab partner walking in the other direction. The two of you first step one way and are still in each other's way. Then you both step the other way and are still in each other's way. Then you both wait a bit, hoping the other person will step aside. You can model this situation as a metastable point and apply the same theory that has been applied to synchronizers and flip-flops. Suppose you create a mathematical model for yourself and your lab partner. You start the unfortunate encounter in the metastable state. The probability that you remain in this state after t seconds is $e^{-\frac{t}{\tau}}$. τ indicates your response rate; today, your brain has been blurred by lack of sleep and has $\tau = 20$ seconds.

(a) How long will it be until you have 99% certainty that you will have resolved from metastability (i.e., figured out how to pass one another)?

(b) You are not only sleepy, but also ravenously hungry. In fact, you will starve to death if you don't get going to the cafeteria within 3 minutes. What is the probability that your lab partner will have to drag you to the morgue?

Exercise 3.39 You have built a synchronizer using flip-flops with $T_0 = 20$ ps and $\tau = 30$ ps. Your boss tells you that you need to increase the MTBF by a factor of 10. By how much do you need to increase the clock period?

Exercise 3.40 Ben Bitdiddle invents a new and improved synchronizer in Figure 3.76 that he claims eliminates metastability in a single cycle. He explains that the circuit in box M is an analog "metastability detector" that produces a HIGH output if the input voltage is in the forbidden zone between V_{IL} and V_{IH}. The metastability detector checks to determine whether the first flip-flop has produced a metastable output on D2. If so, it asynchronously resets the flip-flop to produce a good 0 at D2. The second flip-flop then samples D2, always producing a valid logic level on Q. Alyssa P. Hacker tells Ben that there must be a bug in the circuit, because eliminating metastability is just as impossible as building a perpetual motion machine. Who is right? Explain, showing Ben's error or showing why Alyssa is wrong.

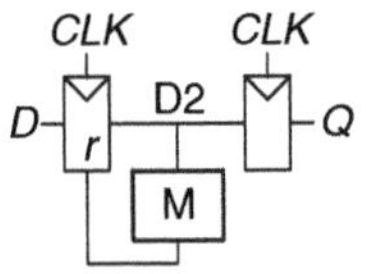

Figure 3.76 "New and improved" synchronizer

Interview Questions

The following exercises present questions that have been asked at interviews for digital design jobs.

Question 3.1 Draw a state machine that can detect when it has received the serial input sequence 01010.

Question 3.2 Design a serial (one bit at a time) two's complementer FSM with two inputs, *Start* and *A*, and one output, *Q*. A binary number of arbitrary length is provided to input *A*, starting with the least significant bit. The corresponding bit of the output appears at *Q* on the same cycle. *Start* is asserted for one cycle to initialize the FSM before the least significant bit is provided.

Question 3.3 What is the difference between a latch and a flip-flop? Under what circumstances is each one preferable?

Question 3.4 Design a 5-bit counter finite state machine.

Question 3.5 Design an edge detector circuit. The output should go HIGH for one cycle after the input makes a $0 \rightarrow 1$ transition.

Question 3.6 Describe the concept of pipelining and why it is used.

Question 3.7 Describe what it means for a flip-flop to have a negative hold time.

Question 3.8 Given signal *A*, shown in Figure 3.77, design a circuit that produces signal *B*.

Figure 3.77 Signal waveforms

Question 3.9 Consider a block of logic between two registers. Explain the timing constraints. If you add a buffer on the clock input of the receiver (the second flip-flop), does the setup time constraint get better or worse?

Hardware Description Languages

4.1 INTRODUCTION

Thus far, we have focused on designing combinational and sequential digital circuits at the schematic level. The process of finding an efficient set of logic gates to perform a given function is labor intensive and error prone, requiring manual simplification of truth tables or Boolean equations and manual translation of finite state machines (FSMs) into gates. In the 1990s, designers discovered that they were far more productive if they worked at a higher level of abstraction, specifying just the logical function and allowing a *computer-aided design* (*CAD*) tool to produce the optimized gates. The specifications are generally given in a *hardware description language* (*HDL*). The two leading hardware description languages are *SystemVerilog* and *VHDL*.

SystemVerilog and VHDL are built on similar principles but have different syntax. Discussion of these languages in this chapter is divided into two columns for literal side-by-side comparison, with SystemVerilog on the left and VHDL on the right. When you read the chapter for the first time, focus on one language or the other. Once you know one, you'll quickly master the other if you need it.

Subsequent chapters show hardware in both schematic and HDL form. If you choose to skip this chapter and not learn one of the HDLs, you will still be able to master the principles of computer organization from the schematics. However, the vast majority of commercial systems are now built using HDLs rather than schematics. If you expect to do digital design at any point in your professional life, we urge you to learn one of the HDLs.

4.1.1 Modules

A block of hardware with inputs and outputs is called a *module*. An AND gate, a multiplexer, and a priority circuit are all examples of hardware modules. The two general styles for describing module functionality are

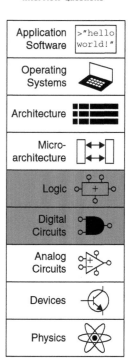

173

behavioral and *structural*. Behavioral models describe what a module does. Structural models describe how a module is built from simpler pieces; it is an application of hierarchy. The SystemVerilog and VHDL code in HDL Example 4.1 illustrate behavioral descriptions of a module that computes the Boolean function from Example 2.6, $y = \overline{a}\,\overline{b}\,\overline{c} + a\overline{b}\,\overline{c} + a\overline{b}c$. In both languages, the module is named `sillyfunction` and has three inputs, a, b, and c, and one output, y.

HDL Example 4.1 COMBINATIONAL LOGIC

SystemVerilog

```
module sillyfunction(input  logic a, b, c,
                     output logic y);

  assign y = ~a & ~b & ~c |
              a & ~b & ~c |
              a & ~b &  c;

endmodule
```

A SystemVerilog module begins with the module name and a listing of the inputs and outputs. The `assign` statement describes combinational logic. ~ indicates NOT, & indicates AND, and | indicates OR.

logic signals such as the inputs and outputs are Boolean variables (0 or 1). They may also have floating and undefined values, as discussed in Section 4.2.8.

The `logic` type was introduced in SystemVerilog. It supersedes the `reg` type, which was a perennial source of confusion in Verilog. `logic` should be used everywhere except on signals with multiple drivers. Signals with multiple drivers are called *nets* and will be explained in Section 4.7.

VHDL

```
library IEEE; use IEEE.STD_LOGIC_1164.all;

entity sillyfunction is
  port(a, b, c: in  STD_LOGIC;
       y:       out STD_LOGIC);
end;

architecture synth of sillyfunction is
begin
  y <= (not a and not b and not c) or
       (a and not b and not c) or
       (a and not b and c);
end;
```

VHDL code has three parts: the `library` use clause, the `entity` declaration, and the `architecture` body. The `library` use clause will be discussed in Section 4.7.2. The `entity` declaration lists the module name and its inputs and outputs. The `architecture` body defines what the module does.

VHDL signals, such as inputs and outputs, must have a *type declaration*. Digital signals should be declared to be `STD_LOGIC` type. `STD_LOGIC` signals can have a value of '0' or '1', as well as floating and undefined values that will be described in Section 4.2.8. The `STD_LOGIC` type is defined in the `IEEE.STD_LOGIC_1164` library, which is why the library must be used.

VHDL lacks a good default order of operations between AND and OR, so Boolean equations should be parenthesized.

A module, as you might expect, is a good application of modularity. It has a well defined interface, consisting of its inputs and outputs, and it performs a specific function. The particular way in which it is coded is unimportant to others that might use the module, as long as it performs its function.

4.1.2 Language Origins

Universities are almost evenly split on which of these languages is taught in a first course. Industry is trending toward SystemVerilog, but many companies still use VHDL and many designers need to be fluent in both.

SystemVerilog

Verilog was developed by Gateway Design Automation as a proprietary language for logic simulation in 1984. Gateway was acquired by Cadence in 1989 and Verilog was made an open standard in 1990 under the control of Open Verilog International. The language became an IEEE standard[1] in 1995. The language was extended in 2005 to streamline idiosyncrasies and to better support modeling and verification of systems. These extensions have been merged into a single language standard, which is now called SystemVerilog (IEEE STD 1800-2009). SystemVerilog file names normally end in .sv.

VHDL

VHDL is an acronym for the *VHSIC Hardware Description Language*. VHSIC is in turn an acronym for the *Very High Speed Integrated Circuits* program of the US Department of Defense.

VHDL was originally developed in 1981 by the Department of Defense to describe the structure and function of hardware. Its roots draw from the Ada programming language. The language was first envisioned for documentation but was quickly adopted for simulation and synthesis. The IEEE standardized it in 1987 and has updated the standard several times since. This chapter is based on the 2008 revision of the VHDL standard (IEEE STD 1076-2008), which streamlines the language in a variety of ways. At the time of this writing, not all of the VHDL 2008 features are supported by CAD tools; this chapter only uses those understood by Synplicity, Altera Quartus, and ModelSim. VHDL file names normally end in .vhd.

To use VHDL 2008 in ModelSim, you may need to set VHDL93 = 2008 in the modelsim.ini configuration file.

Compared to SystemVerilog, VHDL is more verbose and cumbersome, as you might expect of a language developed by committee.

Both languages are fully capable of describing any hardware system, and both have their quirks. The best language to use is the one that is already being used at your site or the one that your customers demand. Most CAD tools today allow the two languages to be mixed, so that different modules can be described in different languages.

4.1.3 Simulation and Synthesis

The two major purposes of HDLs are logic *simulation* and *synthesis*. During simulation, inputs are applied to a module, and the outputs are checked to verify that the module operates correctly. During synthesis, the textual description of a module is transformed into logic gates.

Simulation

Humans routinely make mistakes. Such errors in hardware designs are called *bugs*. Eliminating the bugs from a digital system is obviously important, especially when customers are paying money and lives depend on the correct operation. Testing a system in the laboratory is time-consuming. Discovering the cause of errors in the lab can be extremely difficult, because only signals routed to the chip pins can be observed. There is no way to directly observe what is happening inside a chip. Correcting errors after the system is built can be devastatingly expensive. For example,

The term "bug" predates the invention of the computer. Thomas Edison called the "little faults and difficulties" with his inventions "bugs" in 1878.

The first real computer bug was a moth, which got caught between the relays of the Harvard Mark II electromechanical computer in 1947. It was found by Grace Hopper, who logged the incident, along with the moth itself and the comment "first actual case of bug being found."

Source: Notebook entry courtesy Naval Historical Center, US Navy; photo No. NII 96566-KN)

---

[1] The Institute of Electrical and Electronics Engineers (IEEE) is a professional society responsible for many computing standards including Wi-Fi (802.11), Ethernet (802.3), and floating-point numbers (754).

Figure 4.1 Simulation waveforms

Now:
800 ns

		0 ns 160 320 ns 480 640 ns 800
a	0	
b	0	
c	0	
y	0	

correcting a mistake in a cutting-edge integrated circuit costs more than a million dollars and takes several months. Intel's infamous FDIV (floating point division) bug in the Pentium processor forced the company to recall chips after they had shipped, at a total cost of \$475 million. Logic simulation is essential to test a system before it is built.

Figure 4.1 shows waveforms from a simulation[2] of the previous silly-function module demonstrating that the module works correctly. y is TRUE when a, b, and c are 000, 100, or 101, as specified by the Boolean equation.

Synthesis

Logic synthesis transforms HDL code into a *netlist* describing the hardware (e.g., the logic gates and the wires connecting them). The logic synthesizer might perform optimizations to reduce the amount of hardware required. The netlist may be a text file, or it may be drawn as a schematic to help visualize the circuit. Figure 4.2 shows the results of synthesizing the sillyfunction module.[3] Notice how the three three-input AND gates are simplified into two two-input AND gates, as we discovered in Example 2.6 using Boolean algebra.

The synthesis tool labels each of the synthesized gates. In Figure 4.2, they are un5_y, un8_y, and y.

Circuit descriptions in HDL resemble code in a programming language. However, you must remember that the code is intended to represent hardware. SystemVerilog and VHDL are rich languages with many commands. Not all of these commands can be synthesized into hardware.

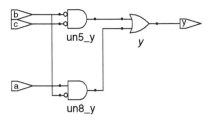

Figure 4.2 Synthesized circuit

---

[2] The simulation was performed with the ModelSim PE Student Edition Version 10.3c. ModelSim was selected because it is used commercially, yet a student version with a capacity of 10,000 lines of code is freely available.

[3] Synthesis was performed with Synplify Premier from Synplicity. The tool was selected because it is the leading commercial tool for synthesizing HDL to field-programmable gate arrays (see Section 5.6.2) and because it is available inexpensively for universities.

For example, a command to print results on the screen during simulation does not translate into hardware. Because our primary interest is to build hardware, we will emphasize a *synthesizable subset* of the languages. Specifically, we will divide HDL code into *synthesizable* modules and a *testbench*. The synthesizable modules describe the hardware. The testbench contains code to apply inputs to a module, check whether the output results are correct, and print discrepancies between expected and actual outputs. Testbench code is intended only for simulation and cannot be synthesized.

One of the most common mistakes for beginners is to think of HDL as a computer program rather than as a shorthand for describing digital hardware. If you don't know approximately what hardware your HDL should synthesize into, you probably won't like what you get. You might create far more hardware than is necessary, or you might write code that simulates correctly but cannot be implemented in hardware. Instead, think of your system in terms of blocks of combinational logic, registers, and finite state machines. Sketch these blocks on paper and show how they are connected before you start writing code.

In our experience, the best way to learn an HDL is by example. HDLs have specific ways of describing various classes of logic; these ways are called *idioms*. This chapter will teach you how to write the proper HDL idioms for each type of block and then how to put the blocks together to produce a working system. When you need to describe a particular kind of hardware, look for a similar example and adapt it to your purpose. We do not attempt to rigorously define all the syntax of the HDLs, because that is deathly boring and because it tends to encourage thinking of HDLs as programming languages, not shorthand for hardware. The IEEE SystemVerilog and VHDL specifications, and numerous dry but exhaustive textbooks, contain all of the details, should you find yourself needing more information on a particular topic. (See the Further Readings section at the back of the book.)

4.2 COMBINATIONAL LOGIC

Recall that we are disciplining ourselves to design synchronous sequential circuits, which consist of combinational logic and registers. The outputs of combinational logic depend only on the current inputs. This section describes how to write behavioral models of combinational logic with HDLs.

4.2.1 Bitwise Operators

Bitwise operators act on single-bit signals or on multi-bit busses. For example, the `inv` module in HDL Example 4.2 describes four inverters connected to 4-bit busses.

HDL Example 4.2 INVERTERS

SystemVerilog

```
module inv(input  logic [3:0] a,
           output logic [3:0] y);

  assign y = ~a:
endmodule
```

a[3:0] represents a 4-bit bus. The bits, from most significant to least significant, are a[3], a[2], a[1], and a[0]. This is called *little-endian* order, because the least significant bit has the smallest bit number. We could have named the bus a[4:1], in which case a[4] would have been the most significant. Or we could have used a[0:3], in which case the bits, from most significant to least significant, would have been a[0], a[1], a[2], and a[3]. This is called *big-endian* order.

VHDL

```
library IEEE; use IEEE.STD_LOGIC_1164.all;

entity inv is
   port(a: in  STD_LOGIC_VECTOR(3 downto 0):
        y: out STD_LOGIC_VECTOR(3 downto 0));
end;

architecture synth of inv is
begin
   y <= not a:
end;
```

VHDL uses STD_LOGIC_VECTOR to indicate busses of STD_LOGIC. STD_LOGIC_VECTOR(3 downto 0) represents a 4-bit bus. The bits, from most significant to least significant, are a(3), a(2), a(1), and a(0). This is called *little-endian* order, because the least significant bit has the smallest bit number. We could have declared the bus to be STD_LOGIC_VECTOR(4 downto 1), in which case bit 4 would have been the most significant. Or we could have written STD_LOGIC_VECTOR(0 to 3), in which case the bits, from most significant to least significant, would have been a(0), a(1), a(2), and a(3). This is called *big-endian* order.

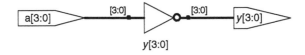

Figure 4.3 inv **synthesized circuit**

The endianness of a bus is purely arbitrary. (See the sidebar in Section 6.2.2 for the origin of the term.) Indeed, endianness is also irrelevant to this example, because a bank of inverters doesn't care what the order of the bits are. Endianness matters only for operators, such as addition, where the sum of one column carries over into the next. Either ordering is acceptable, as long as it is used consistently. We will consistently use the little-endian order, [N − 1:0] in SystemVerilog and (N − 1 downto 0) in VHDL, for an N-bit bus.

After each code example in this chapter is a schematic produced from the SystemVerilog code by the Synplify Premier synthesis tool. Figure 4.3 shows that the inv module synthesizes to a bank of four inverters, indicated by the inverter symbol labeled y[3:0]. The bank of inverters connects to 4-bit input and output busses. Similar hardware is produced from the synthesized VHDL code.

The gates module in HDL Example 4.3 demonstrates bitwise operations acting on 4-bit busses for other basic logic functions.

HDL Example 4.3 LOGIC GATES

SystemVerilog

```
module gates(input  logic [3:0] a, b,
             output logic [3:0] y1, y2,
                                y3, y4, y5);

  /* five different two-input logic
     gates acting on 4-bit busses */
  assign y1 = a & b;    // AND
  assign y2 = a | b;    // OR
  assign y3 = a ^ b;    // XOR
  assign y4 = ~(a & b); // NAND
  assign y5 = ~(a | b); // NOR
endmodule
```

~, ^, and | are examples of SystemVerilog *operators*, whereas a, b, and y1 are *operands*. A combination of operators and operands, such as a & b, or ~(a | b), is called an *expression*. A complete command such as assign y4 = ~(a & b); is called a *statement*.

assign out = in1 op in2; is called a *continuous assignment statement*. Continuous assignment statements end with a semicolon. Anytime the inputs on the right side of the = in a continuous assignment statement change, the output on the left side is recomputed. Thus, continuous assignment statements describe combinational logic.

VHDL

```
library IEEE; use IEEE.STD_LOGIC_1164.all;

entity gates is
port(a, b: in  STD_LOGIC_VECTOR(3 downto 0);
     y1, y2, y3, y4,
     y5:   out STD_LOGIC_VECTOR(3 downto 0));
end;

architecture synth of gates is
begin
  -- five different two-input logic gates
  -- acting on 4-bit busses
  y1 <= a and b;
  y2 <= a or b;
  y3 <= a xor b;
  y4 <= a nand b;
  y5 <= a nor b;
end;
```

not, xor, and or are examples of VHDL *operators*, whereas a, b, and y1 are *operands*. A combination of operators and operands, such as a and b, or a nor b, is called an *expression*. A complete command such as y4 <= a nand b; is called a *statement*.

out <= in1 op in2; is called a *concurrent signal assignment statement*. VHDL assignment statements end with a semicolon. Anytime the inputs on the right side of the <= in a concurrent signal assignment statement change, the output on the left side is recomputed. Thus, concurrent signal assignment statements describe combinational logic.

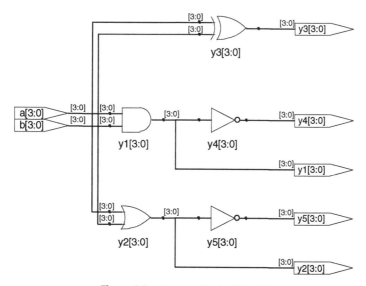

Figure 4.4 gates **synthesized circuit**

4.2.2 Comments and White Space

The `gates` example showed how to format comments. SystemVerilog and VHDL are not picky about the use of white space (i.e., spaces, tabs, and line breaks). Nevertheless, proper indenting and use of blank lines is helpful to make nontrivial designs readable. Be consistent in your use of capitalization and underscores in signal and module names. This text uses all lower case. Module and signal names must not begin with a digit.

SystemVerilog

SystemVerilog comments are just like those in C or Java. Comments beginning with /* continue, possibly across multiple lines, to the next */. Comments beginning with // continue to the end of the line.

SystemVerilog is case-sensitive. y1 and Y1 are different signals in SystemVerilog. However, it is confusing to use multiple signals that differ only in case.

VHDL

Comments beginning with /* continue, possibly across multiple lines, to the next */. Comments beginning with -- continue to the end of the line.

VHDL is not case-sensitive. y1 and Y1 are the same signal in VHDL. However, other tools that may read your file might be case sensitive, leading to nasty bugs if you blithely mix upper and lower case.

4.2.3 Reduction Operators

Reduction operators imply a multiple-input gate acting on a single bus. HDL Example 4.4 describes an eight-input AND gate with inputs a_7, $a_6, \ldots, a_0$. Analogous reduction operators exist for OR, XOR, NAND, NOR, and XNOR gates. Recall that a multiple-input XOR performs parity, returning TRUE if an odd number of inputs are TRUE.

HDL Example 4.4 EIGHT-INPUT AND

SystemVerilog

```
module and8(input  logic [7:0] a,
            output logic       y);

  assign y = &a;

  // &a is much easier to write than
  // assign y = a[7] & a[6] & a[5] & a[4] &
  //            a[3] & a[2] & a[1] & a[0];
endmodule
```

VHDL

```
library IEEE; use IEEE.STD_LOGIC_1164.all;

entity and8 is
  port(a: in  STD_LOGIC_VECTOR(7 downto 0);
       y: out STD_LOGIC);
end;

architecture synth of and8 is
begin
  y <= and a;
  -- and a is much easier to write than
  -- y <= a(7) and a(6) and a(5) and a(4) and
  --      a(3) and a(2) and a(1) and a(0);
end;
```

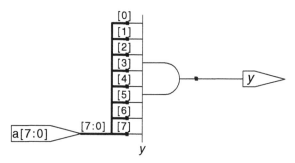

Figure 4.5 and8 **synthesized circuit**

4.2.4 Conditional Assignment

Conditional assignments select the output from among alternatives based on an input called the *condition*. HDL Example 4.5 illustrates a 2:1 multiplexer using conditional assignment.

HDL Example 4.5 2:1 MULTIPLEXER

SystemVerilog

The *conditional operator* ?: chooses, based on a first expression, between a second and third expression. The first expression is called the *condition*. If the condition is 1, the operator chooses the second expression. If the condition is 0, the operator chooses the third expression.

 ?: is especially useful for describing a multiplexer because, based on the first input, it selects between two others. The following code demonstrates the idiom for a 2:1 multiplexer with 4-bit inputs and outputs using the conditional operator.

```
module mux2(input  logic [3:0] d0, d1,
            input  logic       s,
            output logic [3:0] y);

  assign y = s ? d1 : d0;
endmodule
```

If s is 1, then y = d1. If s is 0, then y = d0.

 ?: is also called a *ternary operator*, because it takes three inputs. It is used for the same purpose in the C and Java programming languages.

VHDL

Conditional signal assignments perform different operations depending on some condition. They are especially useful for describing a multiplexer. For example, a 2:1 multiplexer can use conditional signal assignment to select one of two 4-bit inputs.

```
library IEEE; use IEEE.STD_LOGIC_1164.all;

entity mux2 is
  port(d0, d1: in  STD_LOGIC_VECTOR(3 downto 0);
       s:      in  STD_LOGIC;
       y:      out STD_LOGIC_VECTOR(3 downto 0));
end;

architecture synth of mux2 is
begin
  y <= d1 when s else d0;
end;
```

The conditional signal assignment sets y to d1 if s is 1. Otherwise it sets y to d0. Note that prior to the 2008 revision of VHDL, one had to write when s = '1' rather than when s.

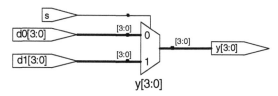

Figure 4.6 mux2 **synthesized circuit**

HDL Example 4.6 shows a 4:1 multiplexer based on the same principle as the 2:1 multiplexer in HDL Example 4.5. Figure 4.7 shows the schematic for the 4:1 multiplexer produced by Synplify Premier. The software uses a different multiplexer symbol than this text has shown so far. The multiplexer has multiple data (d) and one-hot enable (e) inputs. When one of the enables is asserted, the associated data is passed to the output. For example, when s[1] = s[0] = 0, the bottom AND gate, un1_s_5, produces a 1, enabling the bottom input of the multiplexer and causing it to select d0[3:0].

HDL Example 4.6 4:1 MULTIPLEXER

SystemVerilog

A 4:1 multiplexer can select one of four inputs using nested conditional operators.

```
module mux4(input  logic [3:0] d0, d1, d2, d3,
            input  logic [1:0] s,
            output logic [3:0] y);

  assign y = s[1] ? (s[0] ? d3 : d2)
                  : (s[0] ? d1 : d0);
endmodule
```

If s[1] is 1, then the multiplexer chooses the first expression, (s[0] ? d3 : d2). This expression in turn chooses either d3 or d2 based on s[0] (y = d3 if s[0] is 1 and d2 if s[0] is 0). If s[1] is 0, then the multiplexer similarly chooses the second expression, which gives either d1 or d0 based on s[0].

VHDL

A 4:1 multiplexer can select one of four inputs using multiple else clauses in the conditional signal assignment.

```
library IEEE; use IEEE.STD_LOGIC_1164.all;

entity mux4 is
  port(d0, d1,
       d2, d3: in  STD_LOGIC_VECTOR(3 downto 0);
       s:      in  STD_LOGIC_VECTOR(1 downto 0);
       y:      out STD_LOGIC_VECTOR(3 downto 0));
end;

architecture synth1 of mux4 is
begin
  y <= d0 when s = "00" else
       d1 when s = "01" else
       d2 when s = "10" else
       d3;
end;
```

VHDL also supports *selected signal assignment statements* to provide a shorthand when selecting from one of several possibilities. This is analogous to using a switch/case statement in place of multiple if/else statements in some programming languages. The 4:1 multiplexer can be rewritten with selected signal assignment as follows:

```
architecture synth2 of mux4 is
begin
  with s select y <=
    d0 when "00",
    d1 when "01",
    d2 when "10",
    d3 when others;
end;
```

4.2.5 Internal Variables

Often it is convenient to break a complex function into intermediate steps. For example, a full adder, which will be described in Section 5.2.1,

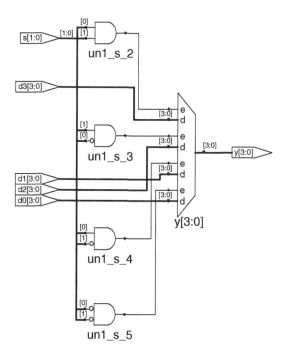

Figure 4.7 mux4 **synthesized circuit**

is a circuit with three inputs and two outputs defined by the following equations:

$$S = A \oplus B \oplus C_{in}$$
$$C_{out} = AB + AC_{in} + BC_{in} \qquad (4.1)$$

If we define intermediate signals, P and G,

$$P = A \oplus B$$
$$G = AB \qquad (4.2)$$

we can rewrite the full adder as follows:

$$S = P \oplus C_{in}$$
$$C_{out} = G + PC_{in} \qquad (4.3)$$

P and G are called *internal variables*, because they are neither inputs nor outputs but are used only internal to the module. They are similar to local variables in programming languages. HDL Example 4.7 shows how they are used in HDLs.

HDL assignment statements (assign in SystemVerilog and <= in VHDL) take place concurrently. This is different from conventional programming languages such as C or Java, in which statements are evaluated in the order in which they are written. In a conventional language, it is

> Check this by filling out the truth table to convince yourself it is correct.

HDL Example 4.7 FULL ADDER

SystemVerilog	**VHDL**

SystemVerilog

In SystemVerilog, internal signals are usually declared as logic.

```
module fulladder(input  logic a, b, cin,
                 output logic s, cout);

  logic p, g;

  assign p=a ^ b;
  assign g=a & b;

  assign s=p ^ cin;
  assign cout=g | (p & cin);
endmodule
```

VHDL

In VHDL, *signals* are used to represent internal variables whose values are defined by *concurrent signal assignment statements* such as p <= a xor b;

```
library IEEE; use IEEE.STD_LOGIC_1164.all;

entity fulladder is
  port(a, b, cin: in  STD_LOGIC;
       s, cout:   out STD_LOGIC);
end;

architecture synth of fulladder is
  signal p, g: STD_LOGIC;
begin
  p <= a xor b;
  g <= a and b;

  s <= p xor cin;
  cout <= g or (p and cin);
end;
```

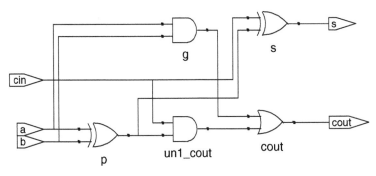

Figure 4.8 fulladder **synthesized circuit**

important that $S = P \oplus C_{in}$ comes after $P = A \oplus B$, because statements are executed sequentially. In an HDL, the order does not matter. Like hardware, HDL assignment statements are evaluated any time the inputs, signals on the right hand side, change their value, regardless of the order in which the assignment statements appear in a module.

4.2.6 Precedence

Notice that we parenthesized the cout computation in HDL Example 4.7 to define the order of operations as $C_{out} = G + (P \cdot C_{in})$, rather than $C_{out} = (G + P) \cdot C_{in}$. If we had not used parentheses, the default operation

HDL Example 4.8 OPERATOR PRECEDENCE

SystemVerilog

Table 4.1 SystemVerilog operator precedence

	Op	Meaning
H i g h e s t	~	NOT
	*, /, %	MUL, DIV, MOD
	+, -	PLUS, MINUS
	<<, >>	Logical Left/Right Shift
	<<<, >>>	Arithmetic Left/Right Shift
	<, <=, >, >=	Relative Comparison
	==, !=	Equality Comparison
L o w e s t	&, ~&	AND, NAND
	^, ~^	XOR, XNOR
	|, ~|	OR, NOR
	?:	Conditional

The operator precedence for SystemVerilog is much like you would expect in other programming languages. In particular, AND has precedence over OR. We could take advantage of this precedence to eliminate the parentheses.

```
assign cout=g | p & cin;
```

VHDL

Table 4.2 VHDL operator precedence

	Op	Meaning
H i g h e s t	not	NOT
	*, /, mod, rem	MUL, DIV, MOD, REM
	+, -	PLUS, MINUS
	rol, ror, srl, sll	Rotate, Shift logical
L o w e s t	<, <=, >, >=	Relative Comparison
	=, /=	Equality Comparison
	and, or, nand, nor, xor, xnor	Logical Operations

Multiplication has precedence over addition in VHDL, as you would expect. However, unlike SystemVerilog, all of the logical operations (and, or, etc.) have equal precedence, unlike what one might expect in Boolean algebra. Thus, parentheses are necessary; otherwise cout <= g or p and cin would be interpreted from left to right as cout <= (g or p) and cin.

order is defined by the language. HDL Example 4.8 specifies operator precedence from highest to lowest for each language. The tables include arithmetic, shift, and comparison operators that will be defined in Chapter 5.

4.2.7 Numbers

Numbers can be specified in binary, octal, decimal, or hexadecimal (bases 2, 8, 10, and 16, respectively). The size, i.e., the number of bits, may optionally be given, and leading zeros are inserted to reach this size. Underscores in numbers are ignored and can be helpful in breaking long numbers into more readable chunks. HDL Example 4.9 explains how numbers are written in each language.

HDL Example 4.9 NUMBERS

SystemVerilog

The format for declaring constants is N'Bvalue, where N is the size in bits, B is a letter indicating the base, and value gives the value. For example, 9'h25 indicates a 9-bit number with a value of $25_{16} = 37_{10} = 000100101_2$. SystemVerilog supports 'b for binary, 'o for octal, 'd for decimal, and 'h for hexadecimal. If the base is omitted, it defaults to decimal.

If the size is not given, the number is assumed to have as many bits as the expression in which it is being used. Zeros are automatically padded on the front of the number to bring it up to full size. For example, if w is a 6-bit bus, assign w = 'b11 gives w the value 000011. It is better practice to explicitly give the size. An exception is that '0 and '1 are SystemVerilog idioms for filling a bus with all 0s and all 1s, respectively.

VHDL

In VHDL, STD_LOGIC numbers are written in binary and enclosed in single quotes: '0' and '1' indicate logic 0 and 1. The format for declaring STD_LOGIC_VECTOR constants is NB"value", where N is the size in bits, B is a letter indicating the base, and value gives the value. For example, 9X"25" indicates a 9-bit number with a value of $25_{16} = 37_{10} = 000100101_2$. VHDL 2008 supports B for binary, O for octal, D for decimal, and X for hexadecimal.

If the base is omitted, it defaults to binary. If the size is not given, the number is assumed to have a size matching the number of bits specified in the value. As of October 2011, Synplify Premier from Synopsys does not yet support specifying the size.

others => '0' and others => '1' are VHDL idioms to fill all of the bits with 0 and 1, respectively.

Table 4.3 SystemVerilog numbers

Numbers	Bits	Base	Val	Stored
3'b101	3	2	5	101
'b11	?	2	3	000 ... 0011
8'b11	8	2	3	00000011
8'b1010_1011	8	2	171	10101011
3'd6	3	10	6	110
6'o42	6	8	34	100010
8'hAB	8	16	171	10101011
42	?	10	42	00 ... 0101010

Table 4.4 VHDL numbers

Numbers	Bits	Base	Val	Stored
3B"101"	3	2	5	101
B"11"	2	2	3	11
8B"11"	8	2	3	00000011
8B"1010_1011"	8	2	171	10101011
3D"6"	3	10	6	110
6O"42"	6	8	34	100010
8X"AB"	8	16	171	10101011
"101"	3	2	5	101
B"101"	3	2	5	101
X"AB"	8	16	171	10101011

4.2.8 Z's and X's

HDLs use z to indicate a floating value. z is particularly useful for describing a tristate buffer, whose output floats when the enable is 0. Recall from Section 2.6.2 that a bus can be driven by several tristate buffers, exactly one of which should be enabled. HDL Example 4.10 shows the idiom for a tristate buffer. If the buffer is enabled, the output is the same as the input. If the buffer is disabled, the output is assigned a floating value (z).

Similarly, HDLs use x to indicate an invalid logic level. If a bus is simultaneously driven to 0 and 1 by two enabled tristate buffers (or other gates), the result is x, indicating contention. If all the tristate buffers driving a bus are simultaneously OFF, the bus will float, indicated by z.

At the start of simulation, state nodes such as flip-flop outputs are initialized to an unknown state (x in SystemVerilog and u in VHDL). This is helpful to track errors caused by forgetting to reset a flip-flop before its output is used.

HDL Example 4.10 TRISTATE BUFFER

SystemVerilog

```
module tristate(input  logic [3:0] a,
                input  logic       en,
                output tri   [3:0] y);

  assign y = en ? a : 4'bz;
endmodule
```

Notice that y is declared as tri rather than logic. logic signals can only have a single driver. Tristate busses can have multiple drivers, so they should be declared as a *net*. Two types of nets in SystemVerilog are called tri and trireg. Typically, exactly one driver on a net is active at a time, and the net takes on that value. If no driver is active, a tri floats (z), while a trireg retains the previous value. If no type is specified for an input or output, tri is assumed. Also note that a tri output from a module can be used as a logic input to another module. Section 4.7 further discusses nets with multiple drivers.

VHDL

```
library IEEE; use IEEE.STD_LOGIC_1164.all;

entity tristate is
    port(a:  in  STD_LOGIC_VECTOR(3 downto 0);
         en: in  STD_LOGIC;
         y:  out STD_LOGIC_VECTOR(3 downto 0));
end;

architecture synth of tristate is
begin
    y <= a when en else "ZZZZ";
end;
```

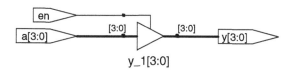

Figure 4.9 tristate **synthesized circuit**

If a gate receives a floating input, it may produce an x output when it can't determine the correct output value. Similarly, if it receives an illegal or uninitialized input, it may produce an x output. HDL Example 4.11

HDL Example 4.11 TRUTH TABLES WITH UNDEFINED AND FLOATING INPUTS

SystemVerilog

SystemVerilog signal values are 0, 1, z, and x. SystemVerilog constants starting with z or x are padded with leading z's or x's (instead of 0's) to reach their full length when necessary.

Table 4.5 shows a truth table for an AND gate using all four possible signal values. Note that the gate can sometimes determine the output despite some inputs being unknown. For example 0 & z returns 0 because the output of an AND gate is always 0 if either input is 0. Otherwise, floating or invalid inputs cause invalid outputs, displayed as x in SystemVerilog.

VHDL

VHDL STD_LOGIC signals are '0', '1', 'z', 'x', and 'u'.

Table 4.6 shows a truth table for an AND gate using all five possible signal values. Notice that the gate can sometimes determine the output despite some inputs being unknown. For example, '0' and 'z' returns '0' because the output of an AND gate is always '0' if either input is '0'. Otherwise, floating or invalid inputs cause invalid outputs, displayed as 'x' in VHDL. Uninitialized inputs cause uninitialized outputs, displayed as 'u' in VHDL.

Table 4.5 SystemVerilog AND gate truth table with z and x

&				A	
		0	1	z	x
	0	0	0	0	0
	1	0	1	x	x
B	z	0	x	x	x
	x	0	x	x	x

Table 4.6 VHDL AND gate truth table with z, x and u

AND				A		
		0	1	z	x	u
	0	0	0	0	0	0
	1	0	1	x	x	u
B	z	0	x	x	x	u
	x	0	x	x	x	u
	u	0	u	u	u	u

HDL Example 4.12 BIT SWIZZLING

SystemVerilog

```
assign y = {c[2:1], {3{d[0]}}, c[0], 3'b101};
```

The {} operator is used to concatenate busses. {3{d[0]}} indicates three copies of d[0].

Don't confuse the 3-bit binary constant 3'b101 with a bus named b. Note that it was critical to specify the length of 3 bits in the constant; otherwise, it would have had an unknown number of leading zeros that might appear in the middle of y.

If y were wider than 9 bits, zeros would be placed in the most significant bits.

VHDL

```
y <= (c(2 downto 1), d(0), d(0), d(0), c(0), 3B"101");
```

The () aggregate operator is used to concatenate busses. y must be a 9-bit STD_LOGIC_VECTOR.

Another example demonstrates the power of VHDL aggregations. Assuming z is an 8-bit STD_LOGIC_VECTOR, z is given the value 10010110 using the following command aggregation.

```
z <= ("10", 4 => '1', 2 downto 1 =>'1', others =>'0')
```

The "10" goes in the leading pair of bits. 1s are also placed into bit 4 and bits 2 and 1. The other bits are 0.

shows how SystemVerilog and VHDL combine these different signal values in logic gates.

Seeing x or u values in simulation is almost always an indication of a bug or bad coding practice. In the synthesized circuit, this corresponds to a floating gate input, uninitialized state, or contention. The x or u may be interpreted randomly by the circuit as 0 or 1, leading to unpredictable behavior.

4.2.9 Bit Swizzling

Often it is necessary to operate on a subset of a bus or to concatenate (join together) signals to form busses. These operations are collectively known as *bit swizzling*. In HDL Example 4.12, y is given the 9-bit value $c_2c_1d_0d_0d_0c_0101$ using bit swizzling operations.

4.2.10 Delays

HDL statements may be associated with delays specified in arbitrary units. They are helpful during simulation to predict how fast a circuit will work (if you specify meaningful delays) and also for debugging purposes to understand cause and effect (deducing the source of a bad output is tricky if all signals change simultaneously in the simulation results). These delays are ignored during synthesis; the delay of a gate produced by the synthesizer depends on its t_{pd} and t_{cd} specifications, not on numbers in HDL code.

HDL Example 4.13 adds delays to the original function from HDL Example 4.1, $y = \overline{a}\,\overline{b}\,\overline{c} + a\overline{b}\,\overline{c} + a\overline{b}c$. It assumes that inverters have a delay of 1 ns, three-input AND gates have a delay of 2 ns, and three-input OR gates have a delay of 4 ns. Figure 4.10 shows the simulation waveforms, with y lagging 7 ns after the inputs. Note that y is initially unknown at the beginning of the simulation.

HDL Example 4.13 LOGIC GATES WITH DELAYS

SystemVerilog

```
'timescale 1ns/1ps

module example(input  logic a, b, c,
               output logic y);

  logic ab, bb, cb, n1, n2, n3;

  assign #1 {ab, bb, cb} = ~{a, b, c};
  assign #2 n1 = ab & bb & cb;
  assign #2 n2 = a & bb & cb;
  assign #2 n3 = a & bb & c;
  assign #4 y = n1 | n2 | n3;
endmodule
```

SystemVerilog files can include a timescale directive that indicates the value of each time unit. The statement is of the form 'timescale unit/precision. In this file, each unit is 1 ns, and the simulation has 1 ps precision. If no timescale directive is given in the file, a default unit and precision (usually 1 ns for both) are used. In SystemVerilog, a # symbol is used to indicate the number of units of delay. It can be placed in assign statements, as well as non-blocking (<=) and blocking (=) assignments, which will be discussed in Section 4.5.4.

VHDL

```
library IEEE; use IEEE.STD_LOGIC_1164.all;

entity example is
  port(a, b, c: in  STD_LOGIC;
       y:       out STD_LOGIC);
end;

architecture synth of example is
  signal ab, bb, cb, n1, n2, n3: STD_LOGIC;
begin
  ab <= not a after 1 ns;
  bb <= not b after 1 ns;
  cb <= not c after 1 ns;
  n1 <= ab and bb and cb after 2 ns;
  n2 <= a and bb and cb after 2 ns;
  n3 <= a and bb and c after 2 ns;
  y  <= n1 or n2 or n3 after 4 ns;
end;
```

In VHDL, the after clause is used to indicate delay. The units, in this case, are specified as nanoseconds.

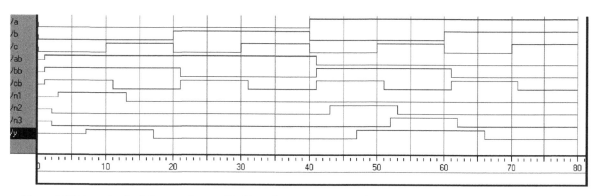

Figure 4.10 Example simulation waveforms with delays (from the ModelSim simulator)

4.3 STRUCTURAL MODELING

The previous section discussed *behavioral* modeling, describing a module in terms of the relationships between inputs and outputs. This section examines *structural* modeling, describing a module in terms of how it is composed of simpler modules.

For example, HDL Example 4.14 shows how to assemble a 4:1 multiplexer from three 2:1 multiplexers. Each copy of the 2:1 multiplexer is called

---

HDL Example 4.14 STRUCTURAL MODEL OF 4:1 MULTIPLEXER

SystemVerilog

```
module mux4(input  logic [3:0] d0, d1, d2, d3,
            input  logic [1:0] s,
            output logic [3:0] y);

  logic [3:0] low, high;

  mux2 lowmux(d0, d1, s[0], low);
  mux2 highmux(d2, d3, s[0], high);
  mux2 finalmux(low, high, s[1], y);
endmodule
```

The three mux2 instances are called lowmux, highmux, and finalmux. The mux2 module must be defined elsewhere in the SystemVerilog code — see HDL Example 4.5, 4.15, or 4.34.

VHDL

```
library IEEE; use IEEE.STD_LOGIC_1164.all;

entity mux4 is
  port(d0, d1,
       d2, d3: in  STD_LOGIC_VECTOR(3 downto 0);
       s:      in  STD_LOGIC_VECTOR(1 downto 0);
       y:      out STD_LOGIC_VECTOR(3 downto 0));
end;

architecture struct of mux4 is
  component mux2
    port(d0,
         d1: in  STD_LOGIC_VECTOR(3 downto 0);
         s:  in  STD_LOGIC;
         y:  out STD_LOGIC_VECTOR(3 downto 0));
  end component;
  signal low, high: STD_LOGIC_VECTOR(3 downto 0);
begin
  lowmux:   mux2 port map(d0, d1, s(0), low);
  highmux:  mux2 port map(d2, d3, s(0), high);
  finalmux: mux2 port map(low, high, s(1), y);
end;
```

The architecture must first declare the mux2 ports using the component declaration statement. This allows VHDL tools to check that the component you wish to use has the same ports as the entity that was declared somewhere else in another entity statement, preventing errors caused by changing the entity but not the instance. However, component declaration makes VHDL code rather cumbersome.

Note that this architecture of mux4 was named struct, whereas architectures of modules with behavioral descriptions from Section 4.2 were named synth. VHDL allows multiple architectures (implementations) for the same entity; the architectures are distinguished by name. The names themselves have no significance to the CAD tools, but struct and synth are common. Synthesizable VHDL code generally contains only one architecture for each entity, so we will not discuss the VHDL syntax to configure which architecture is used when multiple architectures are defined.

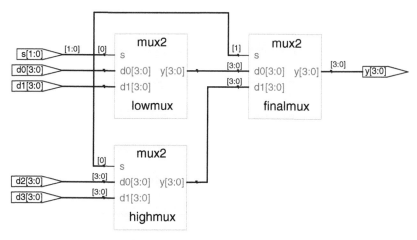

Figure 4.11 mux4 **synthesized circuit**

an *instance*. Multiple instances of the same module are distinguished by distinct names, in this case lowmux, highmux, and finalmux. This is an example of regularity, in which the 2:1 multiplexer is reused many times.

HDL Example 4.15 uses structural modeling to construct a 2:1 multiplexer from a pair of tristate buffers. Building logic out of tristates is not recommended, however.

HDL Example 4.15 STRUCTURAL MODEL OF 2:1 MULTIPLEXER

SystemVerilog

```
module mux2(input  logic [3:0] d0, d1,
            input  logic       s,
            output tri   [3:0] y);

  tristate t0(d0, ~s, y);
  tristate t1(d1, s, y);
endmodule
```

In SystemVerilog, expressions such as ~s are permitted in the port list for an instance. Arbitrarily complicated expressions are legal but discouraged because they make the code difficult to read.

VHDL

```
library IEEE; use IEEE.STD_LOGIC_1164.all;

entity mux2 is
  port(d0, d1: in  STD_LOGIC_VECTOR(3 downto 0);
       s:      in  STD_LOGIC;
       y:      out STD_LOGIC_VECTOR(3 downto 0));
end;

architecture struct of mux2 is
  component tristate
    port(a:  in  STD_LOGIC_VECTOR(3 downto 0);
         en: in  STD_LOGIC;
         y:  out STD_LOGIC_VECTOR(3 downto 0));
  end component;
  signal sbar: STD_LOGIC;
begin
  sbar <= not s;
  t0: tristate port map(d0, sbar, y);
  t1: tristate port map(d1, s, y);
end;
```

In VHDL, expressions such as not s are not permitted in the port map for an instance. Thus, sbar must be defined as a separate signal.

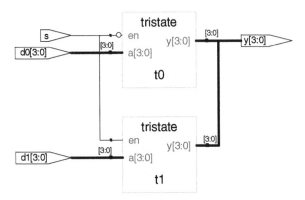

Figure 4.12 mux2 **synthesized circuit**

HDL Example 4.16 shows how modules can access part of a bus. An 8-bit wide 2:1 multiplexer is built using two of the 4-bit 2:1 multiplexers already defined, operating on the low and high nibbles of the byte.

In general, complex systems are designed *hierarchically*. The overall system is described structurally by instantiating its major components. Each of these components is described structurally from its building blocks, and so forth recursively until the pieces are simple enough to describe behaviorally. It is good style to avoid (or at least to minimize) mixing structural and behavioral descriptions within a single module.

HDL Example 4.16 ACCESSING PARTS OF BUSSES

SystemVerilog

```
module mux2_8(input  logic [7:0] d0, d1,
              input  logic       s,
              output logic [7:0] y);

  mux2 lsbmux(d0[3:0], d1[3:0], s, y[3:0]);
  mux2 msbmux(d0[7:4], d1[7:4], s, y[7:4]);
endmodule
```

VHDL

```
library IEEE; use IEEE.STD_LOGIC_1164.all;

entity mux2_8 is
  port(d0, d1: in  STD_LOGIC_VECTOR(7 downto 0);
       s:      in  STD_LOGIC;
       y:      out STD_LOGIC_VECTOR(7 downto 0));
end;

architecture struct of mux2_8 is
  component mux2
    port(d0, d1: in  STD_LOGIC_VECTOR(3 downto 0);
         s:      in  STD_LOGIC;
         y:      out STD_LOGIC_VECTOR(3 downto 0));
  end component;
begin
  lsbmux: mux2
    port map(d0(3 downto 0), d1(3 downto 0),
             s, y(3 downto 0));
  msbmux: mux2
    port map(d0(7 downto 4), d1(7 downto 4),
             s, y(7 downto 4));
end;
```

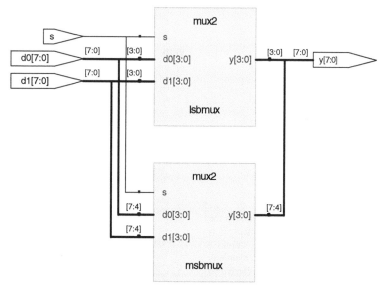

Figure 4.13 mux2_8 **synthesized circuit**

4.4 SEQUENTIAL LOGIC

HDL synthesizers recognize certain idioms and turn them into specific sequential circuits. Other coding styles may simulate correctly but synthesize into circuits with blatant or subtle errors. This section presents the proper idioms to describe registers and latches.

4.4.1 Registers

The vast majority of modern commercial systems are built with registers using positive edge-triggered D flip-flops. HDL Example 4.17 shows the idiom for such flip-flops.

In SystemVerilog always statements and VHDL process statements, signals keep their old value until an event in the sensitivity list takes place that explicitly causes them to change. Hence, such code, with appropriate sensitivity lists, can be used to describe sequential circuits with memory. For example, the flip-flop includes only clk in the sensitive list. It remembers its old value of q until the next rising edge of the clk, even if d changes in the interim.

In contrast, SystemVerilog continuous assignment statements (assign) and VHDL concurrent assignment statements (<=) are reevaluated anytime any of the inputs on the right hand side changes. Therefore, such code necessarily describes combinational logic.

HDL Example 4.17 REGISTER

SystemVerilog

```
module flop(input  logic      clk,
            input  logic [3:0] d,
            output logic [3:0] q);

  always_ff @(posedge clk)
    q <= d;
endmodule
```

In general, a SystemVerilog always **statement is written in the form**

```
always @(sensitivity list)
  statement;
```

The statement is executed only when the event specified in the sensitivity list occurs. In this example, the statement is q <= d (pronounced "q gets d"). Hence, the flip-flop copies d to q on the positive edge of the clock and otherwise remembers the old state of q. Note that sensitivity lists are also referred to as stimulus lists.

<= is called a *nonblocking assignment*. Think of it as a regular = sign for now; we'll return to the more subtle points in Section 4.5.4. Note that <= is used instead of assign inside an always statement.

As will be seen in subsequent sections, always statements can be used to imply flip-flops, latches, or combinational logic, depending on the sensitivity list and statement. Because of this flexibility, it is easy to produce the wrong hardware inadvertently. SystemVerilog introduces always_ff, always_latch, and always_comb to reduce the risk of common errors. always_ff behaves like always but is used exclusively to imply flip-flops and allows tools to produce a warning if anything else is implied.

VHDL

```
library IEEE; use IEEE.STD_LOGIC_1164.all;

entity flop is
  port(clk: in  STD_LOGIC;
       d:   in  STD_LOGIC_VECTOR(3 downto 0);
       q:   out STD_LOGIC_VECTOR(3 downto 0));
end;

architecture synth of flop is
begin
  process(clk) begin
    if rising_edge(clk) then
      q <= d;
    end if;
  end process;
end;
```

A VHDL process is written in the form

```
process(sensitivity list) begin
  statement;
end process;
```

The statement is executed when any of the variables in the sensitivity list change. In this example, the if statement checks if the change was a rising edge on clk. If so, then q <= d (pronounced "q gets d"). Hence, the flip-flop copies d to q on the positive edge of the clock and otherwise remembers the old state of q.

An alternative VHDL idiom for a flip-flop is

```
process(clk) begin
  if clk'event and clk = '1' then
    q <= d;
  end if;
end process;
```

rising_edge(clk) is synonymous with clk'event and clk = '1'.

Figure 4.14 flop **synthesized circuit**

4.4.2 Resettable Registers

When simulation begins or power is first applied to a circuit, the output of a flop or register is unknown. This is indicated with x in SystemVerilog and u in VHDL. Generally, it is good practice to use resettable registers so that on powerup you can put your system in a known state. The reset may be either asynchronous or synchronous. Recall that asynchronous reset occurs immediately, whereas synchronous reset clears the output only on the next rising edge of the clock. HDL Example 4.18 demonstrates the idioms for flip-flops with asynchronous and synchronous resets. Note that distinguishing synchronous and asynchronous reset in a schematic can be difficult. The schematic produced by Synplify Premier places asynchronous reset at the bottom of a flip-flop and synchronous reset on the left side.

HDL Example 4.18 RESETTABLE REGISTER

SystemVerilog

```
module flopr(input  logic       clk,
             input  logic       reset,
             input  logic [3:0] d,
             output logic [3:0] q);

  // asynchronous reset
  always_ff @(posedge clk, posedge reset)
    if (reset) q <= 4'b0;
    else       q <= d;
endmodule

module flopr(input  logic       clk,
             input  logic       reset,
             input  logic [3:0] d,
             output logic [3:0] q);

  // synchronous reset
  always_ff @(posedge clk)
    if (reset) q <= 4'b0;
    else       q <= d;
endmodule
```

Multiple signals in an always statement sensitivity list are separated with a comma or the word or. Notice that posedge reset is in the sensitivity list on the asynchronously resettable flop, but not on the synchronously resettable flop. Thus, the asynchronously resettable flop immediately responds to a rising edge on reset, but the synchronously resettable flop responds to reset only on the rising edge of the clock.

Because the modules have the same name, flopr, you may include only one or the other in your design.

VHDL

```
library IEEE; use IEEE.STD_LOGIC_1164.all;

entity flopr is
  port(clk, reset: in  STD_LOGIC;
       d:          in  STD_LOGIC_VECTOR(3 downto 0);
       q:          out STD_LOGIC_VECTOR(3 downto 0));
end;

architecture asynchronous of flopr is
begin
  process(clk, reset) begin
    if reset then
      q <= "0000";
    elsif rising_edge(clk) then
      q <= d;
    end if;
  end process;
end;

library IEEE; use IEEE.STD_LOGIC_1164.all;

entity flopr is
  port(clk, reset: in  STD_LOGIC;
       d:          in  STD_LOGIC_VECTOR(3 downto 0);
       q:          out STD_LOGIC_VECTOR(3 downto 0));
end;

architecture synchronous of flopr is
begin
  process(clk) begin
    if rising_edge(clk) then
      if reset then q <= "0000";
      else q <= d;
      end if;
    end if;
  end process;
end;
```

Multiple signals in a process sensitivity list are separated with a comma. Notice that reset is in the sensitivity list on the asynchronously resettable flop, but not on the synchronously resettable flop. Thus, the asynchronously resettable flop immediately responds to a rising edge on reset, but the synchronously resettable flop responds to reset only on the rising edge of the clock.

Recall that the state of a flop is initialized to 'u' at startup during VHDL simulation.

As mentioned earlier, the name of the architecture (asynchronous or synchronous, in this example) is ignored by the VHDL tools but may be helpful to the human reading the code. Because both architectures describe the entity flopr, you may include only one or the other in your design.

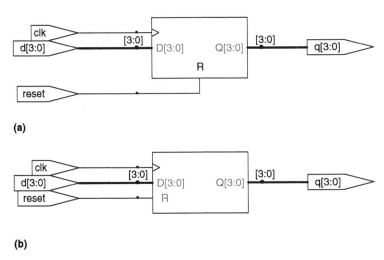

Figure 4.15 flopr **synthesized circuit (a) asynchronous reset, (b) synchronous reset**

4.4.3 Enabled Registers

Enabled registers respond to the clock only when the enable is asserted. HDL Example 4.19 shows an asynchronously resettable enabled register that retains its old value if both reset and en are FALSE.

HDL Example 4.19 RESETTABLE ENABLED REGISTER

SystemVerilog

```
module flopenr(input  logic       clk,
               input  logic       reset,
               input  logic       en,
               input  logic [3:0] d,
               output logic [3:0] q);

  // asynchronous reset
  always_ff @(posedge clk, posedge reset)
    if      (reset) q <= 4'b0;
    else if (en)    q <= d;
endmodule
```

VHDL

```
library IEEE; use IEEE.STD_LOGIC_1164.all;

entity flopenr is
  port(clk,
       reset,
       en: in  STD_LOGIC;
       d:  in  STD_LOGIC_VECTOR(3 downto 0);
       q:  out STD_LOGIC_VECTOR(3 downto 0));
end;

architecture asynchronous of flopenr is
-- asynchronous reset
begin
  process(clk, reset) begin
    if reset then
      q <= "0000";
    elsif rising_edge(clk) then
      if en then
        q <= d;
      end if;
    end if;
  end process;
end;
```

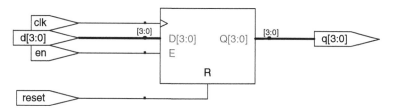

Figure 4.16 flopenr **synthesized circuit**

4.4.4 Multiple Registers

A single always/process statement can be used to describe multiple pieces of hardware. For example, consider the synchronizer from Section 3.5.5 made of two back-to-back flip-flops, as shown in Figure 4.17. HDL Example 4.20 describes the synchronizer. On the rising edge of clk, d is copied to n1. At the same time, n1 is copied to q.

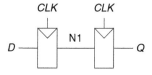

Figure 4.17 Synchronizer circuit

HDL Example 4.20 SYNCHRONIZER

SystemVerilog

```
module sync(input  logic clk,
            input  logic d,
            output logic q);

  logic n1;

  always_ff @(posedge clk)
    begin
      n1 <= d; // nonblocking
      q <= n1; // nonblocking
    end
endmodule
```

Notice that the begin/end construct is necessary because multiple statements appear in the always statement. This is analogous to {} in C or Java. The begin/end was not needed in the flopr example because if/else counts as a single statement.

VHDL

```
library IEEE; use IEEE.STD_LOGIC_1164.all;

entity sync is
  port(clk: in  STD_LOGIC;
       d:   in  STD_LOGIC;
       q:   out STD_LOGIC);
end;

architecture good of sync is
  signal n1: STD_LOGIC;
begin
  process(clk) begin
    if rising_edge(clk) then
      n1 <= d;
      q <= n1;
    end if;
  end process;
end;
```

n1 must be declared as a signal because it is an internal signal used in the module.

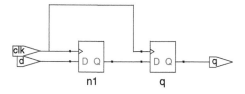

Figure 4.18 sync **synthesized circuit**

4.4.5 Latches

Recall from Section 3.2.2 that a D latch is transparent when the clock is HIGH, allowing data to flow from input to output. The latch becomes opaque when the clock is LOW, retaining its old state. HDL Example 4.21 shows the idiom for a D latch.

Not all synthesis tools support latches well. Unless you know that your tool does support latches and you have a good reason to use them, avoid them and use edge-triggered flip-flops instead. Furthermore, take care that your HDL does not imply any unintended latches, something that is easy to do if you aren't attentive. Many synthesis tools warn you when a latch is created; if you didn't expect one, track down the bug in your HDL. And if you don't know whether you intended to have a latch or not, you are probably approaching HDLs like a programming language and have bigger problems lurking.

4.5 MORE COMBINATIONAL LOGIC

In Section 4.2, we used assignment statements to describe combinational logic behaviorally. SystemVerilog always statements and VHDL process

---

HDL Example 4.21 D LATCH

SystemVerilog

```
module latch(input  logic      clk,
             input  logic [3:0] d,
             output logic [3:0] q);

  always_latch
    if (clk) q <= d;
endmodule
```

always_latch is equivalent to always @(clk, d) and is the preferred idiom for describing a latch in SystemVerilog. It evaluates any time clk or d changes. If clk is HIGH, d flows through to q, so this code describes a positive level sensitive latch. Otherwise, q keeps its old value. SystemVerilog can generate a warning if the always_latch block doesn't imply a latch.

VHDL

```
library IEEE; use IEEE.STD_LOGIC_1164.all;

entity latch is
  port(clk: in  STD_LOGIC;
       d:   in  STD_LOGIC_VECTOR(3 downto 0);
       q:   out STD_LOGIC_VECTOR(3 downto 0));
end;

architecture synth of latch is
begin
  process(clk, d) begin
    if clk = '1' then
      q <= d;
    end if;
  end process;
end;
```

The sensitivity list contains both clk and d, so the process evaluates anytime clk or d changes. If clk is HIGH, d flows through to q.

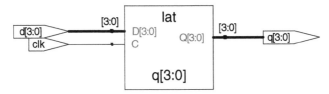

Figure 4.19 latch **synthesized circuit**

HDL Example 4.22 INVERTER USING always/process

SystemVerilog

```
module inv(input  logic [3:0] a,
            output logic [3:0] y);

  always_comb
    y = ~a;
endmodule
```

always_comb reevaluates the statements inside the always statement any time any of the signals on the right hand side of <= or = in the always statement change. In this case, it is equivalent to always @(a), but is better because it avoids mistakes if signals in the always statement are renamed or added. If the code inside the always block is not combinational logic, SystemVerilog will report a warning. always_comb is equivalent to always @(*), but is preferred in SystemVerilog.

The = in the always statement is called a *blocking assignment*, in contrast to the <= nonblocking assignment. In System-Verilog, it is good practice to use blocking assignments for combinational logic and nonblocking assignments for sequential logic. This will be discussed further in Section 4.5.4.

VHDL

```
library IEEE; use IEEE.STD_LOGIC_1164.all;

entity inv is
  port(a: in  STD_LOGIC_VECTOR(3 downto 0);
       y: out STD_LOGIC_VECTOR(3 downto 0));
end;

architecture proc of inv is
begin
  process(all) begin
    y <= not a;
  end process;
end;
```

process(all) reevaluates the statements inside the process any time any of the signals in the process change. It is equivalent to process(a) but is better because it avoids mistakes if signals in the process are renamed or added.

The begin and end process statements are required in VHDL even though the process contains only one assignment.

---

statements are used to describe sequential circuits, because they remember the old state when no new state is prescribed. However, always/process statements can also be used to describe combinational logic behaviorally if the sensitivity list is written to respond to changes in all of the inputs and the body prescribes the output value for every possible input combination. HDL Example 4.22 uses always/process statements to describe a bank of four inverters (see Figure 4.3 for the synthesized circuit).

HDLs support *blocking* and *nonblocking assignments* in an always/process statement. A group of blocking assignments are evaluated in the order in which they appear in the code, just as one would expect in a standard programming language. A group of nonblocking assignments are evaluated concurrently; all of the statements are evaluated before any of the signals on the left hand sides are updated.

HDL Example 4.23 defines a full adder using intermediate signals p and g to compute s and cout. It produces the same circuit from Figure 4.8, but uses always/process statements in place of assignment statements.

These two examples are poor applications of always/process statements for modeling combinational logic because they require more lines than the equivalent approach with assignment statements from HDL Examples 4.2 and 4.7. However, case and if statements are convenient for modeling more complicated combinational logic. case and if statements must appear within always/process statements and are examined in the next sections.

SystemVerilog

In a SystemVerilog always statement, = indicates a blocking assignment and <= indicates a nonblocking assignment (also called a concurrent assignment).

Do not confuse either type with continuous assignment using the assign statement. assign statements must be used outside always statements and are also evaluated concurrently.

VHDL

In a VHDL process statement, := indicates a blocking assignment and <= indicates a nonblocking assignment (also called a concurrent assignment). This is the first section where := is introduced.

Nonblocking assignments are made to outputs and to signals. Blocking assignments are made to variables, which are declared in process statements (see HDL Example 4.23). <= can also appear outside process statements, where it is also evaluated concurrently.

HDL Example 4.23 FULL ADDER USING always/process

SystemVerilog

```
module fulladder(input  logic a, b, cin,
                 output logic s, cout);
  logic p, g;

  always_comb
    begin
      p = a ^ b;           // blocking
      g = a & b;           // blocking

      s = p ^ cin;         // blocking
      cout = g | (p & cin); // blocking
    end
endmodule
```

In this case, always @(a, b, cin) would have been equivalent to always_comb. However, always_comb is better because it avoids common mistakes of missing signals in the sensitivity list.

For reasons that will be discussed in Section 4.5.4, it is best to use blocking assignments for combinational logic. This example uses blocking assignments, first computing p, then g, then s, and finally cout.

VHDL

```
library IEEE; use IEEE.STD_LOGIC_1164.all;

entity fulladder is
  port(a, b, cin: in  STD_LOGIC;
       s, cout:   out STD_LOGIC);
end;

architecture synth of fulladder is
begin
  process(all)
    variable p, g: STD_LOGIC;
  begin
    p := a xor b; -- blocking
    g := a and b; -- blocking
    s <= p xor cin;
    cout <= g or (p and cin);
  end process;
end;
```

In this case, process(a, b, cin) would have been equivalent to process(all). However, process(all) is better because it avoids common mistakes of missing signals in the sensitivity list.

For reasons that will be discussed in Section 4.5.4, it is best to use blocking assignments for intermediate variables in combinational logic. This example uses blocking assignments for p and g so that they get their new values before being used to compute s and cout that depend on them.

Because p and g appear on the left hand side of a blocking assignment (:=) in a process statement, they must be declared to be variable rather than signal. The variable declaration appears before the begin in the process where the variable is used.

4.5.1 Case Statements

A better application of using the `always`/`process` statement for combinational logic is a seven-segment display decoder that takes advantage of the `case` statement that must appear inside an `always`/`process` statement.

As you might have noticed in the seven-segment display decoder of Example 2.10, the design process for large blocks of combinational logic is tedious and prone to error. HDLs offer a great improvement, allowing you to specify the function at a higher level of abstraction, and then automatically synthesize the function into gates. HDL Example 4.24 uses `case` statements to describe a seven-segment display decoder based on its truth table. The `case` statement performs different actions depending on the value of its input. A `case` statement implies combinational logic if all

---

HDL Example 4.24 SEVEN-SEGMENT DISPLAY DECODER

SystemVerilog

```
module sevenseg(input  logic [3:0] data,
                output logic [6:0] segments);
  always_comb
    case(data)
      //                      abc_defg
      0:    segments = 7'b111_1110;
      1:    segments = 7'b011_0000;
      2:    segments = 7'b110_1101;
      3:    segments = 7'b111_1001;
      4:    segments = 7'b011_0011;
      5:    segments = 7'b101_1011;
      6:    segments = 7'b101_1111;
      7:    segments = 7'b111_0000;
      8:    segments = 7'b111_1111;
      9:    segments = 7'b111_0011;
      default: segments = 7'b000_0000;
    endcase
endmodule
```

The `case` statement checks the value of `data`. When `data` is 0, the statement performs the action after the colon, setting `segments` to 1111110. The `case` statement similarly checks other data values up to 9 (note the use of the default base, base 10).

The `default` clause is a convenient way to define the output for all cases not explicitly listed, guaranteeing combinational logic.

In SystemVerilog, `case` statements must appear inside `always` statements.

VHDL

```
library IEEE; use IEEE.STD_LOGIC_1164.all;

entity seven_seg_decoder is
  port(data:     in  STD_LOGIC_VECTOR(3 downto 0);
       segments: out STD_LOGIC_VECTOR(6 downto 0));
end;

architecture synth of seven_seg_decoder is
begin
  process(all) begin
    case data is
      --                                    abcdefg
      when X"0" => segments <= "1111110";
      when X"1" => segments <= "0110000";
      when X"2" => segments <= "1101101";
      when X"3" => segments <= "1111001";
      when X"4" => segments <= "0110011";
      when X"5" => segments <= "1011011";
      when X"6" => segments <= "1011111";
      when X"7" => segments <= "1110000";
      when X"8" => segments <= "1111111";
      when X"9" => segments <= "1110011";
      when others => segments <= "0000000";
    end case;
  end process;
end;
```

The `case` statement checks the value of `data`. When `data` is 0, the statement performs the action after the =>, setting `segments` to 1111110. The `case` statement similarly checks other data values up to 9 (note the use of X for hexadecimal numbers). The `others` clause is a convenient way to define the output for all cases not explicitly listed, guaranteeing combinational logic.

Unlike SystemVerilog, VHDL supports selected signal assignment statements (see HDL Example 4.6), which are much like `case` statements but can appear outside processes. Thus, there is less reason to use processes to describe combinational logic.

Figure 4.20 sevenseg **synthesized circuit**

possible input combinations are defined; otherwise it implies sequential logic, because the output will keep its old value in the undefined cases.

Synplify Premier synthesizes the seven-segment display decoder into a *read-only memory (ROM)* containing the 7 outputs for each of the 16 possible inputs. ROMs are discussed further in Section 5.5.6.

If the default or others clause were left out of the case statement, the decoder would have remembered its previous output anytime data were in the range of 10–15. This is strange behavior for hardware.

Ordinary decoders are also commonly written with case statements. HDL Example 4.25 describes a 3:8 decoder.

4.5.2 If Statements

always/process statements may also contain if statements. The if statement may be followed by an else statement. If all possible input combinations

---

HDL Example 4.25 3:8 DECODER

SystemVerilog

```
module decoder3_8(input  logic [2:0] a,
                  output logic [7:0] y);
  always_comb
    case(a)
      3'b000:  y=8'b00000001;
      3'b001:  y=8'b00000010;
      3'b010:  y=8'b00000100;
      3'b011:  y=8'b00001000;
      3'b100:  y=8'b00010000;
      3'b101:  y=8'b00100000;
      3'b110:  y=8'b01000000;
      3'b111:  y=8'b10000000;
      default: y=8'bxxxxxxxx;
    endcase
endmodule
```

The default statement isn't strictly necessary for logic synthesis in this case because all possible input combinations are defined, but it is prudent for simulation in case one of the inputs is an x or z.

VHDL

```
library IEEE; use IEEE.STD_LOGIC_1164.all;

entity decoder3_8 is
    port(a: in   STD_LOGIC_VECTOR(2 downto 0);
         y: out  STD_LOGIC_VECTOR(7 downto 0));
end;

architecture synth of decoder3_8 is
begin
    process(all) begin
      case a is
        when "000" =>  y <= "00000001";
        when "001" =>  y <= "00000010";
        when "010" =>  y <= "00000100";
        when "011" =>  y <= "00001000";
        when "100" =>  y <= "00010000";
        when "101" =>  y <= "00100000";
        when "110" =>  y <= "01000000";
        when "111" =>  y <= "10000000";
        when others => y <= "XXXXXXXX";
      end case;
    end process;
end;
```

The others clause isn't strictly necessary for logic synthesis in this case because all possible input combinations are defined, but it is prudent for simulation in case one of the inputs is an x, z, or u.

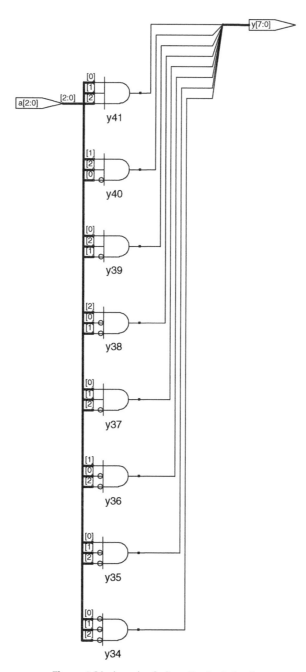

Figure 4.21 decoder3_8 **synthesized circuit**

HDL Example 4.26 PRIORITY CIRCUIT

SystemVerilog

```
module priorityckt(input  logic [3:0] a,
                   output logic [3:0] y);

  always_comb
    if      (a[3]) y = 4'b1000;
    else if (a[2]) y = 4'b0100;
    else if (a[1]) y = 4'b0010;
    else if (a[0]) y = 4'b0001;
    else           y = 4'b0000;
endmodule
```

In SystemVerilog, if statements must appear inside of always statements.

VHDL

```
library IEEE; use IEEE.STD_LOGIC_1164.all;

entity priorityckt is
  port(a: in  STD_LOGIC_VECTOR(3 downto 0);
       y: out STD_LOGIC_VECTOR(3 downto 0));
end;

architecture synth of priorityckt is
begin
  process(all) begin
    if    a(3) then y <= "1000";
    elsif a(2) then y <= "0100";
    elsif a(1) then y <= "0010";
    elsif a(0) then y <= "0001";
    else            y <= "0000";
    end if;
  end process;
end;
```

Unlike SystemVerilog, VHDL supports conditional signal assignment statements (see HDL Example 4.6), which are much like if statements but can appear outside processes. Thus, there is less reason to use processes to describe combinational logic.

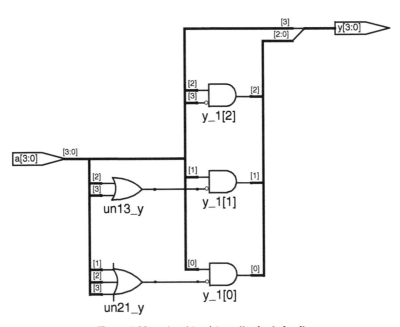

Figure 4.22 priorityckt **synthesized circuit**

are handled, the statement implies combinational logic; otherwise, it produces sequential logic (like the latch in Section 4.4.5).

HDL Example 4.26 uses if statements to describe a priority circuit, defined in Section 2.4. Recall that an *N*-input priority circuit sets the output TRUE that corresponds to the most significant input that is TRUE.

4.5.3 Truth Tables with Don't Cares

As examined in Section 2.7.3, truth tables may include don't care's to allow more logic simplification. HDL Example 4.27 shows how to describe a priority circuit with don't cares.

Synplify Premier synthesizes a slightly different circuit for this module, shown in Figure 4.23, than it did for the priority circuit in Figure 4.22. However, the circuits are logically equivalent.

HDL Example 4.27 PRIORITY CIRCUIT USING DON'T CARES

SystemVerilog

```
module priority_casez(input  logic [3:0] a,
                      output logic [3:0] y);
  always_comb
    casez(a)
      4'b1???: y = 4'b1000;
      4'b01??: y = 4'b0100;
      4'b001?: y = 4'b0010;
      4'b0001: y = 4'b0001;
      default: y = 4'b0000;
    endcase
endmodule
```

The casez statement acts like a case statement except that it also recognizes ? as don't care.

VHDL

```
library IEEE; use IEEE.STD_LOGIC_1164.all;

entity priority_casez is
    port(a: in  STD_LOGIC_VECTOR(3 downto 0);
         y: out STD_LOGIC_VECTOR(3 downto 0));
end;

architecture dontcare of priority_casez is
begin
  process(all) begin
    case? a is
      when "1---" => y <= "1000";
      when "01--" => y <= "0100";
      when "001-" => y <= "0010";
      when "0001" => y <= "0001";
      when others => y <= "0000";
    end case?;
  end process;
end;
```

The case? statement acts like a case statement except that it also recognizes - as don't care.

4.5.4 Blocking and Nonblocking Assignments

The guidelines on page 206 explain when and how to use each type of assignment. If these guidelines are not followed, it is possible to write code that appears to work in simulation but synthesizes to incorrect hardware. The optional remainder of this section explains the principles behind the guidelines.

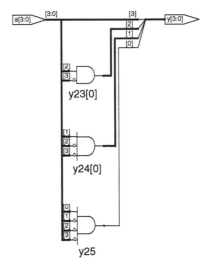

Figure 4.23 `priority_casez` **synthesized circuit**

BLOCKING AND NONBLOCKING ASSIGNMENT GUIDELINES

SystemVerilog

1. Use `always_ff @(posedge clk)` and nonblocking assignments to model synchronous sequential logic.

```
always_ff @(posedge clk)
  begin
    n1 <= d; // nonblocking
    q <= n1; // nonblocking
  end
```

2. Use continuous assignments to model simple combinational logic.

```
assign y = s ? d1 : d0;
```

3. Use `always_comb` and blocking assignments to model more complicated combinational logic where the `always` statement is helpful.

```
always_comb
  begin
    p = a ^ b; // blocking
    g = a & b; // blocking
    s = p ^ cin;
    cout = g | (p & cin);
  end
```

4. Do not make assignments to the same signal in more than one `always` statement or continuous assignment statement.

VHDL

1. Use `process(clk)` and nonblocking assignments to model synchronous sequential logic.

```
process(clk) begin
  if rising_edge(clk) then
    n1 <= d; -- nonblocking
    q <= n1; -- nonblocking
  end if;
end process;
```

2. Use concurrent assignments outside `process` statements to model simple combinational logic.

```
y <= d0 when s = '0' else d1;
```

3. Use `process(all)` to model more complicated combinational logic where the `process` is helpful. Use blocking assignments for internal variables.

```
process(all)
  variable p, g: STD_LOGIC;
begin
  p := a xor b; -- blocking
  g := a and b; -- blocking
  s <= p xor cin;
  cout <= g or (p and cin);
end process;
```

4. Do not make assignments to the same variable in more than one `process` or concurrent assignment statement.

Combinational Logic*

The full adder from HDL Example 4.23 is correctly modeled using blocking assignments. This section explores how it operates and how it would differ if nonblocking assignments had been used.

Imagine that a, b, and cin are all initially 0. p, g, s, and cout are thus 0 as well. At some time, a changes to 1, triggering the always/process statement. The four blocking assignments evaluate in the order shown here. (In the VHDL code, s and cout are assigned concurrently.) Note that p and g get their new values before s and cout are computed because of the blocking assignments. This is important because we want to compute s and cout using the new values of p and g.

1. $p \leftarrow 1 \oplus 0 = 1$

2. $g \leftarrow 1 \cdot 0 = 0$

3. $s \leftarrow 1 \oplus 0 = 1$

4. $cout \leftarrow 0 + 1 \cdot 0 = 0$

In contrast, HDL Example 4.28 illustrates the use of nonblocking assignments.

Now consider the same case of a rising from 0 to 1 while b and cin are 0. The four nonblocking assignments evaluate concurrently:

$p \leftarrow 1 \oplus 0 = 1 \quad g \leftarrow 1 \cdot 0 = 0 \quad s \leftarrow 0 \oplus 0 = 0 \quad cout \leftarrow 0 + 0 \cdot 0 = 0$

HDL Example 4.28 FULL ADDER USING NONBLOCKING ASSIGNMENTS

SystemVerilog

```
// nonblocking assignments (not recommended)
module fulladder(input  logic a, b, cin,
                 output logic s, cout);
  logic p, g;

  always_comb
    begin
      p <= a ^ b; // nonblocking
      g <= a & b; // nonblocking

      s <= p ^ cin;
      cout <= g | (p & cin);
    end
endmodule
```

VHDL

```
-- nonblocking assignments (not recommended)
library IEEE; use IEEE.STD_LOGIC_1164.all;

entity fulladder is
  port(a, b, cin: in  STD_LOGIC;
         s, cout:  out STD_LOGIC);
end;

architecture nonblocking of fulladder is
  signal p, g: STD_LOGIC;
begin
  process(all) begin
    p <= a xor b; -- nonblocking
    g <= a and b; -- nonblocking
    s <= p xor cin;
    cout <= g or (p and cin);
  end process;
end;
```

Because p and g appear on the left hand side of a nonblocking assignment in a process statement, they must be declared to be signal rather than variable. The signal declaration appears before the begin in the architecture, not the process.

Observe that s is computed concurrently with p and hence uses the old value of p, not the new value. Therefore, s remains 0 rather than becoming 1. However, p does change from 0 to 1. This change triggers the always/process statement to evaluate a second time, as follows:

$$p \leftarrow 1 \oplus 0 = 1 \quad g \leftarrow 1 \cdot 0 = 0 \quad s \leftarrow 1 \oplus 0 = 1 \quad cout \leftarrow 0 + 1 \cdot 0 = 0$$

This time, p is already 1, so s correctly changes to 1. The nonblocking assignments eventually reach the right answer, but the always/process statement had to evaluate twice. This makes simulation slower, though it synthesizes to the same hardware.

Another drawback of nonblocking assignments in modeling combinational logic is that the HDL will produce the wrong result if you forget to include the intermediate variables in the sensitivity list.

Worse yet, some synthesis tools will synthesize the correct hardware even when a faulty sensitivity list causes incorrect simulation. This leads to a mismatch between the simulation results and what the hardware actually does.

SystemVerilog

If the sensitivity list of the always statement in HDL Example 4.28 were written as always @(a, b, cin) rather than always_comb, then the statement would not reevaluate when p or g changes. In that case, s would be incorrectly left at 0, not 1.

VHDL

If the sensitivity list of the process statement in HDL Example 4.28 were written as process(a, b, cin) rather than process(all), then the statement would not reevaluate when p or g changes. In that case, s would be incorrectly left at 0, not 1.

Sequential Logic*

The synchronizer from HDL Example 4.20 is correctly modeled using nonblocking assignments. On the rising edge of the clock, d is copied to n1 at the same time that n1 is copied to q, so the code properly describes two registers. For example, suppose initially that d = 0, n1 = 1, and q = 0. On the rising edge of the clock, the following two assignments occur concurrently, so that after the clock edge, n1 = 0 and q = 1.

$$n1 \leftarrow d = 0 \quad q \leftarrow n1 = 1$$

HDL Example 4.29 tries to describe the same module using blocking assignments. On the rising edge of clk, d is copied to n1. Then this new value of n1 is copied to q, resulting in d improperly appearing at both n1 and q. The assignments occur one after the other so that after the clock edge, q = n1 = 0.

1. $n1 \leftarrow d = 0$

2. $q \leftarrow n1 = 0$

HDL Example 4.29 BAD SYNCHRONIZER WITH BLOCKING ASSIGNMENTS

SystemVerilog

```
// Bad implementation of a synchronizer using blocking
// assignments

module syncbad(input  logic clk,
               input  logic d,
               output logic q);
  logic n1;

  always_ff @(posedge clk)
    begin
      n1 = d; // blocking
      q = n1; // blocking
    end
endmodule
```

VHDL

```
-- Bad implementation of a synchronizer using blocking
-- assignment

library IEEE; use IEEE.STD_LOGIC_1164.all;

entity syncbad is
  port(clk: in  STD_LOGIC;
       d:   in  STD_LOGIC;
       q:   out STD_LOGIC);
end;

architecture bad of syncbad is
begin
  process(clk)
    variable n1: STD_LOGIC;
  begin
    if rising_edge(clk) then
      n1 := d; -- blocking
      q <= n1;
    end if;
  end process;
end;
```

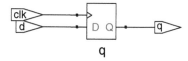

Figure 4.24 syncbad **synthesized circuit**

Because n1 is invisible to the outside world and does not influence the behavior of q, the synthesizer optimizes it away entirely, as shown in Figure 4.24.

The moral of this illustration is to exclusively use nonblocking assignment in always/process statements when modeling sequential logic. With sufficient cleverness, such as reversing the orders of the assignments, you could make blocking assignments work correctly, but blocking assignments offer no advantages and only introduce the risk of unintended behavior. Certain sequential circuits will not work with blocking assignments no matter what the order.

4.6 FINITE STATE MACHINES

Recall that a finite state machine (FSM) consists of a state register and two blocks of combinational logic to compute the next state and the output given the current state and the input, as was shown in Figure 3.22. HDL descriptions of state machines are correspondingly divided into three parts to model the state register, the next state logic, and the output logic.

HDL Example 4.30 DIVIDE-BY-3 FINITE STATE MACHINE

SystemVerilog

```systemverilog
module divideby3FSM(input  logic clk,
                    input  logic reset,
                    output logic y);
  typedef enum logic [1:0] {S0, S1, S2} statetype;
  statetype state, nextstate;

  // state register
  always_ff @(posedge clk, posedge reset)
    if (reset) state <= S0;
    else       state <= nextstate;

  // next state logic
  always_comb
    case (state)
      S0:      nextstate = S1;
      S1:      nextstate = S2;
      S2:      nextstate = S0;
      default: nextstate = S0;
    endcase

  // output logic
  assign y = (state == S0);
endmodule
```

The `typedef` statement defines `statetype` to be a two-bit `logic` value with three possibilities: S0, S1, or S2. `state` and `nextstate` are `statetype` signals.

The enumerated encodings default to numerical order: S0 = 00, S1 = 01, and S2 = 10. The encodings can be explicitly set by the user; however, the synthesis tool views them as suggestions, not requirements. For example, the following snippet encodes the states as 3-bit one-hot values:

```systemverilog
typedef enum logic [2:0] {S0 = 3'b001, S1 = 3'b010, S2 = 3'b100}
statetype;
```

Notice how a `case` statement is used to define the state transition table. Because the next state logic should be combinational, a `default` is necessary even though the state 2'b11 should never arise.

The output, y, is 1 when the state is S0. The *equality comparison* a == b evaluates to 1 if a equals b and 0 otherwise. The *inequality comparison* a != b does the inverse, evaluating to 1 if a does not equal b.

VHDL

```vhdl
library IEEE; use IEEE.STD_LOGIC_1164.all;

entity divideby3FSM is
  port(clk, reset: in  STD_LOGIC;
       y:          out STD_LOGIC);
end;

architecture synth of divideby3FSM is
  type statetype is (S0, S1, S2);
  signal state, nextstate: statetype;
begin
  -- state register
  process(clk, reset) begin
    if reset then state <= S0;
    elsif rising_edge(clk) then
      state <= nextstate;
    end if;
  end process;

  -- next state logic
  nextstate <= S1 when state = S0 else
               S2 when state = S1 else
               S0;

  -- output logic
  y <= '1' when state = S0 else '0';
end;
```

This example defines a new *enumeration* data type, `statetype`, with three possibilities: S0, S1, and S2. `state` and `nextstate` are `statetype` signals. By using an enumeration instead of choosing the state encoding, VHDL frees the synthesizer to explore various state encodings to choose the best one.

The output, y, is 1 when the `state` is S0. The inequality comparison uses /=. To produce an output of 1 when the state is anything but S0, change the comparison to `state /= S0`.

HDL Example 4.30 describes the divide-by-3 FSM from Section 3.4.2. It provides an asynchronous reset to initialize the FSM. The state register uses the ordinary idiom for flip-flops. The next state and output logic blocks are combinational.

The Synplify Premier synthesis tool just produces a block diagram and state transition diagram for state machines; it does not show the logic

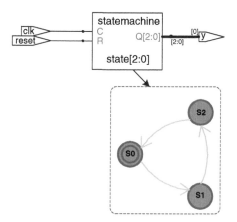

Figure 4.25 dividedby3fsm **synthesized circuit**

gates or the inputs and outputs on the arcs and states. Therefore, be careful that you have specified the FSM correctly in your HDL code. The state transition diagram in Figure 4.25 for the divide-by-3 FSM is analogous to the diagram in Figure 3.28(b). The double circle indicates that S0 is the reset state. Gate-level implementations of the divide-by-3 FSM were shown in Section 3.4.2.

Notice that the states are named with an enumeration data type rather than by referring to them as binary values. This makes the code more readable and easier to change.

If, for some reason, we had wanted the output to be HIGH in states S0 and S1, the output logic would be modified as follows.

Notice that the synthesis tool uses a 3-bit encoding (Q[2:0]) instead of the 2-bit encoding suggested in the SystemVerilog code.

SystemVerilog	**VHDL**
// output logic assign y = (state == S0 | state == S1);	-- output logic y <= '1' when (state = S0 or state = S1) else '0';

The next two examples describe the snail pattern recognizer FSM from Section 3.4.3. The code shows how to use case and if statements to handle next state and output logic that depend on the inputs as well as the current state. We show both Moore and Mealy modules. In the Moore machine (HDL Example 4.31), the output depends only on the current state, whereas in the Mealy machine (HDL Example 4.32), the output logic depends on both the current state and inputs.

HDL Example 4.31 PATTERN RECOGNIZER MOORE FSM

SystemVerilog

```
module patternMoore(input  logic clk,
                    input  logic reset,
                    input  logic a,
                    output logic y);

  typedef enum logic [1:0] {S0, S1, S2} statetype;
  statetype state, nextstate;

  // state register
  always_ff @(posedge clk, posedge reset)
    if (reset) state <= S0;
    else       state <= nextstate;

  // next state logic
  always_comb
    case (state)
      S0: if (a) nextstate = S0;
          else   nextstate = S1;
      S1: if (a) nextstate = S2;
          else   nextstate = S1;
      S2: if (a) nextstate = S0;
          else   nextstate = S1;
      default: nextstate = S0;
    endcase

  // output logic
  assign y = (state == S2);
endmodule
```

Note how nonblocking assignments (<=) are used in the state register to describe sequential logic, whereas blocking assignments (=) are used in the next state logic to describe combinational logic.

VHDL

```
library IEEE; use IEEE.STD_LOGIC_1164.all;

entity patternMoore is
  port(clk, reset: in  STD_LOGIC;
       a:          in  STD_LOGIC;
       y:          out STD_LOGIC);
end;

architecture synth of patternMoore is
  type statetype is (S0, S1, S2);
  signal state, nextstate: statetype;
begin
  -- state register
  process(clk, reset) begin
    if reset then                    state <= S0;
    elsif rising_edge(clk) then state <= nextstate;
    end if;
  end process;

  -- next state logic
  process(all) begin
    case state is
      when S0 =>
        if a then nextstate <= S0;
        else      nextstate <= S1;
        end if;
      when S1 =>
        if a then nextstate <= S2;
        else      nextstate <= S1;
        end if;
      when S2 =>
        if a then nextstate <= S0;
        else      nextstate <= S1;
        end if;
      when others =>
                  nextstate <= S0;
    end case;
  end process;

  --output logic
  y <= '1' when state = S2 else '0';
end;
```

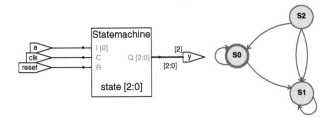

Figure 4.26 patternMoore **synthesized circuit**

HDL Example 4.32 PATTERN RECOGNIZER MEALY FSM

SystemVerilog

```systemverilog
module patternMealy(input  logic clk,
                    input  logic reset,
                    input  logic a,
                    output logic y);

  typedef enum logic {S0, S1} statetype;
  statetype state, nextstate;

  // state register
  always_ff @(posedge clk, posedge reset)
    if (reset) state <= S0;
    else       state <= nextstate;

  // next state logic
  always_comb
    case (state)
      S0: if (a) nextstate = S0;
          else   nextstate = S1;
      S1: if (a) nextstate = S0;
          else   nextstate = S1;
      default: nextstate = S0;
    endcase

  // output logic
  assign y = (a & state==S1);
endmodule
```

VHDL

```vhdl
library IEEE; use IEEE.STD_LOGIC_1164.all;

entity patternMealy is
  port(clk, reset: in  STD_LOGIC;
       a:          in  STD_LOGIC;
       y:          out STD_LOGIC);
end;

architecture synth of patternMealy is
  type statetype is (S0, S1);
  signal state, nextstate: statetype;
begin
  -- state register
  process(clk, reset) begin
    if reset then            state <= S0;
    elsif rising_edge(clk) then state <= nextstate;
    end if;
  end process;

  -- next state logic
  process(all) begin
    case state is
      when S0 =>
        if a then nextstate <= S0;
        else      nextstate <= S1;
        end if;
      when S1 =>
        if a then nextstate <= S0;
        else      nextstate <= S1;
        end if;
      when others =>
                  nextstate <= S0;
    end case;
  end process;

  -- output logic
  y <= '1' when (a = '1' and state = S1) else '0';
end;
```

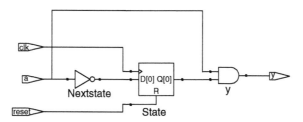

Figure 4.27 `patternMealy` **synthesized circuit**

4.7 DATA TYPES*

This section explains some subtleties about SystemVerilog and VHDL types in more depth.

4.7.1 SystemVerilog

Prior to SystemVerilog, Verilog primarily used two types: reg and wire. Despite its name, a reg signal might or might not be associated with a register. This was a great source of confusion for those learning the language. SystemVerilog introduced the logic type to eliminate the confusion; hence, this book emphasizes the logic type. This section explains the reg and wire types in more detail for those who need to read old Verilog code.

In Verilog, if a signal appears on the left hand side of <= or = in an always block, it must be declared as reg. Otherwise, it should be declared as wire. Hence, a reg signal might be the output of a flip-flop, a latch, or combinational logic, depending on the sensitivity list and statement of an always block.

Input and output ports default to the wire type unless their type is explicitly defined as reg. The following example shows how a flip-flop is described in conventional Verilog. Note that clk and d default to wire, while q is explicitly defined as reg because it appears on the left hand side of <= in the always block.

```
module flop(input          clk,
            input     [3:0] d,
            output reg [3:0] q);
  always @(posedge clk)
    q <= d;
endmodule
```

SystemVerilog introduces the logic type. logic is a synonym for reg and avoids misleading users about whether it is actually a flip-flop. Moreover, SystemVerilog relaxes the rules on assign statements and hierarchical port instantiations so logic can be used outside always blocks where a wire traditionally would have been required. Thus, nearly all SystemVerilog signals can be logic. The exception is that signals with multiple drivers (e.g., a tristate bus) must be declared as a net, as described in HDL Example 4.10. This rule allows SystemVerilog to generate an error message rather than an x value when a logic signal is accidentally connected to multiple drivers.

The most common type of net is called a wire or tri. These two types are synonymous, but wire is conventionally used when a single driver is present and tri is used when multiple drivers are present. Thus, wire is obsolete in SystemVerilog because logic is preferred for signals with a single driver.

When a tri net is driven to a single value by one or more drivers, it takes on that value. When it is undriven, it floats (z). When it is driven to a different value (0, 1, or x) by multiple drivers, it is in contention (x).

There are other net types that resolve differently when undriven or driven by multiple sources. These other types are rarely used, but may be substituted anywhere a tri net would normally appear (e.g., for signals with multiple drivers). Each is described in Table 4.7.

Table 4.7 Net Resolution

Net Type	No Driver	Conflicting Drivers
tri	z	x
trireg	previous value	x
triand	z	0 if there are any 0
trior	z	1 if there are any 1
tri0	0	x
tri1	1	x

4.7.2 VHDL

Unlike SystemVerilog, VHDL enforces a strict data typing system that can protect the user from some errors but that is also clumsy at times.

Despite its fundamental importance, the STD_LOGIC type is not built into VHDL. Instead, it is part of the IEEE.STD_LOGIC_1164 library. Thus, every file must contain the library statements shown in the previous examples.

Moreover, IEEE.STD_LOGIC_1164 lacks basic operations such as addition, comparison, shifts, and conversion to integers for the STD_LOGIC_VECTOR data. These were finally added to the VHDL 2008 standard in the IEEE.NUMERIC_STD_UNSIGNED library.

VHDL also has a BOOLEAN type with two values: true and false. BOOLEAN values are returned by comparisons (such as the equality comparison, s = '0') and are used in conditional statements such as when and if. Despite the temptation to believe a BOOLEAN true value should be equivalent to a STD_LOGIC '1' and BOOLEAN false should mean STD_LOGIC '0', these types were not interchangeable prior to VHDL 2008. For example, in old VHDL code, one must write

```
y <= d1 when (s = '1') else d0;
```

while in VHDL 2008, the when statement automatically converts s from STD_LOGIC to BOOLEAN so one can simply write

```
y <= d1 when s else d0;
```

Even in VHDL 2008, it is still necessary to write

```
q <= '1' when (state = S2) else '0';
```

instead of

```
q <= (state = S2);
```

because (state = S2) returns a BOOLEAN result, which cannot be directly assigned to the STD_LOGIC signal y.

Although we do not declare any signals to be BOOLEAN, they are automatically implied by comparisons and used by conditional statements. Similarly, VHDL has an INTEGER type that represents both positive and negative integers. Signals of type INTEGER span at least the values $-(2^{31} - 1)$ to $2^{31} - 1$. Integer values are used as indices of busses. For example, in the statement

```
y <= a(3) and a(2) and a(1) and a(0);
```

0, 1, 2, and 3 are integers serving as an index to choose bits of the a signal. We cannot directly index a bus with a STD_LOGIC or STD_ LOGIC_ VECTOR signal. Instead, we must convert the signal to an INTEGER. This is demonstrated in the example below for an 8:1 multiplexer that selects one bit from a vector using a 3-bit index. The TO_INTEGER function is defined in the IEEE.NUMERIC_STD_UNSIGNED library and performs the conversion from STD_LOGIC_VECTOR to INTEGER for positive (unsigned) values.

```
library IEEE;
use IEEE.STD_LOGIC_1164.all;
use IEEE.NUMERIC_STD_UNSIGNED.all;
entity mux8 is
  port(d: in  STD_LOGIC_VECTOR(7 downto 0);
       s: in  STD_LOGIC_VECTOR(2 downto 0);
       y: out STD_LOGIC);
end;

architecture synth of mux8 is
begin
  y <= d(TO_INTEGER(s));
end;
```

VHDL is also strict about out ports being exclusively for output. For example, the following code for two- and three-input AND gates is illegal VHDL because v is an output and is also used to compute w.

```
library IEEE; use IEEE.STD_LOGIC_1164.all;

entity and23 is
  port(a, b, c: in STD_LOGIC;
       v, w: out   STD_LOGIC);
end;

architecture synth of and23 is
begin
  v <= a and b;
  w <= v and c;
end;
```

VHDL defines a special port type, buffer, to solve this problem. A signal connected to a buffer port behaves as an output but may also be used within the module. The corrected entity definition follows. Verilog and SystemVerilog do not have this limitation and do not require buffer ports. VHDL 2008 eliminates this restriction by allowing out ports to be readable, but this change is not supported by the Synplify CAD tool at the time of this writing.

```
entity and23 is
  port(a, b, c: in STD_LOGIC;
       v: buffer  STD_LOGIC;
       w: out     STD_LOGIC);
end;
```

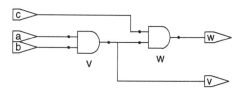

Figure 4.28 and23 **synthesized circuit**

Most operations such as addition, subtraction, and Boolean logic are identical whether a number is signed or unsigned. However, magnitude comparison, multiplication, and arithmetic right shifts are performed differently for signed two's complement numbers than for unsigned binary numbers. These operations will be examined in Chapter 5. HDL Example 4.33 describes how to indicate that a signal represents a signed number.

HDL Example 4.33 (a) UNSIGNED MULTIPLIER (b) SIGNED MULTIPLIER

SystemVerilog

```
// 4.33(a): unsigned multiplier
module multiplier(input  logic [3:0] a, b,
                  output logic [7:0] y);
  assign y = a * b;
endmodule

// 4.33(b): signed multiplier
module multiplier(input  logic signed [3:0] a, b,
                  output logic signed [7:0] y);
  assign y = a * b;
endmodule
```

In SystemVerilog, signals are considered unsigned by default. Adding the signed modifier (e.g., logic signed [3:0] a) causes the signal a to be treated as signed.

VHDL

```
-- 4.33(a): unsigned multiplier
library IEEE; use IEEE.STD_LOGIC_1164.all;
use IEEE.NUMERIC_STD_UNSIGNED.all;

entity multiplier is
  port(a, b: in  STD_LOGIC_VECTOR(3 downto 0);
       y:    out STD_LOGIC_VECTOR(7 downto 0));
end;

architecture synth of multiplier is
begin
  y <= a * b;
end;
```

VHDL uses the NUMERIC_STD_UNSIGNED library to perform arithmetic and comparison operations on STD_LOGIC_VECTORs. The vectors are treated as unsigned.

```
use IEEE.NUMERIC_STD_UNSIGNED.all;
```

VHDL also defines UNSIGNED and SIGNED data types in the IEEE.NUMERIC_STD library, but these involve type conversions beyond the scope of this chapter.

4.8 PARAMETERIZED MODULES*

So far all of our modules have had fixed-width inputs and outputs. For example, we had to define separate modules for 4- and 8-bit wide 2:1 multiplexers. HDLs permit variable bit widths using parameterized modules.

HDL Example 4.34 declares a parameterized 2:1 multiplexer with a default width of 8, then uses it to create 8- and 12-bit 4:1 multiplexers.

HDL Example 4.34 PARAMETERIZED N-BIT 2:1 MULTIPLEXERS

SystemVerilog

```
module mux2
  #(parameter width=8)
  (input  logic [width-1:0] d0, d1,
   input  logic             s,
   output logic [width-1:0] y);

   assign y=s ? d1 : d0;
endmodule
```

SystemVerilog allows a #(parameter . . .) statement before the inputs and outputs to define parameters. The parameter statement includes a default value (8) of the parameter, in this case called width. The number of bits in the inputs and outputs can depend on this parameter.

```
module mux4_8(input  logic [7:0] d0, d1, d2, d3,
              input  logic [1:0] s,
              output logic [7:0] y);

  logic [7:0] low, hi;

  mux2 lowmux(d0, d1, s[0], low);
  mux2 himux(d2, d3, s[0], hi);
  mux2 outmux(low, hi, s[1], y);
endmodule
```

The 8-bit 4:1 multiplexer instantiates three 2:1 multiplexers using their default widths.

In contrast, a 12-bit 4:1 multiplexer, mux4_12, would need to override the default width using #( ) before the instance name, as shown below.

```
module mux4_12(input logic  [11:0] d0, d1, d2, d3,
               input logic  [1:0]  s,
               output logic [11:0] y);

  logic [11:0] low, hi;

  mux2 #(12) lowmux(d0, d1, s[0], low);
  mux2 #(12) himux(d2, d3, s[0], hi);
  mux2 #(12) outmux(low, hi, s[1], y);
endmodule
```

Do not confuse the use of the # sign indicating delays with the use of #(. . .) in defining and overriding parameters.

VHDL

```
library IEEE; use IEEE.STD_LOGIC_1164.all;

entity mux2 is
  generic(width: integer := 8);
  port(d0,
       d1: in  STD_LOGIC_VECTOR(width-1 downto 0);
       s:  in  STD_LOGIC;
       y:  out STD_LOGIC_VECTOR(width-1 downto 0));
end;

architecture synth of mux2 is
begin
  y <= d1 when s else d0;
end;
```

The generic statement includes a default value (8) of width. The value is an integer.

```
library IEEE; use IEEE.STD_LOGIC_1164.all;

entity mux4_8 is
  port(d0, d1, d2,
       d3: in  STD_LOGIC_VECTOR(7 downto 0);
       s:  in  STD_LOGIC_VECTOR(1 downto 0);
       y:  out STD_LOGIC_VECTOR(7 downto 0));
end;

architecture struct of mux4_8 is
  component mux2
    generic(width: integer := 8);
    port(d0,
         d1: in  STD_LOGIC_VECTOR(width-1 downto 0);
         s:  in  STD_LOGIC;
         y:  out STD_LOGIC_VECTOR(width-1 downto 0));
  end component;
  signal low, hi: STD_LOGIC_VECTOR(7 downto 0);
begin
  lowmux: mux2 port map(d0, d1, s(0), low);
  himux:  mux2 port map(d2, d3, s(0), hi);
  outmux: mux2 port map(low, hi, s(1), y);
end;
```

The 8-bit 4:1 multiplexer, mux4_8, instantiates three 2:1 multiplexers using their default widths.

In contrast, a 12-bit 4:1 multiplexer, mux4_12, would need to override the default width using generic map, as shown below.

```
lowmux: mux2 generic map(12)
             port map(d0, d1, s(0), low);
himux:  mux2 generic map(12)
             port map(d2, d3, s(0), hi);
outmux: mux2 generic map(12)
             port map(low, hi, s(1), y);
```

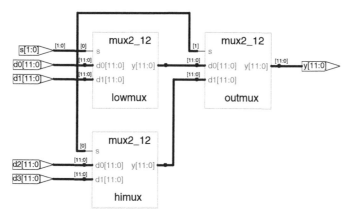

Figure 4.29 mux4_12 **synthesized circuit**

HDL Example 4.35 PARAMETERIZED $N{:}2^N$ DECODER

SystemVerilog

```
module decoder
  #(parameter N=3)
  (input  logic [N-1:0]   a,
   output logic [2**N-1:0] y);

  always_comb
    begin
      y = 0;
      y[a] = 1;
    end
endmodule
```

$2{**}N$ indicates 2^N.

VHDL

```
library IEEE; use IEEE.STD_LOGIC_1164.all;
use IEEE. NUMERIC_STD_UNSIGNED.all;

entity decoder is
  generic(N: integer := 3);
  port(a: in  STD_LOGIC_VECTOR(N-1 downto 0);
       y: out STD_LOGIC_VECTOR(2**N-1 downto 0));
end;

architecture synth of decoder is
begin
  process(all)
  begin
    y <= (OTHERS => '0');
    y(TO_INTEGER(a)) <= '1';
  end process;
end;
```

$2{**}N$ indicates 2^N.

HDL Example 4.35 shows a decoder, which is an even better application of parameterized modules. A large $N{:}2^N$ decoder is cumbersome to specify with case statements, but easy using parameterized code that simply sets the appropriate output bit to 1. Specifically, the decoder uses blocking assignments to set all the bits to 0, then changes the appropriate bit to 1.

HDLs also provide generate statements to produce a variable amount of hardware depending on the value of a parameter. generate supports for loops and if statements to determine how many of what types of hardware to produce. HDL Example 4.36 demonstrates how to use generate statements to produce an N-input AND function from a cascade of two-input AND gates. Of course, a reduction operator would be cleaner and simpler for this application, but the example illustrates the general principle of hardware generators.

Use generate statements with caution; it is easy to produce a large amount of hardware unintentionally!

HDL Example 4.36 PARAMETERIZED N-INPUT AND GATE

SystemVerilog

```
module andN
  #(parameter width=8)
   (input  logic [width-1:0] a,
    output logic            y);

  genvar i;
  logic [width-1:0] x;

  generate
    assign x[0]=a[0];
    for(i=1; i<width; i=i+1) begin: forloop
      assign x[i]=a[i] & x[i-1];
    end
  endgenerate

  assign y=x[width-1];
endmodule
```

The for statement loops through i = 1, 2, ... , width-1 to produce many consecutive AND gates. The begin in a generate for loop must be followed by a : and an arbitrary label (forloop, in this case).

VHDL

```
library IEEE; use IEEE.STD_LOGIC_1164.all;

entity andN is
  generic(width: integer := 8);
  port(a: in  STD_LOGIC_VECTOR(width-1 downto 0);
       y: out STD_LOGIC);
end;

architecture synth of andN is
  signal x: STD_LOGIC_VECTOR(width-1 downto 0);
begin
  x(0) <= a(0);
  gen: for i in 1 to width-1 generate
    x(i) <= a(i) and x(i-1);
  end generate;
  y <= x(width-1);
end;
```

The generate loop variable i does not need to be declared.

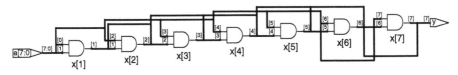

Figure 4.30 andN **synthesized circuit**

4.9 TESTBENCHES

> Some tools also call the module to be tested the *unit under test* (UUT).

A *testbench* is an HDL module that is used to test another module, called the *device under test* (*DUT*). The testbench contains statements to apply inputs to the DUT and, ideally, to check that the correct outputs are produced. The input and desired output patterns are called *test vectors*.

Consider testing the sillyfunction module from Section 4.1.1 that computes $y = \overline{a}\,\overline{b}\,\overline{c} + a\overline{b}\,\overline{c} + a\overline{b}c$. This is a simple module, so we can perform exhaustive testing by applying all eight possible test vectors.

HDL Example 4.37 TESTBENCH

SystemVerilog

```
module testbench1();
  logic a, b, c, y;

  // instantiate device under test
  sillyfunction dut(a, b, c, y);

  // apply inputs one at a time
  initial begin
    a=0; b=0; c=0; #10;
    c=1;          #10;
    b=1; c=0;     #10;
    c=1;          #10;
    a=1; b=0; c=0; #10;
    c=1;          #10;
    b=1; c=0;     #10;
    c=1;          #10;
  end
endmodule
```

The `initial` statement executes the statements in its body at the start of simulation. In this case, it first applies the input pattern 000 and waits for 10 time units. It then applies 001 and waits 10 more units, and so forth until all eight possible inputs have been applied. `initial` statements should be used only in testbenches for simulation, not in modules intended to be synthesized into actual hardware. Hardware has no way of magically executing a sequence of special steps when it is first turned on.

VHDL

```
library IEEE; use IEEE.STD_LOGIC_1164.all;

entity testbench1 is -- no inputs or outputs
end;

architecture sim of testbench1 is
  component sillyfunction
    port(a, b, c: in  STD_LOGIC;
         y:       out STD_LOGIC);
  end component;
  signal a, b, c, y: STD_LOGIC;
begin
  -- instantiate device under test
  dut: sillyfunction port map(a, b, c, y);

  -- apply inputs one at a time
  process begin
    a <= '0'; b <= '0'; c <= '0'; wait for 10 ns;
    c <= '1';                     wait for 10 ns;
    b <= '1'; c <= '0';           wait for 10 ns;
    c <= '1';                     wait for 10 ns;
    a <= '1'; b <= '0'; c <= '0'; wait for 10 ns;
    c <= '1';                     wait for 10 ns;
    b <= '1'; c <= '0';           wait for 10 ns;
    c <= '1';                     wait for 10 ns;
    wait; -- wait forever
  end process;
end;
```

The `process` statement first applies the input pattern 000 and waits for 10 ns. It then applies 001 and waits 10 more ns, and so forth until all eight possible inputs have been applied.

At the end, the process waits indefinitely; otherwise, the process would begin again, repeatedly applying the pattern of test vectors.

HDL Example 4.37 demonstrates a simple testbench. It instantiates the DUT, then applies the inputs. Blocking assignments and delays are used to apply the inputs in the appropriate order. The user must view the results of the simulation and verify by inspection that the correct outputs are produced. Testbenches are simulated the same as other HDL modules. However, they are not synthesizeable.

Checking for correct outputs is tedious and error-prone. Moreover, determining the correct outputs is much easier when the design is fresh in your mind; if you make minor changes and need to retest weeks later, determining the correct outputs becomes a hassle. A much better approach is to write a self-checking testbench, shown in HDL Example 4.38.

Writing code for each test vector also becomes tedious, especially for modules that require a large number of vectors. An even better approach

HDL Example 4.38 SELF-CHECKING TESTBENCH

SystemVerilog

```
module testbench2();
  logic a, b, c, y;

  // instantiate device under test
  sillyfunction dut(a, b, c, y);

  // apply inputs one at a time
  // checking results
  initial begin
    a=0; b=0; c=0; #10;
    assert (y === 1) else $error("000 failed.");
    c=1;  #10;
    assert (y === 0) else $error("001 failed.");
    b=1; c=0;  #10;
    assert (y === 0) else $error("010 failed.");
    c=1;  #10;
    assert (y === 0) else $error("011 failed.");
    a=1; b=0; c=0;  #10;
    assert (y === 1) else $error("100 failed.");
    c=1;  #10;
    assert (y === 1) else $error("101 failed.");
    b=1; c=0;  #10;
    assert (y === 0) else $error("110 failed.");
    c=1;  #10;
    assert (y === 0) else $error("111 failed.");
  end
endmodule
```

The SystemVerilog assert statement checks if a specified condition is true. If not, it executes the else statement. The $error system task in the else statement prints an error message describing the assertion failure. assert is ignored during synthesis.

In SystemVerilog, comparison using == or != is effective between signals that do not take on the values of x and z. Testbenches use the === and !== operators for comparisons of equality and inequality, respectively, because these operators work correctly with operands that could be x or z.

VHDL

```
library IEEE; use IEEE.STD_LOGIC_1164.all;

entity testbench2 is -- no inputs or outputs
end;

architecture sim of testbench2 is
  component sillyfunction
    port(a, b, c: in  STD_LOGIC;
         y:       out STD_LOGIC);
  end component;
  signal a, b, c, y: STD_LOGIC;
begin
  -- instantiate device under test
  dut: sillyfunction port map(a, b, c, y);

  -- apply inputs one at a time
  -- checking results
  process begin
    a <= '0'; b <= '0'; c <= '0'; wait for 10 ns;
      assert y = '1' report "000 failed.";
    c <= '1';               wait for 10 ns;
      assert y = '0' report "001 failed.";
    b <= '1'; c <= '0';     wait for 10 ns;
      assert y = '0' report "010 failed.";
    c <= '1';               wait for 10 ns;
      assert y = '0' report "011 failed.";
    a <= '1'; b <= '0'; c <= '0'; wait for 10 ns;
      assert y = '1' report "100 failed.";
    c <= '1';               wait for 10 ns;
      assert y = '1' report "101 failed.";
    b <= '1'; c <= '0';     wait for 10 ns;
      assert y = '0' report "110 failed.";
    c <= '1';               wait for 10 ns;
      assert y = '0' report "111 failed.";
    wait; -- wait forever
  end process;
end;
```

The assert statement checks a condition and prints the message given in the report clause if the condition is not satisfied. assert is meaningful only in simulation, not in synthesis.

is to place the test vectors in a separate file. The testbench simply reads the test vectors from the file, applies the input test vector to the DUT, waits, checks that the output values from the DUT match the output vector, and repeats until reaching the end of the test vectors file.

HDL Example 4.39 demonstrates such a testbench. The testbench generates a clock using an always/process statement with no sensitivity list, so that it is continuously reevaluated. At the beginning of the simulation, it reads the test vectors from a text file and pulses reset for two cycles. Although the clock and reset aren't necessary to test combinational logic, they are included because they would be important to testing a sequential DUT. example.tv is a text file containing the inputs and expected output written in binary:

```
000_1
001_0
010_0
011_0
100_1
101_1
110_0
111_0
```

HDL Example 4.39 TESTBENCH WITH TEST VECTOR FILE

SystemVerilog

```
module testbench3();
  logic        clk, reset;
  logic        a, b, c, y, yexpected;
  logic [31:0] vectornum, errors;
  logic [3:0]  testvectors[10000:0];

  // instantiate device under test
  sillyfunction dut(a, b, c, y);

  // generate clock
  always
    begin
      clk=1; #5; clk=0; #5;
    end

  // at start of test, load vectors
  // and pulse reset
  initial
    begin
      $readmemb("example.tv", testvectors);
      vectornum=0; errors=0;
      reset=1; #27; reset=0;
    end

  // apply test vectors on rising edge of clk
  always @(posedge clk)
    begin
      #1; {a, b, c, yexpected} = testvectors[vectornum];
    end

  // check results on falling edge of clk
  always @(negedge clk)
    if (~reset) begin // skip during reset
      if (y !== yexpected) begin  // check result
        $display("Error: inputs = %b", {a, b, c});
        $display(" outputs = %b (%b expected)", y, yexpected);
        errors=errors+1;
      end
      vectornum = vectornum+1;
      if (testvectors[vectornum] === 4'bx) begin
        $display("%d tests completed with %d errors",
                 vectornum, errors);
        $finish;
      end
    end
endmodule
```

VHDL

```
library IEEE; use IEEE.STD_LOGIC_1164.all;
use IEEE.STD_LOGIC_TEXTIO.ALL; use STD.TEXTIO.all;

entity testbench3 is -- no inputs or outputs
end;

architecture sim of testbench3 is
  component sillyfunction
    port(a, b, c: in  STD_LOGIC;
         y:       out STD_LOGIC);
  end component;
  signal a, b, c, y:   STD_LOGIC;
  signal y_expected: STD_LOGIC;
  signal clk, reset: STD_LOGIC;
begin
  -- instantiate device under test
  dut: sillyfunction port map(a, b, c, y);

  -- generate clock
  process begin
    clk <= '1'; wait for 5 ns;
    clk <= '0'; wait for 5 ns;
  end process;

  -- at start of test, pulse reset
  process begin
    reset <= '1'; wait for 27 ns; reset <= '0';
    wait;
  end process;

  -- run tests
  process is
    file tv: text;
    variable L: line;
    variable vector_in: std_logic_vector(2 downto 0);
    variable dummy: character;
    variable vector_out: std_logic;
    variable vectornum: integer := 0;
    variable errors: integer := 0;
  begin
    FILE_OPEN(tv, "example.tv", READ_MODE);
    while not endfile(tv) loop

      -- change vectors on rising edge
      wait until rising_edge(clk);

      -- read the next line of testvectors and split into pieces
      readline(tv, L);
      read(L, vector_in);
      read(L, dummy); -- skip over underscore
```

$readmemb reads a file of binary numbers into the testvectors array. $readmemh is similar but reads a file of hexadecimal numbers.

The next block of code waits one time unit after the rising edge of the clock (to avoid any confusion if clock and data change simultaneously), then sets the three inputs (a, b, and c) and the expected output (yexpected) based on the four bits in the current test vector.

The testbench compares the generated output, y, with the expected output, yexpected, and prints an error if they don't match. %b and %d indicate to print the values in binary and decimal, respectively. $display is a system task to print in the simulator window. For example, $display("%b %b", y, yexpected); prints the two values, y and yexpected, in binary. %h prints a value in hexadecimal.

This process repeats until there are no more valid test vectors in the testvectors array. $finish terminates the simulation.

Note that even though the SystemVerilog module supports up to 10,001 test vectors, it will terminate the simulation after executing the eight vectors in the file.

```
      read(L, vector_out);
      (a, b, c) <= vector_in(2 downto 0) after 1 ns;
      y_expected <= vector_out after 1 ns;

      -- check results on falling edge
      wait until falling_edge(clk);

      if y /= y_expected then
        report "Error: y=" & std_logic'image(y);
        errors := errors+1;
      end if;

      vectornum := vectornum+1;
    end loop;

    -- summarize results at end of simulation
    if (errors=0) then
      report "NO ERRORS -- " &
             integer'image(vectornum) &
             " tests completed successfully."
             severity failure;
    else
      report integer'image(vectornum) &
             " tests completed, errors=" &
             integer'image(errors)
             severity failure;
    end if;
  end process;
end;
```

The VHDL code uses file reading commands beyond the scope of this chapter, but it gives the sense of what a self-checking testbench looks like in VHDL.

New inputs are applied on the rising edge of the clock, and the output is checked on the falling edge of the clock. Errors are reported as they occur. At the end of the simulation, the testbench prints the total number of test vectors applied and the number of errors detected.

The testbench in HDL Example 4.39 is overkill for such a simple circuit. However, it can easily be modified to test more complex circuits by changing the example.tv file, instantiating the new DUT, and changing a few lines of code to set the inputs and check the outputs.

4.10 SUMMARY

Hardware description languages (HDLs) are extremely important tools for modern digital designers. Once you have learned SystemVerilog or VHDL, you will be able to specify digital systems much faster than if you had to draw the complete schematics. The debug cycle is also often much faster, because modifications require code changes instead of tedious schematic rewiring. However, the debug cycle can be much *longer* using HDLs if you don't have a good idea of the hardware your code implies.

HDLs are used for both simulation and synthesis. Logic simulation is a powerful way to test a system on a computer before it is turned into hardware. Simulators let you check the values of signals inside your system that might be impossible to measure on a physical piece of hardware. Logic synthesis converts the HDL code into digital logic circuits.

The most important thing to remember when you are writing HDL code is that you are describing real hardware, not writing a computer program. The most common beginner's mistake is to write HDL code without thinking about the hardware you intend to produce. If you don't know what hardware you are implying, you are almost certain not to get what you want. Instead, begin by sketching a block diagram of your system, identifying which portions are combinational logic, which portions are sequential circuits or finite state machines, and so forth. Then write HDL code for each portion, using the correct idioms to imply the kind of hardware you need.

Exercises

The following exercises may be done using your favorite HDL. If you have a simulator available, test your design. Print the waveforms and explain how they prove that it works. If you have a synthesizer available, synthesize your code. Print the generated circuit diagram, and explain why it matches your expectations.

Exercise 4.1 Sketch a schematic of the circuit described by the following HDL code. Simplify the schematic so that it shows a minimum number of gates.

SystemVerilog

```
module exercise1(input  logic a, b, c,
                 output logic y, z);

  assign y = a & b & c | a & b & ~c | a & ~b & c;
  assign z = a & b | ~a & ~b;
endmodule
```

VHDL

```
library IEEE; use IEEE.STD_LOGIC_1164.all;

entity exercise1 is
  port(a, b, c: in   STD_LOGIC;
       y, z:    out  STD_LOGIC);
end;

architecture synth of exercise1 is
begin
  y <= (a and b and c) or (a and b and not c) or
       (a and not b and c);
  z <= (a and b) or (not a and not b);
end;
```

Exercise 4.2 Sketch a schematic of the circuit described by the following HDL code. Simplify the schematic so that it shows a minimum number of gates.

SystemVerilog

```
module exercise2(input  logic [3:0] a,
                 output logic [1:0] y);
  always_comb
    if      (a[0]) y = 2'b11;
    else if (a[1]) y = 2'b10;
    else if (a[2]) y = 2'b01;
    else if (a[3]) y = 2'b00;
    else           y = a[1:0];
endmodule
```

VHDL

```
library IEEE; use IEEE.STD_LOGIC_1164.all;

entity exercise2 is
  port(a: in  STD_LOGIC_VECTOR(3 downto 0);
       y: out STD_LOGIC_VECTOR(1 downto 0));
end;

architecture synth of exercise2 is
begin
  process(all) begin
    if    a(0) then y <= "11";
    elsif a(1) then y <= "10";
    elsif a(2) then y <= "01";
    elsif a(3) then y <= "00";
    else            y <= a(1 downto 0);
    end if;
  end process;
end;
```

Exercise 4.3 Write an HDL module that computes a four-input XOR function. The input is $a_{3:0}$, and the output is y.

Exercise 4.4 Write a self-checking testbench for Exercise 4.3. Create a test vector file containing all 16 test cases. Simulate the circuit and show that it works.

Introduce an error in the test vector file and show that the testbench reports a mismatch.

Exercise 4.5 Write an HDL module called `minority`. It receives three inputs, a, b, and c. It produces one output, y, that is TRUE if at least two of the inputs are FALSE.

Exercise 4.6 Write an HDL module for a hexadecimal seven-segment display decoder. The decoder should handle the digits A, B, C, D, E, and F as well as 0–9.

Exercise 4.7 Write a self-checking testbench for Exercise 4.6. Create a test vector file containing all 16 test cases. Simulate the circuit and show that it works. Introduce an error in the test vector file and show that the testbench reports a mismatch.

Exercise 4.8 Write an 8:1 multiplexer module called `mux8` with inputs $s_{2:0}$, d0, d1, d2, d3, d4, d5, d6, d7, and output y.

Exercise 4.9 Write a structural module to compute the logic function, $y = a\overline{b} + \overline{b}\,\overline{c} + \overline{a}bc$, using multiplexer logic. Use the 8:1 multiplexer from Exercise 4.8.

Exercise 4.10 Repeat Exercise 4.9 using a 4:1 multiplexer and as many NOT gates as you need.

Exercise 4.11 Section 4.5.4 pointed out that a synchronizer could be correctly described with blocking assignments if the assignments were given in the proper order. Think of a simple sequential circuit that cannot be correctly described with blocking assignments, regardless of order.

Exercise 4.12 Write an HDL module for an eight-input priority circuit.

Exercise 4.13 Write an HDL module for a 2:4 decoder.

Exercise 4.14 Write an HDL module for a 6:64 decoder using three instances of the 2:4 decoders from Exercise 4.13 and a bunch of three-input AND gates.

Exercise 4.15 Write HDL modules that implement the Boolean equations from Exercise 2.13.

Exercise 4.16 Write an HDL module that implements the circuit from Exercise 2.26.

Exercise 4.17 Write an HDL module that implements the circuit from Exercise 2.27.

Exercise 4.18 Write an HDL module that implements the logic function from Exercise 2.28. Pay careful attention to how you handle don't cares.

Exercise 4.19 Write an HDL module that implements the functions from Exercise 2.35.

Exercise 4.20 Write an HDL module that implements the priority encoder from Exercise 2.36.

Exercise 4.21 Write an HDL module that implements the modified priority encoder from Exercise 2.37.

Exercise 4.22 Write an HDL module that implements the binary-to-thermometer code converter from Exercise 2.38.

Exercise 4.23 Write an HDL module implementing the days-in-month function from Question 2.2.

Exercise 4.24 Sketch the state transition diagram for the FSM described by the following HDL code.

SystemVerilog

```
module fsm2(input  logic clk, reset,
            input  logic a, b,
            output logic y);

  logic [1:0] state, nextstate;

  parameter  S0 = 2'b00;
  parameter  S1 = 2'b01;
  parameter  S2 = 2'b10;
  parameter  S3 = 2'b11;

  always_ff @(posedge clk, posedge reset)
    if (reset) state <= S0;
    else       state <= nextstate;

  always_comb
    case (state)
      S0: if (a ^ b) nextstate = S1;
          else       nextstate = S0;
      S1: if (a & b) nextstate = S2;
          else       nextstate = S0;
      S2: if (a | b) nextstate = S3;
          else       nextstate = S0;
      S3: if (a | b) nextstate = S3;
          else       nextstate = S0;
    endcase

  assign y = (state == S1) | (state == S2);
endmodule
```

VHDL

```
library IEEE; use IEEE.STD_LOGIC_1164.all;

entity fsm2 is
  port(clk, reset: in  STD_LOGIC;
       a, b:       in  STD_LOGIC;
       y:          out STD_LOGIC);
end;

architecture synth of fsm2 is
  type statetype is (S0, S1, S2, S3);
  signal state, nextstate: statetype;
begin
  process(clk, reset) begin
    if reset then state <= S0;
    elsif rising_edge(clk) then
      state <= nextstate;
    end if;
  end process;

  process(all) begin
    case state is
      when S0 => if (a xor b) then
                      nextstate <= S1;
                 else nextstate <= S0;
                 end if;
      when S1 => if (a and b) then
                      nextstate <= S2;
                 else nextstate <= S0;
                 end if;
      when S2 => if (a or b) then
                      nextstate <= S3;
                 else nextstate <= S0;
                 end if;
      when S3 => if (a or b) then
                      nextstate <= S3;
                 else nextstate <= S0;
                 end if;
    end case;
  end process;

  y <= '1' when ((state = S1) or (state = S2))
       else '0';
end;
```

Exercise 4.25 Sketch the state transition diagram for the FSM described by the following HDL code. An FSM of this nature is used in a branch predictor on some microprocessors.

SystemVerilog

```
module fsm1(input  logic clk, reset,
            input  logic taken, back,
            output logic predicttaken);

  logic [4:0] state, nextstate;

  parameter  S0 = 5'b00001;
  parameter  SI = 5'b00010;
  parameter  S2 = 5'b00100;
  parameter  S3 = 5'b01000;
  parameter  S4 = 5'b10000;

  always_ff @(posedge clk, posedge reset)
    if (reset) state <= S2;
    else       state <= nextstate;

  always_comb
    case (state)
      S0: if (taken)  nextstate = S1;
          else        nextstate = S0;
      S1: if (taken)  nextstate = S2;
          else        nextstate = S0;
      S2: if (taken)  nextstate = S3;
          else        nextstate = S1;
      S3: if (taken)  nextstate = S4;
          else        nextstate = S2;
      S4: if (taken)  nextstate = S4;
          else        nextstate = S3;
      default:        nextstate = S2;
    endcase

  assign predicttaken = (state == S4) |
                        (state == S3) |
                        (state == S2 && back);
endmodule
```

VHDL

```
library IEEE; use IEEE.STD_LOGIC_1164. all;

entity fsm1 is
  port(clk, reset:    in  STD_LOGIC;
       taken, back:   in  STD_LOGIC;
       predicttaken: out STD_LOGIC);
end;

architecture synth of fsm1 is
  type statetype is (S0, S1, S2, S3, S4);
  signal state, nextstate: statetype;
begin
  process(clk, reset) begin
    if reset then state <= S2;
    elsif rising_edge(clk) then
      state <= nextstate;
    end if;
  end process;

process(all) begin
  case state is
    when S0 => if taken then
                    nextstate <= S1;
                 else nextstate <= S0;
                 end if;
    when S1 => if taken then
                    nextstate => S2;
                 else nextstate <= S0;
                 end if;
    when S2 => if taken then
                    nextstate <= S3;
                 else nextstate <= S1;
                 end if;
    when S3 => if taken then
                    nextstate <= S4;
                 else nextstate <= S2;
                 end if;
    when S4 => if taken then
                    nextstate <= S4;
                 else nextstate <= S3;
                 end if;
    when others => nextstate <= S2;
  end case;
end process;

-- output logic
predicttaken <= '1' when
              ((state = S4) or (state = S3) or
               (state = S2 and back = '1'))
  else '0';
end;
```

Exercise 4.26 Write an HDL module for an SR latch.

Exercise 4.27 Write an HDL module for a *JK flip-flop*. The flip-flop has inputs, *clk*, *J*, and *K*, and output *Q*. On the rising edge of the clock, *Q* keeps its old value if $J = K = 0$. It sets *Q* to 1 if $J = 1$, resets *Q* to 0 if $K = 1$, and inverts *Q* if $J = K = 1$.

Exercise 4.28 Write an HDL module for the latch from Figure 3.18. Use one assignment statement for each gate. Specify delays of 1 unit or 1 ns to each gate. Simulate the latch and show that it operates correctly. Then increase the inverter delay. How long does the delay have to be before a race condition causes the latch to malfunction?

Exercise 4.29 Write an HDL module for the traffic light controller from Section 3.4.1.

Exercise 4.30 Write three HDL modules for the factored parade mode traffic light controller from Example 3.8. The modules should be called `controller`, `mode`, and `lights`, and they should have the inputs and outputs shown in Figure 3.33(b).

Exercise 4.31 Write an HDL module describing the circuit in Figure 3.42.

Exercise 4.32 Write an HDL module for the FSM with the state transition diagram given in Figure 3.69 from Exercise 3.22.

Exercise 4.33 Write an HDL module for the FSM with the state transition diagram given in Figure 3.70 from Exercise 3.23.

Exercise 4.34 Write an HDL module for the improved traffic light controller from Exercise 3.24.

Exercise 4.35 Write an HDL module for the daughter snail from Exercise 3.25.

Exercise 4.36 Write an HDL module for the soda machine dispenser from Exercise 3.26.

Exercise 4.37 Write an HDL module for the Gray code counter from Exercise 3.27.

Exercise 4.38 Write an HDL module for the UP/DOWN Gray code counter from Exercise 3.28.

Exercise 4.39 Write an HDL module for the FSM from Exercise 3.29.

Exercise 4.40 Write an HDL module for the FSM from Exercise 3.30.

Exercise 4.41 Write an HDL module for the serial two's complementer from Question 3.2.

Exercise 4.42 Write an HDL module for the circuit in Exercise 3.31.

Exercise 4.43 Write an HDL module for the circuit in Exercise 3.32.

Exercise 4.44 Write an HDL module for the circuit in Exercise 3.33.

Exercise 4.45 Write an HDL module for the circuit in Exercise 3.34. You may use the full adder from Section 4.2.5.

SystemVerilog Exercises
The following exercises are specific to SystemVerilog.

Exercise 4.46 What does it mean for a signal to be declared `tri` in SystemVerilog?

Exercise 4.47 Rewrite the `syncbad` module from HDL Example 4.29. Use nonblocking assignments, but change the code to produce a correct synchronizer with two flip-flops.

Exercise 4.48 Consider the following two SystemVerilog modules. Do they have the same function? Sketch the hardware each one implies.

```
module code1(input  logic clk, a, b, c,
             output logic y);
  logic x;
  always_ff @(posedge clk) begin
    x <= a & b;
    y <= x | c;
  end
endmodule
module code2 (input  logic a, b, c, clk,
              output logic y);
  logic x;
  always_ff @(posedge clk) begin
    y <= x | c;
    x <= a & b;
  end
endmodule
```

Exercise 4.49 Repeat Exercise 4.48 if the `<=` is replaced by `=` in every assignment.

Exercise 4.50 The following SystemVerilog modules show errors that the authors have seen students make in the laboratory. Explain the error in each module and show how to fix it.

(a)
```
module latch(input logic        clk,
             input logic [3:0] d,
             output reg  [3:0] q);
    always @(clk)
      if (clk) q <= d;
endmodule
```

(b)
```
module gates(input  logic [3:0] a, b,
             output logic [3:0] y1, y2, y3, y4, y5);
    always @(a)
      begin
        y1 = a & b;
        y2 = a | b;
        y3 = a ^ b;
        y4 = ~(a & b);
        y5 = ~(a | b);
      end
endmodule
```

(c)
```
module mux2(input  logic [3:0] d0, d1,
            input  logic        s,
            output logic [3:0] y);
    always @(posedge s)
      if (s) y <= d1;
      else   y <= d0;
endmodule
```

(d)
```
module twoflops(input  logic clk,
                input  logic d0, d1,
                output logic q0, q1);
    always @(posedge clk)
      q1 = d1;
      q0 = d0;
endmodule
```

(e)
```
module FSM(input  logic clk,
           input  logic a,
           output logic out1, out2);
    logic state;

    // next state logic and register (sequential)
    always_ff @(posedge clk)
      if (state == 0) begin
          if (a) state  <= 1;
      end else begin
          if (~a) state <= 0;
      end
```

```
     always_comb // output logic (combinational)
        if (state == 0)  out1 = 1;
        else            out2 = 1;
   endmodule
```

(f) module priority(input logic [3:0] a,
                     output logic [3:0] y);

```
     always_comb
        if      (a[3]) y = 4'b1000;
        else if (a[2]) y = 4'b0100;
        else if (a[1]) y = 4'b0010;
        else if (a[0]) y = 4'b0001;
   endmodule
```

(g) module divideby3FSM(input logic clk,
                         input logic reset,
                         output logic out);

```
     logic [1:0] state, nextstate;

     parameter  S0 = 2'b00;
     parameter  S1 = 2'b01;
     parameter  S2 = 2'b10;

     // State Register
     always_ff @(posedge clk, posedge reset)
        if (reset)  state <= S0;
        else        state <= nextstate;

     // Next State Logic
     always @(state)
        case (state)
          S0: nextstate = S1;
          S1: nextstate = S2;
          S2: nextstate = S0;
        endcase

     // Output Logic
     assign out = (state == S2);
   endmodule
```

(h) module mux2tri(input logic [3:0] d0, d1,
                    input logic   s,
                    output tri   [3:0] y);
```
     tristate t0(d0, s, y);
     tristate t1(d1, s, y);
   endmodule
```

(i) module floprsen(input logic   clk,
                     input logic   reset,
                     input logic   set,
                     input logic [3:0] d,
                     output logic [3:0] q);

```
        always_ff @(posedge clk, posedge reset)
          if (reset) q <= 0;
          else        q <= d;
        always @(set)
          if (set)  q <= 1;
      endmodule
```

(j)   module and3(input logic a, b, c,
                    output logic y);

```
        logic tmp;

        always @(a, b, c)
        begin
          tmp <= a & b;
          y   <= tmp & c;
        end
      endmodule
```

VHDL Exercises

The following exercises are specific to VHDL.

Exercise 4.51 In VHDL, why is it necessary to write

```
      q <= '1' when state = S0 else '0';
```

rather than simply

```
      q <= (state = S0);
```

Exercise 4.52 Each of the following VHDL modules contains an error. For brevity, only the architecture is shown; assume that the library use clause and entity declaration are correct. Explain the error and show how to fix it.

(a)   architecture synth of latch is
       begin
         process(clk) begin
           if clk = '1' then q <= d;
           end if;
         end process;
       end;

(b)   architecture proc of gates is
       begin
         process(a) begin
           Y1 <= a and b;
           y2 <= a or b;
           y3 <= a xor b;
           y4 <= a nand b;
           y5 <= a nor b;
         end process;
       end;

(c)
```
architecture synth of flop is
begin
  process(clk)
    if rising_edge(clk) then
      q <= d;
end;
```

(d)
```
architecture synth of priority is
begin
  process(all) begin
    if    a(3) then y <= "1000";
    elsif a(2) then y <= "0100";
    elsif a(1) then y <= "0010";
    elsif a(0) then y <= "0001";
    end if;
  end process;
end;
```

(e)
```
architecture synth of divideby3FSM is
    type statetype is (S0, S1, S2);
    signal state, nextstate: statetype;
begin
  process(clk, reset) begin
    if reset then state <= S0;
    elsif rising_edge(clk) then
      state <= nextstate;
    end if;
  end process;

  process(state) begin
    case state is
      when S0 => nextstate <= S1;
      when S1 => nextstate <= S2;
      when S2 => nextstate <= S0;
    end case;
  end process;

  q <= '1' when state = S0 else '0';
end;
```

(f)
```
architecture struct of mux2 is
    component tristate
      port(a: in   STD_LOGIC_VECTOR(3 downto 0);
           en: in   STD_LOGIC;
           y:  out STD_LOGIC_VECTOR(3 downto 0));
    end component;

begin
  t0: tristate port map(d0, s, y);
  t1: tristate port map(d1, s, y);
end;
```

(g)
```
architecture asynchronous of floprs is
begin
  process(clk, reset) begin
    if reset then
      q <= '0';
    elsif rising_edge(clk) then
      q <= d;
    end if;
  end process;

  process(set) begin
    if set then
      q <= '1';
    end if;
  end process;
end;
```

Interview Questions

The following exercises present questions that have been asked at interviews for digital design jobs.

Question 4.1 Write a line of HDL code that gates a 32-bit bus called `data` with another signal called `sel` to produce a 32-bit `result`. If `sel` is TRUE, `result = data`. Otherwise, `result` should be all 0's.

Question 4.2 Explain the difference between blocking and nonblocking assignments in SystemVerilog. Give examples.

Question 4.3 What does the following SystemVerilog statement do?
```
result = | (data[15:0] & 16'hC820);
```

Digital Building Blocks

5

5.1 INTRODUCTION

Up to this point, we have examined the design of combinational and sequential circuits using Boolean equations, schematics, and HDLs. This chapter introduces more elaborate combinational and sequential building blocks used in digital systems. These blocks include arithmetic circuits, counters, shift registers, memory arrays, and logic arrays. These building blocks are not only useful in their own right, but they also demonstrate the principles of hierarchy, modularity, and regularity. The building blocks are hierarchically assembled from simpler components such as logic gates, multiplexers, and decoders. Each building block has a well-defined interface and can be treated as a black box when the underlying implementation is unimportant. The regular structure of each building block is easily extended to different sizes. In Chapter 7, we use many of these building blocks to build a microprocessor.

5.2 ARITHMETIC CIRCUITS

Arithmetic circuits are the central building blocks of computers. Computers and digital logic perform many arithmetic functions: addition, subtraction, comparisons, shifts, multiplication, and division. This section describes hardware implementations for all of these operations.

5.2.1 Addition

Addition is one of the most common operations in digital systems. We first consider how to add two 1-bit binary numbers. We then extend to N-bit binary numbers. Adders also illustrate trade-offs between speed and complexity.

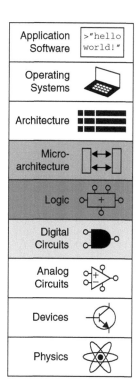

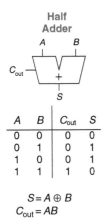

Half
Adder

A B

C_{out} — +

S

A	B	C_{out}	S
0	0	0	0
0	1	0	1
1	0	0	1
1	1	1	0

$S = A \oplus B$
$C_{out} = AB$

Figure 5.1 1-bit half adder

```
  1
0001
+0101
0110
```

Figure 5.2 Carry bit

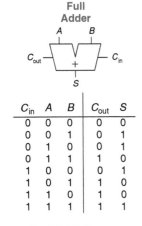

Full
Adder

A B

C_{out} — + — C_{in}

S

C_{in}	A	B	C_{out}	S
0	0	0	0	0
0	0	1	0	1
0	1	0	0	1
0	1	1	1	0
1	0	0	0	1
1	0	1	1	0
1	1	0	1	0
1	1	1	1	1

$S = A \oplus B \oplus C_{in}$
$C_{out} = AB + AC_{in} + BC_{in}$

Figure 5.3 1-bit full adder

Half Adder

We begin by building a 1-bit *half adder*. As shown in Figure 5.1, the half adder has two inputs, A and B, and two outputs, S and C_{out}. S is the sum of A and B. If A and B are both 1, S is 2, which cannot be represented with a single binary digit. Instead, it is indicated with a carry out C_{out} in the next column. The half adder can be built from an XOR gate and an AND gate.

In a multi-bit adder, C_{out} is added or *carried in* to the next most significant bit. For example, in Figure 5.2, the carry bit shown in blue is the output C_{out} of the first column of 1-bit addition and the input C_{in} to the second column of addition. However, the half adder lacks a C_{in} input to accept C_{out} of the previous column. The *full adder*, described in the next section, solves this problem.

Full Adder

A *full adder*, introduced in Section 2.1, accepts the carry in C_{in} as shown in Figure 5.3. The figure also shows the output equations for S and C_{out}.

Carry Propagate Adder

An N-bit adder sums two N-bit inputs, A and B, and a carry in C_{in} to produce an N-bit result S and a carry out C_{out}. It is commonly called a *carry propagate adder* (CPA) because the carry out of one bit propagates into the next bit. The symbol for a CPA is shown in Figure 5.4; it is drawn just like a full adder except that A, B, and S are busses rather than single bits. Three common CPA implementations are called ripple-carry adders, carry-lookahead adders, and prefix adders.

Ripple-Carry Adder

The simplest way to build an N-bit carry propagate adder is to chain together N full adders. The C_{out} of one stage acts as the C_{in} of the next stage, as shown in Figure 5.5 for 32-bit addition. This is called a *ripple-carry adder*. It is a good application of modularity and regularity: the full adder module is reused many times to form a larger system. The ripple-carry adder has the disadvantage of being slow when N is large. S_{31} depends on C_{30}, which depends on C_{29}, which depends on C_{28}, and so forth all the way back to C_{in}, as shown in blue in Figure 5.5. We say that the carry *ripples* through the carry chain. The delay of the adder, t_{ripple},

A B

C_{out} — + — C_{in}

S

Figure 5.4 Carry propagate adder

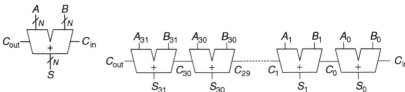

Figure 5.5 32-bit ripple-carry adder

grows directly with the number of bits, as given in Equation 5.1, where t_{FA} is the delay of a full adder.

$$t_{\text{ripple}} = Nt_{FA} \tag{5.1}$$

Carry-Lookahead Adder

The fundamental reason that large ripple-carry adders are slow is that the carry signals must propagate through every bit in the adder. A *carry-lookahead* adder (*CLA*) is another type of carry propagate adder that solves this problem by dividing the adder into *blocks* and providing circuitry to quickly determine the carry out of a block as soon as the carry in is known. Thus it is said to *look ahead* across the blocks rather than waiting to ripple through all the full adders inside a block. For example, a 32-bit adder may be divided into eight 4-bit blocks.

CLAs use *generate* (G) and *propagate* (P) signals that describe how a column or block determines the carry out. The ith column of an adder is said to *generate* a carry if it produces a carry out independent of the carry in. The ith column of an adder is guaranteed to generate a carry C_i if A_i and B_i are both 1. Hence G_i, the generate signal for column i, is calculated as $G_i = A_i B_i$. The column is said to *propagate* a carry if it produces a carry out whenever there is a carry in. The ith column will propagate a carry in, C_{i-1}, if either A_i or B_i is 1. Thus, $P_i = A_i + B_i$. Using these definitions, we can rewrite the carry logic for a particular column of the adder. The ith column of an adder will generate a carry out C_i if it either generates a carry, G_i, or propagates a carry in, $P_i C_{i-1}$. In equation form,

$$C_i = A_i B_i + (A_i + B_i)C_{i-1} = G_i + P_i C_{i-1} \tag{5.2}$$

The generate and propagate definitions extend to multiple-bit blocks. A block is said to generate a carry if it produces a carry out independent of the carry in to the block. The block is said to propagate a carry if it produces a carry out whenever there is a carry in to the block. We define $G_{i:j}$ and $P_{i:j}$ as generate and propagate signals for blocks spanning columns i through j.

A block generates a carry if the most significant column generates a carry, or if the most significant column propagates a carry and the previous column generated a carry, and so forth. For example, the generate logic for a block spanning columns 3 through 0 is

$$G_{3:0} = G_3 + P_3\big(G_2 + P_2(G_1 + P_1 G_0)\big) \tag{5.3}$$

A block propagates a carry if all the columns in the block propagate the carry. For example, the propagate logic for a block spanning columns 3 through 0 is

$$P_{3:0} = P_3 P_2 P_1 P_0 \tag{5.4}$$

Using the block generate and propagate signals, we can quickly compute the carry out of the block, C_i, using the carry in to the block, C_{j-1}.

$$C_i = G_{i:j} + P_{i:j} C_{j-1} \tag{5.5}$$

Schematics typically show signals flowing from left to right. Arithmetic circuits break this rule because the carries flow from right to left (from the least significant column to the most significant column).

Throughout the ages, people have used many devices to perform arithmetic. Toddlers count on their fingers (and some adults stealthily do too). The Chinese and Babylonians invented the abacus as early as 2400 BC. Slide rules, invented in 1630, were in use until the 1970's, when scientific hand calculators became prevalent. Computers and digital calculators are ubiquitous today. What will be next?

Figure 5.6(a) shows a 32-bit carry-lookahead adder composed of eight 4-bit blocks. Each block contains a 4-bit ripple-carry adder and some lookahead logic to compute the carry out of the block given the carry in, as shown in Figure 5.6(b). The AND and OR gates needed to compute the single-bit generate and propagate signals, G_i and P_i, from A_i and B_i are left out for brevity. Again, the carry-lookahead adder demonstrates modularity and regularity.

All of the CLA blocks compute the single-bit and block generate and propagate signals simultaneously. The critical path starts with computing G_0 and $G_{3:0}$ in the first CLA block. C_{in} then advances directly to C_{out} through the AND/OR gate in each block until the last. For a large adder, this is much faster than waiting for the carries to ripple through each consecutive bit of the adder. Finally, the critical path through the last block contains a short ripple-carry adder. Thus, an N-bit adder divided into k-bit blocks has a delay

$$t_{CLA} = t_{pg} + t_{pg\_block} + \left(\frac{N}{k} - 1\right)t_{AND\_OR} + kt_{FA} \tag{5.6}$$

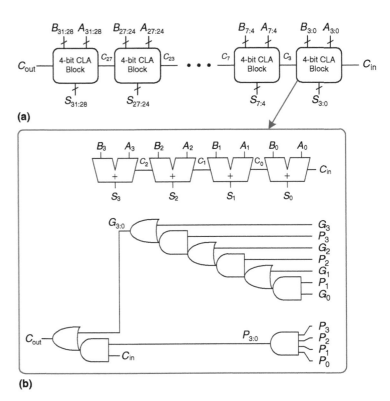

Figure 5.6 (a) 32-bit carry-lookahead adder (CLA), (b) 4-bit CLA block

where t_{pg} is the delay of the individual generate/propagate gates (a single AND or OR gate) to generate P_i and G_i, t_{pg_block} is the delay to find the generate/propagate signals $P_{i:j}$ and $G_{i:j}$ for a k-bit block, and t_{AND_OR} is the delay from C_{in} to C_{out} through the final AND/OR logic of the k-bit CLA block. For $N > 16$, the carry-lookahead adder is generally much faster than the ripple-carry adder. However, the adder delay still increases linearly with N.

Example 5.1 RIPPLE-CARRY ADDER AND CARRY-LOOKAHEAD
ADDER DELAY

Compare the delays of a 32-bit ripple-carry adder and a 32-bit carry-lookahead adder with 4-bit blocks. Assume that each two-input gate delay is 100 ps and that a full adder delay is 300 ps.

Solution: According to Equation 5.1, the propagation delay of the 32-bit ripple-carry adder is 32×300 ps $= 9.6$ ns.

The CLA has $t_{pg} = 100$ ps, $t_{pg\_block} = 6 \times 100$ ps $= 600$ ps, and $t_{AND\_OR} = 2 \times 100$ ps $= 200$ ps. According to Equation 5.6, the propagation delay of the 32-bit carry-lookahead adder with 4-bit blocks is thus 100 ps $+ 600$ ps $+ (32/4 - 1) \times 200$ ps $+ (4 \times 300$ ps$) = 3.3$ ns, almost three times faster than the ripple-carry adder.

Prefix Adder*

Prefix adders extend the generate and propagate logic of the carry-lookahead adder to perform addition even faster. They first compute G and P for pairs of columns, then for blocks of 4, then for blocks of 8, then 16, and so forth until the generate signal for every column is known. The sums are computed from these generate signals.

In other words, the strategy of a prefix adder is to compute the carry in C_{i-1} for each column i as quickly as possible, then to compute the sum, using

$$S_i = (A_i \oplus B_i) \oplus C_{i-1} \tag{5.7}$$

Define column $i = -1$ to hold C_{in}, so $G_{-1} = C_{in}$ and $P_{-1} = 0$. Then $C_{i-1} = G_{i-1:-1}$ because there will be a carry out of column $i-1$ if the block spanning columns $i-1$ through -1 generates a carry. The generated carry is either generated in column $i-1$ or generated in a previous column and propagated. Thus, we rewrite Equation 5.7 as

$$S_i = (A_i \oplus B_i) \oplus G_{i-1:-1} \tag{5.8}$$

Hence, the main challenge is to rapidly compute all the block generate signals $G_{-1:-1}, G_{0:-1}, G_{1:-1}, G_{2:-1}, \ldots, G_{N-2:-1}$. These signals, along with $P_{-1:-1}, P_{0:-1}, P_{1:-1}, P_{2:-1}, \ldots, P_{N-2:-1}$, are called *prefixes*.

Early computers used ripple-carry adders, because components were expensive and ripple-carry adders used the least hardware. Virtually all modern PCs use prefix adders on critical paths, because transistors are now cheap and speed is of great importance.

Figure 5.7 shows an $N = 16$-bit prefix adder. The adder begins with a *precomputation* to form P_i and G_i for each column from A_i and B_i using AND and OR gates. It then uses $\log_2 N = 4$ levels of black cells to form the prefixes of $G_{i:j}$ and $P_{i:j}$. A black cell takes inputs from the upper part of a block spanning bits $i{:}k$ and from the lower part spanning bits $k{-}1{:}j$. It combines these parts to form generate and propagate signals for the entire block spanning bits $i{:}j$ using the equations

$$G_{i:j} = G_{i:k} + P_{i:k}G_{k-1:j} \tag{5.9}$$

$$P_{i:j} = P_{i:k}P_{k-1:j} \tag{5.10}$$

In other words, a block spanning bits $i{:}j$ will generate a carry if the upper part generates a carry or if the upper part propagates a carry generated in the lower part. The block will propagate a carry if both the upper and

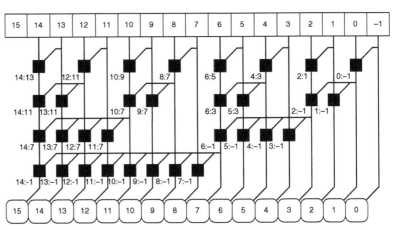

Figure 5.7 16-bit prefix adder

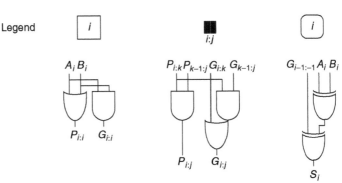

lower parts propagate the carry. Finally, the prefix adder computes the sums using Equation 5.8.

In summary, the prefix adder achieves a delay that grows logarithmically rather than linearly with the number of columns in the adder. This speedup is significant, especially for adders with 32 or more bits, but it comes at the expense of more hardware than a simple carry-lookahead adder. The network of black cells is called a *prefix tree*.

The general principle of using prefix trees to perform computations in time that grows logarithmically with the number of inputs is a powerful technique. With some cleverness, it can be applied to many other types of circuits (see, for example, Exercise 5.7).

The critical path for an N-bit prefix adder involves the precomputation of P_i and G_i followed by $\log_2 N$ stages of black prefix cells to obtain all the prefixes. $G_{i-1:-1}$ then proceeds through the final XOR gate at the bottom to compute S_i. Mathematically, the delay of an N-bit prefix adder is

$$t_{PA} = t_{pg} + \log_2 N(t_{pg-\text{prefix}}) + t_{\text{XOR}} \qquad (5.11)$$

where t_{pg_prefix} is the delay of a black prefix cell.

Example 5.2 PREFIX ADDER DELAY

Compute the delay of a 32-bit prefix adder. Assume that each two-input gate delay is 100 ps.

Solution: The propagation delay of each black prefix cell t_{pg_prefix} is 200 ps (i.e., two gate delays). Thus, using Equation 5.11, the propagation delay of the 32-bit prefix adder is 100 ps + $\log_2(32) \times 200$ ps + 100 ps = 1.2 ns, which is about three times faster than the carry-lookahead adder and eight times faster than the ripple-carry adder from Example 5.1. In practice, the benefits are not quite this great, but prefix adders are still substantially faster than the alternatives.

Putting It All Together

This section introduced the half adder, full adder, and three types of carry propagate adders: ripple-carry, carry-lookahead, and prefix adders. Faster adders require more hardware and therefore are more expensive and power-hungry. These trade-offs must be considered when choosing an appropriate adder for a design.

Hardware description languages provide the + operation to specify a CPA. Modern synthesis tools select among many possible implementations, choosing the cheapest (smallest) design that meets the speed requirements. This greatly simplifies the designer's job. HDL Example 5.1 describes a CPA with carries in and out.

HDL Example 5.1 ADDER

SystemVerilog

```
module adder #(parameter N = 8)
              (input  logic [N-1:0] a, b,
               input  logic         cin,
               output logic [N-1:0] s,
               output logic         cout);

  assign {cout, s} = a + b + cin;
endmodule
```

VHDL

```
library IEEE; use IEEE.STD_LOGIC_1164.ALL;
use IEEE.NUMERIC_STD_UNSIGNED.ALL;

entity adder is
  generic(N: integer := 8);
  port(a, b: in  STD_LOGIC_VECTOR(N-1 downto 0);
       cin:  in  STD_LOGIC;
       s:    out STD_LOGIC_VECTOR(N-1 downto 0);
       cout: out STD_LOGIC);
end;

architecture synth of adder is
  signal result: STD_LOGIC_VECTOR(N downto 0);
begin
  result <= ("0" & a) + ("0" & b) + cin;
  s    <= result(N-1 downto 0);
  cout <= result(N);
end;
```

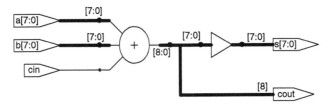

Figure 5.8 **Synthesized adder**

5.2.2 Subtraction

Recall from Section 1.4.6 that adders can add positive and negative numbers using two's complement number representation. Subtraction is almost as easy: flip the sign of the second number, then add. Flipping the sign of a two's complement number is done by inverting the bits and adding 1.

To compute $Y = A - B$, first create the two's complement of B: Invert the bits of B to obtain $\overline{B}$ and add 1 to get $-B = \overline{B} + 1$. Add this quantity to A to get $Y = A + \overline{B} + 1 = A - B$. This sum can be performed with a single CPA by adding $A + \overline{B}$ with $C_{in} = 1$. Figure 5.9 shows the symbol for a subtractor and the underlying hardware for performing $Y = A - B$. HDL Example 5.2 describes a subtractor.

Figure 5.9 **Subtractor: (a) symbol, (b) implementation**

5.2.3 Comparators

A *comparator* determines whether two binary numbers are equal or if one is greater or less than the other. A comparator receives two N-bit binary numbers A and B. There are two common types of comparators.

HDL Example 5.2 SUBTRACTOR

SystemVerilog

```
module subtractor #(parameter N = 8)
                 (input  logic [N-1:0] a, b,
                  output logic [N-1:0] y);

  assign y = a - b;
endmodule
```

VHDL

```
library IEEE; use IEEE.STD_LOGIC_1164.ALL;
use IEEE.NUMERIC_STD_UNSIGNED.ALL;

entity subtractor is
  generic(N: integer := 8);
  port(a, b: in  STD_LOGIC_VECTOR(N-1 downto 0);
       y:    out STD_LOGIC_VECTOR(N-1 downto 0));
end;

architecture synth of subtractor is
begin
  y <= a - b;
end;
```

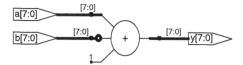

Figure 5.10 Synthesized subtractor

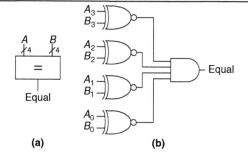

Figure 5.11 4-bit equality comparator: (a) symbol, (b) implementation

An *equality comparator* produces a single output indicating whether A is equal to B ($A == B$). A *magnitude comparator* produces one or more outputs indicating the relative values of A and B.

The equality comparator is the simpler piece of hardware. Figure 5.11 shows the symbol and implementation of a 4-bit equality comparator. It first checks to determine whether the corresponding bits in each column of A and B are equal using XNOR gates. The numbers are equal if all of the columns are equal.

Magnitude comparison of signed numbers is usually done by computing $A - B$ and looking at the sign (most significant bit) of the result as shown in Figure 5.12. If the result is negative (i.e., the sign bit is 1), then A is less than B. Otherwise A is greater than or equal to B. This comparator, however, functions incorrectly upon overflow. Exercises 5.9 and 5.10 explore this limitation and how to fix it.

Figure 5.12 *N*-bit signed comparator

HDL Example 5.3 COMPARATORS

SystemVerilog

```
module comparator #(parameter N = 8)
                   (input  logic [N-1:0] a, b,
                    output logic eq, neq, lt, lte, gt, gte);

   assign eq  = (a == b);
   assign neq = (a != b);
   assign lt  = (a < b);
   assign lte = (a <= b);
   assign gt  = (a > b);
   assign gte = (a >= b);
endmodule
```

VHDL

```
library IEEE; use IEEE.STD_LOGIC_1164.ALL;

entity comparators is
   generic(N: integer : = 8);
   port(a, b: in STD_LOGIC_VECTOR(N-1 downto 0);
        eq, neq, lt, lte, gt, gte: out STD_LOGIC);
end;

architecture synth of comparator is
begin
   eq  <= '1' when (a = b)   else '0';
   neq <= '1' when (a /= b)  else '0';
   lt  <= '1' when (a < b)   else '0';
   lte <= '1' when (a <= b)  else '0';
   gt  <= '1' when (a > b)   else '0';
   gte <= '1' when (a >= b)  else '0';
end;
```

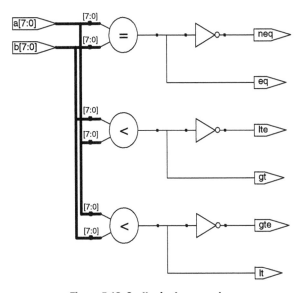

Figure 5.13 **Synthesized comparators**

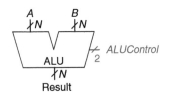

Figure 5.14 **ALU symbol**

HDL Example 5.3 shows how to use various comparison operations for unsigned numbers.

5.2.4 ALU

An *Arithmetic/Logical Unit* (*ALU*) combines a variety of mathematical and logical operations into a single unit. For example, a typical ALU

Table 5.1 **ALU operations**

$ALUControl_{1:0}$	Function
00	Add
01	Subtract
10	AND
11	OR

might perform addition, subtraction, AND, and OR operations. The ALU forms the heart of most computer systems.

Figure 5.14 shows the symbol for an N-bit ALU with N-bit inputs and outputs. The ALU receives a 2-bit control signal *ALUControl* that specifies which function to perform. Control signals will generally be shown in blue to distinguish them from the data. Table 5.1 lists typical functions that the ALU can perform.

Figure 5.15 shows an implementation of the ALU. The ALU contains an N-bit adder and N two-input AND and OR gates. It also contains inverters and a multiplexer to invert input B when $ALUControl_0$ is asserted. A 4:1 multiplexer chooses the desired function based on *ALUControl*.

More specifically, if $ALUControl = 00$, the output multiplexer chooses $A + B$. If $ALUControl = 01$, the ALU computes $A - B$. (Recall from Section 5.2.2 that $\overline{B} + 1 = -B$ in two's complement arithmetic. Because $ALUControl_0$ is 1, the adder receives inputs A and $\overline{B}$ and an asserted carry in, causing

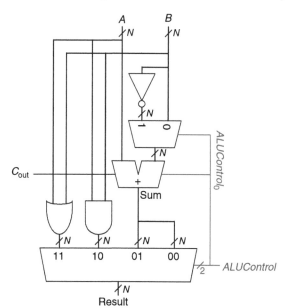

Figure 5.15 **N-bit ALU**

it to perform subtraction: $A + \overline{B} + 1 = A - B$.) If $ALUControl = 10$, the ALU computes A AND B. If $ALUControl = 11$, the ALU performs A OR B.

Some ALUs produce extra outputs, called *flags*, that indicate information about the ALU output. Figure 5.16 shows the ALU symbol with a 4-bit *ALUFlags* output. As shown in the schematic of this ALU in Figure 5.17, the *ALUFlags* output is composed of the N, Z, C, and V flags that indicate, respectively, that the ALU output is negative or zero or that the adder produced a carry out or overflowed. Recall that the most significant bit of a two's complement number is 1 if it is negative and 0 otherwise. Thus, the N flag is connected to the most significant bit of the ALU output, $Result_{31}$. The Z flag is asserted when all of the bits of *Result* are 0, as detected by the N-bit NOR gate in Figure 5.17. The C flag is asserted when the adder produces a carry out *and* the ALU is performing addition or subtraction ($ALUControl_1 = 0$).

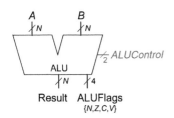

Figure 5.16 ALU symbol with output flags

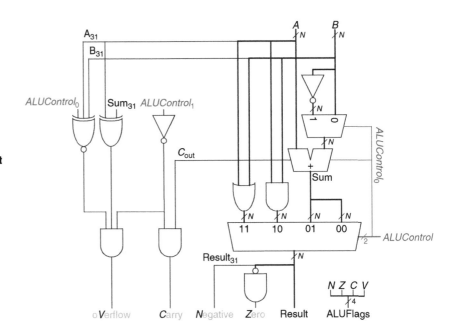

Figure 5.17 N-bit ALU with output flags

Overflow detection, as shown on the left side of Figure 5.17, is trickier. Recall from Section 1.4.6 that overflow occurs when the addition of two same signed numbers produces a result with the opposite sign. So, V is asserted when all three of the following conditions are true: (1) the ALU is performing addition or subtraction ($ALUControl_1 = 0$), (2) A and *Sum* have opposite signs, as detected by the XOR gate, and, as detected by the XNOR gate, (3) either A and B have the same sign and the adder is performing addition ($ALUControl_0 = 0$) or A and B have opposite signs and the adder is performing subtraction ($ALUControl_0 = 1$). The 3-input AND gate detects when all three conditions are true and asserts V.

The HDL for an N-bit ALU with output flags is left to Exercises 5.11 and 5.12. There are many variations on this basic ALU that support other functions, such as XOR or equality comparison.

5.2.5 Shifters and Rotators

Shifters and *rotators* move bits and multiply or divide by powers of 2. As the name implies, a shifter shifts a binary number left or right by a specified number of positions. There are several kinds of commonly used shifters:

▸ **Logical shifter**—shifts the number to the left (LSL) or right (LSR) and fills empty spots with 0's.

  Ex: 11001 LSR 2 = 00110; 11001 LSL 2 = 00100

▸ **Arithmetic shifter**—is the same as a logical shifter, but on right shifts fills the most significant bits with a copy of the old most significant bit (msb). This is useful for multiplying and dividing signed numbers (see Sections 5.2.6 and 5.2.7). Arithmetic shift left (ASL) is the same as logical shift left (LSL).

  Ex: 11001 ASR 2 = 11110; 11001 ASL 2 = 00100

▸ **Rotator**—rotates number in a circle such that empty spots are filled with bits shifted off the other end.

  Ex: 11001 ROR 2 = 01110; 11001 ROL 2 = 00111

An N-bit shifter can be built from N N:1 multiplexers. The input is shifted by 0 to $N - 1$ bits, depending on the value of the $\log_2 N$-bit select lines. Figure 5.18 shows the symbol and hardware of 4-bit shifters. The operators $<<$, $>>$, and $>>>$ typically indicate shift left, logical shift right, and arithmetic shift right, respectively. Depending on the value of the 2-bit shift amount $shamt_{1:0}$, the output Y receives the input A shifted by 0 to 3 bits. For all shifters, when $shamt_{1:0} = 00$, $Y = A$. Exercise 5.18 covers rotator designs.

A left shift is a special case of multiplication. A left shift by N bits multiplies the number by 2^N. For example, $000011_2 << 4 = 110000_2$ is equivalent to $3_{10} \times 2^4 = 48_{10}$.

An arithmetic right shift is a special case of division. An arithmetic right shift by N bits divides the number by 2^N. For example, $11100_2 >>> 2 = 11111_2$ is equivalent to $-4_{10}/2^2 = -1_{10}$.

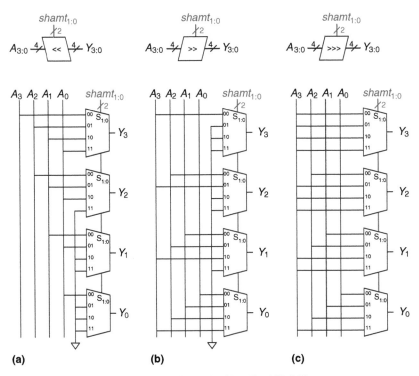

(a)   **(b)**   **(c)**

Figure 5.18 4-bit shifters: (a) shift left, (b) logical shift right, (c) arithmetic shift right

Figure 5.19 Multiplication:
(a) decimal, (b) binary

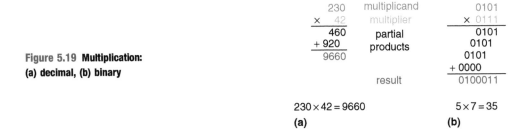

5.2.6 Multiplication*

Multiplication of unsigned binary numbers is similar to decimal multiplication but involves only 1's and 0's. Figure 5.19 compares multiplication in decimal and binary. In both cases, *partial products* are formed by multiplying a single digit of the multiplier with the entire multiplicand. The shifted partial products are summed to form the result.

In general, an $N \times N$ multiplier multiplies two N-bit numbers and produces a $2N$-bit result. The partial products in binary multiplication are either the multiplicand or all 0's. Multiplication of 1-bit binary numbers is equivalent to the AND operation, so AND gates are used to form the partial products.

Signed and unsigned multiplication differ. For example, consider $0xFE \times 0xFD$. If these 8-bit numbers are interpreted as signed integers, they represent -2 and -3, so the 16-bit product is $0x0006$. If these numbers are interpreted as unsigned integers, the 16-bit product is $0xFB06$. Notice that in either case, the least significant byte is $0x06$.

Figure 5.20 shows the symbol, function, and implementation of an unsigned 4×4 multiplier. The unsigned multiplier receives the multiplicand and multiplier, A and B, and produces the product P. Figure 5.20(b) shows how partial products are formed. Each partial product is a single multiplier bit (B_3, B_2, B_1, or B_0) AND the multiplicand bits (A_3, A_2, A_1, A_0). With N-bit operands, there are N partial products and $N-1$ stages of 1-bit adders. For example, for a 4×4 multiplier, the partial product of the first row is B_0 AND (A_3, A_2, A_1, A_0). This partial product is added to the shifted second partial product, B_1 AND (A_3, A_2, A_1, A_0). Subsequent rows of AND gates and adders form and add the remaining partial products.

The HDL for signed and unsigned multipliers is in HDL Example 4.33. As with adders, many different multiplier designs with different speed/cost trade-offs exist. Synthesis tools may pick the most appropriate design given the timing constraints.

A *multiply accumulate* operation multiplies two numbers and adds them to a third number, typically the accumulated value. These operations, also called MACs, are often used in *digital signal processing* (DSP) algorithms such as the Fourier transform, which requires a summation of products.

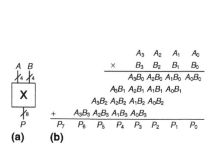

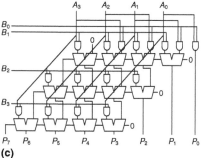

Figure 5.20 4×4 multiplier: (a) symbol, (b) function, (c) implementation

5.2.7 Division*

Binary division can be performed using the following algorithm for N-bit unsigned numbers in the range $[0, 2^{N-1}]$:

```
R' = 0
for i = N-1 to 0
    R = {R' << 1, A_i}
    D = R - B
    if D < 0 then    Q_i = 0, R' = R    // R < B
    else             Q_i = 1, R' = D    // R ≥ B
    R = R'
```

The *partial remainder* R is initialized to 0 $(R' = 0)$, and the most significant bit of the dividend A becomes the least significant bit of R $(R = \{R' << 1, A_i\})$. The divisor B is subtracted from this partial remainder to determine whether it fits $(D = R - B)$. If the difference D is negative (i.e., the sign bit of D is 1), then the quotient bit Q_i is 0 and the difference is discarded. Otherwise, Q_i is 1, and the partial remainder is updated to be the difference. In any event, the partial remainder is then doubled (left-shifted by one column), the next most significant bit of A becomes the least significant bit of R, and the process repeats. The result satisfies $\frac{A}{B} = Q + \frac{R}{B}$.

Figure 5.21 Array divider

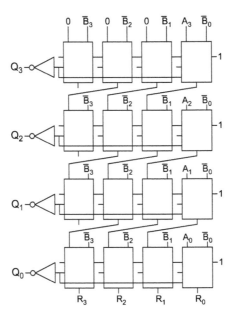

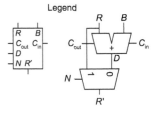

Figure 5.21 shows a schematic of a 4-bit array divider. The divider computes A/B and produces a quotient Q and a remainder R. The legend shows the symbol and schematic for each block in the array divider. Each row performs one iteration of the division algorithm. Specifically, each row calculates the difference $D = R - B$. (Recall that $R + \overline{B} + 1 = R - B$). The signal N indicates whether D is negative. So a row's multiplexer select lines receive the most significant bit of D, which is 1 when the difference is negative. The quotient (Q_i) is 0 when D is negative and 1 otherwise. The multiplexer passes R to the next row if the difference is negative and D otherwise. The following row shifts the new partial remainder left by one bit, appends the next most significant bit of A, and then repeats the process.

The delay of an N-bit array divider increases proportionally to N^2 because the carry must ripple through all N stages in a row before the sign is determined and the multiplexer selects R or D. This repeats for all N rows. Division is a slow and expensive operation in hardware and therefore should be used as infrequently as possible.

5.2.8 Further Reading

Computer arithmetic could be the subject of an entire text. *Digital Arithmetic*, by Ercegovac and Lang, is an excellent overview of the entire field. *CMOS VLSI Design*, by Weste and Harris, covers high-performance circuit designs for arithmetic operations.

5.3 NUMBER SYSTEMS

Computers operate on both integers and fractions. So far, we have only considered representing signed or unsigned integers, as introduced in Section 1.4. This section introduces fixed- and floating-point number systems that can represent rational numbers. Fixed-point numbers are analogous to decimals; some of the bits represent the integer part, and the rest represent the fraction. Floating-point numbers are analogous to scientific notation, with a mantissa and an exponent.

5.3.1 Fixed-Point Number Systems

Fixed-point notation has an implied *binary point* between the integer and fraction bits, analogous to the decimal point between the integer and fraction digits of an ordinary decimal number. For example, Figure 5.22(a) shows a fixed-point number with four integer bits and four fraction bits. Figure 5.22(b) shows the implied binary point in blue, and Figure 5.22(c) shows the equivalent decimal value. The integer bits are called the *high word* and the fraction bits are called the *low word*.

(a) 01101100

(b) 0110.1100

(c) $2^2 + 2^1 + 2^{-1} + 2^{-2} = 6.75$

Figure 5.22 Fixed-point notation of 6.75 with four integer bits and four fraction bits

(a) 0010.0110

(b) 1010.0110

(c) 1101.1010

Figure 5.23 Fixed-point representation of −2.375: (a) absolute value, (b) sign and magnitude, (c) two's complement

Signed fixed-point numbers can use either two's complement or sign/magnitude notation. Figure 5.23 shows the fixed-point representation of −2.375 using both notations with four integer and four fraction bits. The implicit binary point is shown in blue for clarity. In sign/magnitude form, the most significant bit is used to indicate the sign. The two's complement representation is formed by inverting the bits of the absolute value and adding a 1 to the least significant (rightmost) bit. In this case, the least significant bit position is in the 2^{-4} column.

Like all binary number representations, fixed-point numbers are just a collection of bits. There is no way of knowing the existence of the binary point except through agreement of those people interpreting the number.

Example 5.3 ARITHMETIC WITH FIXED-POINT NUMBERS

Compute $0.75 + -0.625$ using fixed-point numbers.

Solution: First convert 0.625, the magnitude of the second number, to fixed-point binary notation. $0.625 \geq 2^{-1}$, so there is a 1 in the 2^{-1} column, leaving $0.625 - 0.5 = 0.125$. Because $0.125 < 2^{-2}$, there is a 0 in the 2^{-2} column. Because $0.125 \geq 2^{-3}$, there is a 1 in the 2^{-3} column, leaving $0.125 - 0.125 = 0$. Thus, there must be a 0 in the 2^{-4} column. Putting this all together, $0.625_{10} = 0000.1010_2$.

Use two's complement representation for signed numbers so that addition works correctly. Figure 5.24 shows the conversion of −0.625 to fixed-point two's complement notation.

Figure 5.25 shows the fixed-point binary addition and the decimal equivalent for comparison. Note that the leading 1 in the binary fixed-point addition of Figure 5.25(a) is discarded from the 8-bit result.

Fixed-point number systems are commonly used for banking and financial applications that require precision but not a large range. Digital signal processing (DSP) applications also often use fixed-point numbers because the computations are faster and consume less power than they would in floating-point.

5.3.2 Floating-Point Number Systems*

Floating-point numbers are analogous to scientific notation. They circumvent the limitation of having a constant number of integer and fraction bits, allowing the representation of very large and very small numbers.

Figure 5.24 Fixed-point two's complement conversion

```
  0000.1010    Binary Magnitude
  1111.0101    One's Complement
+        1    Add 1
  1111.0110    Two's Complement
```

Figure 5.25 Addition: (a) binary fixed-point, (b) decimal equivalent

```
    0000.1100          0.75
  + 1111.0110      + (−0.625)
   10000.0010          0.125
       (a)             (b)
```

Like scientific notation, floating-point numbers have a *sign*, *mantissa* (M), *base* (B), and *exponent* (E), as shown in Figure 5.26. For example, the number 4.1×10^3 is the decimal scientific notation for 4100. It has a mantissa of 4.1, a base of 10, and an exponent of 3. The decimal point *floats* to the position right after the most significant digit. Floating-point numbers are base 2 with a binary mantissa. 32 bits are used to represent 1 sign bit, 8 exponent bits, and 23 mantissa bits.

$$\pm M \times B^E$$

Figure 5.26 Floating-point numbers

Example 5.4 32-BIT FLOATING-POINT NUMBERS

Show the floating-point representation of the decimal number 228.

Solution: First convert the decimal number into binary: $228_{10} = 11100100_2 = 1.11001_2 \times 2^7$. Figure 5.27 shows the 32-bit encoding, which will be modified later for efficiency. The sign bit is positive (0), the 8 exponent bits give the value 7, and the remaining 23 bits are the mantissa.

In binary floating-point, the first bit of the mantissa (to the left of the binary point) is always 1 and therefore need not be stored. It is called the *implicit leading one*. Figure 5.28 shows the modified floating-point representation of $228_{10} = 11100100_2 \times 2^0 = 1.11001_2 \times 2^7$. The implicit leading one is not included in the 23-bit mantissa for efficiency. Only the fraction bits are stored. This frees up an extra bit for useful data.

We make one final modification to the exponent field. The exponent needs to represent both positive and negative exponents. To do so, floating-point uses a *biased* exponent, which is the original exponent plus a constant bias. 32-bit floating-point uses a bias of 127. For example, for the exponent 7, the biased exponent is $7 + 127 = 134 = 10000110_2$. For the exponent -4, the biased exponent is: $-4 + 127 = 123 = 01111011_2$. Figure 5.29 shows $1.11001_2 \times 2^7$ represented in floating-point notation with an implicit leading one and a biased exponent of

As may be apparent, there are many reasonable ways to represent floating-point numbers. For many years, computer manufacturers used incompatible floating-point formats. Results from one computer could not directly be interpreted by another computer.

The Institute of Electrical and Electronics Engineers solved this problem by creating the *IEEE 754 floating-point standard* in 1985 defining floating-point numbers. This floating-point format is now almost universally used and is the one discussed in this section.

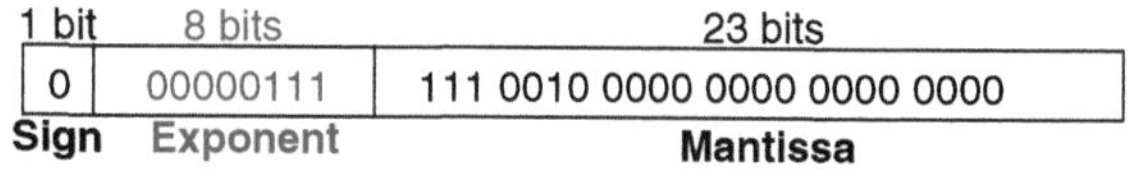

1 bit	8 bits	23 bits
0	00000111	111 0010 0000 0000 0000 0000
Sign	**Exponent**	**Mantissa**

Figure 5.27 32-bit floating-point version 1

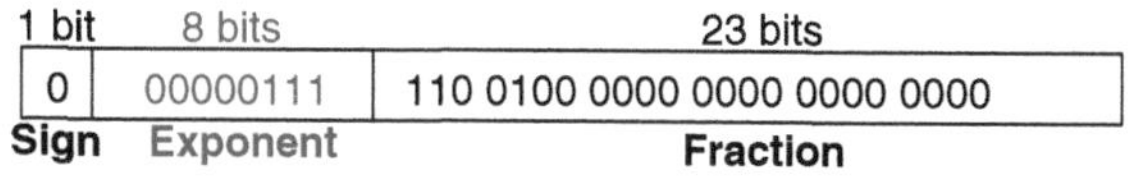

1 bit	8 bits	23 bits
0	00000111	110 0100 0000 0000 0000 0000
Sign	**Exponent**	**Fraction**

Figure 5.28 32-bit floating-point version 2

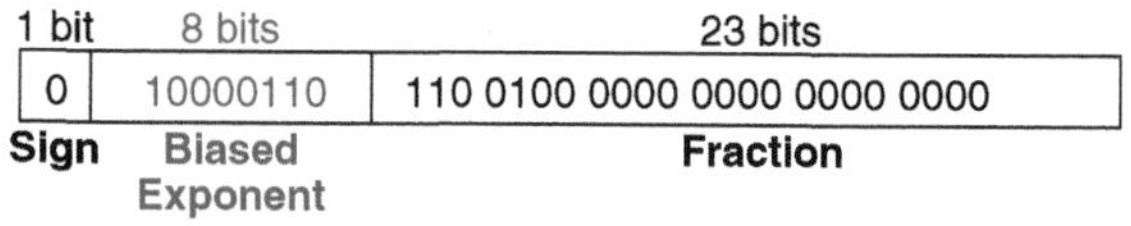

1 bit	8 bits	23 bits
0	10000110	110 0100 0000 0000 0000 0000
Sign	**Biased Exponent**	**Fraction**

Figure 5.29 IEEE 754 floating-point notation

134 $(7 + 127)$. This notation conforms to the IEEE 754 floating-point standard.

Special Cases: 0, $\pm\infty$, and NaN

The IEEE floating-point standard has special cases to represent numbers such as zero, infinity, and illegal results. For example, representing the number zero is problematic in floating-point notation because of the implicit leading one. Special codes with exponents of all 0's or all 1's are reserved for these special cases. Table 5.2 shows the floating-point representations of 0, $\pm\infty$, and NaN. As with sign/magnitude numbers, floating-point has both positive and negative 0. NaN is used for numbers that don't exist, such as $\sqrt{-1}$ or $\log_2(-5)$.

Single- and Double-Precision Formats

So far, we have examined 32-bit floating-point numbers. This format is also called *single-precision*, *single*, or *float*. The IEEE 754 standard also defines 64-bit *double-precision* numbers (also called *doubles*) that provide greater precision and greater range. Table 5.3 shows the number of bits used for the fields in each format.

Excluding the special cases mentioned earlier, normal single-precision numbers span a range of $\pm1.175494 \times 10^{-38}$ to $\pm3.402824 \times 10^{38}$. They have a precision of about seven significant decimal digits (because $2^{-24} \approx 10^{-7}$). Similarly, normal double-precision numbers span a range of $\pm2.22507385850720 \times 10^{-308}$ to $\pm1.79769313486232 \times 10^{308}$ and have a precision of about 15 significant decimal digits.

> Floating-point cannot represent some numbers exactly, like 1.7. However, when you type 1.7 into your calculator, you see exactly 1.7, not 1.69999.... To handle this, some applications, such as calculators and financial software, use *binary coded decimal* (BCD) numbers or formats with a base 10 exponent. BCD numbers encode each decimal digit using four bits with a range of 0 to 9. For example, the BCD fixed-point notation of 1.7 with four integer bits and four fraction bits would be 0001.0111. Of course, nothing is free. The cost is increased complexity in arithmetic hardware and wasted encodings (A–F encodings are not used), and thus decreased performance. So for compute-intensive applications, floating-point is much faster.

Table 5.2 IEEE 754 floating-point notations for 0, $\pm\infty$, and NaN

Number	Sign	Exponent	Fraction
0	X	00000000	00000000000000000000000
∞	0	11111111	00000000000000000000000
$-\infty$	1	11111111	00000000000000000000000
NaN	X	11111111	Non-zero

Table 5.3 Single- and double-precision floating-point formats

Format	Total Bits	Sign Bits	Exponent Bits	Fraction Bits
single	32	1	8	23
double	64	1	11	52

Rounding

Arithmetic results that fall outside of the available precision must round to a neighboring number. The rounding modes are: round down, round up, round toward zero, and round to nearest. The default rounding mode is round to nearest. In the round to nearest mode, if two numbers are equally near, the one with a 0 in the least significant position of the fraction is chosen.

Recall that a number *overflows* when its magnitude is too large to be represented. Likewise, a number *underflows* when it is too tiny to be represented. In round to nearest mode, overflows are rounded up to $\pm\infty$ and underflows are rounded down to 0.

Floating-Point Addition

Addition with floating-point numbers is not as simple as addition with two's complement numbers. The steps for adding floating-point numbers with the same sign are as follows:

1. Extract exponent and fraction bits.

2. Prepend leading 1 to form the mantissa.

3. Compare exponents.

4. Shift smaller mantissa if necessary.

5. Add mantissas.

6. Normalize mantissa and adjust exponent if necessary.

7. Round result.

8. Assemble exponent and fraction back into floating-point number.

Figure 5.30 shows the floating-point addition of 7.875 (1.11111×2^2) and 0.1875 (1.1×2^{-3}). The result is 8.0625 (1.0000001×2^3). After the fraction and exponent bits are extracted and the implicit leading 1 is prepended in steps 1 and 2, the exponents are compared by subtracting the smaller exponent from the larger exponent. The result is the number of bits by which the smaller number is shifted to the right to align the implied binary point (i.e., to make the exponents equal) in step 4. The aligned numbers are added. Because the sum has a mantissa that is greater than or equal to 2.0, the result is normalized by shifting it to the right one bit and incrementing the exponent. In this example, the result is exact, so no rounding is necessary. The result is stored in floating-point notation by removing the implicit leading one of the mantissa and prepending the sign bit.

> Floating-point arithmetic is usually done in hardware to make it fast. This hardware, called the *floating-point unit* (*FPU*), is typically distinct from the *central processing unit* (*CPU*). The infamous *floating-point division* (*FDIV*) bug in the Pentium FPU cost Intel $475 million to recall and replace defective chips. The bug occurred simply because a lookup table was not loaded correctly.

5.4 SEQUENTIAL BUILDING BLOCKS

This section examines sequential building blocks, including counters and shift registers.

Floating-point numbers

0	10000001	111 1100 0000 0000 0000 0000
0	01111100	100 0000 0000 0000 0000 0000

	Exponent	**Fraction**
Step 1	10000001	111 1100 0000 0000 0000 0000
	01111100	100 0000 0000 0000 0000 0000

Step 2	10000001	1.111 1100 0000 0000 0000 0000
	01111100	1.100 0000 0000 0000 0000 0000

Step 3	10000001	1.111 1100 0000 0000 0000 0000
−	01111100	1.100 0000 0000 0000 0000 0000

101 (shift amount)

Step 4	10000001	1.111 1100 0000 0000 0000 0000
	10000001	0.000 0110 0000 0000 0000 0000	00000

Step 5	10000001	1.111 1100 0000 0000 0000 0000
	10000001	+ 0.000 0110 0000 0000 0000 0000

10.000 0010 0000 0000 0000 0000

Step 6	10000001	10.000 0010 0000 0000 0000 0000 >> 1
+	1	
	10000010	1.000 0001 0000 0000 0000 0000

Step 7   (No rounding necessary)

Step 8	0	10000010	000 0001 0000 0000 0000 0000

Figure 5.30 Floating-point addition

Figure 5.31 Counter symbol

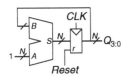

Figure 5.32 N-bit counter

5.4.1 Counters

An N-bit *binary counter*, shown in Figure 5.31, is a sequential arithmetic circuit with clock and reset inputs and an N-bit output Q. *Reset* initializes the output to 0. The counter then advances through all 2^N possible outputs in binary order, incrementing on the rising edge of the clock.

Figure 5.32 shows an N-bit counter composed of an adder and a resettable register. On each cycle, the counter adds 1 to the value stored in the register. HDL Example 5.4 describes a binary counter with asynchronous reset.

Other types of counters, such as Up/Down counters, are explored in Exercises 5.47 through 5.50.

HDL Example 5.4 COUNTER

SystemVerilog	VHDL

```
module counter #(parameter N = 8)
              (input  logic clk,
               input  logic reset,
               output logic [N-1:0] q);

  always_ff @(posedge clk, posedge reset)
    if (reset) q <= 0;
    else       q <= q + 1;
endmodule
```

```
library IEEE; use IEEE.STD_LOGIC_1164.ALL;
use IEEE.NUMERIC_STD_UNSIGNED.ALL;

entity counter is
  generic(N: integer := 8);
  port(clk, reset: in  STD_LOGIC;
           q:           out STD_LOGIC_VECTOR(N-1 downto 0));
end;

architecture synth of counter is
begin
  process(clk, reset) begin
    if reset then                  q <= (OTHERS => '0');
    elsif rising_edge(clk) then q <= q + '1';
    end if;
  end process;
end;
```

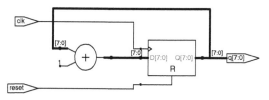

Figure 5.33 Synthesized counter

5.4.2 Shift Registers

A *shift register* has a clock, a serial input S_{in}, a serial output S_{out}, and N parallel outputs $Q_{N-1:0}$, as shown in Figure 5.34. On each rising edge of the clock, a new bit is shifted in from S_{in} and all the subsequent contents are shifted forward. The last bit in the shift register is available at S_{out}. Shift registers can be viewed as *serial-to-parallel converters*. The input is provided serially (one bit at a time) at S_{in}. After N cycles, the past N inputs are available in parallel at Q.

A shift register can be constructed from N flip-flops connected in series, as shown in Figure 5.35. Some shift registers also have a reset signal to initialize all of the flip-flops.

Figure 5.34 Shift register symbol

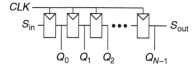

Figure 5.35 Shift register schematic

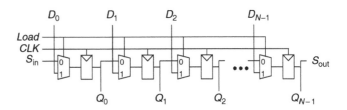

Figure 5.36 Shift register with parallel load

A related circuit is a *parallel-to-serial* converter that loads N bits in parallel, then shifts them out one at a time. A shift register can be modified to perform both serial-to-parallel and parallel-to-serial operations by adding a parallel input $D_{N-1:0}$, and a control signal *Load*, as shown in Figure 5.36. When *Load* is asserted, the flip-flops are loaded in parallel from the D inputs. Otherwise, the shift register shifts normally. HDL Example 5.5 describes such a shift register.

Scan Chains*

Shift registers are often used to test sequential circuits using a technique called *scan chains*. Testing combinational circuits is relatively straightforward. Known inputs called *test vectors* are applied, and the outputs are checked against the expected result. Testing sequential circuits is more difficult, because the circuits have state. Starting from a known initial condition, a large number of cycles of test vectors may be needed to put the circuit into a desired state. For example, testing that the most significant bit of a 32-bit counter advances from 0 to 1 requires resetting the counter, then applying 2^{31} (about two billion) clock pulses!

To solve this problem, designers like to be able to directly observe and control all the state of the machine. This is done by adding a test mode in which the contents of all flip-flops can be read out or loaded with desired values. Most systems have too many flip-flops to dedicate individual pins to read and write each flip-flop. Instead, all the flip-flops in the system are connected together into a shift register called a scan chain. In normal operation, the flip-flops load data from their D input and ignore the scan chain. In test mode, the flip-flops serially shift their contents out and shift in new contents using S_{in} and S_{out}. The load multiplexer is usually integrated into the flip-flop to produce a *scannable flip-flop*. Figure 5.38 shows the schematic and symbol for a scannable flip-flop and illustrates how the flops are cascaded to build an N-bit scannable register.

For example, the 32-bit counter could be tested by shifting in the pattern 011111...111 in test mode, counting for one cycle in normal mode, then shifting out the result, which should be 100000...000. This requires only $32 + 1 + 32 = 65$ cycles.

Don't confuse *shift registers* with the *shifters* from Section 5.2.5. Shift registers are sequential logic blocks that shift in a new bit on each clock edge. Shifters are unclocked combinational logic blocks that shift an input by a specified amount.

HDL Example 5.5 SHIFT REGISTER WITH PARALLEL LOAD

SystemVerilog

```
module shiftreg #(parameter N = 8)
                (input  logic       clk,
                 input  logic       reset, load,
                 input  logic       sin,
                 input  logic [N-1:0] d,
                 output logic [N-1:0] q,
                 output logic        sout);

  always_ff @(posedge clk, posedge reset)
    if (reset)      q <= 0;
    else if (load)  q <= d;
    else            q <= {q[N-2:0], sin};

  assign sout = q[N-1];
endmodule
```

VHDL

```
library IEEE; use IEEE.STD_LOGIC_1164.ALL;

entity shiftreg is
  generic(N: integer := 8);
  port(clk, reset: in  STD_LOGIC;
       load, sin:  in  STD_LOGIC;
       d:          in  STD_LOGIC_VECTOR(N-1 downto 0);
       q:          out STD_LOGIC_VECTOR(N-1 downto 0);
       sout:       out STD_LOGIC);
end;

architecture synth of shiftreg is
begin
  process(clk, reset) begin
    if reset = '1' then   q <= (OTHERS => '0');
    elsif rising_edge(clk) then
      if load then        q <= d;
      else                q <= q(N-2 downto 0) & sin;
      end if;
    end if;
  end process;

  sout <= q(N-1);
end;
```

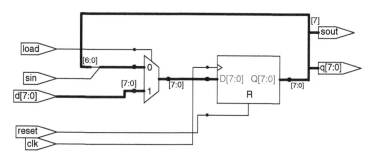

Figure 5.37 Synthesized shiftreg

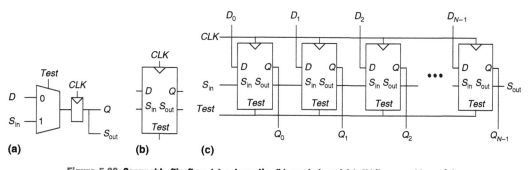

Figure 5.38 Scannable flip-flop: (a) schematic, (b) symbol, and (c) N-bit scannable register

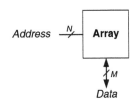

Figure 5.39 Generic memory array symbol

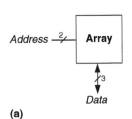

(a)

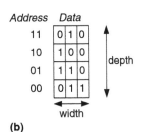

(b)

Figure 5.40 4 × 3 memory array: (a) symbol, (b) function

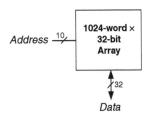

Figure 5.41 32 Kb array: depth = 2^{10} = 1024 words, width = 32 bits

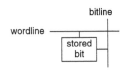

Figure 5.42 Bit cell

5.5 MEMORY ARRAYS

The previous sections introduced arithmetic and sequential circuits for manipulating data. Digital systems also require *memories* to store the data used and generated by such circuits. Registers built from flip-flops are a kind of memory that stores small amounts of data. This section describes *memory arrays* that can efficiently store large amounts of data.

The section begins with an overview describing characteristics shared by all memory arrays. It then introduces three types of memory arrays: dynamic random access memory (DRAM), static random access memory (SRAM), and read only memory (ROM). Each memory differs in the way it stores data. The section briefly discusses area and delay trade-offs and shows how memory arrays are used, not only to store data but also to perform logic functions. The section finishes with the HDL for a memory array.

5.5.1 Overview

Figure 5.39 shows a generic symbol for a memory array. The memory is organized as a two-dimensional array of memory cells. The memory reads or writes the contents of one of the rows of the array. This row is specified by an *Address*. The value read or written is called *Data*. An array with N-bit addresses and M-bit data has 2^N rows and M columns. Each row of data is called a *word*. Thus, the array contains 2^N M-bit words.

Figure 5.40 shows a memory array with two address bits and three data bits. The two address bits specify one of the four rows (data words) in the array. Each data word is three bits wide. Figure 5.40(b) shows some possible contents of the memory array.

The *depth* of an array is the number of rows, and the *width* is the number of columns, also called the word size. The size of an array is given as *depth* × *width*. Figure 5.40 is a 4-word × 3-bit array, or simply 4 × 3 array. The symbol for a 1024-word × 32-bit array is shown in Figure 5.41. The total size of this array is 32 kilobits (Kb).

Bit Cells

Memory arrays are built as an array of *bit cells*, each of which stores 1 bit of data. Figure 5.42 shows that each bit cell is connected to a *wordline* and a *bitline*. For each combination of address bits, the memory asserts a single wordline that activates the bit cells in that row. When the wordline is HIGH, the stored bit transfers to or from the bitline. Otherwise, the bitline is disconnected from the bit cell. The circuitry to store the bit varies with memory type.

To read a bit cell, the bitline is initially left floating (Z). Then the wordline is turned ON, allowing the stored value to drive the bitline to 0 or 1. To write a bit cell, the bitline is strongly driven to the desired value. Then the wordline is turned ON, connecting the bitline to the stored bit. The strongly driven bitline overpowers the contents of the bit cell, writing the desired value into the stored bit.

Organization

Figure 5.43 shows the internal organization of a 4×3 memory array. Of course, practical memories are much larger, but the behavior of larger arrays can be extrapolated from the smaller array. In this example, the array stores the data from Figure 5.40(b).

During a memory read, a wordline is asserted, and the corresponding row of bit cells drives the bitlines HIGH or LOW. During a memory write, the bitlines are driven HIGH or LOW first and then a wordline is asserted, allowing the bitline values to be stored in that row of bit cells. For example, to read *Address* 10, the bitlines are left floating, the decoder asserts *wordline$_2$*, and the data stored in that row of bit cells (100) reads out onto the *Data* bitlines. To write the value 001 to *Address* 11, the bitlines are driven to the value 001, then *wordline$_3$* is asserted and the new value (001) is stored in the bit cells.

Memory Ports

All memories have one or more *ports*. Each port gives read and/or write access to one memory address. The previous examples were all single-ported memories.

Multiported memories can access several addresses simultaneously. Figure 5.44 shows a three-ported memory with two read ports and one write port. Port 1 reads the data from address *A1* onto the read data output *RD1*. Port 2 reads the data from address *A2* onto

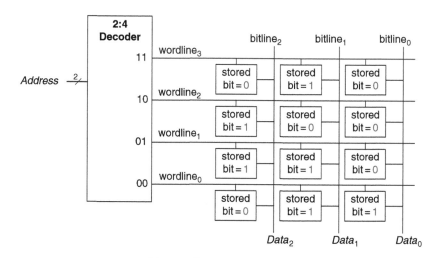

Figure 5.43 4×3 memory array

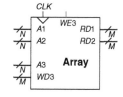

Figure 5.44 **Three-ported memory**

RD2. Port 3 writes the data from the write data input *WD3* into address *A3* on the rising edge of the clock if the write enable *WE3* is asserted.

Memory Types

Memory arrays are specified by their size (depth × width) and the number and type of ports. All memory arrays store data as an array of bit cells, but they differ in how they store bits.

Memories are classified based on how they store bits in the bit cell. The broadest classification is *random access memory (RAM)* versus *read only memory (ROM)*. RAM is *volatile,* meaning that it loses its data when the power is turned off. ROM is *nonvolatile,* meaning that it retains its data indefinitely, even without a power source.

RAM and ROM received their names for historical reasons that are no longer very meaningful. RAM is called *random* access memory because any data word is accessed with the same delay as any other. In contrast, a sequential access memory, such as a tape recorder, accesses nearby data more quickly than faraway data (e.g., at the other end of the tape). ROM is called *read only* memory because, historically, it could only be read but not written. These names are confusing, because ROMs are randomly accessed too. Worse yet, most modern ROMs can be written as well as read! The important distinction to remember is that RAMs are volatile and ROMs are nonvolatile.

The two major types of RAMs are *dynamic RAM (DRAM)* and *static RAM (SRAM)*. Dynamic RAM stores data as a charge on a capacitor, whereas static RAM stores data using a pair of cross-coupled inverters. There are many flavors of ROMs that vary by how they are written and erased. These various types of memories are discussed in the subsequent sections.

5.5.2 Dynamic Random Access Memory (DRAM)

Dynamic RAM (DRAM, pronounced "dee-ram") stores a bit as the presence or absence of charge on a capacitor. Figure 5.45 shows a DRAM bit cell. The bit value is stored on a capacitor. The nMOS transistor behaves as a switch that either connects or disconnects the capacitor from the bitline. When the wordline is asserted, the nMOS transistor turns ON, and the stored bit value transfers to or from the bitline.

As shown in Figure 5.46(a), when the capacitor is charged to V_{DD}, the stored bit is 1; when it is discharged to GND (Figure 5.46(b)), the stored bit is 0. The capacitor node is *dynamic* because it is not actively driven HIGH or LOW by a transistor tied to V_{DD} or GND.

Upon a read, data values are transferred from the capacitor to the bitline. Upon a write, data values are transferred from the bitline to

Robert Dennard, 1932–. Invented DRAM in 1966 at IBM. Although many were skeptical that the idea would work, by the mid-1970s DRAM was in virtually all computers. He claims to have done little creative work until, arriving at IBM, they handed him a patent notebook and said, "put all your ideas in there." Since 1965, he has received 35 patents in semiconductors and microelectronics. (Photo courtesy of IBM.)

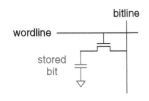

Figure 5.45 DRAM bit cell

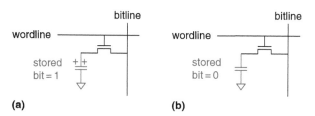

(a)   **(b)**

Figure 5.46 **DRAM stored values**

the capacitor. Reading destroys the bit value stored on the capacitor, so the data word must be restored (rewritten) after each read. Even when DRAM is not read, the contents must be refreshed (read and rewritten) every few milliseconds, because the charge on the capacitor gradually leaks away.

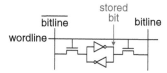

Figure 5.47 **SRAM bit cell**

5.5.3 Static Random Access Memory (SRAM)

Static RAM (*SRAM*, pronounced "es-ram") is *static* because stored bits do not need to be refreshed. Figure 5.47 shows an SRAM bit cell. The data bit is stored on cross-coupled inverters like those described in Section 3.2. Each cell has two outputs, bitline and $\overline{\text{bitline}}$. When the wordline is asserted, both nMOS transistors turn on, and data values are transferred to or from the bitlines. Unlike DRAM, if noise degrades the value of the stored bit, the cross-coupled inverters restore the value.

5.5.4 Area and Delay

Flip-flops, SRAMs, and DRAMs are all volatile memories, but each has different area and delay characteristics. Table 5.4 shows a comparison of these three types of volatile memory. The data bit stored in a flip-flop is available immediately at its output. But flip-flops take at least 20 transistors to build. Generally, the more transistors a device has, the more area, power, and cost it requires. DRAM latency is longer than that of SRAM because its bitline is not actively driven by a transistor. DRAM must wait for charge to move (relatively) slowly from the capacitor to the bitline. DRAM also fundamentally has lower throughput than SRAM, because it must refresh data

Table 5.4 **Memory comparison**

Memory Type	Transistors per Bit Cell	Latency
flip-flop	~20	fast
SRAM	6	medium
DRAM	1	slow

periodically and after a read. DRAM technologies such as *synchronous DRAM (SDRAM)* and *double data rate (DDR)* SDRAM have been developed to overcome this problem. SDRAM uses a clock to pipeline memory accesses. DDR SDRAM, sometimes called simply DDR, uses both the rising and falling edges of the clock to access data, thus doubling the throughput for a given clock speed. DDR was first standardized in 2000 and ran at 100 to 200 MHz. Later standards, DDR2, DDR3, and DDR4, increased the clock speeds, with speeds in 2015 being over 1 GHz.

Memory latency and throughput also depend on memory size; larger memories tend to be slower than smaller ones if all else is the same. The best memory type for a particular design depends on the speed, cost, and power constraints.

5.5.5 Register Files

Digital systems often use a number of registers to store temporary variables. This group of registers, called a *register file*, is usually built as a small, multiported SRAM array, because it is more compact than an array of flip-flops.

Figure 5.48 shows a 16-register × 32-bit three-ported register file built from a three-ported memory similar to that of Figure 5.44. The register file has two read ports (*A1/RD1* and *A2/RD2*) and one write port (*A3/WD3*). The 4-bit addresses, *A1*, *A2*, and *A3*, can each access all $2^4 = 16$ registers. So, two registers can be read and one register written simultaneously.

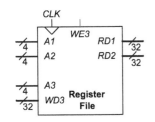

Figure 5.48 16 × 32 register file with two read ports and one write port

5.5.6 Read Only Memory

Read only memory (ROM) stores a bit as the presence or absence of a transistor. Figure 5.49 shows a simple ROM bit cell. To read the cell, the bitline is weakly pulled HIGH. Then the wordline is turned ON. If the transistor is present, it pulls the bitline LOW. If it is absent, the bitline remains HIGH. Note that the ROM bit cell is a combinational circuit and has no state to "forget" if power is turned off.

The contents of a ROM can be indicated using *dot notation*. Figure 5.50 shows the dot notation for a 4-word × 3-bit ROM containing the data from Figure 5.40. A dot at the intersection of a row (wordline) and a column (bitline) indicates that the data bit is 1. For example, the top wordline has a single dot on *Data₁*, so the data word stored at *Address 11* is 010.

Conceptually, ROMs can be built using two-level logic with a group of AND gates followed by a group of OR gates. The AND gates produce all possible minterms and hence form a decoder. Figure 5.51 shows the ROM of Figure 5.50 built using a decoder and OR gates. Each dotted row in Figure 5.50 is an input to an OR gate in Figure 5.51.

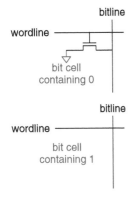

Figure 5.49 ROM bit cells containing 0 and 1

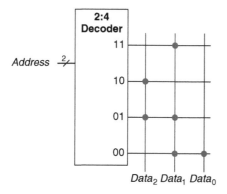

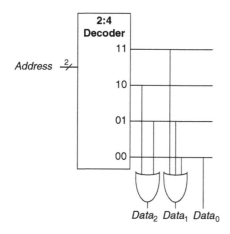

Figure 5.50 **4 × 3 ROM: dot notation**

Figure 5.51 **4 × 3 ROM implementation using gates**

For data bits with a single dot, in this case $Data_0$, no OR gate is needed. This representation of a ROM is interesting because it shows how the ROM can perform any two-level logic function. In practice, ROMs are built from transistors instead of logic gates to reduce their size and cost. Section 5.6.3 explores the transistor-level implementation further.

The contents of the ROM bit cell in Figure 5.49 are specified during manufacturing by the presence or absence of a transistor in each bit cell. A *programmable ROM (PROM*, pronounced like the dance) places a transistor in every bit cell but provides a way to connect or disconnect the transistor to ground.

Figure 5.52 shows the bit cell for a *fuse-programmable ROM*. The user programs the ROM by applying a high voltage to selectively blow

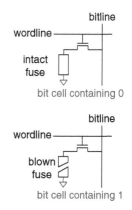

Figure 5.52 **Fuse-programmable ROM bit cell**

Fujio Masuoka, 1944–. Received a Ph.D. in electrical engineering from Tohoku University, Japan. Developed memories and high-speed circuits at Toshiba from 1971 to 1994. Invented Flash memory as an unauthorized project pursued during nights and weekends in the late 1970s. Flash received its name because the process of erasing the memory reminds one of the flash of a camera. Toshiba was slow to commercialize the idea; Intel was first to market in 1988. Flash has grown into a $25 billion per year market. Dr. Masuoka later joined the faculty at Tohoku University and is working to develop a 3-dimensional transistor.

Flash memory drives with Universal Serial Bus (USB) connectors have replaced floppy disks and CDs for sharing files because Flash costs have dropped so dramatically.

fuses. If the fuse is present, the transistor is connected to GND and the cell holds a 0. If the fuse is destroyed, the transistor is disconnected from ground and the cell holds a 1. This is also called a one-time programmable ROM, because the fuse cannot be repaired once it is blown.

Reprogrammable ROMs provide a reversible mechanism for connecting or disconnecting the transistor to GND. *Erasable PROMs* (*EPROMs*, pronounced "e-proms") replace the nMOS transistor and fuse with a *floating-gate transistor*. The floating gate is not physically attached to any other wires. When suitable high voltages are applied, electrons tunnel through an insulator onto the floating gate, turning on the transistor and connecting the bitline to the wordline (decoder output). When the EPROM is exposed to intense ultraviolet (UV) light for about half an hour, the electrons are knocked off the floating gate, turning the transistor off. These actions are called *programming* and *erasing*, respectively. *Electrically erasable PROMs* (*EEPROMs*, pronounced "e-e-proms" or "double-e proms") and *Flash* memory use similar principles but include circuitry on the chip for erasing as well as programming, so no UV light is necessary. EEPROM bit cells are individually erasable; Flash memory erases larger blocks of bits and is cheaper because fewer erasing circuits are needed. In 2015, Flash memory cost about $0.35 per GB, and the price continues to drop by 30 to 40% per year. Flash has become an extremely popular way to store large amounts of data in portable battery-powered systems such as cameras and music players.

In summary, modern ROMs are not really read only; they can be programmed (written) as well. The difference between RAM and ROM is that ROMs take a longer time to write but are nonvolatile.

5.5.7 Logic Using Memory Arrays

Although they are used primarily for data storage, memory arrays can also perform combinational logic functions. For example, the $Data_2$ output of the ROM in Figure 5.50 is the XOR of the two $Address$ inputs. Likewise $Data_0$ is the NAND of the two inputs. A 2^N-word × M-bit memory can perform any combinational function of N inputs and M outputs. For example, the ROM in Figure 5.50 performs three functions of two inputs.

Memory arrays used to perform logic are called *lookup tables* (*LUTs*). Figure 5.53 shows a 4-word × 1-bit memory array used as a lookup table to perform the function $Y = AB$. Using memory to perform logic, the user can look up the output value for a given input combination (address). Each address corresponds to a row in the truth table, and each data bit corresponds to an output value.

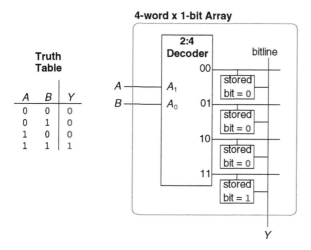

Figure 5.53 **4-word × 1-bit memory array used as a lookup table**

Programmable ROMs can be configured with a device programmer like the one shown below. The device programmer is attached to a computer, which specifies the type of ROM and the data values to program. The device programmer blows fuses or injects charge onto a floating gate on the ROM. Thus the programming process is sometimes called *burning* a ROM.

5.5.8 Memory HDL

HDL Example 5.6 describes a 2^N-word × M-bit RAM. The RAM has a synchronous enabled write. In other words, writes occur on the rising edge of the clock if the write enable *we* is asserted. Reads occur immediately. When power is first applied, the contents of the RAM are unpredictable.

HDL Example 5.7 describes a 4-word × 3-bit ROM. The contents of the ROM are specified in the HDL case statement. A ROM as small as this one may be synthesized into logic gates rather than an array. Note that the seven-segment decoder from HDL Example 4.24 synthesizes into a ROM in Figure 4.20.

5.6 LOGIC ARRAYS

Like memory, gates can be organized into regular arrays. If the connections are made programmable, these *logic arrays* can be configured to perform any function without the user having to connect wires in specific ways. The regular structure simplifies design. Logic arrays are mass produced in large quantities, so they are inexpensive. Software tools allow users to map logic designs onto these arrays. Most logic arrays are also reconfigurable, allowing designs to be modified without replacing the hardware. Reconfigurability is valuable during development and is also useful in the field, because a system can be upgraded by simply downloading the new configuration.

This section introduces two types of logic arrays: programmable logic arrays (PLAs), and field programmable gate arrays (FPGAs). PLAs, the

HDL Example 5.6 RAM

SystemVerilog

```
module ram #(parameter N = 6, M = 32)
           (input  logic        clk,
            input  logic        we,
            input  logic [N-1:0] adr,
            input  logic [M-1:0] din,
            output logic [M-1:0] dout);

  logic [M-1:0] mem [2**N-1:0];

  always_ff @(posedge clk)
    if (we) mem [adr] <= din;

  assign dout = mem[adr];
endmodule
```

VHDL

```
library IEEE; use IEEE.STD_LOGIC_1164.ALL;
use IEEE.NUMERIC_STD_UNSIGNED.ALL;

entity ram_array is
  generic(N: integer := 6; M: integer := 32);
  port(clk,
       we:   in  STD_LOGIC;
       adr:  in  STD_LOGIC_VECTOR(N-1 downto 0);
       din:  in  STD_LOGIC_VECTOR(M-1 downto 0);
       dout: out STD_LOGIC_VECTOR(M-1 downto 0));
end;

architecture synth of ram_array is
  type mem_array is array ((2**N-1) downto 0)
       of STD_LOGIC_VECTOR (M-1 downto 0);
  signal mem: mem_array;
begin
  process(clk) begin
    if rising_edge(clk) then
      if we then mem(TO_INTEGER(adr)) <= din;
      end if;
    end if;
  end process;

  dout <= mem(TO_INTEGER(adr));
end;
```

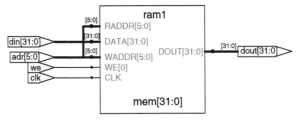

Figure 5.54 Synthesized ram

older technology, perform only combinational logic functions. FPGAs can perform both combinational and sequential logic.

5.6.1 Programmable Logic Array

Programmable logic arrays (*PLAs*) implement two-level combinational logic in sum-of-products (SOP) form. PLAs are built from an AND array followed by an OR array, as shown in Figure 5.55. The inputs (in true and complementary form) drive an AND array, which produces implicants, which in turn are ORed together to form the outputs. An $M \times N \times P$-bit PLA has M inputs, N implicants, and P outputs.

HDL Example 5.7 ROM

SystemVerilog

```
module rom(input  logic [1:0] adr,
           output logic [2:0] dout);
  always_comb
    case(adr)
      2'b00: dout = 3'b011;
      2'b01: dout = 3'b110;
      2'b10: dout = 3'b100;
      2'b11: dout = 3'b010;
    endcase
endmodule
```

VHDL

```
library IEEE; use IEEE.STD_LOGIC_1164.all;

entity rom is
  port(adr:  in  STD_LOGIC_VECTOR(1 downto 0);
       dout: out STD_LOGIC_VECTOR(2 downto 0));
end;

architecture synth of rom is
begin
  process(all) begin
    case adr is
      when "00" => dout <= "011";
      when "01" => dout <= "110";
      when "10" => dout <= "100";
      when "11" => dout <= "010";
    end case;
  end process;
end;
```

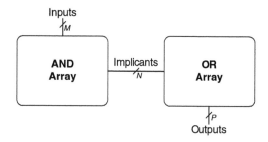

Figure 5.55 $M \times N \times P$-bit PLA

Figure 5.56 shows the dot notation for a $3 \times 3 \times 2$-bit PLA performing the functions $X = \overline{A}\,\overline{B}C + AB\overline{C}$ and $Y = A\overline{B}$. Each row in the AND array forms an implicant. Dots in each row of the AND array indicate which literals comprise the implicant. The AND array in Figure 5.56 forms three implicants: $\overline{A}\,\overline{B}C$, $AB\overline{C}$, and $A\overline{B}$. Dots in the OR array indicate which implicants are part of the output function.

Figure 5.57 shows how PLAs can be built using two-level logic. An alternative implementation is given in Section 5.6.3.

ROMs can be viewed as a special case of PLAs. A 2^M-word $\times$ N-bit ROM is simply an $M \times 2^M \times N$-bit PLA. The decoder behaves as an AND plane that produces all 2^M minterms. The ROM array behaves as an OR plane that produces the outputs. If the function does not depend on all 2^M minterms, a PLA is likely to be smaller than a ROM. For example, an 8-word $\times$ 2-bit ROM is required to perform

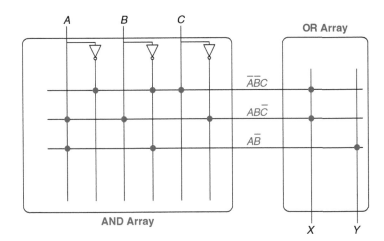

Figure 5.56 3 × 3 × 2-bit PLA: dot notation

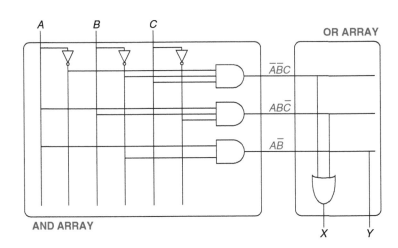

Figure 5.57 3 × 3 × 2-bit PLA using two-level logic

the same functions performed by the $3 \times 3 \times 2$-bit PLA shown in Figures 5.56 and 5.57.

Simple programmable logic devices (SPLDs) are souped-up PLAs that add registers and various other features to the basic AND/OR planes. However, SPLDs and PLAs have largely been displaced by FPGAs, which are more flexible and efficient for building large systems.

5.6.2 Field Programmable Gate Array

A *field programmable gate array* (FPGA) is an array of reconfigurable gates. Using software programming tools, a user can implement designs on the FPGA using either an HDL or a schematic. FPGAs are more powerful and more flexible than PLAs for several reasons. They can implement both combinational and sequential logic. They can also implement multilevel logic functions, whereas PLAs can only implement two-level logic. Modern FPGAs integrate other useful features such as built-in multipliers, high-speed I/Os, data converters including analog-to-digital converters, large RAM arrays, and processors.

FPGAs are built as an array of configurable *logic elements* (*LEs*), also referred to as *configurable logic blocks* (*CLBs*). Each LE can be configured to perform combinational or sequential functions. Figure 5.58 shows a general block diagram of an FPGA. The LEs are surrounded by *input/output elements* (*IOEs*) for interfacing with the outside world. The IOEs connect LE inputs and outputs to pins on the chip package. LEs can connect to other LEs and IOEs through programmable routing channels.

Two of the leading FPGA manufacturers are Altera Corp. and Xilinx, Inc. Figure 5.59 shows a single LE from Altera's Cyclone IV FPGA introduced in 2009. The key elements of the LE are a 4-input lookup table (LUT) and a 1-bit register. The LE also contains configurable multiplexers to route signals through the LE. The FPGA is configured by specifying the contents of the lookup tables and the select signals for the multiplexers.

FPGAs are the brains of many consumer products, including automobiles, medical equipment, and media devices like MP3 players. The Mercedes Benz S-Class series, for example, has over a dozen Xilinx FPGAs or PLDs for uses ranging from entertainment to navigation to cruise control systems. FPGAs allow for quick time to market and make debugging or adding features late in the design process easier.

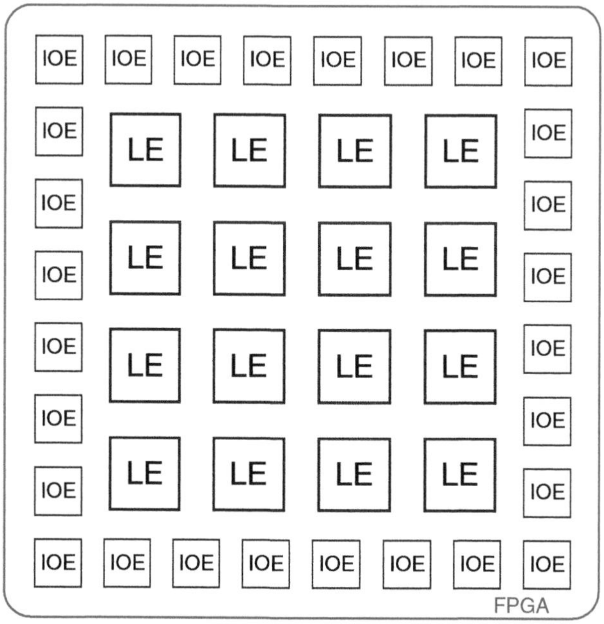

Figure 5.58 General FPGA layout

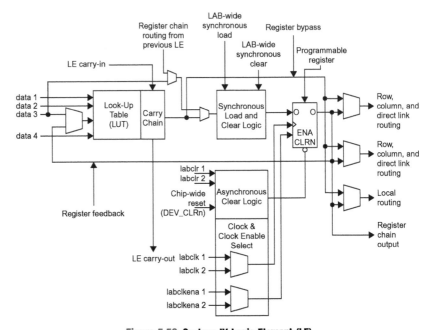

Figure 5.59 Cyclone IV Logic Element (LE)
(Reproduced with permission from the Altera Cyclone™ IV Handbook © 2010
Altera Corporation.)

The Cyclone IV LE has one 4-input LUT and one flip-flop. By loading the appropriate values into the lookup table, the LUT can be configured to perform any function of up to four variables. Configuring the FPGA also involves choosing the select signals that determine how the multiplexers route data through the LE and to neighboring LEs and IOEs. For example, depending on the multiplexer configuration, the LUT may receive one of its inputs from either *data 3* or the output of the LE's own register. The other three inputs always come from *data 1*, *data 2*, and *data 4*. The *data 1-4* inputs come from IOEs or the outputs of other LEs, depending on routing external to the LE. The LUT output either goes directly to the LE output for combinational functions, or it can be fed through the flip-flop for registered functions. The flip-flop input comes from its own LUT output, the *data 3* input, or the register output of the previous LE. Additional hardware includes support for addition using the carry chain hardware, other multiplexers for routing, and flip-flop enable and reset. Altera groups 16 LEs together to create a *logic array block* (*LAB*) and provides local connections between LEs within the LAB.

In summary, the Cyclone IV LE can perform one combinational and/or registered function which can involve up to four variables. Other brands of FPGAs are organized somewhat differently, but the same general principles apply. For example, Xilinx's 7-series FPGAs use 6-input LUTs instead of 4-input LUTs.

The designer configures an FPGA by first creating a schematic or HDL description of the design. The design is then synthesized onto the FPGA. The synthesis tool determines how the LUTs, multiplexers, and routing channels should be configured to perform the specified functions. This configuration information is then downloaded to the FPGA. Because Cyclone IV FPGAs store their configuration information in SRAM, they are easily reprogrammed. The FPGA may download its SRAM contents from a computer in the laboratory or from an EEPROM chip when the system is turned on. Some manufacturers include an EEPROM directly on the FPGA or use one-time programmable fuses to configure the FPGA.

Example 5.5 FUNCTIONS BUILT USING LEs

Explain how to configure one or more Cyclone IV LEs to perform the following functions: (a) $X = \overline{A}\,\overline{B}C + AB\overline{C}$ and $Y = A\overline{B}$ (b) $Y = JKLMPQR$; (c) a divide-by-3 counter with binary state encoding (see Figure 3.29(a)). You may show interconnection between LEs as needed.

Solution: (a) Configure two LEs. One LUT computes X and the other LUT computes Y, as shown in Figure 5.60. For the first LE, inputs *data 1*, *data 2*, and *data 3* are A, B, and C, respectively (these connections are set by the routing channels). *data 4* is a don't care but must be tied to something, so it is tied to 0. For the second LE, inputs *data 1* and *data 2* are A and B; the other LUT inputs are don't cares and are tied to 0. Configure the final multiplexers to select the combinational outputs from the LUTs to produce X and Y. In general, a single LE can compute any function of up to four input variables in this fashion.

(A) data 1	*(B)* data 2	*(C)* data 3	data 4	*(X)* LUT output
0	0	0	X	0
0	0	1	X	1
0	1	0	X	0
0	1	1	X	0
1	0	0	X	0
1	0	1	X	0
1	1	0	X	1
1	1	1	X	0

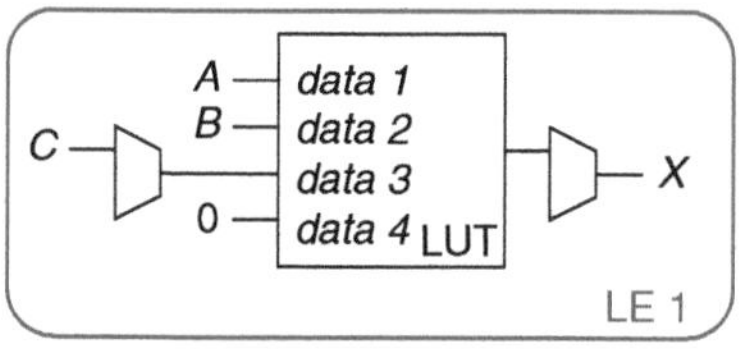

(A) data 1	*(B)* data 2	data 3	data 4	*(Y)* LUT output
0	0	X	X	0
0	1	X	X	0
1	0	X	X	1
1	1	X	X	0

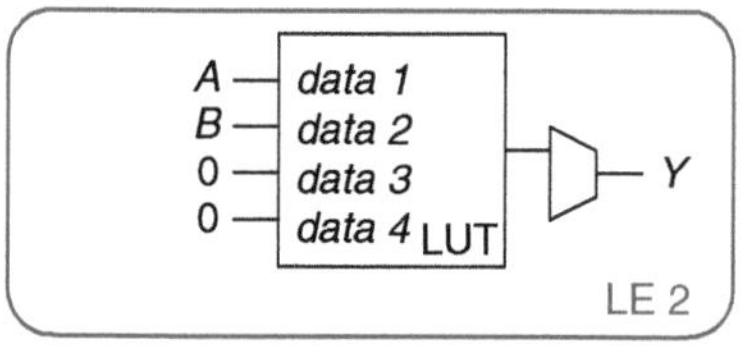

Figure 5.60 **LE configuration for two functions of up to four inputs each**

(b) Configure the LUT of the first LE to compute $X = JKLM$ and the LUT on the second LE to compute $Y = XPQR$. Configure the final multiplexers to select the combinational outputs X and Y from each LE. This configuration is shown in Figure 5.61. Routing channels between LEs, indicated by the dashed blue lines, connect the output of LE 1 to the input of LE 2. In general, a group of LEs can compute functions of N input variables in this manner.

(c) The FSM has two bits of state $(S_{1:0})$ and one output (Y). The next state depends on the two bits of current state. Use two LEs to compute the next state from the current state, as shown in Figure 5.62. Use the two flip-flops, one from

(J)	(K)	(L)	(M)	(X)
data 1	data 2	data 3	data 4	LUT output
0	0	0	0	0
0	0	0	1	0
0	0	1	0	0
0	0	1	1	0
0	1	0	0	0
0	1	0	1	0
0	1	1	0	0
0	1	1	1	0
1	0	0	0	0
1	0	0	1	0
1	0	1	0	0
1	0	1	1	0
1	1	0	0	0
1	1	0	1	0
1	1	1	0	0
1	1	1	1	1

(P)	(Q)	(R)	(X)	(Y)
data 1	data 2	data 3	data 4	LUT output
0	0	0	0	0
0	0	0	1	0
0	0	1	0	0
0	0	1	1	0
0	1	0	0	0
0	1	0	1	0
0	1	1	0	0
0	1	1	1	0
1	0	0	0	0
1	0	0	1	0
1	0	1	0	0
1	0	1	1	0
1	1	0	0	0
1	1	0	1	0
1	1	1	0	0
1	1	1	1	1

Figure 5.61 LE configuration for one function of more than four inputs

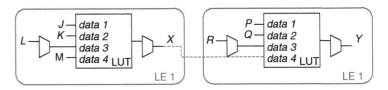

	(S₀)	(S₁)	(S₀')
data 1	data 2	data 3	data 4	LUT output
X	X	0	0	1
X	X	0	1	0
X	X	1	0	0
X	X	1	1	0

Figure 5.62 LE configuration for FSM with two bits of state

	(S₁)	(S₀)	(S₁')
data 1	data 2	data 3	data 4	LUT output
X	X	0	0	0
X	X	0	1	1
X	X	1	0	0
X	X	1	1	0

each LE, to hold this state. The flip-flops have a reset input that can be connected to an external *Reset* signal. The registered outputs are fed back to the LUT inputs using the multiplexer on *data 3* and routing channels between LEs, as indicated by the dashed blue lines. In general, another LE might be necessary to compute the output Y. However, in this case $Y = S_0'$, so Y can come from LE 1. Hence, the entire FSM fits in two LEs. In general, an FSM requires at least one LE for each bit of state, and it may require more LEs for the output or next state logic if they are too complex to fit in a single LUT.

Example 5.6 LE DELAY

Alyssa P. Hacker is building a finite state machine that must run at 200 MHz. She uses a Cyclone IV FPGA with the following specifications: $t_{LE} = 381$ ps per LE, $t_{setup} = 76$ ps, and $t_{pcq} = 199$ ps for all flip-flops. The wiring delay between LEs is 246 ps. Assume the hold time for the flip-flops is 0. What is the maximum number of LEs her design can use?

Solution: Alyssa uses Equation 3.13 to solve for the maximum propagation delay of the logic: $t_{pd} \leq T_c - (t_{pcq} + t_{setup})$.

Thus, $t_{pd} = 5$ ns $- (0.199$ ns $+ 0.076$ ns), so $t_{pd} \leq 4.725$ ns. The delay of each LE plus wiring delay between LEs, $t_{LE+wire}$, is 381 ps $+ 246$ ps $= 627$ ps. The maximum number of LEs, N, is $Nt_{LE+wire} \leq 4.725$ ns. Thus, $N = 7$.

5.6.3 Array Implementations*

To minimize their size and cost, ROMs and PLAs commonly use pseudo-nMOS or dynamic circuits (see Section 1.7.8) instead of conventional logic gates.

Figure 5.63(a) shows the dot notation for a 4×3-bit ROM that performs the following functions: $X = A \oplus B$, $Y = \overline{A} + B$, and $Z = \overline{A}\,\overline{B}$. These are the same functions as those of Figure 5.50, with the address inputs renamed A and B and the data outputs renamed X, Y, and Z. The pseudo-nMOS implementation is given in Figure 5.63(b). Each decoder output is connected to the gates of the nMOS transistors in its row. Remember that in pseudo-nMOS circuits, the weak pMOS transistor pulls the output HIGH *only if* there is no path to GND through the pull-down (nMOS) network.

Pull-down transistors are placed at every junction without a dot. The dots from the dot notation diagram of Figure 5.63(a) are left visible in Figure 5.63(b) for easy comparison. The weak pull-up transistors pull the output HIGH for each wordline without a pull-down transistor. For example, when $AB = 11$, the 11 wordline is HIGH and transistors on X and Z turn on and pull those outputs LOW. The Y output has no

Many ROMs and PLAs use dynamic circuits in place of pseudo-nMOS circuits. Dynamic gates turn the pMOS transistor ON for only part of the time, saving power when the pMOS is OFF and the result is not needed. Aside from this, dynamic and pseudo-nMOS memory arrays are similar in design and behavior.

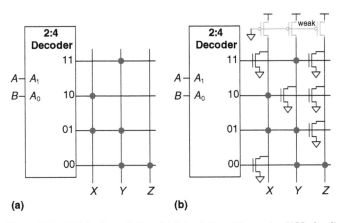

Figure 5.63 ROM implementation: (a) dot notation, (b) pseudo-nMOS circuit

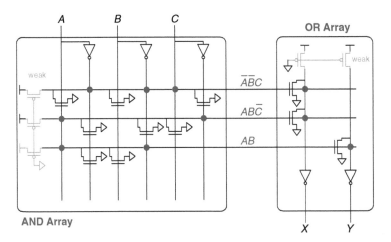

Figure 5.64 $3 \times 3 \times$ 2-bit PLA using pseudo-nMOS circuits

transistor connecting to the 11 wordline, so Y is pulled HIGH by the weak pull-up.

PLAs can also be built using pseudo-nMOS circuits, as shown in Figure 5.64 for the PLA from Figure 5.56. Pull-down (nMOS) transistors are placed on the *complement* of dotted literals in the AND array and on dotted rows in the OR array. The columns in the OR array are sent through an inverter before they are fed to the output bits. Again, the blue dots from the dot notation diagram of Figure 5.56 are left visible in Figure 5.64 for easy comparison.

5.7 SUMMARY

This chapter introduced digital building blocks used in many digital systems. These blocks include arithmetic circuits such as adders, subtractors, comparators, shifters, multipliers, and dividers; sequential circuits such as counters and shift registers; and arrays for memory and logic. The chapter also explored fixed-point and floating-point representations of fractional numbers. In Chapter 7, we use these building blocks to build a microprocessor.

Adders form the basis of most arithmetic circuits. A half adder adds two 1-bit inputs, A and B, and produces a sum and a carry out. A full adder extends the half adder to also accept a carry in. N full adders can be cascaded to form a carry propagate adder (CPA) that adds two N-bit numbers. This type of CPA is called a ripple-carry adder because the carry ripples through each of the full adders. Faster CPAs can be constructed using lookahead or prefix techniques.

A subtractor negates the second input and adds it to the first. A magnitude comparator subtracts one number from another and determines the relative value based on the sign of the result. A multiplier forms partial products using AND gates, then sums these bits using full adders. A divider repeatedly subtracts the divisor from the partial remainder and checks the sign of the difference to determine the quotient bits. A counter uses an adder and a register to increment a running count.

Fractional numbers are represented using fixed-point or floating-point forms. Fixed-point numbers are analogous to decimals, and floating-point numbers are analogous to scientific notation. Fixed-point numbers use ordinary arithmetic circuits, whereas floating-point numbers require more elaborate hardware to extract and process the sign, exponent, and mantissa.

Large memories are organized into arrays of words. The memories have one or more ports to read and/or write the words. Volatile memories, such as SRAM and DRAM, lose their state when the power is turned off. SRAM is faster than DRAM but requires more transistors. A register file is a small multiported SRAM array. Nonvolatile memories, called ROMs, retain their state indefinitely. Despite their names, most modern ROMs can be written.

Arrays are also a regular way to build logic. Memory arrays can be used as lookup tables to perform combinational functions. PLAs are composed of dedicated connections between configurable AND and OR arrays; they only implement combinational logic. FPGAs are composed of many small lookup tables and registers; they implement combinational and sequential logic. The lookup table contents and their interconnections can be configured to perform any logic function. Modern FPGAs are easy to reprogram and are large and cheap enough to build highly sophisticated digital systems, so they are widely used in low- and medium-volume commercial products as well as in education.

Exercises

Exercise 5.1 What is the delay for the following types of 64-bit adders? Assume that each two-input gate delay is 150 ps and that a full adder delay is 450 ps.

(a) a ripple-carry adder

(b) a carry-lookahead adder with 4-bit blocks

(c) a prefix adder

Exercise 5.2 Design two adders: a 64-bit ripple-carry adder and a 64-bit carry-lookahead adder with 4-bit blocks. Use only two-input gates. Each two-input gate is 15 μm^2, has a 50 ps delay, and has 20 fF of total gate capacitance. You may assume that the static power is negligible.

(a) Compare the area, delay, and power of the adders (operating at 100 MHz and 1.2 V).

(b) Discuss the trade-offs between power, area, and delay.

Exercise 5.3 Explain why a designer might choose to use a ripple-carry adder instead of a carry-lookahead adder.

Exercise 5.4 Design the 16-bit prefix adder of Figure 5.7 in an HDL. Simulate and test your module to prove that it functions correctly.

Exercise 5.5 The prefix network shown in Figure 5.7 uses black cells to compute all of the prefixes. Some of the block propagate signals are not actually necessary. Design a "gray cell" that receives G and P signals for bits $i:k$ and $k-1:j$ but produces only $G_{i:j}$, not $P_{i:j}$. Redraw the prefix network, replacing black cells with gray cells wherever possible.

Exercise 5.6 The prefix network shown in Figure 5.7 is not the only way to calculate all of the prefixes in logarithmic time. The *Kogge-Stone* network is another common prefix network that performs the same function using a different connection of black cells. Research Kogge-Stone adders and draw a schematic similar to Figure 5.7 showing the connection of black cells in a Kogge-Stone adder.

Exercise 5.7 Recall that an N-input priority encoder has $\log_2 N$ outputs that encodes which of the N inputs gets priority (see Exercise 2.36).

(a) Design an N-input priority encoder that has delay that increases logarithmically with N. Sketch your design and give the delay of the circuit in terms of the delay of its circuit elements.

(b) Code your design in an HDL. Simulate and test your module to prove that it functions correctly.

Exercise 5.8 Design the following comparators for 32-bit unsigned numbers. Sketch the schematics.

(a) not equal

(b) greater than or equal to

(c) less than

Exercise 5.9 Consider the signed comparator of Figure 5.12.

(a) Give an example of two 4-bit signed numbers A and B for which a 4-bit signed comparator correctly computes $A < B$.

(b) Give an example of two 4-bit signed numbers A and B for which a 4-bit signed comparator incorrectly computes $A < B$.

(c) In general, when does the N-bit signed comparator operate incorrectly?

Exercise 5.10 Modify the N-bit signed comparator of Figure 5.12 to correctly compute $A < B$ for all N-bit signed inputs A and B.

Exercise 5.11 Design the 32-bit ALU shown in Figure 5.15 using your favorite HDL. You can make the top-level module either behavioral or structural.

Exercise 5.12 Design the 32-bit ALU shown in Figure 5.17 using your favorite HDL. You can make the top-level module either behavioral or structural.

Exercise 5.13 Write a testbench to test the 32-bit ALU from Exercise 5.11. Then use it to test the ALU. Include any test vector files necessary. Be sure to test enough corner cases to convince a reasonable skeptic that the ALU functions correctly.

Exercise 5.14 Repeat Exercise 5.13 for the ALU from Exercise 5.12.

Exercise 5.15 Build an Unsigned Comparison Unit that compares two unsigned numbers A and B. The unit's input is the *ALUFlags* signal (N, Z, C, V) from the ALU of Figure 5.16, with the ALU performing subtraction: $A - B$. The unit's outputs are HS, LS, HI, and LO, which indicate that A is higher than or the same as (HS), lower than or the same as (LS), higher (HI), or lower (LO) than B.

(a) Write minimal equations for HS, LS, HI, and LO in terms of N, Z, C, and V.

(b) Sketch circuits for HS, LS, HI, and LO.

Exercise 5.16 Build a Signed Comparison Unit that compares two signed numbers A and B. The unit's input is the *ALUFlags* signal (N, Z, C, V) from the ALU of Figure 5.16, with the ALU performing subtraction: $A - B$. The unit's outputs are GE, LE, GT, and LT, which indicate that A is greater than or equal to (GE), less than or equal to (LE), greater than (GT), or less than (LT) B.

(a) Write minimal equations for GE, LE, GT, and LT in terms of N, Z, C, and V.

(b) Sketch circuits for GE, LE, GT, and LT.

Exercise 5.17 Design a shifter that always shifts a 32-bit input left by 2 bits. The input and output are both 32 bits. Explain the design in words and sketch a schematic. Implement your design in your favorite HDL.

Exercise 5.18 Design 4-bit left and right rotators. Sketch a schematic of your design. Implement your design in your favorite HDL.

Exercise 5.19 Design an 8-bit left shifter using only 24 2:1 multiplexers. The shifter accepts an 8-bit input A and a 3-bit shift amount, $shamt_{2:0}$. It produces an 8-bit output Y. Sketch the schematic.

Exercise 5.20 Explain how to build any N-bit shifter or rotator using only $N\log_2 N$ 2:1 multiplexers.

Exercise 5.21 The *funnel shifter* in Figure 5.65 can perform any N-bit shift or rotate operation. It shifts a $2N$-bit input right by k bits. The output Y is the N least significant bits of the result. The most significant N bits of the input are called B and the least significant N bits are called C. By choosing appropriate values of B, C, and k, the funnel shifter can perform any type of shift or rotate. Explain what these values should be in terms of A, $shamt$, and N for

(a) logical right shift of A by $shamt$

(b) arithmetic right shift of A by $shamt$

(c) left shift of A by $shamt$

(d) right rotate of A by $shamt$

(e) left rotate of A by $shamt$

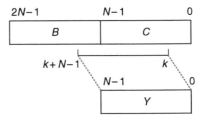

Figure 5.65 Funnel shifter

Exercise 5.22 Find the critical path for the 4×4 multiplier from Figure 5.20 in terms of an AND gate delay (t_{AND}) and an adder delay (t_{FA}) What is the delay of an $N \times N$ multiplier built in the same way?

Exercise 5.23 Find the critical path for the 4×4 divider from Figure 5.21 in terms of a 2:1 mux delay (t_{MUX}), an adder delay (t_{FA}), and an inverter delay (t_{INV}). What is the delay of an $N \times N$ divider built in the same way?

Exercise 5.24 Design a multiplier that handles two's complement numbers.

Exercise 5.25 A *sign extension unit* extends a two's complement number from M to N ($N > M$) bits by copying the most significant bit of the input into the upper bits of the output (see Section 1.4.6). It receives an M-bit input A and produces an N-bit output Y. Sketch a circuit for a sign extension unit with a 4-bit input and an 8-bit output. Write the HDL for your design.

Exercise 5.26 A *zero extension unit* extends an unsigned number from M to N bits ($N > M$) by putting zeros in the upper bits of the output. Sketch a circuit for a zero extension unit with a 4-bit input and an 8-bit output. Write the HDL for your design.

Exercise 5.27 Compute $111001.000_2/001100.000_2$ in binary using the standard division algorithm from elementary school. Show your work.

Exercise 5.28 What is the range of numbers that can be represented by the following number systems?

(a) 24-bit unsigned fixed-point numbers with 12 integer bits and 12 fraction bits

(b) 24-bit sign and magnitude fixed-point numbers with 12 integer bits and 12 fraction bits

(c) 24-bit two's complement fixed-point numbers with 12 integer bits and 12 fraction bits

Exercise 5.29 Express the following base 10 numbers in 16-bit fixed-point sign/magnitude format with eight integer bits and eight fraction bits. Express your answer in hexadecimal.

(a) -13.5625

(b) 42.3125

(c) -17.15625

Exercise 5.30 Express the following base 10 numbers in 12-bit fixed-point sign/magnitude format with six integer bits and six fraction bits. Express your answer in hexadecimal.

(a) −30.5

(b)   16.25

(c) −8.078125

Exercise 5.31 Express the base 10 numbers in Exercise 5.29 in 16-bit fixed-point two's complement format with eight integer bits and eight fraction bits. Express your answer in hexadecimal.

Exercise 5.32 Express the base 10 numbers in Exercise 5.30 in 12-bit fixed-point two's complement format with six integer bits and six fraction bits. Express your answer in hexadecimal.

Exercise 5.33 Express the base 10 numbers in Exercise 5.29 in IEEE 754 single-precision floating-point format. Express your answer in hexadecimal.

Exercise 5.34 Express the base 10 numbers in Exercise 5.30 in IEEE 754 single-precision floating-point format. Express your answer in hexadecimal.

Exercise 5.35 Convert the following two's complement binary fixed-point numbers to base 10. The implied binary point is explicitly shown to aid in your interpretation.

(a) 0101.1000

(b) 1111.1111

(c) 1000.0000

Exercise 5.36 Repeat Exercise 5.35 for the following two's complement binary fixed-point numbers.

(a) 011101.10101

(b) 100110.11010

(c) 101000.00100

Exercise 5.37 When adding two floating-point numbers, the number with the smaller exponent is shifted. Why is this? Explain in words and give an example to justify your explanation.

Exercise 5.38 Add the following IEEE 754 single-precision floating-point numbers.

(a) C0123456 + 81C564B7

(b) D0B10301 + D1B43203

(c) 5EF10324 + 5E039020

Exercise 5.39 Add the following IEEE 754 single-precision floating-point numbers.

(a) C0D20004 + 72407020

(b) C0D20004 + 40DC0004

(c) (5FBE4000 + 3FF80000) + DFDE4000
(Why is the result counterintuitive? Explain.)

Exercise 5.40 Expand the steps in section 5.3.2 for performing floating-point addition to work for negative as well as positive floating-point numbers.

Exercise 5.41 Consider IEEE 754 single-precision floating-point numbers.

(a) How many numbers can be represented by IEEE 754 single-precision floating-point format? You need not count $\pm\infty$ or NaN.

(b) How many additional numbers could be represented if $\pm\infty$ and NaN were not represented?

(c) Explain why $\pm\infty$ and NaN are given special representations.

Exercise 5.42 Consider the following decimal numbers: 245 and 0.0625.

(a) Write the two numbers using single-precision floating-point notation. Give your answers in hexadecimal.

(b) Perform a magnitude comparison of the two 32-bit numbers from part (a). In other words, interpret the two 32-bit numbers as two's complement numbers and compare them. Does the integer comparison give the correct result?

(c) You decide to come up with a new single-precision floating-point notation. Everything is the same as the IEEE 754 single-precision floating-point standard, except that you represent the exponent using two's complement instead of a bias. Write the two numbers using your new standard. Give your answers in hexadecimal.

(e) Does integer comparison work with your new floating-point notation from part (d)?

(f) Why is it convenient for integer comparison to work with floating-point numbers?

Exercise 5.43 Design a single-precision floating-point adder using your favorite HDL. Before coding the design in an HDL, sketch a schematic of your design. Simulate and test your adder to prove to a skeptic that it functions correctly. You may consider positive numbers only and use round toward zero (truncate). You may also ignore the special cases given in Table 5.2.

Exercise 5.44 In this problem, you will explore the design of a 32-bit floating-point multiplier. The multiplier has two 32-bit floating-point inputs and produces a 32-bit floating-point output. You may consider positive numbers only and use round toward zero (truncate). You may also ignore the special cases given in Table 5.2.

(a) Write the steps necessary to perform 32-bit floating-point multiplication.

(b) Sketch the schematic of a 32-bit floating-point multiplier.

(c) Design a 32-bit floating-point multiplier in an HDL. Simulate and test your multiplier to prove to a skeptic that it functions correctly.

Exercise 5.45 In this problem, you will explore the design of a 32-bit prefix adder.

(a) Sketch a schematic of your design.

(b) Design the 32-bit prefix adder in an HDL. Simulate and test your adder to prove that it functions correctly.

(c) What is the delay of your 32-bit prefix adder from part (a)? Assume that each two-input gate delay is 100 ps.

(d) Design a pipelined version of the 32-bit prefix adder. Sketch the schematic of your design. How fast can your pipelined prefix adder run? You may assume a sequencing overhead ($t_{pcq} + t_{setup}$) of 80 ps. Make the design run as fast as possible.

(e) Design the pipelined 32-bit prefix adder in an HDL.

Exercise 5.46 An incrementer adds 1 to an N-bit number. Build an 8-bit incrementer using half adders.

Exercise 5.47 Build a 32-bit synchronous *Up/Down counter*. The inputs are *Reset* and *Up*. When *Reset* is 1, the outputs are all 0. Otherwise, when $Up = 1$, the circuit counts up, and when $Up = 0$, the circuit counts down.

Exercise 5.48 Design a 32-bit counter that adds 4 at each clock edge. The counter has reset and clock inputs. Upon reset, the counter output is all 0.

Exercise 5.49 Modify the counter from Exercise 5.48 such that the counter will either increment by 4 or load a new 32-bit value, D, on each clock edge, depending on a control signal *Load*. When $Load = 1$, the counter loads the new value D.

Exercise 5.50 An N-bit *Johnson counter* consists of an N-bit shift register with a reset signal. The output of the shift register (S_{out}) is inverted and fed back to the input (S_{in}). When the counter is reset, all of the bits are cleared to 0.

(a) Show the sequence of outputs, $Q_{3:0}$, produced by a 4-bit Johnson counter starting immediately after the counter is reset.

(b) How many cycles elapse until an N-bit Johnson counter repeats its sequence? Explain.

(c) Design a decimal counter using a 5-bit Johnson counter, ten AND gates, and inverters. The decimal counter has a clock, a reset, and ten one-hot outputs $Y_{9:0}$. When the counter is reset, Y_0 is asserted. On each subsequent cycle, the next output should be asserted. After ten cycles, the counter should repeat. Sketch a schematic of the decimal counter.

(d) What advantages might a Johnson counter have over a conventional counter?

Exercise 5.51 Write the HDL for a 4-bit scannable flip-flop like the one shown in Figure 5.38. Simulate and test your HDL module to prove that it functions correctly.

Exercise 5.52 The English language has a good deal of redundancy that allows us to reconstruct garbled transmissions. Binary data can also be transmitted in redundant form to allow error correction. For example, the number 0 could be coded as 00000 and the number 1 could be coded as 11111. The value could then be sent over a noisy channel that might flip up to two of the bits. The receiver could reconstruct the original data because a 0 will have at least three of the five received bits as 0's; similarly a 1 will have at least three 1's.

(a) Propose an encoding to send 00, 01, 10, or 11 encoded using five bits of information such that all errors that corrupt one bit of the encoded data can be corrected. Hint: the encodings 00000 and 11111 for 00 and 11, respectively, will not work.

(b) Design a circuit that receives your five-bit encoded data and decodes it to 00, 01, 10, or 11, even if one bit of the transmitted data has been changed.

(c) Suppose you wanted to change to an alternative 5-bit encoding. How might you implement your design to make it easy to change the encoding without having to use different hardware?

Exercise 5.53 Flash EEPROM, simply called Flash memory, is a fairly recent invention that has revolutionized consumer electronics. Research and explain how Flash memory works. Use a diagram illustrating the floating gate. Describe how a bit in the memory is programmed. Properly cite your sources.

Exercise 5.54 The extraterrestrial life project team has just discovered aliens living on the bottom of Mono Lake. They need to construct a circuit to classify the aliens by potential planet of origin based on measured features available from the NASA probe: greenness, brownness, sliminess, and ugliness. Careful consultation with xenobiologists leads to the following conclusions:

- If the alien is green and slimy or ugly, brown, and slimy, it might be from Mars.

- If the critter is ugly, brown, and slimy, or green and neither ugly nor slimy, it might be from Venus.

- If the beastie is brown and neither ugly nor slimy or is green and slimy, it might be from Jupiter.

Note that this is an inexact science; for example, a life form which is mottled green and brown and is slimy but not ugly might be from either Mars or Jupiter.

(a) Program a $4 \times 4 \times 3$ PLA to identify the alien. You may use dot notation.

(b) Program a 16×3 ROM to identify the alien. You may use dot notation.

(c) Implement your design in an HDL.

Exercise 5.55 Implement the following functions using a single 16×3 ROM. Use dot notation to indicate the ROM contents.

(a) $X = AB + B\overline{C}D + \overline{A}\,\overline{B}$

(b) $Y = AB + BD$

(c) $Z = A + B + C + D$

Exercise 5.56 Implement the functions from Exercise 5.55 using a $4 \times 8 \times 3$ PLA. You may use dot notation.

Exercise 5.57 Specify the size of a ROM that you could use to program each of the following combinational circuits. Is using a ROM to implement these functions a good design choice? Explain why or why not.

(a) a 16-bit adder/subtractor with C_{in} and C_{out}

(b) an 8×8 multiplier

(c) a 16-bit priority encoder (see Exercise 2.36)

Exercise 5.58 Consider the ROM circuits in Figure 5.66. For each row, can the circuit in column I be replaced by an equivalent circuit in column II by proper programming of the latter's ROM?

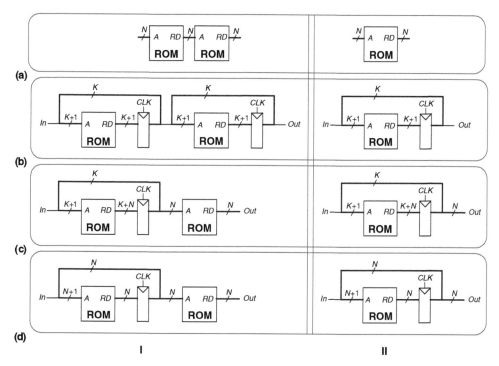

Figure 5.66 ROM circuits

Exercise 5.59 How many Cyclone IV FPGA LEs are required to perform each of the following functions? Show how to configure one or more LEs to perform the function. You should be able to do this by inspection, without performing logic synthesis.

(a) the combinational function from Exercise 2.13(c)

(b) the combinational function from Exercise 2.17(c)

(c) the two-output function from Exercise 2.24

(d) the function from Exercise 2.35

(e) a four-input priority encoder (see Exercise 2.36)

Exercise 5.60 Repeat Exercise 5.59 for the following functions.

(a) an eight-input priority encoder (see Exercise 2.36)

(b) a 3:8 decoder

(c) a 4-bit carry propagate adder (with no carry in or out)

(d) the FSM from Exercise 3.22

(e) the Gray code counter from Exercise 3.27

Exercise 5.61 Consider the Cyclone IV LE shown in Figure 5.59. According to the datasheet, it has the timing specifications given in Table 5.5.

(a) What is the minimum number of Cyclone IV LEs required to implement the FSM of Figure 3.26?

(b) Without clock skew, what is the fastest clock frequency at which this FSM will run reliably?

(c) With 3 ns of clock skew, what is the fastest frequency at which the FSM will run reliably?

Table 5.5 Cyclone IV timing

Name	Value (ps)
t_{pcq}, t_{ccq}	199
t_{setup}	76
t_{hold}	0
t_{pd} (per LE)	381
t_{wire} (between LEs)	246
t_{skew}	0

Exercise 5.62 Repeat Exercise 5.61 for the FSM of Figure 3.31(b).

Exercise 5.63 You would like to use an FPGA to implement an M&M sorter with a color sensor and motors to put red candy in one jar and green candy in another. The design is to be implemented as an FSM using a Cyclone IV FPGA. According to the data sheet, the FPGA has timing characteristics shown in Table 5.5. You would like your FSM to run at 100 MHz. What is the maximum number of LEs on the critical path? What is the fastest speed at which the FSM will run?

Interview Questions

The following exercises present questions that have been asked at interviews for digital design jobs.

Question 5.1 What is the largest possible result of multiplying two unsigned N-bit numbers?

Question 5.2 *Binary coded decimal* (BCD) representation uses four bits to encode each decimal digit. For example, 42_{10} is represented as 01000010_{BCD}. Explain in words why processors might use BCD representation.

Question 5.3 Design hardware to add two 8-bit unsigned BCD numbers (see Question 5.2). Sketch a schematic for your design, and write an HDL module for the BCD adder. The inputs are A, B, and C_{in}, and the outputs are S and C_{out}. C_{in} and C_{out} are 1-bit carries and A, B, and S are 8-bit BCD numbers.

JUMP

FETCH

ADD

Architecture

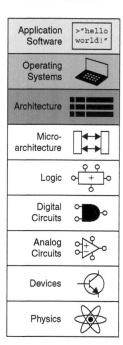

6.1 INTRODUCTION

The previous chapters introduced digital design principles and building blocks. In this chapter, we jump up a few levels of abstraction to define the architecture of a computer. The *architecture* is the programmer's view of a computer. It is defined by the instruction set (language) and operand locations (registers and memory). Many different architectures exist, such as ARM, x86, MIPS, SPARC, and PowerPC.

The first step in understanding any computer architecture is to learn its language. The words in a computer's language are called *instructions*. The computer's vocabulary is called the *instruction set*. All programs running on a computer use the same instruction set. Even complex software applications, such as word processing and spreadsheet applications, are eventually compiled into a series of simple instructions such as add, subtract, and branch. Computer instructions indicate both the operation to perform and the operands to use. The operands may come from memory, from registers, or from the instruction itself.

Computer hardware understands only 1's and 0's, so instructions are encoded as binary numbers in a format called machine language. Just as we use letters to encode human language, computers use binary numbers to encode machine language. The ARM architecture represents each instruction as a 32-bit word. Microprocessors are digital systems that read and execute machine language instructions. However, humans consider reading machine language to be tedious, so we prefer to represent the instructions in a symbolic format called assembly language.

The instruction sets of different architectures are more like different dialects than different languages. Almost all architectures define basic instructions, such as add, subtract, and branch, that operate on memory or registers. Once you have learned one instruction set, understanding others is fairly straightforward.

A computer architecture does not define the underlying hardware implementation. Often, many different hardware implementations of a single architecture exist. For example, Intel and Advanced Micro Devices (AMD) both sell various microprocessors belonging to the same x86 architecture. They all can run the same programs, but they use different underlying hardware and therefore offer trade-offs in performance, price, and power. Some microprocessors are optimized for high-performance servers, whereas others are optimized for long battery life in laptop computers. The specific arrangement of registers, memories, ALUs, and other building blocks to form a microprocessor is called the microarchitecture and will be the subject of Chapter 7. Often, many different microarchitectures exist for a single architecture.

In this text, we introduce the ARM architecture. This architecture was first developed in the 1980s by Acorn Computer Group, which spun off Advanced RISC Machines Ltd., now known as ARM. Over 10 billion ARM processors are sold every year. Almost all cell phones and tablets contain multiple ARM processors. The architecture is used in everything from pinball machines to cameras to robots to cars to rack-mounted servers. ARM is unusual in that it does not sell processors directly, but rather licenses other companies to build its processors, often as part of a larger system-on-chip. For example, Samsung, Altera, Apple, and Qualcomm all build ARM processors, either using microarchitectures purchased from ARM or microarchitectures developed internally under license from ARM. We choose to focus on ARM because it is a commercial leader and because the architecture is clean, with few idiosyncrasies. We start by introducing assembly language instructions, operand locations, and common programming constructs, such as branches, loops, array manipulations, and function calls. We then describe how the assembly language translates into machine language and show how a program is loaded into memory and executed.

Throughout the chapter, we motivate the design of the ARM architecture using four principles articulated by David Patterson and John Hennessy in their text *Computer Organization and Design*: (1) regularity supports simplicity; (2) make the common case fast; (3) smaller is faster; and (4) good design demands good compromises.

> The "ARM architecture" we describe is ARM version 4 (ARMv4), which forms the core of the instruction set. Section 6.7 summarizes new features in versions 5–8 of the architecture. The ARM *Architecture Reference Manual* (ARM), available online, is the authoritative definition of the architecture.

6.2 ASSEMBLY LANGUAGE

Assembly language is the human-readable representation of the computer's native language. Each assembly language instruction specifies both the operation to perform and the operands on which to operate. We introduce simple arithmetic instructions and show how these operations are written in assembly language. We then define the ARM instruction operands: registers, memory, and constants.

This chapter assumes that you already have some familiarity with a high-level programming language such as C, C++, or Java.

(These languages are practically identical for most of the examples in this chapter, but where they differ, we will use C.) Appendix C provides an introduction to C for those with little or no prior programming experience.

6.2.1 Instructions

The most common operation computers perform is addition. Code Example 6.1 shows code for adding variables b and c and writing the result to a. The code is shown on the left in a high-level language (using the syntax of C, C++, and Java) and then rewritten on the right in ARM assembly language. Note that statements in a C program end with a semicolon.

We used Keil's ARM Microcontroller Development Kit (MDK-ARM) to compile, assemble, and simulate the example assembly code in this chapter. The MDK-ARM is a free development tool that comes with a complete ARM compiler. Labs available on this textbook's companion site (see Preface) show how to install and use this tool to write, compile, simulate, and debug both C and assembly programs.

Code Example 6.1 ADDITION

High-Level Code	ARM Assembly Code
a = b + c;	ADD a, b, c

The first part of the assembly instruction, ADD, is called the *mnemonic* and indicates what operation to perform. The operation is performed on b and c, the *source operands*, and the result is written to a, the *destination operand*.

Mnemonic (pronounced ni-mon-ik) comes from the Greek word μιμνΕσκεστηαι, to remember. The assembly language mnemonic is easier to remember than a machine language pattern of 0's and 1's representing the same operation.

Code Example 6.2 SUBTRACTION

High-Level Code	ARM Assembly Code
a = b − c;	SUB a, b, c

Code Example 6.2 shows that subtraction is similar to addition. The instruction format is the same as the ADD instruction except for the operation specification, SUB. This consistent instruction format is an example of the first design principle:

Design Principle 1: Regularity supports simplicity.

Instructions with a consistent number of operands—in this case, two sources and one destination—are easier to encode and handle in hardware. More complex high-level code translates into multiple ARM instructions, as shown in Code Example 6.3.

In the high-level language examples, single-line comments begin with // and continue until the end of the line. Multiline comments begin with /* and end with */. In ARM assembly language, only single-line comments

---

Code Example 6.3 MORE COMPLEX CODE

High-Level Code	ARM Assembly Code

`a = b + c - d;    // single-line comment`
`                 /* multiple-line`
`                    comment */`
	`ADD t, b, c  ; t = b + c`
	`SUB a, t, d  ; a = t - d`

---

are used. They begin with a semicolon (;) and continue until the end of the line. The assembly language program in Code Example 6.3 requires a temporary variable t to store the intermediate result. Using multiple assembly language instructions to perform more complex operations is an example of the second design principle of computer architecture:

Design Principle 2: Make the common case fast.

The ARM instruction set makes the common case fast by including only simple, commonly used instructions. The number of instructions is kept small so that the hardware required to decode the instruction and its operands can be simple, small, and fast. More elaborate operations that are less common are performed using sequences of multiple simple instructions. Thus, ARM is a *reduced instruction set computer* (RISC) architecture. Architectures with many complex instructions, such as Intel's x86 architecture, are *complex instruction set computers* (CISC). For example, x86 defines a "string move" instruction that copies a string (a series of characters) from one part of memory to another. Such an operation requires many, possibly even hundreds, of simple instructions in a RISC machine. However, the cost of implementing complex instructions in a CISC architecture is added hardware and overhead that slows down the simple instructions.

A RISC architecture minimizes the hardware complexity and the necessary instruction encoding by keeping the set of distinct instructions small. For example, an instruction set with 64 simple instructions would need $\log_2 64 = 6$ bits to encode the operation. An instruction set with 256 complex instructions would need $\log_2 256 = 8$ bits of encoding per instruction. In a CISC machine, even though the complex instructions may be used only rarely, they add overhead to all instructions, even the simple ones.

6.2.2 Operands: Registers, Memory, and Constants

An instruction operates on *operands*. In Code Example 6.1, the variables a, b, and c are all operands. But computers operate on 1's and 0's, not variable names. The instructions need a physical location from which to retrieve the binary data. Operands can be stored in registers or memory, or they may be constants stored in the instruction itself. Computers use various locations to hold operands in order to optimize for speed and data capacity. Operands stored as constants or in registers are accessed quickly, but they hold only a small amount of data. Additional data must be accessed from memory, which is large but slow. ARM (prior to ARMv8) is called a 32-bit architecture because it operates on 32-bit data.

Version 8 of the ARM architecture has been extended to 64 bits, but we will focus on the 32-bit version in this book.

Registers

Instructions need to access operands quickly so that they can run fast. But operands stored in memory take a long time to retrieve. Therefore, most architectures specify a small number of registers that hold commonly used operands. The ARM architecture uses 16 registers, called the *register set* or *register file*. The fewer the registers, the faster they can be accessed. This leads to the third design principle:

Design Principle 3: Smaller is faster.

Looking up information from a small number of relevant books on your desk is a lot faster than searching for the information in the stacks at a library. Likewise, reading data from a small register file is faster than reading it from a large memory. A register file is typically built from a small SRAM array (see Section 5.5.3).

Code Example 6.4 shows the ADD instruction with register operands. ARM register names are preceded by the letter 'R'. The variables a, b, and c are arbitrarily placed in R0, R1, and R2. The name R1 is pronounced "register 1" or "R1" or "register R1". The instruction adds the 32-bit values contained in R1 (b) and R2 (c) and writes the 32-bit result to R0 (a). Code Example 6.5 shows ARM assembly code using a register, R4, to store the intermediate calculation of b + c:

Code Example 6.4 REGISTER OPERANDS

High-Level Code	ARM Assembly Code
a = b + c;	; R0 = a, R1 = b, R2 = c ADD R0, R1, R2 ; a = b + c

---

Code Example 6.5 TEMPORARY REGISTERS

High-Level Code	ARM Assembly Code

a = b + c − d;	; R0 = a, R1 = b, R2 = c, R3 = d; R4 = t
	ADD R4, R1, R2 ; t = b + c
	SUB R0, R4, R3 ; a = t − d

**Example 6.1 TRANSLATING HIGH-LEVEL CODE TO ASSEMBLY
                LANGUAGE**

Translate the following high-level code into ARM assembly language. Assume
variables a–c are held in registers R0–R2 and f–j are in R3–R7.

```
a = b - c;
f = (g + h) - (i + j);
```

Solution: The program uses four assembly language instructions.

```
; ARM assembly code
; R0 = a, R1 = b, R2 = c, R3 = f, R4 = g, R5 = h, R6 = i, R7 = j
  SUB R0, R1, R2    ; a = b - c
  ADD R8, R4, R5    ; R8 = g + h
  ADD R9, R6, R7    ; R9 = i + j
  SUB R3, R8, R9    ; f = (g + h) - (i + j)
```

The Register Set

Table 6.1 lists the name and use for each of the 16 ARM registers. R0–R12
are used for storing variables; R0–R3 also have special uses during procedure calls. R13–R15 are also called SP, LR, and PC, and they will be
described later in this chapter.

Constants/Immediates

In addition to register operations, ARM instructions can use constant or
immediate operands. These constants are called immediates, because their
values are immediately available from the instruction and do not require a
register or memory access. Code Example 6.6 shows the ADD instruction
adding an immediate to a register. In assembly code, the immediate is preceded by the # symbol and can be written in decimal or hexadecimal.
Hexadecimal constants in ARM assembly language start with 0x, as they

Table 6.1 ARM register set

Name	Use
R0	Argument / return value / temporary variable
R1–R3	Argument / temporary variables
R4–R11	Saved variables
R12	Temporary variable
R13 (SP)	Stack Pointer
R14 (LR)	Link Register
R15 (PC)	Program Counter

Code Example 6.6 IMMEDIATE OPERANDS

High-Level Code	ARM Assembly Code

`a = a + 4;`
`b = a - 12;`
	`; R7 = a, R8 = b`
	`  ADD R7, R7, #4    ; a = a + 4`
	`  SUB R8, R7, #0xC  ; b = a - 12`

Code Example 6.7 INITIALIZING VALUES USING IMMEDIATES

High-Level Code	ARM Assembly Code

`i = 0;`
`x = 4080;`
	`; R4 = i, R5 = x`
	`  MOV R4, #0       ; i = 0`
	`  MOV R5, #0xFF0   ; x = 4080`

---

do in C. Immediates are unsigned 8- to 12-bit numbers with a peculiar encoding described in Section 6.4.

The move instruction (MOV) is a useful way to initialize register values. Code Example 6.7 initializes the variables i and x to 0 and 4080, respectively. MOV can also take a register source operand. For example, MOV R1, R7 copies the contents of register R7 into R1.

Memory

If registers were the only storage space for operands, we would be confined to simple programs with no more than 15 variables. However, data can also be stored in memory. Whereas the register file is small and fast, memory is larger and slower. For this reason, frequently used variables are kept in registers. In the ARM architecture, instructions operate exclusively on registers, so data stored in memory must be moved to a register before it can be processed. By using a combination of memory and registers, a program can access a large amount of data fairly quickly. Recall from Section 5.5 that memories are organized as an array of data words. The ARM architecture uses 32-bit memory addresses and 32-bit data words.

ARM uses a *byte-addressable* memory. That is, each byte in memory has a unique address, as shown in Figure 6.1(a). A 32-bit word consists of four 8-bit bytes, so each word address is a multiple of 4. The most significant byte (MSB) is on the left and the least significant byte (LSB) is on the right. Both the 32-bit word address and the data value in Figure 6.1(b) are given in hexadecimal. For example, data word 0xF2F1AC07 is stored at memory address 4. By convention, memory is drawn with low memory addresses toward the bottom and high memory addresses toward the top.

ARM provides the *load register* instruction, LDR, to read a data word from memory into a register. Code Example 6.8 loads memory word 2 into a (R7). In C, the number inside the brackets is the *index* or word number,

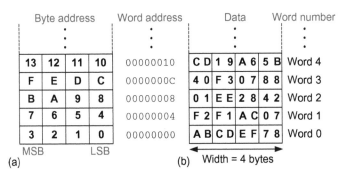

Figure 6.1 ARM byte-addressable memory showing: (a) byte address and (b) data

---

Code Example 6.8 READING MEMORY

High-Level Code	**ARM Assembly Code**

`a = mem[2];`	`; R7 = a`
	`MOV R5, #0      ; base address = 0`
	`LDR R7, [R5, #8]   ; R7 <= data at memory address (R5+8)`

A read from the base address (i.e., index 0) is a special case that requires no offset in the assembly code. For example, a memory read from the base address held in R5 is written as LDR R3, [R5].

ARMv4 requires *word-aligned addresses* for LDR and STR, that is, a word address that is divisible by four. Since ARMv6, this alignment restriction can be removed by setting a bit in the ARM system control register, but performance of *unaligned* loads is usually worse. Some architectures, such as x86, allow non-word-aligned data reads and writes, but others, such as MIPS, require strict alignment for simplicity. Of course, byte addresses for load byte and store byte, LDRB and STRB (discussed in Section 6.3.6), need not be word aligned.

which we discuss further in Section 6.3.6. The LDR instruction specifies the memory address using a *base register* (R5) and an *offset* (8). Recall that each data word is 4 bytes, so word number 1 is at address 4, word number 2 is at address 8, and so on. The word address is four times the word number. The memory address is formed by adding the contents of the base register (R5) and the offset. ARM offers several modes for accessing memory, as will be discussed in Section 6.3.6.

After the load register instruction (LDR) is executed in Code Example 6.8, R7 holds the value 0x01EE2842, which is the data value stored at memory address 8 in Figure 6.1.

ARM uses the *store register* instruction, STR, to write a data word from a register into memory. Code Example 6.9 writes the value 42 from register R9 into memory word 5.

Byte-addressable memories are organized in a big-endian or little-endian fashion, as shown in Figure 6.2. In both formats, a 32-bit word's most significant byte (MSB) is on the left and the least significant byte (LSB) is on the right. Word addresses are the same in both formats and refer to the same four bytes. Only the addresses of bytes within a word

---

Code Example 6.9 WRITING MEMORY

High-Level Code	**ARM Assembly Code**

`mem[5] = 42;`	`MOV R1, #0       ; base address = 0`
	`MOV R9, #42`
	`STR R9, [R1, #0x14]  ; value stored at memory address (R1+20) = 42`

Big-Endian   Little-Endian

| Byte Address | Word Address | Byte Address |

C	D	E	F	C	F	E	D	C
8	9	A	B	8	B	A	9	8
4	5	6	7	4	7	6	5	4
0	1	2	3	0	3	2	1	0

MSB   LSB   MSB   LSB

Figure 6.2 Big-endian and little-endian memory addressing

differ. In *big-endian* machines, bytes are numbered starting with 0 at the big (most significant) end. In *little-endian* machines, bytes are numbered starting with 0 at the little (least significant) end.

IBM's PowerPC (formerly found in Macintosh computers) uses big-endian addressing. Intel's x86 architecture (found in PCs) uses little-endian addressing. ARM prefers little-endian but provides support in some versions for *bi-endian* data addressing, which allows data loads and stores in either format. The choice of endianness is completely arbitrary but leads to hassles when sharing data between big-endian and little-endian computers. In examples in this text, we use little-endian format whenever byte ordering matters.

6.3 PROGRAMMING

Software languages such as C or Java are called high-level programming languages because they are written at a more abstract level than assembly language. Many high-level languages use common software constructs such as arithmetic and logical operations, conditional execution, if/else statements, for and while loops, array indexing, and function calls. See Appendix C for more examples of these constructs in C. In this section, we explore how to translate these high-level constructs into ARM assembly code.

6.3.1 Data-processing Instructions

The ARM architecture defines a variety of *data-processing* instruction (often called logical and arithmetic instructions in other architectures). We introduce these instructions briefly here because they are necessary to implement higher-level constructs. Appendix B provides a summary of ARM instructions.

Logical Instructions

ARM *logical operations* include AND, ORR (OR), EOR (XOR), and BIC (bit clear). These each operate bitwise on two sources and write the result

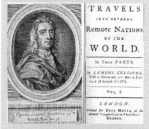

The terms big-endian and little-endian come from Jonathan Swift's *Gulliver's Travels*, first published in 1726 under the pseudonym of Isaac Bickerstaff. In his stories, the Lilliputian king required his citizens (the Little-Endians) to break their eggs on the little end. The Big-Endians were rebels who broke their eggs on the big end.

These terms were first applied to computer architectures by Danny Cohen in his paper "On Holy Wars and a Plea for Peace" published on April Fools Day, 1980 (*USC/ISI IEN 137*). (Photo courtesy of The Brotherton Collection, Leeds University Library.)

Source registers

R1	0100 0110	1010 0001	1111 0001	1011 0111
R2	1111 1111	1111 1111	0000 0000	0000 0000

Figure 6.3 Logical operations

Assembly code

Result

AND R3, R1, R2	R3	0100 0110	1010 0001	0000 0000	0000 0000
ORR R4, R1, R2	R4	1111 1111	1111 1111	1111 0001	1011 0111
EOR R5, R1, R2	R5	1011 1001	0101 1110	1111 0001	1011 0111
BIC R6, R1, R2	R6	0000 0000	0000 0000	1111 0001	1011 0111
MVN R7, R2	R7	0000 0000	0000 0000	1111 1111	1111 1111

to a destination register. The first source is always a register and the second source is either an immediate or another register. Another logical operation, MVN (MoVe and Not), performs a bitwise NOT on the second source (an immediate or register) and writes the result to the destination register. Figure 6.3 shows examples of these operations on the two source values 0x46A1F1B7 and 0xFFFF0000. The figure shows the values stored in the destination register after the instruction executes.

The bit clear (BIC) instruction is useful for masking bits (i.e., forcing unwanted bits to 0). BIC R6, R1, R2 computes R1 AND NOT R2. In other words, BIC clears the bits that are asserted in R2. In this case, the top two bytes of R1 are cleared or *masked*, and the unmasked bottom two bytes of R1, 0xF1B7, are placed in R6. Any subset of register bits can be masked.

The ORR instruction is useful for combining bitfields from two registers. For example, 0x347A0000 ORR 0x000072FC = 0x347A72FC.

Shift Instructions

Shift instructions shift the value in a register left or right, dropping bits off the end. The rotate instruction rotates the value in a register right by up to 31 bits. We refer to both shift and rotate generically as shift operations. ARM shift operations are LSL (logical shift left), LSR (logical shift right), ASR (arithmetic shift right), and ROR (rotate right). There is no ROL instruction because left rotation can be performed with a right rotation by a complementary amount.

As discussed in Section 5.2.5, left shifts always fill the least significant bits with 0's. However, right shifts can be either logical (0's shift into the most significant bits) or arithmetic (the sign bit shifts into the most significant bits). The amount by which to shift can be an immediate or a register.

Figure 6.4 shows the assembly code and resulting register values for LSL, LSR, ASR, and ROR when shifting by an immediate value. R5 is shifted by the immediate amount, and the result is placed in the destination register.

Source register

| R5 | 1111 1111 | 0001 1100 | 0001 0000 | 1110 0111 |

Assembly Code

Result

Figure 6.4 **Shift instructions with immediate shift amounts**

LSL R0, R5, #7	R0	1000 1110	0000 1000	0111 0011	1000 0000
LSR R1, R5, #17	R1	0000 0000	0000 0000	0111 1111	1000 1110
ASR R2, R5, #3	R2	1111 1111	1110 0011	1000 0010	0001 1100
ROR R3, R5, #21	R3	1110 0000	1000 0111	0011 1111	1111 1000

Source registers

| R8 | 0000 1000 | 0001 1100 | 0001 0110 | 1110 0111 |
| R6 | 0000 0000 | 0000 0000 | 0000 0000 | 0001 0100 |

Assembly code

Result

Figure 6.5 **Shift instructions with register shift amounts**

| LSL R4, R8, R6 | R4 | 0110 1110 | 0111 0000 | 0000 0000 | 0000 0000 |
| ROR R5, R8, R6 | R5 | 1100 0001 | 0110 1110 | 0111 0000 | 1000 0001 |

Shifting a value left by N is equivalent to multiplying it by 2^N. Likewise, arithmetically shifting a value right by N is equivalent to dividing it by 2^N, as discussed in Section 5.2.5. Logical shifts are also used to extract or assemble bitfields.

Figure 6.5 shows the assembly code and resulting register values for shift operations where the shift amount is held in a register, R6. This instruction uses the *register-shifted register* addressing mode, where one register (R8) is shifted by the amount (20) held in a second register (R6).

Multiply Instructions*

Multiplication is somewhat different from other arithmetic operations. Multiplying two 32-bit numbers produces a 64-bit product. The ARM architecture provides *multiply instructions* that result in a 32-bit or 64-bit product. Multiply (MUL) multiplies two 32-bit numbers and produces a 32-bit result. MUL R1, R2, R3 multiplies the values in R2 and R3 and places the least significant bits of the product in R1; the most significant 32 bits of the product are discarded. This instruction is useful for multiplying small numbers whose result fits in 32 bits. UMULL (unsigned multiply long) and SMULL (signed multiply long) multiply two 32-bit numbers and produce a 64-bit product. For example, UMULL R1, R2, R3, R4 performs an unsigned multiply of R3 and R4. The least significant 32 bits of the product is placed in R1 and the most significant 32 bits are placed in R2.

Each of these instructions also has a multiply-accumulate variant, MLA, SMLAL, and UMLAL, that adds the product to a running 32- or 64-bit sum. These instructions can boost the math performance in applications such as matrix multiplication and signal processing consisting of repeated multiplies and adds.

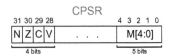

Figure 6.6 Current Program Status Register (CPSR)

The least significant five bits of the CPSR are *mode* bits and will be described in Section 6.6.3.

Other useful instructions for comparing two values are CMN, TST, and TEQ. Each instruction performs an operation, updates the condition flags, and discards the result. CMN (compare negative) compares the first source to the negative of the second source by adding the two sources. As will be shown in Section 6.4, ARM instructions only encode positive immediates. So, CMN R2, #20 is used instead of CMP R2, #-20. TST (test) ANDs the source operands. It is useful for checking if some portion of the register is zero or nonzero. For example, TST R2, #0xFF would set the Z flag if the low byte of R2 is 0. TEQ (test if equal) checks for equivalence by XOR-ing the sources. Thus, the Z flag is set when they are equal and the N flag is set when the signs are different.

6.3.2 Condition Flags

Programs would be boring if they could only run in the same order every time. ARM instructions optionally set *condition flags* based on whether the result is negative, zero, etc. Subsequent instructions then execute *conditionally*, depending on the state of those condition flags. The ARM condition flags, also called *status flags*, are negative (N), zero (Z), carry (C), and overflow (V), as listed in Table 6.2. These flags are set by the ALU (see Section 5.2.4) and are held in the top 4 bits of the 32-bit *Current Program Status Register* (CPSR), as shown in Figure 6.6.

The most common way to set the status bits is with the compare (CMP) instruction, which subtracts the second source operand from the first and sets the condition flags based on the result. For example, if the numbers are equal, the result will be zero and the Z flag is set. If the first number is an unsigned value that is higher than or the same as the second, the subtraction will produce a carry out and the C flag is set.

Subsequent instructions can conditionally execute depending on the state of the flags. The instruction mnemonic is followed by a *condition mnemonic* that indicates when to execute. Table 6.3 lists the 4-bit condition field (*cond*), the condition mnemonic, name, and the state of the condition flags that result in instruction execution (CondEx). For example, suppose a program performs CMP R4, R5, and then ADDEQ R1, R2, R3. The compare sets the Z flag if R4 and R5 are equal, and the ADDEQ executes only if the Z flag is set. The *cond* field will be used in machine language encodings in Section 6.4.

Table 6.2 Condition flags

Flag	Name	Description
N	Negative	Instruction result is negative, i.e., bit 31 of the result is 1
Z	Zero	Instruction result is zero
C	Carry	Instruction causes a carry out
V	oVerflow	Instruction causes an overflow

Table 6.3 Condition mnemonics

cond	Mnemonic	Name	CondEx
0000	EQ	Equal	Z
0001	NE	Not equal	$\overline{Z}$
0010	CS/HS	Carry set / unsigned higher or same	C
0011	CC/LO	Carry clear / unsigned lower	$\overline{C}$
0100	MI	Minus / negative	N
0101	PL	Plus / positive or zero	$\overline{N}$
0110	VS	Overflow / overflow set	V
0111	VC	No overflow / overflow clear	$\overline{V}$
1000	HI	Unsigned higher	$\overline{Z}C$
1001	LS	Unsigned lower or same	Z OR $\overline{C}$
1010	GE	Signed greater than or equal	$\overline{N \oplus V}$
1011	LT	Signed less than	$N \oplus V$
1100	GT	Signed greater than	$\overline{Z}(\overline{N \oplus V})$
1101	LE	Signed less than or equal	Z OR $(N \oplus V)$
1110	AL (or none)	Always / unconditional	Ignored

Condition mnemonics differ for signed and unsigned comparison. For example, ARM provides two forms of greater than or equal comparison: HS (CS) is used for unsigned numbers and GE for signed. For unsigned numbers, $A - B$ will produce a carry out (C) when $A \geq B$. For signed numbers, $A - B$ will make N and V either both 0 or both 1 when $A \geq B$. Figure 6.7 highlights the difference between HS and GE comparisons with two examples using 4-bit numbers for ease of interpretation.

	Unsigned	Signed
$A = 1001_2$	$A = 9$	$A = -7$
$B = 0010_2$	$B = 2$	$B = 2$
$A - B$: 1001		$NZCV = 0011_2$
+ 1110		**HS:** TRUE
(a) 10111		**GE:** FALSE

	Unsigned	Signed
$A = 0101_2$	$A = 5$	$A = 5$
$B = 1101_2$	$B = 13$	$B = -3$
$A - B$: 0101		$NZCV = 1001_2$
+ 0011		**HS:** FALSE
(b) 1000		**GE:** TRUE

Figure 6.7 Signed vs. unsigned comparison: HS vs. GE

Other data-processing instructions will set the condition flags when the instruction mnemonic is followed by "S." For example, SUBS R2, R3, R7 will subtract R7 from R3, put the result in R2, and set the condition flags. Table B.5 in Appendix B summarizes which condition flags are influenced by each instruction. All data-processing instructions will affect the N and Z flags based on whether the result is zero or has the most significant bit set. ADDS and SUBS also influence V and C, and shifts influence C.

Code Example 6.10 shows instructions that execute conditionally. The first instruction, CMP R2, R3, executes unconditionally and sets the condition flags. The remaining instructions execute conditionally, depending on the values of the condition flags. Suppose R2 and R3 contain the values 0x80000000 and 0x00000001. The compare computes R2 – R3 = 0x80000000 – 0x00000001 = 0x80000000 + 0xFFFFFFFF = 0x7FFFFFFF with a carry out ($C = 1$). The sources had opposite signs and the sign of the result differs from the sign of the first source, so the result overflows ($V = 1$). The remaining flags (N and Z) are 0. ANDHS executes

---

Code Example 6.10 CONDITIONAL EXECUTION

ARM Assembly Code

```
CMP    R2, R3
ADDEQ  R4, R5, #78
ANDHS  R7, R8, R9
ORRMI  R10, R11, R12
EORLT  R12, R7, R10
```

---

because $C = 1$. EORLT executes because N is 0 and V is 1 (see Table 6.3). Intuitively, ANDHS and EORLT execute because R2 ≥ R3 (unsigned) and R2 < R3 (signed), respectively. ADDEQ and ORRMI do not execute because the result of R2 − R3 is not zero (i.e., R2 ≠ R3) or negative.

6.3.3 Branching

An advantage of a computer over a calculator is its ability to make decisions. A computer performs different tasks depending on the input. For example, if/else statements, switch/case statements, while loops, and for loops all conditionally execute code depending on some test.

One way to make decisions is to use conditional execution to ignore certain instructions. This works well for simple if statements where a small number of instructions are ignored, but it is wasteful for if statements with many instructions in the body, and it is insufficient to handle loops. Thus, ARM and most other architectures use *branch instructions* to skip over sections of code or repeat code.

A program usually executes in sequence, with the program counter (PC) incrementing by 4 after each instruction to point to the next instruction. (Recall that instructions are 4 bytes long and ARM is a byte-addressed architecture.) Branch instructions change the program counter. ARM includes two types of branches: a simple *branch* (B) and *branch and link* (BL). BL is used for function calls and is discussed in Section 6.3.7. Like other ARM instructions, branches can be unconditional or conditional. Branches are also called *jumps* in some architectures.

Code Example 6.11 shows unconditional branching using the branch instruction B. When the code reaches the B TARGET instruction, the branch is *taken*. That is, the next instruction executed is the SUB instruction just after the *label* called TARGET.

Assembly code uses labels to indicate instruction locations in the program. When the assembly code is translated into machine code, these labels are translated into instruction addresses (see Section 6.4.3). ARM assembly labels cannot be reserved words, such as instruction mnemonics. Most programmers indent their instructions but not the labels, to help

---

Code Example 6.11 UNCONDITIONAL BRANCHING

ARM Assembly Code

```
    ADD R1, R2, #17    ; R1 = R2 + 17
    B   TARGET         ; branch to TARGET
    ORR R1, R1, R3     ; not executed
    AND R3, R1, #0xFF  ; not executed

TARGET
    SUB R1, R1, #78    ; R1 = R1 - 78
```

Code Example 6.12 CONDITIONAL BRANCHING

ARM Assembly Code

```
    MOV R0, #4       ; R0 = 4
    ADD R1, R0, R0   ; R1 = R0 + R0 = 8
    CMP R0, R1       ; set flags based on R0-R1 = -4. NZCV = 1000
    BEQ THERE        ; branch not taken (Z != 1)
    ORR R1, R1, #1   ; R1 = R1 OR 1 = 9

THERE
    ADD R1, R1, #78  ; R1 = R1 + 78 = 87
```

---

make labels stand out. The ARM compiler makes this a requirement: labels must not be indented, and instructions must be preceded by white space. Some compilers, including GCC, require a colon after the label.

Branch instructions can execute conditionally based on the condition mnemonics listed in Table 6.3. Code Example 6.12 illustrates the use of BEQ, branching dependent on equality ($Z = 1$). When the code reaches the BEQ instruction, the Z condition flag is 0 (i.e., R0 $\neq$ R1), so the branch is *not taken*. That is, the next instruction executed is the ORR instruction.

6.3.4 Conditional Statements

if, if/else, and switch/case statements are conditional statements commonly used in high-level languages. They each conditionally execute a *block* of code consisting of one or more statements. This section shows how to translate these high-level constructs into ARM assembly language.

if Statements

An if statement executes a block of code, the *if block*, only when a condition is met. Code Example 6.13 shows how to translate an if statement into ARM assembly code.

Code Example 6.13 IF STATEMENT

High-Level Code	ARM Assembly Code

```
if (apples == oranges)        ; R0 = apples, R1 = oranges, R2 = f, R3 = i
  f = i + 1;                    CMP  R0, R1      ; apples == oranges ?
                                BNE  L1          ; if not equal, skip if block
                                ADD  R2, R3, #1  ; if block: f = i + 1
f = f - i;                   L1
                                SUB  R2, R2, R3  ; f = f - i
```

Recall that != is an inequality comparison and == is an equality comparison in the high-level code.

The assembly code for the if statement tests the opposite condition of the one in the high-level code. In Code Example 6.13, the high-level code tests for apples == oranges. The assembly code tests for apples != oranges using BNE to skip the if block if the condition is **not** satisfied. Otherwise, apples == oranges, the branch is not taken, and the if block is executed.

Because any instruction can be conditionally executed, the ARM assembly code for Code Example 6.13 could also be written more compactly as shown below.

```
CMP   R0, R1        ; apples == oranges ?
ADDEQ R2, R3, #1    ; f = i + 1 on equality (i.e., Z = 1)
SUB   R2, R2, R3    ; f = f - i
```

This solution with conditional execution is shorter and also faster because it involves one fewer instruction. Moreover, we will see in Section 7.5.3 that branches sometimes introduce extra delay, whereas conditional execution is always fast. This example shows the power of conditional execution in the ARM architecture.

In general, when a block of code has a single instruction, it is better to use conditional execution rather than branch around it. As the block becomes longer, the branch becomes valuable because it avoids wasting time fetching instructions that will not be executed.

if/else Statements

if/else statements execute one of two blocks of code depending on a condition. When the condition in the if statement is met, the *if block* is executed. Otherwise, the *else block* is executed. Code Example 6.14 shows an example if/else statement.

Like if statements, if/else assembly code tests the opposite condition of the one in the high-level code. In Code Example 6.14, the high-level code tests for apples == oranges, and the assembly code tests for apples != oranges. If that opposite condition is TRUE, BNE skips the if block and executes the else block. Otherwise, the if block executes and finishes with an unconditional branch (B) past the else block.

Code Example 6.14 IF/ELSE STATEMENT

High-Level Code	**ARM Assembly Code**
`if (apples == oranges)`	`; R0 = apples, R1 = oranges, R2 = f, R3 = i`
`  f = i + 1;`	`    CMP  R0, R1      ; apples == oranges?`
	`    BNE  L1         ; if not equal, skip if block`
	`    ADD  R2, R3, #1 ; if block: f = i + 1`
	`    B    L2         ; skip else block`
`else`	`L1`
`  f = f - i;`	`    SUB  R2, R2, R3 ; else block: f = f - i`
	`L2`

Again, because any instruction can conditionally execute and because the instructions within the if block do not change the condition flags, the ARM assembly code for Code Example 6.14 could also be written much more succinctly as:

```
CMP   R0, R1        ; apples == oranges?
ADDEQ R2, R3, #1    ; f = i + 1 on equality (i.e., Z = 1)
SUBNE R2, R2, R3    ; f = f - i on not equal (i.e., Z = 0)
```

switch/case Statements*

switch/case statements execute one of several blocks of code depending on the conditions. If no conditions are met, the *default block* is executed. A case statement is equivalent to a series of *nested* if/else statements. Code Example 6.15 shows two high-level code snippets with the same

Code Example 6.15 SWITCH/CASE STATEMENT

High-Level Code	**ARM Assembly Code**
`switch (button) {`	`; R0 = button, R1 = amt`
`  case 1:  amt = 20; break;`	`    CMP   R0, #1      ; is button 1 ?`
	`    MOVEQ R1, #20     ; amt = 20 if button is 1`
	`    BEQ   DONE        ; break`
`  case 2:  amt = 50; break;`	`    CMP   R0, #2      ; is button 2 ?`
	`    MOVEQ R1, #50     ; amt = 50 if button is 2`
	`    BEQ   DONE        ; break`
`  case 3:  amt = 100; break;`	`    CMP   R0, #3      ; is button 3?`
	`    MOVEQ R1, #100    ; amt = 100 if button is 3`
	`    BEQ   DONE        ; break`
`  default: amt = 0;`	
`}`	`    MOV   R1, #0      ; default amt = 0`
`// equivalent function using`	`DONE`
`// if/else statements`	
`  if    (button == 1) amt = 20;`	
`  else if (button == 2) amt = 50;`	
`  else if (button == 3) amt = 100;`	
`  else               amt = 0;`	

functionality: they calculate whether to dispense $20, $50, or $100 from an ATM (automatic teller machine) depending on the button pressed. The ARM assembly implementation is the same for both high-level code snippets.

6.3.5 Getting Loopy

Loops repeatedly execute a block of code depending on a condition. while loops and for loops are common loop constructs used by high-level languages. This section shows how to translate them into ARM assembly language, taking advantage of conditional branching.

while Loops

while loops repeatedly execute a block of code until a condition is *not* met. The while loop in Code Example 6.16 determines the value of x such that $2^x = 128$. It executes seven times, until pow = 128.

Like if/else statements, the assembly code for while loops tests the opposite condition of the one in the high-level code. If that opposite condition is TRUE (in this case, R0 == 128), the while loop is finished. If not (R0 $\neq$ 128), the branch isn't taken and the loop body executes.

The int data type in C refers to a word of data representing a two's complement integer. ARM uses 32-bit words, so an int represents a number in the range $[-2^{31}, 2^{31} - 1]$.

Code Example 6.16 WHILE LOOP

High-Level Code	**ARM Assembly Code**

```int pow = 1;```
```int x = 0;```
 	
```while (pow != 128) {```
```   pow = pow * 2;```
```   x = x + 1;```
```}```
	```; R0 = pow, R1 = x```
	``` MOV R0, #1 ; pow = 1```
	``` MOV R1, #0 ; x = 0```
	
	```WHILE```
	``` CMP R0, #128 ; pow != 128 ?```
	``` BEQ DONE ; if pow == 128, exit loop```
	``` LSL R0, R0, #1 ; pow = pow * 2```
	``` ADD R1, R1, #1 ; x = x + 1```
	``` B WHILE ; repeat loop```
	```DONE```

In Code Example 6.16, the while loop compares pow to 128 and exits the loop if it is equal. Otherwise it doubles pow (using a left shift), increments x, and branches back to the start of the while loop.

for Loops

It is very common to initialize a variable before a while loop, check that variable in the loop condition, and change that variable each time through the while loop. for loops are a convenient shorthand that combines the initialization, condition check, and variable change in one place. The format of the for loop is:

```
for (initialization; condition; loop operation)
    statement
```

Code Example 6.17 FOR LOOP

High-Level Code	ARM Assembly Code

```
int i;                          ; R0 = i, R1 = sum
int sum = 0;                      MOV R1, #0      ; sum = 0
                                  MOV R0, #0      ; i = 0          loop initialization

for (i = 0; i < 10; i = i + 1) { FOR
    sum = sum + i;                 CMP R0, #10    ; i < 10 ?       check condition
}                                  BGE DONE       ; if (i >= 10) exit loop
                                   ADD R1, R1, R0 ; sum = sum + i  loop body
                                   ADD R0, R0, #1 ; i = i + 1      loop operation
                                   B   FOR        ; repeat loop
                                 DONE
```

The initialization code executes before the for loop begins. The condition is tested at the beginning of each loop. If the condition is not met, the loop exits. The loop operation executes at the end of each loop.

Code Example 6.17 adds the numbers from 0 to 9. The loop variable, in this case i, is initialized to 0 and is incremented at the end of each loop iteration. The for loop executes as long as i is less than 10. Note that this example also illustrates relative comparisons. The loop checks the < condition to continue, so the assembly code checks the opposite condition, >=, to exit the loop.

Loops are especially useful for accessing large amounts of similar data stored in memory, which is discussed next.

6.3.6 Memory

For ease of storage and access, similar data can be grouped together into an *array*. An array stores its contents at sequential data addresses in memory. Each array element is identified by a number called its *index*. The number of elements in the array is called the *length* of the array.

Figure 6.8 shows a 200-element array of scores stored in memory. Code Example 6.18 is a grade inflation algorithm that adds 10 points to each of the scores. Note that the code for initializing the scores array is not shown. The index into the array is a variable (i) rather than a constant, so we must multiply it by 4 before adding it to the base address.

ARM can *scale* (multiply) the index, add it to the base address, and load from memory in a single instruction. Instead of the LSL and LDR instruction sequence in Code Example 6.18, we can use a single instruction:

```
LDR R3, [R0, R1, LSL #2]
```

R1 is scaled (shifted left by two) then added to the base address (R0). Thus, the memory address is R0 + (R1 × 4).

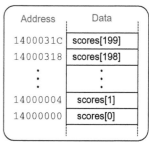

Address	Data
1400031C	scores[199]
14000318	scores[198]
⋮	⋮
14000004	scores[1]
14000000	scores[0]

Main memory

Figure 6.8 Memory holding scores[200] **starting at base address 0x14000000**

Code Example 6.18 ACCESSING ARRAYS USING A FOR LOOP

High-Level Code	ARM Assembly Code

int i;
int scores[200];
...
	; R0 = array base address, R1 = i
	; initialization code ...
	  MOV R0, #0x14000000 ; R0 = base address
	  MOV R1, #0 ; i = 0

for (i = 0; i < 200; i = i + 1)	LOOP
	  CMP R1, #200 ; i < 200?
	  BGE L3 ; if i ≥ 200, exit loop
	  LSL R2, R1, #2 ; R2 = i * 4

scores[i] = scores[i] + 10;	LDR R3, [R0, R2] ; R3 = scores[i]
	  ADD R3, R3, #10 ; R3 = scores[i] + 10
	  STR R3, [R0, R2] ; scores[i] = scores[i] + 10
	  ADD R1, R1, #1 ; i = i + 1
	  B LOOP ; repeat loop
	L3

In addition to scaling the index register, ARM provides offset, pre-indexed, and post-indexed addressing to enable dense and efficient code for array accesses and function calls. Table 6.4 gives examples of each indexing mode. In each case, the base register is R1 and the offset is R2. The offset can be subtracted by writing –R2. The offset may also be an immediate in the range of 0–4095 that can be added (e.g., #20) or subtracted (e.g., #–20).

Offset addressing calculates the address as the base register ± the offset; the base register is unchanged. *Pre-indexed addressing* calculates the address as the base register ± the offset and updates the base register to this new address. *Post-indexed addressing* calculates the address as the base register only and then, after accessing memory, the base register is updated to the base register ± the offset. We have seen many examples of offset indexing mode. Code Example 6.19 shows the for loop from Code Example 6.18 rewritten to use post-indexing, eliminating the ADD to increment i.

Table 6.4 ARM indexing modes

Mode	ARM Assembly	Address	Base Register
Offset	LDR R0, [R1, R2]	R1 + R2	Unchanged
Pre-index	LDR R0, [R1, R2]!	R1 + R2	R1 = R1 + R2
Post-index	LDR R0, [R1], R2	R1	R1 = R1 + R2

Code Example 6.19 FOR LOOP USING POST-INDEXING

High-Level Code	**ARM Assembly Code**

```
int i;
int scores[200];
...


for (i = 0; i < 200; i = i + 1)
     scores[i] = scores[i] + 10;
```

```
; R0 = array base address
; initialization code   ...
    MOV R0, #0x14000000     ; R0 = base address
    ADD R1, R0, #800        ; R1 = base address + (200*4)

LOOP
    CMP R0, R1              ; reached end of array?
    BGE L3                  ; if yes, exit loop
    LDR R2, [R0]            ; R2 = scores[i]
    ADD R2, R2, #10         ; R2 = scores[i] + 10
    STR R2, [R0], #4        ; scores[i] = scores[i] + 10
                           ; then R0 = R0 + 4

    B   LOOP               ; repeat loop
L3
```

Bytes and Characters

Numbers in the range [−128, 127] can be stored in a single byte rather than an entire word. Because there are much fewer than 256 characters on an English language keyboard, English characters are often represented by bytes. The C language uses the type char to represent a byte or character.

Early computers lacked a standard mapping between bytes and English characters, so exchanging text between computers was difficult. In 1963, the American Standards Association published the *American Standard Code for Information Interchange* (*ASCII*), which assigns each text character a unique byte value. Table 6.5 shows these character encodings for printable characters. The ASCII values are given in hexadecimal. Lowercase and uppercase letters differ by 0x20 (32).

ARM provides load byte (LDRB), load signed byte (LDRSB), and store byte (STRB) to access individual bytes in memory. LDRB zero-extends the byte, whereas LDRSB sign-extends the byte to fill the entire 32-bit register. STRB stores the least significant byte of the 32-bit register into the specified byte address in memory. All three are illustrated in Figure 6.9, with

> Other programming languages, such as Java, use different character encodings, most notably Unicode. Unicode uses 16 bits to represent each character, so it supports accents, umlauts, and Asian languages. For more information, see www.unicode.org.

> LDRH, LDRSH, and STRH are similar, but access 16-bit *halfwords*.

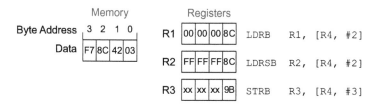

Figure 6.9 Instructions for loading and storing bytes

ASCII codes developed from earlier forms of character encoding. Beginning in 1838, telegraph machines used Morse code, a series of dots (.) and dashes (–), to represent characters. For example, the letters A, B, C, and D were represented as – , – ... , – . – . , and – .. , respectively. The number of dots and dashes varied with each letter. For efficiency, common letters used shorter codes.

In 1874, Jean-Maurice-Emile Baudot invented a 5-bit code called the Baudot code. For example, A, B, C, and D were represented as 00011, 11001, 01110, and 01001.

However, the 32 possible encodings of this 5-bit code were not sufficient for all the English characters, but 8-bit encoding was. Thus, as electronic communication became prevalent, 8-bit ASCII encoding emerged as the standard.

Table 6.5 ASCII encodings

#	Char	#	Char	#	Char	#	Char	#	Char	#	Char
20	space	30	0	40	@	50	P	60	`	70	p
21	!	31	1	41	A	51	Q	61	a	71	q
22	"	32	2	42	B	52	R	62	b	72	r
23	#	33	3	43	C	53	S	63	c	73	s
24	$	34	4	44	D	54	T	64	d	74	t
25	%	35	5	45	E	55	U	65	e	75	u
26	&	36	6	46	F	56	V	66	f	76	v
27	'	37	7	47	G	57	W	67	g	77	w
28	(	38	8	48	H	58	X	68	h	78	x
29	)	39	9	49	I	59	Y	69	i	79	y
2A	*	3A	:	4A	J	5A	Z	6A	j	7A	z
2B	+	3B	;	4B	K	5B	[	6B	k	7B	{
2C	,	3C	<	4C	L	5C	\	6C	l	7C	|
2D	–	3D	=	4D	M	5D	]	6D	m	7D	}
2E	.	3E	>	4E	N	5E	^	6E	n	7E	~
2F	/	3F	?	4F	O	5F	_	6F	o		

the base address R4 being 0. LDRB loads the byte at memory address 2 into the least significant byte of R1 and fills the remaining register bits with 0. LDRSB loads this byte into R2 and sign-extends the byte into the upper 24 bits of the register. STRB stores the least significant byte of R3 (0x9B) into memory byte 3; it replaces 0xF7 with 0x9B. The more significant bytes of R3 are ignored.

A series of characters is called a *string*. Strings have a variable length, so programming languages must provide a way to determine the length or end of the string. In C, the null character (0x00) signifies the end of a string. For example, Figure 6.10 shows the string "Hello!" (0x48 65 6C 6C 6F 21 00) stored in memory. The string is seven bytes long

Example 6.2 USING LDRB AND STRB TO ACCESS A CHARACTER ARRAY

The following high-level code converts a 10-entry array of characters from lower-case to uppercase by subtracting 32 from each array entry. Translate it into ARM assembly language. Remember that the address difference between array elements is now 1 byte, not 4 bytes. Assume that R0 already holds the base address of chararray.

```
// high-level code
// chararray[10] declared and initialized earlier
int i;

for (i = 0; i < 10; i = i + 1)
  chararray[i] = chararray[i] - 32;
```

Solution:
```
; ARM assembly code
; R0 = base address of chararray (initialized earlier), R1 = i
        MOV   R1, #0        ; i = 0
LOOP    CMP   R1, #10       ; i < 10 ?
        BGE   DONE          ; if (i >=10), exit loop
        LDRB  R2, [R0, R1]  ; R2 = mem[R0+R1] = chararray[i]
        SUB   R2, R2, #32   ; R2 = chararray[i] - 32
        STRB  R2, [R0, R1]  ; chararray[i] = R2
        ADD   R1, R1, #1    ; i = i + 1
        B     LOOP          ; repeat loop
DONE
```

and extends from address 0x1522FFF0 to 0x1522FFF6. The first character of the string (H = 0x48) is stored at the lowest byte address (0x1522FFF0).

6.3.7 Function Calls

High-level languages support *functions* (also called *procedures* or *subroutines*) to reuse common code and to make a program more modular and readable. Functions have inputs, called *arguments*, and an output, called the *return value*. Functions should calculate the return value and cause no other unintended side effects.

When one function calls another, the calling function, the *caller*, and the called function, the *callee*, must agree on where to put the arguments and the return value. In ARM, the caller conventionally places up to four arguments in registers R0–R3 before making the function call,

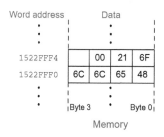

**Figure 6.10 The string "Hello!"
stored in memory**

and the callee places the return value in register R0 before finishing. By following this convention, both functions know where to find the arguments and return value, even if the caller and callee were written by different people.

The callee must not interfere with the behavior of the caller. This means that the callee must know where to return to after it completes and it must not trample on any registers or memory needed by the caller. The caller stores the return address in the link register LR at the same time it jumps to the callee using the branch and link instruction (BL). The callee must not overwrite any architectural state or memory that the caller is depending on. Specifically, the callee must leave the *saved registers* (R4–R11, and LR) and the *stack*, a portion of memory used for temporary variables, unmodified.

This section shows how to call and return from a function. It shows how functions access input arguments and the return value and how they use the stack to store temporary variables.

Function Calls and Returns

ARM uses the branch and link instruction (BL) to call a function and moves the link register to the PC (MOV PC, LR) to return from a function. Code Example 6.20 shows the main function calling the simple function. main is the caller, and simple is the callee. The simple function is called with no input arguments and generates no return value; it just returns to the caller. In Code Example 6.20, instruction addresses are given to the left of each ARM instruction in hexadecimal.

BL (branch and link) and MOV PC, LR are the two essential instructions needed for a function call and return. BL performs two tasks: it stores the *return address* of the next instruction (the instruction

---

Code Example 6.20 simple FUNCTION CALL

High-Level Code

```
int main() {

  simple();
  ...
}

// void means the function returns no value
void simple() {
  return;
}
```

ARM Assembly Code

```
0x00008000 MAIN     ...
...                 ...
0x00008020          BL  SIMPLE   ; call the simple function
...

0x0000902C SIMPLE  MOV PC, LR    ; return
```

after BL) in the link register (LR), and it branches to the target instruction.

In Code Example 6.20, the main function calls the simple function by executing the branch and link instruction (BL). BL branches to the SIMPLE label and stores 0x00008024 in LR. The simple function returns immediately by executing the instruction MOV PC, LR, copying the return address from the LR back to the PC. The main function then continues executing at this address (0x00008024).

Input Arguments and Return Values

The simple function in Code Example 6.20 receives no input from the calling function (main) and returns no output. By ARM convention, functions use R0–R3 for input arguments and R0 for the return value. In Code Example 6.21, the function diffofsums is called with four arguments and returns one result. result is a local variable, which we choose to keep in R4.

According to ARM convention, the calling function, main, places the function arguments from left to right into the input registers, R0–R3. The called function, diffofsums, stores the return value in the return register, R0. When a function with more than four arguments is called, the additional input arguments are placed on the stack, which we discuss next.

Code Example 6.21 FUNCTION CALL WITH ARGUMENTS AND RETURN VALUES

High-Level Code

```
int main() {
  int y;
  . . .
  y = diffofsums(2, 3, 4, 5);
  . . .
}


int diffofsums(int f, int g, int h, int i) {
  int result;

  result = (f + g) - (h + i);
  return result;
}
```

ARM Assembly Code

```
; R4 = y
MAIN
  . . .
  MOV R0, #2        ; argument 0 = 2
  MOV R1, #3        ; argument 1 = 3
  MOV R2, #4        ; argument 2 = 4
  MOV R3, #5        ; argument 3 = 5
  BL  DIFFOFSUMS    ; call function
  MOV R4, R0        ; y = returned value
  . . .

; R4 = result
DIFFOFSUMS
  ADD R8, R0, R1    ; R8 = f + g
  ADD R9, R2, R3    ; R9 = h + i
  SUB R4, R8, R9    ; result = (f + g) - (h + i)
  MOV R0, R4        ; put return value in R0
  MOV PC, LR        ; return to caller
```

Remember that PC and LR are alternative names for R15 and R14, respectively. ARM is unusual in that PC is part of the register set, so a function return can be done with a MOV instruction. Many other instruction sets keep the PC in a special register and use a special return or jump instruction to return from functions.

These days, ARM compilers do a function return using BX LR. The BX branch and exchange instruction is like a branch, but it also can transition between the standard ARM instruction set and the Thumb instruction set described in Section 6.7.1. This chapter doesn't use the Thumb or BX instructions and thus sticks with the ARMv4 MOV PC, LR method.

We will see in Chapter 7 that treating the PC as an ordinary register complicates the implementation of the processor.

Code Example 6.21 has some subtle errors. Code Examples 6.22–6.25 show improved versions of the program.

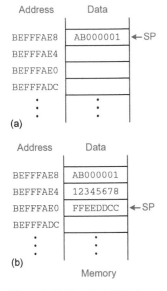

Memory

Figure 6.11 The stack (a) before expansion and (b) after two-word expansion

The stack is typically stored upside down in memory such that the top of the stack is actually the lowest address and the stack grows downward toward lower memory addresses. This is called a *descending stack*. ARM also allows for *ascending stacks* that grow up toward higher memory addresses. The stack pointer typically points to the topmost element on the stack; this is called a *full stack*. ARM also allows for *empty stacks* in which SP points one word beyond the top of the stack. The ARM *Application Binary Interface* (ABI) defines a standard way in which functions pass variables and use the stack so that libraries developed by different compilers can interoperate. It specifies a *full descending* stack, which we will use in this chapter.

The Stack

The stack is memory that is used to save information within a function. The stack expands (uses more memory) as the processor needs more scratch space and contracts (uses less memory) when the processor no longer needs the variables stored there. Before explaining how functions use the stack to store temporary values, we explain how the stack works.

The stack is a last-in-first-out (LIFO) queue. Like a stack of dishes, the last item *pushed* onto the stack (the top dish) is the first one that can be *popped* off. Each function may allocate stack space to store local variables but must deallocate it before returning. The *top of the stack* is the most recently allocated space. Whereas a stack of dishes grows up in space, the ARM stack grows down in memory. The stack expands to lower memory addresses when a program needs more scratch space.

Figure 6.11 shows a picture of the stack. The stack pointer, SP (R13), is an ordinary ARM register that, by convention, *points* to the *top of the stack*. A pointer is a fancy name for a memory address. SP points to (gives the address of) data. For example, in Figure 6.11(a), the stack pointer, SP, holds the address value 0XBEFFFAE8 and points to the data value 0xAB000001.

The stack pointer (SP) starts at a high memory address and decrements to expand as needed. Figure 6.11(b) shows the stack expanding to allow two more data words of temporary storage. To do so, SP decrements by eight to become 0xBEFFFAE0. Two additional data words, 0x12345678 and 0xFFEEDDCC, are temporarily stored on the stack.

One of the important uses of the stack is to save and restore registers that are used by a function. Recall that a function should calculate a return value but have no other unintended side effects. In particular, it should not modify any registers besides R0, the one containing the return value. The diffofsums function in Code Example 6.21 violates this rule because it modifies R4, R8, and R9. If main had been using these registers before the call to diffofsums, their contents would have been corrupted by the function call.

To solve this problem, a function saves registers on the stack before it modifies them, then restores them from the stack before it returns. Specifically, it performs the following steps:

1. Makes space on the stack to store the values of one or more registers

2. Stores the values of the registers on the stack

3. Executes the function using the registers

4. Restores the original values of the registers from the stack

5. Deallocates space on the stack

Code Example 6.22 shows an improved version of diffofsums that saves and restores R4, R8, and R9. Figure 6.12 shows the stack before, during, and after a call to the diffofsums function from Code Example 6.22. The stack starts at 0xBEF0F0FC. diffofsums makes room for three words on the stack by decrementing the stack pointer SP by 12. It then stores the current values held in R4, R8, and R9 in the newly allocated space. It executes the rest of the function, changing the values in these three registers. At the end of the function, diffofsums restores the values of these registers from the stack, deallocates its stack space, and returns. When the function returns, R0 holds the result, but there

Code Example 6.22 FUNCTION SAVING REGISTERS ON THE STACK

ARM Assembly Code

```
;R4 = result
DIFFOFSUMS
    SUB   SP, SP, #12      ; make space on stack for 3 registers
    STR   R9, [SP, #8]     ; save R9 on stack
    STR   R8, [SP, #4]     ; save R8 on stack
    STR   R4, [SP]         ; save R4 on stack

    ADD   R8, R0, R1       ; R8 = f + g
    ADD   R9, R2, R3       ; R9 = h + i
    SUB   R4, R8, R9       ; result = (f + g) - (h + i)
    MOV   R0, R4           ; put return value in R0

    LDR   R4, [SP]         ; restore R4 from stack
    LDR   R8, [SP, #4]     ; restore R8 from stack
    LDR   R9, [SP, #8]     ; restore R9 from stack
    ADD   SP, SP, #12      ; deallocate stack space

    MOV   PC, LR           ; return to caller
```

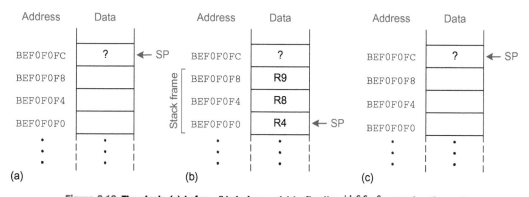

Figure 6.12 The stack: (a) before, (b) during, and (c) after the diffofsums **function call**

are no other side effects: R4, R8, R9, and SP have the same values as they did before the function call.

The stack space that a function allocates for itself is called its *stack frame*. diffofsums's stack frame is three words deep. The principle of modularity tells us that each function should access only its own stack frame, not the frames belonging to other functions.

Loading and Storing Multiple Registers

Saving and restoring registers on the stack is such a common operation that ARM provides Load Multiple and Store Multiple instructions (LDM and STM) that are optimized to this purpose. Code Example 6.23 rewrites diffofsums using these instructions. The stack holds exactly the same information as in the previous example, but the code is much shorter.

Code Example 6.23 SAVING AND RESTORING MULTIPLE REGISTERS

ARM Assembly Code

```
; R4 = result
DIFFOFSUMS
    STMFD  SP!, {R4, R8, R9}     ; push R4/8/9 on full descending stack

    ADD    R8, R0, R1            ; R8 = f + g
    ADD    R9, R2, R3            ; R9 = h + i
    SUB    R4, R8, R9            ; result = (f + g) - (h + i)
    MOV    R0, R4                ; put return value in R0

    LDMFD  SP!, {R4, R8, R9}     ; pop R4/8/9 off full descending stack

    MOV    PC, LR                ; return to caller
```

LDM and STM come in four flavors for full and empty descending and ascending stacks (FD, ED, FA, EA). The SP! in the instructions indicates to store the data relative to the stack pointer and to update the stack pointer after the store or load. PUSH and POP are synonyms for STMFD SP!, {regs} and LDMFD SP!, {regs}, respectively, and are the preferred way to save registers on the conventional full descending stack.

Preserved Registers

Code Examples 6.22 and 6.23 assume that all of the used registers (R4, R8, and R9) must be saved and restored. If the calling function does not use those registers, the effort to save and restore them is wasted. To avoid this waste, ARM divides registers into *preserved* and *nonpreserved* categories. The preserved registers include R4–R11. The nonpreserved registers are R0–R3 and R12. SP and LR (R13 and R14) must also be preserved. A function must save and restore any of the preserved registers that it wishes to use, but it can change the nonpreserved registers freely.

Code Example 6.24 shows a further improved version of diffofsums that saves only R4 on the stack. It also illustrates the preferred PUSH and POP synonyms. The code reuses the nonpreserved argument registers R1 and R3 to hold the intermediate sums when those arguments are no longer necessary.

Code Example 6.24 REDUCING THE NUMBER OF PRESERVED REGISTERS

ARM Assembly Code

```
; R4 = result
DIFFOFSUMS
    PUSH {R4}            ; save R4 on stack
    ADD  R1, R0, R1      ; R1 = f + g
    ADD  R3, R2, R3      ; R3 = h + i
    SUB  R4, R1, R3      ; result = (f + g) - (h + i)
    MOV  R0, R4          ; put return value in R0
    POP  {R4}            ; pop R4 off stack
    MOV  PC, LR          ; return to caller
```

PUSH (and POP) save (and restore) registers on the stack in order of register number from low to high, with the lowest numbered register placed at the lowest memory address, regardless of the order listed in the assembly instruction. For example, PUSH {R8, R1, R3} will store R1 at the lowest memory address, then R3 and finally R8 at the next higher memory addresses on the stack.

Remember that when one function calls another, the former is the caller and the latter is the callee. The callee must save and restore any preserved registers that it wishes to use. The callee may change any of the nonpreserved registers. Hence, if the caller is holding active data in a nonpreserved register, the caller needs to save that nonpreserved register before making the function call and then needs to restore it afterward. For these reasons, preserved registers are also called *callee-save*, and nonpreserved registers are called *caller-save*.

Table 6.6 summarizes which registers are preserved. R4–R11 are generally used to hold local variables within a function, so they must be saved. LR must also be saved, so that the function knows where to return.

Table 6.6 Preserved and nonpreserved registers

Preserved	Nonpreserved
Saved registers: R4–R11	Temporary register: R12
Stack pointer: SP (R13)	Argument registers: R0–R3
Return address: LR (R14)	Current Program Status Register
Stack above the stack pointer	Stack below the stack pointer

The convention of which registers are preserved or not preserved is part of the Procedure Call Standard for the ARM Architecture, rather than of the architecture itself. Alternate procedure call standards exist.

R0–R3 and R12 are used to hold temporary results. These calculations typically complete before a function call is made, so they are not preserved, and it is rare that the caller needs to save them.

R0–R3 are often overwritten in the process of calling a function. Hence, they must be saved by the caller if the caller depends on any of its own arguments after a called function returns. R0 certainly should not be preserved, because the callee returns its result in this register. Recall that the Current Program Status Register (CPSR) holds the condition flags. It is not preserved across function calls.

The stack above the stack pointer is automatically preserved as long as the callee does not write to memory addresses above SP. In this way, it does not modify the stack frame of any other functions. The stack pointer itself is preserved, because the callee deallocates its stack frame before returning by adding back the same amount that it subtracted from SP at the beginning of the function.

The astute reader or an optimizing compiler may notice that the local variable result is immediately returned without being used for anything else. Hence, we can eliminate the variable and simply store it in the return register R0, eliminating the need to push and pop R4 and to move result from R4 to R0. Code Example 6.25 shows this even further optimized diffofsums.

Nonleaf Function Calls

A function that does not call others is called a *leaf function*; diffofsums is an example. A function that does call others is called a *nonleaf function*. As mentioned, nonleaf functions are somewhat more complicated because they may need to save nonpreserved registers on the stack before they call another function and then restore those registers afterward. Specifically:

Caller save rule: Before a function call, the caller must save any non-preserved registers (R0–R3 and R12) that it needs after the call. After the call, it must restore these registers before using them.

Callee save rule: Before a callee disturbs any of the preserved registers (R4–R11 and LR), it must save the registers. Before it returns, it must restore these registers.

Code Example 6.25 OPTIMIZED diffofsums FUNCTION CALL

ARM Assembly Code

```
DIFFOFSUMS
    ADD  R1, R0, R1    ; R1 = f + g
    ADD  R3, R2, R3    ; R3 = h + i
    SUB  R0, R1, R3    ; return (f + g) – (h + i)
    MOV  PC, LR        ; return to caller
```

Code Example 6.26 demonstrates a nonleaf function f1 and a leaf function f2 including all the necessary saving and preserving of registers. Suppose f1 keeps i in R4 and x in R5. f2 keeps r in R4. f1 uses preserved registers R4, R5, and LR, so it initially pushes them on the stack according to the callee save rule. It uses R12 to hold the intermediate result (a − b) so that it does not need to preserve another register for this calculation. Before calling f2, f1 pushes R0 and R1 onto the stack according to the caller save rule because these are nonpreserved registers that f2 might change and that f1 will still need after the call. Although R12 is also a nonpreserved register that f2 could overwrite, f1 no longer needs R12 and doesn't have to save it. f1 then passes the argument to f2 in R0, makes the function call, and uses the result in R0. f1 then restores R0 and R1 because it still needs them. When f1 is done, it puts the return value in R0, restores preserved registers R4, R5, and LR, and returns. f2 saves and restores R4 according to the callee save rule.

A nonleaf function overwrites LR when it calls another function using BL. Thus, a nonleaf function must always save LR on its stack and restore it before returning.

Code Example 6.26 NONLEAF FUNCTION CALL

On careful inspection, one might note that f2 does not modify R1, so f1 did not need to save and restore it. However, a compiler cannot always easily ascertain which nonpreserved registers may be disturbed during a function call. Hence, a simple compiler will always make the caller save and restore any nonpreserved registers that it needs after the call.

High-Level Code	ARM Assembly Code

```
int f1(int a, int b) {        ; R0 = a, R1 = b, R4 = i, R5 = x
  int i, x;               F1
                              PUSH  {R4, R5, LR}   ; save preserved registers used by f1
  x = (a + b)*(a − b);        ADD   R5, R0, R1     ; x = (a + b)
  for (i=0; i<a; i++)         SUB   R12, R0, R1    ; temp = (a − b)
    x = x + f2(b+i);          MUL   R5, R5, R12    ; x = x * temp = (a + b) * (a − b)
  return x;                   MOV   R4, #0         ; i = 0
}                           FOR
                              CMP   R4, R0         ; i < a?
                              BGE   RETURN         ; no: exit loop
                              PUSH  {R0, R1}       ; save nonpreserved registers
                              ADD   R0, R1, R4     ; argument is b + i
                              BL    F2             ; call f2(b+i)
                              ADD   R5, R5, R0     ; x = x + f2(b+i)
                              POP   {R0, R1}       ; restore nonpreserved registers
                              ADD   R4, R4, #1     ; i++
                              B     FOR            ; continue for loop
                            RETURN
                              MOV   R0, R5         ; return value is x
                              POP   {R4, R5, LR}   ; restore preserved registers
                              MOV   PC, LR         ; return from f1

                            ; R0 = p, R4 = r
int f2(int p) {             F2
  int r;                      PUSH  {R4}           ; save preserved registers used by f2
                              ADD   R4, R0, 5      ; r = p + 5
  r = p + 5;                  ADD   R0, R4, R0     ; return value is r + p
  return r + p;               POP   {R4}           ; restore preserved registers
}                             MOV   PC, LR         ; return from f2
```

An optimizing compiler could observe that f2 is a leaf procedure and could allocate r to a nonpreserved register, avoiding the need to save and restore R4.

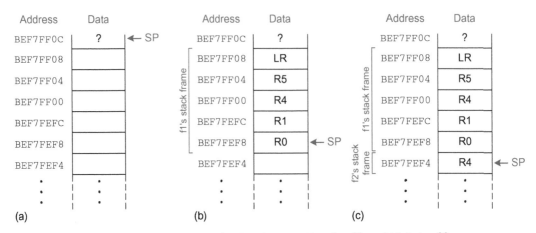

Figure 6.13 The stack: (a) before function calls, (b) during f1, **and (c) during** f2

Figure 6.13 shows the stack during execution of f1. The stack pointer originally starts at 0xBEF7FF0C.

Recursive Function Calls

A *recursive function* is a nonleaf function that calls itself. Recursive functions behave as both caller and callee and must save both preserved and nonpreserved registers. For example, the factorial function can be written as a recursive function. Recall that $factorial(n) = n \times (n - 1) \times (n - 2) \times \cdots \times 2 \times 1$. The factorial function can be rewritten recursively as $factorial(n) = n \times factorial(n - 1)$, as shown in Code Example 6.27. The factorial of 1 is simply 1. To conveniently refer to program addresses, we show the program starting at address 0x8500.

According to the callee save rule, factorial is a nonleaf function and must save LR. According to the caller save rule, factorial will need n after calling itself, so it must save R0. Hence, it pushes both registers onto the stack at the start. It then checks whether n ≤ 1. If so, it puts the return value of 1 in R0, restores the stack pointer, and returns to the caller. It does not have to reload LR and R0 in this case, because they were never modified. If n > 1, the function recursively calls factorial(n - 1). It then restores the value of n and the link register (LR) from the stack, performs the multiplication, and returns this result. Notice that the function cleverly restores n into R1, so as not to overwrite the returned value. The multiply instruction (MUL R0, R1, R0) multiplies n (R1) and the returned value (R0) and puts the result in R0.

Code Example 6.27 `factorial` **RECURSIVE FUNCTION CALL**

High-Level Code

```
int factorial(int n) {
  if (n <= 1)
    return 1;



  else
    return (n * factorial(n - 1));
}
```

ARM Assembly Code

```
0x8500  FACTORIAL  PUSH  {R0, LR}     ; push n and LR on stack
0x8504             CMP   R0, #1       ; R0 <= 1?
0x8508             BGT   ELSE         ; no: branch to else
0x850C             MOV   R0, #1       ; otherwise, return 1
0x8510             ADD   SP, SP, #8   ; restore SP
0x8514             MOV   PC, LR       ; return
0x8518  ELSE       SUB   R0, R0, #1   ; n = n - 1
0x851C             BL    FACTORIAL    ; recursive call
0x8520             POP   {R1, LR}     ; pop n (into R1) and LR
0x8524             MUL   R0, R1, R0   ; R0 = n * factorial(n - 1)
0x8528             MOV   PC, LR       ; return
```

Figure 6.14 shows the stack when executing `factorial(3)`. For illustration, we show SP initially pointing to 0xBEFF0FF0, as shown in Figure 6.14(a). The function creates a two-word stack frame to hold n (R0) and LR. On the first invocation, `factorial` saves R0 (holding n = 3) at 0xBEFF0FE8 and LR at 0xBEFF0FEC, as shown in Figure 6.14(b). The function then changes n to 2 and recursively calls `factorial(2)`, making LR hold 0x8520. On the second invocation, it saves R0 (holding n=2) at 0xBEFF0FE0 and LR at 0xBEFF0FE4. This time, we know that LR contains 0x8520. The function then changes n to 1 and recursively calls `factorial(1)`. On the third invocation, it saves R0 (holding n = 1) at

> For clarity, we will always save registers at the start of a procedure call. An optimizing compiler might observe that there is no need to save R0 and LR when n ≤ 1, and thus push registers only in the ELSE portion of the function.

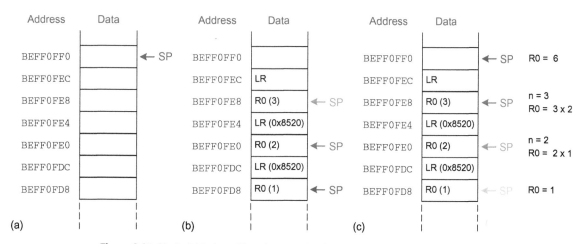

Figure 6.14 Stack: (a) before, (b) during, and (c) after factorial function call with n = 3

0xBEFF0FD8 and LR at 0xBEFF0FDC. This time, LR again contains 0x8520. The third invocation of factorial returns the value 1 in R0 and deallocates the stack frame before returning to the second invocation. The second invocation restores n (into R1) to 2, restores LR to 0x8520 (it happened to already have this value), deallocates the stack frame, and returns R0 = 2 × 1 = 2 to the first invocation. The first invocation restores n (into R1) to 3, restores LR to the return address of the caller, deallocates the stack frame, and returns R0 = 3 × 2 = 6. Figure 6.14(c) shows the stack as the recursively called functions return. When factorial returns to the caller, the stack pointer is in its original position (0xBEFF0FF0), none of the contents of the stack above the pointer have changed, and all of the preserved registers hold their original values. R0 holds the return value, 6.

Additional Arguments and Local Variables*

Functions may have more than four input arguments and may have too many local variables to keep in preserved registers. The stack is used to store this information. By ARM convention, if a function has more than four arguments, the first four are passed in the argument registers as usual. Additional arguments are passed on the stack, just above SP. The caller must expand its stack to make room for the additional arguments. Figure 6.15(a) shows the caller's stack for calling a function with more than four arguments.

A function can also declare local variables or arrays. Local variables are declared within a function and can be accessed only within that function. Local variables are stored in R4–R11; if there are too many local variables, they can also be stored in the function's stack frame. In particular, local arrays are stored on the stack.

Figure 6.15(b) shows the organization of a callee's stack frame. The stack frame holds the temporary registers and link register (if they need to be saved because of a subsequent function call), and any of the saved

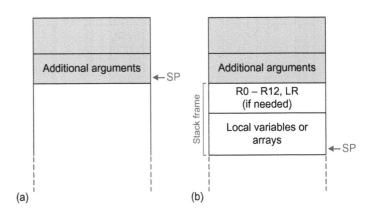

Figure 6.15 Stack usage: (a) before and (b) after call

registers that the function will modify. It also holds local arrays and any excess local variables. If the callee has more than four arguments, it finds them in the caller's stack frame. Accessing additional input arguments is the one exception in which a function can access stack data not in its own stack frame.

6.4 MACHINE LANGUAGE

Assembly language is convenient for humans to read. However, digital circuits understand only 1's and 0's. Therefore, a program written in assembly language is translated from mnemonics to a representation using only 1's and 0's called *machine language*. This section describes ARM machine language and the tedious process of converting between assembly and machine language.

ARM uses 32-bit instructions. Again, regularity supports simplicity, and the most regular choice is to encode all instructions as words that can be stored in memory. Even though some instructions may not require all 32 bits of encoding, variable-length instructions would add complexity. Simplicity would also encourage a single instruction format, but that is too restrictive. However, this issue allows us to introduce the last design principle:

Design Principle 4: Good design demands good compromises.

ARM makes the compromise of defining three main instruction formats: *Data-processing*, *Memory*, and *Branch*. This small number of formats allows for some regularity among instructions, and thus simpler decoder hardware, while also accommodating different instruction needs. Data-processing instructions have a first source register, a second source that is either an immediate or a register, possibly shifted, and a destination register. The Data-processing format has several variations for these second sources. Memory instructions have three operands: a base register, an offset that is either an immediate or an optionally shifted register, and a register that is the destination on an LDR and another source on an STR. Branch instructions take one 24-bit immediate branch offset. This section discusses these ARM instruction formats and shows how they are encoded into binary. Appendix B provides a quick reference for all the ARMv4 instructions.

6.4.1 Data-processing Instructions

The data-processing instruction format is the most common. The first source operand is a register. The second source operand can be an immediate or an optionally shifted register. A third register is the destination. Figure 6.16 shows the data-processing instruction format. The 32-bit instruction has six fields: *cond*, *op*, *funct*, *Rn*, *Rd*, and *Src2*.

Figure 6.16 Data-processing instruction format

Data-processing

31:28	27:26	25:20	19:16	15:12	11:0
cond	op	funct	Rn	Rd	Src2
4 bits	2 bits	6 bits	4 bits	4 bits	12 bits

The operation the instruction performs is encoded in the fields highlighted in blue: *op* (also called the opcode or operation code) and *funct* or function code; the *cond* field encodes conditional execution based on flags described in Section 6.3.2. Recall that $cond = 1110_2$ for unconditional instructions. *op* is 00_2 for data-processing instructions.

The operands are encoded in the three fields: *Rn*, *Rd*, and *Src2*. *Rn* is the first source register and *Src2* is the second source; *Rd* is the destination register.

Figure 6.17 shows the format of the *funct* field and the three variations of *Src2* for data-processing instructions. *funct* has three subfields: *I*, *cmd*, and *S*. The *I*-bit is 1 when *Src2* is an immediate. The *S*-bit is 1 when the instruction sets the condition flags. For example, SUBS R1, R9, #11 has $S = 1$. *cmd* indicates the specific data-processing instruction, as given in Table B.1 in Appendix B. For example, *cmd* is 4 (0100_2) for ADD and 2 (0010_2) for SUB.

> *Rd* is short for "register destination." *Rn* and *Rm* unintuitively indicate the first and second register sources.

Three variations of *Src2* encoding allow the second source operand to be (1) an immediate, (2) a register (*Rm*) optionally shifted by a constant (*shamt5*), or (3) a register (*Rm*) shifted by another register (*Rs*). For the latter two encodings of *Src2*, *sh* encodes the type of shift to perform, as will be shown in Table 6.8.

Data-processing instructions have an unusual immediate representation involving an 8-bit unsigned immediate, *imm8*, and a 4-bit rotation, *rot*. *imm8* is rotated right by $2 \times rot$ to create a 32-bit constant. Table 6.7 gives example rotations and resulting 32-bit constants for the 8-bit immediate 0xFF. This representation is valuable because it

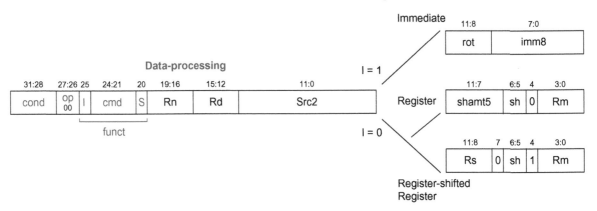

Figure 6.17 Data-processing instruction format showing the *funct* field and *Src2* variations

Table 6.7 Immediate rotations and resulting 32-bit constant for imm8 = 0xFF

rot	32-bit Constant
0000	0000 0000 0000 0000 0000 0000 1111 1111
0001	1100 0000 0000 0000 0000 0000 0011 1111
0010	1111 0000 0000 0000 0000 0000 0000 1111
...	...
1111	0000 0000 0000 0000 0000 0011 1111 1100

If an immediate has multiple possible encodings, the representation with the smallest rotation value *rot* is used. For example, #12 would be represented as (*rot, imm8*) = (0000, 00001100), not (0001, 00110000).

permits many useful constants, including small multiples of any power of two, to be packed into a small number of bits. Section 6.6.1 describes how to generate arbitrary 32-bit constants.

Figure 6.18 shows the machine code for ADD and SUB when *Src2* is a register. The easiest way to translate from assembly to machine code is to write out the values of each field and then convert these values to binary. Group the bits into blocks of four to convert to hexadecimal to make the machine language representation more compact. Beware that the destination is the first register in an assembly language instruction, but it is the second register field (*Rd*) in the machine language instruction. *Rn* and *Rm* are the first and second source operands, respectively. For example, the assembly instruction ADD R5, R6, R7 has *Rn* = 6, *Rd* = 5, and *Rm* = 7.

Figure 6.19 shows the machine code for ADD and SUB with an immediate and two register operands. Again, the destination is the first

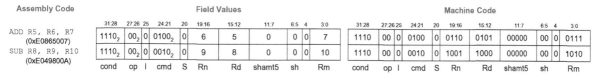

Figure 6.18 Data-processing instructions with three register operands

Assembly Code / Field Values / Machine Code

	31:28	27:26 25	24:21	20	19:16	15:12	11:7	6:5 4	3:0		31:28	27:26 25	24:21	20	19:16	15:12	11:7	6:5 4	3:0
ADD R5, R6, R7 (0xE0865007)	1110₂	00₂ 0	0100₂	0	6	5	0	0 0	7		1110	00 0	0100	0	0110	0101	00000	00 0	0111
SUB R8, R9, R10 (0xE049800A)	1110₂	00₂ 0	0010₂	0	9	8	0	0 0	10		1110	00 0	0010	0	1001	1000	00000	00 0	1010
	cond	op I	cmd	S	Rn	Rd	shamt5	sh	Rm		cond	op I	cmd	S	Rn	Rd	shamt5	sh	Rm

Figure 6.19 Data-processing instructions with an immediate and two register operands

Assembly Code / Field Values / Machine Code

	31:28	27:26 25	24:21	20	19:16	15:12	11:8	7:0		31:28	27:26 25	24:21	20	19:16	15:12	11:8	7:0
ADD R0, R1, #42 (0xE281002A)	1110₂	00₂ 1	0100₂	0	1	0	0	42		1110	00 1	0100	0	0001	0000	0000	00101010
SUB R2, R3, #0xFF0 (0xE2432EFF)	1110₂	00₂ 1	0010₂	0	3	2	14	255		1110	00 1	0010	0	0011	0010	1110	11111111
	cond	op I	cmd	S	Rn	Rd	rot	imm8		cond	op I	cmd	S	Rn	Rd	rot	imm8

register in an assembly language instruction, but it is the second register field (*Rd*) in the machine language instruction. The immediate of the `ADD` instruction (42) can be encoded in 8 bits, so no rotation is needed (*imm8* = 42, *rot* = 0). However, the immediate of `SUB R2, R3, 0xFF0` cannot be encoded directly using the 8 bits of *imm8*. Instead, *imm8* is 255 (0xFF), and it is rotated right by 28 bits (*rot* = 14). This is easiest to interpret by remembering that the right rotation by 28 bits is equivalent to a left rotation by 32−28 = 4 bits.

Shifts are also data-processing instructions. Recall from Section 6.3.1 that the amount by which to shift can be encoded using either a 5-bit immediate or a register.

Figure 6.20 shows the machine code for logical shift left (`LSL`) and rotate right (`ROR`) with immediate shift amounts. The *cmd* field is 13 (1101_2) for all shift instruction, and the shift field (*sh*) encodes the type of shift to perform, as given in Table 6.8. *Rm* (i.e., R5) holds the 32-bit value to be shifted, and *shamt5* gives the number of bits to shift. The shifted result is placed in *Rd*. *Rn* is not used and should be 0.

Figure 6.21 shows the machine code for `LSR` and `ASR` with the shift amount encoded in the least significant 8 bits of *Rs* (R6 and R12). As

Table 6.8 *sh* field encodings

Instruction	sh	Operation
`LSL`	00_2	Logical shift left
`LSR`	01_2	Logical shift right
`ASR`	10_2	Arithmetic shift right
`ROR`	11_2	Rotate right

Field Values

Assembly Code	cond (31:28)	op (27:26)	I (25)	cmd (24:21)	S (20)	Rn (19:16)	Rd (15:12)	shamt5 (11:7)	sh (6:5)	(4)	Rm (3:0)
`LSL R0, R9, #7` (0xE1A00389)	1110_2	00_2	0	1101_2	0	0	0	7	00_2	0	9
`ROR R3, R5, #21` (0xE1A03AE5)	1110_2	00_2	0	1101_2	0	0	3	21	11_2	0	5

Machine Code

Assembly Code	cond (31:28)	op (27:26)	I (25)	cmd (24:21)	S (20)	Rn (19:16)	Rd (15:12)	shamt5 (11:7)	sh (6:5)	(4)	Rm (3:0)
`LSL R0, R9, #7` (0xE1A00389)	1110	00	0	1101	0	0000	0000	00111	00	0	1001
`ROR R3, R5, #21` (0xE1A03AE5)	1110	00	0	1101	0	0000	0011	10101	11	0	0101

Figure 6.20 **Shift instructions with immediate shift amounts**

Field Values

Assembly Code	cond (31:28)	op (27:26)	I (25)	cmd (24:21)	S (20)	Rn (19:16)	Rd (15:12)	Rs (11:8)	(7)	sh (6:5)	(4)	Rm (3:0)
`LSR R4, R8, R6` (0xE1A04638)	1110_2	00_2	0	1101_2	0	0	4	6	0	01_2	1	8
`ASR R5, R1, R12` (0xE1A05C51)	1110_2	00_2	0	1101_2	0	0	5	12	0	10_2	1	1

Machine Code

Assembly Code	cond (31:28)	op (27:26)	I (25)	cmd (24:21)	S (20)	Rn (19:16)	Rd (15:12)	Rs (11:8)	(7)	sh (6:5)	(4)	Rm (3:0)
`LSR R4, R8, R6` (0xE1A04638)	1110	00	0	1101	0	0000	0100	0110	0	01	1	1000
`ASR R5, R1, R12` (0xE1A05C51)	1110	00	0	1101	0	0000	0101	1100	0	10	1	0001

Figure 6.21 **Shift instructions with register shift amounts**

Table 6.9 **Offset type control bits for memory instructions**

Bit	Meaning	
	Ī	U
0	Immediate offset in Src2	Subtract offset from base
1	Register offset in Src2	Add offset to base

before, *cmd* is 13 (1101_2), *sh* encodes the type of shift, *Rm* holds the value to be shifted, and the shifted result is placed in *Rd*. This instruction uses the *register-shifted register* addressing mode, where one register (*Rm*) is shifted by the amount held in a second register (*Rs*). Because the least significant 8 bits of *Rs* are used, *Rm* can be shifted by up to 255 positions. For example, if *Rs* holds the value 0xF001001C, the shift amount is 0x1C (28). A logical shift by more than 31 bits pushes all the bits off the end and produces all 0's. Rotate is cyclical, so a rotate by 50 bits is equivalent to a rotate by 18 bits.

6.4.2 Memory Instructions

Memory instructions use a format similar to that of data-processing instructions, with the same six overall fields: *cond*, *op*, *funct*, *Rn*, *Rd*, and *Src2*, as shown in Figure 6.22. However, memory instructions use a different *funct* field encoding, have two variations of *Src2*, and use an *op* of 01_2. *Rn* is the base register, *Src2* holds the offset, and *Rd* is the destination register in a load or the source register in a store. The offset is either a 12-bit unsigned immediate (*imm12*) or a register (*Rm*) that is optionally shifted by a constant (*shamt5*). *funct* is composed of six control bits: *Ī*, *P*, *U*, *B*, *W*, and *L*. The *Ī* (immediate) and *U* (add) bits determine whether the offset is an immediate or register and whether it should be added or subtracted, according to Table 6.9. The *P* (pre-index) and *W* (writeback) bits specify the index mode according to Table 6.10. The *L* (load) and *B* (byte) bits specify the type of memory operation according to Table 6.11.

Table 6.10 **Index mode control bits for memory instructions**

P	W	Index Mode
0	0	Post-index
0	1	Not supported
1	0	Offset
1	1	Pre-index

Table 6.11 **Memory operation type control bits for memory instructions**

L	B	Instruction
0	0	STR
0	1	STRB
1	0	LDR
1	1	LDRB

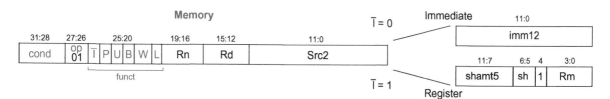

Figure 6.22 **Memory instruction format for** LDR, STR, LDRB, **and** STRB

Example 6.3 TRANSLATING MEMORY INSTRUCTIONS INTO MACHINE LANGUAGE

Translate the following assembly language statement into machine language.

STR R11, [R5], #-26

> Notice the counterintuitive encoding of post-indexing mode.

Solution: STR is a memory instruction, so it has an *op* of 01_2. According to Table 6.11, $L = 0$ and $B = 0$ for STR. The instruction uses post-indexing, so according to Table 6.10, $P = 0$ and $W = 0$. The immediate offset is subtracted from the base, so $\overline{I} = 0$ and $U = 0$. Figure 6.23 shows each field and the machine code. Hence, the machine language instruction is 0xE405B01A.

		Assembly Code				Field Values					Machine Code				
			31:28	27:26	25:20	19:16	15:12	11:0	31:28	27:26	25:20	19:16	15:12	11:0	
STR R11, [R5], #-26			1110_2	01_2	0000000_2	5	11	26	1110	01	000000	0101	1011	0000 0001 1010	
			cond	op	IPUBWL	Rn	Rd	Imm12	E	4	0	5	B	0 1 A	

Figure 6.23 Machine code for the memory instruction of Example 6.3

6.4.3 Branch Instructions

Branch instructions use a single 24-bit signed immediate operand, *imm24*, as shown in Figure 6.24. As with data-processing and memory instructions, branch instructions begin with a 4-bit condition field and a 2-bit *op*, which is 10_2. The *funct* field is only 2 bits. The upper bit of *funct* is always 1 for branches. The lower bit, *L*, indicates the type of branch operation: 1 for BL and 0 for B. The remaining 24-bit two's complement *imm24* field is used to specify an instruction address relative to PC + 8.

Code Example 6.28 shows the use of the branch if less than (BLT) instruction and Figure 6.25 shows the machine code for that instruction. The *branch target address (BTA)* is the address of the next instruction to execute if the branch is taken. The BLT instruction in Figure 6.25 has a BTA of 0x80B4, the instruction address of the THERE label.

The 24-bit immediate field gives the number of instructions between the BTA and PC + 8 (two instructions past the branch). In this case, the value in the immediate field (*imm24*) of BLT is 3 because the BTA (0x80B4) is three instructions past PC + 8 (0x80A8).

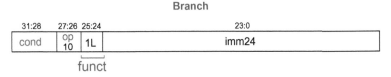

Branch

31:28	27:26	25:24	23:0
cond	op 10	1L	imm24

funct

Figure 6.24 Branch instruction format

Code Example 6.28 CALCULATING THE BRANCH TARGET ADDRESS

ARM Assembly Code

```
0x80A0         BLT THERE
0x80A4         ADD R0, R1, R2
0x80A8         SUB R0, R0, R9
0x80AC         ADD SP, SP, #8
0x80B0         MOV PC, LR
0x80B4 THERE   SUB R0, R0, #1
0x80B8         ADD R3, R3, #0x5
```

Assembly Code		Field Values		Machine Code		
	31:28 27:26 25:24	23:0		31:28 27:26 25:24		23:0
BLT THERE (0xBA000003)	1011_2 10_2 10_2	3		1011 10 10		0000 0000 0000 0000 0000 0011
	cond opfunct	imm24		cond op funct		imm24

Figure 6.25 **Machine code for branch if less than** (BLT)

The processor calculates the BTA from the instruction by sign-extending the 24-bit immediate, shifting it left by 2 (to convert words to bytes), and adding it to PC + 8.

Example 6.4 CALCULATING THE IMMEDIATE FIELD FOR PC-RELATIVE ADDRESSING

Calculate the immediate field and show the machine code for the branch instruction in the following assembly program.

```
0x8040 TEST   LDRB  R5, [R0, R3]
0x8044        STRB  R5, [R1, R3]
0x8048        ADD   R3, R3, #1
0x8044        MOV   PC, LR
0x8050        BL    TEST
0x8054        LDR   R3, [R1], #4
0x8058        SUB   R4, R3, #9
```

Solution: Figure 6.26 shows the machine code for the branch and link instruction (BL). Its branch target address (0x8040) is six instructions behind PC + 8 (0x8058), so the immediate field is -6.

Assembly Code		Field Values		Machine Code		
	31:28 27:26 25:24	23:0		31:28 27:26 25:24		23:0
BL TEST (0xEBFFFFFA)	1110_2 10_2 11_2	-6		1110 10 11		1111 1111 1111 1111 1111 1010
	cond op funct	imm24		cond op funct		imm24

Figure 6.26 BL **machine code**

ARM is unusual among RISC architectures in that it allows the second source operand to be shifted in register and base addressing modes. This requires a shifter in series with the ALU in the hardware implementation but significantly reduces code length in common programs, especially array accesses. For example, in an array of 32-bit data elements, the array index must be left-shifted by 2 to compute the byte offset into the array. Any type of shift is permitted, but left shifts for multiplication are most common.

6.4.4 Addressing Modes

This section summarizes the modes used for addressing instruction operands. ARM uses four main modes: register, immediate, base, and PC-relative addressing. Most other architectures provide similar addressing modes, so understanding these modes helps you easily learn other assembly languages. Register and base addressing have several submodes described below. The first three modes (register, immediate, and base addressing) define modes of reading and writing operands. The last mode (PC-relative addressing) defines a mode of writing the program counter (PC). Table 6.12 summarizes and gives examples of each addressing mode.

Data-processing instructions use register or immediate addressing, in which the first source operand is a register and the second is a register or immediate, respectively. ARM allows the second register to be optionally shifted by an amount specified in an immediate or a third register. Memory instructions use base addressing, in which the base address comes from a register and the offset comes from an immediate, a register, or a register shifted by an immediate. Branches use PC-relative addressing in which the branch target address is computed by adding an offset to PC + 8.

6.4.5 Interpreting Machine Language Code

To interpret machine language, one must decipher the fields of each 32-bit instruction word. Different instructions use different formats, but all

Table 6.12 **ARM operand addressing modes**

Operand Addressing Mode	Example	Description
Register		
Register-only	ADD R3, R2, R1	R3 ← R2 + R1
Immediate-shifted register	SUB R4, R5, R9, LSR #2	R4 ← R5 − (R9 >> 2)
Register-shifted register	ORR R0, R10, R2, ROR R7	R0 ← R10 | (R2 ROR R7)
Immediate	SUB R3, R2, #25	R3 ← R2 − 25
Base		
Immediate offset	STR R6, [R11, #77]	mem[R11+77] ← R6
Register offset	LDR R12, [R1, −R5]	R12 ← mem[R1 − R5]
Immediate-shifted register offset	LDR R8, [R9, R2, LSL #2]	R8 ← mem[R9 + (R2 << 2)]
PC-Relative	B LABEL1	Branch to LABEL1

formats start with a 4-bit condition field and a 2-bit *op*. The best place to begin is to look at the *op*. If it is 00_2, then the instruction is a data-processing instruction; if it is 01_2, then the instruction is a memory instruction; if it is 10_2, then it is a branch instruction. Based on that, the rest of the fields can be interpreted.

Example 6.5 TRANSLATING MACHINE LANGUAGE TO ASSEMBLY LANGUAGE

Translate the following machine language code into assembly language.

```
0xE0475001
0xE5949010
```

Solution: First, we represent each instruction in binary and look at bits 27:26 to find the *op* for each instruction, as shown in Figure 6.27. The *op* fields are 00_2 and 01_2, indicating a data-processing and memory instruction, respectively. Next, we look at the *funct* field of each instruction.

The *cmd* field of the data-processing instruction is 2 (0010_2) and the *I*-bit (bit 25) is 0, indicating that it is a SUB instruction with a register *Src2*. *Rd* is 5, *Rn* is 7, and *Rm* is 1.

The *funct* field for the memory instruction is 011001_2. $B = 0$ and $L = 1$, so this is an LDR instruction. $P = 1$ and $W = 0$, indicating offset addressing. $\bar{I} = 0$, so the offset is an immediate. $U = 1$, so the offset is added. Thus, it is a load register instruction with an immediate offset that is added to the base register. *Rd* is 9, *Rn* is 4, and *imm12* is 16. Figure 6.27 shows the assembly code equivalent of the two machine instructions.

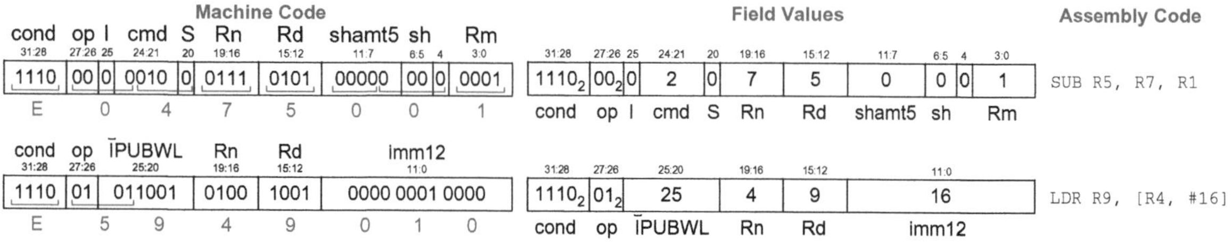

Figure 6.27 Machine code to assembly code translation

6.4.6 The Power of the Stored Program

A program written in machine language is a series of 32-bit numbers representing the instructions. Like other binary numbers, these instructions can be stored in memory. This is called the *stored program* concept, and it is a key reason why computers are so powerful. Running a different

Assembly code	Machine code
MOV R1, #100	0xE3A01064
MOV R2, #69	0xE3A02045
CMP R1, R2	0xE1510002
STRHS R3, [R1, #0x24]	0x25813024

Stored program

Address	Instructions
⋮	⋮
0000800C	2 5 8 1 3 0 2 4
00008008	E 1 5 1 0 0 0 2
00008004	E 3 A 0 2 0 4 5
00008000	E 3 A 0 1 0 6 4	← PC

Main memory

Figure 6.28 Stored program

Ada Lovelace, 1815–1852.
A British mathematician who wrote the first computer program. It calculated the Bernoulli numbers using Charles Babbage's Analytical Engine. She was the daughter of the poet Lord Byron.

program does not require large amounts of time and effort to reconfigure or rewire hardware; it only requires writing the new program to memory. In contrast to dedicated hardware, the stored program offers general-purpose computing. In this way, a computer can execute applications ranging from a calculator to a word processor to a video player simply by changing the stored program.

Instructions in a stored program are retrieved, or *fetched*, from memory and executed by the processor. Even large, complex programs are simply a series of memory reads and instruction executions.

Figure 6.28 shows how machine instructions are stored in memory. In ARM programs, the instructions are normally stored starting at low addresses, in this case 0x00008000. Remember that ARM memory is byte-addressable, so 32-bit (4-byte) instruction addresses advance by 4 bytes, not 1.

To run or execute the stored program, the processor fetches the instructions from memory sequentially. The fetched instructions are then decoded and executed by the digital hardware. The address of the current instruction is kept in a 32-bit register called the program counter (PC), which is register R15. For historical reasons, a read to the PC returns the address of the current instruction plus 8.

To execute the code in Figure 6.28, the PC is initialized to address 0x00008000. The processor fetches the instruction at that memory address and executes the instruction, 0xE3A01064 (MOV R1, #100). The processor then increments the PC by 4 to 0x00008004, fetches and executes that instruction, and repeats.

The *architectural state* of a microprocessor holds the state of a program. For ARM, the architectural state includes the register file and status registers. If the operating system (OS) saves the architectural state at some point in the program, it can interrupt the program, do something else, and then restore the state such that the program continues properly, unaware that it was ever interrupted. The architectural state is also of great importance when we build a microprocessor in Chapter 7.

6.5 LIGHTS, CAMERA, ACTION: COMPILING, ASSEMBLING, AND LOADING*

Until now, we have shown how to translate short high-level code snippets into assembly and machine code. This section describes how to compile and assemble a complete high-level program and how to load the program into memory for execution. We begin by introducing an example ARM *memory map*, which defines where code, data, and stack memory are located.

Figure 6.29 shows the steps required to translate a program from a high-level language into machine language and to start executing that program. First, a *compiler* translates the high-level code into assembly code. The *assembler* translates the assembly code into machine code and puts it in an object file. The *linker* combines the machine code with code from libraries and other files and determines the proper branch addresses and variable locations to produce an entire executable program. In practice, most compilers perform all three steps of compiling, assembling, and linking. Finally, the *loader* loads the program into memory and starts execution. The remainder of this section walks through these steps for a simple program.

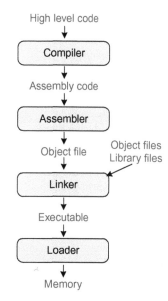

Figure 6.29 Steps for translating and starting a program

6.5.1 The Memory Map

With 32-bit addresses, the ARM address space spans 2^{32} bytes (4 GB). Word addresses are multiples of 4 and range from 0 to 0xFFFFFFFC. Figure 6.30 shows an example memory map. The ARM architecture divides the address space into five parts or segments: the text segment,

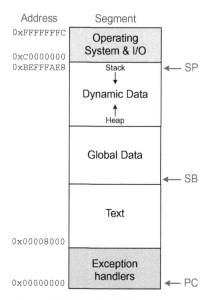

Figure 6.30 Example ARM memory map

We present an example ARM memory map here; however, in ARM, the memory map is somewhat flexible. While the exception vector table must be located at 0x0 and memory-mapped I/O is typically located at the high memory addresses, the user can define where the text (code and constant data), stack, and global data are placed. Moreover, at least historically, most ARM systems have less than 4 GB of memory.

Grace Hopper, 1906–1992.
Graduated from Yale University with a Ph.D. in mathematics. Developed the first compiler while working for the Remington Rand Corporation and was instrumental in developing the COBOL programming language. As a naval officer, she received many awards, including a World War II Victory Medal and the National Defense Service Medal.

global data segment, dynamic data segment, and segments for exception handlers, the operating system (OS) and input/output (I/O). The following sections describe each segment.

The Text Segment

The *text segment* stores the machine language program. ARM also calls this the *read-only* (RO) *segment*. In addition to code, it may include literals (constants) and read-only data.

The Global Data Segment

The *global data segment* stores global variables that, in contrast to local variables, can be accessed by all functions in a program. Global variables are allocated in memory before the program begins executing. ARM also calls this the *read/write* (RW) *segment*. Global variables are typically accessed using a *static base* register that points to the start of the global segment. ARM conventionally uses R9 as the static base pointer (SB).

The Dynamic Data Segment

The *dynamic data segment* holds the stack and the heap. The data in this segment is not known at start-up but is dynamically allocated and deallocated throughout the execution of the program.

Upon start-up, the operating system sets up the stack pointer (SP) to point to the top of the stack. The stack typically grows downward, as shown here. The stack includes temporary storage and local variables, such as arrays, that do not fit in the registers. As discussed in Section 6.3.7, functions also use the stack to save and restore registers. Each stack frame is accessed in last-in-first-out order.

The *heap* stores data that is allocated by the program during runtime. In C, memory allocations are made by the `malloc` function; in C++ and Java, `new` is used to allocate memory. Like a heap of clothes on a dorm room floor, heap data can be used and discarded in any order. The heap typically grows upward from the bottom of the dynamic data segment.

If the stack and heap ever grow into each other, the program's data can become corrupted. The memory allocator tries to ensure that this never happens by returning an out-of-memory error if there is insufficient space to allocate more dynamic data.

The Exception Handler, OS, and I/O Segments

The lowest part of the ARM memory map is reserved for the exception vector table and exception handlers, starting at address 0x0 (see Section 6.6.3). The highest part of the memory map is reserved for the operating system and memory-mapped I/O (see Section 9.2).

6.5.2 Compilation

A compiler translates high-level code into assembly language. The examples in this section are based on GCC, a popular and widely used free compiler, running on the Raspberry Pi single-board computer

---

Code Example 6.29 COMPILING A HIGH-LEVEL PROGRAM

High-Level Code	ARM Assembly Code

```
int f, g, y; // global variables


int sum(int a, int b) {
  return (a + b);
}


int main(void)
{
  f = 2;
  g = 3;
  y = sum(f, g);
  return y;
}
```

```
      .text
      .global sum
      .type   sum, %function
sum:
      add     r0, r0, r1
      bx      lr
      .global main
      .type   main, %function
main:
      push    {r3, lr}
      mov     r0, #2
      ldr     r3, .L3
      str     r0, [r3, #0]
      mov     r1, #3
      ldr     r3, .L3+4
      str     r1, [r3, #0]
      bl      sum
      ldr     r3, .L3+8
      str     r0, [r3, #0]
      pop     {r3, pc}
.L3:
      .word   f
      .word   g
      .word   y
```

In Code Example 6.29, global variables are accessed using two memory instructions: one to load the *address* of the variable, and a second to read or write the variable. The addresses of the global variables are placed after the code, starting at label .L3. LDR R3, .L3 loads the *address* of f into R3, and STR R0, [R3, #0] writes to f; LDR R3, .L3+4 loads the *address* of g into R3, and STR R1, [R3, #0] writes to g, and so on. Section 6.6.1 describes this assembly code construct further.

(see Section 9.3). Code Example 6.29 shows a simple high-level program with three global variables and two functions, along with the assembly code produced by GCC.

To compile, assemble, and link a C program named prog.c with GCC, use the command:

```
gcc -O1 -g prog.c -o prog
```

This command produces an executable output file called prog. The -O1 flag asks the compiler to perform basic optimizations rather than producing grossly inefficient code. The -g flag tells the compiler to include debugging information in the file.

To see the intermediate steps, we can use GCC's -S flag to compile but not assemble or link.

```
gcc -O1 -S prog.c -o prog.s
```

The output, prog.s, is rather verbose, but the interesting parts are shown in Code Example 6.29. Note that GCC requires labels to be followed by a colon. The GCC output is in lowercase and has other assembler directives not discussed here. Observe that sum returns using the BX instruction rather than MOV PC, LR. Also, observe that GCC elected to save and restore R3 even though it is not one of the preserved registers. The addresses of the global variables will be stored in a table starting at label .L3.

6.5.3 Assembling

An assembler turns the assembly language code into an *object file* containing machine language code. GCC can create the object file from either prog.s or directly from prog.c using

```
gcc -c prog.s -o prog.o
```

> or

```
gcc -O1 -g -c prog.c -o prog.o
```

The assembler makes two passes through the assembly code. On the first pass, the assembler assigns instruction addresses and finds all the symbols, such as labels and global variable names. The names and addresses of the symbols are kept in a symbol table. On the second pass through the code, the assembler produces the machine language code. Addresses for labels are taken from the symbol table. The machine language code and symbol table are stored in the object file.

We can *disassemble* the object file using the objdump command to see the assembly language code beside the machine language code. If the code was originally compiled with –g, the disassembler also shows the corresponding lines of C code:

```
objdump -S prog.o
```

The following shows the disassembly of section .text:

```
00000000 <sum>:

int sum(int a, int b) {
    return (a + b);
}
   0:  e0800001   add  r0, r0, r1
   4:  e12fff1e   bx  lr

00000008 <main>:

int f, g, y; // global variables

int sum(int a, int b);

int main(void) {
   8:  e92d4008   push  {r3, lr}
        f = 2;
   c:  e3a00002   mov  r0, #2
  10:  e59f301c   ldr  r3, [pc, #28]   ; 34 <main+0x2c>
  14:  e5830000   str  r0, [r3]
        g = 3;
  18:  e3a01003   mov  r1, #3
  1c:  e59f3014   ldr  r3, [pc, #20]   ; 38 <main+0x30>
  20:  e5831000   str  r1, [r3]
        y = sum(f,g);
  24:  ebfffffe   bl  0 <sum>
```

Recall from Section 6.4.6 that a read to PC returns the address of the current instruction plus 8. So, LDR R3, [PC, #28] loads f's address, which is just after the code at: (PC + 8) + 28 = (0x10 + 0x8) + 0x1C = 0x34.

```
 28:  e59f300c   ldr   r3, [pc, #12]  ; 3c <main+0x34>
 2c:  e5830000   str   r0, [r3]
 return y;
}
 30:  e8bd8008   pop   {r3, pc}
 ...
```

We can also view the symbol table from the object file using `objdump` with the `-t` flag. The interesting parts are shown below. Observe that the `sum` function starts at address 0 and has a size of 8 bytes. `main` starts at address 8 and has size 0x38. The global variable symbols `f`, `g`, and `h` are listed and are 4 bytes each, but they have not yet been assigned addresses.

```
objdump -t prog.o

SYMBOL TABLE:
00000000 l d .text   00000000 .text
00000000 l d .data   00000000 .data
00000000 g F .text   00000008 sum
00000008 g F .text   00000038 main
00000004   O *COM*    00000004 f
00000004   O *COM*    00000004 g
00000004   O *COM*    00000004 y
```

6.5.4 Linking

Most large programs contain more than one file. If the programmer changes only one of the files, it would be wasteful to recompile and reassemble the other files. In particular, programs often call functions in library files; these library files almost never change. If a file of high-level code is not changed, the associated object file need not be updated. Also, a program typically involves some start-up code to initialize the stack, heap, and so forth, that must be executed before calling the `main` function.

The job of the linker is to combine all of the object files and the start-up code into one machine language file called the *executable* and assign addresses for global variables. The linker relocates the data and instructions in the object files so that they are not all on top of each other. It uses the information in the symbol tables to adjust the code based on the new label and global variable addresses. Invoke GCC to link the object file using:

```
gcc prog.o -o prog
```

We can again disassemble the executable using:

```
objdump -S -t prog
```

The start-up code is too lengthy to show, but our program begins at address 0x8390 in the text segment and the global variables are assigned addresses starting at 0x10570 in the global segment. Notice the .word assembler directives defining the addresses of the global variables f, g, and y.

```
00008390 <sum>:
```

```
int sum(int a, int b) {
  return (a + b);
}
  8390:  e0800001  add  r0, r0, r1
  8394:  e12fff1e  bx   lr
```

```
00008398 <main>:
```

```
int f, g, y; // global variables
```

```
int sum(int a, int b);
```

```
int main(void) {
  8398:  e92d4008  push  {r3, lr}
  f = 2;
  839c:  e3a00002  mov   r0, #2
  83a0:  e59f301c  ldr   r3, [pc, #28]  ; 83c4 <main+0x2c>
  83a4:  e5830000  str   r0, [r3]
  g = 3;
  83a8:  e3a01003  mov   r1, #3
  83ac:  e59f3014  ldr   r3, [pc, #20]  ; 83c8 <main+0x30>
  83b0:  e5831000  str   r1, [r3]
  y = sum(f,g);
  83b4:  ebfffff5  bl    8390 <sum>
  83b8:  e59f300c  ldr   r3, [pc, #12]  ; 83cc <main+0x34>
  83bc:  e5830000  str   r0, [r3]
  return y;
}
  83c0:  e8bd8008  pop   {r3, pc}
  83c4:  00010570  .word 0x00010570
  83c8:  00010574  .word 0x00010574
  83cc:  00010578  .word 0x00010578
```

The instruction LDR R3, [PC, #28] in the executable loads from address (PC + 8) + 28 = (0x83A0 + 0x8) + 0x1C = 0x83C4. This memory address contains the value 0x10570, the location of global variable f.

The executable also contains an updated symbol table with the relocated addresses of the functions and global variables.

```
SYMBOL TABLE:
000082e4 l  d .text 00000000        .text
00010564 l  d .data 00000000        .data
00008390 g  F .text 00000008        sum
00008398 g  F .text 00000038        main
00010570 g  O .bss  00000004        f
00010574 g  O .bss  00000004        g
00010578 g  O .bss  00000004        y
```

6.5.5 Loading

The operating system loads a program by reading the text segment of the executable file from a storage device (usually the hard disk) into the text segment of memory. The operating system jumps to the beginning of the program to begin executing. Figure 6.31 shows the memory map at the beginning of program execution.

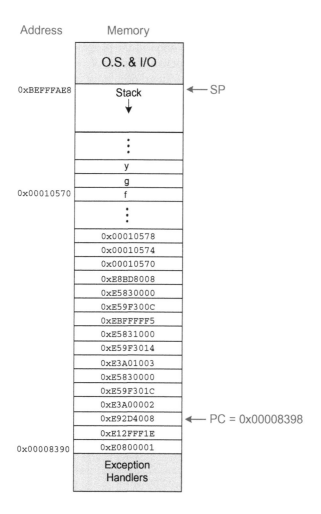

Figure 6.31 **Executable loaded in memory**

6.6 ODDS AND ENDS*

This section covers a few optional topics that do not fit naturally elsewhere in the chapter. These topics include loading 32-bit literals, NOPs, and exceptions.

6.6.1 Loading Literals

Many programs need to load 32-bit literals, such as constants or addresses. MOV only accepts a 12-bit source, so the LDR instruction is used to load these numbers from a *literal pool* in the text segment. ARM assemblers accept loads of the form

```
LDR Rd, =literal
LDR Rd, =label
```

The first loads a 32-bit constant specified by `literal`, and the second loads the address of a variable or pointer in the program specified by `label`. In both cases, the value to load is kept in a *literal pool*, which is a portion of the text segment containing literals. The literal pool must be less than 4096 bytes from the `LDR` instruction so that the load can be performed as `LDR Rd, [PC, #offset_to_literal]`. The program must be careful to branch around the literal pool because executing literals would be nonsensical or worse.

Code Example 6.30 illustrates loading a literal. As shown in Figure 6.32, suppose the `LDR` instruction is at address 0x8110 and the literal is at 0x815C. Remember that reading the PC returns the address 8 bytes beyond the current instruction being executed. Hence, when the `LDR` is executed, reading the PC returns 0x8118. Thus, the `LDR` uses an offset of 0x44 to find the literal pool: `LDR R1, [PC, #0x44]`.

Code Example 6.30 LARGE IMMEDIATE USING A LITERAL POOL

High-level code	ARM Assembly Code

`int a = 0x2B9056F;`	`; R1 = a`
	`LDR R1, =0x2B9056F`
	`. . .`

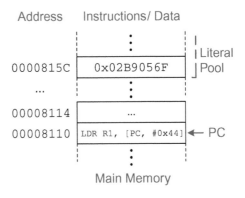

Figure 6.32 Example literal pool

6.6.2 NOP

NOP is a mnemonic for "no operation" and is pronounced "no op." It is a *pseudoinstruction* that does nothing. The assembler translates it to `MOV R0, R0` (0xE1A00000). NOPs are useful to, among other things, achieve some delay or align instructions.

6.6.3 Exceptions

An *exception* is like an unscheduled function call that branches to a new address. Exceptions may be caused by hardware or software. For example, the processor may receive notification that the user pressed a key on a keyboard. The processor may stop what it is doing, determine which key was pressed, save it for future reference, and then resume the program that was running. Such a hardware exception triggered by an input/output (I/O) device such as a keyboard is often called an *interrupt*. Alternatively, the program may encounter an error condition such as an undefined instruction. The program then branches to code in the operating system (OS), which may choose to either emulate the unimplemented instruction or terminate the offending program. Software exceptions are sometimes called *traps*. A particularly important form of a trap is a *system call*, whereby the program invokes a function in the OS running at a higher privilege level. Other causes of exceptions include reset and attempts to read nonexistent memory.

Like any other function call, an exception must save the return address, jump to some address, do its work, clean up after itself, and return to the program where it left off. Exceptions use a *vector* table to determine where to jump to the *exception handler* and use *banked registers* to maintain extra copies of key registers so that they will not corrupt the registers in the active program. Exceptions also change the *privilege level* of the program, allowing the exception handler to access protected parts of memory.

Execution Modes and Privilege Levels

An ARM processor can operate in one of several execution modes with different privilege levels. The different modes allow an exception to take place in an exception handler without corrupting state; for example, an interrupt could occur while the processor is executing operating system code in Supervisor mode, and a subsequent Abort exception could occur if the interrupt attempted to access an invalid memory address. The exception handlers would eventually return and resume the supervisor code. The mode is specified in the bottom bits of the Current Program Status Register (CPSR), as was shown in Figure 6.6. Table 6.13 lists execution modes and their encodings. User mode operates at privilege level PL0, which is unable to access protected portions of memory such as the operating system code. The other modes operate at privilege level PL1, which can access all system resources. Privilege levels are important so that buggy or malicious user code cannot corrupt other programs or crash or infect the system.

Exception Vector Table

When an exception occurs, the processor branches to an offset in the *exception vector table*, depending on the cause of the exception. Table 6.14 describes the vector table, which is normally located starting at address 0x00000000 in memory. For example, when an interrupt occurs, the processor branches to address 0x00000018. Similarly, on

Table 6.13 ARM execution modes

Mode	$CPSR_{4:0}$
User	10000
Supervisor	10011
Abort	10111
Undefined	11011
Interrupt (IRQ)	10010
Fast Interrupt (FIQ)	10001

Table 6.14 Exception vector table

Exception	Address	Mode
Reset	0x00	Supervisor
Undefined Instruction	0x04	Undefined
Supervisor Call	0x08	Supervisor
Prefetch Abort (instruction fetch error)	0x0C	Abort
Data Abort (data load or store error)	0x10	Abort
Reserved	0x14	N/A
Interrupt	0x18	IRQ
Fast Interrupt	0x1C	FIQ

ARM also supports a High Vectors mode in which the exception vector table starts at address 0xFFFF0000. For example, the system may boot using a vector table in ROM at address 0x00000000. Once the system starts up, the OS may write an updated vector table in RAM at 0xFFFF0000 and put the system into High Vectors mode.

power-up, the processor branches to address 0x00000000. Each exception vector offset typically contains a branch instruction to an exception handler, code that handles the exception and then either exits or returns to the user code.

Banked Registers

Before an exception changes the PC, it must save the return address in the LR so that the exception handler knows where to return. However, it must take care not to disturb the value already in the LR, which the program will need later. Therefore, the processor maintains a bank of different registers to use as LR during each of the execution modes. Similarly, the exception handler must not disturb the status register bits.

Hence, a bank of *saved program status registers* (SPSRs) is used to hold a copy of the CPSR during exceptions.

If an exception takes place while a program is manipulating its stack frame, the frame might be in an unstable state (e.g., data has been written onto the stack but the stack pointer is not yet pointing to the top of stack). Hence, each execution mode also uses its own stack and banked copy of SP pointing to the top of its stack. Memory must be reserved for each execution mode's stack and banked versions of the stack pointers must be initialized at start-up.

The first thing that an exception handler must do is to push all of the registers it might change onto the stack. This takes some time. ARM has a *fast interrupt* execution mode FIQ in which R8–R12 are also banked. Thus, the exception handler can immediately begin without saving these registers.

Exception Handling

Now that we have defined execution modes, exception vectors, and banked registers, we can define what occurs during an exception. Upon detecting an exception, the processor:

1. Stores the CPSR into the banked SPSR

2. Sets the execution mode and privilege level based on the type of exception

3. Sets *interrupt mask* bits in the CPSR so that the exception handler will not be interrupted

4. Stores the return address into the banked LR

5. Branches to the exception vector table based on the type of exception

The processor then executes the instruction in the exception vector table, typically a branch to the exception handler. The handler usually pushes other registers onto its stack, takes care of the exception, and pops the registers back off the stack. The exception handler returns using the MOVS PC, LR instruction, a special flavor of MOV that performs the following cleanup:

1. Copies the banked SPSR to the CPSR to restore the status register

2. Copies the banked LR (possibly adjusted for certain exceptions) to the PC to return to the program where the exception occurred

3. Restores the execution mode and privilege level

Exception-Related Instructions

Programs operate at a low privilege level, whereas the operating system has a higher privilege level. To transition between levels in a controlled way, the program places arguments in registers and issues a *supervisor call* (SVC) instruction, which generates an exception and raises the privilege level. The OS examines the arguments and performs the requested function, and then returns to the program.

The OS and other code operating at PL1 can access the banked registers for the various execution modes using the MRS (move to register from special register) and MSR (move to special register from register) instructions. For example, at boot time, the OS will use these instructions to initialize the stacks for exception handlers.

Start-up

On start-up, the processor jumps to the reset vector and begins executing *boot loader* code in supervisor mode. The boot loader typically configures the memory system, initializes the stack pointer, and reads the OS from disk; then it begins a much longer boot process in the OS. The OS eventually will load a program, change to unprivileged user mode, and jump to the start of the program.

6.7 EVOLUTION OF ARM ARCHITECTURE

The ARM1 processor was first developed by Acorn Computer in Britain for the BBC Micro computers in 1985 as an upgrade to the 6502 microprocessor used in many personal computers of the era. It was followed within the year by the ARM2, which went into production in the Acorn Archimedes computer. ARM was an acronym for *Acorn RISC Machine*. The product implemented Version 2 of the ARM instruction set (ARMv2). The address bus was only 26 bits, and the upper 6 bits of the 32-bit PC were used to hold status bits. The architecture included almost all of the instructions described in this chapter, including data-processing, most loads and stores, branches, and multiplies.

ARM soon extended the address bus to a full 32 bits, moving the status bits into a dedicated Current Program Status Register (CPSR). ARMv4, introduced in 1993, added halfword loads and stores and provided both signed and unsigned halfword and byte loads. This is the core of the modern ARM instruction set, and is what we have covered in this chapter.

The ARM instruction set has seen many enhancements described in subsequent sections. The highly successful ARM7TDMI processor in 1995 introduced the 16-bit Thumb instruction set in ARMv4T to improve code density. ARMv5TE added digital signal processing (DSP) and optional floating-point instructions. ARMv6 added multimedia instructions and enhanced the Thumb instruction set. ARMv7 improved the floating-point and multimedia instructions, renaming them Advanced SIMD. ARMv8 introduced a completely new 64-bit architecture. Various other system programming instructions have been introduced as the architecture has evolved.

As of ARMv7, the CPSR is called the Application Program Status Register (APSR).

6.7.1 Thumb Instruction Set

Thumb instructions are 16 bits long to achieve higher code density; they are identical to regular ARM instructions but generally have limitations, including that they:

▸ Access only the bottom eight registers

▸ Reuse a register as both a source and destination

▸ Support shorter immediates

▸ Lack conditional execution

▸ Always write the status flags

Almost all ARM instructions have Thumb equivalents. Because the instructions are less powerful, more are required to write an equivalent program. However, the instructions are half as long, giving overall Thumb code size of about 65% of the ARM equivalent. The Thumb instruction set is valuable not only to reduce the size and cost of code storage memory, but also to allow for an inexpensive 16-bit bus to instruction memory and to reduce the power consumed by fetching instructions from the memory.

ARM processors have an instruction set state register, ISETSTATE, that includes a T bit to indicate whether the processor is in normal mode (T = 0) or Thumb mode (T = 1). This mode determines how instructions should be fetched and interpreted. The BX and BLX branch instructions toggle the T bit to enter or exit Thumb mode.

Thumb instruction encoding is more complex and irregular than ARM instructions to pack as much useful information as possible into 16-bit halfwords. Figure 6.33 shows encodings for common Thumb instructions. The upper bits specify the type of instruction. Data-processing instructions typically specify two registers, one of which is both the first source and the destination. They always write the status flags. Adds, subtracts, and shifts can specify a short immediate. Conditional branches specify a 4-bit condition code and a short offset, whereas unconditional branches allow a longer offset. Note that BX takes a 4-bit register identifier so that it can access the link register LR. Special forms of LDR, STR, ADD, and SUB are defined to operate relative to the stack pointer SP (to access the stack frame during function calls). Another special form of LDR loads relative to the PC (to access a literal pool). Forms of ADD and MOV can access all 16 registers. BL always requires two halfwords to specify a 22-bit destination.

ARM subsequently refined the Thumb instruction set and added a number of 32-bit Thumb-2 instructions to boost performance of common operations and to allow any program to be written in Thumb mode.

The irregular Thumb instruction set encoding and variable-length instructions (1 or 2 halfwords) are characteristic of 16-bit processor architectures that must pack a large amount of information into a short instruction word. The irregularity complicates instruction decoding.

15										0	

0	1	0	0	0	0	funct	Rm	Rdn	\<funct\>S Rdn, Rdn, Rm (data-processing)

| 0 | 0 | 0 | ASR LSR | imm5 | Rm | Rd | LSLS / LSRS / ASRS Rd, Rm, #imm5 |

| 0 | 0 | 0 | 1 | 1 | 1 SUB | imm3 | Rm | Rd | ADDS / SUBS Rd, Rm, #imm3 |

| 0 | 0 | 1 | 1 SUB | Rdn | imm8 | ADDS / SUBS Rdn, Rdn, #imm8 |

| 0 | 1 | 0 | 0 | 0 | 1 | 0 | 0 | Rdn[3] | Rm | Rdn[2:0] | ADD Rdn, Rdn, Rm |

| 1 | 0 | 1 | 1 | 0 | 0 | 0 | 0 | SUB | imm7 | ADD / SUB SP, SP, #imm7 |

| 0 | 0 | 1 | 0 | 1 | Rn | imm8 | CMP Rn, #imm8 |

| 0 | 0 | 1 | 0 | 0 | Rd | imm8 | MOV Rd, #imm8 |

| 0 | 1 | 0 | 0 | 0 | 1 | 1 | 0 | Rdn[3] | Rm | Rdn[2:0] | MOV Rdn, Rm |

| 0 | 1 | 0 | 0 | 0 | 1 | 1 | 1 | L | Rm | 0 | 0 | 0 | BX / BLX Rm |

| 1 | 1 | 0 | 1 | cond | imm8 | B\<cond\> imm8 |

| 1 | 1 | 1 | 0 | 0 | imm8 | B imm11 |

| 0 | 1 | 0 | 1 | L | B | H | Rm | Rn | Rd | STR(B/H) / LDR(B/H) Rd, [Rn, Rm] |

| 0 | 1 | 1 | 0 | L | imm5 | Rn | Rd | STR / LDR Rd, [Rn, #imm5] |

| 1 | 0 | 0 | 1 | L | Rd | imm8 | STR / LDR Rd, [SP, #imm8] |

| 0 | 1 | 0 | 0 | 1 | Rd | imm8 | LDR Rd, [PC, #imm8] |

| 1 | 1 | 1 | 1 | 0 | imm22[21:11] | 1 | 1 | 1 | 1 | 1 | imm22[10:0] | BL imm22 |

Figure 6.33 **Thumb instruction encoding examples**

Thumb-2 instructions are identified by their most significant 5 bits being 11101, 11110, or 11111. The processor then fetches a second halfword containing the remainder of the instruction. The Cortex-M series of processors operates exclusively in Thumb state.

6.7.2 DSP Instructions

The Fast Fourier Transform (FFT), the most common DSP algorithm, is both complicated and performance-critical. The DSP instructions in computer architectures are intended to perform efficient FFTs, especially on 16-bit fractional data.

Digital signal processors (DSPs) are designed to efficiently handle signal processing algorithms such as the Fast Fourier Transform (FFT) and Finite/Infinite Impulse Response filters (FIR/IIR). Common applications include audio and video encoding and decoding, motor control, and speech recognition. ARM provides a number of DSP instructions for these purposes. DSP instructions include multiply, add, and multiply-accumulate (MAC)—multiply and add the result to a running sum: sum = sum + src1 × src2. MAC is a distinguishing feature separating DSP instruction sets from regular instruction sets. It is very commonly used in DSP algorithms and doubles the performance relative to separate multiply and add instructions. However, MAC requires specifying an extra register to hold the running sum.

The basic multiply instructions, listed in Appendix B, are part of ARMv4. ARMv5TE added the saturating math instructions and packed and fractional multiplies to support DSP algorithms.

DSP instructions often operate on short (16-bit) data representing samples read from a sensor by an analog-to-digital converter. However, the intermediate results are held to greater precision (e.g., 32 or 64 bits)

Table 6.15 DSP data types

Type	Sign Bit	Integer Bits	Fractional Bits
short	1	15	0
unsigned short	0	16	0
long	1	31	0
unsigned long	0	32	0
long long	1	63	0
unsigned long long	0	64	0
Q15	1	0	15
Q31	1	0	31

or saturated to prevent overflow. In *saturated arithmetic*, results larger than the most positive number are treated as the most positive, and results smaller than the most negative are treated as the most negative. For example, in 32-bit arithmetic, results greater than $2^{31} - 1$ saturate at $2^{31} - 1$, and results less than -2^{31} saturate at -2^{31}. Common DSP data types are given in Table 6.15. Two's complement numbers are indicated as having one sign bit. The 16-, 32-, and 64-bit types are also known as *half*, *single*, and *double* precision, not to be confused with single and double-precision floating-point numbers. For efficiency, two half-precision numbers are packed in a single 32-bit word.

The *integer* types come in signed and unsigned flavors with the sign bit in the msb. *Fractional* types (Q15 and Q31) represent a signed fractional number; for example, Q31 spans the range $[-1, 1-2^{-31}]$ with a step of 2^{-31} between consecutive numbers. These types are not defined in the C standard but are supported by some libraries. Q31 can be converted to Q15 by truncation or rounding. In truncation, the Q15 result is just the upper half. In rounding, 0x00008000 is added to the Q31 value and then the result is truncated. When a computation involves many steps, rounding is useful because it avoids accumulating multiple small truncation errors into a significant error.

ARM added a Q flag to the status registers to indicate that overflow or saturation has occurred in DSP instructions. For applications where accuracy is critical, the program can clear the Q flag before a computation, do the computation in single-precision, and check the Q flag afterward. If it is set, overflow occurred and the computation can be repeated in double precision if necessary.

Saturated arithmetic is an important way to gracefully degrade accuracy in DSP algorithms. Commonly, single-precision arithmetic is sufficient to handle most inputs, but pathological cases can overflow the single-precision range. An overflow causes an abrupt sign change to a radically wrong answer, which may appear to the user as a click in an audio stream or a strangely colored pixel in a video stream. Going to double-precision arithmetic prevents overflow but degrades performance and increases power consumption in the typical case. Saturated arithmetic clips the overflow at the maximum or minimum value, which is usually close to the desired value and causes little inaccuracy.

Addition and subtraction are performed identically no matter which format is used. However, multiplication depends on the type. For example, with 16-bit numbers, the number 0xFFFF is interpreted as 65535 for unsigned short, −1 for short, and -2^{-15} for Q15 numbers. Hence, 0xFFFF × 0xFFFF has a very different value for each representation (4,294,836,225; 1; and 2^{-30}, respectively). This leads to different instructions for signed and unsigned multiplication.

A Q15 number A can be viewed as $a \times 2^{-15}$, where a is its interpretation in the range $[-2^{15}, 2^{15}-1]$ as a signed 16-bit number. Hence, the product of two Q15 numbers is:

$$A \times B = a \times b \times 2^{-30} = 2 \times a \times b \times 2^{-31}$$

This means that to multiply two Q15 numbers and get a Q31 result, do ordinary signed multiplication and then double the product. The product can then be truncated or rounded to put it back into Q15 format if necessary.

The rich assortment of multiply and multiply-accumulate instructions are summarized in Table 6.16. MACs require up to four registers: *RdHi*, *RdLo*, *Rn*, and *Rm*. For double-precision operations, *RdHi* and *RdLo* hold the most and least significant 32 bits, respectively. For example, UMLAL RdLo, RdHi, Rn, Rm computes {*RdHi*, *RdLo*} = {*RdHi*, *RdLo*} + *Rn* × *Rm*. Half-precision multiplies come in various flavors denoted in braces to choose the operands from the top or bottom half of the word, and in *dual* forms where both the top and bottom halves are multiplied. MACs involving half-precision inputs and a single-precision accumulator (SMLA*, SMLAW*, SMUAD, SMUSD, SMLAD, SMLSD) will set the Q flag if the accumulator overflows. The most significant word (MSW) multiplies also come in forms with an R suffix that round rather than truncate.

The DSP instructions also include saturated add (QADD) and subtract (QSUB) of 32-bit words that saturate the results instead of overflowing. They also include QDADD and QDSUB, which double the second operand before adding/subtracting it to/from the first with saturation; we will shortly find these valuable in fractional MACs. They set the Q flag if saturation occurs.

Finally, the DSP instructions include LDRD and STRD that load and store an even/odd pair of registers in a 64-bit memory double word. These instructions increase the efficiency of moving double-precision values between memory and registers.

Table 6.17 summarizes how to use the DSP instructions to multiply or MAC various types of data. The examples assume halfword data is in the bottom half of a register and that the top half is zero; use the T flavor of SMUL when the data is in the top instead. The result is stored in R2, or in {R3, R2} for double-precision. Fractional operations (Q15/Q31) double the result using saturated adds to prevent overflow when multiplying −1 × −1.

Table 6.16 **Multiply and multiply-accumulate instructions**

Instruction	Function	Description
Ordinary 32-bit multiplication works for both signed and unsigned		
MUL	$32 = 32 \times 32$	Multiply
MLA	$32 = 32 + 32 \times 32$	Multiply-accumulate
MLS	$32 = 32 - 32 \times 32$	Multiply-subtract
unsigned long long = unsigned long × unsigned long		
UMULL	$64 = 32 \times 32$	Unsigned multiply long
UMLAL	$64 = 64 + 32 \times 32$	Unsigned multiply-accumulate long
UMAAL	$64 = 32 + 32 \times 32 + 32$	Unsigned multiply-accumulate-add long
long long = long × long		
SMULL	$64 = 32 \times 32$	Signed multiply long
SMLAL	$64 = 64 + 32 \times 32$	Signed multiply-accumulate long
Packed arithmetic: short × short		
SMUL{BB/BT/TB/TT}	$32 = 16 \times 16$	Signed multiply {bottom/top}
SMLA{BB/BT/TB/TT}	$32 = 32 + 16 \times 16$	Signed multiply-accumulate {bottom/top}
SMLAL{BB/BT/TB/TT}	$64 = 64 + 16 \times 16$	Signed multiply-accumulate long {bottom/top}
Fractional multiplication (Q31 / Q15)		
SMULW{B/T}	$32 = (32 \times 16) \gg 16$	Signed multiply word-halfword {bottom/top}
SMLAW{B/T}	$32 = 32 + (32 \times 16) \gg 16$	Signed multiply-add word-halfword {bottom/top}
SMMUL{R}	$32 = (32 \times 32) \gg 32$	Signed MSW multiply {round}
SMMLA{R}	$32 = 32 + (32 \times 32) \gg 32$	Signed MSW multiply-accumulate {round}
SMMLS{R}	$32 = 32 - (32 \times 32) \gg 32$	Signed MSW multiply-subtract {round}
long or long long = short × short + short × short		
SMUAD	$32 = 16 \times 16 + 16 \times 16$	Signed dual multiply-add
SMUSD	$32 = 16 \times 16 - 16 \times 16$	Signed dual multiply-subtract
SMLAD	$32 = 32 + 16 \times 16 + 16 \times 16$	Signed multiply-accumulate dual
SMLSD	$32 = 32 + 16 \times 16 - 16 \times 16$	Signed multiply-subtract dual
SMLALD	$64 = 64 + 16 \times 16 + 16 \times 16$	Signed multiply-accumulate long dual
SMLSLD	$64 = 64 + 16 \times 16 - 16 \times 16$	Signed multiply-subtract long dual

Table 6.17 **Multiply and MAC code for various data types**

First Operand (R0)	Second Operand (R1)	Product (R3/R2)	Multiply	MAC
short	short	short	SMULBB R2, R0, R1 LDR R3, =0x0000FFFF AND R2, R3, R2	SMLABB R2, R0, R1 LDR R3, =0x0000FFFF AND R2, R3, R2
short	short	long	SMULBB R2, R0, R1	SMLABB R2, R0, R1, R2

short	short	long long	MOV R2, #0
			MOV R3, #0
			SMLALBB R2, R3, R0, R1
				SMLALBB R2, R3, R0, R1

long	short	long	SMULWB R2, R0, R1	SMLAWB R2, R0, R1, R2
long	long	long	MUL R2, R0, R1	MLA R2, R0, R1, R2
long	long	long long	SMULL R2, R3, R0, R1	SMLAL R2, R3, R0, R1

unsigned short	unsigned short	unsigned short	MUL R2, R0, R1
			LDR R3, =0x0000FFFF
			AND R2, R3, R2
				MLA R2, R0, R1, R2
				LDR R3, =0x0000FFFF
				AND R2, R3, R2

unsigned short	unsigned short	unsigned long	MUL R2, R0, R1	MLA R2, R0, R1, R2
unsigned long	unsigned short	unsigned long	MUL R2, R0, R1	MLA R2, R0, R1, R2
unsigned long	unsigned long	unsigned long	MUL R2, R0, R1	MLA R2, R0, R1, R2
unsigned long	unsigned long	unsigned long long	UMULL R2, R3, R0, R1	UMLAL R2, R3, R0, R1
Q15	Q15	Q15	SMULBB R2, R0, R1 QADD R2, R2, R2 LSR R2, R2, #16	SMLABB R2, R0, R1, R2 SSAT R2, 16, R2
Q15	Q15	Q31	SMULBB R2, R0, R1 QADD R2, R2, R2	SMULBB R3, R0, R1 QDADD R2, R2, R3
Q31	Q15	Q31	SMULWB R2, R0, R1 QADD R2, R2, R2	SMULWB R3, R0, R1 QDADD R2, R2, R3
Q31	Q31	Q31	SMMUL R2, R0, R1 QADD R2, R2, R2	SMMUL R3, R0, R1 QDADD R2, R2, R3

6.7.3 Floating-Point Instructions

Floating-point is more flexible than the fixed-point numbers favored in DSP and makes programming easier. Floating-point is widely used in graphics, scientific applications, and control algorithms. Floating-point arithmetic can be performed with a series of ordinary data-processing instructions but is faster and consumes less power using dedicated floating-point instructions and hardware.

The ARMv5 instruction set includes optional floating-point instructions. These instructions access at least 16 64-bit double-precision registers separate from the ordinary registers. These registers can also be treated as pairs of 32-bit single-precision registers. The registers are named D0–D15 as double-precision or S0–S31 as single-precision. For example, VADD.F32 S2, S0, S1 and VADD.F64 D2, D0, D1 perform single and double-precision floating-point adds, respectively. Floating-point instructions, listed in Table 6.18, are suffixed with .F32 or .F64 to indicate single- or double-precision floating-point.

Table 6.18 **ARM floating-point instructions**

Instruction	Function
VABS Rd, Rm	Rd = |Rm|
VADD Rd, Rn, Rm	Rd = Rn + Rm
VCMP Rd, Rm	Compare and set floating-point status flags
VCVT Rd, Rm	Convert between int and float
VDIV Rd, Rn, Rm	Rd = Rn / Rm
VMLA Rd, Rn, Rm	Rd = Rd + Rn * Rm
VMLS Rd, Rn, Rm	Rd = Rd − Rn * Rm
VMOV Rd, Rm or #const	Rd = Rm or constant
VMUL Rd, Rn, Rm	Rd = Rn * Rm
VNEG Rd, Rm	Rd = −Rm
VNMLA Rd, Rn, Rm	Rd = −(Rd + Rn * Rm)
VNMLS Rd, Rn, Rm	Rd = −(Rd − Rn * Rm)
VNMUL Rd, Rn, Rm	Rd = −Rn * Rm
VSQRT Rd, Rm	Rd = sqrt(Rm)
VSUB Rd, Rn, Rm	Rd = Rn − Rm

The `MRC` and `MCR` instructions are used to transfer data between the ordinary registers and the floating-point coprocessor registers.

ARM defines the Floating-Point Status and Control Register (FPSCR). Like the ordinary status register, it holds *N*, *Z*, *C*, and *V* flags for floating-point operations. It also specifies rounding modes, exceptions, and special conditions such as overflow, underflow, and divide-by-zero. The `VMRS` and `VMSR` instructions transfer information between a regular register and the FPSCR.

6.7.4 Power-Saving and Security Instructions

Battery-powered devices save power by spending most of their time in sleep mode. ARMv6K introduced instructions to support such power savings. The wait for interrupt (`WFI`) instruction allows the processor to enter a low-power state until an interrupt occurs. The system may generate interrupts based on user events (such as touching a screen) or on a periodic timer. The wait for event (`WFE`) instruction is similar but is helpful in multiprocessor systems (see Section 7.7.8) so that a processor can go to sleep until notified by another processor. It wakes up either during an interrupt or when another processor sends an event using the `SEV` instruction.

ARMv7 enhances the exception handling to support virtualization and security. In *virtualization*, multiple operating systems can run concurrently on the same processor, unaware of each other's existence. A hypervisor switches between the operating systems. The hypervisor operates at privilege level PL2. It is invoked with a hypervisor trap exception. With *security* extensions, the processor defines a secure state with limited means of entry and restricted access to secure portions of memory. Even if an attacker compromises the operating system, the secure kernel may resist tampering. For example, the secure kernel may be used to disable a stolen phone or to enforce digital rights management such that a user can't duplicate copyrighted content.

6.7.5 SIMD Instructions

The term SIMD (pronounced "sim-dee") stands for *single instruction multiple data*, in which a single instruction acts on multiple pieces of data in parallel. A common application of SIMD is to perform many short arithmetic operations at once, especially for graphics processing. This is also called *packed* arithmetic.

Short data elements often appear in graphics processing. For example, a pixel in a digital photo may use 8 bits to store each of the red, green, and blue color components. Using an entire 32-bit word to process one of these components wastes the upper 24 bits. Moreover, when the components from 16 adjacent pixels are packed into a 128-bit quadword, the processing can be performed 16 times faster. Similarly, coordinates in a 3-dimensional graphics space are generally represented with 32-bit (single-precision) floating-point numbers. Four of these coordinates can be packed into a 128-bit quadword.

Most modern architectures offer SIMD arithmetic operations with wide SIMD registers packing multiple narrower operands. For example, the ARMv7 Advanced SIMD instructions share the registers from the floating-point unit. Moreover, these registers can also be paired to act as eight 128-bit quad words Q0–Q7. The registers pack together several 8-, 16-, 32-, or 64-bit integer or floating-point values. The instructions are suffixed with .I8, .I16, .I32, .I64, .F32, or .F64 to indicate how the registers should be treated.

Figure 6.34 shows the VADD.I8 D2, D1, D0 vector add instruction operating on eight pairs of 8-bit integers packed into 64-bit double words. Similarly VADD.I32 Q2, Q1, Q0 adds four pairs of 32-bit integers packed into 128-bit quad words and VADD.F32, D2, D1, D0 adds two pairs of 32-bit single-precision floating-point numbers packed into 64-bit double words. Performing packed arithmetic requires modifying the ALU to eliminate carries between the smaller data elements. For example, a carry out of $a_0 + b_0$ must not affect the result of $a_1 + b_1$.

Advanced SIMD instructions begin with V. They include the following categories:

▸ Basic arithmetic functions also defined for floating-point

▸ Loads and stores of multiple elements, including deinterleaving and interleaving

▸ Bitwise logical operations

▸ Comparisons

▸ Many flavors of shifts, additions, and subtractions with and without saturation

▸ Many flavors of multiply and MAC

▸ Miscellaneous instructions

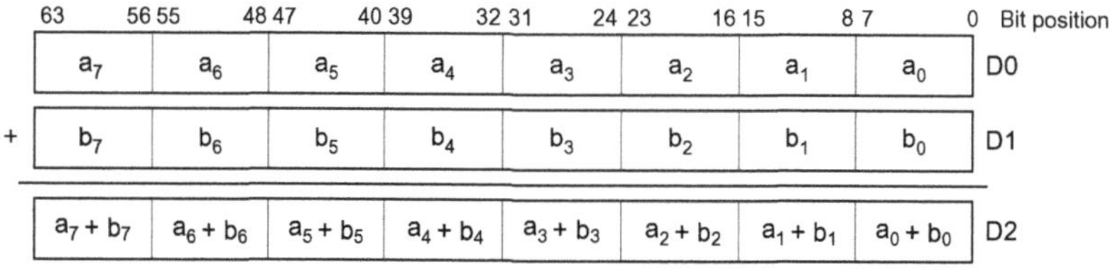

63	56 55	48 47	40 39	32 31	24 23	16 15	8 7	0	Bit position
a_7	a_6	a_5	a_4	a_3	a_2	a_1	a_0		D0
b_7	b_6	b_5	b_4	b_3	b_2	b_1	b_0		D1
$a_7 + b_7$	$a_6 + b_6$	$a_5 + b_5$	$a_4 + b_4$	$a_3 + b_3$	$a_2 + b_2$	$a_1 + b_1$	$a_0 + b_0$		D2

Figure 6.34 **Packed arithmetic: eight simultaneous 8-bit additions**

ARMv6 also defined a more limited set of SIMD instructions operating on the regular 32-bit registers. These include 8- and 16-bit addition and subtraction, and instructions to efficiently pack and unpack bytes and halfwords into a word. These instructions are useful to manipulate 16-bit data in DSP code.

6.7.6 64-bit Architecture

32-bit architectures allow a program to directly access at most 2^{32} bytes = 4 GB of memory. Large computer servers led the transition to 64-bit architectures that can access vast amounts of memory. Personal computers and then mobile devices followed. 64-bit architectures can sometimes be faster as well because they move more information with a single instruction.

Many architectures simply extend their general-purpose registers from 32 to 64 bits, but ARMv8 introduced a new instruction set as well to streamline idiosyncrasies. The classic instruction set lacks enough general-purpose registers for complex programs, forcing costly movement of data between registers and memory. Keeping the PC in R15 and SP in R13 also complicates the processor implementation, and programs often need a register containing the value 0.

The ARMv8 instructions are still 32 bits long and the instruction set looks very much like ARMv7, but with some problems cleaned up. In ARMv8, the register file is expanded to 31 64-bit registers (called X0–X30) and the PC and SP are no longer part of the general-purpose registers. X30 serves as the link register. Note that there is no X31 register; instead, it is called the zero register (ZR) and is hardwired to 0. Data-processing instructions can operate on 32- or 64-bit values, whereas loads and stores always use 64-bit addresses. To make room for the extra bits to specify source and destination registers, the condition field is removed from most instructions. However, branches can still be conditional. ARMv8 also streamlines exception handling, doubles the number of advanced SIMD registers, and adds instructions for AES and SHA cryptography. The instruction encodings are rather complex and do not classify into a handful of categories.

On reset, ARMv8 processors boot in 64-bit mode. The processor can drop into 32-bit mode by setting a bit in a system register and invoking an exception. It returns to 64-bit mode when the exception returns.

6.8 ANOTHER PERSPECTIVE: x86 ARCHITECTURE

Almost all personal computers today use x86 architecture microprocessors. x86, also called IA-32, is a 32-bit architecture originally developed by Intel. AMD also sells x86 compatible microprocessors.

The x86 architecture has a long and convoluted history dating back to 1978, when Intel announced the 16-bit 8086 microprocessor. IBM selected the 8086 and its cousin, the 8088, for IBM's first personal computers. In 1985, Intel introduced the 32-bit 80386 microprocessor, which was backward compatible with the 8086, so it could run software developed for earlier PCs. Processor architectures compatible with the 80386 are called x86 processors. The Pentium, Core, and Athlon processors are well known x86 processors.

Various groups at Intel and AMD over many years have shoehorned more instructions and capabilities into the antiquated architecture. The result is far less elegant than ARM. However, software compatibility is far more important than technical elegance, so x86 has been the *de facto* PC standard for more than two decades. More than 100 million x86 processors are sold every year. This huge market justifies more than $5 billion of research and development annually to continue improving the processors.

x86 is an example of a Complex Instruction Set Computer (CISC) architecture. In contrast to RISC architectures such as ARM, each CISC instruction can do more work. Programs for CISC architectures usually require fewer instructions. The instruction encodings were selected to be more compact, so as to save memory, when RAM was far more expensive than it is today; instructions are of variable length and are often less than 32 bits. The trade-off is that complicated instructions are more difficult to decode and tend to execute more slowly.

This section introduces the x86 architecture. The goal is not to make you into an x86 assembly language programmer, but rather to illustrate some of the similarities and differences between x86 and ARM. We think it is interesting to see how x86 works. However, none of the material in this section is needed to understand the rest of the book. Major differences between x86 and ARM are summarized in Table 6.19.

Table 6.19 **Major differences between ARM and x86**

Feature	ARM	x86
# of registers	15 general purpose	8, some restrictions on purpose
# of operands	3–4 (2–3 sources, 1 destination)	2 (1 source, 1 source/destination)
operand location	registers or immediates	registers, immediates, or memory
operand size	32 bits	8, 16, or 32 bits
condition flags	yes	yes
instruction types	simple	simple and complicated
instruction encoding	fixed, 4 bytes	variable, 1–15 bytes

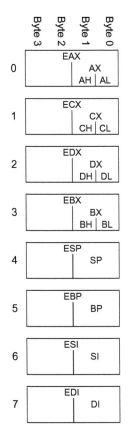

Figure 6.35 x86 registers

6.8.1 x86 Registers

The 8086 microprocessor provided eight 16-bit registers. It could separately access the upper and lower eight bits of some of these registers. When the 32-bit 80386 was introduced, the registers were extended to 32 bits. These registers are called EAX, ECX, EDX, EBX, ESP, EBP, ESI, and EDI. For backward compatibility, the bottom 16 bits and some of the bottom 8-bit portions are also usable, as shown in Figure 6.35.

The eight registers are almost, but not quite, general purpose. Certain instructions cannot use certain registers. Other instructions always put their results in certain registers. Like SP in ARM, ESP is normally reserved for the stack pointer.

The x86 program counter is called the EIP (the *extended instruction pointer*). Like the ARM PC, it advances from one instruction to the next or can be changed with branch and function call instructions.

6.8.2 x86 Operands

ARM instructions always act on registers or immediates. Explicit load and store instructions are needed to move data between memory and the registers. In contrast, x86 instructions may operate on registers, immediates, or memory. This partially compensates for the small set of registers.

ARM instructions generally specify three operands: two sources and one destination. x86 instructions specify only two operands. The first is a source. The second is both a source and the destination. Hence, x86 instructions always overwrite one of their sources with the result. Table 6.20 lists the combinations of operand locations in x86. All combinations are possible except memory to memory.

Table 6.20 Operand locations

Source/ Destination	Source	Example	Meaning
register	register	add EAX, EBX	EAX <− EAX + EBX
register	immediate	add EAX, 42	EAX <− EAX + 42
register	memory	add EAX, [20]	EAX <− EAX + Mem[20]
memory	register	add [20], EAX	Mem[20] <− Mem[20] + EAX
memory	immediate	add [20], 42	Mem[20] <− Mem[20] + 42

Table 6.21 Memory addressing modes

Example	Meaning	Comment
add EAX, [20]	EAX <— EAX + Mem[20]	displacement
add EAX, [ESP]	EAX <— EAX + Mem[ESP]	base addressing
add EAX, [EDX+40]	EAX <— EAX + Mem[EDX+40]	base + displacement
add EAX, [60+EDI*4]	EAX <— EAX + Mem[60+EDI*4]	displacement + scaled index
add EAX, [EDX+80+EDI*2]	EAX <— EAX + Mem[EDX+80+EDI*2]	base + displacement + scaled index

Table 6.22 Instructions acting on 8-, 16-, or 32-bit data

Example	Meaning	Data Size
add AH, BL	AH <— AH + BL	8-bit
add AX, —1	AX <— AX + 0xFFFF	16-bit
add EAX, EDX	EAX <— EAX + EDX	32-bit

Like ARM, x86 has a 32-bit memory space that is byte-addressable. However, x86 supports a wider variety of memory indexing modes. Memory locations are specified with any combination of a *base register*, *displacement*, and a *scaled index register*. Table 6.21 illustrates these combinations. The displacement can be an 8-, 16-, or 32-bit value. The scale multiplying the index register can be 1, 2, 4, or 8. The base + displacement mode is equivalent to the ARM base addressing mode for loads and stores. Like ARM, x86 also provides a scaled index. In x86, the scaled index provides an easy way to access arrays or structures of 2-, 4-, or 8-byte elements without having to issue a sequence of instructions to generate the address.

While ARM always acts on 32-bit words, x86 instructions can operate on 8-, 16-, or 32-bit data. Table 6.22 illustrates these variations.

6.8.3 Status Flags

x86, like many CISC architectures, uses condition flags (also called *status flags*) to make decisions about branches and to keep track of carries and arithmetic overflow. x86 uses a 32-bit register, called EFLAGS, that stores the status flags. Some of the bits of the EFLAGS register are given in Table 6.23. Other bits are used by the operating system.

ARM's use of condition flags sets it apart from other RISC architectures.

Table 6.23 **Selected EFLAGS**

Name	Meaning
CF (Carry Flag)	Carry out generated by last arithmetic operation. Indicates overflow in unsigned arithmetic. Also used for propagating the carry between words in multiple-precision arithmetic
ZF (Zero Flag)	Result of last operation was zero
SF (Sign Flag)	Result of last operation was negative (msb = 1)
OF (Overflow Flag)	Overflow of two's complement arithmetic

The architectural state of an x86 processor includes EFLAGS as well as the eight registers and the EIP.

6.8.4 x86 Instructions

x86 has a larger set of instructions than ARM. Table 6.24 describes some of the general purpose instructions. x86 also has instructions for floating-point arithmetic and for arithmetic on multiple short data elements packed into a longer word. D indicates the destination (a register or memory location), and S indicates the source (a register, memory location, or immediate).

Note that some instructions always act on specific registers. For example, 32×32-bit multiplication always takes one of the sources from EAX and always puts the 64-bit result in EDX and EAX. LOOP always stores the loop counter in ECX. PUSH, POP, CALL, and RET use the stack pointer, ESP.

Conditional jumps check the flags and branch if the appropriate condition is met. They come in many flavors. For example, JZ jumps if the zero flag (ZF) is 1. JNZ jumps if the zero flag is 0. Like ARM, the jumps usually follow an instruction, such as the compare instruction (CMP), that sets the flags. Table 6.25 lists some of the conditional jumps and how they depend on the flags set by a prior compare operation.

6.8.5 x86 Instruction Encoding

The x86 instruction encodings are truly messy, a legacy of decades of piecemeal changes. Unlike ARMv4, whose instructions are uniformly 32 bits, x86 instructions vary from 1 to 15 bytes, as shown in Figure 6.36.[1]

---

[1] It is possible to construct 17-byte instructions if all the optional fields are used. However, x86 places a 15-byte limit on the length of legal instructions.

Table 6.24 Selected x86 instructions

Instruction	Meaning	Function
ADD/SUB	add/subtract	$D = D + S$ / $D = D - S$
ADDC	add with carry	$D = D + S + CF$
INC/DEC	increment/decrement	$D = D + 1$ / $D = D - 1$
CMP	compare	Set flags based on $D - S$
NEG	negate	$D = -D$
AND/OR/XOR	logical AND/OR/XOR	$D = D$ op S
NOT	logical NOT	$D = \overline{D}$
IMUL/MUL	signed/unsigned multiply	$EDX:EAX = EAX \times D$
IDIV/DIV	signed/unsigned divide	$EDX:EAX/D$ EAX = Quotient; EDX = Remainder
SAR/SHR	arithmetic/logical shift right	$D = D >>> S$ / $D = D >> S$
SAL/SHL	left shift	$D = D << S$
ROR/ROL	rotate right/left	Rotate D by S
RCR/RCL	rotate right/left with carry	Rotate CF and D by S
BT	bit test	$CF = D[S]$ (the S*th* bit of D)
BTR/BTS	bit test and reset/set	$CF = D[S]$; $D[S] = 0$ / 1
TEST	set flags based on masked bits	Set flags based on D AND S
MOV	move	$D = S$
PUSH	push onto stack	$ESP = ESP - 4$; $Mem[ESP] = S$
POP	pop off stack	$D = MEM[ESP]$; $ESP = ESP + 4$
CLC, STC	clear/set carry flag	$CF = 0$ / 1
JMP	unconditional jump	relative jump: $EIP = EIP + S$ absolute jump: $EIP = S$
Jcc	conditional jump	if (flag) $EIP = EIP + S$
LOOP	loop	$ECX = ECX - 1$ if ($ECX \neq 0$) $EIP = EIP + imm$
CALL	function call	$ESP = ESP - 4$; $MEM[ESP] = EIP$; $EIP = S$
RET	function return	$EIP = MEM[ESP]$; $ESP = ESP + 4$

Table 6.25 Selected branch conditions

Instruction	Meaning	Function after CMP D, S
JZ/JE	jump if ZF = 1	jump if D = S
JNZ/JNE	jump if ZF = 0	jump if D ≠ S
JGE	jump if SF = OF	jump if D ≥ S
JG	jump if SF = OF and ZF = 0	jump if D >S
JLE	jump if SF ≠ OF or ZF = 1	jump if D ≤ S
JL	jump if SF ≠ OF	jump if D <S
JC/JB	jump if CF = 1	
JNC	jump if CF = 0	
JO	jump if OF = 1	
JNO	jump if OF = 0	
JS	jump if SF = 1	
JNS	jump if SF = 0	

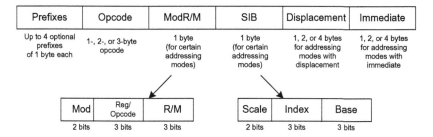

Figure 6.36 x86 instruction encodings

The *opcode* may be 1, 2, or 3 bytes. It is followed by four optional fields: *ModR/M*, *SIB*, *Displacement*, and *Immediate*. *ModR/M* specifies an addressing mode. *SIB* specifies the scale, index, and base registers in certain addressing modes. *Displacement* indicates a 1-, 2-, or 4-byte displacement in certain addressing modes. And *Immediate* is a 1-, 2-, or 4-byte constant for instructions using an immediate as the source operand. Moreover, an instruction can be preceded by up to four optional byte-long prefixes that modify its behavior.

The *ModR/M* byte uses the 2-bit *Mod* and 3-bit *R/M* field to specify the addressing mode for one of the operands. The operand can come from one of the eight registers, or from one of 24 memory addressing modes. Due to artifacts in the encodings, the ESP and EBP registers are not available for use as the base or index register in certain addressing modes. The *Reg* field specifies the register used as the other operand. For certain instructions that do not require a second operand, the *Reg* field is used to specify three more bits of the *opcode*.

In addressing modes using a scaled index register, the *SIB* byte specifies the index register and the scale (1, 2, 4, or 8). If both a base and index are used, the *SIB* byte also specifies the base register.

ARM fully specifies the instruction in the *cond*, *op*, and *funct* fields of the instruction. x86 uses a variable number of bits to specify different instructions. It uses fewer bits to specify more common instructions, decreasing the average length of the instructions. Some instructions even have multiple opcodes. For example, add AL, imm8 performs an 8-bit add of an immediate to AL. It is represented with the 1-byte opcode, 0x04, followed by a 1-byte immediate. The A register (AL, AX, or EAX) is called the *accumulator*. On the other hand, add D, imm8 performs an 8-bit add of an immediate to an arbitrary destination, *D* (memory or a register). It is represented with the 1-byte *opcode* 0x80 followed by one or more bytes specifying *D*, followed by a 1-byte immediate. Many instructions have shortened encodings when the destination is the accumulator.

In the original 8086, the *opcode* specified whether the instruction acted on 8- or 16-bit operands. When the 80386 introduced 32-bit operands, no new opcodes were available to specify the 32-bit form. Instead, the same opcode was used for both 16- and 32-bit forms. An additional bit in the *code segment descriptor* used by the OS specifies which form the processor should choose. The bit is set to 0 for backward compatibility with 8086 programs, defaulting the *opcode* to 16-bit operands. It is set to 1 for programs to default to 32-bit operands. Moreover, the programmer can specify prefixes to change the form for a particular instruction. If the *prefix* 0x66 appears before the *opcode*, the alternative size operand is used (16 bits in 32-bit mode, or 32 bits in 16-bit mode).

6.8.6 Other x86 Peculiarities

The 80286 introduced *segmentation* to divide memory into segments of up to 64 KB in length. When the OS enables segmentation, addresses are computed relative to the beginning of the segment. The processor checks for addresses that go beyond the end of the segment and indicates an error, thus preventing programs from accessing memory outside their own segment. Segmentation proved to be a hassle for programmers and is not used in modern versions of the Windows operating system.

Intel and Hewlett-Packard jointly developed a new 64-bit architecture called IA-64 in the mid 1990's. It was designed from a clean slate, bypassing the convoluted history of x86, taking advantage of 20 years of new research in computer architecture, and providing a 64-bit address space. However, IA-64 has yet to become a market success. Most computers needing the large address space now use the 64-bit extensions of x86.

x86 contains string instructions that act on entire strings of bytes or words. The operations include moving, comparing, or scanning for a specific value. In modern processors, these instructions are usually slower than performing the equivalent operation with a series of simpler instructions, so they are best avoided.

As mentioned earlier, the 0x66 *prefix* is used to choose between 16- and 32-bit operand sizes. Other prefixes include ones used to lock the bus (to control access to shared variables in a multiprocessor system), to predict whether a branch will be taken or not, and to repeat the instruction during a string move.

The bane of any architecture is to run out of memory capacity. With 32-bit addresses, x86 can access 4 GB of memory. This was far more than the largest computers had in 1985, but by the early 2000's it had become limiting. In 2003, AMD extended the address space and register sizes to 64 bits, calling the enhanced architecture AMD64. AMD64 has a compatibility mode that allows it to run 32-bit programs unmodified while the OS takes advantage of the bigger address space. In 2004, Intel gave in and adopted the 64-bit extensions, renaming them Extended Memory 64 Technology (EM64T). With 64-bit addresses, computers can access 16 exabytes (16 billion GB) of memory.

For those curious about more details of the x86 architecture, the x86 Intel Architecture Software Developer's Manual is freely available on Intel's Web site.

6.8.7 The Big Picture

ARM strikes a balance between simple instructions and dense code by including features such as condition flags and shifted register operands. Thease features make ARM code more compact than other RISC architectures.

This section has given a taste of some of the differences between the ARM RISC architecture and the x86 CISC architecture. x86 tends to have shorter programs, because a complex instruction is equivalent to a series of simple ARM instructions and because the instructions are encoded to minimize memory use. However, the x86 architecture is a hodgepodge of features accumulated over the years, some of which are no longer useful but must be kept for compatibility with old programs. It has too few registers, and the instructions are difficult to decode. Merely explaining the instruction set is difficult. Despite all these failings, x86 is firmly entrenched as the dominant computer architecture for PCs, because the value of software compatibility is so great and because the huge market justifies the effort required to build fast x86 microprocessors.

6.9 SUMMARY

To command a computer, you must speak its language. A computer architecture defines how to command a processor. Many different computer architectures are in widespread commercial use today, but once you understand one, learning others is much easier. The key questions to ask when approaching a new architecture are:

▸ What is the data word length?

▸ What are the registers?

▸ How is memory organized?

▸ What are the instructions?

ARM is a 32-bit architecture because it operates on 32-bit data. The ARM architecture has 16 registers which include 15 general-purpose registers and the PC. In principle, any of the general-purpose registers can be used in any code. However, by convention, certain registers are reserved for certain purposes for ease of programming and so that functions written by different programmers can communicate easily. For example, R14 (the link register LR) holds the return address after a BL instruction, and R0–R3 hold the arguments of a function. ARM has a byte-addressable memory system with 32-bit addresses. Instructions are 32 bits long and are word-aligned for efficient access. This chapter discussed the most commonly used ARM instructions.

The power of defining a computer architecture is that a program written for any given architecture can run on many different implementations of that architecture. For example, programs written for the Intel Pentium processor in 1993 will generally still run (and run much faster) on the Intel Xeon or AMD Phenom processors in 2015.

In the first part of this book, we learned about the circuit and logic levels of abstraction. In this chapter, we jumped up to the architecture level. In the next chapter, we study microarchitecture, the arrangement of digital building blocks that implement a processor architecture. Microarchitecture is the link between hardware and software engineering. And, we believe it is one of the most exciting topics in all of engineering: You will learn to build your own microprocessor!

Exercises

Exercise 6.1 Give three examples from the ARM architecture of each of the architecture design principles: (1) regularity supports simplicity; (2) make the common case fast; (3) smaller is faster; and (4) good design demands good compromises. Explain how each of your examples exhibits the design principle.

Exercise 6.2 The ARM architecture has a register set that consists of 16 32-bit registers. Is it possible to design a computer architecture without a register set? If so, briefly describe the architecture, including the instruction set. What are advantages and disadvantages of this architecture over the ARM architecture?

Exercise 6.3 Consider memory storage of a 32-bit word stored at memory word 42 in a byte-addressable memory.

(a) What is the byte address of memory word 42?

(b) What are the byte addresses that memory word 42 spans?

(c) Draw the number 0xFF223344 stored at word 42 in both big-endian and little-endian machines. Clearly label the byte address corresponding to each data byte value.

Exercise 6.4 Repeat Exercise 6.3 for memory storage of a 32-bit word stored at memory word 15 in a byte-addressable memory.

Exercise 6.5 Explain how the following ARM program can be used to determine whether a computer is big-endian or little-endian:

```
MOV  R0, #100
LDR  R1, =0xABCD876     ; R1 = 0xABCD876
STR  R1, [R0]
LDRB R2, [R0, #1]
```

Exercise 6.6 Write the following strings using ASCII encoding. Write your final answers in hexadecimal.

(a) SOS

(b) Cool

(c) boo!

Exercise 6.7 Repeat Exercise 6.6 for the following strings.

(a) howdy

(b) lions

(c) To the rescue!

Exercise 6.8 Show how the strings in Exercise 6.6 are stored in a byte-addressable memory on a little-endian machine starting at memory address 0x00001050C. Clearly indicate the memory address of each byte.

Exercise 6.9 Repeat Exercise 6.8 for the strings in Exercise 6.7.

Exercise 6.10 Convert the following ARM assembly code into machine language. Write the instructions in hexadecimal.

```
MOV R10, #63488
LSL R9, R6, #7
STR R4, [R11, R8]
ASR R6, R7, R3
```

Exercise 6.11 Repeat Exercise 6.10 for the following ARM assembly code:

```
ADD R8, R0, R1
LDR R11, [R3, #4]
SUB R5, R7, #0x58
LSL R3, R2, #14
```

Exercise 6.12 Consider data-processing instructions with an immediate *Src2*.

(a) Which instructions from Exercise 6.10 are in this format?

(b) Write out the 12-bit immediate field (*imm12*) of the instructions from part (a), then write them as 32-bit immediates.

Exercise 6.13 Repeat Exercise 6.12 for the instructions in Exercise 6.11.

Exercise 6.14 Convert the following program from machine language into ARM assembly language. The numbers on the left are the instruction addresses in memory, and the numbers on the right give the instruction at that address. Then reverse engineer a high-level program that would compile into this assembly language routine and write it. Explain in words what the program does. R0 and R1 are the input, and they initially contain positive numbers, a and b. At the end of the program, R0 is the output.

```
0x00008008   0xE3A02000
0x0000800C   0xE1A03001
0x00008010   0xE1510000
0x00008014   0x8A000002
0x00008018   0xE2822001
0x0000801C   0xE0811003
0x00008020   0xEAFFFFFA
0x00008024   0xE1A00002
```

Exercise 6.15 Repeat Exercise 6.14 for the following machine code. R0 and R1 are the inputs. R0 contains a 32-bit number and R1 is the address of a 32-element array of characters (char).

```
0x00008104   0xE3A0201F
0x00008108   0xE1A03230
0x0000810C   0xE2033001
0x00008110   0xE4C13001
0x00008114   0xE2522001
0x00008118   0x5AFFFFFA
0x0000811C   0xE1A0F00E
```

Exercise 6.16 The NOR instruction is not part of the ARM instruction set, because the same functionality can be implemented using existing instructions. Write a short assembly code snippet that has the following functionality: R0 = R1 NOR R2. Use as few instructions as possible.

Exercise 6.17 The NAND instruction is not part of the ARM instruction set, because the same functionality can be implemented using existing instructions. Write a short assembly code snippet that has the following functionality: R0 = R1 NAND R2. Use as few instructions as possible.

Exercise 6.18 Consider the following high-level code snippets. Assume the (signed) integer variables g and h are in registers R0 and R1, respectively.

(i)
```
if (g >= h)
    g = g + h;
else
    g = g - h;
```

(ii)
```
if (g < h)
    h = h + 1;
else
    h = h * 2;
```

(a) Write the code snippets in ARM assembly language assuming conditional execution is available for branch instructions only. Use as few instructions as possible (within these parameters).

(b) Write the code snippets in ARM assembly language with conditional execution available for all instructions. Use as few instructions as possible.

(c) Compare the difference in code density (i.e., number of instructions) between (a) and (b) for each code snippet and discuss any advantages or disadvantages.

Exercise 6.19 Repeat Exercise 6.18 for the following code snippets.

(i)
```
if (g > h)
    g = g + 1;
else
    h = h - 1;
```

(ii)
```
if (g <= h)
    g = 0;
else
    h = 0;
```

Exercise 6.20 Consider the following high-level code snippet. Assume that the base addresses of array1 and array2 are held in R1 and R2 and that array2 is initialized before it is used.

```
int i;
int array1[100];
int array2[100];
...
for (i=0; i<100; i=i+1)
    array1[i] = array2[i];
```

(a) Write the code snippet in ARM assembly without using pre- or post-indexing or a scaled register. Use as few instructions as possible (given the constraints).

(b) Write the code snippet in ARM assembly with pre- or post-indexing and a scaled register available. Use as few instructions as possible.

(c) Compare the difference in code density (i.e., number of instructions) between (a) and (b). Discuss any advantages or disadvantages.

Exercise 6.21 Repeat Exercise 6.20 for the following high-level code snippet. Assume that temp is initialized before it is used and that R3 holds the base address of temp.

```
int i;
int temp[100];
...
for (i=0; i<100; i=i+1)
  temp[i] = temp[i] * 128;
```

Exercise 6.22 Consider the following two code snippets. Assume R1 holds i and that R0 holds the base address of the vals array.

(i)
```
int i;
int vals[200];

for (i=0; i < 200; i=i+1)
  vals[i] = i;
```

(ii)
```
int i;
int vals[200];

for (i=199; i >= 0; i = i-1)
    vals[i] = i;
```

(a) Are the code snippets functionally equivalent?

(b) Write each code snippet using ARM assembly language. Use as few instructions as possible.

(c) Discuss any advantages or disadvantages of one construct over the other.

Exercise 6.23 Repeat Exercise 6.22 for the following high-level code snippets. Assume R1 holds i, R0 holds the base address of the nums array, and that the array is initialized before use.

(i)
```
int i;
int nums[10];

. . .
for (i=0; i < 10; i=i+1)
    nums[i] = nums[i]/2;
```

(ii)
```
int i;
int nums[10];

. . .
for (i=9; i >= 0; i = i-1)
    nums[i] = nums[i]/2;
```

Exercise 6.24 Write a function in a high-level language for int find42(int array[], int size). size specifies the number of elements in array, and array specifies the base address of the array. The function should return the index number of the first array entry that holds the value 42. If no array entry is 42, it should return the value –1.

Exercise 6.25 The high-level function strcpy copies the character string src to the character string dst.

```
// C code
void strcpy(char dst[], char src[]) {
  int i = 0;
  do {
    dst[i] = src[i];
  } while (src[i++]);
}
```

This simple string copy function has a serious flaw: it has no way of knowing that dst has enough space to receive src. If a malicious programmer were able to execute strcpy with a long string src, the programmer might be able to write bytes all over memory, possibly even modifying code stored in subsequent memory locations. With some cleverness, the modified code might take over the machine. This is called a buffer overflow attack; it is employed by several nasty programs, including the infamous Blaster worm, which caused an estimated $525 million in damages in 2003.

(a) Implement the strcpy function in ARM assembly code. Use R4 for i.

(b) Draw a picture of the stack before, during, and after the strcpy function call.

Assume SP = 0xBEFFF000 just before strcpy is called.

Exercise 6.26 Convert the high-level function from Exercise 6.24 into ARM assembly code.

Exercise 6.27 Consider the ARM assembly code below. func1, func2, and func3 are non-leaf functions. func4 is a leaf function. The code is not shown for each function, but the comments indicate which registers are used within each function.

```
0x00091000 func1 ...   ; func1 uses R4-R10
0x00091020 BL func2
. . .
0x00091100 func2 ...   ; func2 uses R0-R5
0x0009117C BL func3
. . .
0x00091400 func3 ...   ; func3 uses R3, R7-R9
0x00091704 BL func4
. . .
0x00093008 func4 ...   ; func4 uses R11-R12
0x00093118 MOV PC, LR
```

(a) How many words are the stack frames of each function?

(b) Sketch the stack after func4 is called. Clearly indicate which registers are stored where on the stack and mark each of the stack frames. Give values where possible.

Exercise 6.28 Each number in the Fibonacci series is the sum of the previous two numbers. Table 6.26 lists the first few numbers in the series, $fib(n)$.

(a) What is $fib(n)$ for $n = 0$ and $n = -1$?

(b) Write a function called fib in a high-level language that returns the Fibonacci number for any nonnegative value of n. Hint: You probably will want to use a loop. Clearly comment your code.

(c) Convert the high-level function of part (b) into ARM assembly code. Add comments after every line of code that explain clearly what it does. Use the Keil MDK-ARM simulator to test your code on $fib(9)$. (See the Preface for how to install the Keil MDK-ARM simulator.)

Table 6.26 Fibonacci series

n	1	2	3	4	5	6	7	8	9	10	11	...
$fib(n)$	1	1	2	3	5	8	13	21	34	55	89	...

Exercise 6.29 Consider Code Example 6.27. For this exercise, assume *factorial*(*n*) is called with input argument $n = 5$.

(a) What value is in R0 when `factorial` returns to the calling function?

(b) Suppose you replace the instructions at addresses 0x8500 and 0x8520 with PUSH {R0, R1} and POP {R1, R2}, respectively. Will the program:
   (1) enter an infinite loop but not crash;
   (2) crash (cause the stack to grow or shrink beyond the dynamic data segment or the PC to jump to a location outside the program);
   (3) produce an incorrect value in R0 when the program returns to loop (if so, what value?); or
   (4) run correctly despite the deleted lines?

(c) Repeat part (b) with the following instruction modifications:
   (i) replace the instructions at addresses 0x8500 and 0x8520 with PUSH {R3, LR} and POP {R3, LR}, respectively.
   (ii) replace the instructions at addresses 0x8500 and 0x8520 with PUSH {LR} and POP {LR}, respectively.
   (iii) delete the instruction at address 0x8510.

Exercise 6.30 Ben Bitdiddle is trying to compute the function $f(a, b) = 2a + 3b$ for nonnegative *b*. He goes overboard in the use of function calls and recursion and produces the following high-level code for functions f and g.

```
// high-level code for functions f and g
int f(int a, int b) {
  int j;

  j = a;

  return j + a + g(b);
}
int g(int x) {
  int k;
  k = 3;

  if (x == 0) return 0;
  else return k + g(x - 1);
}
```

Ben then translates the two functions into assembly language as follows. He also writes a function, test, that calls the function f(5, 3).

```
; ARM assembly code
; f: R0 = a, R1 = b, R4 = j;
; g: R0 = x, R4 = k

0x00008000 test   MOV   R0, #5            ; a = 5
0x00008004        MOV   R1, #3            ; b = 3
0x00008008        BL    f                 ; call f(5, 3)
0x0000800C loop   B     loop              ; and loop forever
0x00008010 f      PUSH {R1,R0,LR,R4}      ; save registers on stack
0x00008014        MOV   R4, R0            ; j = a
0x00008018        MOV   R0, R1            ; place b as argument for g
0x0000801C        BL    g                 ; call g(b)
0x00008020        MOV   R2, R0            ; place return value in R2
0x00008024        POP   {R1,R0}           ; restore a and b after call
0x00008028        ADD   R0, R2, R0        ; R0 = g(b) + a
0x0000802C        ADD   R0, R0, R4        ; R0 = (g(b) + a) + j
0x00008030        POP   {R4,LR}           ; restore R4, LR
0x00008034        MOV   PC, LR            ; return
0x00008038 g      PUSH {R4,LR}            ; save registers on stack
0x0000803C        MOV   R4, #3            ; k = 3
0x00008040        CMP   R0, #0            ; x == 0?
0x00008044        BNE   else              ; branch when not equal
0x00008048        MOV   R0, #0            ; if equal, return value = 0
0x0000804C        B     done              ; and clean up
0x00008050 else   SUB   R0, R0, #1        ; x = x - 1
0x00008054        BL    g                 ; call g(x - 1)
0x00008058        ADD   R0, R0, R4        ; R0 = g(x - 1) + k
0x0000805C done   POP   {R4,LR}           ; restore R0,R4,LR from stack
0x00008060        MOV   PC, LR            ; return
```

You will probably find it useful to make drawings of the stack similar to the one in Figure 6.14 to help you answer the following questions.

(a) If the code runs starting at test, what value is in R0 when the program gets to loop? Does his program correctly compute $2a + 3b$?

(b) Suppose Ben changes the instructions at addresses 0x00008010 and 0x00008030 to PUSH {R1,R0,R4} and POP {R4}, respectively. Will the program

   (1) enter an infinite loop but not crash;

   (2) crash (cause the stack to grow beyond the dynamic data segment or the PC to jump to a location outside the program);

   (3) produce an incorrect value in R0 when the program returns to loop (if so, what value?), or

   (4) run correctly despite the deleted lines?

(c) Repeat part (b) when the following instructions are changed. Note that labels aren't changed, only instructions.

    (i)   instructions at 0x00008010 and 0x00008024 change to PUSH {R1,LR, R4} and POP {R1}, respectively.

    (ii)   instructions at 0x00008010 and 0x00008024 change to PUSH {R0,LR, R4} and POP {R0}, respectively.

    (iii)   instructions at 0x00008010 and 0x00008030 change to PUSH {R1,R0, LR} and POP {LR}, respectively.

    (iv)   instructions at 0x00008010, 0x00008024, and 0x00008030 are deleted.

    (v)   instructions at 0x00008038 and 0x0000805C change to PUSH {R4} and POP {R4}, respectively.

    (vi)   instructions at 0x00008038 and 0x0000805C change to PUSH {LR} and POP {LR}, respectively.

    (vii)   instructions at 0x00008038 and 0x0000805C are deleted.

Exercise 6.31 Convert the following branch instructions into machine code. Instruction addresses are given to the left of each instruction.

```
(a)    0x0000A000       BEQ LOOP
       0x0000A004       ...
       0x0000A008       ...
       0x0000A00C LOOP ...

(b)    0x00801000       BGE DONE
       ...
       0x00802040 DONE ...

(c)    0x0000B10C BACK ...
       ...              ...
       0x0000D000       BHI BACK

(d)    0x00103000       BL  FUNC
       ...              ...
       0x0011147C FUNC ...

(e)    0x00008004 L1    ...
       ...              ...
       0x0000F00C       B L1
```

Exercise 6.32 Consider the following ARM assembly language snippet. The numbers to the left of each instruction indicate the instruction address.

```
0x000A0028 FUNC1       MOV R4, R1
0x000A002C             ADD R5, R3, R5, LSR #2
0x000A0030             SUB R4, R0, R3, ROR R4
0x000A0034             BL  FUNC2
...                    ...
0x000A0038 FUNC2       LDR R2, [R0, #4]
0x000A003C             STR R2, [R1, -R2]
```

```
0x000A0040                    CMP R3, #0
0x000A0044                    BNE ELSE
0x000A0048                    MOV PC, LR
0x000A004C ELSE               SUB R3, R3, #1
0x000A0050                    B FUNC2
```

(a) Translate the instruction sequence into machine code. Write the machine code instructions in hexadecimal.

(b) List the addressing mode used at each line of code.

Exercise 6.33 Consider the following C code snippet.

```
// C code
void setArray(int num) {
  int i;
  int array[10];

  for (i = 0; i < 10; i = i + 1)
    array[i] = compare(num, i);
}
int compare(int a, int b) {
  if (sub(a, b) >= 0)
    return 1;
  else
    return 0;
}
int sub(int a, int b) {
  return a - b;
}
```

(a) Implement the C code snippet in ARM assembly language. Use R4 to hold the variable i. Be sure to handle the stack pointer appropriately. The array is stored on the stack of the setArray function (see the end of Section 6.3.7).

(b) Assume setArray is the first function called. Draw the status of the stack before calling setArray and during each function call. Indicate the names of registers and variables stored on the stack, mark the location of SP, and clearly mark each stack frame.

(c) How would your code function if you failed to store LR on the stack?

Exercise 6.34 Consider the following high-level function.

```
// C code
int f(int n, int k) {
  int b;

  b = k + 2;
  if (n == 0) b = 10;
  else b = b + (n * n) + f(n - 1, k + 1);
  return b * k;
}
```

(a) Translate the high-level function f into ARM assembly language. Pay particular attention to properly saving and restoring registers across function calls and using the ARM preserved register conventions. Clearly comment your code. You can use the ARM MUL instruction. The function starts at instruction address 0x00008100. Keep local variable b in R4.

(b) Step through your function from part (a) by hand for the case of f(2, 4). Draw a picture of the stack similar to the one in Figure 6.14, and assume that SP is equal to 0xBFF00100 when f is called. Write the register name and data value stored at each location in the stack and keep track of the stack pointer value (SP). Clearly mark each stack frame. You might also find it useful to keep track of the values in R0, R1, and R4 throughout execution. Assume that when f is called, R4 = 0xABCD and LR = 0x00008010. What is the final value of R0?

Exercise 6.35 Give an example of the worst case for a forward branch (i.e., a branch to a higher instruction address). The worst case is when the branch cannot branch far. Show instructions and instruction addresses.

Exercise 6.36 The following questions examine the limitations of the branch instruction, B. Give your answer in number of instructions relative to the branch instruction.

(a) In the worst case, how far can B branch forward (i.e., to higher addresses)? (The worst case is when the branch instruction cannot branch far.) Explain using words and examples, as needed.

(b) In the best case, how far can B branch forward? (The best case is when the branch instruction can branch the farthest.) Explain.

(c) In the worst case, how far can B branch backward (to lower addresses)? Explain.

(d) In the best case, how far can B branch backward? Explain.

Exercise 6.37 Explain why it is advantageous to have a large immediate field, *imm24*, in the machine format for the branch instructions, B and BL.

Exercise 6.38 Write assembly code that branches to an instruction 32 Minstructions from the first instruction. Recall that 1 Minstruction = 2^{20} instructions =1,048,576 instructions. Assume that your code begins at address 0x00008000. Use a minimum number of instructions.

Exercise 6.39 Write a function in high-level code that takes a 10-entry array of 32-bit integers stored in little-endian format and converts it to big-endian format. After writing the high-level code, convert it to ARM assembly code. Comment all your code and use a minimum number of instructions.

Exercise 6.40 Consider two strings: string1 and string2.

(a) Write high-level code for a function called concat that concatenates (joins together) the two strings: void concat(char string1[], char string2[], char stringconcat[]). The function does not return a value. It concatenates string1 and string2 and places the resulting string in stringconcat. You may assume that the character array stringconcat is large enough to accommodate the concatenated string.

(b) Convert the function from part (a) into ARM assembly language.

Exercise 6.41 Write an ARM assembly program that adds two positive single-precision floating point numbers held in R0 and R1. Do not use any of the ARM floating-point instructions. You need not worry about any of the encodings that are reserved for special purposes (e.g., 0, NANs, etc.) or numbers that overflow or underflow. Use the Keil MDK-ARM simulator to test your code. (See the Preface for how to install the Keil MDK-ARM simulator.) You will need to manually set the values of R0 and R1 to test your code. Demonstrate that your code functions reliably.

Exercise 6.42 Consider the following ARM program. Assume the instructions are placed starting at memory address 0x8400 and that L1 is at memory address 0x10024.

```
; ARM assembly code
MAIN
    PUSH {LR}
    LDR  R2, =L1   ; this is translated into a PC-relative load
    LDR  R0, [R2]
    LDR  R1, [R2, #4]
    BL   DIFF
    POP  {LR}
    MOV  PC, LR
DIFF
    SUB  R0, R0, R1
    MOV  PC, LR
    . . .
L1
```

(a) First show the instruction address next to each assembly instruction.

(b) Describe the symbol table: i.e., list the address of each of the labels.

(c) Convert all instructions into machine code.

(d) How big (how many bytes) are the data and text segments?

(e) Sketch a memory map showing where data and instructions are stored, similar to Figure 6.31.

Exercise 6.43 Repeat Exercise 6.42 for the following ARM code. Assume the instructions are placed starting at memory address 0x8534 and that L2 is at memory address 0x1305C.

```
; ARM assembly code
MAIN
  PUSH {R4,LR}
  MOV  R4, #15
  LDR  R3, =L2  ; this is translated into a PC-relative load
  STR  R4, [R3]
  MOV  R1, #27
  STR  R1, [R3, #4]
  LDR  R0, [R3]
  BL   GREATER
  POP  {R4,LR}
  MOV  PC, LR
GREATER
  CMP  R0, R1
  MOV  R0, #0
  MOVGT R0, #1
  MOV  PC, LR
  ...
L2
```

Exercise 6.44 Name two ARM instructions that can increase code density (i.e., decrease the number of instructions in a program). Give examples of each, showing equivalent ARM assembly code with and without using the instructions.

Exercise 6.45 Explain the advantages and disadvantages of conditional execution.

Interview Questions

The following exercises present questions that have been asked at interviews for digital design jobs (but are usually open to any assembly language).

Question 6.1 Write ARM assembly code for swapping the contents of two registers, R0 and R1. You may not use any other registers.

Question 6.2 Suppose you are given an array of both positive and negative integers. Write ARM assembly code that finds the subset of the array with the largest sum. Assume that the array's base address and the number of array elements are in R0 and R1, respectively. Your code should place the resulting subset of the array starting at the base address in R2. Write code that runs as fast as possible.

Question 6.3 You are given an array that holds a C string. The string forms a sentence. Design an algorithm for reversing the words in the sentence and storing the new sentence back in the array. Implement your algorithm using ARM assembly code.

Question 6.4 Design an algorithm for counting the number of 1's in a 32-bit number. Implement your algorithm using ARM assembly code.

Question 6.5 Write ARM assembly code to reverse the bits in a register. Use as few instructions as possible. Assume the register of interest is R3.

Question 6.6 Write ARM assembly code to test whether overflow occurs when R2 and R3 are added. Use a minimum number of instructions.

Question 6.7 Design an algorithm for testing whether a given string is a palindrome. (Recall that a palindrome is a word that is the same forward and backward. For example, the words "wow" and "racecar" are palindromes.) Implement your algorithm using ARM assembly code

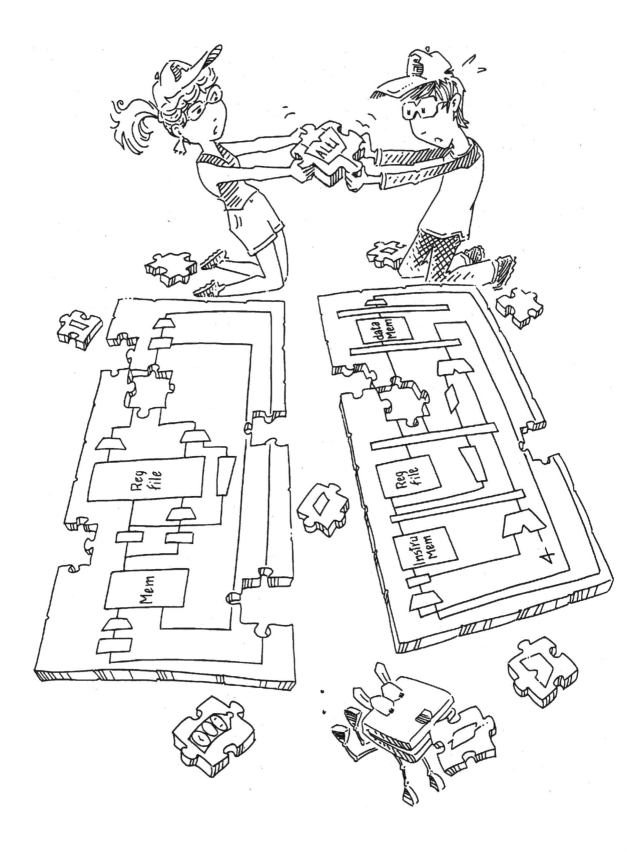

Microarchitecture

7.1 INTRODUCTION

In this chapter, you will learn how to piece together a microprocessor. Indeed, you will puzzle out three different versions, each with different trade-offs between performance, cost, and complexity.

To the uninitiated, building a microprocessor may seem like black magic. But it is actually relatively straightforward, and by this point you have learned everything you need to know. Specifically, you have learned to design combinational and sequential logic given functional and timing specifications. You are familiar with circuits for arithmetic and memory. And you have learned about the ARM architecture, which specifies the programmer's view of the ARM processor in terms of registers, instructions, and memory.

This chapter covers *microarchitecture*, which is the connection between logic and architecture. Microarchitecture is the specific arrangement of registers, ALUs, finite state machines (FSMs), memories, and other logic building blocks needed to implement an architecture. A particular architecture, such as ARM, may have many different microarchitectures, each with different trade-offs of performance, cost, and complexity. They all run the same programs, but their internal designs vary widely. We design three different microarchitectures in this chapter to illustrate the trade-offs.

7.1.1 Architectural State and Instruction Set

Recall that a computer architecture is defined by its instruction set and architectural state. The *architectural state* for the ARM processor consists of 16 32-bit registers and the status register. Any ARM microarchitecture must contain all of this state. Based on the current architectural state, the processor executes a particular instruction with a particular set of data to produce a new architectural state. Some microarchitectures contain

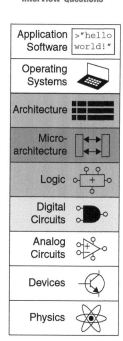

additional *nonarchitectural state* to either simplify the logic or improve performance; we point this out as it arises.

To keep the microarchitectures easy to understand, we consider only a subset of the ARM instruction set. Specifically, we handle the following instructions:

▸ Data-processing instructions: ADD, SUB, AND, ORR (with register and immediate addressing modes but no shifts)

▸ Memory instructions: LDR, STR (with positive immediate offset)

▸ Branches: B

These particular instructions were chosen because they are sufficient to write many interesting programs. Once you understand how to implement these instructions, you can expand the hardware to handle others.

7.1.2 Design Process

We divide our microarchitectures into two interacting parts: the *datapath* and the *control unit*. The datapath operates on words of data. It contains structures such as memories, registers, ALUs, and multiplexers. We are implementing the 32-bit ARM architecture, so we use a 32-bit datapath. The control unit receives the current instruction from the datapath and tells the datapath how to execute that instruction. Specifically, the control unit produces multiplexer select, register enable, and memory write signals to control the operation of the datapath.

A good way to design a complex system is to start with hardware containing the state elements. These elements include the memories and the architectural state (the program counter, registers, and status register). Then, add blocks of combinational logic between the state elements to compute the new state based on the current state. The instruction is read from part of memory; load and store instructions then read or write data from another part of memory. Hence, it is often convenient to partition the overall memory into two smaller memories, one containing instructions and the other containing data. Figure 7.1 shows a block diagram with the five state elements: the program counter, register file, status register, and instruction and data memories.

In Figure 7.1, heavy lines are used to indicate 32-bit data busses. Medium lines are used to indicate narrower busses, such as the 4-bit address busses on the register file. Narrow lines indicate 1-bit buses, and blue lines are used for control signals, such as the register file write enable. We use this convention throughout the chapter to avoid cluttering diagrams with bus widths. Also, state elements usually have a reset input to put them into a known state at start-up. Again, to save clutter, this reset is not shown.

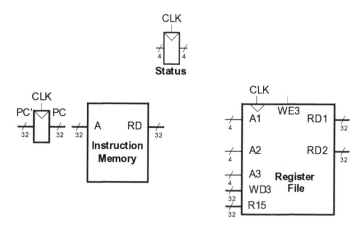

Figure 7.1 **State elements of ARM processor**

Although the *program counter* (PC) is logically part of the register file, it is read and written on every cycle independent of the normal register file operation and is more naturally built as a stand-alone 32-bit register. Its output, *PC*, points to the current instruction. Its input, *PC′*, indicates the address of the next instruction.

The *instruction memory* has a single read port.[1] It takes a 32-bit instruction address input, *A*, and reads the 32-bit data (i.e., instruction) from that address onto the read data output, *RD*.

The 15-element × 32-bit register file holds registers R0–R14 and has an additional input to receive R15 from the PC. The register file has two read ports and one write port. The read ports take 4-bit address inputs, *A1* and *A2*, each specifying one of $2^4 = 16$ registers as source operands. They read the 32-bit register values onto read data outputs *RD1* and *RD2*, respectively. The write port takes a 4-bit address input, *A3*; a 32-bit write data input, *WD3*; a write enable input, *WE3*; and a clock. If the write enable is asserted, then the register file writes the data into the specified register on the rising edge of the clock. A read of R15 returns the value from the PC plus 8, and writes to R15 must be specially handled to update the PC because it is separate from the register file.

The *data memory* has a single read/write port. If its write enable, *WE*, is asserted, then it writes data *WD* into address *A* on the rising edge of the clock. If its write enable is 0, then it reads address *A* onto *RD*.

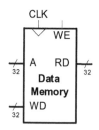

Resetting the PC

At the very least, the program counter must have a reset signal to initialize its value when the processor turns on. ARM processors normally initialize the PC to 0x00000000 on reset, and we start our programs there.

Treating the PC as part of the register file complicates the system design, and complexity ultimately means more gates and higher power consumption. Most other architectures treat the PC as a special register that is only updated by branches, not by ordinary data-processing instructions. As described in Section 6.7.6, ARM's 64-bit ARMv8 architecture also makes the PC a special register separate from the register file.

---

[1] This is an oversimplification used to treat the instruction memory as a ROM; in most real processors, the instruction memory must be writable so that the OS can load a new program into memory. The multicycle microarchitecture described in Section 7.4 is more realistic in that it uses a combined memory for instructions and data that can be both read and written.

The instruction memory, register file, and data memory are all read *combinationally*. In other words, if the address changes, then the new data appears at *RD* after some propagation delay; no clock is involved. They are written only on the rising edge of the clock. In this fashion, the state of the system is changed only at the clock edge. The address, data, and write enable must setup before the clock edge and must remain stable until a hold time after the clock edge.

Because the state elements change their state only on the rising edge of the clock, they are synchronous sequential circuits. The microprocessor is built of clocked state elements and combinational logic, so it too is a synchronous sequential circuit. Indeed, the processor can be viewed as a giant finite state machine, or as a collection of simpler interacting state machines.

7.1.3 Microarchitectures

In this chapter, we develop three microarchitectures for the ARM architecture: single-cycle, multicycle, and pipelined. They differ in the way that the state elements are connected together and in the amount of nonarchitectural state.

The *single-cycle microarchitecture* executes an entire instruction in one cycle. It is easy to explain and has a simple control unit. Because it completes the operation in one cycle, it does not require any nonarchitectural state. However, the cycle time is limited by the slowest instruction. Moreover, the processor requires separate instruction and data memories, which is generally unrealistic.

The *multicycle microarchitecture* executes instructions in a series of shorter cycles. Simpler instructions execute in fewer cycles than complicated ones. Moreover, the multicycle microarchitecture reduces the hardware cost by reusing expensive hardware blocks such as adders and memories. For example, the adder may be used on different cycles for several purposes while carrying out a single instruction. The multicycle microprocessor accomplishes this by adding several nonarchitectural registers to hold intermediate results. The multicycle processor executes only one instruction at a time, but each instruction takes multiple clock cycles. The multicycle processor requires only a single memory, accessing it on one cycle to fetch the instruction and on another to read or write data. Therefore, multicycle processors were the historical choice for inexpensive systems.

The *pipelined microarchitecture* applies pipelining to the single-cycle microarchitecture. It therefore can execute several instructions simultaneously, improving the throughput significantly. Pipelining must add logic to handle dependencies between simultaneously executing instructions. It also requires nonarchitectural pipeline registers. Pipelined processors must access instructions and data in the same cycle; they generally use separate instruction and data caches for this purpose, as discussed

Examples of classic multicycle processors include the 1947 MIT Whirlwind, the IBM System/360, the Digital Equipment Corporation VAX, the 6502 used in the Apple II, and the 8088 used in the IBM PC. Multicycle microarchitectures are still used in inexpensive microcontrollers such as the 8051, the 68HC11, and the PIC16-series found in appliances, toys, and gadgets.

Intel processors have been pipelined since the 80486 was introduced in 1989. Nearly all RISC microprocessors are also pipelined. ARM processors have been pipelined since the original ARM1 in 1985. A pipelined ARM Cortex-M0 requires only about 12,000 logic gates, so in a modern integrated circuit it is so small that one needs a microscope to see it and the manufacturing cost is a fraction of a penny. Combined with memory and peripherals, a commercial Cortex-M0 chip such as the Freescale Kinetis still costs less than 50 cents. Thus, pipelined processors are replacing their slower multicycle siblings in even the most cost-sensitive applications.

in Chapter 8. The added logic and registers are worthwhile; all commercial high-performance processors use pipelining today.

We explore the details and trade-offs of these three microarchitectures in the subsequent sections. At the end of the chapter, we briefly mention additional techniques that are used to achieve even more speed in modern high-performance microprocessors.

7.2 PERFORMANCE ANALYSIS

As we mentioned, a particular processor architecture can have many microarchitectures with different cost and performance trade-offs. The cost depends on the amount of hardware required and the implementation technology. Precise cost calculations require detailed knowledge of the implementation technology but, in general, more gates and more memory mean more dollars.

This section lays the foundation for analyzing performance. There are many ways to measure the performance of a computer system, and marketing departments are infamous for choosing the method that makes their computer look fastest, regardless of whether the measurement has any correlation to real-world performance. For example, microprocessor makers often market their products based on the clock frequency and the number of cores. However, they gloss over the complications that some processors accomplish more work than others in a clock cycle and that this varies from program to program. What is a buyer to do?

The only gimmick-free way to measure performance is by measuring the execution time of a program of interest to you. The computer that executes your program fastest has the highest performance. The next best choice is to measure the total execution time of a collection of programs that are similar to those you plan to run; this may be necessary if you have not written your program yet or if somebody else who does not have your program is making the measurements. Such collections of programs are called *benchmarks*, and the execution times of these programs are commonly published to give some indication of how a processor performs.

Equation 7.1 gives the execution time of a program, measured in seconds.

$$Execution\ Time = \left(\#instructions \right) \left(\frac{cycles}{instruction} \right) \left(\frac{seconds}{cycle} \right) \quad (7.1)$$

The number of instructions in a program depends on the processor architecture. Some architectures have complicated instructions that do more work per instruction, thus reducing the number of instructions in a program. However, these complicated instructions are often slower to

Dhrystone, CoreMark, and SPEC are three popular benchmarks. The first two are *synthetic benchmarks* comprising important common pieces of programs. Dhrystone was developed in 1984 and remains commonly used for embedded processors, although the code is somewhat unrepresentative of real-life programs. CoreMark is an improvement over Dhrystone and involves matrix multiplications that exercise the multiplier and adder, linked lists to exercise the memory system, state machines to exercise the branch logic, and cyclical redundancy checks that involve many parts of the processor. Both benchmarks are less than 16 KB in size and do not stress the instruction cache.

The SPEC CINT2006 benchmark from the Standard Performance Evaluation Corporation is composed of real programs, including h264ref (video compression), sjeng (an artificial intelligence chess player), hmmer (protein sequence analysis), and gcc (a C compiler). The benchmark is widely used for high-performance processors because it stresses the entire CPU in a representative way.

execute in hardware. The number of instructions also depends enormously on the cleverness of the programmer. For the purposes of this chapter, we assume that we are executing known programs on an ARM processor, so the number of instructions for each program is constant, independent of the microarchitecture. The *cycles per instruction (CPI)* is the number of clock cycles required to execute an average instruction. It is the reciprocal of the throughput (*instructions per cycle*, or *IPC*). Different microarchitectures have different CPIs. In this chapter, we assume we have an ideal memory system that does not affect the CPI. In Chapter 8, we examine how the processor sometimes has to wait for the memory, which increases the CPI.

The number of seconds per cycle is the clock period, T_c. The clock period is determined by the critical path through the logic on the processor. Different microarchitectures have different clock periods. Logic and circuit designs also significantly affect the clock period. For example, a carry-lookahead adder is faster than a ripple-carry adder. Manufacturing advances have historically doubled transistor speeds every 4–6 years, so a microprocessor built today will be faster than one from last decade, even if the microarchitecture and logic are unchanged.

The challenge of the microarchitect is to choose the design that minimizes the execution time while satisfying constraints on cost and/or power consumption. Because microarchitectural decisions affect both CPI and T_c and are influenced by logic and circuit designs, determining the best choice requires careful analysis.

Many other factors affect overall computer performance. For example, the hard disk, the memory, the graphics system, and the network connection may be limiting factors that make processor performance irrelevant. The fastest microprocessor in the world does not help surfing the Internet on a dial-up connection. But these other factors are beyond the scope of this book.

7.3 SINGLE-CYCLE PROCESSOR

We first design a microarchitecture that executes instructions in a single cycle. We begin constructing the datapath by connecting the state elements from Figure 7.1 with combinational logic that can execute the various instructions. Control signals determine which specific instruction is performed by the datapath at any given time. The control unit contains combinational logic that generates the appropriate control signals based on the current instruction. We conclude by analyzing the performance of the single-cycle processor.

7.3.1 Single-Cycle Datapath

This section gradually develops the single-cycle datapath, adding one piece at a time to the state elements from Figure 7.1. The new connections are emphasized in black (or blue, for new control signals), whereas the hardware that has already been studied is shown in gray. The status register is part of the controller and will be omitted while we focus on the datapath.

The program counter contains the address of the instruction to execute. The first step is to read this instruction from instruction memory. Figure 7.2 shows that the PC is simply connected to the address input of the instruction memory. The instruction memory reads out, or *fetches*, the 32-bit instruction, labeled *Instr*.

The processor's actions depend on the specific instruction that was fetched. First, we will work out the datapath connections for the LDR instruction with positive immediate offset. Then, we will consider how to generalize the datapath to handle other instructions.

LDR

For the LDR instruction, the next step is to read the source register containing the base address. This register is specified in the *Rn* field of the instruction, $Instr_{19:16}$. These bits of the instruction are connected to the address input of one of the register file ports, *A1*, as shown in Figure 7.3. The register file reads the register value onto *RD1*.

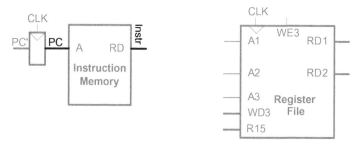
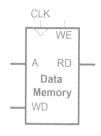

Figure 7.2 Fetch instruction from memory

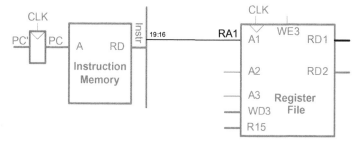
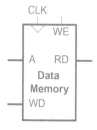

Figure 7.3 Read source operand from register file

The LDR instruction also requires an offset. The offset is stored in the immediate field of the instruction, $Instr_{11:0}$. It is an unsigned value, so it must be zero-extended to 32 bits, as shown in Figure 7.4. The 32-bit value is called *ExtImm*. Zero extension simply means prepending leading zeros: $ImmExt_{31:12} = 0$ and $ImmExt_{11:0} = Instr_{11:0}$.

The processor must add the base address to the offset to find the address to read from memory. Figure 7.5 introduces an ALU to perform this addition. The ALU receives two operands, *SrcA* and *SrcB*. *SrcA* comes from the register file, and *SrcB* comes from the extended immediate. The ALU can perform many operations, as was described in Section 5.2.4. The 2-bit *ALUControl* signal specifies the operation. The ALU generates a 32-bit *ALUResult*. For an LDR instruction, *ALUControl* should be set to 00 to perform addition. *ALUResult* is sent to the data memory as the address to read, as shown in Figure 7.5.

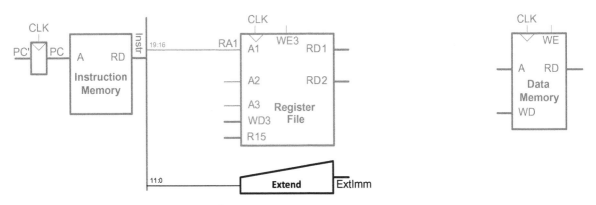

Figure 7.4 Zero-extend the immediate

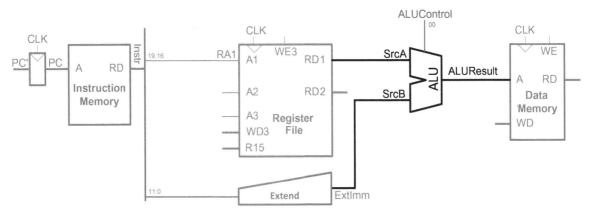

Figure 7.5 Compute memory address

The data is read from the data memory onto the *ReadData* bus and then written back to the destination register at the end of the cycle, as shown in Figure 7.6. Port 3 of the register file is the write port. The destination register for the LDR instruction is specified in the *Rd* field, *Instr*$_{15:12}$, which is connected to the port 3 address input, *A3*, of the register file. The *ReadData* bus is connected to the port 3 write data input, *WD3*, of the register file. A control signal called *RegWrite* is connected to the port 3 write enable input, *WE3*, and is asserted during an LDR instruction so that the data value is written into the register file. The write takes place on the rising edge of the clock at the end of the cycle.

While the instruction is being executed, the processor must compute the address of the next instruction, *PC'*. Because instructions are 32 bits (4 bytes), the next instruction is at *PC* + 4. Figure 7.7 uses an adder to

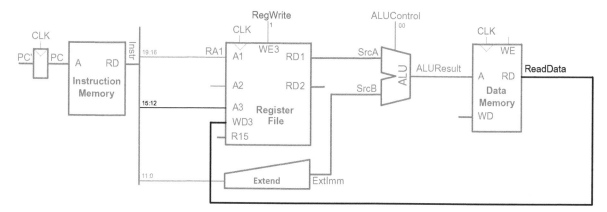

Figure 7.6 Write data back to register file

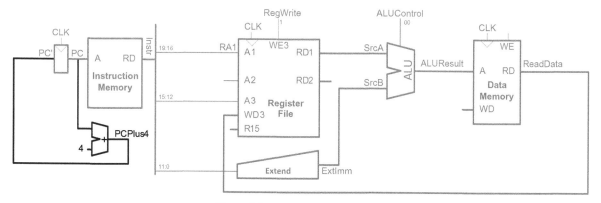

Figure 7.7 Increment program counter

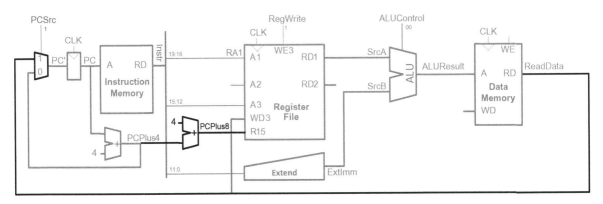

Figure 7.8 Read or write program counter as R15

increment the PC by 4. The new address is written into the program counter on the next rising edge of the clock. This completes the datapath for the LDR instruction, except for a sneaky case of the base or destination register being R15.

Recall from Section 6.4.6 that in the ARM architecture, reading register R15 returns $PC + 8$. Therefore, another adder is needed to further increment the PC and pass this sum to the *R15* port of the register file. Similarly, writing register R15 updates the PC. Therefore, *PC* may come from the result of the instruction (*ReadData*) rather than *PCPlus4*. A multiplexer chooses between these two possibilities. The *PCSrc* control signal is set to 0 to choose *PCPlus4* or 1 to choose *ReadData*. These PC-related features are highlighted in Figure 7.8.

STR

Next, let us extend the datapath to also handle the STR instruction. Like LDR, STR reads a base address from port 1 of the register file and zero-extends the immediate. The ALU adds the base address to the immediate to find the memory address. All of these functions are already supported in the datapath.

The STR instruction also reads a second register from the register file and writes it to the data memory. Figure 7.9 shows the new connections for this function. The register is specified in the *Rd* field, $Instr_{15:12}$, which is connected to the *A2* port of the register file. The register value is read onto the *RD2* port. It is connected to the write data (*WD*) port of the data memory. The write enable port of the data memory, *WE*, is controlled by *MemWrite*. For an STR instruction: *MemWrite* = 1 to write the data to memory; *ALUControl* = 00 to add the base address and offset; and *RegWrite* = 0, because nothing should be written to the register file. Note that data is still read from the address given to the data memory, but that this *ReadData* is ignored because *RegWrite* = 0.

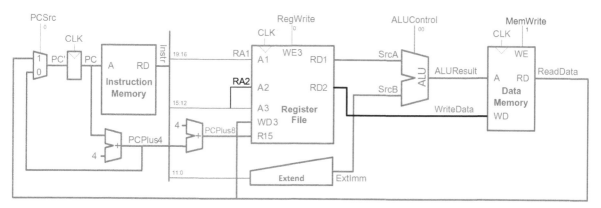

Figure 7.9 Write data to memory for STR instruction

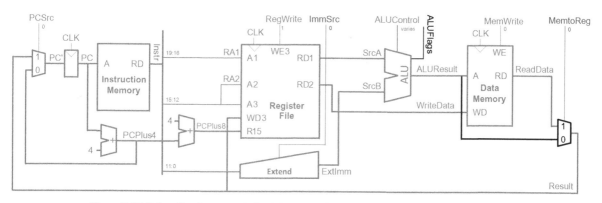

Figure 7.10 Datapath enhancements for data-processing instructions with immediate addressing

Data-Processing Instructions with Immediate Addressing

Next, consider extending the datapath to handle the data-processing instructions, ADD, SUB, AND, and ORR, using the immediate addressing mode. All of these instructions read a source register from the register file and an immediate from the low bits of the instruction, perform some ALU operation on them, and write the result back to a third register. They differ only in the specific ALU operation. Hence, they can all be handled with the same hardware using different *ALUControl* signals. As described in Section 5.2.4, *ALUControl* is 00 for ADD, 01 for SUB, 10 for AND, or 11 for ORR. The ALU also produces four flags, $ALUFlags_{3:0}$ (Zero, Negative, Carry, oVerflow), that are sent back to the controller.

Figure 7.10 shows the enhanced datapath handling data-processing instructions with an immediate second source. Like LDR, the datapath reads the first ALU source from port 1 of the register file and extends the immediate from the low bits of *Instr*. However, data-processing instructions use only an 8-bit immediate rather than a 12-bit immediate. Therefore, we provide the *ImmSrc* control signal to the Extend block. When it is 0, *ExtImm* is zero-extended from $Instr_{7:0}$ for data-processing instructions. When it is 1, *ExtImm* is zero-extended from $Instr_{11:0}$ for LDR or STR.

For LDR, the register file received its write data from the data memory. However, data-processing instructions write *ALUResult* to the register file. Therefore, we add another multiplexer to choose between *ReadData* and *ALUResult*. We call its output *Result*. The multiplexer is controlled by another new signal, *MemtoReg*. *MemtoReg* is 0 for data-processing instructions to choose *Result* from *ALUResult*; it is 1 for LDR to choose *ReadData*. We do not care about the value of *MemtoReg* for STR because STR does not write the register file.

Data-Processing Instructions with Register Addressing

Data-processing instructions with register addressing receive their second source from *Rm*, specified by $Instr_{3:0}$, rather than from the immediate. Thus, we must add multiplexers on the inputs of the register file and ALU to select this second source register, as shown in Figure 7.11.

RA2 is chosen from the *Rd* field ($Instr_{15:12}$) for STR and the *Rm* field ($Instr_{3:0}$) for data-processing instructions with register addressing based on the *RegSrc* control signal. Similarly, based on the *ALUSrc* control signal, the second source to the ALU is selected from *ExtImm* for instructions using immediates and from the register file for data-processing instructions with register addressing.

B

Finally, we extend the datapath to handle the B instruction, as shown in Figure 7.12. The branch instruction adds a 24-bit immediate to $PC + 8$ and writes the result back to the PC. The immediate is multiplied by 4

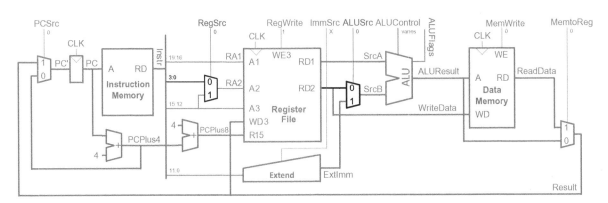

Figure 7.11 Datapath enhancements for data-processing instructions with register addressing

and sign extended. Therefore, the Extend logic needs yet another mode. *ImmSrc* is increased to 2 bits, with the encoding given in Table 7.1.

$PC + 8$ is read from the first port of the register file. Therefore, a multiplexer is needed to choose R15 as the *RA1* input. This multiplexer is controlled by another bit of *RegSrc*, choosing $Instr_{19:16}$ for most instructions but 15 for B.

MemtoReg is set to 0 and *PCSrc* is set to 1 to select the new PC from *ALUResult* for the branch.

This completes the design of the single-cycle processor datapath. We have illustrated not only the design itself but also the design process in which the state elements are identified, and the combinational logic connecting the state elements is systematically added. In the next section, we consider how to compute the control signals that direct the operation of our datapath.

7.3.2 Single-Cycle Control

The control unit computes the control signals based on the *cond*, *op*, and *funct* fields of the instruction ($Instr_{31:28}$, $Instr_{27:26}$, and $Instr_{25:20}$) as well as the flags and whether the destination register is the PC. The controller also stores the current status flags and updates them appropriately. Figure 7.13 shows the entire single-cycle processor with the control unit attached to the datapath.

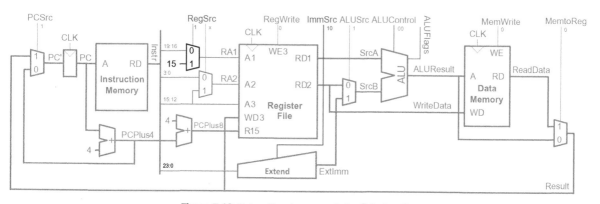

Figure 7.12 Datapath enhancements for B instruction

Table 7.1 ImmSrc Encoding

ImmSrc	ExtImm	Description
00	{24 0s} $Instr_{7:0}$	8-bit unsigned immediate for data-processing
01	{20 0s} $Instr_{11:0}$	12-bit unsigned immediate for LDR/STR
10	{6 $Instr_{23}$} $Instr_{23:0}$ 00	24-bit signed immediate multiplied by 4 for B

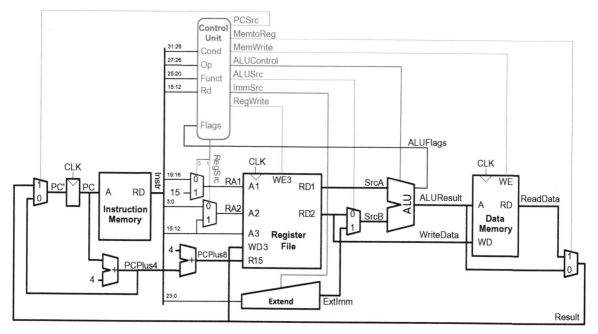

Figure 7.13 Complete single-cycle processor

Figure 7.14 shows a detailed diagram of the controller. We partition the controller into two main parts: the Decoder, which generates control signals based on *Instr*, and the Conditional Logic, which maintains the status flags and only enables updates to architectural state when the instruction should be conditionally executed. The Decoder, shown in Figure 7.14(b), is composed of a Main Decoder that produces most of the control signals, an ALU Decoder that uses the *Funct* field to determine the type of data-processing instruction, and PC Logic to determine whether the PC needs updating due to a branch or a write to R15.

The behavior of the Main Decoder is given by the truth table in Table 7.2. The Main Decoder determines the type of instruction: Data-Processing Register, Data-Processing Immediate, STR, LDR, or B. It produces the appropriate control signals to the datapath. It sends *MemtoReg*, *ALUSrc*, *ImmSrc*$_{1:0}$, and *RegSrc*$_{1:0}$ directly to the datapath. However, the write enables *MemW* and *RegW* must pass through the Conditional Logic before becoming datapath signals *MemWrite* and *RegWrite*. These write enables may be killed (reset to 0) by the Conditional Logic if the condition is not satisfied. The Main Decoder also generates the *Branch* and *ALUOp* signals, which are used within the controller to indicate that the instruction is B or data-processing, respectively. The logic for the Main Decoder can be developed from the truth table using your favorite techniques for combinational logic design.

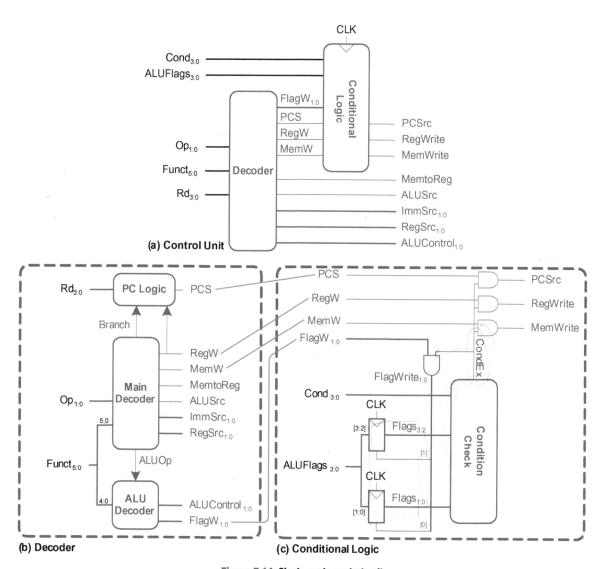

(a) Control Unit

(b) Decoder

(c) Conditional Logic

Figure 7.14 Single-cycle control unit

The behavior of the ALU Decoder is given by the truth tables in Table 7.3. For data-processing instructions, the ALU Decoder chooses *ALUControl* based on the type of instruction (ADD, SUB, AND, ORR). Moreover, it asserts *FlagW* to update the status flags when the *S*-bit is set. Note that ADD and SUB update all flags, whereas AND and ORR only update the *N* and *Z* flags, so two bits of *FlagW* are needed: $FlagW_1$ for updating *N* and *Z* ($Flags_{3:2}$), and $FlagW_0$ for updating *C* and *V* ($Flags_{1:0}$). $FlagW_{1:0}$ is killed by the Conditional Logic when the condition is not satisfied ($CondEx = 0$).

Table 7.2 Main Decoder truth table

Op	Funct$_5$	Funct$_0$	Type	Branch	MemtoReg	MemW	ALUSrc	ImmSrc	RegW	RegSrc	ALUOp
00	0	X	DP Reg	0	0	0	0	XX	1	00	1
00	1	X	DP Imm	0	0	0	1	00	1	X0	1
01	X	0	STR	0	X	1	1	01	0	10	0
01	X	1	LDR	0	1	0	1	01	1	X0	0
10	X	X	B	1	0	0	1	10	0	X1	0

Table 7.3 ALU Decoder truth table

ALUOp	Funct$_{4:1}$ (cmd)	Funct$_0$ (S)	Type	ALUControl$_{1:0}$	FlagW$_{1:0}$
0	X	X	Not DP	00 (Add)	00
1	0100	0	ADD	00 (Add)	00
		1			11
	0010	0	SUB	01 (Sub)	00
		1			11
	0000	0	AND	10 (And)	00
		1			10
	1100	0	ORR	11 (Or)	00
		1			10

The PC Logic checks if the instruction is a write to R15 or a branch such that the PC should be updated. The logic is:

$$PCS = ((Rd == 15) \,\&\, RegW)\,|\,Branch$$

PCS may be killed by the Conditional Logic before it is sent to the datapath as *PCSrc*.

The Conditional Logic, shown in Figure 7.14(c), determines whether the instruction should be executed (*CondEx*) based on the *cond* field and the current values of the *N*, *Z*, *C*, and *V* flags (*Flags$_{3:0}$*), as was described in Table 6.3. If the instruction should not be executed, the write enables and *PCSrc* are forced to 0 so that the instruction does not change the architectural state. The Conditional Logic also updates some or all of the flags from the *ALUFlags* when *FlagW* is asserted by the ALU Decoder and the instruction's condition is satisfied (*CondEx* = 1).

Example 7.1 SINGLE-CYCLE PROCESSOR OPERATION

Determine the values of the control signals and the portions of the datapath that are used when executing an ORR instruction with register addressing mode.

Solution: Figure 7.15 illustrates the control signals and flow of data during execution of the ORR instruction. The PC points to the memory location holding the instruction, and the instruction memory returns this instruction.

The main flow of data through the register file and ALU is represented with a heavy blue line. The register file reads the two source operands specified by $Instr_{19:16}$ and $Instr_{3:0}$, so $RegSrc$ must be 00. $SrcB$ should come from the second port of the register file (not $ExtImm$), so $ALUSrc$ must be 0. The ALU performs a bitwise OR operation, so $ALUControl$ must be 11. The result comes from the ALU, so $MemtoReg$ is 0. The result is written to the register file, so $RegWrite$ is 1. The instruction does not write memory, so $MemWrite = 0$.

The updating of PC with $PCPlus4$ is shown with a heavy gray line. $PCSrc$ is 0 to select the incremented PC.

Note that data certainly does flow through the nonhighlighted paths, but that the value of that data is unimportant for this instruction. For example, the immediate is extended and data is read from memory, but these values do not influence the next state of the system.

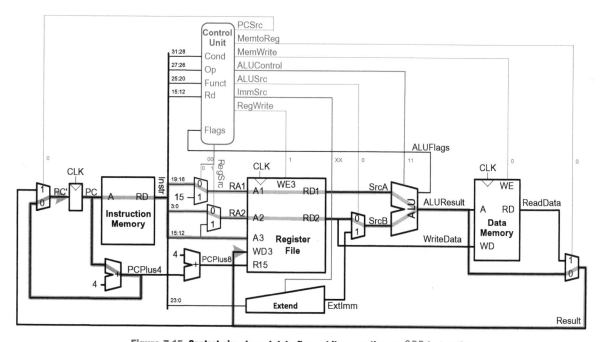

Figure 7.15 Control signals and data flow while executing an ORR instruction

7.3.3 More Instructions

We have considered a limited subset of the full ARM instruction set. In this section, we add support for the compare (CMP) instruction and for addressing modes in which the second source is a shifted register. These examples illustrate the principle of how to handle new instructions; with enough effort, you could extend the single-cycle processor to handle every ARM instruction. Moreover, we will see that supporting some instructions simply requires enhancing the decoders, whereas supporting others also requires new hardware in the datapath.

Example 7.2 CMP INSTRUCTION

The compare instruction, CMP, subtracts $SrcB$ from $SrcA$ and sets the flags but does not write the difference to a register. The datapath is already capable of this task. Determine the necessary changes to the controller to support CMP.

Solution: Introduce a new control signal called *NoWrite* to prevent writing Rd during CMP. (This signal would also be helpful for other instructions such as TST that do not write a register.) We extend the ALU Decoder to produce this signal and the *RegWrite* logic to accept it, as highlighted in blue in Figure 7.16. The enhanced ALU Decoder truth table is given in Table 7.4, with the new instruction and signal also highlighted.

Example 7.3 ENHANCED ADDRESSING MODE: REGISTERS WITH CONSTANT SHIFTS

So far, we assumed that data-processing instructions with register addressing did not shift the second source register. Enhance the single-cycle processor to support a shift by an immediate.

Solution: Insert a shifter before the ALU. Figure 7.17 shows the enhanced datapath. The shifter uses $Instr_{11:7}$ to specify the shift amount and $Instr_{6:5}$ to specify the shift type.

7.3.4 Performance Analysis

Each instruction in the single-cycle processor takes one clock cycle, so the CPI is 1. The critical paths for the LDR instruction are shown in Figure 7.18 with a heavy blue line. It starts with the PC loading a new address on the rising edge of the clock. The instruction memory reads the new instruction. The Main Decoder computes $RegSrc_0$, which drives the multiplexer to choose $Instr_{19:16}$ as $RA1$, and the register file reads this register as $SrcA$. While the register file is reading, the immediate field is zero-extended and selected at the *ALUSrc* multiplexer to determine $SrcB$. The ALU adds $SrcA$ and $SrcB$ to find the effective address. The data memory reads from this address. The *MemtoReg* multiplexer selects *ReadData*.

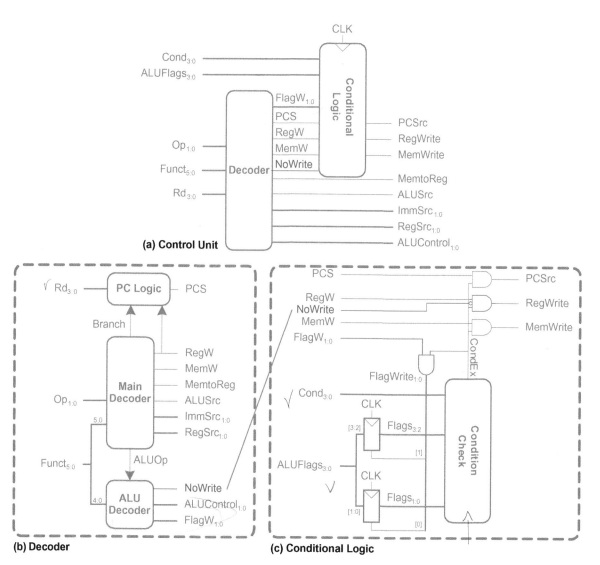

Figure 7.16 Controller modification for CMP

Finally, *Result* must set up at the register file before the next rising clock edge so that it can be properly written. Hence, the cycle time is:

$$T_{c1} = t_{pcq\_PC} + t_{mem} + t_{dec} + \max[t_{mux} + t_{RFread}, t_{ext} + t_{mux}]$$
$$+ t_{ALU} + t_{mem} + t_{mux} + t_{RFsetup} \qquad (7.2)$$

We use the subscript 1 to distinguish this cycle time from that of subsequent processor designs. In most implementation technologies, the

Table 7.4 **ALU Decoder truth table enhanced for** CMP

$ALUOp$	$Funct_{4:1}$ (cmd)	$Funct_0$ (S)	Notes	$ALUControl_{1:0}$	$FlagW_{1:0}$	$NoWrite$
0	X	X	Not DP	00	00	0
1	0100	0	ADD	00	00	0
		1			11	0
	0010	0	SUB	01	00	0
		1			11	0
	0000	0	AND	10	00	0
		1			10	0
	1100	0	ORR	11	00	0
		1			10	0
	1010	1	CMP	01	11	1

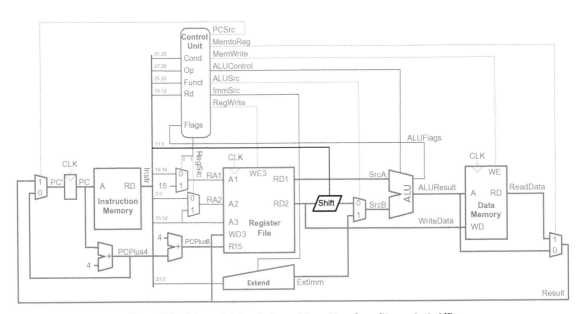

Figure 7.17 **Enhanced datapath for register addressing with constant shifts**

ALU, memory, and register file are substantially slower than other combinational blocks. Therefore, the cycle time simplifies to:

$$T_{c1} = t_{pcq\_PC} + 2t_{mem} + t_{dec} + t_{RFread} + t_{ALU} + 2t_{mux} + t_{RFsetup} \qquad (7.3)$$

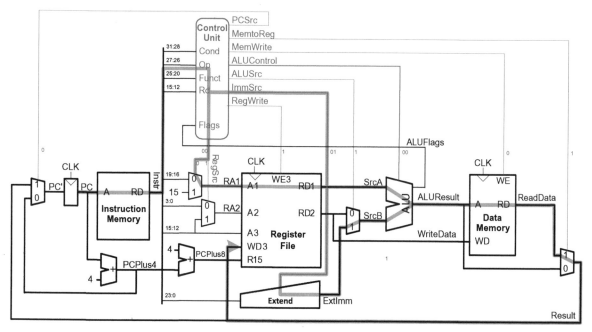

Figure 7.18 LDR **critical path**

The numerical values of these times will depend on the specific implementation technology.

Other instructions have shorter critical paths. For example, data-processing instructions do not need to access data memory. However, we are disciplining ourselves to synchronous sequential design, so the clock period is constant and must be long enough to accommodate the slowest instruction.

Example 7.4 SINGLE-CYCLE PROCESSOR PERFORMANCE

Ben Bitdiddle is contemplating building the single-cycle processor in a 16-nm CMOS manufacturing process. He has determined that the logic elements have the delays given in Table 7.5. Help him compute the execution time for a program with 100 billion instructions.

Solution: According to Equation 7.3, the cycle time of the single-cycle processor is $T_{c1} = 40 + 2(200) + 70 + 100 + 120 + 2(25) + 60 = 840$ ps. According to Equation 7.1, the total execution time is $T_1 = (100 \times 10^9$ instruction) (1 cycle/instruction) $(840 \times 10^{-12}$ s/cycle) = 84 seconds.

Table 7.5 Delay of circuit elements

Element	Parameter	Delay (ps)
Register clk-to-Q	t_{pcq}	40
Register setup	t_{setup}	50
Multiplexer	t_{mux}	25
ALU	t_{ALU}	120
Decoder	t_{dec}	70
Memory read	t_{mem}	200
Register file read	t_{RFread}	100
Register file setup	$t_{RFsetup}$	60

7.4 MULTICYCLE PROCESSOR

The single-cycle processor has three notable weaknesses. First, it requires separate memories for instructions and data, whereas most processors only have a single external memory holding both instructions and data. Second, it requires a clock cycle long enough to support the slowest instruction (LDR), even though most instructions could be faster. Finally, it requires three adders (one in the ALU and two for the PC logic); adders are relatively expensive circuits, especially if they must be fast.

The multicycle processor addresses these weaknesses by breaking an instruction into multiple shorter steps. In each short step, the processor can read or write the memory or register file or use the ALU. The instruction is read in one step and data can be read or written in a later step, so the processor can use a single memory for both. Different instructions use different numbers of steps, so simpler instructions can complete faster than more complex ones. And the processor needs only one adder, which is reused for different purposes on different steps.

We design a multicycle processor following the same procedure we used for the single-cycle processor. First, we construct a datapath by connecting the architectural state elements and memories with combinational logic. But, this time, we also add nonarchitectural state elements to hold intermediate results between the steps. Then, we design the controller. The controller produces different signals on different steps during execution of a single instruction, so now it is a finite state machine rather than combinational logic. Finally, we analyze the performance of the multicycle processor and compare it with the single-cycle processor.

7.4.1 Multicycle Datapath

Again, we begin our design with the memory and architectural state of the processor, as shown in Figure 7.19. In the single-cycle design, we used separate instruction and data memories because we needed to read the instruction memory and read or write the data memory all in one cycle. Now, we choose to use a combined memory for both instructions and data. This is more realistic, and it is feasible because we can read the instruction in one cycle, then read or write the data in a separate cycle. The PC and register file remain unchanged. As with the single-cycle processor, we gradually build the datapath by adding components to handle each step of each instruction.

The PC contains the address of the instruction to execute. The first step is to read this instruction from instruction memory. Figure 7.20 shows that the PC is simply connected to the address input of the memory. The instruction is read and stored in a new nonarchitectural instruction register (IR) so that it is available for future cycles. The IR receives an enable signal, called *IRWrite*, which is asserted when the IR should be loaded with a new instruction.

LDR

As we did with the single-cycle processor, we first work out the datapath connections for the LDR instruction. After fetching LDR, the next step is

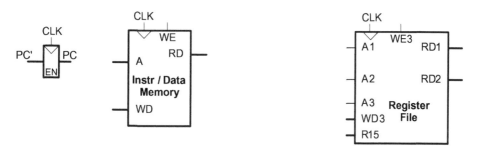

Figure 7.19 State elements with unified instruction/data memory

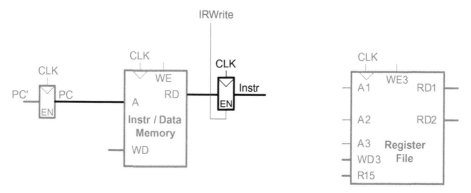

Figure 7.20 Fetch instruction from memory

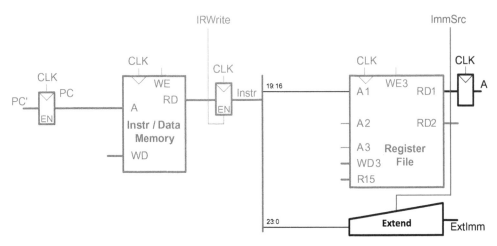

Figure 7.21 Read one source from register file and extend the second source from the immediate field

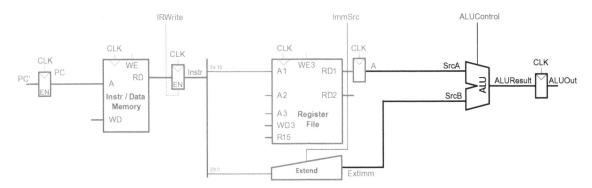

Figure 7.22 Add base address to offset

to read the source register containing the base address. This register is specified in the *Rn* field, *Instr*$_{19:16}$. These bits of the instruction are connected to address input *A1* of the register file, as shown in Figure 7.21. The register file reads the register into *RD1*. This value is stored in another nonarchitectural register, *A*.

The LDR instruction also requires a 12-bit offset, found in the immediate field of the instruction, *Instr*$_{11:0}$, which must be zero-extended to 32 bits, as shown in Figure 7.21. As in the single-cycle processor, the Extend block takes an *ImmSrc* control signal to specify an 8-, 12-, or 24-bit immediate to extend for various types of instructions. The 32-bit extended immediate is called *ExtImm*. To be consistent, we might store *ExtImm* in another nonarchitectural register. However, *ExtImm* is a combinational function of *Instr* and will not change while the current instruction is being processed, so there is no need to dedicate a register to hold the constant value.

The address of the load is the sum of the base address and offset. We use an ALU to compute this sum, as shown in Figure 7.22. *ALUControl* should be set to 00 to perform the addition. *ALUResult* is stored in a non-architectural register called *ALUOut*.

The next step is to load the data from the calculated address in the memory. We add a multiplexer in front of the memory to choose the memory address, *Adr*, from either the PC or *ALUOut* based on the *AdrSrc* select, as shown in Figure 7.23. The data read from memory is stored in another nonarchitectural register, called *Data*. Note that the address multiplexer permits us to reuse the memory during the LDR instruction. On a first step, the address is taken from the PC to fetch the instruction. On a later step, the address is taken from *ALUOut* to load the data. Hence, *AdrSrc* must have different values on different steps. In Section 7.4.2, we develop the FSM controller that generates these sequences of control signals.

Finally, the data is written back to the register file, as shown in Figure 7.24. The destination register is specified by the *Rd* field of the instruction, *Instr*$_{15:12}$. The result comes from the *Data* register. Instead of

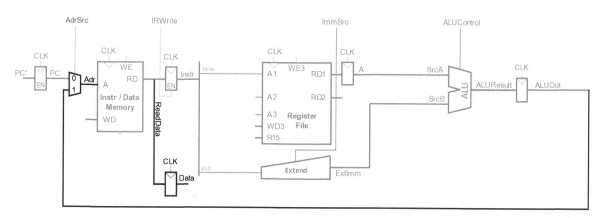

Figure 7.23 Load data from memory

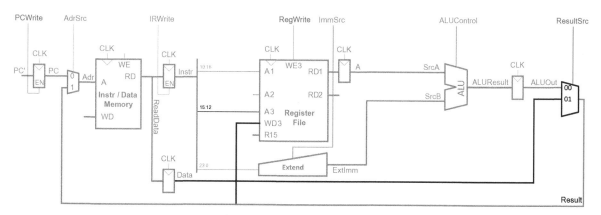

Figure 7.24 Write data back to register file

connecting the *Data* register directly to the register file *WD3* write port, let us add a multiplexer on the *Result* bus to choose either *ALUOut* or *Data* before feeding *Result* back to the register file write port. This will be helpful because other instructions will need to write a result from the ALU. The *RegWrite* signal is 1 to indicate that the register file should be updated.

While all this is happening, the processor must update the program counter by adding 4 to the old *PC*. In the single-cycle processor, a separate adder was needed. In the multicycle processor, we can use the existing ALU during the fetch step because it is not busy. To do so, we must insert source multiplexers to choose *PC* and the constant 4 as ALU inputs, as shown in Figure 7.25. A multiplexer controlled by *ALUSrcA* chooses either *PC* or register *A* as *SrcA*. Another multiplexer chooses either 4 or *ExtImm* as *SrcB*. To update the PC, the ALU adds *SrcA* (PC) to *SrcB* (4), and the result is written into the program counter. The *ResultSrc* multiplexer chooses this sum from *ALUResult* rather than *ALUOut*; this requires a third input. The *PCWrite* control signal enables the PC to be written only on certain cycles.

Again, we face the ARM architecture idiosyncrasy that reading R15 returns *PC* + 8 and writing R15 updates the PC. First, consider R15 reads. We already computed *PC* + 4 during the fetch step, and the sum is available in the PC register. Thus, during the second step, we obtain *PC* + 8 by adding four to the updated PC using the ALU. *ALUResult* is selected as the *Result* and fed to the R15 input port of the register file. Figure 7.26 shows the completed LDR datapath with this new connection. Thus, a read of R15, which also occurs during the second step, produces the value *PC* + 8 on the read data output of the register file. Writes to R15 require writing the PC register instead of the register file. Thus, in the final step of the instruction, *Result* must be routed to the PC register (instead of to the register file) and *PCWrite* must be asserted (instead of *RegWrite*). The datapath already accommodates this, so no datapath changes are required.

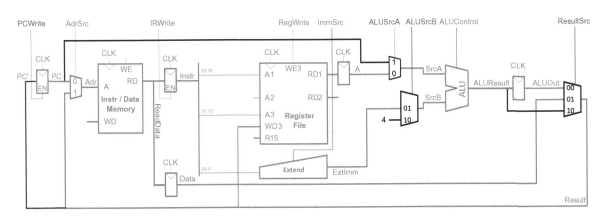

Figure 7.25 Increment PC by 4

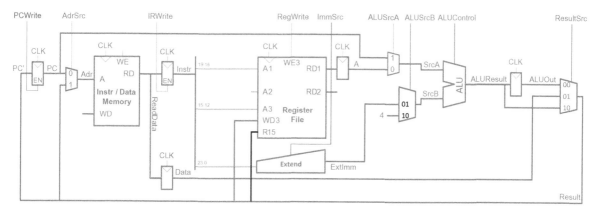

Figure 7.26 Handle R15 reads and writes

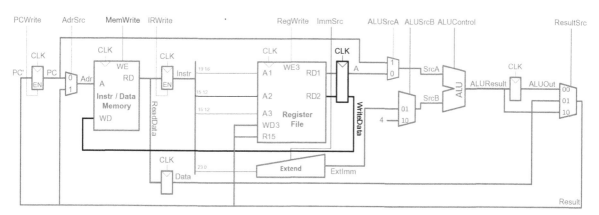

Figure 7.27 Enhanced datapath for STR **instruction**

STR

Next, let us extend the datapath to handle the STR instruction. Like LDR, STR reads a base address from port 1 of the register file and extends the immediate. The ALU adds the base address to the immediate to find the memory address. All of these functions are already supported by existing hardware in the datapath.

The only new feature of STR is that we must read a second register from the register file and write it into the memory, as shown in Figure 7.27. The register is specified in the *Rd* field of the instruction, *Instr*$_{15:12}$, which is connected to the second port of the register file. When the register is read, it is stored in a nonarchitectural register, *WriteData*. On the next step, it is sent to the write data port (*WD*) of the data memory to be written.

The memory receives the *MemWrite* control signal to indicate that the write should occur.

Data-Processing Instructions with Immediate Addressing

Data-processing instructions with immediate addressing read the first source from *Rn* and extend the second source from an 8-bit immediate. They operate on these two sources and then write the result back to the register file. The datapath already contains all the connections necessary for these steps. The ALU uses the *ALUControl* signal to determine the type of data-processing instruction to execute. The *ALUFlags* are sent back to the controller to update the *Status* register.

Data-Processing Instructions with Register Addressing

Data-processing instructions with register addressing select the second source from the register file. The register is specified in the *Rm* field, $Instr_{3:0}$, so we insert a multiplexer to choose this field as *RA2* for the register file. We also extend the *SrcB* multiplexer to accept the value read from the register file, as shown in Figure 7.28. Otherwise, the behavior is the same as for data-processing instructions with immediate addressing.

B

The branch instruction B reads $PC + 8$ and a 24-bit immediate, sums them, and adds the result to the PC. Recall from Section 6.4.6 that a read to R15 returns $PC + 8$, so we add a multiplexer to choose R15 as *RA1* for the register file, as shown in Figure 7.29. The rest of the hardware to perform the addition and write the PC is already present in the datapath.

This completes the design of the multicycle datapath. The design process is much like that of the single-cycle processor in that hardware is systematically connected between the state elements to handle each instruction. The main difference is that the instruction is executed in several steps. Nonarchitectural registers are inserted to hold the results

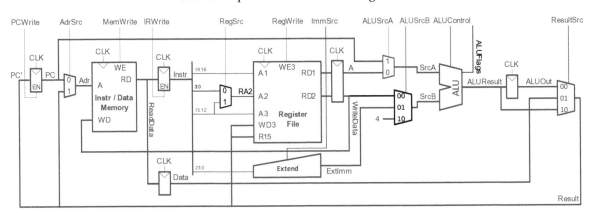

Figure 7.28 Enhanced datapath for data-processing instructions with register addressing

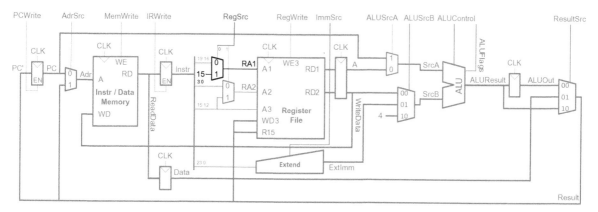

Figure 7.29 Enhanced datapath for the B instruction

of each step. In this way, the memory can be shared for instructions and data and the ALU can be reused several times, reducing hardware costs. In the next section, we develop an FSM controller to deliver the appropriate sequence of control signals to the datapath on each step of each instruction.

7.4.2 Multicycle Control

As in the single-cycle processor, the control unit computes the control signals based on the *cond*, *op*, and *funct* fields of the instruction ($Instr_{31:28}$, $Instr_{27:26}$, and $Instr_{25:20}$) as well as the flags and whether the destination register is the PC. The controller also stores the current status flags and updates them appropriately. Figure 7.30 shows the entire multicycle processor with the control unit attached to the datapath. The datapath is shown in black and the control unit is shown in blue.

As in the single-cycle processor, the control unit is partitioned into Decoder and Conditional Logic blocks, as shown in Figure 7.31(a). The Decoder is decomposed further in Figure 7.31(b). The combinational Main Decoder of the single-cycle processor is replaced with a Main FSM in the multicycle processor to produce a sequence of control signals on the appropriate cycles. We design the Main FSM as a Moore machine so that the outputs are only a function of the current state. However, we will see during the state machine design that *ImmSrc* and *RegSrc* are a function of *Op* rather than the current state, so we also use a small Instruction Decoder to compute these signals, as will be described in Table 7.6. The ALU Decoder and PC Logic are identical to those in the single-cycle processor. The Conditional Logic is almost identical to that of the single-cycle processor. We add a *NextPC* signal to force a write to the PC when we compute $PC + 4$. We also delay *CondEx* by one cycle

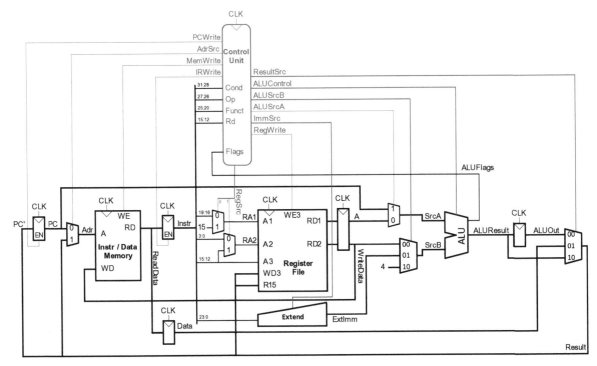

Figure 7.30 Complete multicycle processor

before sending it to *PCWrite*, *RegWrite*, and *MemWrite* so that updated condition flags are not seen until the end of an instruction. The remainder of this section develops the state transition diagram for the Main FSM.

The Main FSM produces multiplexer select, register enable, and memory write enable signals for the datapath. To keep the following state transition diagrams readable, only the relevant control signals are listed. Select signals are listed only when their value matters; otherwise, they are don't care. Enable signals (*RegW*, *MemW*, *IRWrite*, and *NextPC*) are listed only when they are asserted; otherwise, they are 0.

The first step for any instruction is to fetch the instruction from memory at the address held in the PC and to increment the PC to the next instruction. The FSM enters this Fetch state on reset. The control signals are shown in Figure 7.32. The data flow on this step is shown in Figure 7.33, with the instruction fetch highlighted in blue and the PC increment highlighted in gray. To read memory, *AdrSrc* = 0, so the address is taken from the PC. *IRWrite* is asserted to write the instruction into the instruction register, *IR*. Meanwhile, the PC should be incremented by 4 to point to the next instruction. Because the ALU is not being used for anything else, the processor can

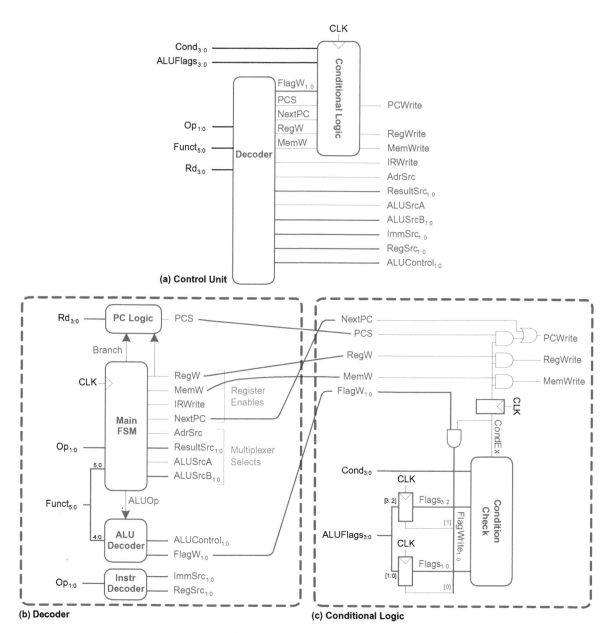

Figure 7.31 Multicycle control unit

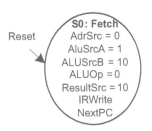

Figure 7.32 Fetch

Table 7.6 Instr Decoder logic for *RegSrc* and *ImmSrc*

Instruction	*Op*	*Funct$_5$*	*Funct$_0$*	*RegSrc$_1$*	*RegSrc$_0$*	*ImmSrc$_{1:0}$*
LDR	01	X	1	X	0	01
STR	01	X	0	1	0	01
DP immediate	00	1	X	X	0	00
DP register	00	0	X	0	0	00
B	10	X	X	X	1	10

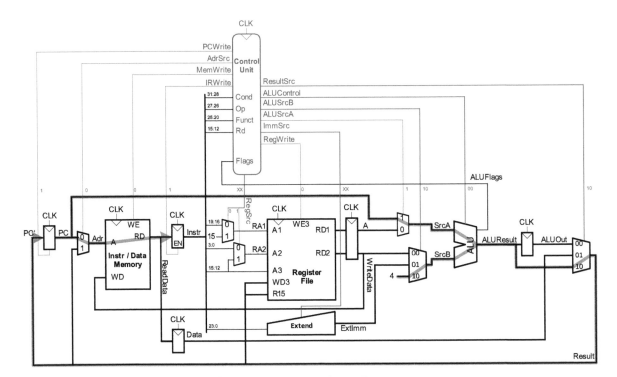

Figure 7.33 Data flow during the fetch step

use it to compute $PC + 4$ at the same time that it fetches the instruction. $ALUSrcA = 1$, so $SrcA$ comes from the PC. $ALUSrcB = 10$, so $SrcB$ is the constant 4. $ALUOp = 0$, so the ALU produces $ALUControl = 00$ to make the ALU add. To update the PC with $PC + 4$, $ResultSrc = 10$ to choose the $ALUResult$ and $NextPC = 1$ to enable $PCWrite$.

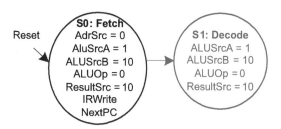

Figure 7.34 **Decode**

The second step is to read the register file and/or immediate and decode the instructions. The registers and immediate are selected based on *RegSrc* and *ImmSrc*, which are computed by the Instr Decoder based on *Instr*. $RegSrc_0$ should be 1 for branches to read $PC + 8$ as *SrcA*. $RegSrc_1$ should be 1 for stores to read the store value as *SrcB*. *ImmSrc* should be 00 for data-processing instructions to select an 8-bit immediate, 01 for loads and stores to select a 12-bit immediate, and 10 for branches to select a 24-bit immediate. Because the multicycle FSM is a Moore machine whose outputs depend only on the current state, the FSM cannot directly produce these selects that depend on *Instr*. The FSM could be organized as a Mealy machine whose outputs depend on *Instr* as well as the state, but this would be messy. Instead, we choose the simplest solution, which is to make these selects combinational functions of *Instr*, as given in Table 7.6. Taking advantage of don't cares, the Instr Decoder logic can be simplified to:

$RegSrc_1 = (Op == 01)$

$RegSrc_0 = (Op == 10)$

$ImmSrc_{1:0} = Op$

Meanwhile, the ALU is reused to compute $PC + 8$ by adding 4 more to the PC that was incremented in the Fetch step. Control signals are applied to select *PC* as the first ALU input ($ALUSrcA = 1$) and 4 as the second input ($ALUSrcB = 10$) and to perform addition ($ALUOp = 0$). This sum is selected as the *Result* ($ResultSrc = 10$) and provided to the *R15* input of the register file so that R15 reads as $PC + 8$. The FSM Decode step is shown in Figure 7.34 and the data flow is shown in Figure 7.35, highlighting the R15 computation and the register file read.

Now the FSM proceeds to one of several possible states, depending on *Op* and *Funct* that are examined during the Decode step. If the instruction is a memory load or store (LDR or STR, $Op = 01$), then the multicycle processor computes the address by adding the base address to the zero-extended offset. This requires $ALUSrcA = 0$ to select the base address from the register file and $ALUSrcB = 01$ to select *ExtImm*. $ALUOp = 0$ so the ALU adds. The effective address is stored in the

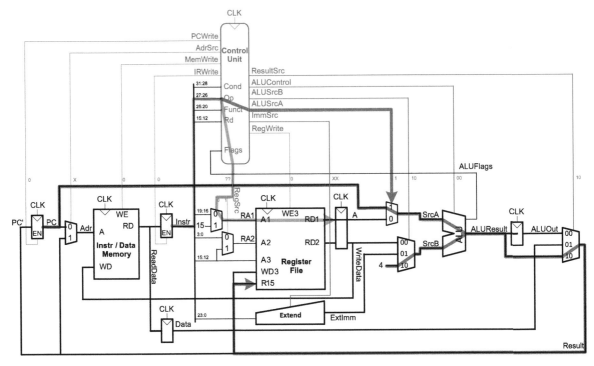

Figure 7.35 Data flow during the Decode step

ALUOut register for use on the next step. The FSM MemAdr state is shown in Figure 7.36 and the data flow is highlighted in Figure 7.37.

If the instruction is LDR ($Funct_0 = 1$), then the multicycle processor must next read data from the memory and write it to the register file. These two steps are shown in Figure 7.38. To read from the memory, $ResultSrc = 00$ and $AdrSrc = 1$ to select the memory address that was just computed and saved in *ALUOut*. This address in memory is read and saved in the *Data* register during the MemRead step. Then, in the memory writeback step MemWB, *Data* is written to the register file. $ResultSrc = 01$ to choose *Result* from *Data* and *RegW* is asserted to write the register file, completing the LDR instruction. Finally, the FSM returns to the Fetch state to start the next instruction. For these and subsequent steps, try to visualize the data flow on your own.

From the MemAdr state, if the instruction is STR ($Funct_0 = 0$), the data read from the second port of the register file is simply written to memory. In this MemWrite state, $ResultSrc = 00$ and $AdrSrc = 1$ to select the address computed in the MemAdr state and saved in *ALUOut*. *MemW* is asserted to write the memory. Again, the FSM returns to the Fetch state. The state is shown in Figure 7.39.

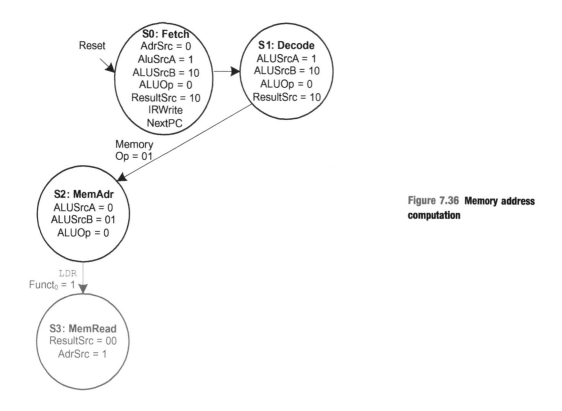

Figure 7.36 **Memory address computation**

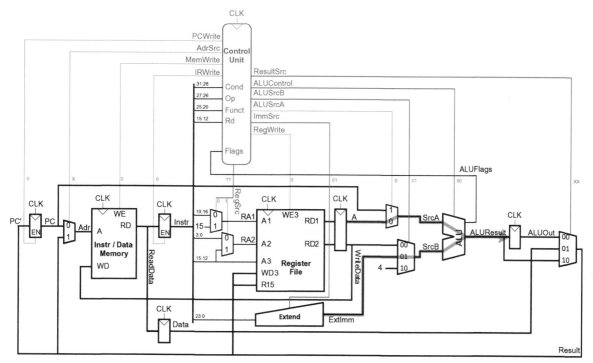

Figure 7.37 **Data flow during memory address computation**

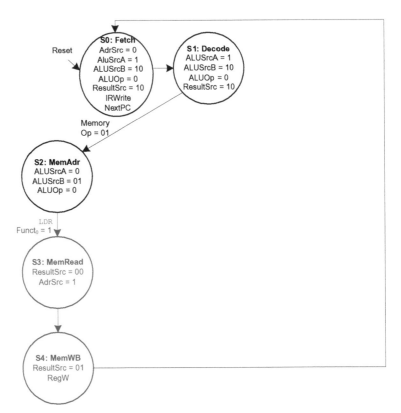

Figure 7.38 Memory read

For data-processing instructions $(Op = 00)$, the multicycle processor must calculate the result using the ALU and write that result to the register file. The first source always comes from the register $(ALUSrcA = 0)$. $ALUOp = 1$ so the ALU Decoder chooses the appropriate $ALUControl$ for the specific instruction based on *cmd* $(Funct_{4:1})$. The second source comes from the register file for register instructions $(ALUSrcB = 00)$ or from *ExtImm* for immediate instructions $(ALUSrcB = 01)$. Thus, the FSM needs ExecuteR and ExecuteI states to cover these two possibilities. In either case, the data-processing instruction advances to the ALU Write-back state (ALUWB), in which the result is selected from $ALUOut$ $(ResultSrc = 00)$ and written to the register file $(RegW = 1)$. All of these states are shown in Figure 7.40.

For a branch instruction, the processor must calculate the destination address $(PC + 8 + \text{offset})$ and write it to the PC. During the Decode state, $PC + 8$ was already computed and read from the register file onto *RD1*. Therefore, during the Branch state, the controller uses $ALUSrcA = 0$ to choose R15 $(PC + 8)$, $ALUSrcB = 01$ to choose *ExtImm*, and $ALUOp = 0$

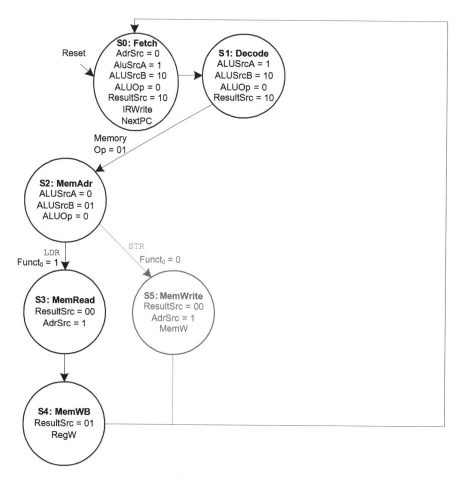

Figure 7.39 Memory write

to add. The *Result* multiplexer chooses *ALUResult* (*ResultSrc* = 10). *Branch* is asserted to write the result to the PC.

Putting these steps together, Figure 7.41 shows the complete Main FSM state transition diagram for the multicycle processor. The function of each state is summarized below the figure. Converting the diagram to hardware is a straightforward but tedious task using the techniques of Chapter 3. Better yet, the FSM can be coded in an HDL and synthesized using the techniques of Chapter 4.

7.4.3 Performance Analysis

The execution time of an instruction depends on both the number of cycles it uses and the cycle time. Whereas the single-cycle processor

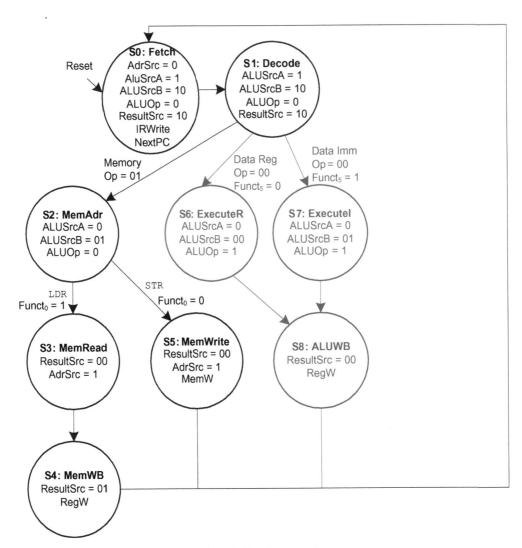

Figure 7.40 Data-processing

performed all instructions in one cycle, the multicycle processor uses varying numbers of cycles for the various instructions. However, the multicycle processor does less work in a single cycle and, thus, has a shorter cycle time.

The multicycle processor requires three cycles for branches, four for data-processing instructions and stores, and five for loads. The CPI depends on the relative likelihood that each instruction is used.

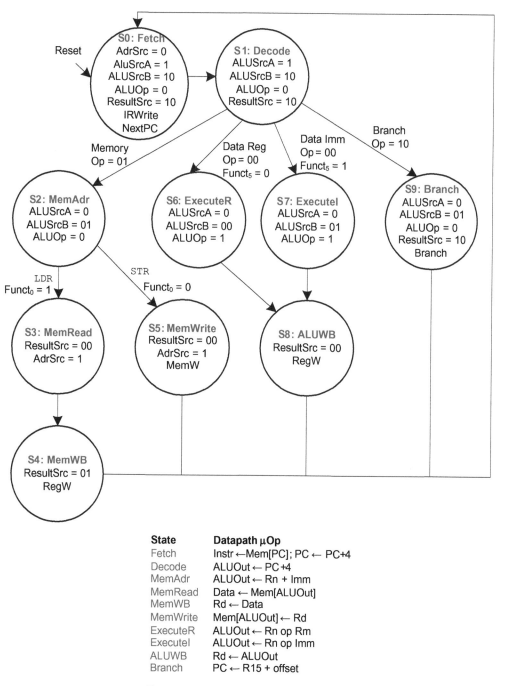

State	Datapath μOp
Fetch	Instr ←Mem[PC]; PC ← PC+4
Decode	ALUOut ← PC+4
MemAdr	ALUOut ← Rn + Imm
MemRead	Data ← Mem[ALUOut]
MemWB	Rd ← Data
MemWrite	Mem[ALUOut] ← Rd
ExecuteR	ALUOut ← Rn op Rm
ExecuteI	ALUOut ← Rn op Imm
ALUWB	Rd ← ALUOut
Branch	PC ← R15 + offset

Figure 7.41 Complete multicycle control FSM

Example 7.5 MULTICYCLE PROCESSOR CPI

The SPECINT2000 benchmark consists of approximately 25% loads, 10% stores, 13% branches, and 52% data-processing instructions.[2] Determine the average CPI for this benchmark.

Solution: The average CPI is the sum over each instruction of the CPI for that instruction multiplied by the fraction of the time that instruction is used. For this benchmark, average CPI $= (0.13)(3) + (0.52 + 0.10)(4) + (0.25)(5) = 4.12$. This is better than the worst-case CPI of 5, which would be required if all instructions took the same time.

Recall that we designed the multicycle processor so that each cycle involved one ALU operation, memory access, or register file access. Let us assume that the register file is faster than the memory and that writing memory is faster than reading memory. Examining the datapath reveals two possible critical paths that would limit the cycle time:

1. From the PC through the *SrcA* multiplexer, ALU, and result multiplexer to the *R15* port of the register file to the *A* register

2. From *ALUOut* through the *Result* and *Adr* muxes to read memory into the *Data* register

$$T_{c2} = t_{pcq} + 2t_{mux} + \max[t_{ALU} + t_{mux}, t_{mem}] + t_{setup} \qquad (7.4)$$

The numerical values of these times will depend on the specific implementation technology.

Example 7.6 PROCESSOR PERFORMANCE COMPARISON

Ben Bitdiddle is wondering whether the multicycle processor would be faster than the single-cycle processor. For both designs, he plans on using the 16-nm CMOS manufacturing process with the delays given in Table 7.5. Help him compare each processor's execution time for 100 billion instructions from the SPECINT2000 benchmark (see Example 7.5).

Solution: According to Equation 7.4, the cycle time of the multicycle processor is $T_{c2} = 40 + 2(25) + 200 + 50 = 340$ ps. Using the CPI of 4.12 from Example 7.5, the total execution time is $T_2 = (100 \times 10^9$ instructions)(4.12 cycles/instruction) $(340 \times 10^{-12}$ s/cycle) $= 140$ seconds. According to Example 7.4, the single-cycle processor had a total execution time of 84 seconds.

[2] Data from Patterson and Hennessy, *Computer Organization and Design*, 4th Edition, Morgan Kaufmann, 2011.

One of the original motivations for building a multicycle processor was to avoid making all instructions take as long as the slowest one. Unfortunately, this example shows that the multicycle processor is slower than the single-cycle processor given the assumptions of CPI and circuit element delays. The fundamental problem is that even though the slowest instruction, LDR, was broken into five steps, the multicycle processor cycle time was not nearly improved five-fold. This is partly because not all of the steps are exactly the same length, and partly because the 90-ps sequencing overhead of the register clock-to-Q and setup time must now be paid on every step, not just once for the entire instruction. In general, engineers have learned that it is difficult to exploit the fact that some computations are faster than others unless the differences are large.

Compared with the single-cycle processor, the multicycle processor is likely to be less expensive because it shares a single memory for instructions and data and because it eliminates two adders. It does, however, require five nonarchitectural registers and additional multiplexers.

7.5 PIPELINED PROCESSOR

Pipelining, introduced in Section 3.6, is a powerful way to improve the throughput of a digital system. We design a pipelined processor by subdividing the single-cycle processor into five pipeline stages. Thus, five instructions can execute simultaneously, one in each stage. Because each stage has only one-fifth of the entire logic, the clock frequency is almost five times faster. Hence, the latency of each instruction is ideally unchanged, but the throughput is ideally five-times better. Microprocessors execute millions or billions of instructions per second, so throughput is more important than latency. Pipelining introduces some overhead, so the throughput will not be quite as high as we might ideally desire, but pipelining nevertheless gives such great advantage for so little cost that all modern high-performance microprocessors are pipelined.

Reading and writing the memory and register file and using the ALU typically constitute the biggest delays in the processor. We choose five pipeline stages so that each stage involves exactly one of these slow steps. Specifically, we call the five stages *Fetch*, *Decode*, *Execute*, *Memory*, and *Writeback*. They are similar to the five steps that the multicycle processor used to perform LDR. In the *Fetch* stage, the processor reads the instruction from instruction memory. In the *Decode* stage, the processor reads the source operands from the register file and decodes the instruction to produce the control signals. In the *Execute* stage, the processor performs a computation with the ALU. In the *Memory* stage, the processor reads or writes data memory. Finally, in the *Writeback* stage, the processor writes the result to the register file, when applicable.

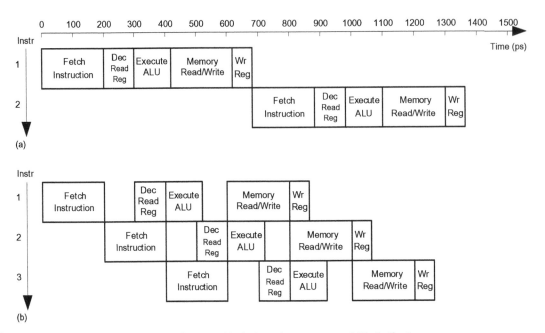

Figure 7.42 Timing diagrams: (a) single-cycle processor and (b) pipelined processor

Figure 7.42 shows a timing diagram comparing the single-cycle and pipelined processors. Time is on the horizontal axis, and instructions are on the vertical axis. The diagram assumes the logic element delays from Table 7.5 but ignores the delays of multiplexers and registers. In the single-cycle processor (Figure 7.42(a)), the first instruction is read from memory at time 0; next, the operands are read from the register file; and, then, the ALU executes the necessary computation. Finally, the data memory may be accessed, and the result is written back to the register file by 680 ps. The second instruction begins when the first completes. Hence, in this diagram, the single-cycle processor has an instruction latency of $200 + 100 + 120 + 200 + 60 = 680$ ps and a throughput of 1 instruction per 680 ps (1.47 billion instructions per second).

In the pipelined processor (Figure 7.42(b)), the length of a pipeline stage is set at 200 ps by the slowest stage, the memory access (in the Fetch or Memory stage). At time 0, the first instruction is fetched from memory. At 200 ps, the first instruction enters the Decode stage, and a second instruction is fetched. At 400 ps, the first instruction executes, the second instruction enters the Decode stage, and a third instruction is fetched. And so forth, until all the instructions complete. The instruction latency is $5 \times 200 = 1000$ ps. The throughput is 1 instruction per 200 ps (5 billion instructions per second). Because the stages are not perfectly balanced with equal amounts of logic, the latency is longer for the pipelined

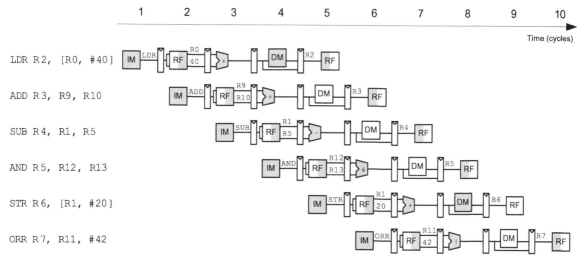

Figure 7.43 Abstract view of pipeline in operation

processor than for the single-cycle processor. Similarly, the throughput is not quite five-times as great for a five-stage pipeline as for the single-cycle processor. Nevertheless, the throughput advantage is substantial.

Figure 7.43 shows an abstracted view of the pipeline in operation in which each stage is represented pictorially. Each pipeline stage is represented with its major component—instruction memory (IM), register file (RF) read, ALU execution, data memory (DM), and register file write-back—to illustrate the flow of instructions through the pipeline. Reading across a row shows the clock cycles in which a particular instruction is in each stage. For example, the SUB instruction is fetched in cycle 3 and executed in cycle 5. Reading down a column shows what the various pipeline stages are doing on a particular cycle. For example, in cycle 6, the ORR instruction is being fetched from instruction memory, whereas R1 is being read from the register file, the ALU is computing R12 AND R13, the data memory is idle, and the register file is writing a sum to R3. Stages are shaded to indicate when they are used. For example, the data memory is used by LDR in cycle 4 and by STR in cycle 8. The instruction memory and ALU are used in every cycle. The register file is written by every instruction except STR. In the pipelined processor, the register file is written in the first part of a cycle and read in the second part, as suggested by the shading. This way, data can be written and read back within a single cycle.

A central challenge in pipelined systems is handling hazards that occur when the results of one instruction are needed by a subsequent instruction before the former instruction has completed. For example, if the ADD in Figure 7.43 used R2 rather than R10, a hazard would occur because the R2 register has not been written by the LDR by the time it is read by the ADD. After designing the pipelined datapath and control, this section explores *forwarding*, *stalls*, and *flushes* as methods to resolve hazards. Finally, this section revisits performance analysis considering sequencing overhead and the impact of hazards.

7.5.1 Pipelined Datapath

The pipelined datapath is formed by chopping the single-cycle datapath into five stages separated by pipeline registers.

Figure 7.44(a) shows the single-cycle datapath stretched out to leave room for the pipeline registers. Figure 7.44(b) shows the pipelined datapath formed by inserting four pipeline registers to separate the datapath into five stages. The stages and their boundaries are indicated in blue. Signals are given a suffix (F, D, E, M, or W) to indicate the stage in which they reside.

The register file is peculiar because it is read in the Decode stage and written in the Writeback stage. It is drawn in the Decode stage, but the write address and data come from the Writeback stage. This feedback will lead to pipeline hazards, which are discussed in Section 7.5.3. The register file in the pipelined processor writes on the falling edge of CLK so that it

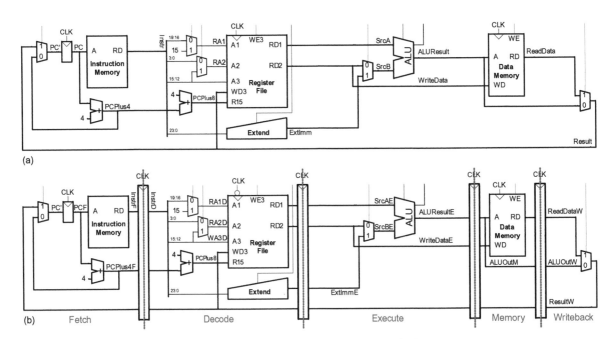

Figure 7.44 Datapaths: (a) single-cycle and (b) pipelined

can write a result in the first half of a cycle and read that result in the second half of the cycle for use in a subsequent instruction.

One of the subtle but critical issues in pipelining is that all signals associated with a particular instruction must advance through the pipeline in unison. Figure 7.44(b) has an error related to this issue. Can you find it?

The error is in the register file write logic, which should operate in the Writeback stage. The data value comes from *ResultW*, a Writeback stage signal. But the write address comes from $InstrD_{15:12}$ (also known as *WA3D*), which is a Decode stage signal. In the pipeline diagram of Figure 7.43, during cycle 5, the result of the LDR instruction would be incorrectly written to R5 rather than R2.

Figure 7.45 shows a corrected datapath, with the modification in black. The *WA3* signal is now pipelined along through the Execution, Memory, and Writeback stages, so it remains in sync with the rest of the instruction. *WA3W* and *ResultW* are fed back together to the register file in the Writeback stage.

The astute reader may note that the *PC'* logic is also problematic, because it might be updated with a Fetch or a Writeback stage signal (*PCPlus4F* or *ResultW*). This control hazard will be fixed in Section 7.5.3.

Figure 7.46 shows another optimization to save a 32-bit adder and register in the PC logic. Observe in Figure 7.45 that each time the program counter is incremented, *PCPlus4F* is simultaneously written to the PC and the pipeline register between the Fetch and Decode stages. Moreover, on the subsequent cycle, the value in both of these registers is incremented by 4 again. Thus, *PCPlus4F* for the instruction in the Fetch stage is logically equivalent to *PCPlus8D* for the instruction in the Decode stage. Sending this signal ahead saves the pipeline register and second adder.[3]

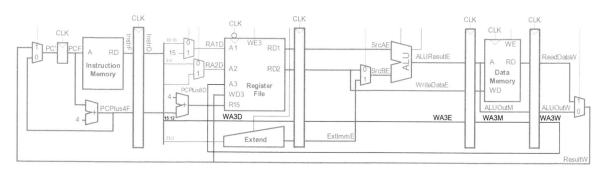

Figure 7.45 Corrected pipelined datapath

---

[3] There is a potential problem with this simplification when the PC is written with *ResultW* rather than *PCPlus4F*. However, this case is handled in Section 7.5.3 by flushing the pipeline, so *PCPlus8D* becomes a don't care and the pipeline still operates correctly.

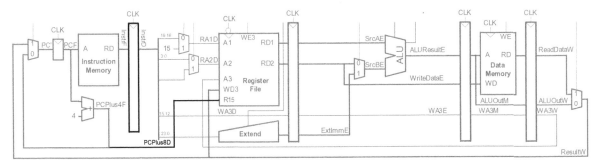

Figure 7.46 Optimized PC logic eliminating a register and adder

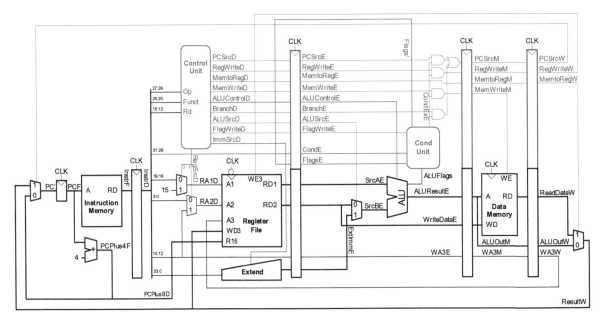

Figure 7.47 Pipelined processor with control

7.5.2 Pipelined Control

The pipelined processor takes the same control signals as the single-cycle processor and therefore uses the same control unit. The control unit examines the *Op* and *Funct* fields of the instruction in the Decode stage to produce the control signals, as was described in Section 7.3.2. These control signals must be pipelined along with the data so that they remain synchronized with the instruction. The control unit also examines the *Rd* field to handle writes to R15 (PC).

The entire pipelined processor with control is shown in Figure 7.47. *RegWrite* must be pipelined into the Writeback stage before it feeds back to the register file, just as *WA3* was pipelined in Figure 7.45.

7.5.3 Hazards

In a pipelined system, multiple instructions are handled concurrently. When one instruction is *dependent* on the results of another that has not yet completed, a *hazard* occurs.

The register file can be read and written in the same cycle. The write takes place during the first half of the cycle and the read takes place during the second half of the cycle, so a register can be written and read back in the same cycle without introducing a hazard.

Figure 7.48 illustrates hazards that occur when one instruction writes a register (R1) and subsequent instructions read this register. This is called a *read after write* (RAW) *hazard*. The ADD instruction writes a result into R1 in the first half of cycle 5. However, the AND instruction reads R1 on cycle 3, obtaining the wrong value. The ORR instruction reads R1 on cycle 4, again obtaining the wrong value. The SUB instruction reads R1 in the second half of cycle 5, obtaining the correct value, which was written in the first half of cycle 5. Subsequent instructions also read the correct value of R1. The diagram shows that hazards may occur in this pipeline when an instruction writes a register and either of the two subsequent instructions reads that register. Without special treatment, the pipeline will compute the wrong result.

A software solution would be to require the programmer or compiler to insert NOP instructions between the ADD and AND instructions so that the dependent instruction does not read the result (R1) until it is available in the register file, as shown in Figure 7.49. Such a *software interlock* complicates programming as well as degrading performance, so it is not ideal.

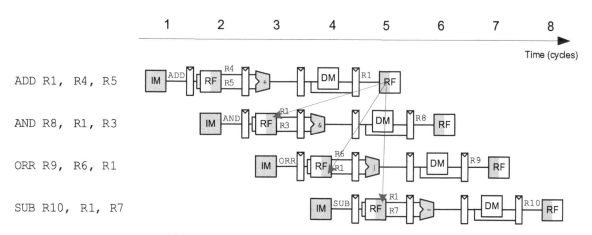

Figure 7.48 Abstract pipeline diagram illustrating hazards

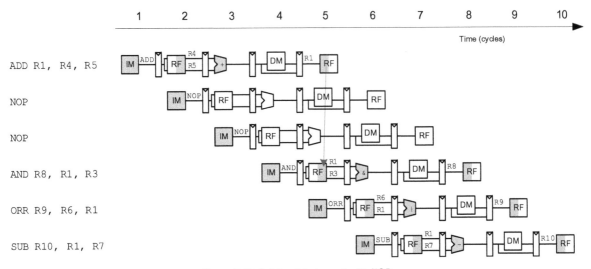

Figure 7.49 Solving data hazard with NOP

On closer inspection, observe from Figure 7.48 that the sum from the ADD instruction is computed by the ALU in cycle 3 and is not strictly needed by the AND instruction until the ALU uses it in cycle 4. In principle, we should be able to forward the result from one instruction to the next to resolve the RAW hazard without waiting for the result to appear in the register file and without slowing down the pipeline. In other situations explored later in this section, we may have to stall the pipeline to give time for a result to be produced before the subsequent instruction uses the result. In any event, something must be done to solve hazards so that the program executes correctly despite the pipelining.

Hazards are classified as data hazards or control hazards. A *data hazard* occurs when an instruction tries to read a register that has not yet been written back by a previous instruction. A *control hazard* occurs when the decision of what instruction to fetch next has not been made by the time the fetch takes place. In the remainder of this section, we enhance the pipelined processor with a Hazard Unit that detects hazards and handles them appropriately, so that the processor executes the program correctly.

Solving Data Hazards with Forwarding

Some data hazards can be solved by *forwarding* (also called *bypassing*) a result from the Memory or Writeback stage to a dependent instruction in

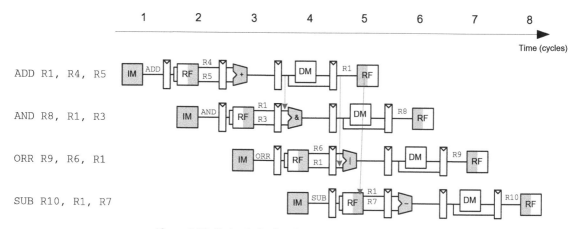

Figure 7.50 Abstract pipeline diagram illustrating forwarding

the Execute stage. This requires adding multiplexers in front of the ALU to select the operand from either the register file or the Memory or Writeback stage. Figure 7.50 illustrates this principle. In cycle 4, R1 is forwarded from the Memory stage of the ADD instruction to the Execute stage of the dependent AND instruction. In cycle 5, R1 is forwarded from the Writeback stage of the ADD instruction to the Execute stage of the dependent ORR instruction.

Forwarding is necessary when an instruction in the Execute stage has a source register matching the destination register of an instruction in the Memory or Writeback stage. Figure 7.51 modifies the pipelined processor to support forwarding. It adds a *Hazard Unit* and two *forwarding multiplexers*. The Hazard Unit receives four match signals from the datapath (abbreviated to *Match* in Figure 7.51) that indicate whether the source registers in the Execute stage match the destination registers in the Memory and Execute stages:

```
Match_1E_M = (RA1E == WA3M)
Match_1E_W = (RA1E == WA3W)
Match_2E_M = (RA2E == WA3M)
Match_2E_W = (RA2E == WA3W)
```

The Hazard Unit also receives the *RegWrite* signals from the Memory and Writeback stages to know whether the destination register will actually be written (e.g., the STR and B instructions do not write results to the register file and, hence, do not need to have their results forwarded).

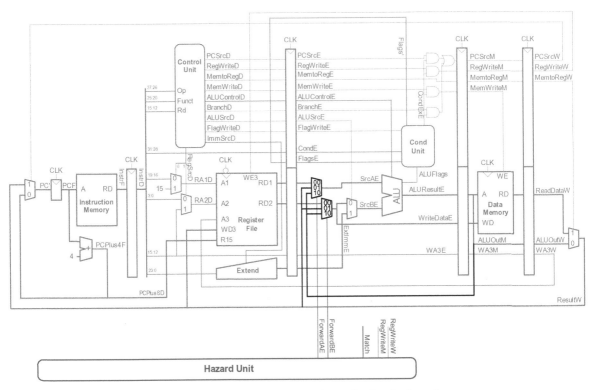

Figure 7.51 Pipelined processor with forwarding to solve hazards

Note that these signals are *connected by name*. In other words, rather than cluttering up the diagram with long wires running from the control signals at the top to the Hazard Unit at the bottom, the connections are indicated by a short stub of wire labeled with the control signal name to which it is connected. The Match signal logic and pipeline registers for *RA1E* and *RA2E* are also left out to limit clutter.

The Hazard Unit computes control signals for the forwarding multiplexers to choose operands from the register file or from the results in the Memory or Writeback stage (*ALUOutM* or *ResultW*). It should forward from a stage if that stage will write a destination register and the destination register matches the source register. If both the Memory and Writeback stages contain matching destination registers, then the Memory stage should have priority, because it contains the more recently executed instruction. In summary, the function of the forwarding logic for *SrcAE* is given here. The forwarding logic for *SrcBE* (*ForwardBE*) is identical except that it checks *Match_2E*.

```
if      (Match_1E_M • RegWriteM)   ForwardAE = 10;   // SrcAE = ALUOutM
else if (Match_1E_W • RegWriteW)   ForwardAE = 01;   // SrcAE = ResultW
else                               ForwardAE = 00;   // SrcAE from regfile
```

Solving Data Hazards with Stalls

Forwarding is sufficient to solve RAW data hazards when the result is computed in the Execute stage of an instruction, because its result can then be forwarded to the Execute stage of the next instruction. Unfortunately, the LDR instruction does not finish reading data until the end of the Memory stage, so its result cannot be forwarded to the Execute stage of the next instruction. We say that the LDR instruction has a *two-cycle latency*, because a dependent instruction cannot use its result until two cycles later. Figure 7.52 shows this problem. The LDR instruction receives data from memory at the end of cycle 4. But the AND instruction needs that data as a source operand at the beginning of cycle 4. There is no way to solve this hazard with forwarding.

The alternative solution is to *stall* the pipeline, holding up operation until the data is available. Figure 7.53 shows stalling the dependent instruction (AND) in the Decode stage. AND enters the Decode stage in cycle 3 and stalls there through cycle 4. The subsequent instruction (ORR) must remain in the Fetch stage during both cycles as well, because the Decode stage is full.

In cycle 5, the result can be forwarded from the Writeback stage of LDR to the Execute stage of AND. Also in cycle 5, source R1 of the ORR instruction is read directly from the register file, with no need for forwarding.

Note that the Execute stage is unused in cycle 4. Likewise, Memory is unused in cycle 5 and Writeback is unused in cycle 6. This unused stage propagating through the pipeline is called a *bubble*, and it behaves like

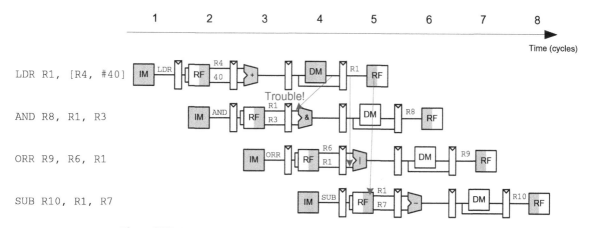

Figure 7.52 Abstract pipeline diagram illustrating trouble forwarding from LDR

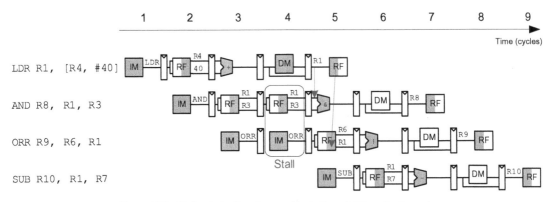

Figure 7.53 Abstract pipeline diagram illustrating stall to solve hazards

a NOP instruction. The bubble is introduced by zeroing out the Execute stage control signals during a Decode stall so that the bubble performs no action and changes no architectural state.

In summary, stalling a stage is performed by disabling the pipeline register, so that the contents do not change. When a stage is stalled, all previous stages must also be stalled, so that no subsequent instructions are lost. The pipeline register directly after the stalled stage must be cleared (flushed) to prevent bogus information from propagating forward. Stalls degrade performance, so they should be used only when necessary.

Figure 7.54 modifies the pipelined processor to add stalls for LDR data dependencies. The Hazard Unit examines the instruction in the Execute stage. If it is an LDR and its destination register (*WA3E*) matches either source operand of the instruction in the Decode stage (*RA1D* or *RA2D*), then that instruction must be stalled in the Decode stage until the source operand is ready.

Stalls are supported by adding enable inputs (*EN*) to the Fetch and Decode pipeline registers and a synchronous reset/clear (*CLR*) input to the Execute pipeline register. When an LDR stall occurs, *StallD* and *StallF* are asserted to force the Decode and Fetch stage pipeline registers to hold their old values. *FlushE* is also asserted to clear the contents of the Execute stage pipeline register, introducing a bubble.

The *MemtoReg* signal is asserted for the LDR instruction. Hence, the logic to compute the stalls and flushes is

```
Match_12D_E = (RA1D == WA3E) + (RA2D == WA3E)
LDRstall = Match_12D_E • MemtoRegE
StallF = StallD = FlushE = LDRstall
```

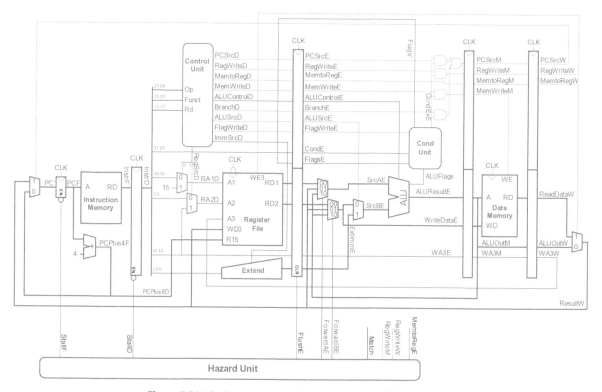

Figure 7.54 Pipelined processor with stalls to solve LDR **data hazard**

Solving Control Hazards

The B instruction presents a control hazard: the pipelined processor does not know what instruction to fetch next, because the branch decision has not been made by the time the next instruction is fetched. Writes to R15 (PC) present a similar control hazard.

One mechanism for dealing with the control hazard is to stall the pipeline until the branch decision is made (i.e., *PCSrcW* is computed). Because the decision is made in the Writeback stage, the pipeline would have to be stalled for four cycles at every branch. This would severely degrade the system performance if it occurs often.

An alternative is to predict whether the branch will be taken and begin executing instructions based on the prediction. Once the branch decision is available, the processor can throw out the instructions if the prediction was wrong. In the pipeline presented so far (Figure 7.54), the processor predicts that branches are not taken and simply continues executing the program in order until *PCSrcW* is asserted to select the next PC from *ResultW* instead. If the branch should have been taken, then the

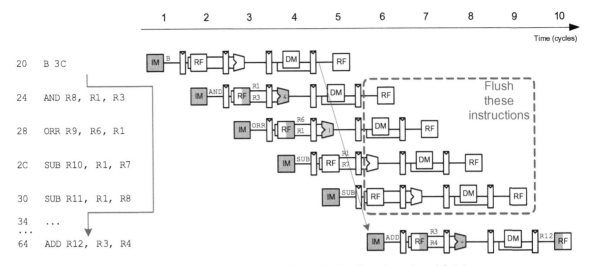

Figure 7.55 Abstract pipeline diagram illustrating flushing when a branch is taken

four instructions following the branch must be *flushed* (discarded) by clearing the pipeline registers for those instructions. These wasted instruction cycles are called the *branch misprediction penalty*.

Figure 7.55 shows such a scheme in which a branch from address 0x20 to address 0x64 is taken. The PC is not written until cycle 5, by which point the AND, ORR, and both SUB instructions at addresses 0x24, 0x28, 0x2C, and 0x30 have already been fetched. These instructions must be flushed, and the ADD instruction is fetched from address 0x64 in cycle 6. This is somewhat of an improvement, but flushing so many instructions when the branch is taken still degrades performance.

We could reduce the branch misprediction penalty if the branch decision could be made earlier. Observe that the branch decision can be made in the Execute stage when the destination address has been computed and *CondEx* is known. Figure 7.56 shows the pipeline operation with the early branch decision being made in cycle 3. In cycle 4, the AND and ORR instructions are flushed and the ADD instruction is fetched. Now the branch misprediction penalty is reduced to only two instructions rather than four.

Figure 7.57 modifies the pipelined processor to move the branch decision earlier and handle control hazards. A branch multiplexer is added before the PC register to select the branch destination from *ALUResultE*. The *BranchTakenE* signal controlling this multiplexer is asserted on branches whose condition is satisfied. *PCSrcW* is now only asserted for writes to the PC, which still occur in the Writeback stage.

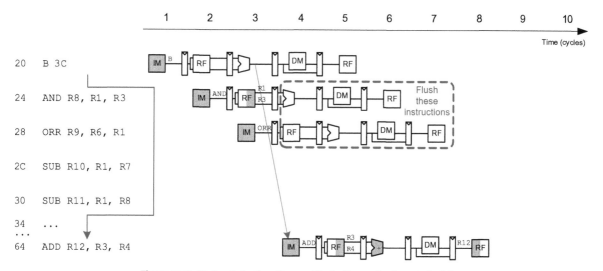

```
20    B 3C

24    AND R8, R1, R3

28    ORR R9, R6, R1

2C    SUB R10, R1, R7

30    SUB R11, R1, R8

34    ...
...
64    ADD R12, R3, R4
```

Figure 7.56 Abstract pipeline diagram illustrating earlier branch decision

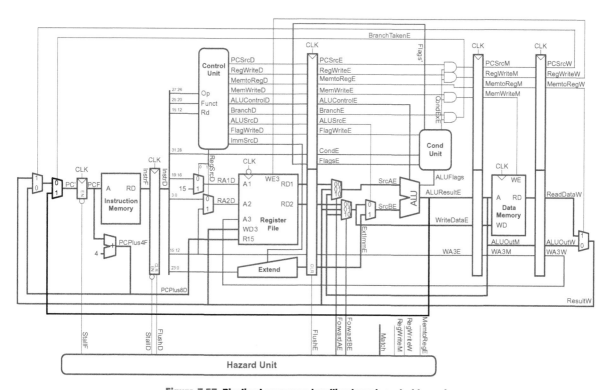

Figure 7.57 Pipelined processor handling branch control hazard

Finally, we must work out the stall and flush signals to handle branches and PC writes. It is common to goof this part of a pipelined processor design because the conditions are rather complicated. When a branch is taken, the subsequent two instructions must be flushed from the pipeline registers of the Decode and Execute stages. When a write to the PC is in the pipeline, the pipeline should be stalled until the write completes. This is done by stalling the Fetch stage. Recall that stalling one stage also requires flushing the next to prevent the instruction from being executed repeatedly. The logic to handle these cases is given here. *PCWrPending* is asserted when a PC write is in progress (in the Decode, Execute, or Memory stage). During this time, the Fetch stage is stalled and the Decode stage is flushed. When the PC write reaches the Writeback stage (*PCSrcW* asserted), *StallF* is released to allow the write to occur, but *FlushD* is still asserted so that the undesired instruction in the Fetch stage does not advance.

To reduce clutter, the Hazard Unit connections of *PCSrcD*, *PCSrcE*, *PCSrcM*, and *BranchTakenE* from the datapath are not shown in Figures 7.57 and 7.58.

```
PCWrPendingF = PCSrcD + PCSrcE + PCSrcM;
StallD = LDRstall;
StallF = LDRstall + PCWrPendingF;
FlushE = LDRstall + BranchTakenE;
FlushD = PCWrPendingF + PCSrcW + BranchTakenE;
```

Branches are very common, and even a two-cycle misprediction penalty still impacts performance. With a bit more work, the penalty could be reduced to one cycle for many branches. The destination address must be computed in the Decode stage as *PCBranchD = PCPlus8D + ExtImmD*. *BranchTakenD* must also be computed in the Decode stage based on *ALUFlagsE* generated by the previous instruction. This might increase the cycle time of the processor if these flags arrive late. These changes are left as an exercise to the reader (see Exercise 7.36).

Hazard Summary

In summary, RAW data hazards occur when an instruction depends on the result of another instruction that has not yet been written into the register file. The data hazards can be resolved by forwarding if the result is computed soon enough; otherwise, they require stalling the pipeline until the result is available. Control hazards occur when the decision of what instruction to fetch has not been made by the time the next instruction must be fetched. Control hazards are solved by predicting which instruction should be fetched and flushing the pipeline if the prediction is later determined to be wrong or by stalling the pipeline until the decision is made. Moving the decision as early as possible minimizes the number of instructions that are flushed on a misprediction. You may have observed

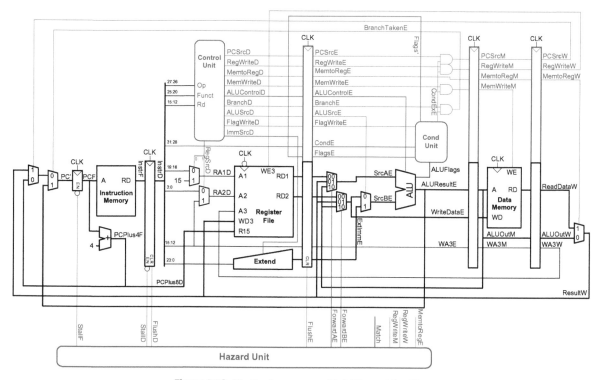

Figure 7.58 Pipelined processor with full hazard handling

by now that one of the challenges of designing a pipelined processor is to understand all the possible interactions between instructions and to discover all the hazards that may exist. Figure 7.58 shows the complete pipelined processor handling all of the hazards.

7.5.4 Performance Analysis

The pipelined processor ideally would have a CPI of 1, because a new instruction is issued every cycle. However, a stall or a flush wastes a cycle, so the CPI is slightly higher and depends on the specific program being executed.

Example 7.7 PIPELINED PROCESSOR CPI

The SPECINT2000 benchmark considered in Example 7.5 consists of approximately 25% loads, 10% stores, 13% branches, and 52% data-processing instructions. Assume that 40% of the loads are immediately followed by an instruction that uses the result, requiring a stall, and that 50% of the branches are taken (mis-predicted), requiring a flush. Ignore other hazards. Compute the average CPI of the pipelined processor.

Solution: The average CPI is the sum over each instruction of the CPI for that instruction multiplied by the fraction of time that instruction is used. Loads take one clock cycle when there is no dependency and two cycles when the processor must stall for a dependency, so they have a CPI of $(0.6)(1) + (0.4)(2) = 1.4$. Branches take one clock cycle when they are predicted properly and three when they are not, so they have a CPI of $(0.5)(1) + (0.5)(3) = 2.0$. All other instructions have a CPI of 1. Hence, for this benchmark, average CPI $= (0.25)(1.4) + (0.1)(1) + (0.13)(2.0) + (0.52)(1) = 1.23$.

We can determine the cycle time by considering the critical path in each of the five pipeline stages shown in Figure 7.58. Recall that the register file is written in the first half of the Writeback cycle and read in the second half of the Decode cycle. Therefore, the cycle time of the Decode and Writeback stages is twice the time necessary to do the half-cycle of work.

$$T_{c3} = max \begin{bmatrix} t_{pcq} + t_{mem} + t_{setup} & Fetch \\ 2(t_{RFread} + t_{setup}) & Decode \\ t_{pcq} + 2t_{mux} + t_{ALU} + t_{setup} & Execute \\ t_{pcq} + t_{mem} + t_{setup} & Memory \\ 2(t_{pcq} + t_{mux} + t_{RFsetup}) & Writeback \end{bmatrix} \qquad (7.5)$$

Example 7.8 PROCESSOR PERFORMANCE COMPARISON

Ben Bitdiddle needs to compare the pipelined processor performance with that of the single-cycle and multicycle processors considered in Example 7.6. The logic delays were given in Table 7.5. Help Ben compare the execution time of 100 billion instructions from the SPECINT2000 benchmark for each processor.

Solution: According to Equation 7.5, the cycle time of the pipelined processor is $T_{c3} = max[40 + 200 + 50, 2(100 + 50), 40 + 2(25) + 120 + 50, 40 + 200 + 50, 2(40 + 25 + 60)] = 300$ ps. According to Equation 7.1, the total execution time is $T_3 = (100 \times 10^9$ instructions$)(1.23$ cycles/instruction$)(300 \times 10^{-12}$ s/cycle$) = 36.9$ seconds. This compares with 84 seconds for the single-cycle processor and 140 seconds for the multicycle processor.

The pipelined processor is substantially faster than the others. However, its advantage over the single-cycle processor is nowhere near the five-fold speed-up one might hope to get from a five-stage pipeline. The pipeline hazards introduce a small CPI penalty. More significantly, the sequencing overhead (clk-to-Q and setup times) of the registers applies to every pipeline stage, not just once to the overall datapath. Sequencing overhead limits the benefits one can hope to achieve from pipelining. The pipelined processor is similar in hardware requirements to the single-cycle processor, but it adds eight 32-bit pipeline registers, along with multiplexers, smaller pipeline registers, and control logic to resolve hazards.

7.6 HDL REPRESENTATION*

This section presents HDL code for the single-cycle processor supporting the instructions discussed in this chapter. The code illustrates good coding practices for a moderately complex system. HDL code for the multicycle processor and pipelined processor are left to Exercises 7.25 and 7.40.

In this section, the instruction and data memories are separated from the datapath and connected by address and data busses. In practice, most processors pull instructions and data from separate caches. However, to handle literal pools, a more complete processor must also be able to read data from the instruction memory. Chapter 8 will revisit memory systems, including the interaction of the caches with main memory.

The processor is composed of a datapath and a controller. The controller, in turn, is composed of the Decoder and the Conditional Logic. Figure 7.59 shows a block diagram of the single-cycle processor interfaced to external memories.

The HDL code is partitioned into several sections. Section 7.6.1 provides HDL for the single-cycle processor datapath and controller. Section 7.6.2 presents the generic building blocks, such as registers and multiplexers, which are used by any microarchitecture. Section 7.6.3 introduces the testbench and external memories. The HDL is available in electronic form on this book's website (see the Preface).

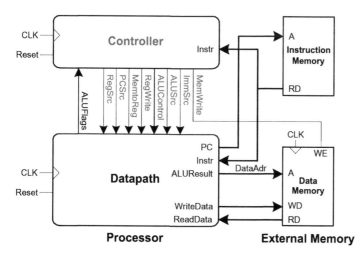

Figure 7.59 Single-cycle processor interfaced to external memory

7.6.1 Single-Cycle Processor

The main modules of the single-cycle processor module are given in the following HDL examples.

HDL Example 7.1 SINGLE-CYCLE PROCESSOR

SystemVerilog

```
module arm(input  logic          clk, reset,
           output logic  [31:0]  PC,
           input  logic  [31:0]  Instr,
           output logic          MemWrite,
           output logic  [31:0]  ALUResult, WriteData,
           input  logic  [31:0]  ReadData);

  logic  [3:0]  ALUFlags;
  logic         RegWrite,
                ALUSrc, MemtoReg, PCSrc;
  logic  [1:0]  RegSrc, ImmSrc, ALUControl;

  controller c(clk, reset, Instr[31:12], ALUFlags,
               RegSrc, RegWrite, ImmSrc,
               ALUSrc, ALUControl,
               MemWrite, MemtoReg, PCSrc);
  datapath dp(clk, reset,
               RegSrc, RegWrite, ImmSrc,
               ALUSrc, ALUControl,
               MemtoReg, PCSrc,
               ALUFlags, PC, Instr,
               ALUResult, WriteData, ReadData);
endmodule
```

VHDL

```
library IEEE; use IEEE.STD_LOGIC_1164.all;
entity arm is -- single cycle processor
  port(clk, reset:            in  STD_LOGIC;
       PC:                    out STD_LOGIC_VECTOR(31 downto 0);
       Instr:                 in  STD_LOGIC_VECTOR(31 downto 0);
       MemWrite:              out STD_LOGIC;
       ALUResult, WriteData: out STD_LOGIC_VECTOR(31 downto 0);
       ReadData:              in  STD_LOGIC_VECTOR(31 downto 0));
end;

architecture struct of arm is
  component controller
  port(clk, reset:     in  STD_LOGIC;
       Instr:          in  STD_LOGIC_VECTOR(31 downto 12);
       ALUFlags:       in  STD_LOGIC_VECTOR(3 downto 0);
       RegSrc:         out STD_LOGIC_VECTOR(1 downto 0);
       RegWrite:       out STD_LOGIC;
       ImmSrc:         out STD_LOGIC_VECTOR(1 downto 0);
       ALUSrc:         out STD_LOGIC;
       ALUControl:     out STD_LOGIC_VECTOR(1 downto 0);
       MemWrite:       out STD_LOGIC;
       MemtoReg:       out STD_LOGIC;
       PCSrc:          out STD_LOGIC);
  end component;
  component datapath
    port(clk, reset:        in    STD_LOGIC;
         RegSrc:            in    STD_LOGIC_VECTOR(1 downto 0);
         RegWrite:          in    STD_LOGIC;
         ImmSrc:            in    STD_LOGIC_VECTOR(1 downto 0);
         ALUSrc:            in    STD_LOGIC;
         ALUControl:        in    STD_LOGIC_VECTOR(1 downto 0);
         MemtoReg:          in    STD_LOGIC;
         PCSrc:             in    STD_LOGIC;
         ALUFlags:          out   STD_LOGIC_VECTOR(3 downto 0);
         PC:                buffer STD_LOGIC_VECTOR(31 downto 0);
         Instr:             in    STD_LOGIC_VECTOR(31 downto 0);
         ALUResult, WriteData:buffer STD_LOGIC_VECTOR(31 downto 0);
         ReadData:          in    STD_LOGIC_VECTOR(31 downto 0));
    end component;
    signal RegWrite, ALUSrc, MemtoReg, PCSrc: STD_LOGIC;
    signal RegSrc, ImmSrc, ALUControl: STD_LOGIC_VECTOR
                                       (1 downto 0);
    signal ALUFlags: STD_LOGIC_VECTOR(3 downto 0);
begin
  cont: controller port map(clk, reset, Instr(31 downto 12),
                            ALUFlags, RegSrc, RegWrite,
                            ImmSrc, ALUSrc, ALUControl,
                            MemWrite, MemtoReg, PCSrc);
  dp: datapath port map(clk, reset, RegSrc, RegWrite, ImmSrc,
                        ALUSrc, ALUControl, MemtoReg, PCSrc,
                        ALUFlags, PC, Instr, ALUResult,
                        WriteData, ReadData);
end;
```

HDL Example 7.2 CONTROLLER

SystemVerilog

```
module controller(input  logic          clk, reset,
                  input  logic [31:12]  Instr,
                  input  logic [3:0]    ALUFlags,
                  output logic [1:0]    RegSrc,
                  output logic          RegWrite,
                  output logic [1:0]    ImmSrc,
                  output logic          ALUSrc,
                  output logic [1:0]    ALUControl,
                  output logic          MemWrite, MemtoReg,
                  output logic          PCSrc);
  logic [1:0] FlagW;
  logic       PCS, RegW, MemW;

  decoder dec(Instr[27:26], Instr[25:20], Instr[15:12],
              FlagW, PCS, RegW, MemW,
              MemtoReg, ALUSrc, ImmSrc, RegSrc, ALUControl);
  condlogic cl(clk, reset, Instr[31:28], ALUFlags,
               FlagW, PCS, RegW, MemW,
               PCSrc, RegWrite, MemWrite);
endmodule
```

VHDL

```
library IEEE; use IEEE.STD_LOGIC_1164.all;
entity controller is -- single cycle control
  port(clk, reset:  in  STD_LOGIC;
       Instr:       in  STD_LOGIC_VECTOR(31 downto 12);
       ALUFlags:    in  STD_LOGIC_VECTOR(3 downto 0);
       RegSrc:      out STD_LOGIC_VECTOR(1 downto 0);
       RegWrite:    out STD_LOGIC;
       ImmSrc:      out STD_LOGIC_VECTOR(1 downto 0);
       ALUSrc:      out STD_LOGIC;
       ALUControl:  out STD_LOGIC_VECTOR(1 downto 0);
       MemWrite:    out STD_LOGIC;
       MemtoReg:    out STD_LOGIC;
       PCSrc:       out STD_LOGIC);
end;

architecture struct of controller is
  component decoder
    port(Op:                in  STD_LOGIC_VECTOR(1 downto 0);
         Funct:             in  STD_LOGIC_VECTOR(5 downto 0);
         Rd:                in  STD_LOGIC_VECTOR(3 downto 0);
         FlagW:             out STD_LOGIC_VECTOR(1 downto 0);
         PCS, RegW, MemW:   out STD_LOGIC;
         MemtoReg, ALUSrc:  out STD_LOGIC;
         ImmSrc, RegSrc:    out STD_LOGIC_VECTOR(1 downto 0);
         ALUControl:        out STD_LOGIC_VECTOR(1 downto 0));
  end component;
  component condlogic
    port(clk, reset:         in  STD_LOGIC;
         Cond:               in  STD_LOGIC_VECTOR(3 downto 0);
         ALUFlags:           in  STD_LOGIC_VECTOR(3 downto 0);
         FlagW:              in  STD_LOGIC_VECTOR(1 downto 0);
         PCS, RegW, MemW:    in  STD_LOGIC;
         PCSrc, RegWrite:    out STD_LOGIC;
         MemWrite:           out STD_LOGIC);
  end component;
  signal FlagW: STD_LOGIC_VECTOR(1 downto 0);
  signal PCS, RegW, MemW: STD_LOGIC;
begin
  dec: decoder port map(Instr(27 downto 26), Instr(25 downto 20),
                        Instr(15 downto 12), FlagW, PCS,
                        RegW, MemW, MemtoReg, ALUSrc, ImmSrc,
                        RegSrc, ALUControl);
  cl: condlogic port map(clk, reset, Instr(31 downto 28),
                         ALUFlags, FlagW, PCS, RegW, MemW,
                         PCSrc, RegWrite, MemWrite);
end;
```

HDL Example 7.3 DECODER

SystemVerilog

```
module decoder(input  logic [1:0] Op,
               input  logic [5:0] Funct,
               input  logic [3:0] Rd,
               output logic [1:0] FlagW,
               output logic       PCS, RegW, MemW,
               output logic       MemtoReg, ALUSrc,
               output logic [1:0] ImmSrc, RegSrc, ALUControl);

  logic [9:0] controls;
  logic       Branch, ALUOp;

  // Main Decoder
  always_comb
    casex(Op)
                              // Data-processing immediate
      2'b00: if (Funct[5]) controls = 10'b0000101001;
                              // Data-processing register
             else          controls = 10'b0000001001;
                              // LDR
      2'b01: if (Funct[0]) controls = 10'b0001111000;
                              // STR
             else          controls = 10'b1001110100;
                              // B
      2'b10:               controls = 10'b0110100010;
                              // Unimplemented
      default:             controls = 10'bx;
    endcase

  assign {RegSrc, ImmSrc, ALUSrc, MemtoReg,
    RegW, MemW, Branch, ALUOp} = controls;

  // ALU Decoder
  always_comb
  if (ALUOp) begin              // which DP Instr?
    case(Funct[4:1])
        4'b0100: ALUControl = 2'b00;  // ADD
        4'b0010: ALUControl = 2'b01;  // SUB
        4'b0000: ALUControl = 2'b10;  // AND
        4'b1100: ALUControl = 2'b11;  // ORR
        default: ALUControl = 2'bx;   // unimplemented
    endcase

    // update flags if S bit is set (C & V only for arith)
    FlagW[1]    = Funct[0];
    FlagW[0]    = Funct[0] &
      (ALUControl == 2'b00 | ALUControl == 2'b01);
  end else begin
    ALUControl = 2'b00;  // add for non-DP instructions
    FlagW      = 2'b00;  // don't update Flags
  end

  // PC Logic
  assign PCS = ((Rd == 4'b1111) & RegW) | Branch;
endmodule
```

VHDL

```
library IEEE; use IEEE.STD_LOGIC_1164.all;
entity decoder is -- main control decoder
  port(Op:                in  STD_LOGIC_VECTOR(1 downto 0);
       Funct:             in  STD_LOGIC_VECTOR(5 downto 0);
       Rd:                in  STD_LOGIC_VECTOR(3 downto 0);
       FlagW:             out STD_LOGIC_VECTOR(1 downto 0);
       PCS, RegW, MemW:   out STD_LOGIC;
       MemtoReg, ALUSrc:  out STD_LOGIC;
       ImmSrc, RegSrc:    out STD_LOGIC_VECTOR(1 downto 0);
       ALUControl:        out STD_LOGIC_VECTOR(1 downto 0));
end;
architecture behave of decoder is
  signal controls:       STD_LOGIC_VECTOR(9 downto 0);
  signal ALUOp, Branch:  STD_LOGIC;
  signal op2:            STD_LOGIC_VECTOR(3 downto 0);
begin
  op2 <= (Op, Funct(5), Funct(0));
  process(all) begin -- Main Decoder
    case? (op2) is
      when "000-" => controls <= "0000001001";
      when "001-" => controls <= "0000101001";
      when "01-0" => controls <= "1001110100";
      when "01-1" => controls <= "0001111000";
      when "10--" => controls <= "0110100010";
      when others => controls <= "----------";
    end case?;
  end process;

  (RegSrc, ImmSrc, ALUSrc, MemtoReg, RegW, MemW,
  Branch, ALUOp) <= controls;

  process(all) begin -- ALU Decoder
  if (ALUOp) then
    case Funct(4 downto 1) is
      when "0100" => ALUControl <= "00"; -- ADD
      when "0010" => ALUControl <= "01"; -- SUB
      when "0000" => ALUControl <= "10"; -- AND
      when "1100" => ALUControl <= "11"; -- ORR
      when others => ALUControl <= "--"; -- unimplemented
    end case;
    FlagW(1) <= Funct(0);
    FlagW(0) <= Funct(0) and (not ALUControl(1));
  else
    ALUControl <= "00";
    FlagW <= "00";
  end if;
  end process;

  PCS <= ((and Rd) and RegW) or Branch;
end;
```

HDL Example 7.4 CONDITIONAL LOGIC

SystemVerilog

```
module condlogic(input   logic        clk, reset,
                 input   logic [3:0]  Cond,
                 input   logic [3:0]  ALUFlags,
                 input   logic [1:0]  FlagW,
                 input   logic        PCS, RegW, MemW,
                 output  logic        PCSrc, RegWrite,
                                      MemWrite);

  logic [1:0]  FlagWrite;
  logic [3:0]  Flags;
  logic        CondEx;

  flopenr #(2)flagreg1(clk, reset, FlagWrite[1],
                       ALUFlags[3:2], Flags[3:2]);
  flopenr #(2)flagreg0(clk, reset, FlagWrite[0],
                       ALUFlags[1:0], Flags[1:0]);

  // write controls are conditional
  condcheck cc(Cond, Flags, CondEx);
  assign FlagWrite = FlagW  & {2{CondEx}};
  assign RegWrite  = RegW   & CondEx;
  assign MemWrite  = MemW   & CondEx;
  assign PCSrc     = PCS    & CondEx;
endmodule

module condcheck(input  logic [3:0]  Cond,
                 input  logic [3:0]  Flags,
                 output logic        CondEx);

  logic neg, zero, carry, overflow, ge;

  assign {neg, zero, carry, overflow} = Flags;
  assign ge = (neg == overflow);

  always_comb
    case(Cond)
      4'b0000: CondEx = zero;              // EQ
      4'b0001: CondEx = ~zero;             // NE
      4'b0010: CondEx = carry;             // CS
      4'b0011: CondEx = ~carry;            // CC
      4'b0100: CondEx = neg;               // MI
      4'b0101: CondEx = ~neg;              // PL
      4'b0110: CondEx = overflow;          // VS
      4'b0111: CondEx = ~overflow;         // VC
      4'b1000: CondEx = carry & ~zero;     // HI
      4'b1001: CondEx = ~(carry & ~zero);  // LS
      4'b1010: CondEx = ge;                // GE
      4'b1011: CondEx = ~ge;               // LT
      4'b1100: CondEx = ~zero & ge;        // GT
      4'b1101: CondEx = ~(~zero & ge);     // LE
      4'b1110: CondEx = 1'b1;              // Always
      default: CondEx = 1'bx;              // undefined
    endcase
endmodule
```

VHDL

```
library IEEE; use IEEE.STD_LOGIC_1164.all;
entity condlogic is -- Conditional logic
  port(clk, reset:       in  STD_LOGIC;
       Cond:             in  STD_LOGIC_VECTOR(3 downto 0);
       ALUFlags:         in  STD_LOGIC_VECTOR(3 downto 0);
       FlagW:            in  STD_LOGIC_VECTOR(1 downto 0);
       PCS, RegW, MemW:  in  STD_LOGIC;
       PCSrc, RegWrite:  out STD_LOGIC;
       MemWrite:         out STD_LOGIC);
end;

architecture behave of condlogic is
  component condcheck
    port(Cond:   in  STD_LOGIC_VECTOR(3 downto 0);
         Flags:  in  STD_LOGIC_VECTOR(3 downto 0);
         CondEx: out STD_LOGIC);
  end component;
  component flopenr generic(width: integer);
    port(clk, reset, en: in  STD_LOGIC;
         d:  in  STD_LOGIC_VECTOR (width-1 downto 0);
         q:  out STD_LOGIC_VECTOR (width-1 downto 0));
  end component;
  signal FlagWrite: STD_LOGIC_VECTOR(1 downto 0);
  signal Flags:     STD_LOGIC_VECTOR(3 downto 0);
  signal CondEx:    STD_LOGIC;
begin
  flagreg1: flopenr generic map(2)
    port map(clk, reset, FlagWrite(1),
             ALUFlags(3 downto 2), Flags(3 downto 2));
  flagreg0: flopenr generic map(2)
    port map(clk, reset, FlagWrite(0),
             ALUFlags(1 downto 0), Flags(1 downto 0));
  cc: condcheck port map(Cond, Flags, CondEx);

  FlagWrite <= FlagW and (CondEx, CondEx);
  RegWrite  <= RegW  and CondEx;
  MemWrite  <= MemW  and CondEx;
  PCSrc     <= PCS   and CondEx;
end;

library IEEE; use IEEE.STD_LOGIC_1164.all;
entity condcheck is
  port(Cond:   in  STD_LOGIC_VECTOR(3 downto 0);
       Flags:  in  STD_LOGIC_VECTOR(3 downto 0);
       CondEx: out STD_LOGIC);
end;

architecture behave of condcheck is
  signal neg, zero, carry, overflow, ge: STD_LOGIC;
begin
  (neg, zero, carry, overflow) <= Flags;
  ge <= (neg xnor overflow);

  process(all) begin -- Condition checking
    case Cond is
      when "0000" => CondEx <= zero;
      when "0001" => CondEx <= not zero;
      when "0010" => CondEx <= carry;
      when "0011" => CondEx <= not carry;
      when "0100" => CondEx <= neg;
      when "0101" => CondEx <= not neg;
      when "0110" => CondEx <= overflow;
```

```
              when "0111"  =>  CondEx  <=  not overflow;
              when "1000"  =>  CondEx  <=  carry and (not zero);
              when "1001"  =>  CondEx  <=  not(carry and (not zero));
              when "1010"  =>  CondEx  <=  ge;
              when "1011"  =>  CondEx  <=  not ge;
              when "1100"  =>  CondEx  <=  (not zero) and ge;
              when "1101"  =>  CondEx  <=  not ((not zero) and ge);
              when "1110"  =>  CondEx  <=  '1';
              when others  =>  CondEx  <=  '-';
           end case;
        end process;
     end;
```

HDL Example 7.5 DATAPATH

SystemVerilog

```systemverilog
module datapath(input  logic        clk, reset,
                input  logic [1:0]  RegSrc,
                input  logic        RegWrite,
                input  logic [1:0]  ImmSrc,
                input  logic        ALUSrc,
                input  logic [1:0]  ALUControl,
                input  logic        MemtoReg,
                input  logic        PCSrc,
                output logic [3:0]  ALUFlags,
                output logic [31:0] PC,
                input  logic [31:0] Instr,
                output logic [31:0] ALUResult, WriteData,
                input  logic [31:0] ReadData);

  logic [31:0] PCNext, PCPlus4, PCPlus8;
  logic [31:0] ExtImm, SrcA, SrcB, Result;
  logic [3:0]  RA1, RA2;

  // next PC logic
  mux2 #(32)  pcmux(PCPlus4, Result, PCSrc, PCNext);
  flopr #(32) pcreg(clk, reset, PCNext, PC);
  adder #(32) pcadd1(PC, 32'b100, PCPlus4);
  adder #(32) pcadd2(PCPlus4, 32'b100, PCPlus8);

  // register file logic
  mux2 #(4)  ra1mux(Instr[19:16], 4'b1111, RegSrc[0], RA1);
  mux2 #(4)  ra2mux(Instr[3:0], Instr[15:12], RegSrc[1], RA2);
  regfile    rf(clk, RegWrite, RA1, RA2,
               Instr[15:12], Result, PCPlus8,
               SrcA, WriteData);
  mux2 #(32) resmux(ALUResult, ReadData, MemtoReg, Result);
  extend     ext(Instr[23:0], ImmSrc, ExtImm);

  // ALU logic
  mux2 #(32) srcbmux(WriteData, ExtImm, ALUSrc, SrcB);
  alu        alu(SrcA, SrcB, ALUControl, ALUResult, ALUFlags);
endmodule
```

VHDL

```vhdl
library IEEE; use IEEE.STD_LOGIC_1164.all;
entity datapath is
   port(clk, reset:       in     STD_LOGIC;
        RegSrc:           in     STD_LOGIC_VECTOR(1 downto 0);
        RegWrite:         in     STD_LOGIC;
        ImmSrc:           in     STD_LOGIC_VECTOR(1 downto 0);
        ALUSrc:           in     STD_LOGIC;
        ALUControl:       in     STD_LOGIC_VECTOR(1 downto 0);
        MemtoReg:         in     STD_LOGIC;
        PCSrc:            in     STD_LOGIC;
        ALUFlags:         out    STD_LOGIC_VECTOR(3 downto 0);
        PC:               buffer STD_LOGIC_VECTOR(31 downto 0);
        Instr:            in     STD_LOGIC_VECTOR(31 downto 0);
        ALUResult, WriteData:buffer STD_LOGIC_VECTOR(31 downto 0);
        ReadData:         in     STD_LOGIC_VECTOR(31 downto 0));
end;

architecture struct of datapath is
   component alu
   port(a, b:          in     STD_LOGIC_VECTOR(31 downto 0);
        ALUControl:    in     STD_LOGIC_VECTOR(1 downto 0);
        Result:        buffer STD_LOGIC_VECTOR(31 downto 0);
        ALUFlags:      out    STD_LOGIC_VECTOR(3 downto 0));
   end component;
   component regfile
   port(clk:           in  STD_LOGIC;
        we3:           in  STD_LOGIC;
        ra1, ra2, wa3: in  STD_LOGIC_VECTOR(3 downto 0);
        wd3, r15:      in  STD_LOGIC_VECTOR(31 downto 0);
        rd1, rd2:      out STD_LOGIC_VECTOR(31 downto 0));
   end component;
   component adder
   port(a, b: in  STD_LOGIC_VECTOR(31 downto 0);
        y:    out STD_LOGIC_VECTOR(31 downto 0));
   end component;
   component extend
   port(Instr: in  STD_LOGIC_VECTOR(23 downto 0);
        ImmSrc: in  STD_LOGIC_VECTOR(1 downto 0);
        ExtImm: out STD_LOGIC_VECTOR(31 downto 0));
   end component;
```

```
                               component flopr generic(width: integer);
                               port(clk, reset:  in  STD_LOGIC;
                                        d:           in  STD_LOGIC_VECTOR(width-1 downto 0);
                                        q:           out STD_LOGIC_VECTOR(width-1 downto 0));
                               end component;
                               component mux2 generic(width: integer);
                               port(d0, d1:  in  STD_LOGIC_VECTOR(width-1 downto 0);
                                        s:       in  STD_LOGIC;
                                        y:       out STD_LOGIC_VECTOR(width-1 downto 0));
                               end component;
                               signal PCNext, PCPlus4,
                                       PCPlus8:         STD_LOGIC_VECTOR(31 downto 0);
                               signal ExtImm, Result:   STD_LOGIC_VECTOR(31 downto 0);
                               signal SrcA, SrcB:       STD_LOGIC_VECTOR(31 downto 0);
                               signal RA1, RA2:         STD_LOGIC_VECTOR(3 downto 0);
                             begin
                               -- next PC logic
                               pcmux:  mux2 generic map(32)
                                        port map(PCPlus4, Result, PCSrc, PCNext);
                               pcreg: flopr generic map(32) port map(clk, reset, PCNext, PC);
                               pcadd1: adder port map(PC, X"00000004", PCPlus4);
                               pcadd2: adder port map(PCPlus4, X"00000004", PCPlus8);

                               -- register file logic
                               ra1mux: mux2 generic map (4)
                                  port map(Instr(19 downto 16), "1111", RegSrc(0), RA1);
                               ra2mux: mux2 generic map (4) port map(Instr(3 downto 0),
                                               Instr(15 downto 12), RegSrc(1), RA2);
                               rf: regfile port map(clk, RegWrite, RA1, RA2,
                                            Instr(15 downto 12), Result,
                                            PCPlus8, SrcA, WriteData);
                               resmux: mux2 generic map(32)
                                  port map(ALUResult, ReadData, MemtoReg, Result);
                               ext: extend port map(Instr(23 downto 0), ImmSrc, ExtImm);

                               -- ALU logic
                               srcbmux: mux2 generic map(32)
                                  port map(WriteData, ExtImm, ALUSrc, SrcB);
                               i_alu:  alu port map(SrcA, SrcB, ALUControl, ALUResult,
                                            ALUFlags);
                             end;
```

7.6.2 Generic Building Blocks

This section contains generic building blocks that may be useful in any digital system, including a register file, adder, flip-flops, and a 2:1 multiplexer. The HDL for the ALU is left to Exercises 5.11 and 5.12.

HDL Example 7.6 REGISTER FILE

SystemVerilog

```systemverilog
module regfile(input  logic        clk,
               input  logic        we3,
               input  logic [3:0]  ra1, ra2, wa3,
               input  logic [31:0] wd3, r15,
               output logic [31:0] rd1, rd2);

  logic [31:0] rf[14:0];

  // three ported register file
  // read two ports combinationally
  // write third port on rising edge of clock
  // register 15 reads PC + 8 instead

  always_ff @(posedge clk)
    if (we3) rf[wa3] <= wd3;

  assign rd1 = (ra1 == 4'b1111) ? r15 : rf[ra1];
  assign rd2 = (ra2 == 4'b1111) ? r15 : rf[ra2];
endmodule
```

VHDL

```vhdl
library IEEE; use IEEE.STD_LOGIC_1164.all;
use IEEE.NUMERIC_STD_UNSIGNED.all;
entity regfile is -- three-port register file
  port(clk:          in  STD_LOGIC;
       we3:          in  STD_LOGIC;
       ra1, ra2, wa3: in  STD_LOGIC_VECTOR(3 downto 0);
       wd3, r15:     in  STD_LOGIC_VECTOR(31 downto 0);
       rd1, rd2:     out STD_LOGIC_VECTOR(31 downto 0));
end;

architecture behave of regfile is
  type ramtype is array (31 downto 0) of
       STD_LOGIC_VECTOR(31 downto 0);
  signal mem: ramtype;
begin
  process(clk) begin
    if rising_edge(clk) then
      if we3 = '1' then mem(to_integer(wa3)) <= wd3;
      end if;
    end if;
  end process;
  process(all) begin
    if (to_integer(ra1) = 15) then rd1 <= r15;
    else rd1 <= mem(to_integer(ra1));
    end if;
    if (to_integer(ra2) = 15) then rd2 <= r15;
    else rd2 <= mem(to_integer(ra2));
    end if;
  end process;
end;
```

HDL Example 7.7 ADDER

SystemVerilog

```systemverilog
module adder #(parameter WIDTH = 8)
              (input  logic [WIDTH-1:0] a, b,
               output logic [WIDTH-1:0] y);

  assign y = a + b;
endmodule
```

VHDL

```vhdl
library IEEE; use IEEE.STD_LOGIC_1164.all;
use IEEE.NUMERIC_STD_UNSIGNED.all;
entity adder is -- adder
  port(a, b: in  STD_LOGIC_VECTOR(31 downto 0);
       y:    out STD_LOGIC_VECTOR(31 downto 0));
end;

architecture behave of adder is
begin
  y <= a + b;
end;
```

HDL Example 7.8 IMMEDIATE EXTENSION

SystemVerilog

```
module extend(input  logic  [23:0]  Instr,
              input  logic  [1:0]   ImmSrc,
              output logic  [31:0]  ExtImm);

  always_comb
    case(ImmSrc)
              // 8-bit unsigned immediate
      2'b00:  ExtImm = {24'b0, Instr[7:0]};
              // 12-bit unsigned immediate
      2'b01:  ExtImm = {20'b0, Instr[11:0]};
              // 24-bit two's complement shifted branch
      2'b10:  ExtImm = {{6{Instr[23]}}, Instr[23:0], 2'b00};
      default: ExtImm = 32'bx; // undefined
    endcase
endmodule
```

VHDL

```
library IEEE; use IEEE.STD_LOGIC_1164.all;
entity extend is
  port(Instr:   in  STD_LOGIC_VECTOR(23 downto 0);
       ImmSrc:  in  STD_LOGIC_VECTOR(1 downto 0);
       ExtImm:  out STD_LOGIC_VECTOR(31 downto 0));
end;

architecture behave of extend is
begin
  process(all) begin
    case ImmSrc is
      when "00"  => ExtImm <= (X"000000", Instr(7 downto 0));
      when "01"  => ExtImm <= (X"00000", Instr(11 downto 0));
      when "10"  => ExtImm <= (Instr(23), Instr(23),
                              Instr(23), Instr(23),
                              Instr(23), Instr(23),
                              Instr(23 downto 0), "00");
      when others  => ExtImm  <= X"--------";
    end case;
  end process;
end;
```

HDL Example 7.9 RESETTABLE FLIP-FLOP

SystemVerilog

```
module flopr #(parameter WIDTH = 8)
              (input  logic              clk, reset,
               input  logic  [WIDTH-1:0] d,
               output logic  [WIDTH-1:0] q);

  always_ff @(posedge clk, posedge reset)
    if (reset) q <= 0;
    else       q <= d;
endmodule
```

VHDL

```
library IEEE; use IEEE.STD_LOGIC_1164.all;
entity flopr is -- flip-flop with synchronous reset
  generic(width: integer);
  port(clk, reset:  in  STD_LOGIC;
       d:           in  STD_LOGIC_VECTOR(width-1 downto 0);
       q:           out STD_LOGIC_VECTOR(width-1 downto 0));
end;

architecture asynchronous of flopr is
begin
  process(clk, reset) begin
    if reset then  q <= (others => '0');
    elsif rising_edge(clk) then
          q <= d;
    end if;
  end process;
end;
```

HDL Example 7.10 RESETTABLE FLIP-FLOP WITH ENABLE

SystemVerilog

```
module flopenr #(parameter WIDTH = 8)
               (input  logic              clk, reset, en,
                input  logic [WIDTH-1:0]  d,
                output logic [WIDTH-1:0]  q);

  always_ff @(posedge clk, posedge reset)
    if (reset)   q <= 0;
    else if (en) q <= d;
endmodule
```

VHDL

```
library IEEE; use IEEE.STD_LOGIC_1164.all;
entity flopenr is -- flip-flop with enable and synchronous reset
  generic(width: integer);
  port(clk, reset, en: in  STD_LOGIC;
       d:             in  STD_LOGIC_VECTOR(width-1 downto 0);
       q:             out STD_LOGIC_VECTOR(width-1 downto 0));
end;

architecture asynchronous of flopenr is
begin
  process(clk, reset) begin
    if reset then  q <= (others => '0');
    elsif rising_edge(clk) then
      if en then
        q <= d;
      end if;
    end if;
  end process;
end;
```

HDL Example 7.11 2:1 MULTIPLEXER

SystemVerilog

```
module mux2 #(parameter WIDTH = 8)
            (input  logic [WIDTH-1:0]  d0, d1,
             input  logic              s,
             output logic [WIDTH-1:0]  y);

  assign y = s ? d1 : d0;
endmodule
```

VHDL

```
library IEEE; use IEEE.STD_LOGIC_1164.all;
entity mux2 is -- two-input multiplexer
  generic(width: integer);
  port(d0, d1: in  STD_LOGIC_VECTOR(width-1 downto 0);
       s:      in  STD_LOGIC;
       y:      out STD_LOGIC_VECTOR(width-1 downto 0));
end;

architecture behave of mux2 is
begin
  y <= d1 when s else d0;
end;
```

7.6.3 Testbench

The testbench loads a program into the memories. The program in Figure 7.60 exercises all of the instructions by performing a computation that should produce the correct result only if all of the instructions are functioning correctly. Specifically, the program will write the value 7 to address 100 if it runs correctly, but it is unlikely to do so if the hardware is buggy. This is an example of *ad hoc* testing.

The machine code is stored in a hexadecimal file called memfile.dat, which is loaded by the testbench during simulation. The file consists of the machine code for the instructions, one instruction per line. The testbench, top-level ARM module, and external memory HDL code are given in the following examples. The memories in this example hold 64 words each.

ADDR		PROGRAM	; COMMENTS	BINARY MACHINE CODE	HEX CODE
00	MAIN	SUB R0, R15, R15	; R0 = 0	1110 000 0010 0 1111 0000 0000 0000 1111	E04F000F
04		ADD R2, R0, #5	; R2 = 5	1110 001 0100 0 0000 0010 0000 0000 0101	E2802005
08		ADD R3, R0, #12	; R3 = 12	1110 001 0100 0 0000 0011 0000 0000 1100	E280300C
0C		SUB R7, R3, #9	; R7 = 3	1110 001 0010 0 0011 0111 0000 0000 1001	E2437009
10		ORR R4, R7, R2	; R4 = 3 OR 5 = 7	1110 000 1100 0 0111 0100 0000 0000 0010	E1874002
14		AND R5, R3, R4	; R5 = 12 AND 7 = 4	1110 000 0000 0 0011 0101 0000 0000 0100	E0035004
18		ADD R5, R5, R4	; R5 = 4 + 7 = 11	1110 000 0100 0 0101 0101 0000 0000 0100	E0855004
1C		SUBS R8, R5, R7	; R8 = 11 - 3 = 8, set Flags	1110 000 0010 1 0101 1000 0000 0000 0111	E0558007
20		BEQ END	; shouldn't be taken	0000 1010 0000 0000 0000 0000 0000 1100	0A00000C
24		SUBS R8, R3, R4	; R8 = 12 - 7 = 5	1110 000 0010 1 0011 1000 0000 0000 0100	E0538004
28		BGE AROUND	; should be taken	1010 1010 0000 0000 0000 0000 0000 0000	AA000000
2C		ADD R5, R0, #0	; should be skipped	1110 001 0100 0 0000 0101 0000 0000 0000	E2805000
30	AROUND	SUBS R8, R7, R2	; R8 = 3 - 5 = -2, set Flags	1110 000 0010 1 0111 1000 0000 0000 0010	E0578002
34		ADDLT R7, R5, #1	; R7 = 11 + 1 = 12	1011 001 0100 0 0101 0111 0000 0000 0001	B2857001
38		SUB R7, R7, R2	; R7 = 12 - 5 = 7	1110 000 0010 0 0111 0111 0000 0000 0010	E0477002
3C		STR R7, [R3, #84]	; mem[12+84] = 7	1110 010 1100 0 0011 0111 0000 0101 0100	E5837054
40		LDR R2, [R0, #96]	; R2 = mem[96] = 7	1110 010 1100 1 0000 0010 0000 0110 0000	E5902060
44		ADD R15, R15, R0	; PC = PC+8 (skips next)	1110 000 0100 0 1111 1111 0000 0000 0000	E08FF000
48		ADD R2, R0, #14	; shouldn't happen	1110 001 0100 0 0000 0010 0000 0000 0001	E280200E
4C		B END	; always taken	1110 1010 0000 0000 0000 0000 0000 0001	EA000001
50		ADD R2, R0, #13	; shouldn't happen	1110 001 0100 0 0000 0010 0000 0000 0001	E280200D
54		ADD R2, R0, #10	; shouldn't happen	1110 001 0100 0 0000 0010 0000 0000 0001	E280200A
58	END	STR R2, [R0, #100]	; mem[100] = 7	1110 010 1100 0 0000 0010 0000 0101 0100	E5802064

Figure 7.60 Assembly and machine code for test program

HDL Example 7.12 TESTBENCH

SystemVerilog

```
module testbench();
  logic        clk;
  logic        reset;
  logic [31:0] WriteData, DataAdr;
  logic        MemWrite;

  // instantiate device to be tested
  top dut(clk, reset, WriteData, DataAdr, MemWrite);

  // initialize test
  initial
  begin
    reset <= 1; # 22; reset <= 0;
  end

  // generate clock to sequence tests
  always
  begin
    clk <= 1; # 5; clk <= 0; # 5;
  end
```

VHDL

```
library IEEE;
use IEEE.STD_LOGIC_1164.all; use IEEE.NUMERIC_STD_UNSIGNED.all;
entity testbench is
end;

architecture test of testbench is
  component top
    port(clk, reset:           in  STD_LOGIC;
         WriteData, DataAdr: out STD_LOGIC_VECTOR(31 downto 0);
         MemWrite:           out STD_LOGIC);
  end component;
  signal WriteData, DataAdr:   STD_LOGIC_VECTOR(31 downto 0);
  signal clk, reset, MemWrite: STD_LOGIC;
begin
  -- instantiate device to be tested
  dut: top port map(clk, reset, WriteData, DataAdr, MemWrite);

  -- generate clock with 10 ns period
  process begin
    clk <= '1';
    wait for 5 ns;
    clk <= '0';
    wait for 5 ns;
  end process;
```

```
// check that 7 gets written to address 0x64
// at end of program
always @(negedge clk)
begin
  if(MemWrite) begin
    if(DataAdr === 100 & WriteData === 7) begin
      $display("Simulation succeeded");
      $stop;
    end else if (DataAdr !== 96) begin
      $display("Simulation failed");
      $stop;
    end
  end
end
endmodule
```

```
-- generate reset for first two clock cycles
process begin
  reset <= '1';
  wait for 22 ns;
  reset <= '0';
  wait;
end process;

-- check that 7 gets written to address 0x64
-- at end of program
process (clk) begin
  if (clk'event and clk = '0' and MemWrite = '1') then
    if (to_integer(DataAdr) = 100 and
        to_integer(WriteData) = 7) then
      report "NO ERRORS: Simulation succeeded" severity
        failure;
    elsif (DataAdr /= 96) then
      report "Simulation failed" severity failure;
    end if;
  end if;
end process;
end;
```

HDL Example 7.13 TOP-LEVEL MODULE

SystemVerilog

```
module top(input  logic         clk, reset,
           output logic [31:0]  WriteData, DataAdr,
           output logic         MemWrite);

  logic [31:0] PC, Instr, ReadData;

  // instantiate processor and memories
  arm arm(clk, reset, PC, Instr, MemWrite, DataAdr,
          WriteData, ReadData);
  imem imem(PC, Instr);
  dmem dmem(clk, MemWrite, DataAdr, WriteData, ReadData);
endmodule
```

VHDL

```
library IEEE;
use IEEE.STD_LOGIC_1164.all; use IEEE.NUMERIC_STD_UNSIGNED.all;
entity top is -- top-level design for testing
  port(clk, reset:          in    STD_LOGIC;
       WriteData, DataAdr:  buffer STD_LOGIC_VECTOR(31 downto 0);
       MemWrite:            buffer STD_LOGIC);
end;

architecture test of top is
  component arm
    port(clk, reset:        in  STD_LOGIC;
         PC:                out STD_LOGIC_VECTOR(31 downto 0);
         Instr:             in  STD_LOGIC_VECTOR(31 downto 0);
         MemWrite:          out STD_LOGIC;
         ALUResult, WriteData:out STD_LOGIC_VECTOR(31 downto 0);
         ReadData:          in  STD_LOGIC_VECTOR(31 downto 0));
  end component;
  component imem
  port(a:  in  STD_LOGIC_VECTOR(31 downto 0);
       rd: out STD_LOGIC_VECTOR(31 downto 0));
  end component;
  component dmem
  port(clk, we: in    STD_LOGIC;
       a, wd:   in    STD_LOGIC_VECTOR(31 downto 0);
       rd:      out   STD_LOGIC_VECTOR(31 downto 0));
  end component;
  signal PC, Instr,
         ReadData: STD_LOGIC_VECTOR(31 downto 0);
begin
  -- instantiate processor and memories
  i_arm: arm port map(clk, reset, PC, Instr, MemWrite, DataAdr,
                      WriteData, ReadData);
  i_imem: imem port map(PC, Instr);
  i_dmem: dmem port map(clk, MemWrite, DataAdr,
                        WriteData, ReadData);
end;
```

HDL Example 7.14 DATA MEMORY

SystemVerilog

```
module dmem(input  logic        clk, we,
            input  logic [31:0] a, wd,
            output logic [31:0] rd);

  logic [31:0] RAM[63:0];

  assign rd = RAM[a[31:2]]; // word aligned

  always_ff @(posedge clk)
    if (we) RAM[a[31:2]] <= wd;
endmodule
```

VHDL

```
library IEEE;
use IEEE.STD_LOGIC_1164.all; use STD.TEXTIO.all;
use IEEE.NUMERIC_STD_UNSIGNED.all;
entity dmem is -- data memory
  port(clk, we: in  STD_LOGIC;
       a, wd:   in  STD_LOGIC_VECTOR(31 downto 0);
       rd:      out STD_LOGIC_VECTOR(31 downto 0));
end;

architecture behave of dmem is
begin
  process is
    type ramtype is array (63 downto 0) of
                    STD_LOGIC_VECTOR(31 downto 0);
    variable mem: ramtype;
  begin -- read or write memory
    loop
      if clk'event and clk = '1' then
        if (we = '1') then
          mem(to_integer(a(7 downto 2))) := wd;
        end if;
      end if;
      rd <= mem(to_integer(a(7 downto 2)));
      wait on clk, a;
    end loop;
  end process;
end;
```

HDL Example 7.15 INSTRUCTION MEMORY

SystemVerilog

```
module imem(input  logic [31:0] a,
            output logic [31:0] rd);

  logic [31:0] RAM[63:0];

  initial
    $readmemh("memfile.dat",RAM);

  assign rd = RAM[a[31:2]]; // word aligned
endmodule
```

VHDL

```
library IEEE;
use IEEE.STD_LOGIC_1164.all; use STD.TEXTIO.all;
use IEEE.NUMERIC_STD_UNSIGNED.all;
entity imem is -- instruction memory
  port(a:  in  STD_LOGIC_VECTOR(31 downto 0);
       rd: out STD_LOGIC_VECTOR(31 downto 0));
end;
architecture behave of imem is -- instruction memory
begin
  process is
    file mem_file: TEXT;
    variable L: line;
    variable ch: character;
    variable i, index, result: integer;
    type ramtype is array (63 downto 0) of
                    STD_LOGIC_VECTOR(31 downto 0);
    variable mem: ramtype;
  begin
    -- initialize memory from file
    for i in 0 to 63 loop -- set all contents low
      mem(i) := (others => '0');
    end loop;
```

```
index := 0;
FILE_OPEN(mem_file, "memfile.dat", READ_MODE);
while not endfile(mem_file) loop
  readline(mem_file, L);
  result := 0;
  for i in 1 to 8 loop
    read(L, ch);
    if '0' <= ch and ch <= '9' then
      result := character'pos(ch) - character'pos('0');
    elsif 'a' <= ch and ch <= 'f' then
      result := character'pos(ch) - character'pos('a') + 10;
    elsif 'A' <= ch and ch <= 'F' then
      result := character'pos(ch) - character'pos('A') + 10;
    else report "Format error on line " & integer'image(index)
      severity error;
    end if;
    mem(index)(35-i*4 downto 32-i*4) :=
      to_std_logic_vector(result,4);
  end loop;
  index := index + 1;
end loop;

-- read memory
loop
  rd <= mem(to_integer(a(7 downto 2)));
  wait on a;
end loop;
end process;
end;
```

7.7 ADVANCED MICROARCHITECTURE*

High-performance microprocessors use a wide variety of techniques to run programs faster. Recall that the time required to run a program is proportional to the period of the clock and to the number of clock cycles per instruction (CPI). Thus, to increase performance, we would like to speed-up the clock and/or reduce the CPI. This section surveys some existing speed-up techniques. The implementation details become quite complex, so we focus on the concepts. Hennessy & Patterson's *Computer Architecture* text is a definitive reference if you want to fully understand the details.

Advances in integrated circuit manufacturing have steadily reduced transistor sizes. Smaller transistors are faster and generally consume less power. Thus, even if the microarchitecture does not change, the clock frequency can increase because all the gates are faster. Moreover, smaller transistors enable placing more transistors on a chip. Microarchitects use the additional transistors to build more complicated processors or to put more processors on a chip. Unfortunately, power consumption increases with the number of transistors and the speed at which they operate (see Section 1.8). Power consumption is now an essential concern. Microprocessor designers have a challenging task juggling the trade-offs among speed, power, and cost for chips with billions of transistors in some of the most complex systems that humans have ever built.

7.7.1 Deep Pipelines

Aside from advances in manufacturing, the easiest way to speed up the clock is to chop the pipeline into more stages. Each stage contains less logic, so it can run faster. This chapter has considered a classic five-stage pipeline, but 10–20 stages are now commonly used.

The maximum number of pipeline stages is limited by pipeline hazards, sequencing overhead, and cost. Longer pipelines introduce more dependencies. Some of the dependencies can be solved by forwarding but others require stalls, which increase the CPI. The pipeline registers between each stage have sequencing overhead from their setup time and clk-to-Q delay (as well as clock skew). This sequencing overhead makes adding more pipeline stages give diminishing returns. Finally, adding more stages increases the cost because of the extra pipeline registers and hardware required to handle hazards.

Example 7.9

Consider building a pipelined processor by chopping up the single-cycle processor into N stages. The single-cycle processor has a propagation delay of 740 ps through the combinational logic. The sequencing overhead of a register is 90 ps. Assume that the combinational delay can be arbitrarily divided into any number of stages and that pipeline hazard logic does not increase the delay. The five-stage pipeline in Example 7.7 has a CPI of 1.23. Assume that each additional stage increases the CPI by 0.1 because of branch mispredictions and other pipeline hazards. How many pipeline stages should be used to make the processor execute programs as fast as possible?

Solution: The cycle time for an N-stage pipeline is $T_c = (740/N + 90)$ ps. The CPI is $1.23 + 0.1(N–5)$. The time per instruction, or instruction time, is the product of the cycle time and the CPI. Figure 7.61 plots the cycle time and instruction time versus the number of stages. The instruction time has a minimum of 279 ps at $N = 8$ stages. This minimum is only slightly better than the 293 ps per instruction achieved with a five-stage pipeline.

In the late 1990s and early 2000s, microprocessors were marketed largely based on clock frequency ($1/T_c$). This pushed microprocessors to use very deep pipelines (20–31 stages on the Pentium 4) to maximize the clock frequency, even if the benefits for overall performance were questionable. Power is proportional to clock frequency and also increases with the number of pipeline registers, so now that power consumption is so important, pipeline depths are decreasing.

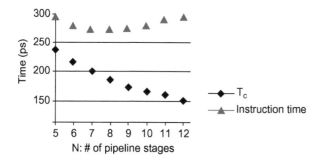

Figure 7.61 Cycle time and instruction time vs. the number of pipeline stages

7.7.2 Micro-Operations

Recall our design principles of "regularity supports simplicity" and "make the common case fast." Pure reduced instruction set computer (RISC) architectures such as MIPS contain only simple instructions, typically those that can be executed in a single cycle on a simple, fast datapath with a three-ported register file, single ALU, and single data memory access like the ones we have developed in this chapter. Complex instruction set computer (CISC) architectures generally include instructions requiring more registers, more additions, or more than one memory access per instruction. For example, the x86 instruction ADD [ESP], [EDX + 80 + EDI*2] involves reading the three registers, adding the base, displacement, and scaled index, reading two memory locations, summing their values, and writing the result back to memory. A microprocessor that could perform all of these functions at once would be unnecessarily slow on more common, simpler instructions.

Computer architects make the common case fast by defining a set of simple *micro-operations* (also known as *micro-ops* or *μops*) that can be executed on simple datapaths. Each real instruction is decoded into one or more micro-ops. For example, if we defined *μops* resembling basic ARM instructions and some temporary registers T1 and T2 for holding intermediate results, then the x86 instruction could become seven *μops*:

```
ADD  T1, [EDX + 80] ; T1 <- EDX + 80
LSL  T2, EDI, 2     ; T2 <- EDI*2
ADD  T1, T2, T2     ; T1 <- EDX + 80 + EDI*2
LDR  T1, [T1]       ; T1 <- MEM[EDX + 80 + EDI*2]
LDR  T2, [ESP]      ; T2 <- MEM[ESP]
ADD  T1, T2, T1     ; T1 <- MEM[ESP] + MEM[EDX + 80 + EDI*2]
STR  T1, [ESP]      ; MEM[ESP]<- MEM[ESP] + MEM[EDX + 80 + EDI*2]
```

Although most ARM instructions are simple, some are decomposed into multiple micro-ops as well. For example, loads with postindexed addressing (such as LDR R1, [R2], #4) require a second write port on the register file. Data-processing instructions with register-shifted register addressing (such as ORR R3, R4, R5, LSL R6) require a third read port on the register file. Instead of providing a larger five-port register file, the ARM datapath may decode these complex instructions into pairs of simpler instructions:

Complex Op	Micro-op Sequence
LDR R1, [R2], #4	LDR R1, [R2]
	ADD R2, R2, #4
ORR R3, R4, R5 LSL R6	LSL T1, R5, R6
	ORR R3, R4, T1

Although the programmer could have written the simpler instructions directly and the program may have run just as fast, a single complex instruction takes less memory than the pair of simpler instructions. Reading instructions from external memory can consume significant power, so the complex instruction also can save power. The ARM instruction set is so successful in part because of the architects' judicious choice of instructions that give better code density than pure RISC instructions sets such as MIPS, yet more efficient decoding than CISC instruction sets such as x86.

Microarchitects make the decision of whether to provide hardware to implement a complex operation directly or break it into micro-op sequences. They make similar decisions about other options described later in this section. These choices lead to different points in the performance-power-cost design space.

7.7.3 Branch Prediction

An ideal pipelined processor would have a CPI of 1.0. The branch misprediction penalty is a major reason for increased CPI. As pipelines get deeper, branches are resolved later in the pipeline. Thus, the branch misprediction penalty gets larger because all the instructions issued after the mispredicted branch must be flushed. To address this problem, most pipelined processors use a *branch predictor* to guess whether the branch should be taken. Recall that our pipeline from Section 7.5.3 simply predicted that branches are never taken.

Some branches occur when a program reaches the end of a loop and branches back to repeat the loop (e.g., in a for or while loop). Loops tend to be executed many times, so these backward branches are usually taken. The simplest form of branch prediction checks the direction of the branch and predicts that backward branches should be taken. This is called *static branch prediction*, because it does not depend on the history of the program.

Forward branches are difficult to predict without knowing more about the specific program. Therefore, most processors use *dynamic branch predictors*, which use the history of program execution to guess whether a branch should be taken. Dynamic branch predictors maintain a table of the last several hundred (or thousand) branch instructions that the processor has executed. The table, called a *branch target buffer*, includes the destination of the branch and a history of whether the branch was taken.

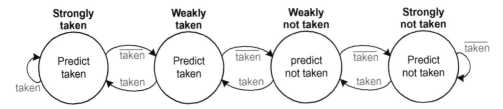

Figure 7.62 Two-bit branch predictor state transition diagram

To see the operation of dynamic branch predictors, consider the following loop from Code Example 6.17. The loop repeats 10 times, and the BGE out of the loop is taken only on the last iteration.

```
    MOV  R1,  #0
    MOV  R0,  #0

FOR
    CMP  R0,  #10
    BGE  DONE
    ADD  R1,  R1,  R0
    ADD  R0,  R0,  #1
    B    FOR
DONE
```

A *one-bit dynamic branch predictor* remembers whether the branch was taken the last time and predicts that it will do the same thing the next time. While the loop is repeating, it remembers that the BGE was not taken last time and predicts that it should not be taken next time. This is a correct prediction until the last branch of the loop, when the branch does get taken. Unfortunately, if the loop is run again, the branch predictor remembers that the last branch was taken. Therefore, it incorrectly predicts that the branch should be taken when the loop is first run again. In summary, a 1-bit branch predictor mispredicts the first and last branches of a loop.

A *two-bit dynamic branch predictor* solves this problem by having four states: *strongly taken*, *weakly taken*, *weakly not taken*, and *strongly not taken*, as shown in Figure 7.62. When the loop is repeating, it enters the "strongly not taken" state and predicts that the branch should not be taken next time. This is correct until the last branch of the loop, which is taken and moves the predictor to the "weakly not taken" state. When the loop is first run again, the branch predictor correctly predicts that the branch should not be taken and re-enters the "strongly not taken" state. In summary, a two-bit branch predictor mispredicts only the last branch of a loop.

The branch predictor operates in the Fetch stage of the pipeline so that it can determine which instruction to execute on the next cycle. When it predicts that the branch should be taken, the processor fetches the next instruction from the branch destination stored in the branch target buffer.

As one can imagine, branch predictors may be used to track even more history of the program to increase the accuracy of predictions. Good branch predictors achieve better than 90% accuracy on typical programs.

7.7.4 Superscalar Processor

A *superscalar processor* contains multiple copies of the datapath hardware to execute multiple instructions simultaneously. Figure 7.63 shows a block diagram of a two-way superscalar processor that fetches and executes two instructions per cycle. The datapath fetches two instructions at a time from the instruction memory. It has a six-ported register file to read four source operands and write two results back in each cycle. It also contains two ALUs and a two-ported data memory to execute the two instructions at the same time.

Figure 7.64 shows a pipeline diagram illustrating the two-way superscalar processor executing two instructions on each cycle. For this program, the processor has a CPI of 0.5. Designers commonly refer to the reciprocal of the CPI as the *instructions per cycle*, or IPC. This processor has an IPC of 2 on this program.

Executing many instructions simultaneously is difficult because of dependencies. For example, Figure 7.65 shows a pipeline diagram running a program with data dependencies. The dependencies in the code are shown in blue. The ADD instruction is dependent on R8, which is produced by the LDR instruction, so it cannot be issued at the same time as LDR. The ADD instruction stalls for yet another cycle so that LDR can forward R8 to ADD in cycle 5. The other dependencies (between SUB and

A *scalar* processor acts on one piece of data at a time.

A *vector* processor acts on several pieces of data with a single instruction.

A *superscalar* processor issues several instructions at a time, each of which operates on one piece of data.

Our ARM pipelined processor is a scalar processor. Vector processors were popular for supercomputers in the 1980s and 1990s because they efficiently handled the long vectors of data common in scientific computations, and they are heavily used now in *graphics processing units* (GPUs). Modern high-performance microprocessors are superscalar, because issuing several independent instructions is more flexible than processing vectors.

However, modern processors also include hardware to handle short vectors of data that are common in multimedia and graphics applications. These are called *single instruction multiple data* (SIMD) units and are discussed in Section 6.7.5.

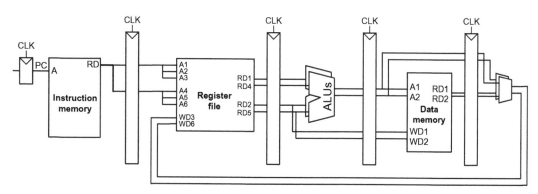

Figure 7.63 Superscalar datapath

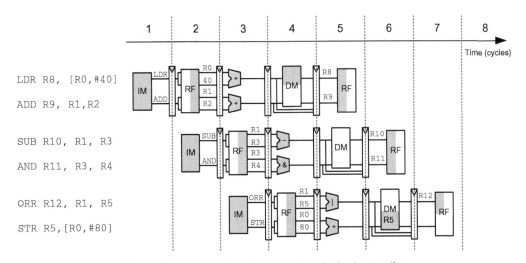

Figure 7.64 Abstract view of a superscalar pipeline in operation

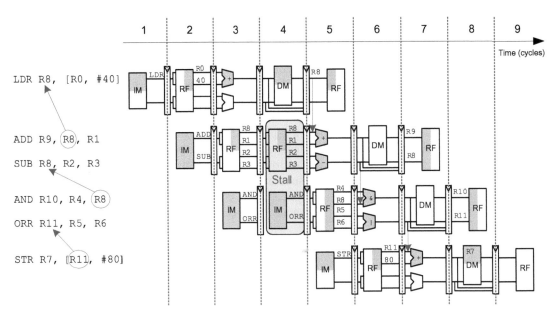

Figure 7.65 Program with data dependencies

AND based on R8, and between ORR and STR based on R11) are handled by forwarding results produced in one cycle to be consumed in the next. This program requires five cycles to issue six instructions, for an IPC of 1.2.

Recall that parallelism comes in temporal and spatial forms. Pipelining is a case of temporal parallelism. Multiple execution units is a case of spatial parallelism. Superscalar processors exploit both forms of parallelism to squeeze out performance far exceeding that of our single-cycle and multicycle processors.

Commercial processors may be three-, four-, or even six-way superscalar. They must handle control hazards such as branches as well as data hazards. Unfortunately, real programs have many dependencies, so wide superscalar processors rarely fully utilize all of the execution units. Moreover, the large number of execution units and complex forwarding networks consume vast amounts of circuitry and power.

7.7.5 Out-of-Order Processor

To cope with the problem of dependencies, an out-of-order processor looks ahead across many instructions to *issue*, or begin executing, independent instructions as rapidly as possible. The instructions can issue in a different order than that written by the programmer, as long as dependencies are honored so that the program produces the intended result.

Consider running the same program from Figure 7.65 on a two-way superscalar out-of-order processor. The processor can issue up to two instructions per cycle from anywhere in the program, as long as dependencies are observed. Figure 7.66 shows the data dependencies and the

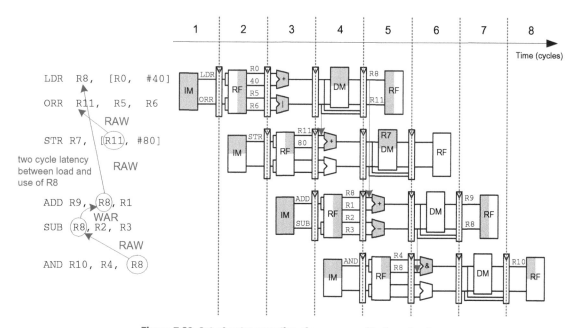

Figure 7.66 Out-of-order execution of a program with dependencies

operation of the processor. The classifications of dependencies as RAW and WAR will be discussed soon. The constraints on issuing instructions are:

▶ Cycle 1
  - The LDR instruction issues.
  - The ADD, SUB, and AND instructions are dependent on LDR by way of R8, so they cannot issue yet. However, the ORR instruction is independent, so it also issues.

▶ Cycle 2
  - Remember that there is a two-cycle latency between issuing an LDR instruction and a dependent instruction, so ADD cannot issue yet because of the R8 dependence. SUB writes R8, so it cannot issue before ADD, lest ADD receive the wrong value of R8. AND is dependent on SUB.
  - Only the STR instruction issues.

▶ Cycle 3
  - On cycle 3, R8 is available, so the ADD issues. SUB issues simultaneously, because it will not write R8 until after ADD consumes R8.

▶ Cycle 4
  - The AND instruction issues. R8 is forwarded from SUB to AND.

The out-of-order processor issues the six instructions in four cycles, for an IPC of 1.5.

The dependence of ADD on LDR by way of R8 is a *read after write* (*RAW*) hazard. ADD must not read R8 until after LDR has written it. This is the type of dependency we are accustomed to handling in the pipelined processor. It inherently limits the speed at which the program can run, even if infinitely many execution units are available. Similarly, the dependence of STR on ORR by way of R11 and of AND on SUB by way of R8 are RAW dependencies.

The dependence between SUB and ADD by way of R8 is called a *write after read* (*WAR*) hazard or an *antidependence*. SUB must not write R8 before ADD reads R8, so that ADD receives the correct value according to the original order of the program. WAR hazards could not occur in the simple pipeline, but they may happen in an out-of-order processor if the dependent instruction (in this case, SUB) is moved too early.

A WAR hazard is not essential to the operation of the program. It is merely an artifact of the programmer's choice to use the same register for two unrelated instructions. If the SUB instruction had written R12 instead of R8, then the dependency would disappear and SUB could be issued before ADD. The ARM architecture only has 16 registers, so sometimes the programmer is forced to reuse a register and introduce a hazard just because all the other registers are in use.

A third type of hazard, not shown in the program, is called a *write after write* (WAW) hazard or an *output dependence*. A WAW hazard occurs if an instruction attempts to write a register after a subsequent instruction has already written it. The hazard would result in the wrong value being written to the register. For example, in the following code, LDR and ADD both write R8. The final value in R8 should come from ADD according to the order of the program. If an out-of-order processor attempted to execute ADD first, then a WAW hazard would occur.

```
LDR  R8,  [R3]
ADD  R8,  R1,  R2
```

WAW hazards are not essential either; again, they are artifacts caused by the programmer's using the same destination register for two unrelated instructions. If the ADD instruction were issued first, then the program could eliminate the WAW hazard by discarding the result of the LDR instead of writing it to R8. This is called *squashing* the LDR.[4]

Out-of-order processors use a table to keep track of instructions waiting to issue. The table, sometimes called a *scoreboard*, contains information about the dependencies. The size of the table determines how many instructions can be considered for issue. On each cycle, the processor examines the table and issues as many instructions as it can, limited by the dependencies and by the number of execution units (e.g., ALUs, memory ports) that are available.

The *instruction level parallelism* (ILP) is the number of instructions that can be executed simultaneously for a particular program and microarchitecture. Theoretical studies have shown that the ILP can be quite large for out-of-order microarchitectures with perfect branch predictors and enormous numbers of execution units. However, practical processors seldom achieve an ILP greater than two or three, even with six-way superscalar datapaths with out-of-order execution.

7.7.6 Register Renaming

Out-of-order processors use a technique called *register renaming* to eliminate WAR and WAW hazards. Register renaming adds some nonarchitectural renaming registers to the processor. For example, a processor might add 20 renaming registers, called T0–T19. The

---

[4] You might wonder why the LDR needs to be issued at all. The reason is that out-of-order processors must guarantee that all of the same exceptions occur that would have occurred if the program had been executed in its original order. The LDR potentially may produce a Data Abort exception, so it must be issued to check for the exception, even though the result can be discarded.

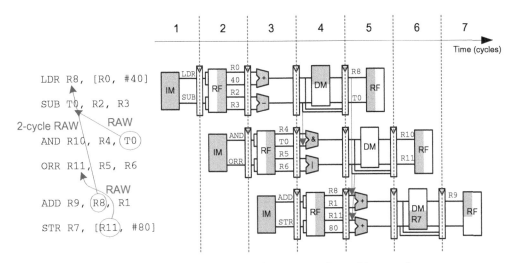

LDR R8, [R0, #40]

SUB T0, R2, R3

2-cycle RAW   RAW
AND R10, R4, (T0)

ORR R11, R5, R6

                   RAW
ADD R9, (R8), R1

STR R7, [R11], #80]

Figure 7.67 Out-of-order execution of a program using register renaming

programmer cannot use these registers directly, because they are not part of the architecture. However, the processor is free to use them to eliminate hazards.

For example, in the previous section, a WAR hazard occurred between the SUB and ADD instructions based on reusing R8. The out-of-order processor could rename R8 to T0 for the SUB instruction. Then, SUB could be executed sooner, because T0 has no dependency on the ADD instruction. The processor keeps a table of which registers were renamed so that it can consistently rename registers in subsequent dependent instructions. In this example, R8 must also be renamed to T0 in the AND instruction, because it refers to the result of SUB.

Figure 7.67 shows the same program from Figure 7.65 executing on an out-of-order processor with register renaming. R8 is renamed to T0 in SUB and AND to eliminate the WAR hazard. The constraints on issuing instructions are:

▶   Cycle 1
   –   The LDR instruction issues.
   –   The ADD instruction is dependent on LDR by way of R8, so it cannot issue yet. However, the SUB instruction is independent now that its destination has been renamed to T0, so SUB also issues.

▶   Cycle 2
   –   Remember that there is a two-cycle latency between issuing an LDR instruction and a dependent instruction, so ADD cannot issue yet because of the R8 dependence.

- – The AND instruction is dependent on SUB, so it can issue. T0 is forwarded from SUB to AND.
- – The ORR instruction is independent, so it also issues.

▸ Cycle 3
- – On cycle 3, R8 is available, so the ADD issues.
- – R11 is also available, so STR issues.

The out-of-order processor with register renaming issues the six instructions in three cycles, for an IPC of 2.

7.7.7 Multithreading

Because the ILP of real programs tends to be fairly low, adding more execution units to a superscalar or out-of-order processor gives diminishing returns. Another problem, discussed in Chapter 8, is that memory is much slower than the processor. Most loads and stores access a smaller and faster memory, called a *cache*. However, when the instructions or data are not available in the cache, the processor may stall for 100 or more cycles while retrieving the information from the main memory. Multithreading is a technique that helps keep a processor with many execution units busy even if the ILP of a program is low or the program is stalled waiting for memory.

To explain multithreading, we need to define a few new terms. A program running on a computer is called a *process*. Computers can run multiple processes simultaneously; for example, you can play music on a PC while surfing the web and running a virus checker. Each process consists of one or more *threads* that also run simultaneously. For example, a word processor may have one thread handling the user typing, a second thread spell-checking the document while the user works, and a third thread printing the document. In this way, the user does not have to wait, for example, for a document to finish printing before being able to type again. The degree to which a process can be split into multiple threads that can run simultaneously defines its level of *thread level parallelism* (TLP).

In a conventional processor, the threads only give the illusion of running simultaneously. The threads actually take turns being executed on the processor under control of the OS. When one thread's turn ends, the OS saves its architectural state, loads the architectural state of the next thread, and starts executing that next thread. This procedure is called *context switching*. As long as the processor switches through all the threads fast enough, the user perceives all of the threads as running at the same time.

A multithreaded processor contains more than one copy of its architectural state, so that more than one thread can be active at a time. For example, if we extended a processor to have four program counters and 64 registers, four threads could be available at one time. If one thread stalls while waiting for data from main memory, then the processor could context switch to another thread without any delay, because the program counter and registers are already available. Moreover, if one thread lacks sufficient parallelism to keep all the execution units busy in a superscalar design, then another thread could issue instructions to the idle units.

Multithreading does not improve the performance of an individual thread, because it does not increase the ILP. However, it does improve the overall throughput of the processor, because multiple threads can use processor resources that would have been idle when executing a single thread. Multithreading is also relatively inexpensive to implement, because it replicates only the PC and register file, not the execution units and memories.

7.7.8 Multiprocessors

With contributions from Matthew Watkins

Modern processors have enormous numbers of transistors available. Using them to increase the pipeline depth or to add more execution units to a superscalar processor gives little performance benefit and is wasteful of power. Around the year 2005, computer architects made a major shift to building multiple copies of the processor on the same chip; these copies are called *cores*.

A *multiprocessor* system consists of multiple processors and a method for communication between the processors. Three common classes of multiprocessors include *symmetric* (or *homogeneous*) multiprocessors, *heterogeneous* multiprocessors, and *clusters*.

Symmetric Multiprocessors

Symmetric multiprocessors include two or more identical processors sharing a single main memory. The multiple processors may be separate chips or multiple cores on the same chip.

Multiprocessors can be used to run more threads simultaneously or to run a particular thread faster. Running more threads simultaneously is easy; the threads are simply divided up among the processors. Unfortunately, typical PC users need to run only a small number of threads at any given time. Running a particular thread faster is much more challenging. The programmer must divide the existing thread into multiple threads to execute on each processor. This becomes tricky when the processors need to communicate with each other. One of the major challenges for computer designers and programmers is to effectively use large numbers of processor cores.

Symmetric multiprocessors have a number of advantages. They are relatively simple to design because the processor can be designed once and then replicated multiple times to increase performance. Programming for and executing code on a symmetric multiprocessor is also relatively straightforward because any program can run on any processor in the system and achieve approximately the same performance.

Heterogeneous Multiprocessors

Unfortunately, continuing to add more and more symmetric cores is not guaranteed to provide continued performance improvement. As of 2015, consumer applications used few threads at any given time, and a typical consumer might be expected to have a couple of applications actually computing simultaneously. Although this is enough to keep dual-core and quad-core systems busy, unless programs start incorporating significantly more parallelism, continuing to add more cores beyond this point will provide diminishing benefits. As an added issue, because general-purpose processors are designed to provide good average performance, they are generally not the most power-efficient option for performing a given operation. This energy inefficiency is especially important in highly power-constrained systems such as mobile phones.

Heterogeneous multiprocessors aim to address these issues by incorporating different types of cores and/or specialized hardware in a single system. Each application uses those resources that provide the best performance, or power-performance ratio, for that application. Because transistors are fairly plentiful these days, the fact that not every application will make use of every piece of hardware is of lesser concern. Heterogeneous systems can take a number of forms. A heterogeneous system can incorporate cores with different microarchitectures that have different power, performance, and area trade-offs.

One heterogeneous strategy popularized by ARM is *big.LITTLE*, in which a system contains both energy-efficient and high-performance cores. "LITTLE" cores such as the Cortex-A53 are single-issue or dual-issue in-order processors with good energy efficiency that handle routine tasks. "big" cores such as the Cortex-A57 are more complex superscalar out-of-order cores delivering high performance for peak loads.

Another heterogeneous strategy is accelerators, in which a system contains special-purpose hardware optimized for performance or energy efficiency on specific types of tasks. For example, a mobile system-on-chip (SoC) presently may contain dedicated accelerators for graphics processing, video, wireless communication, real-time tasks, and cryptography. These accelerators can be 10–100x more efficient than general-purpose processors for the same tasks. Digital signal processors are another class of accelerators. These processors have a specialized instruction set optimized for math-intensive tasks.

Heterogeneous systems are not without their drawbacks. They add complexity in terms of both designing the different heterogeneous elements and the additional programming effort to decide when and how to make use of the varying resources. Symmetric and heterogeneous

Scientists searching for signs of extraterrestrial intelligence use the world's largest clustered multiprocessors to analyze radio telescope data for patterns that might be signs of life in other solar systems. The cluster, operational since 1999, consists of personal computers owned by more than 6 million volunteers around the world.

When a computer in the cluster is idle, it fetches a piece of the data from a centralized server, analyzes the data, and sends the results back to the server. You can volunteer your computer's idle time for the cluster by visiting setiathome.berkeley.edu.

systems both have their places in modern systems. Symmetric multi-processors are good for situations like large data centers that have lots of thread level parallelism available. Heterogeneous systems are good for cases that have more varying or special-purpose workloads.

Clusters

In *clustered* multiprocessors, each processor has its own local memory system. One type of cluster is a group of personal computers connected together on the network running software to jointly solve a large problem. Another type of cluster that has become very important is the *data center*, in which racks of computers and disks are networked together and share power and cooling. Major Internet companies including Google, Amazon, and Facebook have driven the rapid development of data centers to support millions of users around the world.

7.8 REAL-WORLD PERSPECTIVE: EVOLUTION OF ARM MICROARCHITECTURE*

This section traces the development of the ARM architecture and microarchitecture since its inception in 1985. Table 7.7 summarizes the highlights, showing 10x improvement in IPC and 250x increase in

DMIPS (Dhrystone millions of instructions per second) measures performance.

Table 7.7 Evolution of ARM processors

Microarchitecture	Year	Architecture	Pipeline Depth	DMIPS/ MHz	Representative Frequency (MHz)	L1 Cache	Relative Size
ARM1	1985	v1	3	0.33	8	N/A	0.1
ARM6	1992	v3	3	0.65	30	4 KB unified	0.6
ARM7	1994	v4T	3	0.9	100	0–8 KB unified	1
ARM9E	1999	v5TE	5	1.1	300	0–16 KB I + D	3
ARM11	2002	v6	8	1.25	700	4–64 KB I + D	30
Cortex-A9	2009	v7	8	2.5	1000	16–64 KB I + D	100
Cortex-A7	2011	v7	8	1.9	1500	8–64 KB I + D	40
Cortex-A15	2011	v7	15	3.5	2000	32 KB I + D	240
Cortex-M0 +	2012	v7M	2	0.93	60–250	None	0.3
Cortex-A53	2012	v8	8	2.3	1500	8–64 KB I + D	50
Cortex-A57	2012	v8	15	4.1	2000	48 KB I + 32 KB D	300

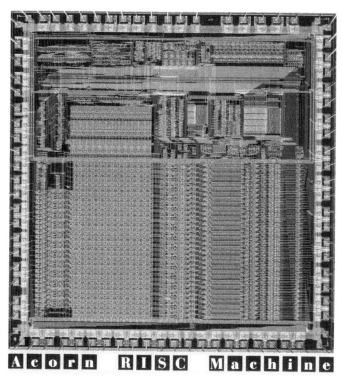

Figure 7.68 ARM1 die photograph
(Reproduced with permission from ARM. © 1985 ARM Ltd.)

frequency over three decades and eight revisions of the architecture. Frequency, area, and power will vary with manufacturing process and the goals, schedule, and capabilities of the design team. The representative frequencies are quoted for a fabrication process at the time of product introduction, so much of the frequency gain comes from transistors rather than microarchitecture. The relative size is normalized by the transistor feature size and can vary widely depending on cache size and other factors.

Figure 7.68 shows a die photograph of the ARM1 processor, which contained 25,000 transistors in a three-stage pipeline. If you count carefully, you can observe the 32 bits of the datapath at the bottom. The register file is on the left and the ALU is on the right. At the very left is the program counter; observe that the two least significant bits at the bottom are empty (tied to 0) and the six at the top are different because they are used for status bits. The controller sits on top of the datapath. Some of the rectangular blocks are PLAs implementing control logic. The rectangles around the edge are I/O pads, with tiny gold bond wires visible leading out of the picture.

In 1990, Acorn spun off the processor design team to establish a new
company, Advanced RISC Machines (later named ARM Holdings),
which began licensing the ARMv3 architecture. The ARMv3 architecture
moved the status bits from the PC to the Current Program Status Register
and extended the PC to 32 bits. Apple bought a major stake in ARM and
used the ARM 610 in the Newton computer, the world's first Personal
Digital Assistant (PDA) and one of the first commercial applications of
handwriting recognition. Newton proved to be ahead of its time, but it
laid the foundation for more successful PDAs and later for smart phones
and tablets.

ARM achieved huge success with the ARM7 line in 1994, especially the
ARM7TDMI, which became one of the mostly widely used RISC processors
in embedded systems over the next 15 years. The ARM7TDMI used the
ARMv4T instruction set, which introduced the Thumb instruction set for
better code density and defined halfword and signed byte load and store
instructions. TDMI stood for Thumb, JTAG Debug, fast Multiply, and In-
Circuit Debug. The various debug features help programmers write code
on the hardware and test it from a PC using a simple cable, an important
advance at the time. ARM7 used a simple three-stage pipeline with Fetch,
Decode, and Execute stages. The processor had a unified cache containing
both instructions and data. Because the cache in a pipelined processor is
usually busy every cycle fetching instructions, ARM7 stalled memory
instructions in the Execute stage to make time for the cache to access the
data. Figure 7.69 shows a block diagram of the processor. Rather than manufacturing a chip directly, ARM licensed the processor to other companies
that put them into their larger system-on-chip (SoC). Customers could buy
the processor as a hard macro (a complete and efficient but inflexible layout
that could be dropped directly into a chip) or as a soft macro (Verilog code
that could be synthesized by the customer). The ARM7 was used in a vast
number of products, including mobile phones, the Apple iPod, Lego Mind-
storms NXT, Nintendo game machines, and automobiles. Since then, nearly
all mobile phones have been built around ARM processors.

The ARM9E line improved on ARM7 with a five-stage pipeline similar to the one described in this chapter, separate instruction and data
caches, and new Thumb and digital signal processing instructions in the
ARMv5TE architecture. Figure 7.70 shows a block diagram of the
ARM9 containing many of the same components as we encountered in
this chapter but adding the multiplier and shifter. The IA/ID/DA/DD signals are the Instruction and Data Address and Data busses to the memory
system, and the IAreg is the PC. The next-generation ARM11 extended
the pipeline further to eight stages to boost frequency and defined
Thumb2 and SIMD instructions.

The ARMv7 instruction set added Advanced SIMD instructions operating on double- and quad-word registers. It also defined a v7-M variant

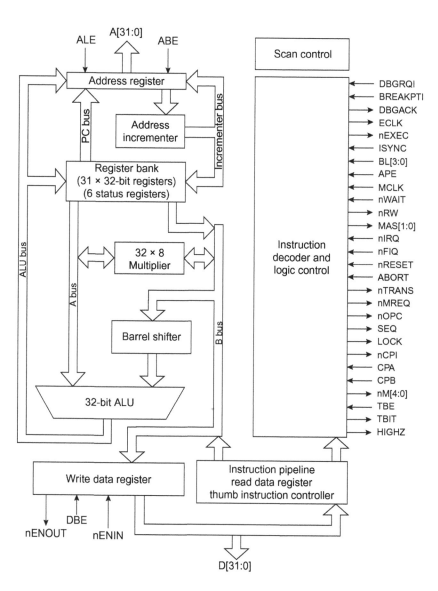

Figure 7.69 ARM7 block diagram
(Reproduced with permission from ARM. © 1998 ARM Ltd.)

Steve Furber (1953–) was born in Manchester, England, and received a PhD in aerodynamics from the University of Cambridge. He joined Acorn Computer, where he codesigned the BBC Micro and ARM1 microprocessor for Acorn Computer. In 1990, he joined the faculty of the University of Manchester, where his research has focused on asynchronous computing and neural systems.

(Photograph © 2012 The University of Manchester. Reproduced with permission.)

supporting only Thumb instructions. ARM introduced the Cortex-A and Cortex-M families of processors. The Cortex-A family of high-performance processors are now used in virtually all smart phones and tablets. The Cortex-M family, running the Thumb instruction set, are tiny and inexpensive microcontrollers used in embedded systems. For example, the Cortex-M0+ uses a two-stage pipeline and only 12,000 gates, compared with hundreds of thousands in an A-series processor. It costs well under a dollar as a stand-alone chip, or under a penny when integrated

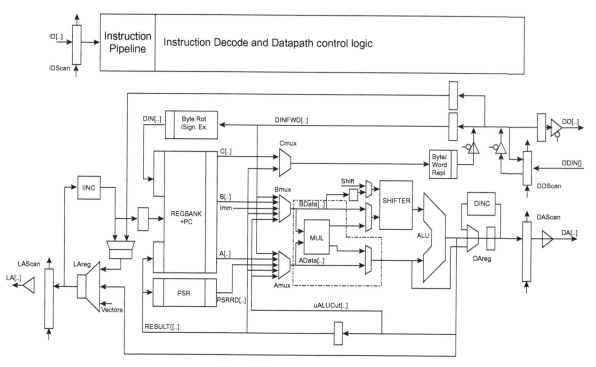

Figure 7.70 ARM9 block diagram

(Reproduced with permission from the ARM9TDMI Technical Reference Manual. © 1999 ARM Ltd.)

on a larger SoC. The power consumption is roughly 3 μW/MHz, so the processor powered by a watch battery could run continuously for nearly a year at 10 MHz.

Higher-end ARMv7 processors captured the cell phone and tablet markets. The Cortex-A9 was widely used in mobile phones, often as part of a dual-core SoC containing two Cortex-A9 processors, a graphics accelerator, a cellular modem, and other peripherals. Figure 7.71 shows a block diagram of the Cortex-A9. The processor decodes two instructions per cycle, performs register renaming, and issues them to out-of-order execution units.

Energy efficiency and performance are both critical for mobile devices, so ARM has been promoting the big.LITTLE architecture combining several high-performance "big" cores for peak workloads with energy-efficient "LITTLE" cores that handle most routine processes. For example, the Samsung Exynos 5 Octa in the Galaxy S5 phone contains four Cortex-A15 big cores running up to 2.1 GHz and four Cortex-A7 LITTLE cores running at up to 1.5 GHz. Figure 7.72 shows pipeline diagrams for the two types of cores. The Cortex-A7 is an in-order processor that can decode and issue up to one memory instruction and

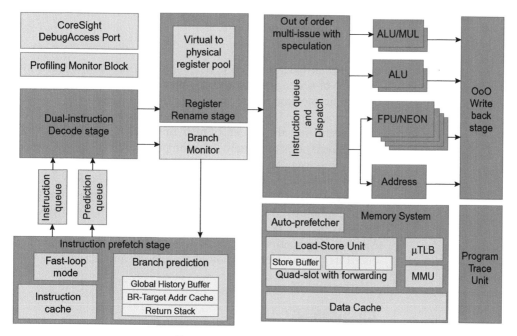

Figure 7.71 Cortex-A9 block diagram
(This image has been sourced by the authors and does not imply ARM endorsement.)

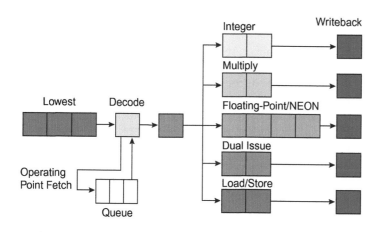

Figure 7.72 Cortex-A7 and -A15 block diagrams
(This image has been sourced by the authors and does not imply ARM endorsement.)

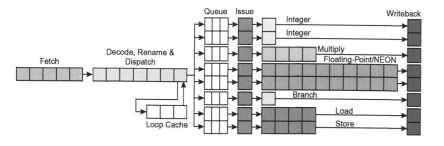

one other instruction each cycle. The Cortex-A15 is a much more complex out-of-order processor that can decode up to three instructions each cycle. The pipeline length almost doubles to handle the complexity and boost clock speed, so a more accurate branch predictor is necessary to compensate for the larger branch misprediction penalty. The Cortex-A15 delivers approximately 2.5x the performance of the Cortex-A7, but at 6x the power. Smart phones can only run the big cores briefly before the chip will begin to overheat and throttle itself back.

The ARMv8 architecture is a streamlined 64-bit architecture. ARM's Cortex-A53 and -A57 have pipelines similar to the Cortex-A7 and -A15, respectively, but boost the registers and datapaths to 64 bits to handle ARMv8. Apple popularized the 64-bit architecture in 2013, when it introduced its own implementation in the iPhone and iPad.

7.9 SUMMARY

This chapter has described three ways to build processors, each with different performance and cost trade-offs. We find this topic almost magical: how can such a seemingly complicated device as a microprocessor actually be simple enough to fit in a half-page schematic? Moreover, the inner workings, so mysterious to the uninitiated, are actually reasonably straightforward.

The microarchitectures have drawn together almost every topic covered in the text so far. Piecing together the microarchitecture puzzle illustrates the principles introduced in previous chapters, including the design of combinational and sequential circuits (covered in Chapters 2 and 3), the application of many of the building blocks (described in Chapter 5), and the implementation of the ARM architecture (introduced in Chapter 6). The microarchitectures can be described in a few pages of HDL using the techniques from Chapter 4.

Building the microarchitectures has also heavily used our techniques for managing complexity. The microarchitectural abstraction forms the link between the logic and architecture abstractions, forming the crux of this book on digital design and computer architecture. We also use the abstractions of block diagrams and HDL to succinctly describe the arrangement of components. The microarchitectures exploit regularity and modularity, reusing a library of common building blocks such as ALUs, memories, multiplexers, and registers. Hierarchy is used in numerous ways. The microarchitectures are partitioned into the datapath and control units. Each of these units is built from logic blocks, which can be built from gates, which in turn can be built from transistors using the techniques developed in the first five chapters.

This chapter has compared single-cycle, multicycle, and pipelined microarchitectures for the ARM processor. All three microarchitectures implement the same subset of the ARM instruction set and have the same architectural state. The single-cycle processor is the most straightforward and has a CPI of 1.

The multicycle processor uses a variable number of shorter steps to execute instructions. It thus can reuse the ALU, rather than requiring several adders. However, it does require several nonarchitectural registers to store results between steps. The multicycle design in principle could be faster, because not all instructions must be equally long. In practice, it is generally slower, because it is limited by the slowest steps and by the sequencing overhead in each step.

The pipelined processor divides the single-cycle processor into five relatively fast pipeline stages. It adds pipeline registers between the stages to separate the five instructions that are simultaneously executing. It nominally has a CPI of 1, but hazards force stalls or flushes that increase the CPI slightly. Hazard resolution also costs some extra hardware and design complexity. The clock period ideally could be five times shorter than that of the single-cycle processor. In practice, it is not that short, because it is limited by the slowest stage and by the sequencing overhead in each stage. Nevertheless, pipelining provides substantial performance benefits. All modern high-performance microprocessors use pipelining today.

Although the microarchitectures in this chapter implement only a subset of the ARM architecture, we have seen that supporting more instructions involves straightforward enhancements of the datapath and controller.

A major limitation of this chapter is that we have assumed an ideal memory system that is fast and large enough to store the entire program and data. In reality, large fast memories are prohibitively expensive. The next chapter shows how to get most of the benefits of a large fast memory with a small fast memory that holds the most commonly used information and one or more larger but slower memories holding the rest of the information.

Exercises

Exercise 7.1 Suppose that one of the following control signals in the single-cycle ARM processor has a *stuck-at-0 fault*, meaning that the signal is always 0, regardless of its intended value. What instructions would malfunction? Why?

(a) *RegW*

(b) *ALUOp*

(c) *MemW*

Exercise 7.2 Repeat Exercise 7.1, assuming that the signal has a stuck-at-1 fault.

Exercise 7.3 Modify the single-cycle ARM processor to implement one of the following instructions. See Appendix B for a definition of the instructions. Mark up a copy of Figure 7.13 to indicate the changes to the datapath. Name any new control signals. Mark up a copy of Tables 7.2 and 7.3 to show the changes to the Main Decoder and ALU Decoder. Describe any other changes that are required.

(a) TST

(b) LSL

(c) CMN

(d) ADC

Exercise 7.4 Repeat Exercise 7.3 for the following ARM instructions.

(a) EOR

(b) LSR

(c) TEQ

(d) RSB

Exercise 7.5 ARM includes LDR with post-indexing, which updates the base register after completing the load. LDR Rd,[Rn],Rm is equivalent to the following two instructions:

```
LDR  Rd,[Rn]
ADD  Rn,Rn,Rm
```

Repeat Exercise 7.3 for LDR with post-indexing. Is it possible to add the instruction without modifying the register file?

Exercise 7.6 ARM includes LDR with pre-indexing, which updates the base register after completing the load. LDR Rd,[Rn,Rm]! is equivalent to the following two instructions:

```
LDR  Rd,[Rn, Rm]
ADD  Rn,Rn,Rm
```

Repeat Exercise 7.3 for LDR with pre-indexing. Is it possible to add the instruction without modifying the register file?

Exercise 7.7 Your friend is a crack circuit designer. She has offered to redesign one of the units in the single-cycle ARM processor to have half the delay. Using the delays from Table 7.5, which unit should she work on to obtain the greatest speedup of the overall processor, and what would the cycle time of the improved machine be?

Exercise 7.8 Consider the delays given in Table 7.5. Ben Bitdiddle builds a prefix adder that reduces the ALU delay by 20 ps. If the other element delays stay the same, find the new cycle time of the single-cycle ARM processor and determine how long it takes to execute a benchmark with 100 billion instructions.

Exercise 7.9 Modify the HDL code for the single-cycle ARM processor, given in Section 7.6.1, to handle one of the new instructions from Exercise 7.3. Enhance the testbench, given in Section 7.6.3, to test the new instruction.

Exercise 7.10 Repeat Exercise 7.9 for the new instructions from Exercise 7.4.

Exercise 7.11 Suppose one of the following control signals in the multicycle ARM processor has a stuck-at-0 fault, meaning that the signal is always 0, regardless of its intended value. What instructions would malfunction? Why?

(a) $RegSrc_1$

(b) $AdrSrc$

(c) $NextPC$

Exercise 7.12 Repeat Exercise 7.11, assuming that the signal has a stuck-at-1 fault.

Exercise 7.13 Modify the multicycle ARM processor to implement one of the following instructions. See Appendix B for a definition of the instructions. Mark up a copy of Figure 7.30 to indicate the changes to the datapath. Name any new control signals. Mark up a copy of Figure 7.41 to show the changes to the controller FSM. Describe any other changes that are required.

(a) ASR

(b) TST

(c) SBC

(d) ROR

Exercise 7.14 Repeat Exercise 7.13 for the following ARM instructions.

(a) BL

(b) LDR (with positive or negative immediate offset)

(c) LDRB (with positive immediate offset only)

(d) BIC

Exercise 7.15 Repeat Exercise 7.5 for the multicycle ARM processor. Show the changes to the multicycle datapath and control FSM. Is it possible to add the instruction without modifying the register file?

Exercise 7.16 Repeat Exercise 7.6 for the multicycle ARM processor. Show the changes to the multicycle datapath and control FSM. Is it possible to add the instruction without modifying the register file?

Exercise 7.17 Repeat Excercise 7.7 for the multicycle ARM processor. Assume the instruction mix of Example 7.5.

Exercise 7.18 Repeat Exercise 7.8 for the multicycle ARM processor. Assume the instruction mix of Example 7.5.

Exercise 7.19 Your friend, the crack circuit designer, has offered to redesign one of the units in the multicycle ARM processor to be much faster. Using the delays from Table 7.5, which unit should she work on to obtain the greatest speedup of the overall processor? How fast should it be? (Making it faster than necessary is a waste of your friend's effort.) What is the cycle time of the improved processor?

Exercise 7.20 Goliath Corp claims to have a patent on a three-ported register file. Rather than fighting Goliath in court, Ben Bitdiddle designs a new register file that has only a single read/write port (like the combined instruction and data memory). Redesign the ARM multicycle datapath and controller to use his new register file.

Exercise 7.21 Suppose the multicycle ARM processor has the component delays given in Table 7.5. Alyssa P. Hacker designs a new register file that has 40% less power but twice as much delay. Should she switch to the slower but lower power register file for her multicycle processor design?

Exercise 7.22 What is the CPI of the redesigned multicycle ARM processor from Exercise 7.20? Use the instruction mix from Example 7.5.

Exercise 7.23 How many cycles are required to run the following program on the multicycle ARM processor? What is the CPI of this program?

```
    MOV  R0,  #5             ; result = 5
    MOV  R1,  #0             ; R1 = 0
L1
    CMP  R0,  R1
    BEQ  DONE                ; if result > 0, loop
    SUB  R0,  R0,  #1        ; result = result-1
    B    L1
DONE
```

Exercise 7.24 Repeat Exercise 7.23 for the following program.

```
    MOV  R0,  #0             ; i = 0
    MOV  R1,  #0             ; sum = 0
    MOV  R2,  #10            ; R2 = 10

LOOP
    CMP  R2,  R0            ; R2 == R0?
    BEQ  L2
    ADD  R1,  R1,  R0        ; sum = sum + i
    ADD  R0,  R0,  #1        ; increment i
    B
    LOOP
L2
```

Exercise 7.25 Write HDL code for the multicycle ARM processor. The processor should be compatible with the following top-level module. The mem module is used to hold both instructions and data. Test your processor using the testbench from Section 7.6.3.

```
module top(input    logic          clk, reset,
           output   logic  [31:0]  WriteData, Adr,
           output   logic          MemWrite);

  logic [31:0] ReadData;

  // instantiate processor and shared memory
  arm arm(clk, reset, MemWrite, Adr,
          WriteData, ReadData);
  mem mem(clk, MemWrite, Adr, WriteData, ReadData);
endmodule

module mem(input    logic          clk, we,
           input    logic  [31:0]  a, wd,
           output   logic  [31:0]  rd);

  logic [31:0] RAM[63:0];
  initial
     $readmemh("memfile.dat",RAM);
```

```
        assign rd = RAM[a[31:2]];  // word aligned
    always_ff @(posedge clk)
        if (we) RAM[a[31:2]] <= wd;
endmodule
```

Exercise 7.26 Extend your HDL code for the multicycle ARM processor from Exercise 7.25 to handle one of the new instructions from Exercise 7.14. Enhance the testbench to test the new instruction.

Exercise 7.27 Repeat Exercise 7.26 for one of the new instructions from Exercise 7.13.

Exercise 7.28 The pipelined ARM processor is running the following code snippet. Which registers are being written, and which are being read on the fifth cycle? Recall that the pipelined ARM processor has a Hazard Unit.

```
MOV  R1,  #42
SUB  R0,  R1,  #5
LDR  R3,  [R0, #18]
STR  R4,  [R1, #63]
ORR  R2,  R0,  R3
```

Exercise 7.29 Repeat Exercise 7.28 for the following ARM code snippet.

```
ADD  R0,  R4,  R5
SUB  R1,  R6,  R7
AND  R2,  R0,  R1
ORR  R3,  R2,  R5
LSL  R4,  R2,  R3
```

Exercise 7.30 Using a diagram similar to Figure 7.53, show the forwarding and stalls needed to execute the following instructions on the pipelined ARM processor.

```
ADD  R0,  R4,  R9
SUB  R0,  R0,  R2
LDR  R1,  [R0, #60]
AND  R2,  R1, R0
```

Exercise 7.31 Repeat Exercise 7.30 for the following instructions.

```
ADD  R0,  R11,  R5
LDR  R2,  [R1, #45]
SUB  R5,  R0,  R2
AND  R5,  R2,  R5
```

Exercise 7.32 How many cycles are required for the pipelined ARM processor to issue all of the instructions for the program in Exercise 7.24? What is the CPI of the processor on this program?

Exercise 7.33 Repeat Exercise 7.32 for the instructions of the program in Exercise 7.23.

Exercise 7.34 Explain how to extend the pipelined ARM processor to handle the EOR instruction.

Exercise 7.35 Explain how to extend the pipelined processor to handle the CMN instruction.

Exercise 7.36 Section 7.5.3 points out that the pipelined processor performance might be better if branches take place during the Decode stage rather than the Execute stage. Show how to modify the pipelined processor from Figure 7.58 to branch in the Decode stage. How do the stall, flush, and forwarding signals change? Redo Examples 7.7 and 7.8 to find the new CPI, cycle time, and overall time to execute the program.

Exercise 7.37 Your friend, the crack circuit designer, has offered to redesign one of the units in the pipelined ARM processor to be much faster. Using the delays from Table 7.5, which unit should she work on to obtain the greatest speedup of the overall processor? How fast should it be? (Making it faster than necessary is a waste of your friend's effort.) What is the cycle time of the improved processor?

Exercise 7.38 Consider the delays from Table 7.5. Now suppose that the ALU were 20% faster. Would the cycle time of the pipelined ARM processor change? What if the ALU were 20% slower?

Exercise 7.39 Suppose the ARM pipelined processor is divided into 10 stages of 400 ps each, including sequencing overhead. Assume the instruction mix of Example 7.7. Also assume that 50% of the loads are immediately followed by an instruction that uses the result, requiring six stalls, and that 30% of the branches are mispredicted. The target address of a branch instruction is not computed until the end of the second stage. Calculate the average CPI and execution time of computing 100 billion instructions from the SPECINT2000 benchmark for this 10-stage pipelined processor.

Exercise 7.40 Write HDL code for the pipelined ARM processor. The processor should be compatible with the top-level module from HDL Example 7.13. It should support the seven instructions described in this chapter: ADD, SUB, AND, ORR (with register and immediate addressing modes but no shifts), LDR, STR (with positive immediate offset), and B. Test your design using the testbench from HDL Example 7.12.

Exercise 7.41 Design the Hazard Unit shown in Figure 7.58 for the pipelined ARM processor. Use an HDL to implement your design. Sketch the hardware that a synthesis tool might generate from your HDL.

Interview Questions

The following exercises present questions that have been asked at interviews for digital design jobs.

Question 7.1 Explain the advantages of pipelined microprocessors?

Question 7.2 If additional pipeline stages allow a processor to go faster, why don't processors have 100 pipeline stages?

Question 7.3 Describe what a hazard is in a microprocessor and explain ways in which it can be resolved. What are the pros and cons of each way?

Question 7.4 Describe the concept of a superscalar processor and its pros and cons?

Memory Systems

8.1 INTRODUCTION

Computer system performance depends on the memory system as well as the processor microarchitecture. Chapter 7 assumed an ideal memory system that could be accessed in a single clock cycle. However, this would be true only for a very small memory—or a very slow processor! Early processors were relatively slow, so memory was able to keep up. But processor speed has increased at a faster rate than memory speeds. DRAM memories are currently 10 to 100 times slower than processors. The increasing gap between processor and DRAM memory speeds demands increasingly ingenious memory systems to try to approximate a memory that is as fast as the processor. This chapter investigates memory systems and considers trade-offs of speed, capacity, and cost.

The processor communicates with the memory system over a *memory interface*. Figure 8.1 shows the simple memory interface used in our multi-cycle ARM processor. The processor sends an address over the *Address* bus to the memory system. For a read, *MemWrite* is 0 and the memory returns the data on the *ReadData* bus. For a write, *MemWrite* is 1 and the processor sends data to memory on the *WriteData* bus.

The major issues in memory system design can be broadly explained using a metaphor of books in a library. A library contains many books on the shelves. If you were writing a term paper on the meaning of dreams, you might go to the library[1] and pull Freud's *The Interpretation of Dreams* off the shelf and bring it to your cubicle. After skimming it, you might put it back and pull out Jung's *The Psychology of the Unconscious*. You might then go back for another quote from *Interpretation of Dreams*, followed by yet another trip to the stacks for Freud's *The Ego and the Id*. Pretty soon

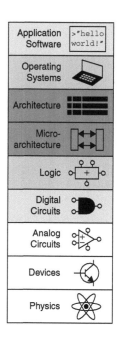

---

[1] We realize that library usage is plummeting among college students because of the Internet. But we also believe that libraries contain vast troves of hard-won human knowledge that are not electronically available. We hope that Web searching does not completely displace the art of library research.

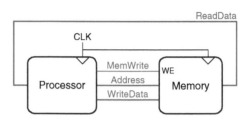

Figure 8.1 The memory interface

you would get tired of walking from your cubicle to the stacks. If you are clever, you would save time by keeping the books in your cubicle rather than schlepping them back and forth. Furthermore, when you pull a book by Freud, you could also pull several of his other books from the same shelf.

This metaphor emphasizes the principle, introduced in Section 6.2.1, of making the common case fast. By keeping books that you have recently used or might likely use in the future at your cubicle, you reduce the number of time-consuming trips to the stacks. In particular, you use the principles of *temporal* and *spatial locality*. Temporal locality means that if you have used a book recently, you are likely to use it again soon. Spatial locality means that when you use one particular book, you are likely to be interested in other books on the same shelf.

The library itself makes the common case fast by using these principles of locality. The library has neither the shelf space nor the budget to accommodate all of the books in the world. Instead, it keeps some of the lesser-used books in deep storage in the basement. Also, it may have an interlibrary loan agreement with nearby libraries so that it can offer more books than it physically carries.

In summary, you obtain the benefits of both a large collection and quick access to the most commonly used books through a hierarchy of storage. The most commonly used books are in your cubicle. A larger collection is on the shelves. And an even larger collection is available, with advanced notice, from the basement and other libraries. Similarly, memory systems use a hierarchy of storage to quickly access the most commonly used data while still having the capacity to store large amounts of data.

Memory subsystems used to build this hierarchy were introduced in Section 5.5. Computer memories are primarily built from dynamic RAM (DRAM) and static RAM (SRAM). Ideally, the computer memory system is fast, large, and cheap. In practice, a single memory only has two of these three attributes; it is either slow, small, or expensive. But computer systems can approximate the ideal by combining a fast small cheap memory and a slow large cheap memory. The fast memory stores the most commonly used data and instructions, so on average the memory system appears fast. The large memory stores the remainder of the data and instructions, so the overall capacity is large. The combination of two cheap memories is much less

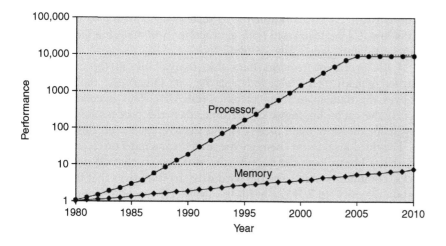

Figure 8.2 Diverging processor and memory performance
Adapted with permission from Hennessy and Patterson, *Computer Architecture: A Quantitative Approach,* 5th ed., Morgan Kaufmann, 2011.

expensive than a single large fast memory. These principles extend to using an entire hierarchy of memories of increasing capacity and decreasing speed.

Computer memory is generally built from DRAM chips. In 2015, a typical PC had a *main memory* consisting of 8 to 16 GB of DRAM, and DRAM cost about $7 per gigabyte (GB). DRAM prices have declined at about 25% per year for the last three decades, and memory capacity has grown at the same rate, so the total cost of the memory in a PC has remained roughly constant. Unfortunately, DRAM speed has improved by only about 7% per year, whereas processor performance has improved at a rate of 25 to 50% per year, as shown in Figure 8.2. The plot shows memory (DRAM) and processor speeds with the 1980 speeds as a baseline. In about 1980, processor and memory speeds were the same. But performance has diverged since then, with memories badly lagging.[2]

DRAM could keep up with processors in the 1970s and early 1980's, but it is now woefully too slow. The DRAM access time is one to two orders of magnitude longer than the processor cycle time (tens of nanoseconds, compared to less than one nanosecond).

To counteract this trend, computers store the most commonly used instructions and data in a faster but smaller memory, called a *cache*. The cache is usually built out of SRAM on the same chip as the processor. The cache speed is comparable to the processor speed, because SRAM is inherently faster than DRAM, and because the on-chip memory eliminates lengthy delays caused by traveling to and from a separate chip. In 2015, on-chip SRAM costs were on the order of $5,000/GB, but the

---

[2] Although recent single processor performance has remained approximately constant, as shown in Figure 8.2 for the years 2005–2010, the increase in multi-core systems (not depicted on the graph) only worsens the gap between processor and memory performance.

cache is relatively small (kilobytes to several megabytes), so the overall cost is low. Caches can store both instructions and data, but we will refer to their contents generically as "data."

If the processor requests data that is available in the cache, it is returned quickly. This is called a cache *hit*. Otherwise, the processor retrieves the data from main memory (DRAM). This is called a cache *miss*. If the cache hits most of the time, then the processor seldom has to wait for the slow main memory, and the average access time is low.

The third level in the memory hierarchy is the hard drive. In the same way that a library uses the basement to store books that do not fit in the stacks, computer systems use the hard drive to store data that does not fit in main memory. In 2015, a hard disk drive (HDD), built using magnetic storage, cost less than $0.05/GB and had an access time of about 5 ms. Hard disk costs have decreased at 60%/year but access times scarcely improved. Solid state drives (SSDs), built using flash memory technology, are an increasingly common alternative to HDDs. SSDs have been used by niche markets for over two decades, and they were introduced into the mainstream market in 2007. SSDs overcome some of the mechanical failures of HDDs, but they cost about ten times as much at $0.40/GB.

The hard drive provides an illusion of more capacity than actually exists in the main memory. It is thus called virtual memory. Like books in the basement, data in virtual memory takes a long time to access. Main memory, also called physical memory, holds a subset of the virtual memory. Hence, the main memory can be viewed as a cache for the most commonly used data from the hard drive.

Figure 8.3 summarizes the memory hierarchy of the computer system discussed in the rest of this chapter. The processor first seeks data in a small but fast cache that is usually located on the same chip. If the data is not available in the cache, the processor then looks in main memory. If the data is not there either, the processor fetches the data from virtual memory on the large but slow hard disk. Figure 8.4 illustrates this capacity and speed trade-off in the memory hierarchy and lists typical costs, access times, and bandwidth in 2015 technology. As access time decreases, speed increases.

Section 8.2 introduces memory system performance analysis. Section 8.3 explores several cache organizations, and Section 8.4 delves into virtual memory systems.

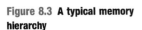

Figure 8.3 A typical memory hierarchy

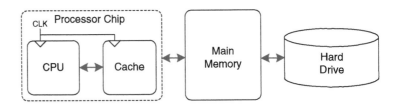

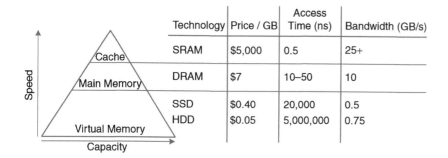

Technology	Price / GB	Access Time (ns)	Bandwidth (GB/s)
SRAM	$5,000	0.5	25+
DRAM	$7	10–50	10
SSD	$0.40	20,000	0.5
HDD	$0.05	5,000,000	0.75

Figure 8.4 Memory hierarchy components, with typical characteristics in 2015

8.2 MEMORY SYSTEM PERFORMANCE ANALYSIS

Designers (and computer buyers) need quantitative ways to measure the performance of memory systems to evaluate the cost-benefit trade-offs of various alternatives. Memory system performance metrics are *miss rate* or *hit rate* and *average memory access time*. Miss and hit rates are calculated as:

$$Miss\ Rate = \frac{Number\ of\ misses}{Number\ of\ total\ memory\ accesses} = 1 - Hit\ Rate$$

$$(8.1)$$

$$Hit\ Rate = \frac{Number\ of\ hits}{Number\ of\ total\ memory\ accesses} = 1 - Miss\ Rate$$

Example 8.1 CALCULATING CACHE PERFORMANCE

Suppose a program has 2000 data access instructions (loads or stores), and 1250 of these requested data values are found in the cache. The other 750 data values are supplied to the processor by main memory or disk memory. What are the miss and hit rates for the cache?

Solution: The miss rate is $750/2000 = 0.375 = 37.5\%$. The hit rate is $1250/2000 = 0.625 = 1 - 0.375 = 62.5\%$.

Average memory access time (*AMAT*) is the average time a processor must wait for memory per load or store instruction. In the typical computer system from Figure 8.3, the processor first looks for the data in the cache. If the cache misses, the processor then looks in main memory. If the main memory misses, the processor accesses virtual memory on the hard disk. Thus, *AMAT* is calculated as:

$$AMAT = t_{cache} + MR_{cache}(t_{MM} + MR_{MM}t_{VM}) \qquad (8.2)$$

where t_{cache}, t_{MM}, and t_{VM} are the access times of the cache, main memory, and virtual memory, and MR_{cache} and MR_{MM} are the cache and main memory miss rates, respectively.

Example 8.2 CALCULATING AVERAGE MEMORY ACCESS TIME

Suppose a computer system has a memory organization with only two levels of hierarchy, a cache and main memory. What is the average memory access time given the access times and miss rates in Table 8.1?

Solution: The average memory access time is $1 + 0.1(100) = 11$ cycles.

Table 8.1 Access times and miss rates

Memory Level	Access Time (Cycles)	Miss Rate
Cache	1	10%
Main Memory	100	0%

Example 8.3 IMPROVING ACCESS TIME

An 11-cycle average memory access time means that the processor spends ten cycles waiting for data for every one cycle actually using that data. What cache miss rate is needed to reduce the average memory access time to 1.5 cycles given the access times in Table 8.1?

Solution: If the miss rate is m, the average access time is $1 + 100m$. Setting this time to 1.5 and solving for m requires a cache miss rate of 0.5%.

Gene Amdahl, 1922–. Most famous for Amdahl's Law, an observation he made in 1965. While in graduate school, he began designing computers in his free time. This side work earned him his Ph.D. in theoretical physics in 1952. He joined IBM immediately after graduation, and later went on to found three companies, including one called Amdahl Corporation in 1970.

As a word of caution, performance improvements might not always be as good as they sound. For example, making the memory system ten times faster will not necessarily make a computer program run ten times as fast. If 50% of a program's performance is due to loads and stores, a tenfold memory system improvement only means a 1.82-fold improvement in program performance. This general principle is called *Amdahl's Law*, which says that the effort spent on increasing the performance of a subsystem is worthwhile only if the subsystem affects a large percentage of the overall performance.

8.3 CACHES

A cache holds commonly used memory data. The number of data words that it can hold is called the *capacity*, *C*. Because the capacity of the cache is smaller than that of main memory, the computer system designer must choose what subset of the main memory is kept in the cache.

When the processor attempts to access data, it first checks the cache for the data. If the cache hits, the data is available immediately. If the cache misses, the processor fetches the data from main memory and places it in the cache for future use. To accommodate the new data, the cache must *replace* old data. This section investigates these issues in cache design by answering the following questions: (1) What data is held in the cache? (2) How is data found? and (3) What data is replaced to make room for new data when the cache is full?

When reading the next sections, keep in mind that the driving force in answering these questions is the inherent spatial and temporal locality of data accesses in most applications. Caches use spatial and temporal locality to predict what data will be needed next. If a program accesses data in a random order, it would not benefit from a cache.

As we explain in the following sections, caches are specified by their capacity (*C*), number of sets (*S*), block size (*b*), number of blocks (*B*), and degree of associativity (*N*).

Although we focus on data cache loads, the same principles apply for fetches from an instruction cache. Data cache store operations are similar and are discussed further in Section 8.3.4.

Cache: a hiding place especially for concealing and preserving provisions or implements.
– Merriam Webster Online Dictionary, 2015. www.merriam-webster.com

8.3.1 What Data is Held in the Cache?

An ideal cache would anticipate all of the data needed by the processor and fetch it from main memory ahead of time so that the cache has a zero miss rate. Because it is impossible to predict the future with perfect accuracy, the cache must guess what data will be needed based on the past pattern of memory accesses. In particular, the cache exploits temporal and spatial locality to achieve a low miss rate.

Recall that temporal locality means that the processor is likely to access a piece of data again soon if it has accessed that data recently. Therefore, when the processor loads or stores data that is not in the cache, the data is copied from main memory into the cache. Subsequent requests for that data hit in the cache.

Recall that spatial locality means that, when the processor accesses a piece of data, it is also likely to access data in nearby memory locations. Therefore, when the cache fetches one word from memory, it may also fetch several adjacent words. This group of words is called a *cache block* or *cache line*. The number of words in the cache block, *b*, is called the *block size*. A cache of capacity *C* contains $B = C/b$ blocks.

The principles of temporal and spatial locality have been experimentally verified in real programs. If a variable is used in a program, the same variable is likely to be used again, creating temporal locality. If an element in an array is used, other elements in the same array are also likely to be used, creating spatial locality.

8.3.2 How is Data Found?

A cache is organized into *S sets*, each of which holds one or more blocks of data. The relationship between the address of data in main memory and the location of that data in the cache is called the *mapping*. Each memory address maps to exactly one set in the cache. Some of the address bits are used to determine which cache set contains the data. If the set contains more than one block, the data may be kept in any of the blocks in the set.

Caches are categorized based on the number of blocks in a set. In a *direct mapped* cache, each set contains exactly one block, so the cache has $S = B$ sets. Thus, a particular main memory address maps to a unique block in the cache. In an *N-way set associative* cache, each set contains N blocks. The address still maps to a unique set, with $S = B/N$ sets. But the data from that address can go in any of the N blocks in that set. A *fully associative* cache has only $S = 1$ set. Data can go in any of the B blocks in the set. Hence, a fully associative cache is another name for a B-way set associative cache.

To illustrate these cache organizations, we will consider an ARM memory system with 32-bit addresses and 32-bit words. The memory is byte-addressable, and each word is four bytes, so the memory consists of 2^{30} words aligned on word boundaries. We analyze caches with an eight-word capacity (C) for the sake of simplicity. We begin with a one-word block size (b), then generalize later to larger blocks.

Direct Mapped Cache

A *direct mapped* cache has one block in each set, so it is organized into $S = B$ sets. To understand the mapping of memory addresses onto cache blocks, imagine main memory as being mapped into *b*-word blocks, just as the cache is. An address in block 0 of main memory maps to set 0 of the cache. An address in block 1 of main memory maps to set 1 of the cache, and so forth until an address in block $B - 1$ of main memory maps to block $B - 1$ of the cache. There are no more blocks of the cache, so the mapping wraps around, such that block B of main memory maps to block 0 of the cache.

This mapping is illustrated in Figure 8.5 for a direct mapped cache with a capacity of eight words and a block size of one word. The cache has eight sets, each of which contains a one-word block. The bottom two bits of the address are always 00, because they are word aligned. The next $\log_2 8 = 3$ bits indicate the set onto which the memory address maps. Thus, the data at addresses 0x00000004, 0x00000024, . . . , 0xFFFFFFE4 all

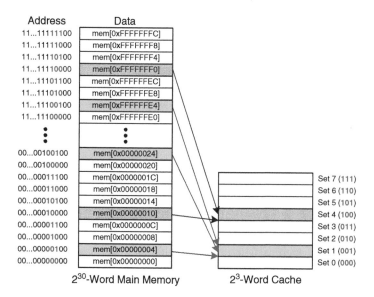

Figure 8.5 Mapping of main memory to a direct mapped cache

map to set 1, as shown in blue. Likewise, data at addresses 0x00000010, . . . , 0xFFFFFFF0 all map to set 4, and so forth. Each main memory address maps to exactly one set in the cache.

Example 8.4 CACHE FIELDS

To what cache set in Figure 8.5 does the word at address 0x00000014 map? Name another address that maps to the same set.

Solution: The two least significant bits of the address are 00, because the address is word aligned. The next three bits are 101, so the word maps to set 5. Words at addresses 0x34, 0x54, 0x74, . . . , 0xFFFFFFF4 all map to this same set.

Because many addresses map to a single set, the cache must also keep track of the address of the data actually contained in each set. The least significant bits of the address specify which set holds the data. The remaining most significant bits are called the *tag* and indicate which of the many possible addresses is held in that set.

In our previous examples, the two least significant bits of the 32-bit address are called the *byte offset*, because they indicate the byte within the word. The next three bits are called the *set bits*, because they indicate the set to which the address maps. (In general, the number of set bits is $\log_2 S$.) The remaining 27 tag bits indicate the memory address of the data stored in a given cache set. Figure 8.6 shows the cache fields for address 0xFFFFFFE4. It maps to set 1 and its tag is all 1's.

Figure 8.6 Cache fields for address 0xFFFFFFE4 when mapping to the cache in Figure 8.5

Example 8.5 CACHE FIELDS

Find the number of set and tag bits for a direct mapped cache with 1024 (2^{10}) sets and a one-word block size. The address size is 32 bits.

Solution: A cache with 2^{10} sets requires $\log_2(2^{10}) = 10$ set bits. The two least significant bits of the address are the byte offset, and the remaining $32 - 10 - 2 = 20$ bits form the tag.

Sometimes, such as when the computer first starts up, the cache sets contain no data at all. The cache uses a *valid bit* for each set to indicate whether the set holds meaningful data. If the valid bit is 0, the contents are meaningless.

Figure 8.7 shows the hardware for the direct mapped cache of Figure 8.5. The cache is constructed as an eight-entry SRAM. Each entry, or set, contains one line consisting of 32 bits of data, 27 bits of tag, and 1 valid bit. The cache is accessed using the 32-bit address. The two least significant bits, the byte offset bits, are ignored for word accesses. The next three bits, the set bits, specify the entry or set in the cache. A load instruction reads the specified entry from the cache and checks the tag and valid bits. If the tag matches the most significant 27 bits of the

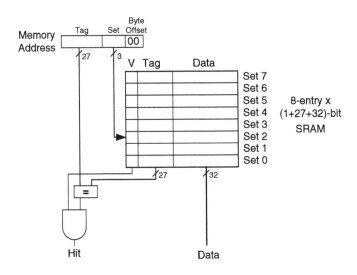

Figure 8.7 Direct mapped cache with 8 sets

address and the valid bit is 1, the cache hits and the data is returned to the processor. Otherwise, the cache misses and the memory system must fetch the data from main memory.

Example 8.6 TEMPORAL LOCALITY WITH A DIRECT MAPPED CACHE

Loops are a common source of temporal and spatial locality in applications. Using the eight-entry cache of Figure 8.7, show the contents of the cache after executing the following silly loop in ARM assembly code. Assume that the cache is initially empty. What is the miss rate?

```
        MOV R0, #5
        MOV R1, #0
LOOP    CMP R0, #0
        BEQ DONE
        LDR R2, [R1, #4]
        LDR R3, [R1, #12]
        LDR R4, [R1, #8]
        SUB R0, R0, #1
        B    LOOP
DONE
```

Solution: The program contains a loop that repeats for five iterations. Each iteration involves three memory accesses (loads), resulting in 15 total memory accesses. The first time the loop executes, the cache is empty and the data must be fetched from main memory locations 0x4, 0xC, and 0x8 into cache sets 1, 3, and 2, respectively. However, the next four times the loop executes, the data is found in the cache. Figure 8.8 shows the contents of the cache during the last request to memory address 0x4. The tags are all 0 because the upper 27 bits of the addresses are 0. The miss rate is $3/15 = 20\%$.

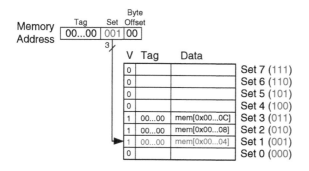

Figure 8.8 Direct mapped cache contents

When two recently accessed addresses map to the same cache block, a *conflict* occurs, and the most recently accessed address *evicts* the previous one from the block. Direct mapped caches have only one block in each set, so two addresses that map to the same set always cause a conflict. Example 8.7 illustrates conflicts.

Example 8.7 CACHE BLOCK CONFLICT

What is the miss rate when the following loop is executed on the eight-word direct mapped cache from Figure 8.7? Assume that the cache is initially empty.

```
        MOV R0, #5
        MOV R1, #0
LOOP    CMP R0, #0
        BEQ DONE
        LDR R2, [R1, #0x4]
        LDR R3, [R1, #0x24]
        SUB R0, R0, #1
        B   LOOP
DONE
```

Solution: Memory addresses 0x4 and 0x24 both map to set 1. During the initial execution of the loop, data at address 0x4 is loaded into set 1 of the cache. Then data at address 0x24 is loaded into set 1, evicting the data from address 0x4. Upon the second execution of the loop, the pattern repeats and the cache must refetch data at address 0x4, evicting data from address 0x24. The two addresses conflict, and the miss rate is 100%.

Multi-way Set Associative Cache

An *N-way set associative* cache reduces conflicts by providing N blocks in each set where data mapping to that set might be found. Each memory address still maps to a specific set, but it can map to any one of the N blocks

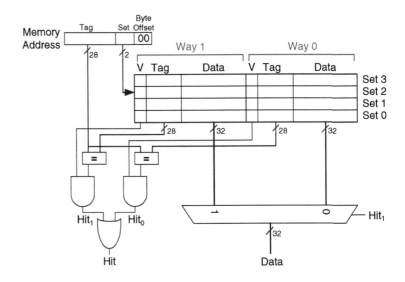

Figure 8.9 Two-way set associative cache

in the set. Hence, a direct mapped cache is another name for a one-way set associative cache. N is also called the *degree of associativity* of the cache.

Figure 8.9 shows the hardware for a $C = 8$-word, $N = 2$-way set associative cache. The cache now has only $S = 4$ sets rather than 8. Thus, only $\log_2 4 = 2$ set bits rather than 3 are used to select the set. The tag increases from 27 to 28 bits. Each set contains two *ways* or degrees of associativity. Each way consists of a data block and the valid and tag bits. The cache reads blocks from both ways in the selected set and checks the tags and valid bits for a hit. If a hit occurs in one of the ways, a multiplexer selects data from that way.

Set associative caches generally have lower miss rates than direct mapped caches of the same capacity, because they have fewer conflicts. However, set associative caches are usually slower and somewhat more expensive to build because of the output multiplexer and additional comparators. They also raise the question of which way to replace when both ways are full; this is addressed further in Section 8.3.3. Most commercial systems use set associative caches.

Example 8.8 SET ASSOCIATIVE CACHE MISS RATE

Repeat Example 8.7 using the eight-word two-way set associative cache from Figure 8.9.

Solution: Both memory accesses, to addresses 0x4 and 0x24, map to set 1. However, the cache has two ways, so it can accommodate data from both addresses. During the first loop iteration, the empty cache misses both addresses and loads both words of data into the two ways of set 1, as shown in Figure 8.10. On the next four iterations, the cache hits. Hence, the miss rate is $2/10 = 20\%$. Recall that the direct mapped cache of the same size from Example 8.7 had a miss rate of 100%.

	Way 1			Way 0		
V	Tag	Data	V	Tag	Data	
0			0			Set 3
0			0			Set 2
1	00...00	mem[0x00...24]	1	00...10	mem[0x00...04]	Set 1
0			0			Set 0

Figure 8.10 Two-way set associative cache contents

Fully Associative Cache

A *fully associative* cache contains a single set with B ways, where B is the number of blocks. A memory address can map to a block in any of these ways. A fully associative cache is another name for a B-way set associative cache with one set.

Figure 8.11 shows the SRAM array of a fully associative cache with eight blocks. Upon a data request, eight tag comparisons (not shown) must be made, because the data could be in any block. Similarly, an 8:1

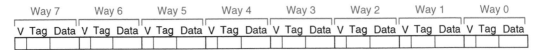

Figure 8.11 Eight-block fully associative cache

multiplexer chooses the proper data if a hit occurs. Fully associative caches tend to have the fewest conflict misses for a given cache capacity, but they require more hardware for additional tag comparisons. They are best suited to relatively small caches because of the large number of comparators.

Block Size

The previous examples were able to take advantage only of temporal locality, because the block size was one word. To exploit spatial locality, a cache uses larger blocks to hold several consecutive words.

The advantage of a block size greater than one is that when a miss occurs and the word is fetched into the cache, the adjacent words in the block are also fetched. Therefore, subsequent accesses are more likely to hit because of spatial locality. However, a large block size means that a fixed-size cache will have fewer blocks. This may lead to more conflicts, increasing the miss rate. Moreover, it takes more time to fetch the missing cache block after a miss, because more than one data word is fetched from main memory. The time required to load the missing block into the cache is called the *miss penalty*. If the adjacent words in the block are not accessed later, the effort of fetching them is wasted. Nevertheless, most real programs benefit from larger block sizes.

Figure 8.12 shows the hardware for a $C = 8$-word direct mapped cache with a $b = 4$-word block size. The cache now has only $B = C/b = 2$ blocks. A direct mapped cache has one block in each set, so this cache

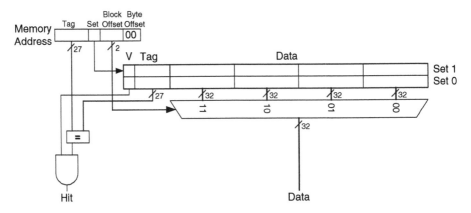

Figure 8.12 Direct mapped cache with two sets and a four-word block size

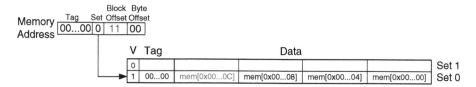

is organized as two sets. Thus, only $\log_2 2 = 1$ bit is used to select the set. A multiplexer is now needed to select the word within the block. The multiplexer is controlled by the $\log_2 4 = 2$ *block offset bits* of the address. The most significant 27 address bits form the tag. Only one tag is needed for the entire block, because the words in the block are at consecutive addresses.

Figure 8.13 shows the cache fields for address 0x8000009C when it maps to the direct mapped cache of Figure 8.12. The byte offset bits are always 0 for word accesses. The next $\log_2 b = 2$ block offset bits indicate the word within the block. And the next bit indicates the set. The remaining 27 bits are the tag. Therefore, word 0x8000009C maps to set 1, word 3 in the cache. The principle of using larger block sizes to exploit spatial locality also applies to associative caches.

Example 8.9 SPATIAL LOCALITY WITH A DIRECT MAPPED CACHE

Repeat Example 8.6 for the eight-word direct mapped cache with a four-word block size.

Solution: Figure 8.14 shows the contents of the cache after the first memory access. On the first loop iteration, the cache misses on the access to memory address 0x4. This access loads data at addresses 0x0 through 0xC into the cache block. All subsequent accesses (as shown for address 0xC) hit in the cache. Hence, the miss rate is $1/15 = 6.67\%$.

Memory Address

	Tag	Set	Block Offset	Byte Offset
	00...00	0	11	00

V	Tag	Data				
0						Set 1
1	00...00	mem[0x00...0C]	mem[0x00...08]	mem[0x00...04]	mem[0x00...00]	Set 0

Figure 8.14 Cache contents with a block size *b* of four words

Putting it All Together

Caches are organized as two-dimensional arrays. The rows are called sets, and the columns are called ways. Each entry in the array

Table 8.2 **Cache organizations**

Organization	Number of Ways (N)	Number of Sets (S)
Direct Mapped	1	B
Set Associative	$1 < N < B$	B/N
Fully Associative	B	1

consists of a data block and its associated valid and tag bits. Caches are characterized by

▸ capacity C

▸ block size b (and number of blocks, $B = C/b$)

▸ number of blocks in a set (N)

Table 8.2 summarizes the various cache organizations. Each address in memory maps to only one set but can be stored in any of the ways.

Cache capacity, associativity, set size, and block size are typically powers of 2. This makes the cache fields (tag, set, and block offset bits) subsets of the address bits.

Increasing the associativity N usually reduces the miss rate caused by conflicts. But higher associativity requires more tag comparators. Increasing the block size b takes advantage of spatial locality to reduce the miss rate. However, it decreases the number of sets in a fixed sized cache and therefore could lead to more conflicts. It also increases the miss penalty.

8.3.3 What Data is Replaced?

In a direct mapped cache, each address maps to a unique block and set. If a set is full when new data must be loaded, the block in that set is replaced with the new data. In set associative and fully associative caches, the cache must choose which block to evict when a cache set is full. The principle of temporal locality suggests that the best choice is to evict the least recently used block, because it is least likely to be used again soon. Hence, most associative caches have a *least recently used* (*LRU*) replacement policy.

In a two-way set associative cache, a *use bit*, U, indicates which way within a set was least recently used. Each time one of the ways is used, U is adjusted to indicate the other way. For set associative caches with more than two ways, tracking the least recently used way becomes complicated. To simplify the problem, the ways are often divided into two groups and U indicates which *group* of ways was least recently used. Upon replacement, the new block replaces a random block within the least recently used group. Such a policy is called *pseudo-LRU* and is good enough in practice.

Example 8.10 LRU REPLACEMENT

Show the contents of an eight-word two-way set associative cache after executing the following code. Assume LRU replacement, a block size of one word, and an initially empty cache.

```
MOV R0, #0
LDR R1, [R0, #4]
LDR R2, [R0, #0x24]
LDR R3, [R0, #0x54]
```

Solution: The first two instructions load data from memory addresses 0x4 and 0x24 into set 1 of the cache, shown in Figure 8.15(a). $U = 0$ indicates that data in way 0 was the least recently used. The next memory access, to address 0x54, also maps to set 1 and replaces the least recently used data in way 0, as shown in Figure 8.15(b). The use bit U is set to 1 to indicate that data in way 1 was the least recently used.

V	U	Tag	Data	V	Tag	Data	
0	0			0			Set 3 (11)
0	0			0			Set 2 (10)
1	0	00...010	mem[0x00...24]	1	00...000	mem[0x00...04]	Set 1 (01)
0	0			0			Set 0 (00)

Way 1 spans Tag, Data (first). Way 0 spans V, Tag, Data.

(a)

V	U	Tag	Data	V	Tag	Data	
0	0			0			Set 3 (11)
0	0			0			Set 2 (10)
1	1	00...010	mem[0x00...24]	1	00...101	mem[0x00...54]	Set 1 (01)
0	0			0			Set 0 (00)

(b)

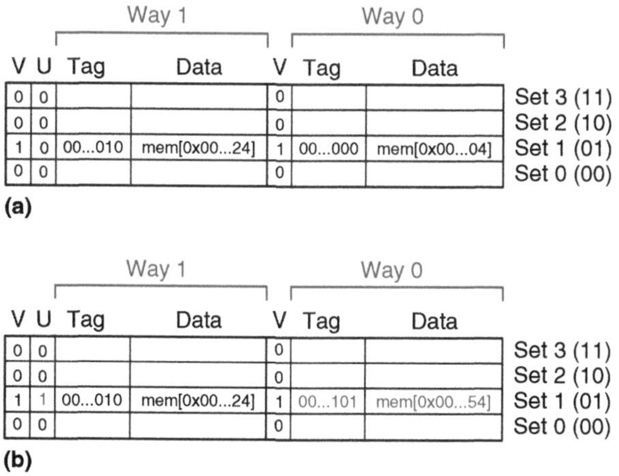

Figure 8.15 Two-way associative cache with LRU replacement

8.3.4 Advanced Cache Design*

Modern systems use multiple levels of caches to decrease memory access time. This section explores the performance of a two-level caching system and examines how block size, associativity, and cache capacity affect miss rate. The section also describes how caches handle stores, or writes, by using a write-through or write-back policy.

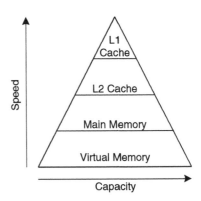

Figure 8.16 Memory hierarchy with two levels of cache

Multiple-Level Caches

Large caches are beneficial because they are more likely to hold data of interest and therefore have lower miss rates. However, large caches tend to be slower than small ones. Modern systems often use at least two levels of caches, as shown in Figure 8.16. The first-level (L1) cache is small enough to provide a one- or two-cycle access time. The second-level (L2) cache is also built from SRAM but is larger, and therefore slower, than the L1 cache. The processor first looks for the data in the L1 cache. If the L1 cache misses, the processor looks in the L2 cache. If the L2 cache misses, the processor fetches the data from main memory. Many modern systems add even more levels of cache to the memory hierarchy, because accessing main memory is so slow.

Example 8.11 SYSTEM WITH AN L2 CACHE

Use the system of Figure 8.16 with access times of 1, 10, and 100 cycles for the L1 cache, L2 cache, and main memory, respectively. Assume that the L1 and L2 caches have miss rates of 5% and 20%, respectively. Specifically, of the 5% of accesses that miss the L1 cache, 20% of those also miss the L2 cache. What is the average memory access time (*AMAT*)?

Solution: Each memory access checks the L1 cache. When the L1 cache misses (5% of the time), the processor checks the L2 cache. When the L2 cache misses (20% of the time), the processor fetches the data from main memory. Using Equation 8.2, we calculate the average memory access time as follows: 1 cycle + 0.05[10 cycles + 0.2(100 cycles)] = 2.5 cycles

The L2 miss rate is high because it receives only the "hard" memory accesses, those that miss in the L1 cache. If all accesses went directly to the L2 cache, the L2 miss rate would be about 1%.

Reducing Miss Rate

Cache misses can be reduced by changing capacity, block size, and/or associativity. The first step to reducing the miss rate is to understand the causes of the misses. The misses can be classified as compulsory, capacity, and conflict. The first request to a cache block is called a *compulsory miss*, because the block must be read from memory regardless of the cache design. *Capacity misses* occur when the cache is too small to hold all concurrently used data. *Conflict misses* are caused when several addresses map to the same set and evict blocks that are still needed.

Changing cache parameters can affect one or more type of cache miss. For example, increasing cache capacity can reduce conflict and capacity misses, but it does not affect compulsory misses. On the other hand, increasing block size could reduce compulsory misses (due to spatial locality) but might actually *increase* conflict misses (because more addresses would map to the same set and could conflict).

Memory systems are complicated enough that the best way to evaluate their performance is by running benchmarks while varying cache parameters. Figure 8.17 plots miss rate versus cache size and degree of associativity for the SPEC2000 benchmark. This benchmark has a small number of compulsory misses, shown by the dark region near the x-axis. As expected, when cache size increases, capacity misses decrease. Increased associativity, especially for small caches, decreases the number of conflict misses shown along the top of the curve. Increasing associativity beyond four or eight ways provides only small decreases in miss rate.

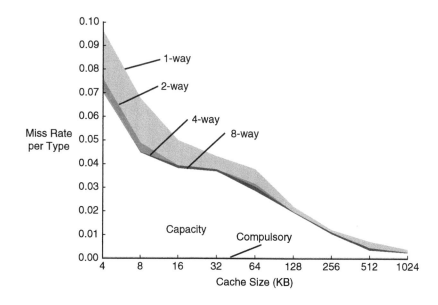

Figure 8.17 Miss rate versus cache size and associativity on SPEC2000 benchmark (Adapted with permission from Hennessy and Patterson, *Computer Architecture: A Quantitative Approach*, 5th ed., Morgan Kaufmann, 2012.)

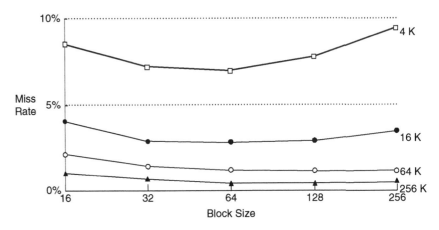

Figure 8.18 Miss rate versus block size and cache size on SPEC92 benchmark
(Adapted with permission from Hennessy and Patterson, *Computer Architecture: A Quantitative Approach*, 5th ed., Morgan Kaufmann, 2012.)

As mentioned, miss rate can also be decreased by using larger block sizes that take advantage of spatial locality. But as block size increases, the number of sets in a fixed-size cache decreases, increasing the probability of conflicts. Figure 8.18 plots miss rate versus block size (in number of bytes) for caches of varying capacity. For small caches, such as the 4-KB cache, increasing the block size beyond 64 bytes *increases* the miss rate because of conflicts. For larger caches, increasing the block size beyond 64 bytes does not change the miss rate. However, large block sizes might still increase execution time because of the larger miss penalty, the time required to fetch the missing cache block from main memory.

Write Policy

The previous sections focused on memory loads. Memory stores, or writes, follow a similar procedure as loads. Upon a memory store, the processor checks the cache. If the cache misses, the cache block is fetched from main memory into the cache, and then the appropriate word in the cache block is written. If the cache hits, the word is simply written to the cache block.

Caches are classified as either write-through or write-back. In a *write-through* cache, the data written to a cache block is simultaneously written to main memory. In a *write-back* cache, a *dirty bit* (D) is associated with each cache block. D is 1 when the cache block has been written and 0 otherwise. Dirty cache blocks are written back to main memory only when they are evicted from the cache. A write-through cache requires no dirty bit but usually requires more main memory writes than a write-back cache. Modern caches are usually write-back, because main memory access time is so large.

Example 8.12 WRITE-THROUGH VERSUS WRITE-BACK

Suppose a cache has a block size of four words. How many main memory accesses are required by the following code when using each write policy: write-through or write-back?

```
MOV R5, #0
STR R1, [R5]
STR R2, [R5, #12]
STR R3, [R5, #8]
STR R4, [R5, #4]
```

Solution: All four store instructions write to the same cache block. With a write-through cache, each store instruction writes a word to main memory, requiring four main memory writes. A write-back policy requires only one main memory access, when the dirty cache block is evicted.

8.3.5 The Evolution of ARM Caches*

Table 8.3 traces the evolution of cache organizations used by the ARM processor from 1985 to 2012. The major trends are the introduction of multiple levels of cache, larger cache capacity, and separation of instruction and data L1 caches. These trends are driven by the growing disparity between CPU frequency and main memory speed and the decreasing cost

Table 8.3 ARM cache evolution

Year	CPU	MHz	L1 Cache	L2 Cache
1985	ARM1	8	None	None
1992	ARM6	30	4 KB, unified	None
1994	ARM7	100	8 KB, unified	None
1999	ARM9E	300	0–128 KB, I/D	None
2002	ARM11	700	4–64 KB, I/D	0–128 KB, off-chip
2009	Cortex-A9	1000	16–64 KB, I/D	0–8 MB
2011	Cortex-A7	1500	32 KB, I/D	0–4 MB
2011	Cortex-A15	2000	32 KB, I/D	0–4 MB
2012	Cortex-M0+	60–250	None	None
2012	Cortex-A53	1500	8–64 KB, I/D	128 KB–2 MB
2012	Cortex-A57	2000	48 KB I / 32 KB D	512 KB–2 MB

of transistors. The increasing difference between CPU and memory speeds necessitates a lower miss rate to avoid the main memory bottleneck, and the decreasing cost of transistors allows larger cache sizes.

8.4 VIRTUAL MEMORY

Most modern computer systems use a *hard drive* made of magnetic or solid state storage as the lowest level in the memory hierarchy (see Figure 8.4). Compared with the ideal large, fast, cheap memory, a hard drive is large and cheap but terribly slow. It provides a much larger capacity than is possible with a cost-effective main memory (DRAM). However, if a significant fraction of memory accesses involve the hard drive, performance is dismal. You may have encountered this on a PC when running too many programs at once.

Figure 8.19 shows a hard drive made of magnetic storage, also called a *hard disk*, with the lid of its case removed. As the name implies, the hard disk contains one or more rigid disks or *platters*, each of which has a *read/write head* on the end of a long triangular arm. The head

Figure 8.19 Hard disk

moves to the correct location on the disk and reads or writes data magnetically as the disk rotates beneath it. The head takes several milliseconds to *seek* the correct location on the disk, which is fast from a human perspective but millions of times slower than the processor. Hard disk drives are increasingly being replaced by solid state drives because reading is orders of magnitude faster (see Figure 8.4) and they are not as susceptible to mechanical failures.

The objective of adding a hard drive to the memory hierarchy is to inexpensively give the illusion of a very large memory while still providing the speed of faster memory for most accesses. A computer with only 128 MB of DRAM, for example, could effectively provide 2 GB of memory using the hard drive. This larger 2-GB memory is called *virtual memory*, and the smaller 128-MB main memory is called *physical memory*. We will use the term physical memory to refer to main memory throughout this section.

A computer with 32-bit addresses can access a maximum of 2^{32} bytes = 4 GB of memory. This is one of the motivations for moving to 64-bit computers, which can access far more memory.

Programs can access data anywhere in virtual memory, so they must use *virtual addresses* that specify the location in virtual memory. The physical memory holds a subset of most recently accessed virtual memory. In this way, physical memory acts as a cache for virtual memory. Thus, most accesses hit in physical memory at the speed of DRAM, yet the program enjoys the capacity of the larger virtual memory.

Virtual memory systems use different terminologies for the same caching principles discussed in Section 8.3. Table 8.4 summarizes the analogous terms. Virtual memory is divided into *virtual pages*, typically 4 KB in size. Physical memory is likewise divided into *physical pages* of the same size. A virtual page may be located in physical memory (DRAM) or on the hard drive. For example, Figure 8.20 shows a virtual memory that is larger than physical memory. The rectangles indicate pages. Some virtual pages are present in physical memory, and some are located on the hard drive. The process of determining the physical address from the virtual address is called *address translation*. If the processor attempts to access a virtual address that is not in physical memory, a *page fault*

Table 8.4 Analogous cache and virtual memory terms

Cache	Virtual Memory
Block	Page
Block size	Page size
Block offset	Page offset
Miss	Page fault
Tag	Virtual page number

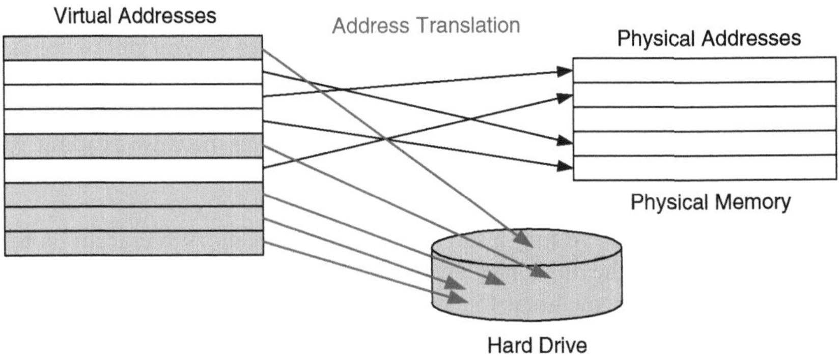

Figure 8.20 **Virtual and physical pages**

occurs, and the operating system loads the page from the hard drive into physical memory.

To avoid page faults caused by conflicts, any virtual page can map to any physical page. In other words, physical memory behaves as a fully associative cache for virtual memory. In a conventional fully associative cache, every cache block has a comparator that checks the most significant address bits against a tag to determine whether the request hits in the block. In an analogous virtual memory system, each physical page would need a comparator to check the most significant virtual address bits against a tag to determine whether the virtual page maps to that physical page.

A realistic virtual memory system has so many physical pages that providing a comparator for each page would be excessively expensive. Instead, the virtual memory system uses a page table to perform address translation. A page table contains an entry for each virtual page, indicating its location in physical memory or that it is on the hard drive. Each load or store instruction requires a page table access followed by a physical memory access. The page table access translates the virtual address used by the program to a physical address. The physical address is then used to actually read or write the data.

The page table is usually so large that it is located in physical memory. Hence, each load or store involves two physical memory accesses: a page table access, and a data access. To speed up address translation, a translation lookaside buffer (TLB) caches the most commonly used page table entries.

The remainder of this section elaborates on address translation, page tables, and TLBs.

8.4.1 Address Translation

In a system with virtual memory, programs use virtual addresses so that they can access a large memory. The computer must translate these virtual

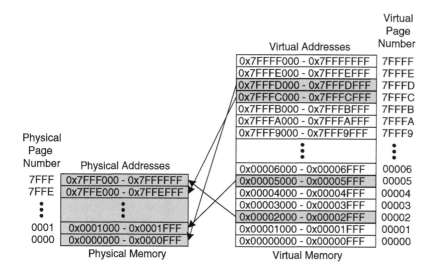

Figure 8.21 **Physical and virtual pages**

addresses to either find the address in physical memory or take a page fault and fetch the data from the hard drive.

Recall that virtual memory and physical memory are divided into pages. The most significant bits of the virtual or physical address specify the virtual or physical *page number*. The least significant bits specify the word within the page and are called the *page offset*.

Figure 8.21 illustrates the page organization of a virtual memory system with 2 GB of virtual memory and 128 MB of physical memory divided into 4-KB pages. MIPS accommodates 32-bit addresses. With a 2-GB $= 2^{31}$-byte virtual memory, only the least significant 31 virtual address bits are used; the 32nd bit is always 0. Similarly, with a 128-MB $= 2^{27}$-byte physical memory, only the least significant 27 physical address bits are used; the upper 5 bits are always 0.

Because the page size is 4 KB $= 2^{12}$ bytes, there are $2^{31}/2^{12} = 2^{19}$ virtual pages and $2^{27}/2^{12} = 2^{15}$ physical pages. Thus, the virtual and physical page numbers are 19 and 15 bits, respectively. Physical memory can only hold up to 1/16th of the virtual pages at any given time. The rest of the virtual pages are kept on the hard drive.

Figure 8.21 shows virtual page 5 mapping to physical page 1, virtual page 0x7FFFC mapping to physical page 0x7FFE, and so forth. For example, virtual address 0x53F8 (an offset of 0x3F8 within virtual page 5) maps to physical address 0x13F8 (an offset of 0x3F8 within physical page 1). The least significant 12 bits of the virtual and physical addresses are the same (0x3F8) and specify the page offset within the virtual and physical pages. Only the page number needs to be translated to obtain the physical address from the virtual address.

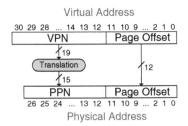

Figure 8.22 Translation from virtual address to physical address

Figure 8.22 illustrates the translation of a virtual address to a physical address. The least significant 12 bits indicate the page offset and require no translation. The upper 19 bits of the virtual address specify the *virtual page number* (VPN) and are translated to a 15-bit *physical page number* (PPN). The next two sections describe how page tables and TLBs are used to perform this address translation.

Example 8.13 VIRTUAL ADDRESS TO PHYSICAL ADDRESS TRANSLATION

Find the physical address of virtual address 0x247C using the virtual memory system shown in Figure 8.21.

Solution: The 12-bit page offset (0x47C) requires no translation. The remaining 19 bits of the virtual address give the virtual page number, so virtual address 0x247C is found in virtual page 0x2. In Figure 8.21, virtual page 0x2 maps to physical page 0x7FFF. Thus, virtual address 0x247C maps to physical address 0x7FFF47C.

8.4.2 The Page Table

The processor uses a *page table* to translate virtual addresses to physical addresses. The page table contains an entry for each virtual page. This entry contains a physical page number and a valid bit. If the valid bit is 1, the virtual page maps to the physical page specified in the entry. Otherwise, the virtual page is found on the hard drive.

Because the page table is so large, it is stored in physical memory. Let us assume for now that it is stored as a contiguous array, as shown in Figure 8.23. This page table contains the mapping of the memory system of Figure 8.21. The page table is indexed with the virtual page number (VPN). For example, entry 5 specifies that virtual page 5 maps to physical page 1. Entry 6 is invalid ($V = 0$), so virtual page 6 is located on the hard drive.

V	Physical Page Number	Virtual Page Number
0		7FFFF
0		7FFFE
1	0x0000	7FFFD
1	0x7FFE	7FFFC
0		7FFFB
0		7FFFA
⋮	⋮	⋮
0		00007
0		00006
1	0x0001	00005
0		00004
0		00003
1	0x7FFF	00002
0		00001
0		00000

Page Table

Figure 8.23 The page table for Figure 8.21

Example 8.14 USING THE PAGE TABLE TO PERFORM ADDRESS TRANSLATION

Find the physical address of virtual address 0x247C using the page table shown in Figure 8.23.

Solution: Figure 8.24 shows the virtual address to physical address translation for virtual address 0x247C. The 12-bit page offset requires no translation. The remaining 19 bits of the virtual address are the virtual page number, 0x2, and give the index into the page table. The page table maps virtual page 0x2 to physical page 0x7FFF. So, virtual address 0x247C maps to physical address 0x7FFF47C. The least significant 12 bits are the same in both the physical and the virtual address.

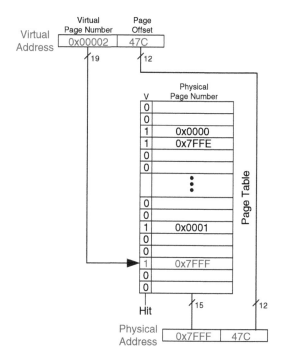

Figure 8.24 Address translation using the page table

The page table can be stored anywhere in physical memory, at the discretion of the OS. The processor typically uses a dedicated register, called the *page table register*, to store the base address of the page table in physical memory.

To perform a load or store, the processor must first translate the virtual address to a physical address and then access the data at that physical address. The processor extracts the virtual page number from the virtual address and adds it to the page table register to find the physical address of the page table entry. The processor then reads this page table entry from physical memory to obtain the physical page number. If the entry is valid, it merges this physical page number with the page offset to create the physical address. Finally, it reads or writes data at this physical address. Because the page table is stored in physical memory, each load or store involves two physical memory accesses.

8.4.3 The Translation Lookaside Buffer

Virtual memory would have a severe performance impact if it required a page table read on every load or store, doubling the delay of loads and stores. Fortunately, page table accesses have great temporal locality. The temporal and spatial locality of data accesses and the large page size mean that many consecutive loads or stores are likely to reference the same page. Therefore, if the processor remembers the last page table entry that it read, it can probably reuse this translation without rereading the page table. In general, the processor can keep the last several page table entries in a small cache called a *translation lookaside buffer (TLB)*. The processor "looks aside" to find the translation in the TLB before having to access the page table in physical memory. In real programs, the vast majority of accesses hit in the TLB, avoiding the time-consuming page table reads from physical memory.

A TLB is organized as a fully associative cache and typically holds 16 to 512 entries. Each TLB entry holds a virtual page number and its corresponding physical page number. The TLB is accessed using the virtual page number. If the TLB hits, it returns the corresponding physical page number. Otherwise, the processor must read the page table in physical memory. The TLB is designed to be small enough that it can be accessed in less than one cycle. Even so, TLBs typically have a hit rate of greater than 99%. The TLB decreases the number of memory accesses required for most load or store instructions from two to one.

Example 8.15 USING THE TLB TO PERFORM ADDRESS TRANSLATION

Consider the virtual memory system of Figure 8.21. Use a two-entry TLB or explain why a page table access is necessary to translate virtual addresses 0x247C and 0x5FB0 to physical addresses. Suppose the TLB currently holds valid translations of virtual pages 0x2 and 0x7FFFD.

Solution: Figure 8.25 shows the two-entry TLB with the request for virtual address 0x247C. The TLB receives the virtual page number of the incoming address, 0x2, and compares it to the virtual page number of each entry. Entry 0 matches and is valid, so the request hits. The translated physical address is the physical page number of the matching entry, 0x7FFF, concatenated with the page offset of the virtual address. As always, the page offset requires no translation.

The request for virtual address 0x5FB0 misses in the TLB. So, the request is forwarded to the page table for translation.

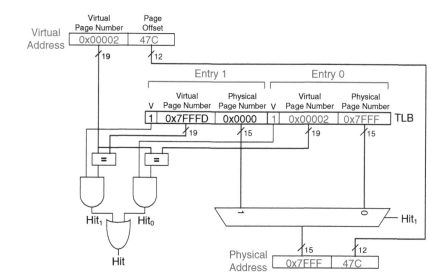

Figure 8.25 **Address translation using a two-entry TLB**

8.4.4 Memory Protection

So far, this section has focused on using virtual memory to provide a fast, inexpensive, large memory. An equally important reason to use virtual memory is to provide protection between concurrently running programs.

As you probably know, modern computers typically run several programs or *processes* at the same time. All of the programs are simultaneously present in physical memory. In a well-designed computer system, the programs should be protected from each other so that no program can crash or hijack another program. Specifically, no program should be able to access another program's memory without permission. This is called *memory protection*.

Virtual memory systems provide memory protection by giving each program its own *virtual address space*. Each program can use as much memory as it wants in that virtual address space, but only a portion of the virtual address space is in physical memory at any given time. Each program can use its entire virtual address space without having to worry about where other programs are physically located. However, a program can access only those physical pages that are mapped in its page table. In this way, a program cannot accidentally or maliciously access another program's physical pages, because they are not mapped in its page table. In some cases, multiple programs access common instructions or data. The operating system adds control bits to each page table entry to determine which programs, if any, can write to the shared physical pages.

8.4.5 Replacement Policies*

Virtual memory systems use write-back and an approximate least recently used (LRU) replacement policy. A write-through policy, where each write to physical memory initiates a write to the hard drive, would be impractical. Store instructions would operate at the speed of the hard drive instead of the speed of the processor (milliseconds instead of nanoseconds). Under the writeback policy, the physical page is written back to the hard drive only when it is evicted from physical memory. Writing the physical page back to the hard drive and reloading it with a different virtual page is called *paging*, and the hard drive in a virtual memory system is sometimes called *swap space*. The processor pages out one of the least recently used physical pages when a page fault occurs, then replaces that page with the missing virtual page. To support these replacement policies, each page table entry contains two additional status bits: a dirty bit *D* and a use bit *U*.

The dirty bit is 1 if any store instructions have changed the physical page since it was read from the hard drive. When a physical page is paged out, it needs to be written back to the hard drive only if its dirty bit is 1; otherwise, the hard drive already holds an exact copy of the page.

The use bit is 1 if the physical page has been accessed recently. As in a cache system, exact LRU replacement would be impractically complicated. Instead, the OS approximates LRU replacement by periodically resetting all the use bits in the page table. When a page is accessed, its use bit is set to 1. Upon a page fault, the OS finds a page with $U = 0$ to page out of physical memory. Thus, it does not necessarily replace the least recently used page, just one of the least recently used pages.

8.4.6 Multilevel Page Tables*

Page tables can occupy a large amount of physical memory. For example, the page table from the previous sections for a 2 GB virtual memory with 4 KB pages would need 2^{19} entries. If each entry is 4 bytes, the page table is $2^{19} \times 2^2$ bytes $= 2^{21}$ bytes $= 2$ MB.

To conserve physical memory, page tables can be broken up into multiple (usually two) levels. The first-level page table is always kept in physical memory. It indicates where small second-level page tables are stored in virtual memory. The second-level page tables each contain the actual translations for a range of virtual pages. If a particular range of translations is not actively used, the corresponding second-level page table can be paged out to the hard drive so it does not waste physical memory.

In a two-level page table, the virtual page number is split into two parts: the *page table number* and the *page table offset*, as shown in Figure 8.26. The page table number indexes the first-level page table, which must reside in physical memory. The first-level page table entry gives the base address of the second-level page table or indicates that it must be fetched from the

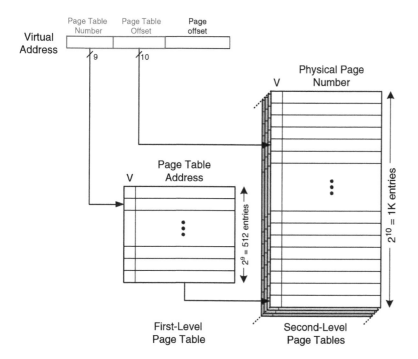

Virtual
Address

Page Table
Number

Page Table
Offset

Page
offset

9

10

Physical Page
V   Number

Page Table
V   Address

2^{10} = 1K entries

2^9 = 512 entries

First-Level
Page Table

Second-Level
Page Tables

Figure 8.26 Hierarchical page tables

hard drive when *V* is 0. The page table offset indexes the second-level page table. The remaining 12 bits of the virtual address are the page offset, as before, for a page size of $2^{12} = 4$ KB.

In Figure 8.26 the 19-bit virtual page number is broken into 9 and 10 bits, to indicate the page table number and the page table offset, respectively. Thus, the first-level page table has $2^9 = 512$ entries. Each of these 512 second-level page tables has $2^{10} = 1$ K entries. If each of the first- and second-level page table entries is 32 bits (4 bytes) and only two second-level page tables are present in physical memory at once, the hierarchical page table uses only $(512 \times 4 \text{ bytes}) + 2 \times (1 \text{ K} \times 4 \text{ bytes}) = 10$ KB of physical memory. The two-level page table requires a fraction of the physical memory needed to store the entire page table (2 MB). The drawback of a two-level page table is that it adds yet another memory access for translation when the TLB misses.

Example 8.16 USING A MULTILEVEL PAGE TABLE FOR ADDRESS
TRANSLATION

Figure 8.27 shows the possible contents of the two-level page table from Figure 8.26. The contents of only one second-level page table are shown. Using this two-level page table, describe what happens on an access to virtual address 0x003FEFB0.

Solution: As always, only the virtual page number requires translation. The most significant nine bits of the virtual address, 0x0, give the page table number, the index into the first-level page table. The first-level page table at entry 0x0 indicates that the second-level page table is resident in memory ($V = 1$) and its physical address is 0x2375000.

The next ten bits of the virtual address, 0x3FE, are the page table offset, which gives the index into the second-level page table. Entry 0 is at the bottom of the second-level page table, and entry 0x3FF is at the top. Entry 0x3FE in the second-level page table indicates that the virtual page is resident in physical memory ($V = 1$) and that the physical page number is 0x23F1. The physical page number is concatenated with the page offset to form the physical address, 0x23F1FB0.

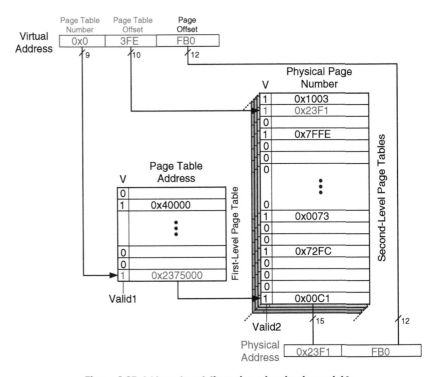

Figure 8.27 Address translation using a two-level page table

8.5 SUMMARY

Memory system organization is a major factor in determining computer performance. Different memory technologies, such as DRAM, SRAM, and hard drives, offer trade-offs in capacity, speed, and cost. This chapter introduced cache and virtual memory organizations that use a hierarchy of memories to approximate an ideal large, fast, inexpensive memory. Main memory is typically built from DRAM, which is significantly slower than the processor. A cache reduces access time by keeping commonly used data in fast SRAM. Virtual memory increases the memory capacity by using a hard drive to store data that does not fit in the main memory. Caches and virtual memory add complexity and hardware to a computer system, but the benefits usually outweigh the costs. All modern personal computers use caches and virtual memory.

EPILOGUE

This chapter brings us to the end of our journey together into the realm of digital systems. We hope this book has conveyed the beauty and thrill of the art as well as the engineering knowledge. You have learned to design combinational and sequential logic using schematics and hardware description languages. You are familiar with larger building blocks such as multiplexers, ALUs, and memories. Computers are one of the most fascinating applications of digital systems. You have learned how to program an ARM processor in its native assembly language and how to build the processor and memory system using digital building blocks. Throughout, you have seen the application of abstraction, discipline, hierarchy, modularity, and regularity. With these techniques, we have pieced together the puzzle of a microprocessor's inner workings. From cell phones to digital television to Mars rovers to medical imaging systems, our world is an increasingly digital place.

Imagine what Faustian bargain Charles Babbage would have made to take a similar journey a century and a half ago. He merely aspired to calculate mathematical tables with mechanical precision. Today's digital systems are yesterday's science fiction. Might Dick Tracy have listened to iTunes on his cell phone? Would Jules Verne have launched a constellation of global positioning satellites into space? Could Hippocrates have cured illness using high-resolution digital images of the brain? But at the same time, George Orwell's nightmare of ubiquitous government surveillance becomes closer to reality each day. Hackers and governments wage undeclared cyberwarfare, attacking industrial infrastructure and financial networks. And rogue states develop nuclear weapons using laptop computers more powerful than the room-sized supercomputers that simulated Cold War bombs. The microprocessor revolution continues to accelerate. The changes in the coming decades will surpass those of the past. You now have the tools to design and build these new systems that will shape our future. With your newfound power comes profound responsibility. We hope that you will use it, not just for fun and riches, but also for the benefit of humanity.

Exercises

Exercise 8.1 In less than one page, describe four everyday activities that exhibit temporal or spatial locality. List two activities for each type of locality, and be specific.

Exercise 8.2 In one paragraph, describe two short computer applications that exhibit temporal and/or spatial locality. Describe how. Be specific.

Exercise 8.3 Come up with a sequence of addresses for which a direct mapped cache with a size (capacity) of 16 words and block size of 4 words outperforms a fully associative cache with least recently used (LRU) replacement that has the same capacity and block size.

Exercise 8.4 Repeat Exercise 8.3 for the case when the fully associative cache outperforms the direct mapped cache.

Exercise 8.5 Describe the trade-offs of increasing each of the following cache parameters while keeping the others the same:

(a) block size

(b) associativity

(c) cache size

Exercise 8.6 Is the miss rate of a two-way set associative cache always, usually, occasionally, or never better than that of a direct mapped cache of the same capacity and block size? Explain.

Exercise 8.7 Each of the following statements pertains to the miss rate of caches. Mark each statement as true or false. Briefly explain your reasoning; present a counterexample if the statement is false.

(a) A two-way set associative cache always has a lower miss rate than a direct mapped cache with the same block size and total capacity.

(b) A 16-KB direct mapped cache always has a lower miss rate than an 8-KB direct mapped cache with the same block size.

(c) An instruction cache with a 32-byte block size usually has a lower miss rate than an instruction cache with an 8-byte block size, given the same degree of associativity and total capacity.

Exercise 8.8 A cache has the following parameters: b, block size given in numbers of words; S, number of sets; N, number of ways; and A, number of address bits.

(a) In terms of the parameters described, what is the cache capacity, C?

(b) In terms of the parameters described, what is the total number of bits required to store the tags?

(c) What are S and N for a fully associative cache of capacity C words with block size b?

(d) What is S for a direct mapped cache of size C words and block size b?

Exercise 8.9 A 16-word cache has the parameters given in Exercise 8.8. Consider the following repeating sequence of LDR addresses (given in hexadecimal):

40 44 48 4C 70 74 78 7C 80 84 88 8C 90 94 98 9C 0 4 8 C 10 14 18 1C 20

Assuming least recently used (LRU) replacement for associative caches, determine the effective miss rate if the sequence is input to the following caches, ignoring startup effects (i.e., compulsory misses).

(a) direct mapped cache, $b = 1$ word

(b) fully associative cache, $b = 1$ word

(c) two-way set associative cache, $b = 1$ word

(d) direct mapped cache, $b = 2$ words

Exercise 8.10 Repeat Exercise 8.9 for the following repeating sequence of LDR addresses (given in hexadecimal) and cache configurations. The cache capacity is still 16 words.

74 A0 78 38C AC 84 88 8C 7C 34 38 13C 388 18C

(a) direct mapped cache, $b = 1$ word

(b) fully associative cache, $b = 2$ words

(c) two-way set associative cache, $b = 2$ words

(d) direct mapped cache, $b = 4$ words

Exercise 8.11 Suppose you are running a program with the following data access pattern. The pattern is executed only once.

0x0 0x8 0x10 0x18 0x20 0x28

(a) If you use a direct mapped cache with a cache size of 1 KB and a block size of 8 bytes (2 words), how many sets are in the cache?

(b) With the same cache and block size as in part (a), what is the miss rate of the direct mapped cache for the given memory access pattern?

(c) For the given memory access pattern, which of the following would decrease the miss rate the most? (Cache capacity is kept constant.) Circle one.

(i)   Increasing the degree of associativity to 2.

(ii) Increasing the block size to 16 bytes.

(iii) Either (i) or (ii).

(iv) Neither (i) nor (ii).

Exercise 8.12 You are building an instruction cache for an ARM processor. It has a total capacity of $4C = 2^{c+2}$ bytes. It is $N = 2^n$-way set associative ($N \geq 8$), with a block size of $b = 2^{b'}$ bytes ($b \geq 8$). Give your answers to the following questions in terms of these parameters.

(a) Which bits of the address are used to select a word within a block?

(b) Which bits of the address are used to select the set within the cache?

(c) How many bits are in each tag?

(d) How many tag bits are in the entire cache?

Exercise 8.13 Consider a cache with the following parameters:
N (associativity) $= 2$, b (block size) $= 2$ words, W (word size) $= 32$ bits, C (cache size) $= 32$ K words, A (address size) $= 32$ bits. You need consider only word addresses.

(a) Show the tag, set, block offset, and byte offset bits of the address. State how many bits are needed for each field.

(b) What is the size of *all* the cache tags in bits?

(c) Suppose each cache block also has a valid bit (V) and a dirty bit (D). What is the size of each cache set, including data, tag, and status bits?

(d) Design the cache using the building blocks in Figure 8.28 and a small number of two-input logic gates. The cache design must include tag storage, data

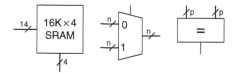

Figure 8.28 **Building blocks**

storage, address comparison, data output selection, and any other parts you feel are relevant. Note that the multiplexer and comparator blocks may be any size (n or p bits wide, respectively), but the SRAM blocks must be $16K \times 4$ bits. Be sure to include a neatly labeled block diagram. You need only design the cache for reads.

Exercise 8.14 You've joined a hot new Internet startup to build wrist watches with a built-in pager and Web browser. It uses an embedded processor with a multilevel cache scheme depicted in Figure 8.29. The processor includes a small on-chip cache in addition to a large off-chip second-level cache. (Yes, the watch weighs 3 pounds, but you should see it surf!)

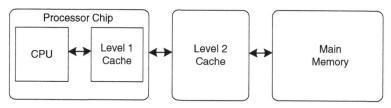

Figure 8.29 **Computer system**

Assume that the processor uses 32-bit physical addresses but accesses data only on word boundaries. The caches have the characteristics given in Table 8.5. The DRAM has an access time of t_m and a size of 512 MB.

Table 8.5 **Memory characteristics**

Characteristic	On-chip Cache	Off-chip Cache
Organization	Four-way set associative	Direct mapped
Hit rate	A	B
Access time	t_a	t_b
Block size	16 bytes	16 bytes
Number of blocks	512	256K

(a) For a given word in memory, what is the total number of locations in which it might be found in the on-chip cache and in the second-level cache?

(b) What is the size, in bits, of each tag for the on-chip cache and the second-level cache?

(c) Give an expression for the average memory read access time. The caches are accessed in sequence.

(d) Measurements show that, for a particular problem of interest, the on-chip cache hit rate is 85% and the second-level cache hit rate is 90%. However, when the on-chip cache is disabled, the second-level cache hit rate shoots up to 98.5%. Give a brief explanation of this behavior.

Exercise 8.15 This chapter described the least recently used (LRU) replacement policy for multiway associative caches. Other, less common, replacement policies include first-in-first-out (FIFO) and random policies. FIFO replacement evicts the block that has been there the longest, regardless of how recently it was accessed. Random replacement randomly picks a block to evict.

(a) Discuss the advantages and disadvantages of each of these replacement policies.

(b) Describe a data access pattern for which FIFO would perform better than LRU.

Exercise 8.16 You are building a computer with a hierarchical memory system that consists of separate instruction and data caches followed by main memory. You are using the ARM multicycle processor from Figure 7.30 running at 1 GHz.

(a) Suppose the instruction cache is perfect (i.e., always hits) but the data cache has a 5% miss rate. On a cache miss, the processor stalls for 60 ns to access main memory, then resumes normal operation. Taking cache misses into account, what is the average memory access time?

(b) How many clock cycles per instruction (CPI) on average are required for load and store word instructions considering the non-ideal memory system?

(c) Consider the benchmark application of Example 7.5 that has 25% loads, 10% stores, 13% branches, and 52% data-processing instructions. Taking the non-ideal memory system into account, what is the average CPI for this benchmark?

(d) Now suppose that the instruction cache is also non-ideal and has a 7% miss rate. What is the average CPI for the benchmark in part (c)? Take into account both instruction and data cache misses.

Exercise 8.17 Repeat Exercise 8.16 with the following parameters.

(a) The instruction cache is perfect (i.e., always hits) but the data cache has a 15% miss rate. On a cache miss, the processor stalls for 200 ns to access main memory, then resumes normal operation. Taking cache misses into account, what is the average memory access time?

(b) How many clock cycles per instruction (CPI) on average are required for load and store word instructions considering the non-ideal memory system?

(c) Consider the benchmark application of Example 7.5 that has 25% loads, 10% stores, 13% branches, and 52% data-processing instructions. Taking the non-ideal memory system into account, what is the average CPI for this benchmark?

(d) Now suppose that the instruction cache is also non-ideal and has a 10% miss rate. What is the average CPI for the benchmark in part (c)? Take into account both instruction and data cache misses.

Exercise 8.18 If a computer uses 64-bit virtual addresses, how much virtual memory can it access? Note that 2^{40} bytes = 1 *terabyte*, 2^{50} bytes = 1 *petabyte*, and 2^{60} bytes = 1 *exabyte*.

Exercise 8.19 A supercomputer designer chooses to spend $1 million on DRAM and the same amount on hard disks for virtual memory. Using the prices from Figure 8.4, how much physical and virtual memory will the computer have? How many bits of physical and virtual addresses are necessary to access this memory?

Exercise 8.20 Consider a virtual memory system that can address a total of 2^{32} bytes. You have unlimited hard drive space, but are limited to only 8 MB of semiconductor (physical) memory. Assume that virtual and physical pages are each 4 KB in size.

(a) How many bits is the physical address?

(b) What is the maximum number of virtual pages in the system?

(c) How many physical pages are in the system?

(d) How many bits are the virtual and physical page numbers?

(e) Suppose that you come up with a direct mapped scheme that maps virtual pages to physical pages. The mapping uses the least significant bits of the virtual page number to determine the physical page number. How many virtual pages are mapped to each physical page? Why is this "direct mapping" a bad plan?

(f)   Clearly, a more flexible and dynamic scheme for translating virtual addresses into physical addresses is required than the one described in part (e). Suppose you use a page table to store mappings (translations from virtual page number to physical page number). How many page table entries will the page table contain?

(g)   Assume that, in addition to the physical page number, each page table entry also contains some status information in the form of a valid bit (V) and a dirty bit (D). How many bytes long is each page table entry? (Round up to an integer number of bytes.)

(h)   Sketch the layout of the page table. What is the total size of the page table in bytes?

Exercise 8.21 Consider a virtual memory system that can address a total of 2^{50} bytes. You have unlimited hard drive space, but are limited to 2 GB of semiconductor (physical) memory. Assume that virtual and physical pages are each 4 KB in size.

(a)   How many bits is the physical address?

(b)   What is the maximum number of virtual pages in the system?

(c)   How many physical pages are in the system?

(d)   How many bits are the virtual and physical page numbers?

(e)   How many page table entries will the page table contain?

(f)   Assume that, in addition to the physical page number, each page table entry also contains some status information in the form of a valid bit (V) and a dirty bit (D). How many bytes long is each page table entry? (Round up to an integer number of bytes.)

(g)   Sketch the layout of the page table. What is the total size of the page table in bytes?

Exercise 8.22 You decide to speed up the virtual memory system of Exercise 8.20 by using a translation lookaside buffer (TLB). Suppose your memory system has the characteristics shown in Table 8.6. The TLB and cache miss rates indicate how

Table 8.6 **Memory characteristics**

Memory Unit	Access Time (Cycles)	Miss Rate
TLB	1	0.05%
Cache	1	2%
Main memory	100	0.0003%
Hard drive	1,000,000	0%

often the requested entry is not found. The main memory miss rate indicates how often page faults occur.

(a) What is the average memory access time of the virtual memory system before and after adding the TLB? Assume that the page table is always resident in physical memory and is never held in the data cache.

(b) If the TLB has 64 entries, how big (in bits) is the TLB? Give numbers for data (physical page number), tag (virtual page number), and valid bits of each entry. Show your work clearly.

(c) Sketch the TLB. Clearly label all fields and dimensions.

(d) What size SRAM would you need to build the TLB described in part (c)? Give your answer in terms of depth × width.

Exercise 8.23 You decide to speed up the virtual memory system of Exercise 8.21 by using a translation lookaside buffer (TLB) with 128 entries.

(a) How big (in bits) is the TLB? Give numbers for data (physical page number), tag (virtual page number), and valid bits of each entry. Show your work clearly.

(b) Sketch the TLB. Clearly label all fields and dimensions.

(c) What size SRAM would you need to build the TLB described in part (b)? Give your answer in terms of depth × width.

Exercise 8.24 Suppose the ARM multicycle processor described in Section 7.4 uses a virtual memory system.

(a) Sketch the location of the TLB in the multicycle processor schematic.

(b) Describe how adding a TLB affects processor performance.

Exercise 8.25 The virtual memory system you are designing uses a single-level page table built from dedicated hardware (SRAM and associated logic). It supports 25-bit virtual addresses, 22-bit physical addresses, and 2^{16}-byte (64 KB) pages. Each page table entry contains a physical page number, a valid bit (V), and a dirty bit (D).

(a) What is the total size of the page table, in bits?

(b) The operating system team proposes reducing the page size from 64 to 16 KB, but the hardware engineers on your team object on the grounds of added hardware cost. Explain their objection.

(c) The page table is to be integrated on the processor chip, along with the on-chip cache. The on-chip cache deals only with physical (not virtual) addresses. Is it possible to access the appropriate set of the on-chip cache concurrently with the page table access for a given memory access? Explain briefly the relationship that is necessary for concurrent access to the cache set and page table entry.

(d) Is it possible to perform the tag comparison in the on-chip cache concurrently with the page table access for a given memory access? Explain briefly.

Exercise 8.26 Describe a scenario in which the virtual memory system might affect how an application is written. Be sure to include a discussion of how the page size and physical memory size affect the performance of the application.

Exercise 8.27 Suppose you own a personal computer (PC) that uses 32-bit virtual addresses.

(a) What is the maximum amount of virtual memory space each program can use?

(b) How does the size of your PC's hard drive affect performance?

(c) How does the size of your PC's physical memory affect performance?

Interview Questions

The following exercises present questions that have been asked on interviews.

Question 8.1 Explain the difference between direct mapped, set associative, and fully associative caches. For each cache type, describe an application for which that cache type will perform better than the other two.

Question 8.2 Explain how virtual memory systems work.

Question 8.3 Explain the advantages and disadvantages of using a virtual memory system.

Question 8.4 Explain how cache performance might be affected by the virtual page size of a memory system.

I/O Systems

9.1 INTRODUCTION

Input/Output (I/O) systems are used to connect a computer with external devices called peripherals. In a personal computer, the devices typically include keyboards, monitors, printers, and wireless networks. In embedded systems, devices could include a toaster's heating element, a doll's speech synthesizer, an engine's fuel injector, a satellite's solar panel positioning motors, and so forth. A processor accesses an I/O device using the address and data busses in the same way that it accesses memory.

This chapter provides concrete examples of I/O devices. Section 9.2 shows the basic principles of interfacing an I/O device to a processor and accessing it from a program. Section 9.3 examines I/O in the context of embedded systems, showing how to use an ARM-based Raspberry Pi single-board computer to access on-board peripherals including general-purpose, serial, and analog I/O as well as timers. Section 9.4 gives examples of interfacing with other common devices such as character LCDs, VGA monitors, Bluetooth radios, and motors. Section 9.5 describes bus interfaces and illustrates the popular AHB-Lite bus. Section 9.6 surveys the major I/O systems used in PCs.

The rest of this chapter is available online as a downloadable PDF from the book's companion site: http://booksite.elsevier.com/9780128000564.

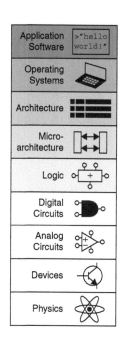

Digital System Implementation

A.1 INTRODUCTION

This appendix introduces practical issues in the design of digital systems. The material is not necessary for understanding the rest of the book, however, it seeks to demystify the process of building real digital systems. Moreover, we believe that the best way to understand digital systems is to build and debug them yourself in the laboratory.

Digital systems are usually built using one or more chips. One strategy is to connect together chips containing individual logic gates or larger elements such as arithmetic/logical units (ALUs) or memories. Another is to use programmable logic, which contains generic arrays of circuitry that can be programmed to perform specific logic functions. Yet a third is to design a custom integrated circuit containing the specific logic necessary for the system. These three strategies offer trade-offs in cost, speed, power consumption, and design time that are explored in the following sections. This appendix also examines the physical packaging and assembly of circuits, the transmission lines that connect the chips, and the economics of digital systems.

The rest of this chapter is available online as a downloadable PDF from the book's companion site: http://booksite.elsevier.com/9780128000564.

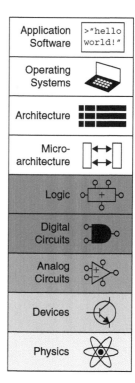

ARM Instructions

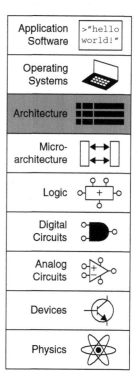

This appendix summarizes ARMv4 instructions used in this book. Condition encodings are given in Table 6.3.

B.1 DATA-PROCESSING INSTRUCTIONS

Standard data-processing instructions use the encoding in Figure B.1. The 4-bit *cmd* field specifies the type of instruction as given in Table B.1. When the *S*-bit is 1, the status register is updated with the condition flags produced by the instruction. The *I*-bit and bits 4 and 7 specify one of three encodings for the second source operand, *Src2*, as described in Section 6.4.2. The *cond* field specifies which condition codes to check, as given in Section 6.3.2.

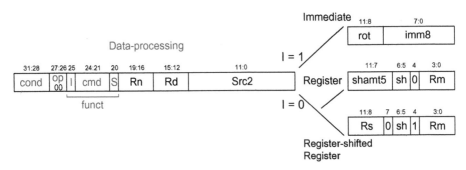

Figure B.1 Data-processing instruction encodings

Table B.1 Data-processing instructions

cmd	Name	Description	Operation
0000	AND Rd, Rn, Src2	Bitwise AND	Rd ← Rn & Src2
0001	EOR Rd, Rn, Src2	Bitwise XOR	Rd ← Rn ^ Src2
0010	SUB Rd, Rn, Src2	Subtract	Rd ← Rn - Src2
0011	RSB Rd, Rn, Src2	Reverse Subtract	Rd ← Src2 - Rn
0100	ADD Rd, Rn, Src2	Add	Rd ← Rn+Src2
0101	ADC Rd, Rn, Src2	Add with Carry	Rd ← Rn+Src2+C
0110	SBC Rd, Rn, Src2	Subtract with Carry	Rd ← Rn - Src2 - $\overline{C}$
0111	RSC Rd, Rn, Src2	Reverse Sub w/ Carry	Rd ← Src2 - Rn - $\overline{C}$
1000 ($S = 1$)	TST Rd, Rn, Src2	Test	Set flags based on Rn & Src2
1001 ($S = 1$)	TEQ Rd, Rn, Src2	Test Equivalence	Set flags based on Rn ^ Src2
1010 ($S = 1$)	CMP Rn, Src2	Compare	Set flags based on Rn - Src2
1011 ($S = 1$)	CMN Rn, Src2	Compare Negative	Set flags based on Rn+Src2
1100	ORR Rd, Rn, Src2	Bitwise OR	Rd ← Rn | Src2
1101 $I = 1$ OR (instr$_{11:4}$ = 0)	**Shifts:** MOV Rd, Src2	Move	Rd ← Src2
$I = 0$ AND ($sh = 00$; instr$_{11:4} \neq 0$)	LSL Rd, Rm, Rs/shamt5	Logical Shift Left	Rd ← Rm << Src2
$I = 0$ AND ($sh = 01$)	LSR Rd, Rm, Rs/shamt5	Logical Shift Right	Rd ← Rm >> Src2

(continued)

Table B.1 Data-processing instructions—Cont'd

cmd	Name	Description	Operation
$I = 0$ AND $(sh = 10)$	ASR Rd, Rm, Rs/shamt5	Arithmetic Shift Right	Rd ← Rm>>>Src2
$I = 0$ AND $(sh = 11;$ $instr_{11:7, 4} = 0)$	RRX Rd, Rm, Rs/shamt5	Rotate Right Extend	{Rd, C} ← {C, Rd}
$I = 0$ AND $(sh = 11;$ $instr_{11:7} \neq 0)$	ROR Rd, Rm, Rs/shamt5	Rotate Right	Rd ← Rn ror Src2
1110	BIC Rd, Rn, Src2	Bitwise Clear	Rd ← Rn & ~Src2
1111	MVN Rd, Rn, Src2	Bitwise NOT	Rd ← ~Rn

NOP (no operation) is typically encoded as 0xE1A000, which is equivalent to MOV R0, R0.

B.1.1 Multiply Instructions

Multiply instructions use the encoding in Figure B.2 The 3-bit *cmd* field specifies the type of multiply, as given in Table B.2.

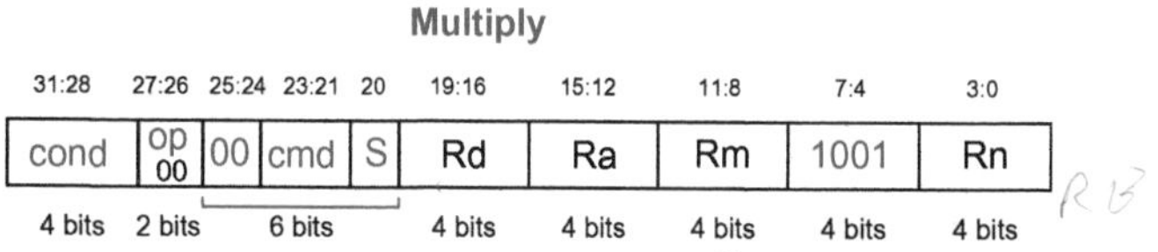

Multiply

31:28	27:26	25:24	23:21	20	19:16	15:12	11:8	7:4	3:0
cond	op 00	00	cmd	S	Rd	Ra	Rm	1001	Rn
4 bits	2 bits		6 bits		4 bits	4 bits	4 bits	4 bits	4 bits

Figure B.2 Multiply instruction encoding

Table B.2 Multiply instructions

cmd	Name	Description	Operation
000	MUL Rd, Rn, Rm	Multiply	Rd ← Rn × Rm (low 32 bits)
001	MLA Rd, Rn, Rm, Ra	Multiply Accumulate	Rd ← (Rn × Rm)+Ra (low 32 bits)
100	UMULL Rd, Rn, Rm, Ra	Unsigned Multiply Long	{Rd, Ra} ← Rn × Rm (all 64 bits, Rm/Rn unsigned)
101	UMLAL Rd, Rn, Rm, Ra	Unsigned Multiply Accumulate Long	{Rd, Ra} ← (Rn × Rm)+{Rd, Ra} (all 64 bits, Rm/Rn unsigned)
110	SMULL Rd, Rn, Rm, Ra	Signed Multiply Long	{Rd, Ra} ← Rn × Rm (all 64 bits, Rm/Rn signed)
111	SMLAL Rd, Rn, Rm, Ra	Signed Multiply Accumulate Long	{Rd, Ra} ← (Rn × Rm)+{Rd, Ra} (all 64 bits, Rm/Rn signed)

B.2 MEMORY INSTRUCTIONS

The most common memory instructions (LDR, STR, LDRB, and STRB) oper-ate on words or bytes and are encoded with $op = 01$. Extra memory instructions operating on halfwords or signed bytes are encoded with $op = 00$ and have less flexibility generating $Src2$. The immediate offset is only 8 bits and the register offset cannot be shifted. LDRB and LDRH zero-extend the bits to fill a word, while LDRSB and LDRSH sign-extend the bits. Also see memory indexing modes in Section 6.3.6.

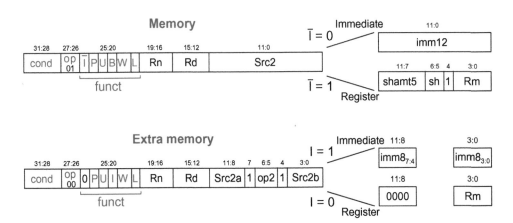

Figure B.3 Memory instruction encodings

Table B.3 Memory instructions

op	B	op2	L	Name	Description	Operation
01	0	N/A	0	STR Rd, [Rn, ±Src2]	Store Register	Mem[Adr] ← Rd
01	0	N/A	1	LDR Rd, [Rn, ±Src2]	Load Register	Rd ← Mem[Adr]
01	1	N/A	0	STRB Rd, [Rn, ±Src2]	Store Byte	Mem[Adr] ← Rd$_{7:0}$
01	1	N/A	1	LDRB Rd, [Rn, ±Src2]	Load Byte	Rd ← Mem[Adr]$_{7:0}$
00	N/A	01	0	STRH Rd, [Rn, ±Src2]	Store Halfword	Mem[Adr] ← Rd$_{15:0}$
00	N/A	01	1	LDRH Rd, [Rn, ±Src2]	Load Halfword	Rd ← Mem[Adr]$_{15:0}$
00	N/A	10	1	LDRSB Rd, [Rn, ±Src2]	Load Signed Byte	Rd ← Mem[Adr]$_{7:0}$
00	N/A	11	1	LDRSH Rd, [Rn, ±Src2]	Load Signed Half	Rd ← Mem[Adr]$_{15:0}$

B.3 BRANCH INSTRUCTIONS

Figure B.4 shows the encoding for branch instructions (B and BL) and Table B.4 describes their operation.

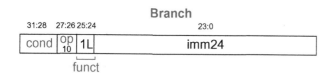

Branch

Figure B.4 Branch instruction encoding

Table B.4 Branch instructions

L	Name	Description	Operation
0	B label	Branch	PC ← (PC+8)+imm24 << 2
1	BL label	Branch with Link	LR ← (PC+8) - 4; PC ← (PC+8)+imm24 << 2

B.4 MISCELLANEOUS INSTRUCTIONS

The ARMv4 instruction set includes the following miscellaneous instructions. Consult the ARM Architecture Reference Manual for details.

Instructions	Description	Purpose
LDM, STM	Load/store multiple	Save and recall registers in subroutine calls
SWP / SWPB	Swap (byte)	Atomic load and store for process synchronization
LDRT, LDRBT, STRT, STRBT	Load/store word/byte with translation	Allow operating system to access memory in user virtual memory space
SWI[1]	Software Interrupt	Create an exception, often used to call the operating system
CDP, LDC, MCR, MRC, STC	Coprocessor access	Communicate with optional coprocessor
MRS, MSR	Move from/to status register	Save status register during exceptions

[1] SWI was renamed SVC (supervisor call) in ARMv7.

B.5 CONDITION FLAGS

Condition flags are changed by data-processing instructions with $S = 1$ in the machine code. All instructions except CMP, CMN, TEQ, and TST must have an "S" appended to the instruction mnemonic to make $S = 1$. Table B.5 shows which condition flags are affected by each instruction.

Table B.5 **Instructions that affect condition flags**

Type	Instructions	Condition Flags
Add	ADDS, ADCS	N, Z, C, V
Subtract	SUBS, SBCS, RSBS, RSCS	N, Z, C, V
Compare	CMP, CMN	N, Z, C, V
Shifts	ASRS, LSLS, LSRS, RORS, RRXS	N, Z, C
Logical	ANDS, ORRS, EORS, BICS	N, Z, C
Test	TEQ, TST	N, Z, C
Move	MOVS, MVNS	N, Z, C
Multiply	MULS, MLAS, SMLALS, SMULLS, UMLALS, UMULLS	N, Z

C Programming

C.1 INTRODUCTION

The overall goal of this book is to give a picture of how computers work on many levels, from the transistors by which they are constructed all the way up to the software they run. The first five chapters of this book work up through the lower levels of abstraction, from transistors to gates to logic design. Chapters 6 through 8 jump up to architecture and work back down to microarchitecture to connect the hardware with the software. This Appendix on C programming fits logically between Chapters 5 and 6, covering C programming as the highest level of abstraction in the text. It motivates the architecture material and links this book to programming experience that may already be familiar to the reader. This material is placed in the Appendix so that readers may easily cover or skip it depending on previous experience.

The rest of this chapter is available online as a downloadable PDF from the book's companion site: http://booksite.elsevier.com/9780128000564.

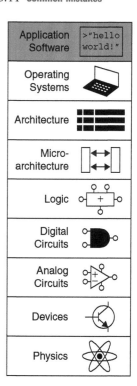

Index

Edwards Brothers Malloy
Ann Arbor MI. USA
December 28, 2016